OECD Employment Outlook

Towards More and Better Jobs

2003

OECD

ORGANISATION FOR ECONOMIC CO-OPERATION AND DEVELOPMENT

The OECD Employment Outlook

provides an annual assessment of labour market developments and prospects in member countries. Each issue contains an overall analysis of the latest labour market trends and short-term forecasts, and examines key labour market developments. Reference statistics are also included.

The **OECD Employment Outlook** is the joint work of members of the Directorate for Employment, Labour and Social Affairs, and is published on the responsibility of the Secretary-General of the OECD. This report is based on draft contributions from Glenda Quintini and Paul Swaim (Chapters 1 and 2), Anne Saint-Martin and Peter Whiteford (Chapter 3), David Grubb and Koji Miyamoto (Chapter 4), Andrea Bassanini and Wooseok Ok (Chapter 5). Raymond Torres coordinated the report. The assessments of countries' labour market prospects do not necessarily correspond to those of the national authorities concerned.

THE ORGANISATION FOR ECONOMIC CO-OPERATION AND DEVELOPMENT (OECD)

was set up under a Convention signed in Paris on 14th December 1960, which provides that the OECD shall promote policies designed:

- *to achieve the highest sustainable economic growth and employment and a rising standard of living in member countries, while maintaining financial stability, and thus to contribute to the development of the world economy;*
- *to contribute to sound economic expansion in member as well as non-member countries in the process of economic development; and*
- *to contribute to the expansion of world trade on a multilateral, non-discriminatory basis in accordance with international obligations.*

The original member countries of the OECD are Austria, Belgium, Canada, Denmark, France, Germany, Greece, Iceland, Ireland, Italy, Luxembourg, the Netherlands, Norway, Portugal, Spain, Sweden, Switzerland, Turkey, the United Kingdom and the United States. The following countries became members subsequently through accession at the dates indicated hereafter: Japan (28th April 1964), Finland (28th January 1969), Australia (7th June 1971), New Zealand 29th May 1973), Mexico (18th May 1994), the Czech Republic (21st December 1995), Hungary (7th May 1996), Poland (22nd November 1996), Korea (12th December 1996) and Slovak Republic (14th December 2000). The Commission of the European Communities takes part in the work of the OECD (Article 13 of the OECD Convention).

Publié en français sous le titre :
Perspectives de l'emploi de l'OCDE : 2003
Vers des emplois plus nombreux et meilleurs

© OECD 2003

Permission to reproduce a portion of this work for non-commercial purposes or classroom use should be obtained through the Centre français d'exploitation du droit de copie (CFC), 20,rue des Grands-Augustins, 75006 Paris, France, tel. (33-1) 44 07 477 0, fax (33-1) 46 34 67 19, for every country except the United States. In the United States permission should be obtained through the Copyright Clearance Center, Customer Service, (508)750-8400, 222 Rosewood Drive, Danvers, MA 01923 USA, or CCC Online: *www.copyright.com*. All other applications for permission to reproduce or translate all or part of this book should be made to OECD Publications, 2,rue André-Pascal, 75775 Paris Cedex 16, France.

Table of Contents

Introduction: Towards More and Better Jobs 11

Chapter 1. **More and Better Jobs? Aggregate Performance During the Past Decade** ... 17
    Introduction 18
    Main findings 19
    1. How much has aggregate performance improved? 21
        A. Latest developments and short-term prospects 21
        B. Progress at raising employment over the past decade 25
        C. Were the gains widely shared? 27
    2. Is the progress sustainable? 30
        A. The NAIRU has tended to fall 30
        B. Matching of unemployed with jobs shows little improvement 31
        C. Wage setting has reflected greater restraint 36
        D. Increased dynamism for private sector employment growth 39
        E. Overall assessment of structural progress 40
    3. More and better jobs? 40
        A. Do new jobs pay well? 41
        B. Long hours and headaches: some indicators of working conditions 45
        C. Growth in part-time and temporary jobs 49
        D. Is employment insecurity on the rise? 51
    Conclusions 55
    Annex 1. Supplementary Evidence 59

    Bibliography 64

Chapter 2. **The Labour Mobilisation Challenge: Combating Inactivity Traps
and Barriers to Moving Up Job Ladders** 67
    Introduction 68
    Main findings 69
    1. Raising employment by mobilising potential labour supply 70
        A. Why increase aggregate labour supply and employment? 70
        B. The demographic challenge: adapting to population ageing 72
        C. Estimating potential labour supply 74
    2. The many faces of non-employment 81
        A. Women are still significantly under-represented in the labour market 81
        B. About 15% of youths are neither working nor studying in the OECD
           as a whole 82
        C. Withdrawal from the labour market starts well before the official
           retirement age 82
        D. Fewer than one-half of the less educated are employed in the OECD
           as a whole 86

		E. Immigrants: a very heterogeneous group	86
		F. Few persons with disabilities are in work	89
	3.	Getting into work, staying there and moving up job ladders	90
		A. Inactivity traps from a multi-year perspective	90
		B. Low-pay traps and unstable employment	93
		C. The intertwined risks of non-employment, low pay and poverty	95
Conclusions			102
Annex 1. Supplementary Evidence			107
Bibliography			111

Chapter 3. **Making Work Pay – Making Work Possible** 113

Introduction			114
Main findings			115
1.	Financial incentive schemes: making work pay and facilitating access to employment		116
	A. Encouraging labour supply by making work pay: employment-conditional benefits		117
	B. Supporting labour demand by lowering labour costs		123
	C. Subsidising workers or employers? Relevance and drawbacks of each option		128
2.	Promoting employment while taking specific situations into account		131
	A. Mothers with young children		131
	B. Working-age disabled persons		138
	C. Improving employment prospects of older workers		147
Conclusions			152
Annex 1. Tables 3.A1.1 to 3.A1.4			157
Bibliography			166

Chapter 4. **Benefits and Employment, Friend or Foe? Interactions Between Passive and Active Social Programmes** 171

Introduction		172
Main findings		172
1. Trends in benefit dependency		174
	A. Analysis of benefit recipiency rates	174
	B. Long adjustment lags to policy changes	182
2. The meaning and measurement of the "active" content of policy		192
	A. Spending on "active" vs. "passive" labour market programmes	193
	B. PES interventions in the unemployment spell	194
	C. Benefit eligibility criteria and benefit sanctions	195
	D. Compulsory vs. voluntary participation in labour market programmes	196
	E. Institutional arrangements	197
	F. Activating "inactive" benefits and gatekeeping in inactive programmes	199
3. Outcomes from "active" policies		201
	A. The role of activation strategies in reducing benefit dependency	202
	B. Substitution between benefits	208
	C. The effect on employment, earnings and career prospects	210
Conclusions		214
Annex 1. Definition and Measurement of Benefit Recipiency Rates		221
Annex 2. How Long Adjustment Lags Arise from Interaction and Feedback		230
Bibliography		232

Chapter 5. **Upgrading Workers' Skills and Competencies** 237
    Introduction 238
    Main findings 239
    1. Continuous vocational training: a glance at the data 240
    2. Not enough and not equal? A closer look at the determinants
        of training patterns 245
        A. Market failures affecting training outcomes 246
        B. Disentangling employers' supply from employees' demand 249
        C. The impact of workers' opportunity costs on training participation 253
    3. Policy approaches to improve training outcomes 256
        A. From diagnosis to remedies 256
        B. Strategies for addressing economic and financial barriers 260
        C. Framework conditions 273
    Conclusions 275
    Annex 1. Data Description and Detailed Estimation Results 280
    Annex 2. Identification and Estimation of Training Demand and Supply 290
    Bibliography 293

Statistical Annex 297
    Sources and definitions 297
    Conventional signs 298

List of Tables

Chapter 1.
1.1. Employment and labour force growth in OECD countries 22
1.2. Unemployment in OECD countries 23
1.3. The NAIRU has declined in a majority of countries 31
1.4. Contribution of part-time and temporary work to employment growth, 1991-2001   49
1.5. Perceptions of insecurity are on the rise 52
1.6. Wage losses following unemployment and dismissal are usually small 53

Annex
1.A1.1. Productivity and real wage growth and wage share in OECD countries, 1970-2002 60
1.A1.2. Growth in real labour costs in excess of productivity growth in OECD countries,
        1970-2001 61
1.A1.3. Growth in multi-factor productivity and the employment to population
        ratio in selected countries, 1980-1990 and 1990-2000 62

Chapter 2.
2.1. Older workers follow multiple pathways out of the labour market 85
2.2. Big differences in how easily non-employed groups move into employment 91

Annex
2.A1.1. Inactive persons of working age who would like to work (now or at some time
        in the future), 1997 108
2.A1.2. Inactive persons of working age who have worked previously and the reasons
        why they stopped working, 1997 109

Chapter 3.
3.1. In-work benefits and their effects on labour-market participation and
       employment: lone parents, a highly receptive group 119

3.2. Examples of broad reductions in social insurance contributions for low-paid jobs.... 124
3.3. Targeted employment subsidies account for a significant share of expenditure on active labour market programmes 126
3.4. Targeted employment subsidies: recipient outcomes and employers' views (examples drawn from recent evaluations) 127
3.5. Near unanimous support for the right to paid maternity leave 132
3.6. Non-employment among lone-parents: a factor behind child poverty 138
3.7. Disability benefits: some disabled who are excluded, some recipients who do not acknowledge that they have any disabilities and very low exit rates 140
3.8. Employment, a real asset for the economic integration of disabled persons 141
3.9. Sheltered employment remains the most common employment assistance scheme for disabled persons 144
3.10. Subsidised and supported jobs: examples of good practice 145

Annex

3.A1.1. Non-employment among young women, older workers and disabled persons: a low level of education as a common factor 158
3.A1.2. Examples of employment-conditional benefits 159
3.A1.3. Main features of progressive retirement schemes 161
3.A1.4. Employment subsidy schemes for older workers in selected OECD countries ... 164

Chapter 4.

4.1. Employment rates and benefit dependency rates in the working-age population, 1980 to 1999 175
4.2. Indicators for spending on active labour market programmes 193
4.3. Elements in the activation strategies of Denmark, Ireland, the Netherlands and the United Kingdom 204
4.4. Decline in welfare recipiency and increase in employment for single mothers in the United States 211

Annex

4.A1.1. Recipiency rates by type of benefit in the population of working age: average, trends and standard deviation, 1980 to 1999 224

Chapter 5.

5.1. Cross-country variation of training outcomes is large 242
5.2. Workers in small firms receive relatively little training 245
5.3. Training supply and demand vary across firms and individuals 251
5.4. A quarter of all workers would like to take more training 254
5.5. From evidence to policy 257
5.6. Corporate tax deductions for training expenditures in selected OECD countries 261
5.7. Individual learning accounts in OECD countries 270
5.8. Training-leave schemes in selected OECD countries 272

Annex

5.A1.1. Probit and Tobit estimates of the determinants of training 282
5.A1.2. Training demand and supply 285
5.A1.3. Training supply and demand: the effect of literacy 288
5.A2.1. Samples and dependent variables 291
5.A2.2. Estimating supply differences across groups from demand and equilibrium estimates 292

Statistical Annex

A.	Standardised unemployment rates in 27 OECD countries	299
B.	Employment/population ratios, activity and unemployment rates	300
C.	Employment/population ratios, activity and unemployment rates by selected age groups	304
D.	Employment/population ratios, activity and unemployment rates by educational attainment, 2001	316
E.	Incidence and composition of part-time employment	320
F.	Average annual hours actually worked per person in employment	322
G.	Incidence of long-term unemployment	325
H.	Public expenditure and participant inflows in labour market programmes in OECD countries	328

List of Figures

Chapter 1.

1.1.	Strong gains preceded the current slowdown in the EU and Oceania	24
1.2.	Employment has been more resilient in the current slowdown	25
1.3.	Reductions in inactivity often contributed most to employment growth	26
1.4.	Employment gains during the past decade were broadly shared	28
1.5.	Limited evidence for an improvement in the matching process	32
1.6.	Productivity has grown more rapidly than real labour costs, favouring employment growth	38
1.7.	Business sector employment shows dynamism	40
1.8.	Growth in high-paid jobs has been relatively strong	41
1.9.	Rising employment is compatible with strong productivity growth	43
1.10.	Earnings inequality has tended to increase in some countries	44
1.11.	Physical hazards and stress are on the rise	46
1.12.	A growing number of people work very long hours in some countries	47
1.13.	Long hours and intense work disrupt family life and cause stress	48
1.14.	Part-time is mostly a voluntary choice but temporary workers look for permanent jobs	50
1.15.	After dismissal, the low-skilled, youth and women find it more difficult to exit unemployment	54

Annex

1.A1.1.	Trends in the incidence of low pay, 1979-2001	63

Chapter 2.

2.1.	The ageing challenge	73
2.2.	Population ageing and the labour force: recent experience and a demographic-driven scenario in selected OECD areas	75
2.3.	Some groups are significantly under-represented in employment	77
2.4.	Raising participation among women and older persons is key	79
2.5.	Many inactive individuals (but few retirees) want to work	80
2.6.	Women's participation rates vary widely across OECD countries	83
2.7.	Withdrawal from work starts well in advance of age 65 in most OECD countries	84
2.8.	Low skilled account for half of total non-employment in the OECD area	87
2.9.	Employment gap is small for immigrant men in all but a few countries	88

2.10. Employment rate of disabled persons varies widely across OECD countries 89
2.11. Considerable turnover in non-employment 92
2.12. Time in non-employment accumulates strongly 94
2.13. Low-pay incidence highest for youths and less educated workers 96
2.14. Low pay harder to escape for women, older workers (in Europe) and less educated workers (in the United States) 97
2.15. Low-paid employment often alternates with non-employment 98
2.16. Poverty risk is high for lone-parent families and jobless households 100
2.17. Chronic poverty is closely linked to persistence in non-employment and low-paid employment 101

Annex

2.A1.1. Four-year earnings mobility of low-paid workers in Europe and the United States 110

Chapter 3

3.1. Women working and family life: differing opinions 132
3.2. Female labour force participation and child care 135
3.3. Part-time work: a bridge to female labour market participation 137
3.4. Too few resources devoted to vocational rehabilitation 142
3.5. Effective age of retirement: lower than the official age in many OECD countries 148

Chapter 4

4.1. In some countries, most non-employed adults receive a benefit 176
4.2. Employment and benefit dependency: a complex link 177
4.3. Trends in benefit recipiency 179
4.4. Index of unemployment benefit entitlements 184
4.5. Long adjustment lags for special unemployment benefit schemes in Belgium, Italy and Spain, 1979-2002 187
4.6. Long adjustement lags for assistance benefits 189
4.7. Recipiency rate for disability insurance and assistance benefits in the Netherlands, 1969-2001 191
4.8. Disability prevalance and disability benefit recipiency rates in the late 1990s 192
4.9. Unemployment beneficiaries and LFS unemployment have tended to diverge in Ireland since 1986 206
4.10. Is there substitution between active and inactive benefits? 209

Chapter 5

5.1. CVT courses account for more than two thirds of formal adult learning 241
5.2. Older workers and women receive less training 243
5.3. Native and skilled workers receive more training 244
5.4. Most training is entirely paid by employers 247
5.5. Employer-paid CVT less frequently imparts firm-specific skills 247
5.6. Workers with better literacy skills receive more training 252
5.7. Time is the most frequently reported reason for which training costs may be too high for the workers 255
5.8. Cost factors vary across worker groups 256
5.9. Training participation is greater in firms with a joint CVT agreement 275

Annex

5.A2.1. Demand and supply of training: solving the identification problem 290

List of Boxes

Chapter 1.
1.1. What is the Beveridge curve? 34
1.2. What factors shift the Beveridge curve? 35
1.3. What influences wage setting? 36
1.4. Employment and productivity growth: a macroeconomic trade-off? 42
1.5. Consequences of long hours on health and life quality 47

Chapter 3
3.1. Canada's Self-Sufficiency Project (SSP): promoting employment and reducing poverty among lone parents 120
3.2. Making work pay policies: different costs for different goals 122
3.3. Combining training, job-search assistance and financial incentives to strengthen job attachment 130
3.4. The impact of the length of maternity/parental leave on wages and employment: some recent studies 134
3.5. Lone parents and employment: towards a work-oriented safety net 139
3.6. Promoting employment among disabled persons: involving employers in the process 146

Chapter 4
4.1. Aggregate benefit dependency rates compared with employment and education participation 178
4.2. Trends in entitlements for unemployment and disability benefits 183
4.3. Adjustment lags for three European unemployment benefit schemes 185
4.4. Adjustment lags for the main unemployment assistance and social assistance schemes in four countries 188
4.5. Lone-parent benefits in two countries 190
4.6. National *versus* regional financing and management of insurance and assistance benefits in Canada 198
4.7. Sweden's Activity Guarantee and the "carousel" effect 203
4.8. The impact of activation measures in Ireland 205
4.9. The content of welfare reform in the United States 207

Chapter 5
5.1. The impact of CVT on earnings and employment security 242
5.2. Non-labour market sources of market failures: theoretical aspects 249
5.3. Corporate tax deductions training expenditures in Austria 262
5.4. The Geneva Training Voucher 268

Introduction

Towards More and Better Jobs

Towards More and Better Jobs

Mobilising under-represented groups into jobs has become a key policy objective…

Unemployment is on the rise in a majority of member countries, reminding us that the fight against high and persistent unemployment should remain at the top of the policy agenda. The deterioration of labour market conditions could affect disproportionately some groups, such as older workers, women, lone parents, people with disabilities, immigrants and disadvantaged youth. As stressed in this edition of the *Employment Outlook*, these groups are already under-represented in employment, and mobilising them into jobs should now be a key policy objective for OECD countries. This requires a broader approach of reducing *non-employment*, which embraces both unemployment and inactivity.

… because this serves both economic and social goals

Adopting the broader target of reducing non-employment – and not just unemployment – has three main advantages. First, it serves a social objective. The shift towards an employment-oriented social policy reflects the judgement that many working-age recipients of social benefits could work with the proper encouragement and assistance, and that both they and society would benefit from their greater integration into the labour market. Second, policies that have attempted to reduce unemployment through subsidising the withdrawal of people from the labour market have proven to be counter-productive. Third, population ageing requires urgent action to better mobilise under-represented groups. Unless their participation rates are increased, population ageing will lead to a significant slowdown in labour force growth, with adverse consequences for future growth prospects. In sum, the economic and social returns to fostering greater participation are very high.

To some extent, participation patterns reflect a personal choice

However, one has to recognise that non-employment sometimes reflects individuals' work-leisure preferences. For instance, some parents – especially those with young children – prefer to take care of their children rather than participate in the labour market. Similarly, retirement is sometimes a household decision: when one partner retires, it is often the case that the other partner withdraws from the labour market, even if this means a loss of income. Clearly, governments should respect these differences in life situations and personal preferences.

But in many cases under-represented groups face demand- and supply-side barriers to work…

But non-employment is often due to the presence of barriers to labour market participation – on both sides of the market. High minimum wages and regulations setting minimum quality thresholds for jobs have the potential to limit employment opportunities, especially for certain groups. The tax/transfer system may also influence the decision to participate in the labour market, thereby creating "inactivity traps". Another example is that many public pension systems and early retirement schemes often create strong financial disincentives to remain in employment until the official retirement age.

… and find it hard to progress up the career ladder if they get a job

In addition, some under-represented groups have difficulties moving up the career ladder even when they find a job. The result is that they often drop back into unemployment or inactivity. Therefore, consideration should be given to issues of career progression, as well as helping the under-represented groups get into work.

This volume examines how to provide more and better jobs for all

The first part of this volume examines the employment challenge facing OECD policy makers. It documents labour market developments since the early 1990s (Chapter 1) and looks at the labour market situation of groups which are under-represented in employment (Chapter 2). The second part analyses a range of policies to improve the employment position of these groups (Chapters 3 to 5). Such specific policies should, of course, be accompanied by support to aggregate labour demand and, more generally, higher economic growth – issues which go beyond the scope of this volume.

It starts by noting a mixed employment situation…

Chapter 1 reports some encouraging signs of structural improvement in OECD labour markets. An important portion of the employment gains registered over the past decade was structural, and thus sustainable. Though the employment situation has deteriorated since 2000-2001 in all member countries, the rise in unemployment to date is less pronounced than was the case in earlier periods of economic weakness. This chapter also reviews trends in the quality of jobs, looking at indicators of job precariousness, work intensification and stress at work. No clear pattern of improvement or deterioration in job quality is found.

... in which certain groups are finding it hard to progress

Chapter 2 documents the considerable scope for improving the employment position of under-represented groups. When they get into work, many women, older workers and low-educated persons are at risk of getting trapped in low-paid jobs. And they are also subject to considerable employment instability. Indeed, in both Europe and the United States, those who are low-paid in a given year are likely to spend nearly four of the following five years in either low-paid employment or non-employment. This suggests that policies that help people move up career ladders should become an important component in any medium-term employment strategy.

It then considers a comprehensive policy strategy, including making work pay and facilitating access to employment,...

Addressing these problems requires a comprehensive strategy to reduce demand- and supply-side barriers to employment. In particular, work should be financially attractive (Chapter 3). This is especially important for low-skilled individuals who have a limited earnings capacity, as well as low-income families and lone parents who receive an income-replacement benefit. Various countries have used in-work benefits and tax credits (so-called "making work pay" policies) to improve the financial incentives for welfare recipients accepting work. But pay must also be affordable by employers. Reduced social security contributions on low wages have proven effective in supporting labour demand in some countries.

But financial incentives, on their own, are not enough: access to work should also be facilitated by a variety of services and flexible working arrangements such as part-time jobs. This may help reconcile work and family life, or help disabled persons make the most of their reduced work capacity. For older workers, flexible retirement schemes, encouragement of second careers, together with action to ensure that disincentives to hire or retain these workers are removed, provide interesting reform avenues.

... effective activation policies,...

Greater efforts to move beneficiaries of unemployment and other non-employment benefits into jobs are also needed. Activation policies can play an important role here. Chapter 4 shows that several common principles underlie effective activation strategies. First, to receive benefits the recipient has to search actively for a job and/or be willing to take steps to improve his/her employability. Second, a range of re-employment services should be available for the job-seeker. Third, the public employment service or related agency should maintain effective contact with people on benefits in order to deliver adequate support services, monitor their job-search behaviour and ensure constant efforts to return to work.

... and job-related training which pays attention to existing learning inequalities

Job-related training is essential to improve career prospects. Once in jobs, some workers may fall into low-wage traps, and training may reduce this risk by helping them realise their productivity and earnings potential. Yet, Chapter 5 shows that under-represented groups receive relatively little training. The nature of this inequality varies considerably from one group to the other. In some cases employers lack the incentive to invest in the human capital of the groups. In other cases, it is the workers themselves who lack interest in participating in learning activities. This is why policies should improve the incentives to invest in lifelong learning on the part of both employers and individuals. And the thorny issue of who should pay for job-related training should also be addressed in co-operation with the social partners and other stakeholders.

OECD Employment and Labour Ministers will discuss the policy dilemmas posed by such a medium-term strategy

This edition provides the analytical background for the meeting of OECD Employment and Labour Ministers to be held on the 29-30 September 2003, entitled "Towards More and Better Jobs". Ministers will discuss some of the policy trade-offs involved in mobilising under-represented groups. In particular, they will discuss whether policy priority should be given to the groups which suffer the greatest labour market disadvantage (*e.g.* persons with disabilities), or those offering the largest labour resource potential (*e.g.* women and older workers). The extent to which it is sufficient to get more people from under-represented groups into work or whether policy makers need to give consideration to low-wage traps and employment instability is another key question for Ministers. They will also examine how to extend existing employment policies, which have been designed to deal with unemployment, to groups on the margins of the labour market. They will exchange views on what works and what doesn't, while paying special attention to the cost-effectiveness of the measures – at a time of very tight fiscal constraints.

More fundamentally, the Ministerial discussions will provide an opportunity to highlight that mobilising under-represented groups serves economic objectives, while also promoting a more inclusive society.

John P. Martin
Director for Employment, Labour and Social affairs

ISBN 92-64-10061-X
OECD Employment Outlook: 2003
Towards More and Better Jobs
© OECD 2003

Chapter 1

More and Better Jobs? Aggregate Performance During the Past Decade

The share of the working-age population in employment rose in two thirds of all OECD countries during the past decade. However, the OECD average hides a wide diversity of experiences, ranging from dramatic increases in employment rates in a few countries to rising unemployment or greater labour market inactivity in others. Are employment gains registered during the past decade sustainable? How do employment losses recorded in the current economic slowdown compare with previous recessions? Is there evidence that progress in increasing employment has been accompanied by improvements in "job quality", notably as regards earnings inequality, job insecurity and working conditions?

Introduction 18
Main findings 19
1. How much has aggregate performance improved? 21
2. Is the progress sustainable? 30
3. More and better jobs? 40
Conclusions 55
Annex 1. Supplementary evidence 59
Bibliography 64

Introduction

The comparative resiliency of the labour market in the current economic slowdown provides some hope that structural reforms may have begun to pay-off in a long-run improvement of employment performance.[1] However, the improvement in aggregate performance that has been observed for the OECD area as a whole during the past decade is modest and masks important differences across member countries. Furthermore, even in those OECD countries where significant improvements in employment performance have been registered, concerns remain about the sustainability of these gains. In particular, it is not yet clear whether structural reforms have produced a durable reduction in unemployment, once cyclical fluctuations and other transitory factors (*e.g.* the Internet bubble of the late 1990s) are accounted for.

Another concern is how broadly recent employment gains have been shared across the working-age population. Distributional concerns focus on groups within the working-age population whose members tend to be found on the margins of the labour market, even when employment is robust overall. Often, the employment to population ratios of women, older workers, low-skilled workers, and persons with partial disabilities or who live in economically depressed regions remain relatively low, with potentially adverse consequences for their living standards and the long-term fiscal viability of important social programmes (see Chapter 2 for a detailed analysis of the employment situation and career prospects of these groups).

Discussions about the structural performance of labour markets also touch upon the broader issue of job "quality." One such debate concerns the relationship between the quantity and quality of employment, including whether some of the policies intended to expand employment may also tend to increase the segmentation of the labour market between "good" career jobs, which are available to workers with skills that are in demand, and low-paid, precarious jobs which are available to those on the margins of the labour market. In some countries, rising incidences of non-standard forms of employment (short-term contracts, temporary jobs, casual employment, etc., see OECD, 2002a) or in-work poverty (OECD, 2001a) provide some support for this concern. But other commentators argue that these jobs may represent valuable stepping stones to moving up the job ladder and, in any case, are better than no job at all.[2] A second debate concerns the possibility that new patterns of work organisation are resulting in a more "intense" pace of work, which may create health problems, make it more difficult to reconcile work with family life, or tend to push older workers into withdrawing from the labour market earlier than otherwise would be the case (Green, 2002; Green and Gallie, 2002).

This chapter documents recent trends in labour market performance in both quantitative and qualitative terms in order to throw some light on these debates. Section 1 establishes the essential baseline by documenting the recent evolution of employment, unemployment and inactivity. Some attention is devoted to current macroeconomic conditions, but the emphasis is placed on assessing progress in expanding aggregate employment during the past decade and identifying which population groups benefited most from these gains. Section 2 analyses whether employment gains – where they occurred – are structural in nature and, hence, likely to prove sustainable. The final section looks at a number of aspects of job quality, including pay, working conditions and employment security.

Main findings

- Unemployment has risen by approximately 1 percentage point in the OECD area since its recent low in 2000-2001, as global economic activity has slowed, reversing approximately two-thirds of the decline during the second half of the 1990s. However, these averages mask important differences across OECD countries in both the severity of the current slowdown and the trend evolution of unemployment rates during the previous decade. Unemployment rates have trended upward since 1990 in Japan and Central and Eastern European (CEE) countries, but downwards in the European Union, North America and, particularly, Oceania.[3] In the latter three regions, a significant share of the improvement in employment and unemployment that was registered during the 1990s expansion has been maintained through the current slowdown, suggestive of increased labour market resiliency in the face of negative shocks. Nonetheless, the prospects for economic recovery remain uncertain and the slowdown highlights the potential reversibility of the improvements in labour market performance that were registered in a number of OECD countries during the past decade.

- The employment to population ratio rose during 1991-2001 in two-thirds of all OECD countries, consistent with a trend improvement in overall labour market performance. Although the average increase in the employment rate was small (1.1 percentage point), the increase exceeded 2 percentage points in one-half of these countries and exceeded 10 percentage points in Ireland and the Netherlands. However, large reductions in employment rates occurred in the CEE countries, associated with the transition from centrally-planned to market-based economies. Among other OECD countries, significant reductions in employment were registered in Turkey (10.2 percentage points) and Sweden (5.8 percentage points). Changes in both unemployment and, especially, participation rates contributed to changing the employment rate in most countries.

- In countries where the aggregate employment to population ratio rose during 1991-2001, those gains were widely shared across workforce groups. The increase in employment was especially strong for women and often quite strong for older workers, for whom rising participation reinforced the impact of declining unemployment: the secular increase in female participation continued in almost all countries, while improving labour market conditions and cuts in incentives for early retirement resulted in a reversal of the secular decrease in participation among older workers in quite a few countries. By contrast, the employment to population ratios for youths and less educated persons fell over the past decade in a large majority of OECD countries. In the case of youths, this was partly due to a rise in the proportion of young people in school and hence is not necessarily indicative of growing labour market difficulties for youths generally, but declining employment for low-skilled persons probably reflects a further deterioration of labour market opportunities for this group.

- It is difficult to assess the relative importance of cyclical and structural factors in the improvements in labour market performance during the past decade, where they occurred. Nonetheless, the evidence suggests that a considerable share of the progress observed may be structural in nature and, hence, potentially sustainable. OECD estimates of the equilibrium rate of unemployment (*i.e.* the non-accelerating inflation rate of unemployment or NAIRU) indicate a downward trend for the large majority of countries. Direct evidence is also found for increased wage restraint, including the fall in the wage share in a number of European countries and Japan. The more muted rise of real labour costs in many European countries may have helped labour demand. Indeed, the private business sector has accounted for a rising share of employment growth over the 1990s in marked contrast with the experience in the two previous decades. However, Beveridge curves shifted favourably, signalling an improvement in the *matching* of unemployed persons to vacancies, in only a few OECD countries.

- The overall picture with regard to recent trends in job quality is mixed. Recent trends provide some support for concerns that the policies and institutional configurations that facilitated strong employment growth may also have tended to cause overall wage inequality to increase. However, the proportion of workers in low-paid employment has increased significantly in only a few countries and there is little support for the fears sometimes expressed that recent increases in employment are mainly due to a proliferation of low-paying jobs, or that reforms intended to mobilise groups at the margins of the labour market have resulted in lower productivity growth.

- Changes in working conditions, another important dimension of job quality, also give a mixed picture. The share of European workers reporting that they are exposed to health and safety risks at work has fallen, but the proportion reporting that they are working at very high speed or to tight deadlines is on the rise. Those working long hours or at an intense work pace also report a greater number of stress-related health problems and greater difficulty in reconciling work and family life.

- Part-time jobs accounted for half or more of total employment growth over the past decade in one-half of all OECD countries, and for a considerable share of new jobs in quite a few more. Part-time work accounted for a particularly large share of total employment gains for women and youths in most countries – and also for older workers in a smaller number of countries – suggesting that shorter working hours are often useful for reconciling paid employment with other activities, such as parenting, study or a form of phased retirement. Temporary employment also grew in two-thirds of OECD countries, but accounted for half or more of total job gains in only five countries. Although temporary employment generally was less dynamic than part-time employment, its expansion raises particular concerns because the majority of temporary workers would prefer permanent jobs and the spread of temporary jobs may account, in part, for the decline in subjective appraisals of job security.

- Survey evidence shows that perceptions of employment insecurity are on the rise. This is somewhat paradoxical as job tenures have not become shorter and average wage reductions following job loss are relatively small for workers finding another job. Fears of becoming long-term unemployed after dismissal may account for the perception of insecurity, particularly among low-skilled workers.

1. How much has aggregate performance improved?

A. Latest developments and short-term prospects

As a result of the economic slowdown, employment growth in the OECD area almost came to a halt in 2002, after growing 1 percentage point per year on average between 1990 and 2000 (Table 1.1). The latest OECD projections suggest that the hesitant recovery already underway for some time in the United States will solidify, leading the way for a broader recovery throughout the OECD area. As a result, employment growth is projected to resume slowly this year and return to 1.1% in 2004. Although a sluggish recovery appears to be the most likely short-term scenario, the world economic outlook is characterised by an unusual degree of uncertainty, with down-side risks predominating.

Labour force growth has slowed in response to worsening job prospects, but not enough to prevent unemployment from rising. Unemployment increased by 0.5 percentage points (or 3.1 million persons) in the OECD area in 2002, reaching 6.7% (or 36.4 million persons unemployed), and is projected to increase further to 7% in 2003, before easing to 6.8% in 2004 (Table 1.2). Unemployment rose by a relatively large 1 percentage point to 5.8% in the United States in 2002 – only Turkey and Poland registered larger increases – and it is projected to rise further in 2003 before moderating slightly in 2004. The effects of the slowdown have been slower to manifest themselves in EU labour markets, but the descending path of unemployment reversed in 2002 and the EU unemployment rate is projected to rise to about 8.0% in 2003-2004. In Australia and New Zealand, the unemployment rate declined slightly in 2002 and is expected to remain stable or decline slightly through 2003-2004.

Under these projections, the current slowdown will only partially reverse the gains in aggregate employment and unemployment that occurred during the second half of the 1990s (Chart 1.1). Unemployment is projected to rise by approximately 1 percentage point in the OECD area during 2000-2003, reversing approximately two-thirds of its decline during the late-1990s expansion, while the employment to population ratio is projected to surrender 58% of its earlier 1.8 percentage-points rise. However, the overall resilience of OECD labour markets in the current slowdown masks highly diverse experiences across OECD regions in the evolution of employment during both the current slowdown and the previous business cycle. A common business cycle component – with labour market conditions worsening in the early 1990s, improving in the late 1990s and then worsening again after 2000 – is visible in all regions. However, it is superimposed over a worsening trend in labour market performance in the CEE and Asian members of the OECD, but over an improving trend in the European Union, North America and Oceania.

Chart 1.2 compares the responsiveness of employment to cyclical variations in GDP for 1989-93 and 2000-2002, demonstrating that the employment response to the current slowdown appears to have been more muted than was the case during the slowdown of the early 1990s, particularly in EU countries. This finding is consistent with speculation among some observers that structural reforms may have made labour markets more resilient to external shocks, particularly in the European Union (European Commission, 2002). However, it would be premature to draw a strong conclusion on this point, since the current slowdown is recent and relatively shallow in most of the OECD. Another reason for caution is that this finding needs to be reconciled

Table 1.1. Employment and labour force growth in OECD countries[a]
Annual percentage change

	\multicolumn{6}{c}{Employment}	\multicolumn{6}{c}{Labour force}
	Level in 2001 (000s)	Average 1990-2000	2001	2002	Projections 2003	Projections 2004	Level in 2001 (000s)	Average 1990-2000	2001	2002	Projections 2003	Projections 2004
North America												
Canada	15 076	1.3	1.1	2.2	2.1	1.7	16 249	1.2	1.5	2.6	1.8	1.3
Mexico	39 386	2.9	−0.3	1.4	2.0	2.7	40 351	2.8	−0.1	1.7	2.0	2.4
United States	136 941	1.4	0.0	−0.3	0.9	1.4	143 783	1.3	0.8	0.8	1.1	1.2
Asia												
Japan	64 121	0.3	−0.5	−1.3	−0.6	−0.2	67 518	0.6	−0.2	−0.9	−0.3	−0.2
Korea	21 362	1.5	1.4	2.4	1.3	1.7	22 181	1.7	1.1	1.7	1.5	1.5
Europe												
Austria	4 077	0.4	0.7	−0.4	−0.4	0.3	4 282	0.4	0.8	0.2	0.2	0.2
Belgium	4 198	0.5	1.4	−0.2	−0.1	0.7	4 498	0.6	1.2	0.4	0.5	0.6
Czech Republic[b]	4 707	−0.4	0.7	1.2	0.1	0.1	5 128	0.3	0.0	0.2	0.0	0.0
Denmark	2 721	0.2	0.2	0.1	0.0	0.5	2 845	0.0	0.1	0.2	0.2	0.2
Finland	2 359	−0.7	1.4	0.2	0.0	0.5	2 597	0.0	0.7	0.1	0.1	0.3
France	24 517	0.6	1.6	0.4	−0.1	0.7	26 838	0.7	0.7	0.7	0.4	0.5
Germany[c]	38 917	0.4	0.4	−0.6	−1.0	0.0	41 991	0.5	0.4	−0.1	−0.4	0.1
Greece	3 921	0.6	−0.3	−0.1	0.6	0.9	4 378	1.0	−1.1	−0.6	0.0	0.4
Hungary[d]	3 803	−0.8	0.5	−0.2	−0.3	−0.2	4 036	−1.2	−0.3	−0.1	−0.2	0.2
Iceland	159	1.3	1.7	−0.2	0.5	1.5	163	1.3	1.7	0.6	0.8	1.2
Ireland	1 741	3.8	2.9	1.4	0.6	1.3	1 812	2.9	2.5	1.7	1.5	1.5
Italy	21 300	−0.1	2.0	1.5	0.5	1.2	23 567	0.1	0.8	0.9	0.5	0.8
Luxembourg	277	3.4	5.6	3.1	0.7	1.7	282	3.5	5.5	3.4	1.4	1.6
Netherlands	7 064	2.1	2.1	0.7	−0.6	0.1	7 210	1.7	1.5	1.2	1.1	1.0
Norway	2 278	1.1	0.4	0.2	0.0	0.3	2 362	0.9	0.5	0.6	0.6	0.4
Poland[d]	14 207	−0.8	−2.2	−3.0	−1.0	1.0	17 376	−0.4	0.4	−0.9	−0.4	0.4
Portugal	5 063	1.0	1.6	0.3	−0.4	1.1	5 279	0.9	1.7	1.3	1.1	0.9
Slovak Republic[e]	2 124	−0.1	1.0	0.2	0.6	0.8	2 632	1.0	1.7	−0.7	−0.5	−0.3
Spain	15 946	1.7	3.7	2.0	1.4	2.1	17 815	1.7	3.1	3.0	2.2	1.8
Sweden	4 239	−0.8	2.0	0.1	−0.3	0.4	4 415	−0.4	1.3	0.1	0.2	0.2
Switzerland	4 154	0.3	1.7	0.6	−0.5	0.6	4 221	0.4	1.6	1.3	0.4	0.4
Turkey	20 367	0.8	−1.0	−0.4	1.1	1.2	22 269	0.6	1.1	1.9	1.0	1.3
United Kingdom	27 505	0.2	0.8	0.7	0.2	0.5	28 976	0.2	0.3	0.8	0.4	0.3
Oceania												
Australia	9 188	1.4	1.1	2.0	1.7	1.8	9 854	1.3	1.5	1.5	1.5	1.5
New Zealand	1 823	1.8	2.5	2.9	1.1	1.0	1 925	1.7	1.8	2.8	1.0	1.2
European Union	163 845	0.5	1.4	0.5	0.0	0.7	176 784	0.5	0.9	0.7	0.5	0.6
OECD Europe[f]	215 642	0.5	0.9	0.2	0.0	0.7	234 970	0.6	0.8	0.7	0.4	0.6
Total OECD[f]	503 539	1.0	0.4	0.1	0.5	1.1	536 832	1.0	0.7	0.7	0.8	0.9

a) The OECD Secretariat's projection methods and underlying statistical concepts and sources are described in detail in "Sources and Methods: OECD Economic Outlook" which can be downloaded from the OECD Internet site (www.oecd.org/EN/document/0,,EN-document-0-nodirectorate-no-2-26100-0,00.html).
b) The average growth rate has been calculated for 1993-2000.
c) The average growth rate has been calculated by chaining the data for the whole of Germany to the corresponding data for western Germany prior to 1992.
d) The average growth rate has been calculated for 1992-2000.
e) The average growth rate has been calculated for 1994-2000.
f) The average growth rate for 1990-2000 excluded the Czech Republic, Hungary, Poland and the Slovak Republic.

Source: OECD Economic Outlook, No. 73, April 2003.

Table 1.2. Unemployment in OECD countries[a]

| | \multicolumn{4}{c}{Percentage of labour force} | | \multicolumn{4}{c}{Millions} |
	Average 1990-2000	2001	2002	Projections 2003	Projections 2004	Average 1990-2000	2001	2002	Projections 2003	Projections 2004
North America										
Canada	9.3	7.2	7.7	7.3	7.0	1.4	1.2	1.3	1.2	1.2
Mexico	3.5	2.4	2.7	2.7	2.4	1.3	1.0	1.1	1.1	1.0
United States	5.6	4.8	5.8	6.0	5.8	7.4	6.8	8.4	8.8	8.6
Asia										
Japan	3.2	5.0	5.4	5.7	5.7	2.1	3.4	3.6	3.8	3.8
Korea	3.3	3.7	3.0	3.2	3.0	0.7	0.8	0.7	0.7	0.7
Europe										
Austria	5.1	4.8	5.3	5.9	5.9	0.2	0.2	0.2	0.3	0.3
Belgium	8.3	6.7	7.3	7.8	7.7	0.4	0.3	0.3	0.4	0.4
Czech Republic[b]	5.7	8.2	7.3	7.2	7.2	0.3	0.4	0.4	0.4	0.4
Denmark	6.7	4.3	4.5	4.7	4.4	0.2	0.1	0.1	0.1	0.1
Finland	11.7	9.2	9.1	9.2	9.0	0.3	0.2	0.2	0.2	0.2
France	10.9	8.6	8.9	9.3	9.2	2.8	2.3	2.4	2.5	2.5
Germany[c]	7.5	7.3	7.8	8.3	8.3	3.1	3.1	3.3	3.5	3.5
Greece	9.6	10.4	10.0	9.5	9.1	0.4	0.5	0.4	0.4	0.4
Hungary[d]	9.3	5.8	5.9	6.0	6.4	0.4	0.2	0.2	0.2	0.3
Iceland	3.5	2.3	3.1	3.3	3.0	0.0	0.0	0.0	0.0	0.0
Ireland	11.3	3.9	4.2	5.0	5.2	0.2	0.1	0.1	0.1	0.1
Italy	10.7	9.6	9.1	9.2	8.9	2.4	2.3	2.2	2.2	2.1
Luxembourg	1.9	1.7	2.0	2.7	2.6	0.0	0.0	0.0	0.0	0.0
Netherlands	5.5	2.0	2.5	4.1	5.0	0.4	0.1	0.2	0.3	0.4
Norway	4.7	3.5	4.0	4.5	4.6	0.1	0.1	0.1	0.1	0.1
Poland[d]	13.2	18.2	19.9	20.4	19.9	2.3	3.2	3.4	3.5	3.4
Portugal	5.5	4.1	5.1	6.4	6.3	0.3	0.2	0.3	0.3	0.3
Slovak Republic[e]	14.0	19.3	18.6	17.7	16.8	0.4	0.5	0.5	0.5	0.4
Spain	14.8	10.5	11.4	12.0	11.7	2.3	1.9	2.1	2.2	2.2
Sweden	6.1	4.0	4.0	4.5	4.3	0.3	0.2	0.2	0.2	0.2
Switzerland	2.9	1.6	2.3	3.1	2.9	0.1	0.1	0.1	0.1	0.1
Turkey	7.4	8.5	10.6	10.5	10.6	1.6	1.9	2.4	2.4	2.5
United Kingdom	7.7	5.1	5.2	5.4	5.2	2.2	1.5	1.5	1.6	1.5
Oceania										
Australia	8.4	6.8	6.3	6.1	5.8	0.8	0.7	0.6	0.6	0.6
New Zealand	7.8	5.3	5.2	5.1	5.3	0.1	0.1	0.1	0.1	0.1
European Union	9.0	7.3	7.6	8.0	7.9	15.3	12.9	13.5	14.4	14.3
OECD Europe[f]	8.7	8.2	8.7	9.1	9.0	17.1	19.3	20.6	21.6	21.5
Total OECD[f]	6.4	6.2	6.7	7.0	6.8	30.8	33.3	36.4	38.0	37.5

a) See note to Table 1.1.
b) The average has been calculated for 1993-2000.
c) The average growth rate has been calculated by chaining the data for the whole of Germany to the corresponding data for western Germany prior to 1992.
d) The average has been calculated for 1992-2000.
e) The average has been calculated for 1994-2000.
f) The average for 1990-2000 excluded the Czech Republic, Hungary, Poland and the Slovak Republic.

Source: OECD Economic Outlook, No. 73, April 2003.

1. MORE AND BETTER JOBS? AGGREGATE PERFORMANCE DURING THE PAST DECADE

Chart 1.1. **Strong gains preceded the current slowdown in the EU and Oceania**

Evolution of employment and unemployment in selected OECD areas,[a] 1990-2004[b]

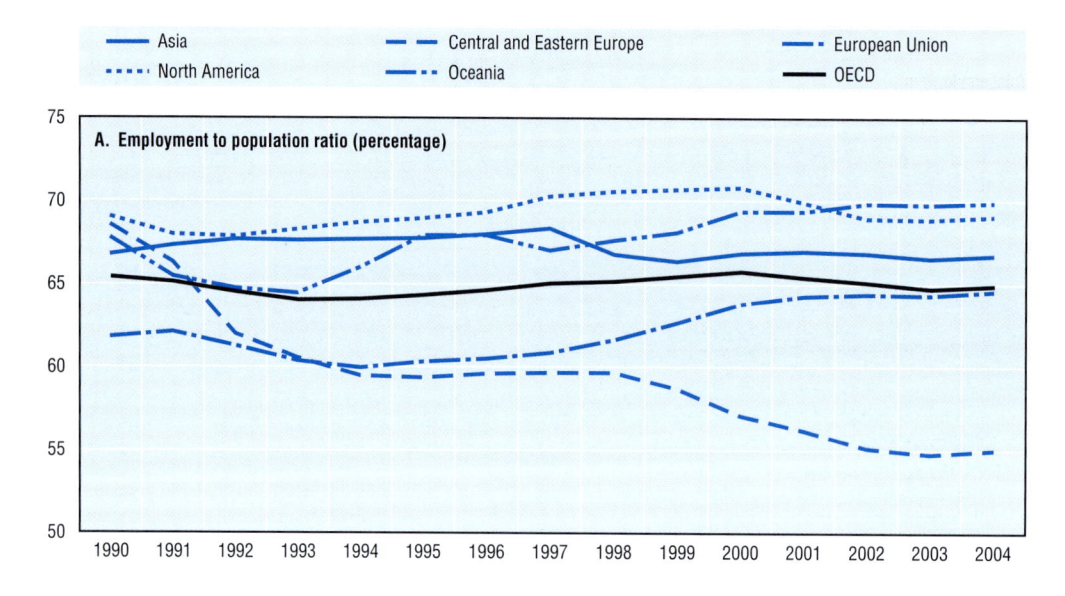

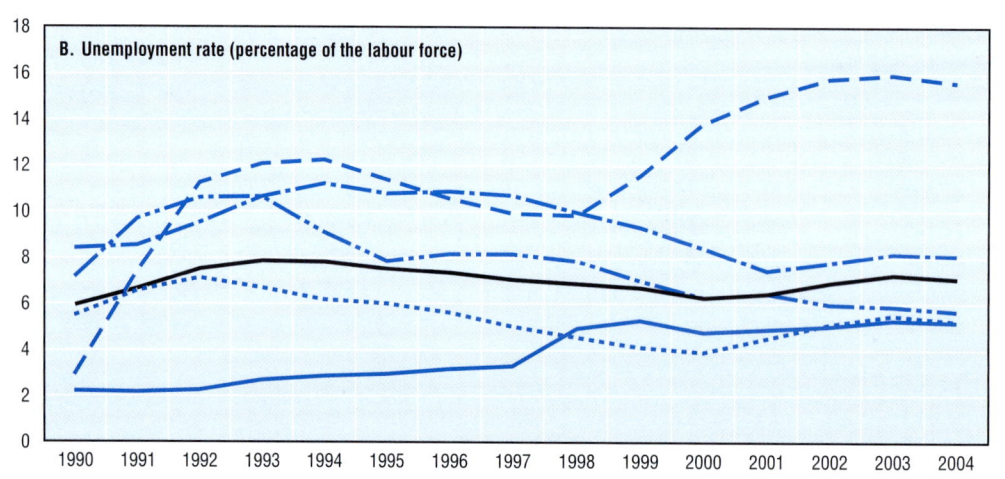

Legend: Asia — Central and Eastern Europe — European Union — North America — Oceania — OECD

A. Employment to population ratio (percentage)

B. Unemployment rate (percentage of the labour force)

a) Population-weighted values for the areas shown. The regional groupings are defined as follows: Central and Eastern Europe (the Czech Republic, Hungary, Poland and the Slovak Republic), European Union (15 EU member countries as of 2002), Asia (Korea and Japan), North America (Canada, Mexico and the United States), Oceania (Australia and New Zealand).
b) Data for 2003-2004 are projections.
Source: OECD database on Labour Force Statistics (supplemented by *OECD Economic Outlook*, No. 73, April 2003).

with those in other quite recent studies (albeit not recent enough to incorporate data from the current slowdown) concluding that employment has become more, not less, responsive to the economic cycle.[4]

Chart 1.2. **Employment has been more resilient in the current slowdown**
Cyclical variation in employment and GDP: early 1990s compared with the current slowdown,
OECD and European Union countries
Percentage deviation of employment and GDP from their respective trends[a, b]

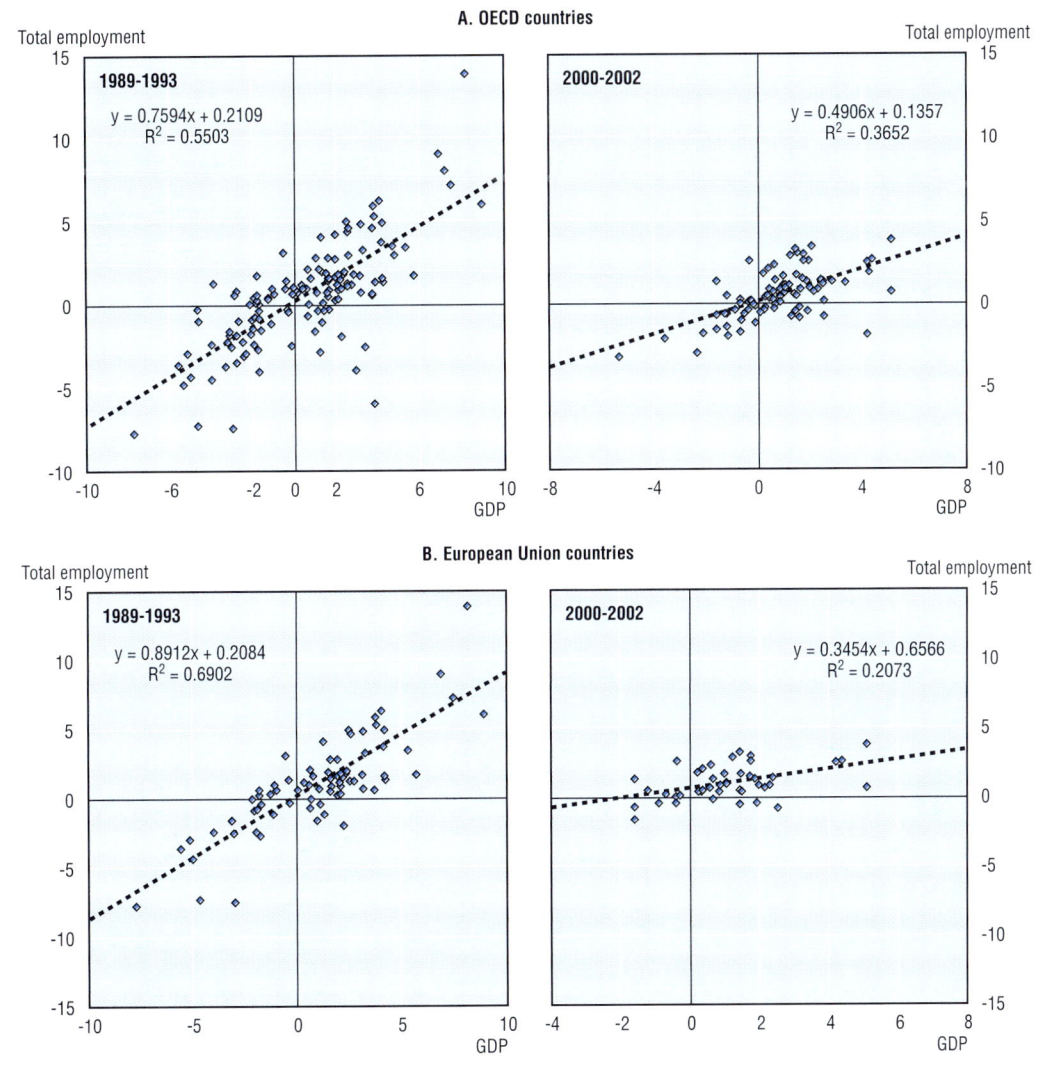

A. OECD countries

1989-1993: $y = 0.7594x + 0.2109$, $R^2 = 0.5503$

2000-2002: $y = 0.4906x + 0.1357$, $R^2 = 0.3652$

B. European Union countries

1989-1993: $y = 0.8912x + 0.2084$, $R^2 = 0.6902$

2000-2002: $y = 0.3454x + 0.6566$, $R^2 = 0.2073$

a) Each point in the chart represents a country-year observation of the percentage deviation of employment and GDP from their respective trends.
b) The trends have been established by the Hodrick-Prescott filter imposing identical smoothing factors for total employment and GDP in all countries.
Source: OECD Analytical Database.

B. Progress at raising employment over the past decade

Nearly a decade has passed since the OECD proposed a comprehensive blueprint for labour market reform, the so-called "Jobs Strategy" (OECD, 1994a). Progress in implementing this agenda has been uneven. Nonetheless, the 1990s were a decade of notable policy initiatives, as many countries responded to chronically high unemployment, high inactivity rates among certain groups in the working-age population and other labour market problems by introducing important structural reforms. An assessment of the progress achieved in raising employment rates and lowering unemployment and better mobilising potential labour supply is thus timely. This sub-section presents such an assessment. The central question posed is the extent to which OECD countries have increased the share of the working-age population that is employed over the course of the past decade, either by lowering unemployment or by increasing participation rates.[5] No attempt is made to identify the contribution of policies to the progress (or lack of progress) in different countries.

This medium-term analysis emphasises changes in employment performance between 1991 and 2001, the most recent complete business cycle for which labour force data were available at the time this analysis was undertaken.[6] This choice increases the probability that observed changes in employment outcomes are largely structural in nature. Ten years may also represent a sufficiently long period for some of the effects of recent structural reforms to have become evident, although this is unlikely to be the case for those most recently enacted.[7]

Employment improved during the past cycle but this masks major country difference

The employment to population ratio for the OECD area[8] rose by only 1.1 percentage points during 1991-2001 (Chart 1.3). The modest gain in employment for the OECD area as

Chart 1.3. **Reductions in inactivity often contributed most to employment growth**
Contributions of reductions in inactivity and unemployment to employment growth in OECD countries,[a] 1991 2001[b]

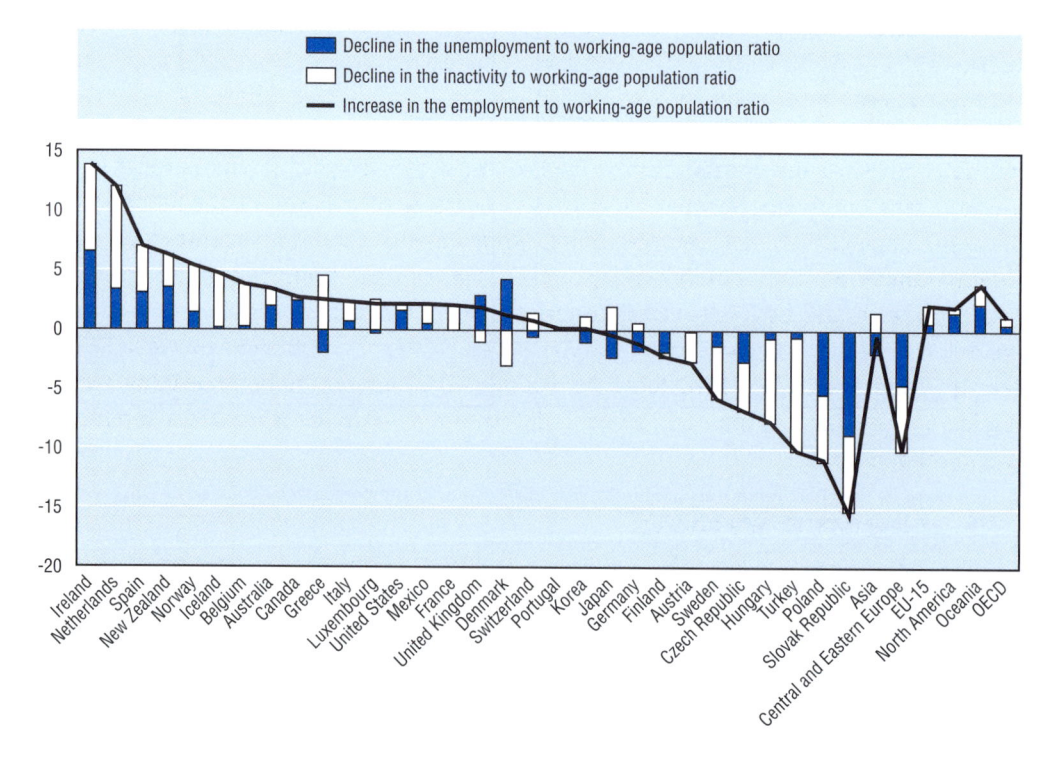

OECD: Population-weighted average of all countries shown except the Czech Republic, Hungary, Poland and the Slovak Republic.
a) The increase in the employment to population ratio for persons between the ages of 15 and 64 years is shown as the vertical sum of the decreases in the ratios of unemployment and inactivity to population.
b) 1992-2001 for Hungary and Poland; 1993-2001 for the Czech Republic; 1994-2001 for the Slovak Republic; 1995-2001 for Austria.
Source: OECD database on Labour Force Statistics.

a whole during the past decade left the employment to population ratio at 65.4% for the OECD area as a whole, unemployment at 4.5% (of the working-age population), and the inactivity rate at 30.1% (2001 values). However, these averages hide widely divergent experiences in different OECD countries. Two-thirds of the countries registered an increase in the employment rate, but a few countries registered large decreases (particularly, the CEE countries, Sweden and Turkey).[9] The two countries with the biggest increases were Ireland (13.9 percentage points) and the Netherlands (12 percentage points). Other European countries where the employment rate grew strongly include Spain (which started from a low rate) and Norway (where employment was already high at the beginning of the 1990s). Except for Germany, where the employment rate fell by 1.2 percentage points,[10] the other large West European economies – France, Italy and the United Kingdom – performed quite well with gains around 2 percentage points.

Significant increases in the employment ratio have also been registered outside OECD Europe. In New Zealand, the employment rate rose by 6.2 percentage points, over half of which was due to a strong decline in unemployment. Employment gains were smaller but still substantial in Australia, Canada and the United States, all countries which had relatively high employment rates at the beginning of the 1990s. The employment rate fell by a modest 0.4 percentage points in Japan, where a significant increase in unemployment was largely neutralised by rising participation.

Reductions in unemployment and inactivity contributed to rising employment

The increase in the employment rate achieved by about two-thirds of OECD countries during 1991-2001 usually reflected the combined impact of reductions in both unemployment and inactivity rates (Chart 1.3).[11] However, there is considerable international variation in the relative importance of changes in unemployment or inactivity rates to the overall change in the employment rate. In the European Union, where raising employment rates has become a prominent policy goal, the fall in inactivity (1.8 percentage points) contributed three times as much as the 0.6 percentage-point fall in the unemployment to population ratio to the 2.4 percentage-point rise in the employment rate. Even within the EU area, the numerical contribution of changes in unemployment exceeded those of changes in inactivity rates in four countries (Denmark, Finland, Germany and the United Kingdom), as was also the case in English-speaking countries outside of the EU area, Japan and several CEE countries which experienced steep increases in unemployment.[12]

C. Were the gains widely shared?

This sub-section looks at the extent to which different workforce groups – particularly groups whose members are often found on the margins of the labour market – have benefited from the increase in aggregate employment over the past ten years. The groups considered are women, youths, older workers and less educated workers; they are not mutually exclusive.[13]

The employment rate of women has tended to improve

In almost all countries, the employment rate rose more (or fell less) during 1991-2001 for women than for men, with this differential averaging 3.7 percentage points (Chart 1.4, Panel A). Employment growth for women outpaced that for men by substantial margins in a number of EU countries, including the three countries with the strongest overall

1. MORE AND BETTER JOBS? AGGREGATE PERFORMANCE DURING THE PAST DECADE

Chart 1.4. **Employment gains during the past decade were broadly shared**
Percentage-point change in employment/population ratios, 1991 to 2001[a]

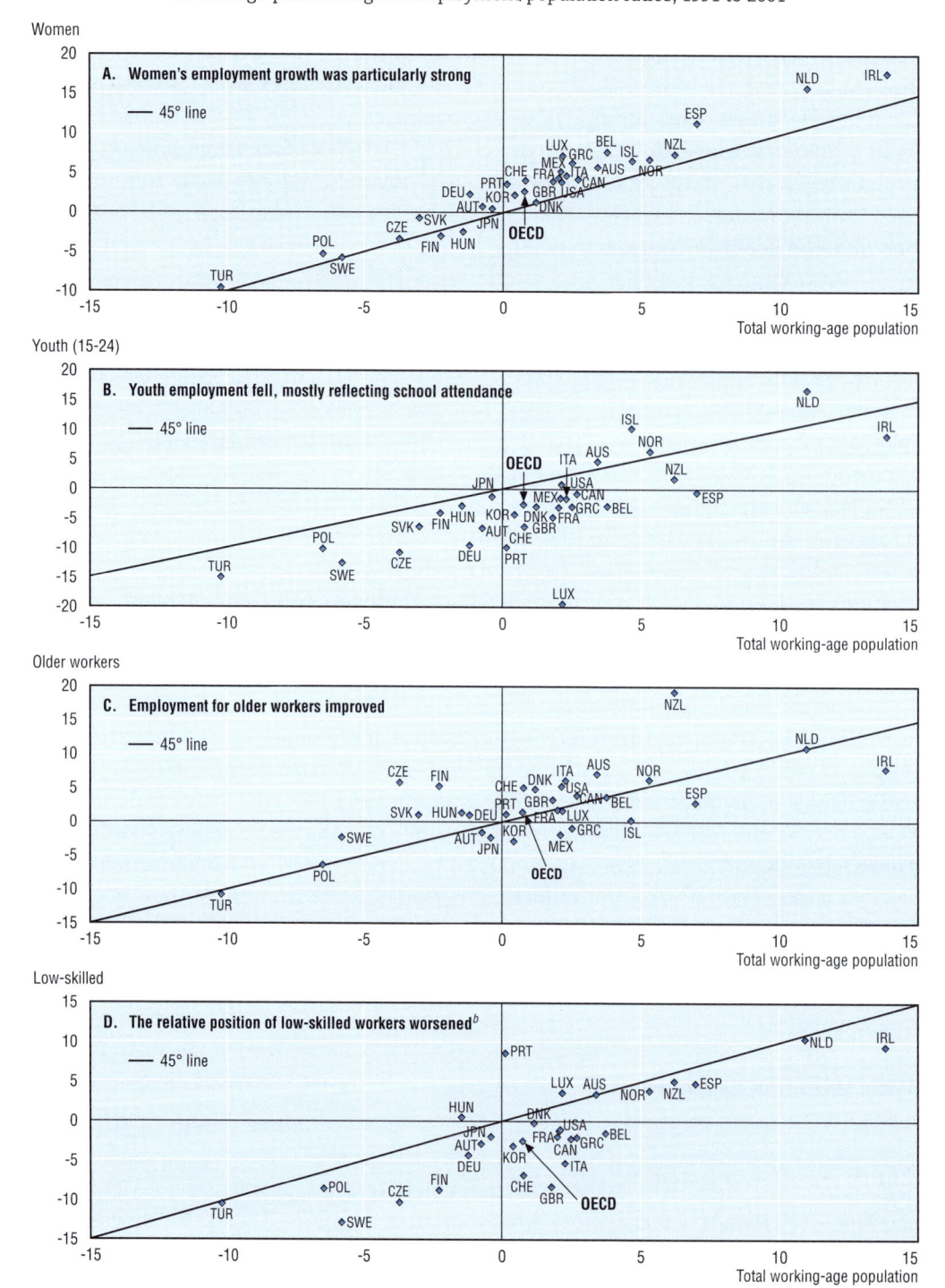

A. Women's employment growth was particularly strong

B. Youth employment fell, mostly reflecting school attendance

C. Employment for older workers improved

D. The relative position of low-skilled workers worsened[b]

OECD: Population-weighted average for the countries shown.
a) 1992-2001 for Hungary and Poland; 1993-2001 for the Czech Republic; 1994-2001 for the Slovak Republic; 1995-2001 for Austria; except that in Panel D; 1991-2000 for the Netherlands; 1994-2001 for the Czech Republic and Greece; 1995-2001 for Korea and Poland; 1996-2001 for Hungary and Iceland; 1997-2001 for Japan and Mexico; 1999-2001 for Luxembourg.
b) Low-skilled corresponds to individuals not having finished upper secondary schooling (ISCED-76).
Source: OECD database on Labour Force Statistics and OECD, *Education at a Glance – OECD Indicators 2002* (for data on low-skilled employment).

employment performance in the OECD (*i.e.* Ireland, the Netherlands and Spain). Part of the explanation for the strong employment performance of women is that the secular increase in female participation rates continued in most countries, while a secular decrease in male participation may have continued in a considerable number of countries, albeit at a slower pace.[14] As a consequence, the OECD inactivity rate for women fell 2.2 percentage points, while that of men fell by 1.4 percentage points (which largely reflected the cyclical pattern, in which more robust hiring encourages higher participation). Women also tended to benefit more than men in countries where unemployment fell. For the OECD area as a whole, unemployment fell by about 1 percentage point for women, but remained approximately unchanged for men.

Youth employment rates fell, reflecting longer school attendance

The youth employment rate for the OECD area as a whole decreased by almost 3 percentage points during 1991-2001 (Chart 1.4, Panel B). This was in sharp contrast to the overall increase in the employment rate rose by about 1 percentage point. The fall in youth employment is due to a rising rate of inactivity (3.5 percentage points), since unemployment fell strongly for this group in most countries where overall unemployment declined, resulting in an average decline of 0.7 percentage point in the OECD area. These patterns suggest that youths generally have benefited from the improvement in overall labour market conditions and that the tendency for youth employment rates to fall reflects the fact that more youths are staying in school longer. Indeed, the share of youths neither employed nor in education – a better indicator of difficulties in the labour market for this age group than standard unemployment and inactivity rates – has trended downwards during the past two decades (OECD, 2002a).

Employment of older workers increased somewhat…

For the OECD area as a whole, the employment rate for persons aged 55 to 64 years rose by 1.4 percentage points during 1991-2001, slightly outpacing employment growth for the total working-age population (Chart 1.4, Panel C). The rise in older worker employment rates is mostly attributable to the 1.6 percentage-point fall in the inactivity rate for this group, which was larger than the 0.7 figure for the prime-age population and represented a break with the historic trend towards retirement at younger ages.[15] The unemployment rate for the 55-64 age group remained roughly unchanged. The largest increase in employment rates for older workers occurred in New Zealand, where there was a nearly 20 percentage-point reduction in the inactivity rate for persons between the ages of 55 and 64 years, mainly in response to a substantial increase in the retirement age in the national pension system (see Chapter 3).

… but the relative employment position of low-skilled workers continued to deteriorate

Chart 1.4, Panel D shows that the employment rate for persons not having completed upper secondary schooling (hereafter referred to as "low-skilled") fell by 2.4 percentage points, despite the overall rise in employment. The weak employment performance of low-skilled workers reflected a tendency for labour market participation to decline strongly for the low skilled, even where aggregate employment opportunities expanded, consistent with the hypothesis that skill-biased technical change and shifts in international trade patterns reduced the relative demand for low-skilled workers in OECD countries. However, low-skilled workers fared even worse where overall employment was weak, with the

1. MORE AND BETTER JOBS? AGGREGATE PERFORMANCE DURING THE PAST DECADE

sharpest reductions in the employment rate for low-skilled people occurring in the Czech Republic, Sweden and Turkey.

2. Is the progress sustainable?

This section examines the extent to which *sustainable* progress has been made in improving the overall functioning of labour markets in OECD countries. The assessment begins with a "bottom-line" indicator of structural progress, namely, whether econometric estimates of the "equilibrium" unemployment rate indicate that lower unemployment rates can now be maintained without causing inflation to worsen.[16] Since the OECD's estimates of the NAIRU do, in fact, confirm a tendency for equilibrium unemployment to have fallen during the past decade, attention then turns to whether structural factors can be identified that would account for this apparent progress (and its unevenness across OECD countries). Accordingly, a number of the institutional factors emphasised in research on the determinants of the NAIRU are examined, to check whether they changed in ways that would support an inference that structural progress has occurred.[17] A major theme in this literature is that appropriate policies and institutional arrangements can reduce equilibrium unemployment by improving the *matching* between vacant posts and unemployed individuals.[18] This possibility is analysed here using so-called "Beveridge curves." A second way that structural reforms could have contributed to lowering the NAIRU would be to have improved the *wage-setting environment*, so as to moderate upward pressure on wages and render them more sensitive to market conditions. Accordingly, the evolution of real wages and labour costs over the past decade is analysed. Finally, evidence is presented concerning whether employment growth has become more dynamic in the private business sector.

A. The NAIRU has tended to fall

Table 1.3 presents data on the evolution of equilibrium unemployment rates over the past decade in the 21 countries for which OECD estimates of the NAIRU are available. A broad, but not universal, decreasing trend is evident, with the NAIRU falling in 12 countries, stable in four, and rising in five. Another encouraging development is that progress in lowering the NAIRU tended to be concentrated in countries beginning the 1990s with a relatively high level of equilibrium unemployment. The mean 1991 NAIRU in the 12 countries where it fell over the course of the following decade was 8.4%, compared with 5.3% where the NAIRU was stable and 5.1% where it rose.[19]

Within the Euro area, the fall in the NAIRU was especially large in Ireland and the Netherlands (8 and 3 percentage points, respectively), but was much smaller or nonexistent in France, Germany and Italy. Canada, Denmark and the United Kingdom experienced the largest reductions in equilibrium unemployment among OECD countries outside the Euro area. The fall was also significant, albeit smaller, in Australia and New Zealand. The NAIRU fell slightly in the United States from a relatively low level. Increases in the NAIRU of 1.5 to 2 percentage points were recorded in Finland, Greece, Iceland and Japan.

The estimation of equilibrium unemployment rates raises major conceptual and empirical difficulties (Richardson *et al.*, 2000). Accordingly, the evidence for structural progress would be appreciably stronger if it can be shown that the declines in the estimated NAIRUs coincided with improvements in important determinants of aggregate labour market performance. The following sub-sections investigate whether this is the case.

Table 1.3. **The NAIRU has declined in a majority of countries**
OECD estimates of the structural rate of unemployment[a] in selected countries[b], 1991 and 2001

	1991	2001	1991-2001 change
Falling NAIRU average 1991 = 8.4			
Ireland	14.3	6.4	−7.9
Netherlands	7.1	4.0	−3.1
United Kingdom	8.2	5.5	−2.6
Denmark	7.3	4.9	−2.4
Spain	13.4	11.5	−1.9
Canada	8.8	6.9	−1.9
Belgium	8.8	7.2	−1.6
New Zealand	7.0	5.4	−1.5
Norway	4.9	3.6	−1.4
Portugal	4.7	3.8	−1.0
Australia	6.8	6.2	−0.7
France	9.7	9.3	−0.4
Stable NAIRU average 1991 = 5.3			
United States	5.4	5.1	−0.2
Italy	9.3	9.2	−0.1
Switzerland	1.7	1.8	0.0
Austria	4.8	4.9	0.1
Rising NAIRU average 1991 = 5.1			
Germany	6.7	7.3	0.6
Greece	8.3	9.8	1.5
Japan	2.4	3.9	1.5
Finland	6.8	8.6	1.8
Iceland	1.5	3.5	2.0
Euro zone[c]	8.6	8.3	−0.3
OECD[d]	6.3	6.1	−0.2

a) The structural rate of unemployment is the OECD's estimate of the non-accelarating inflation rate of unemployment (NAIRU), which is estimated using a Kalman-filtering approach that embodies a reduced-form Phillips curve, as described in Richardson *et al.* (2000). The estimated levels of the NAIRU are subject to significant margins of error, but the margin is significantly less than what is obtained using standard univariate filtering techniques, such as the Hodrick-Prescott filter.
b) Countries ordered by 1991-2001 change in the NAIRU.
c) Labour-force weighted average of European countries.
d) Labour-force weighted average of countries shown.
Source: OECD Economic Outlook, No. 72, June 2002.

B. *Matching of unemployed with jobs shows little improvement*

For most countries, the Beveridge curves shifted rightwards until the 1980s, suggesting a growing mismatch between vacancies and those looking for work, as unemployment trended upwards from the lows recorded in the 1960s (see Box 1.1 for an explanation of the Beveridge curve). Chart 1.5 plots national unemployment and vacancy data from 1980 onwards, in order to assess whether OECD countries experienced a turn-around more recently, with their Beveridge Curves moving back to the left.[20] Such a reversal is visible at the beginning or middle of the 1980s for four countries: Canada, the Netherlands, Portugal, and the United States.[21] In New Zealand, Switzerland and Spain, conditions continued to worsen through the 1980s before beginning to improve towards the end of the 1990s. However, no improvement is evident for the majority of the countries shown, nor for the Euro area as a whole. Indeed, the Beveridge curve appears to have continued shifting in an adverse direction in a number of countries, including Austria,

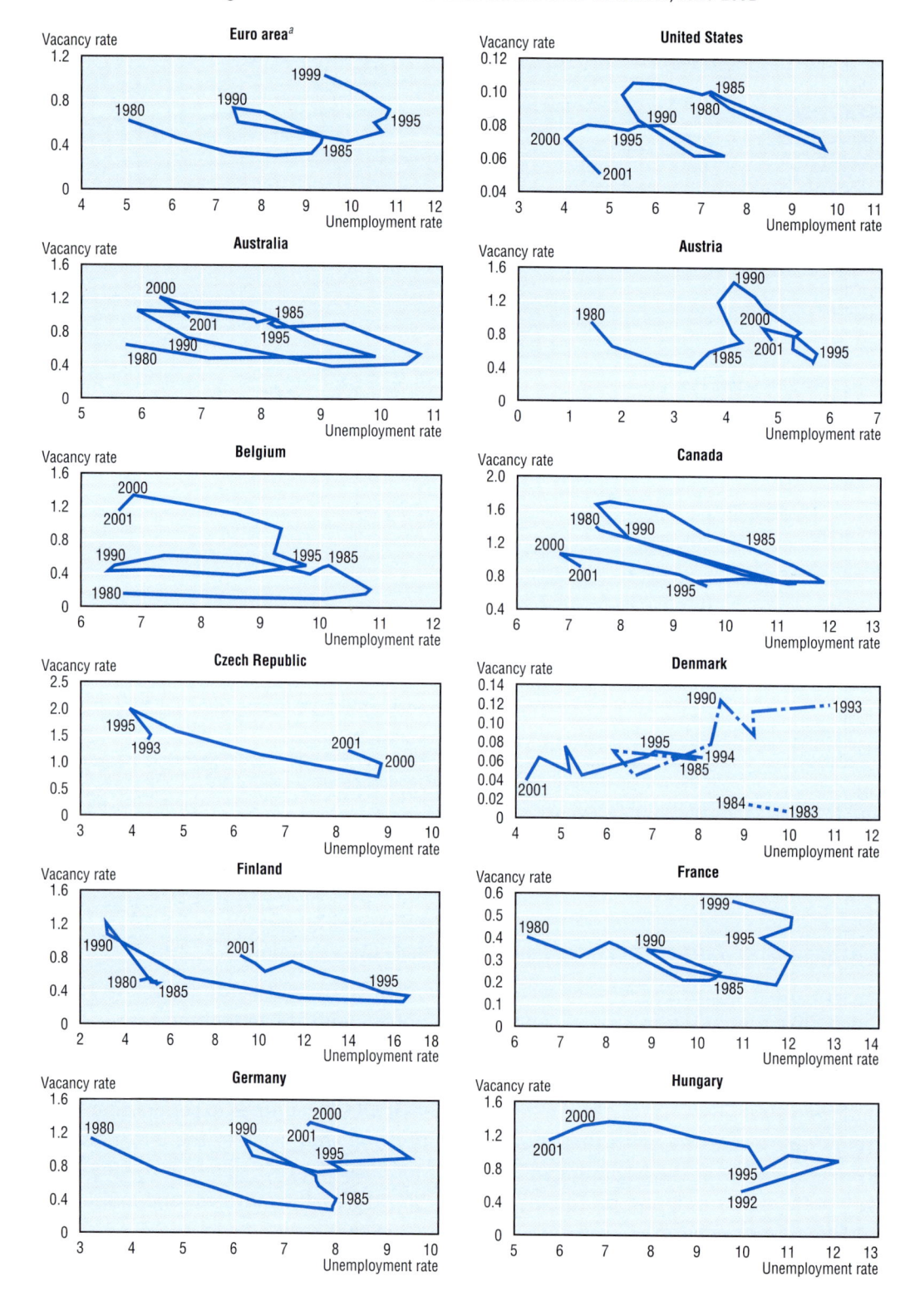

1. MORE AND BETTER JOBS? AGGREGATE PERFORMANCE DURING THE PAST DECADE

Chart 1.5. **Limited evidence for an improvement in the matching process**
Beveridge curves for the euro area and selected OECD countries, 1980-2001

1. MORE AND BETTER JOBS? AGGREGATE PERFORMANCE DURING THE PAST DECADE

Chart 1.5. **Limited evidence for an improvement in the matching process** (cont.)
Beveridge curves for the euro area and selected OECD countries, 1980-2001

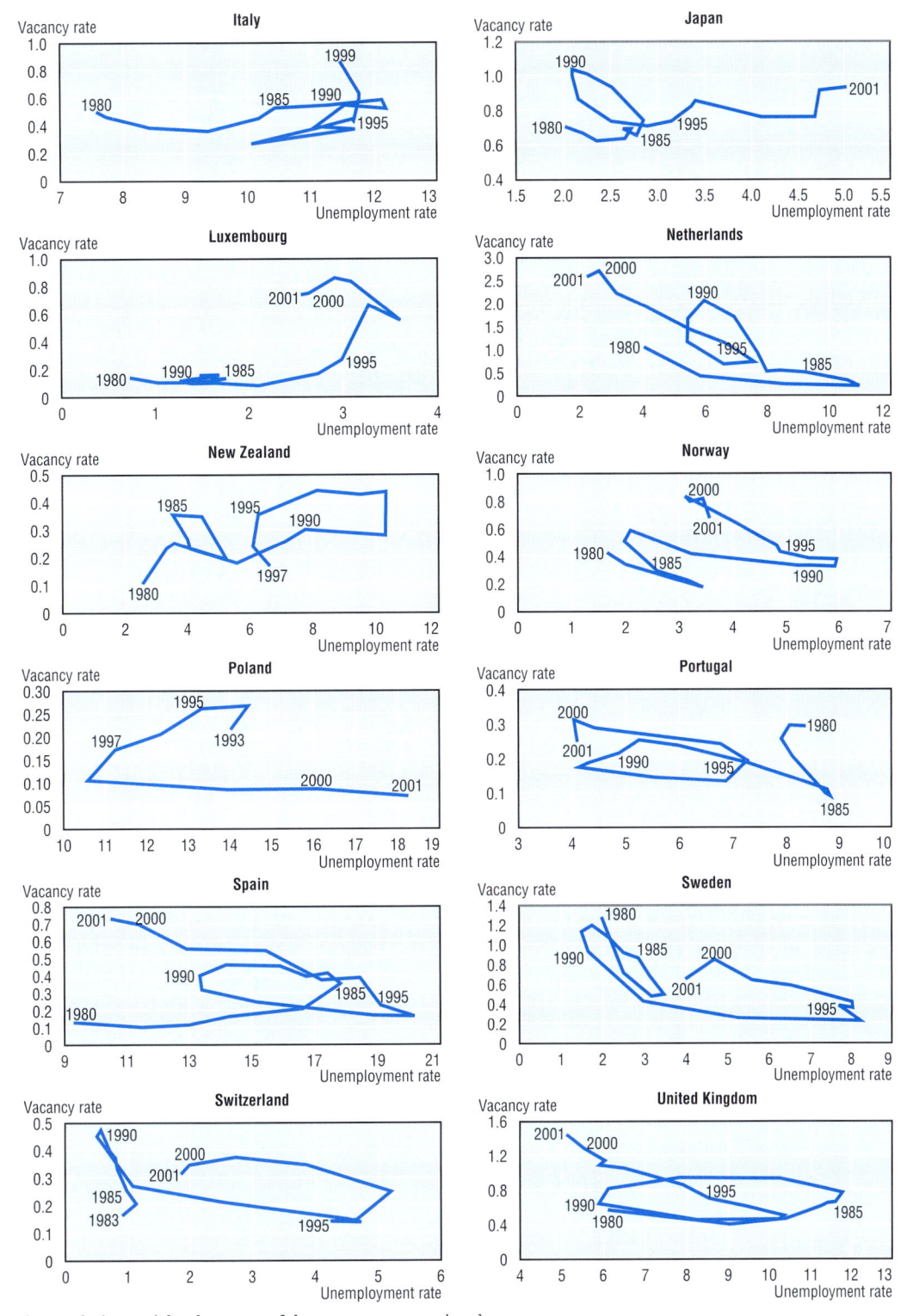

a) Population-weighted average of the euro area countries shown.

Source: OECD Analytical Database; Secretariat calculations based on data provided by the National Labour Market Authority for Denmark; by the *Istituto per lo Sviluppo della FOrmazione professionale dei Lavoratori* (ISFOL) for Italy; and Nickell *et al.* (2003) for France.

> Box 1.1. **What is the Beveridge curve?**
>
> The reallocation of workers normally takes place with the coexistence of unemployment and vacancies, reflecting the presence of frictions in the labour market and the fact that it takes time to achieve a satisfactory worker-job match. The plot of unemployment and vacancies is known as the Beveridge curve or U-V curve (see Blanchard and Diamond, 1989; and Nickell et al., 2003). The position of the Beveridge curve in U-V space influences the long-run equilibrium level of unemployment: a curve that lies far to the left (i.e. close to the vertical axis) indicates that unemployed workers are easily matched to vacant jobs, consistent with a low NAIRU, while a curve far to the right indicates severe mismatch and high equilibrium unemployment. However, limitations in the availability and quality of data on vacancies present considerable difficulties for conducting empirical analysis of these patterns.[a]
>
> As *unemployment* and vacancies change with fluctuations in aggregate activity, the position on the curve can indicate where the economy is in the business cycle. Recessions, for example, are generally times of high unemployment and few job vacancies, corresponding to points on the lower right end of the curve, while in expansions the opposite is true, corresponding to points on the higher left end. However, the Beveridge curve is not a straight diagonal line, but rather a loop that is traced out by the counter-clockwise movements of unemployment and vacancies over the business cycle, due to the fact that cyclical movements of unemployment typically lags those of vacancies.
>
> The Beveridge curve can also change its position in response to structural factors. A shift of the curve to the right would indicate an increase in equilibrium unemployment, while a movement to the left implies a fall in the equilibrium unemployment rate. Visual inspection of U-V pairs over the course of the past two decades, as shown in Chart 1.5, provides a first indication of whether the Beveridge curves have shifted. However, more formal statistical analysis is required to verify impressions based on "eye-balling" the data. Following Nickell et al. (2003), shifts in the Beveridge curve can be captured by the trend terms in a regression of the form:
>
> $$\ln u_t = \alpha_0 + \alpha_1 \ln u_{t-1} + \alpha_2 \ln v_t + \alpha_3 t + \alpha_4 t^2 + \alpha_5 t^3$$
>
> where u is the unemployment rate, v is the vacancy rate and t is a time trend. For example, a visual impression that the Beveridge curve has shifted to the left (right) would be confirmed if the regression estimates indicate a declining (increasing) time trend. Although the results are not reported here, this method was used to verify statements in the text distinguishing countries on the basis of movements of the U-V locus over the past two decades.
>
> a) Data on vacancies are not available for a considerable number of OECD countries and raise difficult issues of comparability when available (see also OECD 2001a). In the majority of the countries included in Chart 1.5, the vacancy data are based on the number of unfilled vacancies listed with public employment offices. However, Canada, the United States and Italy measure vacancies by the number of "help-wanted" advertisements that employers place in leading newspapers in a sample of large cities. Data for France refer to a labour shortage index.

Belgium, Germany, Japan, and Norway. Other countries are more difficult to classify, since it is not evident that cyclical and structural movements can be differentiated.

The simple regression method described in Box 1.1 suggests that in a modest number of OECD countries the matching process between the unemployed and vacancies became more efficient recently, with the timing of this improvement varying considerably across the countries considered. It is also plausible that these improvement represent, at least in part, the fruits of structural reforms (see Box 1.2 for a summary of the ways in which certain policies may be expected to influence the position of the Beveridge curve). By making out-of-work individuals more employable, these reforms help reduce labour shortages and thus decrease unemployment, without creating inflationary pressures.

> ### Box 1.2. **What factors shift the Beveridge curve?**
>
> - The *benefit system* directly affects the readiness of the unemployed to fill vacancies. Its most important aspects are the generosity and duration of benefits, the coverage, the strictness with which the system is operated, and the extent to which unemployed individuals receive adequate counselling and support from public employment services (see Nickell, 1997a; Nickell and Layard, 1997b; Nickell and Van Ours, 2000; Lalive *et al.*, 2002; and Chapter 4.
>
> - *Active labour market policies* (ALMPs) may also facilitate the matching between unemployed and vacancies. The purpose of ALMPs is to provide active assistance to the unemployed which will improve their chances of obtaining work (see Chapter 4). For example, the public employment service can help to bring job seekers together with employers posting suitable vacancies ("job brokerage"). Existing vacancies may require skills different from those that can be provided by the unemployed, necessitating training. Skills mismatch may be a particular problem for the long-term unemployed, whose generic skills may have deteriorated from lack of use and/or specific job skills may not be transferable to prospective employers. A similar mismatch may affect young people leaving school without the skills required of them by the labour market.
>
> - *Employment protection legislation* (EPL), which consists of the regulations determining the level of employment security, including rules for fixed-term contracts, temporary placement agencies and other forms of temporary employment, can affect matching efficiency. Strict EPL makes firms more cautious about filling vacancies which slows the speed at which the unemployed move into work, reducing the efficiency of job matching. Another complication is that some countries have retained strict EPL for regular employees while relaxing rules for temporary contracts. This combination has led to a rapid expansion of temporary jobs in some countries, which generates increased flows of new vacancies and newly unemployed workers, as temporary positions are regularly re-staffed (OECD, 2002a; Boeri *et al.*, 2000; Blanchard and Giavazzi, 2000; Saint-Paul, 1999).
>
> - *Limited geographical mobility* constitutes another barrier to matching job seekers with available jobs (Oswald, 1997). Locational preferences, home ownership or family responsibilities constrain the areas where many workers are prepared to work. This immobility explains the co-existence, often for long periods of time, of labour shortages in some regions of a country and high unemployment rates in others.

C. Wage setting has reflected greater restraint

The previous sub-section presented some evidence that structural reforms may have helped improve the matching between the unemployed and vacancies over the past decade in a few OECD countries, and thereby contribute to a better labour market performance. Another factor that may have lowered equilibrium unemployment rates is increased restraint in wage setting, particularly in countries where real wage growth previously had outpaced productivity growth. The institutional and policy factors that are likely to shift the Beveridge curve are also likely to have an impact on wage-setting behaviour, either directly or indirectly (i.e. through their effect on unemployment). Additionally, some features of wage-setting institutions affect wages directly, without having a direct effect on the matching process. These include unionisation, co-ordination in wage bargaining, minimum wages, labour taxation and the vigour of product market competition (see Box 1.3). This sub-section analyses data on real wage growth, productivity and unit labour costs, in order to assess whether diminished wage pressures in countries where the wage share had risen to very high levels have brought down the structural rate of unemployment.[22]

Box 1.3. **What influences wage setting?**

The institutional factors that improve the matching between job seekers and vacancies (Box 1.2) are also likely to influence wages. In addition to these policies, the wage-setting environment has an important role in shaping wage growth and therefore labour market performance.

- *Union bargaining power* is expected to exert upward pressure on wages, raising equilibrium unemployment. (Layard *et al.*, 1991). This effect is likely to be strengthened if monopoly power is present in product markets which leads to a significant price mark-up on production costs (Nicoletti *et al.*, 2001). However, the upward wage pressure exerted by unions may be offset where wage bargaining is *co-ordinated* across sectors or firms. Wage negotiations may be considered to be co-ordinated if the parties take into account the consequences of any wage settlement on the rest of the economy. Co-ordination can be achieved through centralization of bargaining at the national level, but centralization is not a necessary condition. Co-ordination can also be achieved where wages are negotiated at the industry level or enterprise level, through the presence of co-ordinating institutions, such as national trade union congresses and employers' federations, which assist bargainers to act in concert (Ochel, 2000).

- Union power can also raise equilibrium unemployment if it compresses relative wages too much, as can *statutory minimum wages* in cases where they are set too high. For example, a uniform national pay scale may result in high unemployment in regions where productivity lags. Allowing for decentralised wage bargaining might reduce the large regional imbalances that are characteristic of many European countries, since setting wages according to productivity would generate incentives for job creation in lagging regions and for unemployed workers to migrate to high-wage regions (OECD, 1997). Similar problems will arise if wage differentials by skill level are compressed to the point that employers are reluctant to hire the least skilled workers. Special minimum wages for low-productivity workers, such as school leavers, can minimize this latter problem (OECD, 1998a; Dolado *et al.*, 1996).

Box 1.3. **What influences wage setting?** *(cont.)*

- *Taxes on labour* may also raise equilibrium unemployment. The taxes that most matter for employment are those that form a "wedge" between the real product wage (labour costs per employee normalised on the output price) and the real consumption wage (after-tax pay normalised on the consumer price index), namely, payroll taxes, income taxes and consumption taxes. Economic theory indicates that the impact of such a tax wedge depends on the extent to which the tax is shifted onto wages which, in turn, depend on many, potentially offsetting factors (*e.g.* whether there is a minimum wage and the organisation of wage bargaining). The empirical literature studying the impact of labour taxation on equilibrium unemployment has reported mixed results. However, several recent studies suggest that these taxes raise unemployment, with the size of this effect depending on national wage-setting institutions: Daveri and Tabellini (2000) and Nickell *et al.* (2003) find that employment taxes raise equilibrium unemployment, but that this effect is smaller in economies with co-ordinated wage bargaining.[a] Put somewhat differently, labour taxation may have had a particularly harmful effect on unemployment in Belgium, France, Germany, Italy, the Netherlands (before the Wassenaar agreement)[b] and Spain, while taxation had less effect in raising unemployment in the Nordic countries, such as Finland, Norway and Sweden, where wage bargaining was co-ordinated so as to reduce the adverse impact on employment.

- The concept of *real wage resistance* is useful for understanding the impact of wage-bargaining structures on the equilibrium rate of unemployment and its evolution. The idea is that workers may attempt to sustain recent rates of real wage growth, even when the rate consistent with stable employment drops due to a negative shock (*e.g.* a rise in the price of oil, a slowdown of the growth of productivity, a rise in real interest rates, an increase in the tax wedge or a worsening of the terms of trade). In the presence of real wage resistance, real labour costs rise in the aftermath of these shocks because employers are not able to shift any of the burden onto employees by reducing the rate of wage growth. This may be particularly likely to occur in highly unionised environments or where wages are automatically linked with a retail price index. In some theoretical models, real wage resistance only has a *temporary* effect on unemployment, because the initial increase in unemployment eventually pushes wages down enough that labour costs return to their original level. However, Mortensen and Pissarides (1999) show that an increase in payroll taxes can lead to a *permanent* increase in equilibrium unemployment in a general equilibrium model of bilateral search.

a) The Nickell *et al.* (2003) estimates suggests that a 10 percentage point increase in the employment tax rate leads to around a 1.5 percentage point rise in unemployment in the long run at average levels of co-ordination. These recent findings represent a turnaround from previous research by Nickell and a range of co-authors, where the effects of employment taxes were found to be non-existent or fairly slight (see Bean *et al.*, 1986; Layard *et al.*, 1991; and Nickell and Layard, 1999).

b) Under the tripartite Wassenaar agreement, which was signed in 1982, Dutch unions gave up price indexation of wages and committed themselves to moderate future wage claims in exchange for a series of commitments by the employers' federation and the government, including working-time reductions and improved conditions for part-time workers. Nickell and Van Ours (2000) discuss the so-called "Dutch miracle" after Wassenaar.

Real wage growth in the business sector has been moderate in relation to productivity growth during the 1990s, as reflected in a falling wage share in a majority of countries for which data are available (Annex Table 1.A1.1). The decline in the wage

Chart 1.6. **Productivity has grown more rapidly than real labour costs, favouring employment growth**

Growth in real labour costs, labour productivity and employment, 1970-2001
Index 1970 = 100

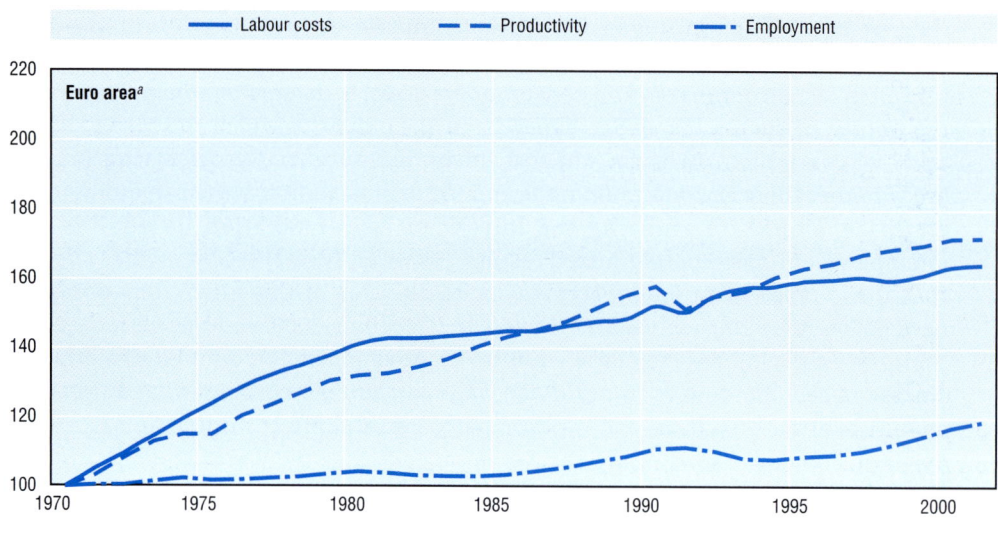

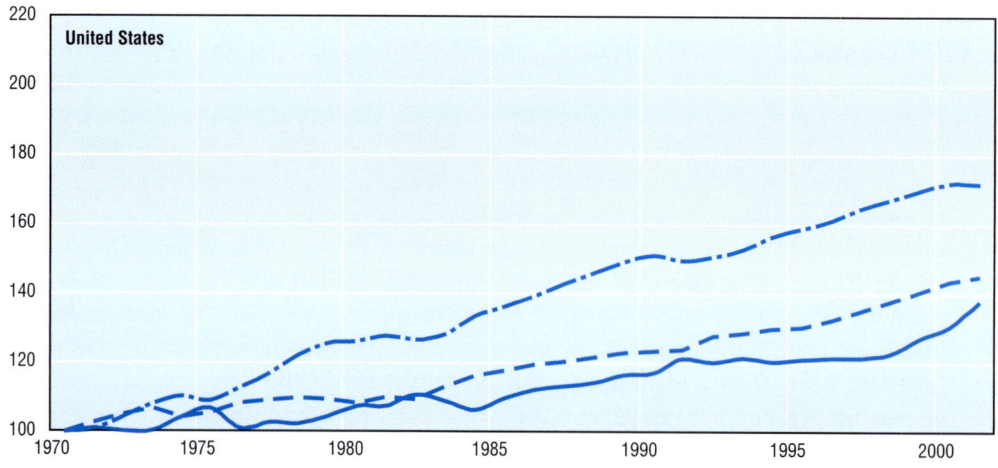

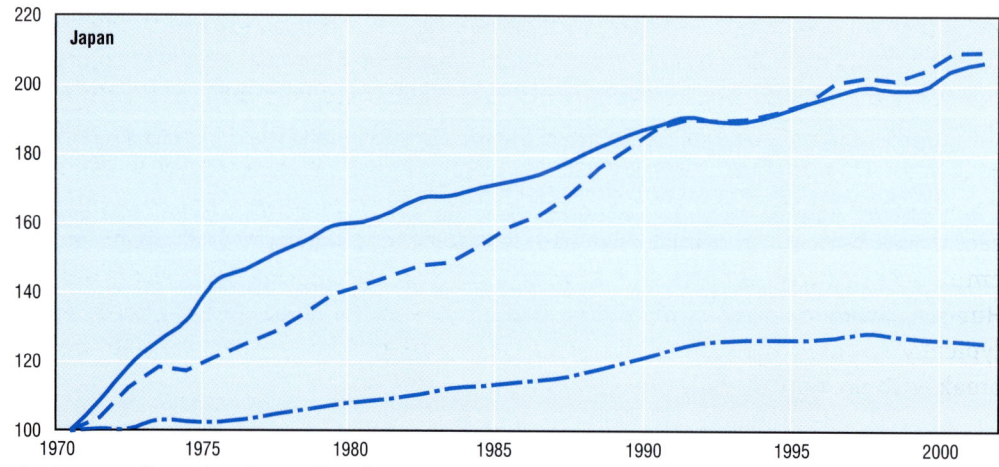

a) The European figures have been adjusted to remove the impact of German reunification.
Source: OECD Economic Outlook, No. 72, June 2002.

share between 1990 and 2002 was especially large in Finland and Korea, where it exceeded 10 percentage points, and also sizeable in Australia, France, Ireland, Italy, Sweden. Declines in the wage share were more pronounced in the first half of the 1990s, when high levels of labour market slack reinforced the effect of policy initiatives to restrain wage growth. As labour markets tightened in the second half of the decade, the picture became more mixed, with the wage share rising in nearly as many countries as where it fell. Norway and the United Kingdom experienced particularly sharp increases in the wage share between 1995 and 2002 (11 and 8 percentage points, respectively).

From the standpoint of economic efficiency, real wage restraint is desirable only if real wages have risen faster than productivity in the past, such that excessive wage levels have become a barrier to job creation. The data presented in Annex Table 1.A1.1 show that wage shares rose sharply in many OECD countries during the 1970s (with the notable exception of the United States), but the wage share reversed course and began to fall during the 1980s in many of these countries.[23] However, wages are only one component of *total real labour cost* per employee. If the share of non-wage costs in total compensation should increase, trends in the wage share will overstate the extent of wage restraint. Chart 1.6 shows that total real labour costs outpaced gains in labour productivity during the 1970s in the Euro area and Japan, but that productivity growth caught up with labour costs during the 1980s and even moved ahead of labour costs during the 1990s in the Euro area. By contrast, labour productivity growth outpaced the growth in total labour costs in the United States throughout the past two decades, perhaps contributing to the relatively stronger employment growth in that country, but also to the relative stagnation in compensation levels (Mishel *et al.*, 2003). Labour costs (and wage) growth accelerated markedly in the United States after 1995, in marked contrast to the deceleration observed in the Euro area. The recent shift toward slower growth in real labour costs was also quite pronounced in Japan, Korea and Turkey (see Annex Table 1.A1.2).

D. *Increased dynamism for private sector employment growth*

If wage setting has become more responsive to market conditions, this change should be particularly important for facilitating employment growth in the business sector. Indeed, the diagnosis of the causes of high unemployment that was put forward in the *OECD Jobs Study* (OECD, 1994b) emphasised the fact that net job growth in the business sector had been weak, or even negative, in a significant number of OECD countries in the 1970s and 1980s. Chart 1.7 shows that the 1990s were very different, with most of the employment gains having occurred in the private sector in the majority of OECD countries. This was the case in most EU countries, where the contrast with previous decades (particularly the 1970s) is striking.[24] Even as employment growth in the private sector has been more robust over the past decade, significant reductions in public employment have occurred in several European countries, including Germany, Hungary, Sweden and the United Kingdom. Private sector employment growth was also typically stronger than its public sector counterpart outside of Europe, although the break with previous decades tended to be less pronounced.

Chart 1.7. **Business sector employment shows dynamism**
Total employment growth in the public and private sectors, 1991-2001[a, b]
Percentage change

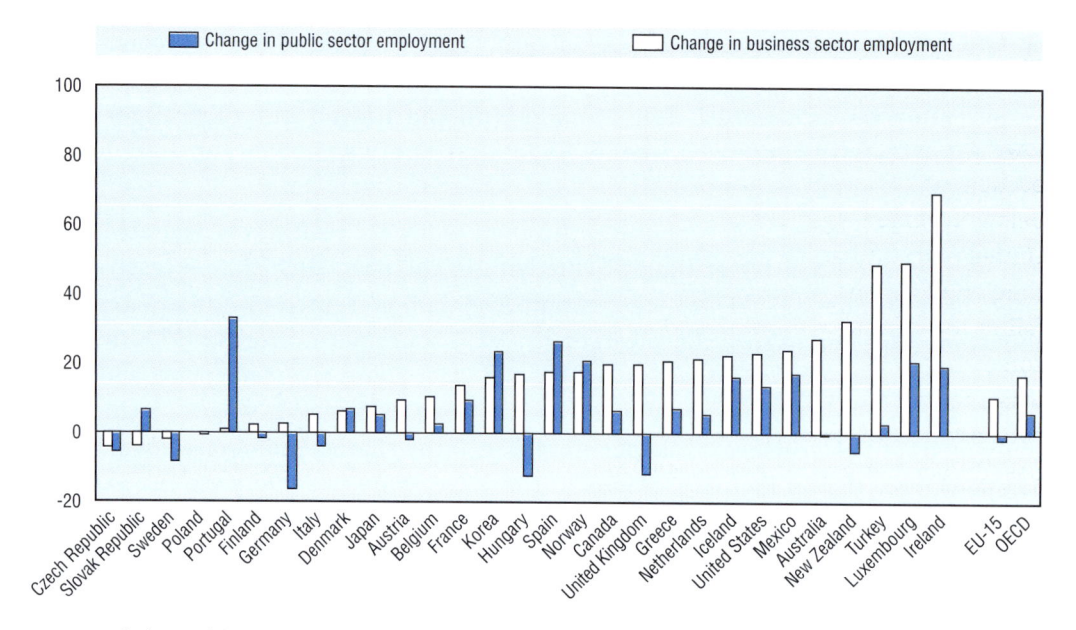

OECD: Population-weighted average of countries shown.
a) Countries in ascending order by growth in business sector employment.
b) 1993-2001 for the Czech Republic and Poland; 1994-2001 for Hungary and the Slovak Republic.
Source: OECD Economic Outlook, No. 72, June 2002.

E. Overall assessment of structural progress

The evidence considered in this section is somewhat mixed, but overall suggests that an important share of the improvement in labour market performance over the past decade is structural and, hence, potentially sustainable. The strongest evidence of structural progress is provided by the tendency for estimates of the NAIRU to fall, as well as the concordance of this trend with the evidence that the upward pressure on wages has eased and job growth in the private business sector has become more dynamic. By contrast, the analysis of the Beveridge curves provided less support for structural progress, suggesting that the matching of job seekers to job vacancies has become more efficient in only a few countries (although the problematic nature of job vacancies data should be born in mind when weighing this evidence).

3. More and better jobs?

Has the improvement in employment performance documented above been accompanied by similar progress with improving job quality? No consensus exists on this question. Some analysts have emphasised that the tight labour markets of the late 1990s were good for job quality and were especially beneficial for less advantaged groups in the labour force (Mishel *et al.*, 2003), but others have raised concerns that the job-rich growth achieved in some countries during the 1990s was characterised by a proliferation of "low-quality" jobs (Gregg and Wadsworth, 2000). In order to shed light on this question, this section assembles evidence on diverse aspects of job quality and how they evolved during the past decade: the incidence of low-paid employment and overall earnings inequality;

the incidence of dangerous and high-stress jobs; the incidence of part-time and temporary work; and the extent of employment insecurity.

A. Do new jobs pay well?

The number of high-paid jobs has grown relatively rapidly...

Contrary to the common impression that recent job growth has been concentrated in low-paying service jobs, employment has tended to grow more rapidly in industries and occupations that pay relatively well, than in industries and occupations with average or below-average wages. This pattern holds for both the EU countries as a group and the United States (Chart 1.8).[25] Keating (2003) finds a similar pattern in Australia, where full-time employment grew strongly in the 1990s in the most highly skilled occupations, and fell in the middle and lower skilled occupations.[26] However, several EU countries deviate somewhat from this general pattern. In Portugal, employment growth over the past decade was the strongest for the medium-paid category and employment in the high-paid category fell, while in the Netherlands and the United Kingdom job creation during the past decade has been characterised by relatively strong growth in low-paying jobs.

There is no evident relationship between the strength of overall employment growth in a country and the share of low-paid jobs in employment growth. In particular, job growth

Chart 1.8. Growth in high-paid jobs has been relatively strong
Employment growth by wage level[a] in Europe and the United States, 1993-2001[b]
Index (1993 = 100)

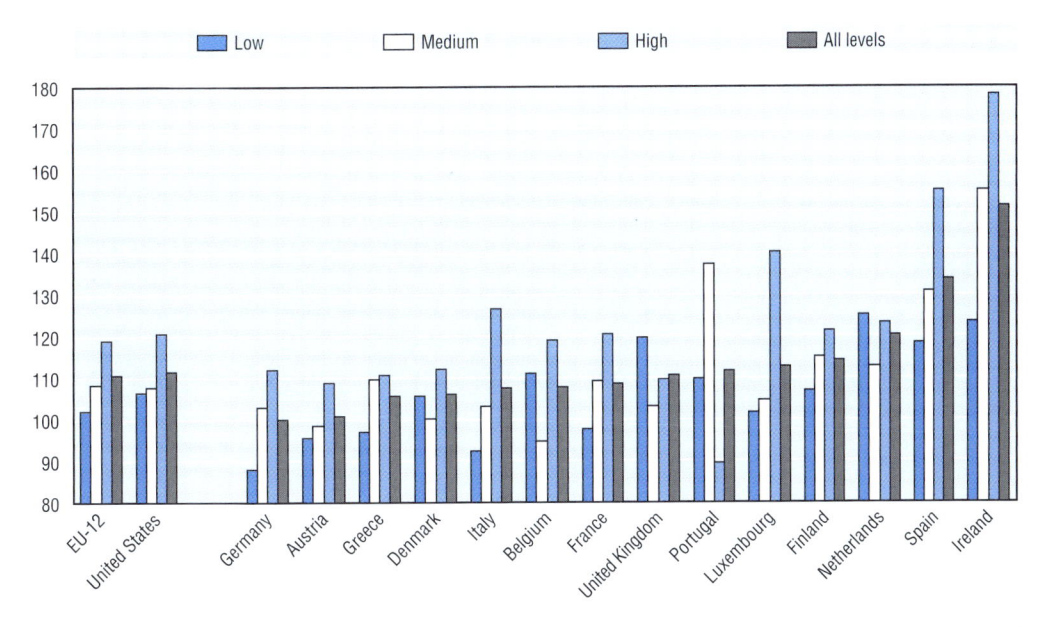

a) For each country, jobs (*i.e.* employment in 76 industry/occupation cells) are ranked on the basis of average hourly earnings in 1996 and then placed into three groups of equal size in terms of employment shares. The growth in employment in the same jobs at each level is then calculated.
b) The EU-12 average excludes Austria and Finland; 1995-2001 for Austria; 1997-2001 for Finland; 1993-1999 for the United States.
Source: Secretariat calculations based on the European Union Labour Force Survey and the European Community Household Panel for EU countries and on data from the Current Population Survey (Outgoing Rotation Group file) for the United States.

was relatively strong in high-paying industries and occupations in the United States and the two EU countries with the fastest employment growth, Ireland and Spain. These findings are confirmed by macroeconomic analysis of employment and productivity growth (see Box 1.4).

... but earnings inequality has also tended to increase

Neither the evidence on the sectoral and occupational mix of recent job growth nor the evidence on recent productivity growth confirms fears that structural policies raising employment rates resulted principally in the creation of low-pay/low-productivity jobs. Nonetheless, it is still possible that policies designed to increase labour market "flexibility" – including flexibility in setting relative wages – may have caused earnings inequality to grow along with employment. Recent trends in overall earnings distributions provide some support

---

Box 1.4. Employment and productivity growth: a macroeconomic trade-off?

Some of the policy reforms intended to increase employment rates (*e.g.* those advocated in the OECD, 1994a) influence labour supply and demand, and wage bargaining in ways that may tend to lower average wages or increase wage inequality. For example, activation measures for persons on unemployment and other benefits are intended to increase aggregate labour supply. These and other supply-side measures will tend to depress average wages by shifting the economy down the labour demand curve, unless they are accompanied by a compensating rightward shift of the labour demand curve. Since labour force entrants mobilised by these policies will tend to be relatively low skilled, wage inequality may also increase as many in this group will become employed at a wage substantially below the mean wage, at least initially. Complementary reforms intended to assure adequate demand could reinforce these impacts on the wage structure. For example, decentralisation of wage bargaining and trimming back of high minimum wages may tend to lower wages, at least in the lower ranges of the earnings distribution. Similarly, relaxing employment protection legislation and regulations limiting product market competition may encourage expansion of low-productivity/low-pay jobs in services (*e.g.* in retail trade, lodging and food services). However, offsetting effects may also be in play. For example, greater flexibility of labour and product markets could stimulate innovation and productivity growth, creating the economic conditions for increasing wages and living standards (Nicoletti *et al.*, 2001).

Chart 1.9 shows that high employment growth and strong growth in labour productivity were compatible during the past decade, as illustrated by Ireland. Nonetheless, the cross-country correlation between the increase in the employment to population ratio during the 1990s and the increase in labour productivity is weakly negative, suggesting that a weak trade-off may exist between gains in employment and productivity.

There may be even less of a trade-off between raising employment rates and technological progress, as proxied by multi-factor productivity (MFP) growth. The data presented in Annex Table 1.A1.3 show that Australia, Ireland, New Zealand and Norway all experienced simultaneous accelerations in employment growth and MFP in the 1990s. However, MFP growth slowed in a similar number of countries where employment growth accelerated.

Chart 1.9. **Rising employment is compatible with strong productivity growth**
Trend series, average annual percentage change, 1990-2000

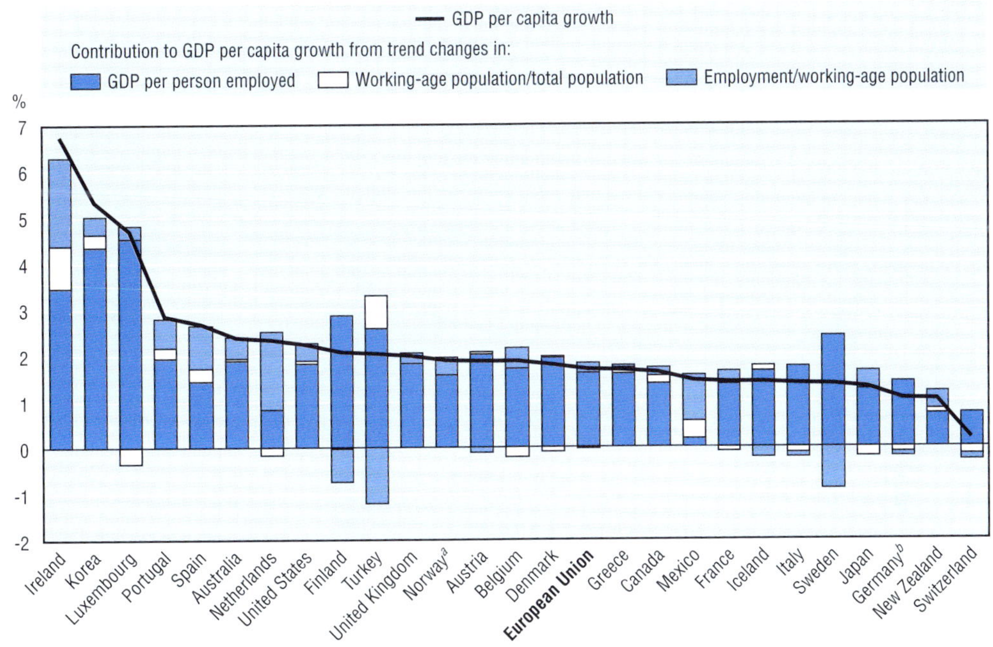

— GDP per capita growth

Contribution to GDP per capita growth from trend changes in:
GDP per person employed   Working-age population/total population   Employment/working-age population

a) Mainland only.
b) 1991-2000.
Source: OECD (2003), *The Sources of Economic Growth in OECD countries*, Paris.

for this argument in some countries (Chart 1.10). For example, wage dispersion has increased steadily since the 1980s in the United Kingdom, where wage setting became considerably more decentralised and market driven over the past two decades. Similarly, wage dispersion has increased strongly over the past two decades in the United States, despite starting from an already high level, and more recently (albeit from a lower initial level) in Central European economies. Earnings inequality has also tended to increase in Australia and New Zealand, and in the Netherlands, albeit only since the mid-1990s. On the other hand, wage inequality remained roughly stable, and often quite low, in many EU countries and Japan.

An increase in overall earnings dispersion probably raises greater social concerns if it is associated with an increase in the share of the workforce earning substantially less than does a typical worker. Data on the proportion of workers in low-paid employment (defined as earning less than two-thirds of the median wage) suggest that the incidence of low pay has shown, at most, a weak tendency to rise during the past decade (Annex Chart 1.A1.1). The incidence of low-paid employment increased strongly in the United States and the United Kingdom in the 1980s, but tended to stabilise more recently – even showing some slight reversal during the second half of the 1990s, as wages rose in response to very tight labour markets. The incidence of low pay also rose in the Netherlands and in several Central European economies. For the latter, the rise probably reflected the continuing transition from the compressed wage structures of the central planning era to a market-driven wage structure. The incidence of low-paid employment tended to fall in Japan and Germany, which also experienced rather weak employment growth, while not showing any clear trend in the other OECD countries for which data are available.

1. MORE AND BETTER JOBS? AGGREGATE PERFORMANCE DURING THE PAST DECADE

Chart 1.10. **Earnings inequality has tended to increase in some countries**
Trends in wage rate dispersion,[a] 1979-2001[b]

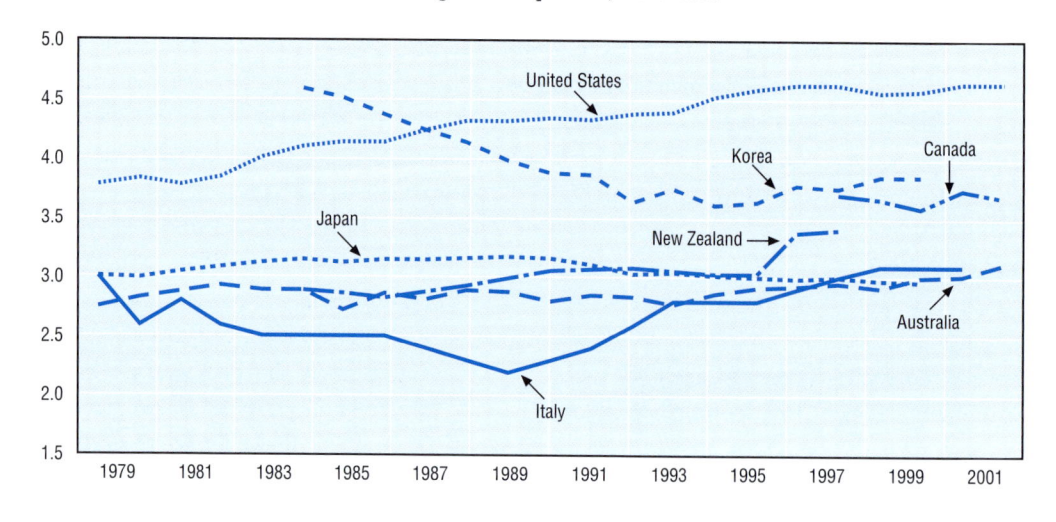

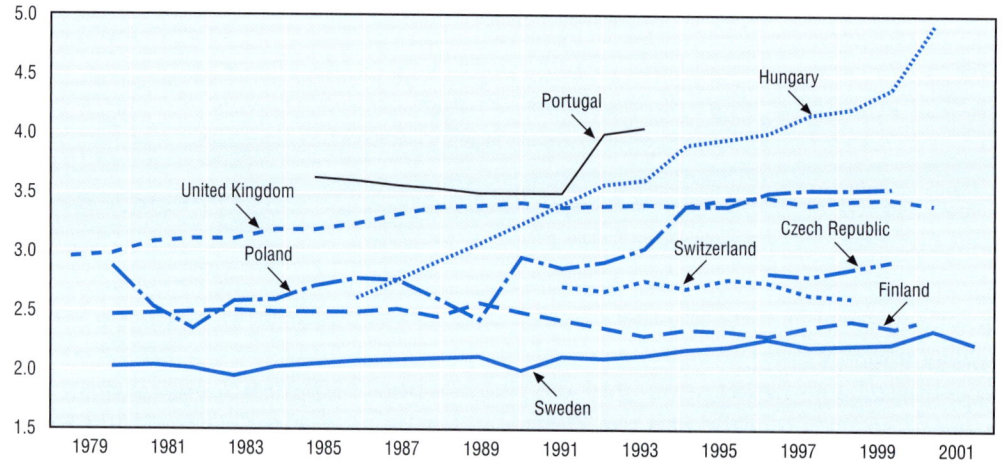

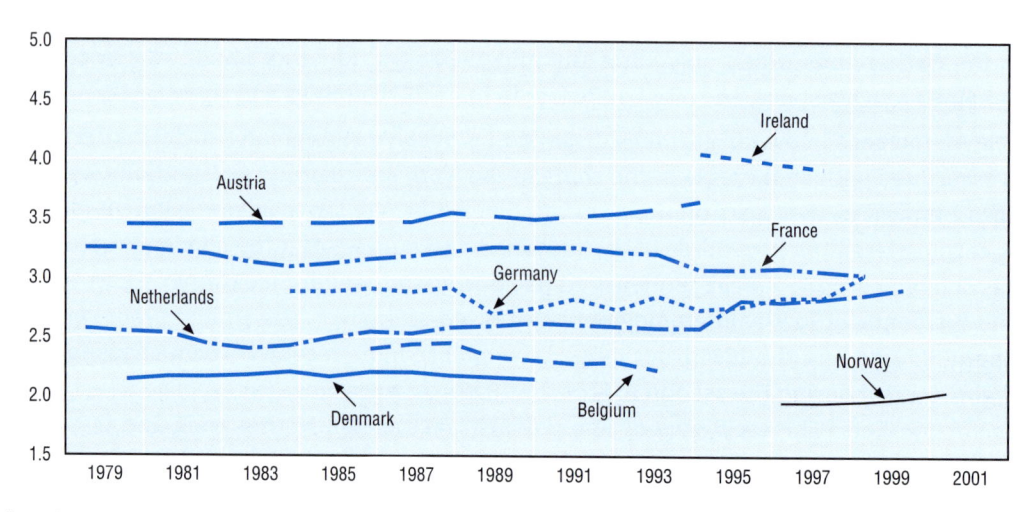

a) D9/D1 ratio, defined as the ratio of gross wage rates at the breakpoint between the ninth and the tenth deciles and the breakpoint between the first and second deciles, except that the data for France and Italy refer to net wages.
b) The data have been interpolated for missing years for Austria, Canada, Finland, Hungary, Ireland, New Zealand and Portugal.
Source: OECD database on Earnings.

To conclude, there is some evidence to support the view that policies and institutions that facilitated strong growth in employment have been accompanied by a tendency for wage inequality to increase. However, it is less clear that the incidence of low-paid employment has risen and it is not the case that the rise in employment has happened mainly in low-paying occupations and industries, or has been detrimental to productivity growth. Furthermore, the welfare implications of increases in wage inequality will be less controversial to the extent that they are associated with increased employment opportunities for low-skill individuals and do not result in a corresponding widening of income inequality.

B. Long hours and headaches: some indicators of working conditions

In the past few years, a renewed interest in working conditions has emerged. This includes concerns that changes in work practices, more flexible work arrangements, atypical contracts and work up-skilling may be degrading certain aspects of the quality of working life (Green *et al.*, 2002; and Green, 2002). In order to investigate changes in working conditions over the past decade, this section analyses data from the European Survey of Working Conditions (ESWC) for the 15 EU countries in 1990, 1995 and 2000. In the ESWC, workers are asked about various aspects of their work environment, including the nature of the tasks performed, health problems and the degree of job autonomy. These and similar "subjective" indicators of working conditions provide a portrait of how workers' perceptions of their jobs evolved during the past decade, but differences in responses over time or across workforce groups or countries may not represent real differences in objective conditions.

Some work-related health problems such as physical hazards and stress are on the rise...

The ESWC data provide a mixed picture of how health risks at work evolved during the past decade. When asked directly, a declining share of workers reported that their jobs posed a risk to their health or safety: the share reporting exposure to such risks fell about 3 percentage points between 1990 and 2000 (Chart 1.11, Panel A). However, workers' responses to separate and more detailed questions about specific hazardous conditions or health problems related to work suggested a worsening situation (Chart 1.11, Panel B).[27] Similarly, increasing numbers of workers report work-related health problems, both overall and with respect to a number of specific conditions including headaches, backaches, muscular pains in the neck and shoulders, overall fatigue and stress. Finally, 42% of the workers consider their jobs as non-sustainable, stating that they do not think they will be able to or want to do the same job when they are 60 years old.

The nature of the tasks carried out on the job also influences the quality of working life. For example, if a job involves frequent repetition of the same short tasks, working at high speed, respecting tight deadlines or working long hours, high stress levels may result. Again, the ESWC data provide a mixed picture of how these aspects of work have evolved. In 2000, 31% of workers reported performing repetitive movements on a continuous basis, slightly lower than in 1995. In contrast, work intensity appears to have increased during the past decade: in 2000, 56% of respondents said that they worked at "very high speed," up from 48% in 1990, and 60% said that they were working to "tight deadlines," up 10 percentage points (Chart 1.11, Panel C). On a more positive note, workers also reported increased autonomy on their jobs (Chart 1.11, Panel D).

1. MORE AND BETTER JOBS? AGGREGATE PERFORMANCE DURING THE PAST DECADE

Chart 1.11. **Physical hazards and stress are on the rise**
Selected working conditions in Europe,[a] 1990-2001

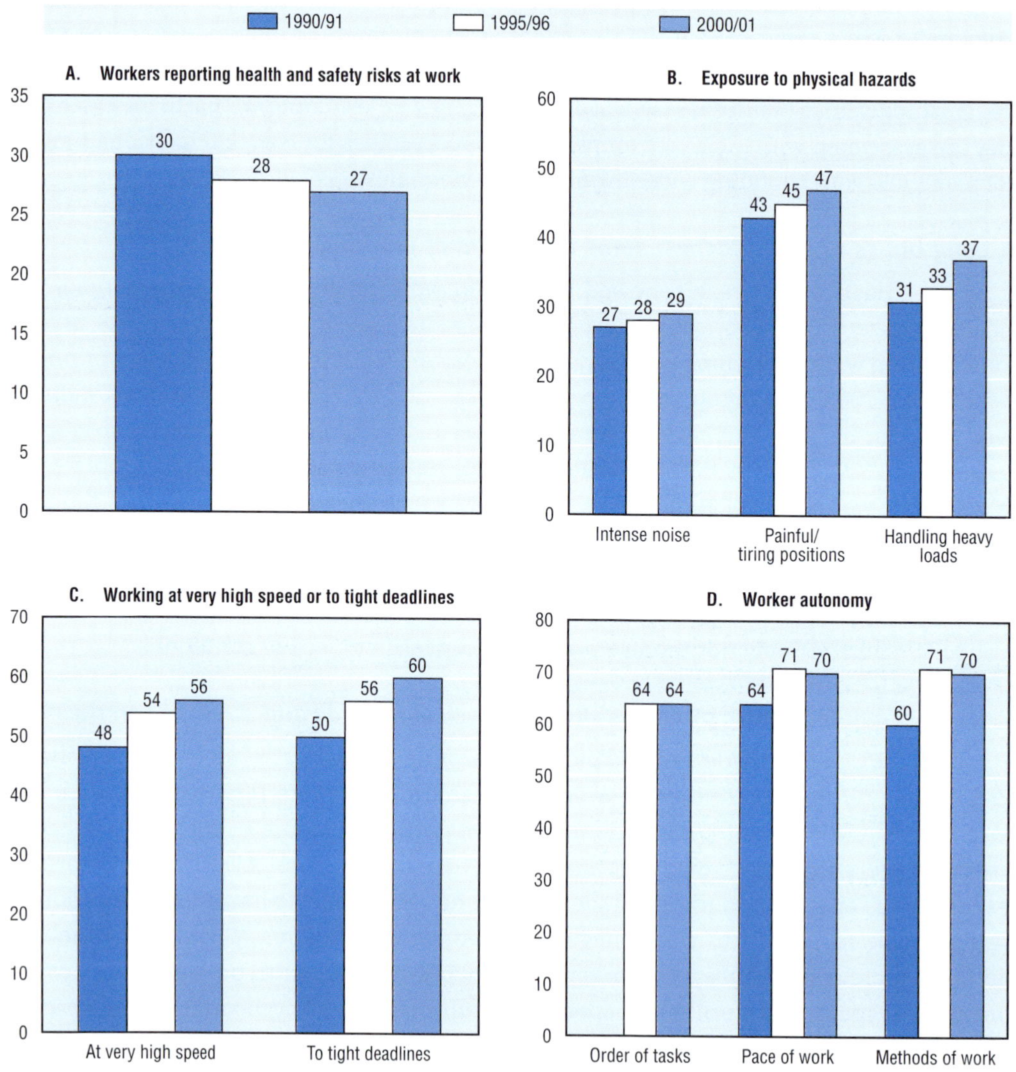

■ 1990/91   □ 1995/96   ■ 2000/01

A. Workers reporting health and safety risks at work
- 1990/91: 30
- 1995/96: 28
- 2000/01: 27

B. Exposure to physical hazards
- Intense noise: 27, 28, 29
- Painful/tiring positions: 43, 45, 47
- Handling heavy loads: 31, 33, 37

C. Working at very high speed or to tight deadlines
- At very high speed: 48, 54, 56
- To tight deadlines: 50, 56, 60

D. Worker autonomy
- Order of tasks: 64, 64, 64
- Pace of work: 64, 71, 70
- Methods of work: 60, 71, 70

a) Population-weighted averages for Austria, Belgium, Denmark, Finland, France, Germany, Greece, Ireland, Italy, Luxembourg, the Netherlands, Portugal, Spain, Sweden and the United Kingdom.
Source: European Survey on Working Conditions, waves 1 to 3 (1990/91, 1995/96 and 2000).

... and a growing number of individuals work very long hours in some countries

Long hours of work can be onerous and may place a worker's health at risk or interfere with family commitments (see Box 1.5). While there has been a century long trend towards a shorter workweek, this historic trend has slowed in recent decades and appears to have stopped in a few countries (OECD, 1998a). The most typical weekly schedule is around 38 hours, but the proportion of individuals working more than 45 hours per week is quite large, exceeding 40% of working men in Greece, Iceland, and the United Kingdom (Chart 1.12). The share of men working very long hours appears to have increased over the past decade in nearly half of the OECD countries for which data are available. The largest increases in the share of men working 45 or more hours per week occurred in Iceland, Denmark, Finland and

Belgium. Working very long hours is a little less frequent for women than for men. However, the share of women working very long hours also increased over the past decade in some countries including, notably, Denmark, Finland, Iceland and the United Kingdom.

To conclude, although working conditions overall may seem to have improved slightly over the past decade, some hazards or stress-related illnesses are reported to be more common now than they were in 1990. The nature of tasks carried out, another indicator of job quality, also presents a mixed picture, with work intensity on the rise but autonomy also increasing. Overall, there does not seem to be clear evidence of an overall shift towards worse working conditions.

Chart 1.12. **A growing number of people work very long hours in some countries**
Individuals working 45 hours and over per week,[a] 1991 and 2001

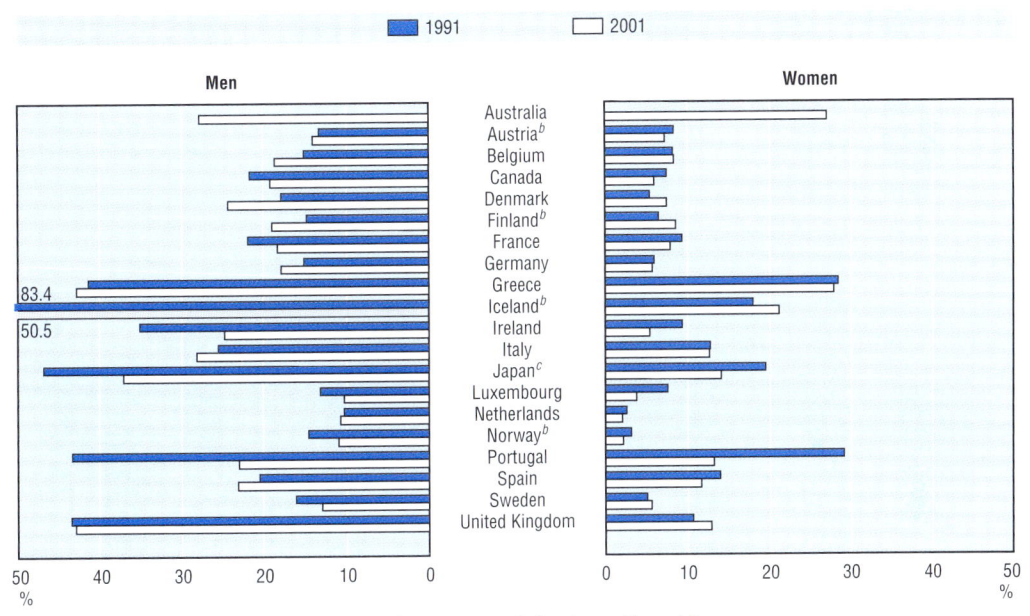

a) Usual weekly hours, except actual hours in survey week for Australia and Japan.
b) Data refer to 1995 instead of 1991.
c) Data refer to 49+ hours.
Source: OECD database on Usual Hours Worked.

Box 1.5. **Consequences of long hours on health and life quality**

Chart 1.13 shows the relationship between two stress factors – long work hours and an intense work pace – and two adverse consequences that potentially could result from these working conditions – an increase in the number of stress-related health problems and self-assessed conflict between working hours and family or social obligations. Panel A confirms that both increased working hours and an increasingly intense pace of work are associated with an increase in the number of stress-related health problems that workers experience and identify as being related to their jobs. Similarly, Panel B documents that an intense work pace and long hours are also associated with an increased level of the perceived conflict between work on the one hand and family and social life on the other.

1. MORE AND BETTER JOBS? AGGREGATE PERFORMANCE DURING THE PAST DECADE

Chart 1.13. **Long hours and intense work disrupt family life and cause stress**
Life quality consequences of long hours and intense work, 2000/2001
Percentage of dependent employees in the identified group[a]

A. Number of stress-related symptoms[b] that workers attribute to their jobs by weekly hours and intensity of work

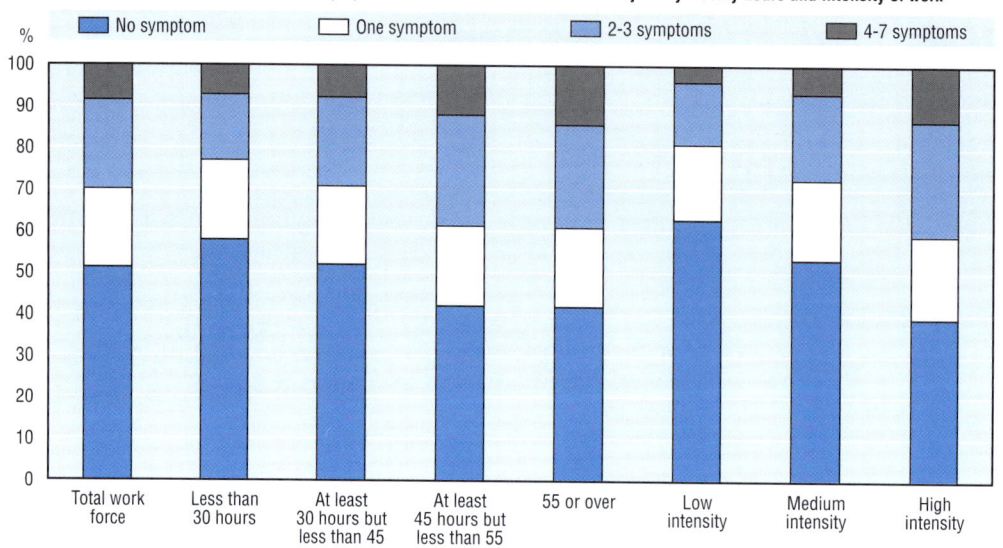

B. Conflict between working hours and family or social commitments by weekly hours and intensity of work

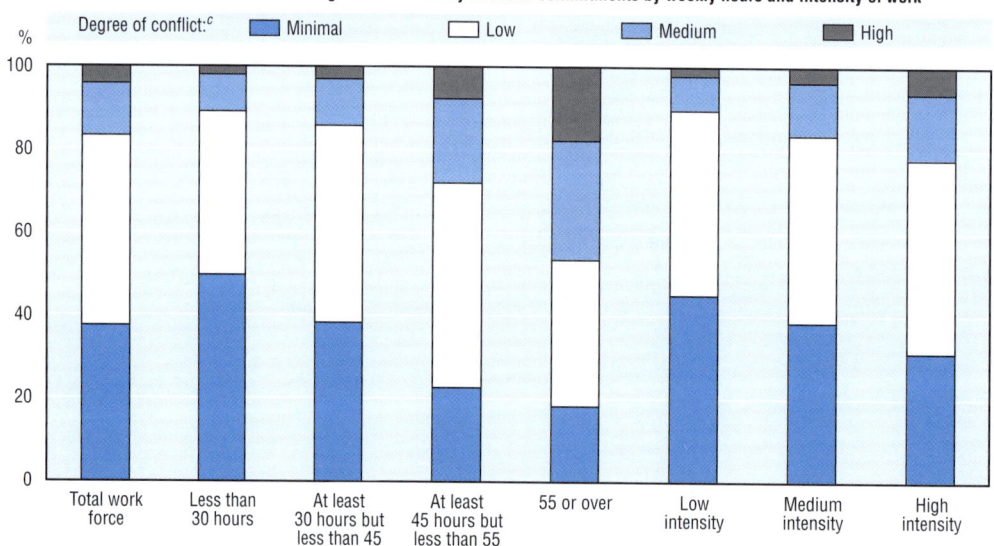

a) Unweighted averages for 15 European countries (Austria, Belgium, Denmark, Finland, France, Germany, Greece, Ireland, Italy, Luxembourg, the Netherlands, Portugal, Spain, Sweden and the United Kingdom).
b) Based on workers responses to question 35, which asks them to identify health problems caused by their jobs. Among a larger number of symptoms, seven were selected as being closely associated with stress: headaches, stomach ache, muscular pains in shoulders and neck, stress, overall fatigue, sleeping problems and anxiety.
c) The classification by degree of conflict is based on question 20 which asks workers to assess how well their work hours "fit" with their family or social commitments outside work, with the responses "very well", "fairly well", "not very well" and "not at all well" being interpreted as indicating minimal, low, medium and high conflict, respectively.

Source: Secretariat calculations based on microdata from the Third European Working Conditions Survey 2000/2001, collected by the European Foundation in Dublin.

C. Growth in part-time and temporary jobs

Part-time work has been an important factor behind employment growth of under-represented groups

Part-time work accounted for a substantial share of overall employment growth in a considerable number of OECD countries (Table 1.4). Rising part-time employment offset declining full-time employment in four countries (Austria, Finland, Italy and Japan). It also accounted for over half of total employment growth in nine other countries. Disaggregation of these data (not shown) reveal that part-time work has been an especially important factor behind employment growth for women, youths and, to a lesser extent, older workers

Table 1.4. **Contribution of part-time[a] and temporary work[b] to employment growth, 1991-2001**

	Share of part-time in total employment 2001	Annual average change as a percentage of total employment		Share of temporary in total employment 2001	Annual average change as a percentage of total employment	
		Full-time	Part-time		Permanent	Temporary
Australia	27.2	1.1	0.9	5.7	..	..
Austria	12.4	−0.1	0.2	8.0	−0.1	0.4
Belgium	17.6	0.1	0.3	8.8	0.7	0.5
Canada	18.1	1.4	0.3	12.8	2.2	0.7
Czech Republic	3.2	−0.1	−0.1	9.0	−1.4	0.3
Denmark	14.5	0.8	−0.3	9.4	0.7	−0.2
Finland	10.5	−0.2	0.3	16.4	2.9	0.0
France	13.8	0.6	0.3	14.9	0.7	0.7
Germany	17.6	−0.8	0.6	12.7	−0.5	0.3
Greece	4.8	1.0	−0.2	12.9	2.1	0.1
Hungary	2.8	1.1	0.0	7.5	1.6	0.4
Iceland	20.4	1.5	0.1	9.9	2.4	−0.2
Ireland	18.4	3.0	1.7	4.7	5.1	−0.2
Italy	12.2	−0.2	0.4	9.5	−0.4	0.4
Japan	24.9	−0.4	0.5	12.8	0.4	0.3
Korea	7.5	1.0	0.4	17.0	..	..
Luxembourg	13.1	0.4	0.6	4.4	1.7	0.2
Mexico	13.8	3.0	−0.1	19.7	4.2	0.3
Netherlands	33.0	1.3	1.3	14.3	1.5	1.0
New Zealand	22.4	1.7	0.7	..	..	..
Norway	20.1	1.3	0.1	9.3	2.4	−0.6
Poland	11.6	0.1	−0.1	11.9	−4.5	1.9
Portugal	9.2	0.5	0.2	20.3	0.2	0.6
Slovak Republic	1.9	0.3	−0.1	5.0	−0.5	0.3
Spain	7.9	1.2	0.5	31.5	1.8	0.7
Sweden	13.9	1.7	0.4	14.8	1.9	0.4
Switzerland	24.8	0.1	0.4	11.6	0.3	−0.1
Turkey	8.0	0.7	−0.3	15.2	3.4	0.5
United Kingdom	23.0	0.1	0.4	6.7	0.7	0.2
United States	13.0	1.5	0.1	4.0	2.0	−0.1

.. Data not available.

a) Part-time employment refers to persons who usually work less than 30 hours per week in their main job. 1991-2000 for Germany and the Netherlands; 1992-2001 for Poland; 1993-2001 for the Czech Republic; 1994-2001 for the Slovak Republic; 1995-2001 for Austria, Hungary and Mexico.
b) 1991-2000 for Germany and Ireland; 1993-2001 for the Czech Republic; 1994-2001 for the Slovak Republic; 1995-2001 for Austria, Mexico and the United States; 1996-2000 for Norway; 1997-2001 for Canada, Finland, Hungary and Sweden; 1998-2001 for Poland; 1997 for Australia; and 2001 for Korea.

Source: OECD databases on Part-time and Temporary Employment.

1. MORE AND BETTER JOBS? AGGREGATE PERFORMANCE DURING THE PAST DECADE

Chart 1.14, Panel A shows that in the OECD as a whole, about 13% of part-time women and 16% of part-time men would prefer a full-time job, if one was available. This suggests that part-time work most often reflects a preference for a shorter work week and suggests that countries with very little part-time employment could foster increased participation

Chart 1.14. **Part-time is mostly a voluntary choice but temporary workers look for permanent jobs**

Voluntary and involuntary incidence of part-time and temporary employment by gender and age, 2001
Percentages of total employment

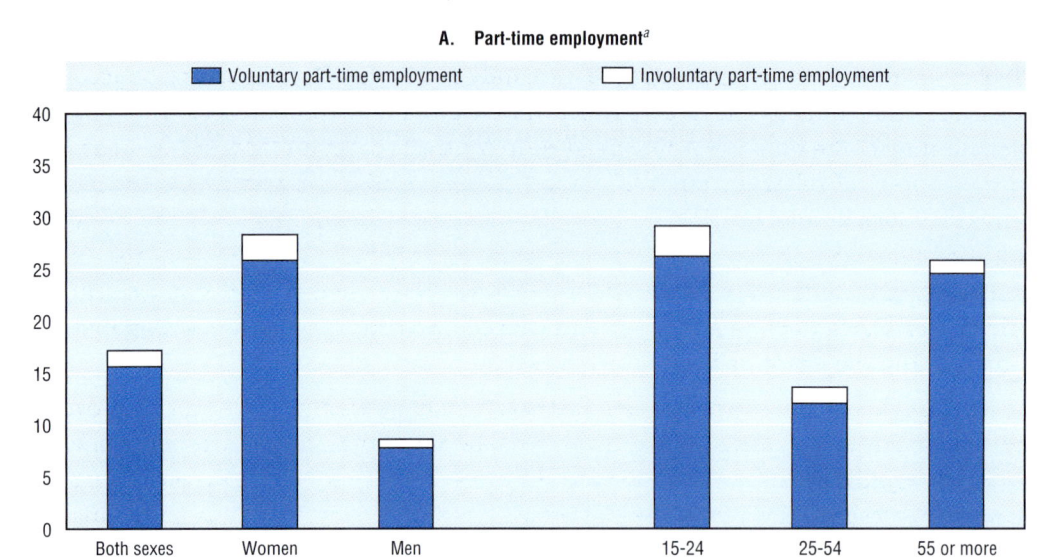

A. Part-time employment[a]

B. Temporay employment[b]

a) Population-weighted averages of the following countries: Australia, Austria, Belgium, Canada, the Czech Republic, Denmark, Finland, France, Germany, Greece, Hungary, Iceland, Ireland, Italy, Japan, Luxembourg, the Netherlands, New Zealand, Norway, Poland, Portugal, the Slovak Republic, Spain, Sweden, Switzerland, Turkey, the United Kingdom and the United States.
b) Population-weighted averages of the following countries: Austria, Belgium, the Czech Republic, Denmark, Finland, Germany, Greece, Hungary, Iceland, Ireland, Italy, Luxembourg, the Netherlands, Norway, Poland, Portugal, the Slovak Republic, Spain, Sweden and the United Kingdom.

Source: Secretariat estimates based on OECD database on Part-time Employment and the European Union Labour Force Survey, data provided by Eurostat.

and employment of women with children – and perhaps other groups – by policies that promote the availability of part-time positions or make them more attractive (*e.g.* by providing part-time workers with pay parity and access to fringe benefits and social insurance on a pro-rata basis). The extent to which part-time work can help improve the employment prospects of under-represented groups is discussed in Chapter 3.

... while temporary jobs have been less dynamic

Temporary employment has been a less dynamic component of total employment growth over the past decade than part-time employment, accounting for one-fourth or more of total job gains in only ten of the 24 countries where total employment rose (Table 1.4). In four countries (Austria, France, Italy and Portugal), temporary jobs accounted for more than half of the growth in total employment, probably as a response to liberalisation of the rules governing fixed-term contracts or temporary placement agencies in the context of relatively strict job protection for regular workers. While the share of temporary jobs in total employment rose in a majority of countries, temporary work was not the main contributor to employment growth. Only in 7 out of 27 countries did the contribution of temporary employment surpass that or permanent employment. The temporary share declined modestly in Spain, the country where the expansion of temporary employment had gone the furthest.

Although temporary employment has been less dynamic than part-time employment, its expansion raises particular concerns because more than four out of ten workers in temporary jobs indicate that they would prefer a permanent contract (Chart 1.14, Panel B).[28] Despite many workers not viewing temporary contracts as an intrinsically attractive employment condition, temporary jobs may make it easier for non-employed persons to enter employment by increasing the willingness of employers to hire job searchers whose productivity is difficult to assess (*e.g.* persons with little prior work experience) or whose commitment to a long-term employment relationship is doubted. However, any such gains in easing the entry into employment would need to be offset against the possible disadvantages of temporary jobs in terms of employment retention and access to training (OECD, 2002a, see also Chapter 5).

D. Is employment insecurity on the rise?

Another important feature of jobs is their *stability*. This has both an objective dimensions (*i.e.* how many workers experience job loss and what are the consequences?) and a subjective dimensions (*i.e.* workers' perceptions of how stable their current job is). In this sub-section, data are presented on both of these dimensions of employment insecurity.

Perceptions of insecurity are on the rise in a number of countries...

Table 1.5 analyses changes in workers' perceptions of job security using data from the 1989 and 1997 waves of the International Social Survey Programme.[29] The percentage of employees perceiving that their job was at least somewhat insecure (more precisely, not strongly agreeing that their job was secure) rose in all seven countries with data for both of these years, often quite sharply.[30] While subjective data, such as these, are always difficult to interpret, some recent empirical evidence shows that subjective job-loss expectations have significant predictive power in explaining future job losses, and that higher subjective job-loss probabilities are correlated with an increased expectation of future earnings declines (Stephens, 2003). Moreover, these perceptions are important in their own right. First, some researchers argue that subjective job security is closely tied to individual well-being (see *e.g.* Bohle et al., 2001). Second, higher levels of perceived insecurity have implications for the macro-economy, being linked to lower levels of consumer expenditure and greater wage restraint.[31] Finally, perceived insecurity can influence the employer-employee relationship, for example, by reducing productivity levels through low satisfaction and motivation at work.[32]

Table 1.5. **Perceptions of insecurity are on the rise**
Perceptions of job insecurity in OECD countries, 1989 and 1997
Percentage of employees not strongly agreeing that "my job is secure"

	Both sexes 1989	Both sexes 1997	Men 1989	Men 1997	Women 1989	Women 1997
Austria	47	..	48	..	46	..
Canada	..	80	..	75	..	84
Czech Republic	..	82	..	84	..	79
Denmark	..	46	..	45	..	47
East Germany	..	94	..	94	..	94
France	..	75	..	82	..	69
Hungary	82	88	81	88	83	88
Ireland	77	..	72	..	85	..
Italy	49	70	47	72	50	67
Japan	..	55	..	55	..	55
Netherlands	76	81	74	80	78	83
Norway	67	76	68	80	65	72
Poland	..	87	..	87	..	86
Portugal	..	65	..	65	..	65
Sweden	..	83	..	82	..	84
Switzerland	..	83	..	83	..	82
United Kingdom	83	87	83	88	83	86
United States	73	77	73	81	72	75
West Germany	63	68	61	70	66	66
Germany	..	76	..	77	..	74
OECD	**70**	**78**	**70**	**80**	**71**	**77**

OECD: Unweighted average of the seven countries with data for both years.
Source: Secretariat estimates based on the International Social Survey Programme, 1989 and 1997.

... but objective measures of insecurity are mixed

The most obvious explanation for an increased perception of insecurity would be that the risk of job loss has increased. Although internationally comparable data on the risk of involuntary layoffs are not available, the overall stability of the distribution of job tenures casts doubt on this explanation.[33] Another possibility is that economic consequences may have worsened for workers who lose their job. The remainder of this sub-section presents two measures of the cost of job loss: average wage losses once re-employed and the probability of experiencing a dismissal leading to long-term unemployment.

Unemployment and dismissal cause losses in real wages but these are usually small

Table 1.6 reports results from a simple regression analysis of average wage losses following unemployment and dismissal, once re-employed.[34] The starting point is a standard log-wage equation relating individual earnings to a set of human capital variables. This standard model is augmented to include controls for having experienced unemployment or a dismissal. Separate versions of the model are estimated for the two types of events, with dummy variables being used to capture the impacts of unemployment (dismissal) on gross hourly earnings. Two dummy variables are used in each case: one variable taking the value of one if the spell of unemployment ended (or job loss occurred) within 12 months of the earnings observation, and zero otherwise; the second taking the value of one if the spell of unemployment ended (or job loss occurred) more than 12 months before the earnings observation, and zero otherwise. This structure makes it simple to evaluate not only the effect of unemployment (dismissal) on earnings but also whether this effect fades as experience is accumulated on the new job. These models were estimated by OLS using data from the European Community Household Panel (ECHP), which provides detailed labour market histories for representative samples of workers in EU countries. The effect of unemployment (job loss) on earnings is estimated separately by country and for a pooled sample of all EU countries.[35]

Table 1.6. **Wage losses following unemployment and dismissal are usually small**
Average wage losses following an unemployment spell or dismissal by country, 1994-1998

	Percentage change in gross hourly earnings following an unemployment spell[a]		Percentage change in gross hourly earnings following dismissal[b]	
	Within the 12 past months	More than 12 months ago	Within the 12 past months	More than 12 months ago
Austria	..	..	−9.0	..
Belgium	−6.0	−7.0	−5.6	..
Denmark	..	..	−4.0	..
Finland	..	−9.0	..	..
France	−3.5	−10.9	−5.4	−7.8
Germany	..	..	..	..
Greece	..	−4.4	..	−6.1
Ireland	−4.4	−10.6	..	−3.6
Italy	−4.3	−3.4	−3.9	..
Netherlands	−5.3	..	..	..
Portugal	−2.4	−1.8	..	−5.1
Spain	−6.3	−2.2	−5.3	−3.6
United Kingdom	−3.9	−10.9	..	..
ECHP[c]	**−3.7**	**−2.0**	**−4.6**	**−3.5**

.. Not statistically significant at 10% level.
a) OLS coefficients of dummy variables for experiencing, respectively, a spell of unemployment within the 12 past months or a spell of unemployment more than 12 months earlier. The dependent variable is the logarithm of the gross hourly wage and the sample is all wage and salary workers. The explanatory variables also include dummy variables for age, educational attainment, job tenure and time.
b) OLS coefficients of dummy variables for experiencing, respectively, a dismissal within the 12 past months or a dismissal more than 12 months earlier. The dependent variable is the logarithm of the gross hourly wage and the sample is all wage and salary workers. The explanatory variables also include dummy variables for age, educational attainment, job tenure and time.
c) OLS coefficients from a pooled regression which also incorporates country fixed effects.
Source: Secretariat estimates based on the European Community Household Panel, wave 1 to 5 (1994-1998).

The estimation results indicate that average wage losses are quite small (Table 1.6), which is consistent with the literature on insecurity (Farber, 2003). The variation across countries in wage losses following a spell of unemployment during the previous year is quite narrow, with the losses ranging from 4% to just above 6%, with the sole exception of Portugal where the estimated wage loss is only 2.4%. The largest earnings losses following unemployment are observed in the United Kingdom and in Belgium, where hourly wages in the year following unemployment are about 6% less than they would have been in the absence of an unemployment spell. Average wage losses in the year following dismissal are a little larger overall and somewhat more variable across countries, ranging from about 4% in the Netherlands and Italy to over 9% in Austria. The size of the wage loss diminishes with the passage of time in some countries, but rises in Belgium, France, Ireland and the United Kingdom.

The regression analysis was also carried out separately for different age and gender groups, but very few significant differences emerged and these results are not reported. More interesting differences emerged when changes in gross *monthly* earnings were used to assess the impacts of unemployment and dismissals on earnings. Rankings of countries are not much affected. However, the estimated average percentage losses are significantly larger for monthly than for hourly earnings, because the monthly estimates reflect reductions in both hourly earnings and hours worked.

The low skilled, youths, and women find it difficult to exit unemployment after dismissal

Although the estimated wage losses discussed above do not show marked differences across demographic groups, it is possible that individuals belonging to some groups may find it more difficult to regain employment and, hence, tend to be omitted from the analysis of earnings losses among re-employed persons. Chart 1.15 reports incidence rates of dismissal leading to long-term unemployment for European workers disaggregated by gender, age and educational attainment. This incidence measure sheds some light on demographic differences in the ease of re-employment following dismissal, while also serving as a proxy for the total expected costs of job loss, since it combines the probability of job loss with an indication of the magnitude of the resulting costs.[36] On average for

Chart 1.15. **After dismissal, the low-skilled, youth and women find it more difficult to exit unemployment**

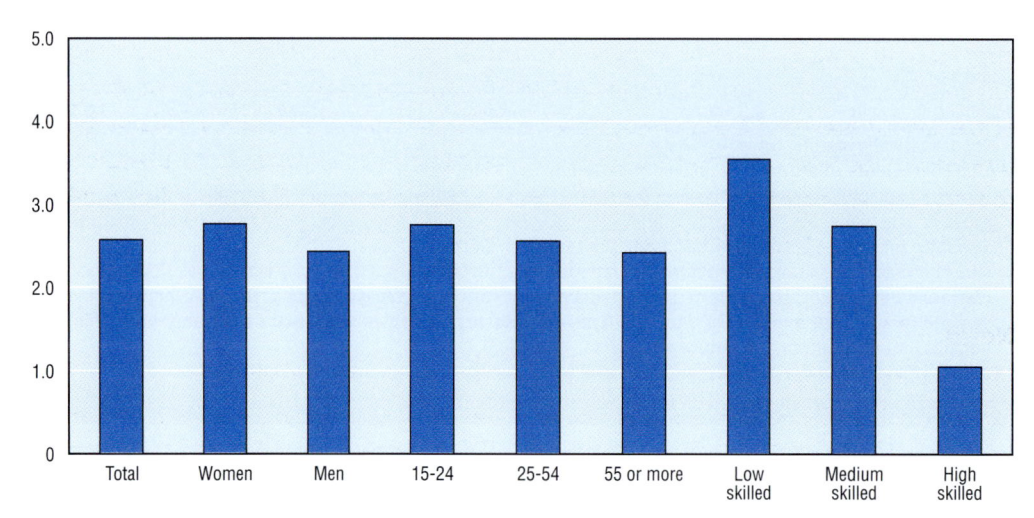

Incidence of long-term unemployment following dismissal by gender, age and educational attainment,[a] 2001
Percentage[b]

a) Low educational attainment corresponds to not having completed upper secondary schooling and high educational attainment to having completed a university or tertiary degree.
b) Population-weighted average for the following countries: Austria, Belgium, the Czech Republic, Denmark, Finland, France, Germany, Greece, Hungary, Iceland, Ireland, Italy, Luxembourg, the Netherlands, Norway, Poland, Portugal, the Slovak Republic, Spain, Sweden and the United Kingdom.

Source: Secretariat calculations based on the European Labour Force Survey, data provided by Eurostat.

22 European countries in 2001, these incidence rates are above the overall average of 2.6% for women (2.8%), youths (2.8%) and, especially, low-educated workers (3.6%). Farber (2003) finds similar patterns among displaced workers in the United States, with youths and low-educated workers having above-average incidences of dismissal, and women, youths and low-educated workers having above-average probabilities of remaining jobless for an extended period of time following dismissal.[37]

Conclusions

This chapter's analysis provides some support for the view that there has been a modest improvement in overall labour market performance in the OECD area during the past decade. It also appears likely that a considerable share of these gains are structural. However, OECD averages hide a wide diversity of experience across countries, ranging from dramatic increases in employment rates in a few countries to rising unemployment in others. Furthermore, progress in increasing employment has not been accompanied by systematic changes in indicators of job quality, which provide a mixed picture including some evidence for upward pressures on earnings inequality, job insecurity and the intensity of work, but also evidence that a strong employment performance need not imply a degradation of job standards or productivity growth. In sum, some progress has been achieved in generating more and better jobs, but plenty of scope for improvement remains.

The chapter's analysis of aggregate labour market performance during the past decade points to three areas where further analysis is required. First, our understanding of the linkages between structural reforms and sustained improvements in performance remains incomplete. Recent experience suggests that the broad policy framework laid-out in the *OECD Jobs Strategy* generally has proven to be effective (OECD, 1999b). However, a comprehensive reappraisal would be timely. Second, a longer-run perspective on labour market reforms and employment performance is required to supplement the medium-term analysis in this chapter. As is discussed in Chapter 2, a key criterion for judging policy choices should be whether they foster the necessary, long-term adaptations to population ageing. Finally, this analysis of aggregate employment performance also needs to be supplemented with a more finely grained analysis of the supply and demand-side factors affecting the participation choices and employment experiences of groups on the margins of the labour market. Strong overall labour demand is a precondition for these groups to fare well in the labour market, but policy makers also need to address the specific barriers to full integration into employment which affect these groups. The rest of this publication addresses some of these barriers, as well as policies to overcome them.

Notes

1. This chapter's analysis of labour market conditions reflects data available as of June 2003.
2. Longitudinal analysis is required to resolve these issues. Research to date, while far from having achieved a definitive resolution, has revealed a complex reality that conforms to neither the most pessimistic nor the most optimistic accounts (OECD, 1996, 1997, 2002a; and Chapter 2 of this publication).
3. In this publication, the terms "European Union" and "EU" refer to the 15 member countries of the European Union as of 2002 and "Oceania" refers to Australia and New Zealand.
4. IMF (2001), European Commission (2001 and 2002) and Pehkonen (2000) investigated possible changes in the responsiveness of employment to growth in the 1990s and concluded that employment became more "cyclical" in the past decade in some EU countries. The IMF study finds

that this is true for Spain, Italy and France, but not for Germany, while the European Commission finds this result applies to the European Union as a whole. A possible explanation for increased responsiveness of employment to output growth is provided by the wider use of fixed-term contracts and other non-standard forms of employment, while the quicker response of unemployment rates to changes in hiring could also reflect a downward trend in the pool of workers having left the labour force due to discouragement effects following job loss (Bentolilla and Bertola, 1990; and Bentolilla and Saint-Paul, 1992, present some theoretical support for this argument). As noted in the text, however, the current economic slowdown appears to confound these expectations.

5. Chapter 2 argues that the increased prominence of increased employment rates as a policy goal is to be welcomed, especially in the context of population ageing.

6. The years 1991 and 2001 correspond to the on-set of a recession (or slowdown) for the OECD area as a whole, but not for all OECD countries (Chart 1.1).

7. The length of time necessary for the full effects of structural reforms to become visible is likely to be long and is rather uncertain (Elmeskov *et al.*, 1998; OECD, 1999b). The analysis of benefit recipiency rates in Chapter 4 also illustrates the potential importance of long lags in behavioural responses to policy changes.

8. Population-weighted average for the OECD, excluding the Czech Republic, Hungary, Poland and the Slovak Republic (due to missing data in the early 1990s).

9. The CEE countries represent a special case, since the transition from centrally-planned economies (in which open unemployment hardly existed) to market-based economies has resulted in a sharp fall in employment that is irrelevant for assessing the efficacy of labour market reforms in other countries. In Sweden, the early 1990s crisis caused a strong reduction in employment that has not been fully recovered yet: the 2001 employment to population ratio was still 5.7 percentage points below its 1991 level. One reason behind this only partial recovery is the strong increase in enrolment in Active Labour Market (ALMP) schemes and education programs. In 1999, a total of 7% of the labour force was in active labour market policy and extraordinary education programmes (OECD, 1999c). The 10 percentage-points fall in the employment rate in Turkey is due to strong labour force withdrawal during a decade of economic turbulence.

10. The poor performance of Germany appears to have been related to the difficulties of absorbing the former Eastern Germany and is associated with large regional differences in employment outcomes. The Finnish economy was also strongly adversely affected by the break-up of the Soviet economic block and the employment rate fell a little more strongly during 1991 to 2001 in Finland than in Germany. However, Finland experienced a far steeper initial drop in employment, followed by a strong recovery.

11. Note that in the decomposition of changes in the total employment/population ratio in Chart 1.3 into the numerical contributions of changes in unemployment and inactivity rates, unemployment is measured as a share of the total working-age population rather than as a share of the labour force. In comparing the numerical contributions of reductions in inactivity and unemployment to increased employment, it should also be borne in mind that the practical significance of the statistical distinction between certain forms of inactivity and unemployment may not be very pronounced. An example is provided by "discouraged workers" (*i.e.* individuals who would like to work, but are not searching for a job because they believe that none are available). However, the analysis reported here is not much affected by alternative treatments of these measurement issues. In particular, an analysis of 1991-2001 trends using an "augmented" unemployment rate – which incorporates discouraged and involuntary part-time workers (with a weight of one-half) – yields similar results to those discussed in the text based on standard employment, unemployment and inactivity rates.

12. Although reductions in unemployment and inactivity rates contributed to a similar degree to increasing employment rates during the 1990s, future increases in employment rates that would be sufficient to stabilise dependency ratios in the context of population ageing or to allow low-employment countries to close the gap with high-employment countries would have to come mostly from reductions in inactivity (see Chapter 2 for a more detailed analysis).

13. This section makes use of scatter plots juxtaposing the percentage-point changes in the employment rates of these four workforce groups with employment rate changes for the total working-age population. Points lying above the 45-degree line indicate above-average employment growth for the marginal group in the associated countries.

14. Since the 1960s, participation rates for men, over the life cycle, have dropped dramatically due to rising educational attainment (*i.e.* later labour market entry) and falling effective ages of

15. retirement (OECD, 1998b). This secular decline appears to have slowed during the 1990s, as retirement ages have stabilised or even risen in some countries, but the extent of this slowing is difficult to judge since improving cyclical conditions also encouraged greater participation.

16. This probably reflects both the impact of important pension reforms in a number of countries and the fact that improved labour market conditions made it easier and more attractive for older workers to remain in the labour force.

17. Macroeconomists define the equilibrium unemployment rate – often referred to by its acronym "NAIRU" (*i.e.* the non-accelerating inflation rate of unemployment) – as the rate of unemployment consistent with stable inflation and a balance of payments in equilibrium. Estimates of the NAIRU provide a useful point of reference for both short-run stabilisation policy (which aims to reduce fluctuations around the NAIRU) and long-run structural policy (which aims to achieve a low NAIRU).

18. Layard *et al.* (1991) developed a theoretical framework in which equilibrium unemployment is determined by the interplay of a U-V curve (reflecting matching between unemployed job seekers and job vacancies) and a wage curve (reflecting wage pressure). This framework continues to underpin much theoretical and empirical research, as is evidenced by Blanchard and Katz's (1997) survey article. Several empirical studies have adopted this framework (*e.g.* Nickell and Layard, 1997b; Elmeskov *et al.*, 1998; OECD, 1999b; Nicoletti *et al.*, 1999; Belot and Van Ours. (2000); Daveri and Tabellini, 2000; Blanchard and Wolfers, 2002; and Nickell *et al.*, 2003), providing important insights into the factors affecting the level of structural unemployment. Several of these studies conclude that changes over time in a few of the structural factors highlighted by the theoretical framework provide a reasonably satisfactory explanation of the broad evolution of unemployment in OECD countries during the past several decades.

19. For example, improvements in public employment services (Chapter 4) or policies to upgrade workers' skills (Chapter 5) may increase matching efficiency, by facilitating the reintegration of unemployed individuals.

20. The cross-country standard deviation of the NAIRU values in Table 1.3 fell from 3.3 in 1991 to 2.5 in 2001. Chart 1.1 shows that *actual* unemployment rates also converged (aside from the CEE countries).

21. The results discussed here are consistent overall with the evidence presented in Nickell *et al.* (2003), although the analysis has been extended to incorporate two additional years of data.

22. Nickell *et al.* (2003) also classify the United Kingdom as a "successful" country where the Beveridge Curve shifted leftwards from the mid-1980s. As is evident in Chart 1.8, this classification is called into question when data through 2001 (which incorporate recent revisions to the historical series on vacancies), are plotted. However, if alternative data on labour shortages (collected by the Confederation of British Industry) are used instead, a favourable shift of the UK Beveridge curve is confirmed (Nickell, 2002).

23. See Estevão and Nargis (2002) for an exhaustive analysis of the topic using micro-data for France.

24. Real wage shares can be interpreted as the ratio of the real wage to labour productivity.

25. Business-sector employment growth in EU countries had began to recover in the 1980s, but that trend strengthened in the 1990s.

26. In this analysis, jobs are classified by broad wage levels (low, medium, high) as follows (see OECD, 2001a, for more details). First, employment in each country is divided into 13 sectors and into a number of broad occupations, varying from four to seven depending on the sector. In total, 76 separate sector/occupation categories are identified. These categories are then ranked on the basis of average hourly earnings for workers in each category in 1995 and assigned to three groups (low, medium, high paid) of equal size on the basis of employment shares. Employment changes between 1993 and 2001 are then traced out for each group of jobs.

27. Keating also shows that changes in the structure of labour demand in favour of more skilled jobs were the main cause behind the increase in the dispersion of earnings in Australia over the past decade. The Commonwealth government presented similar findings regarding the pattern of employment growth, and showed in the 2001-2002 Safety Net Review report that growth in hours worked has been strongest amongst high-paid occupations and weakest amongst low-paid occupations.

28. For example, the proportions of workers reporting working in painful and tiring positions increased by 4 percentage points, exposure to intense noise rose by 2 percentage points and the share of workers reporting that they lift heavy weights rose by 6 percentage points.

28. Gender differences in involuntary temporary work are muted, but age differences are quite large. Over one-half of prime-age workers in temporary jobs would prefer a permanent job, as compared to 29% of younger workers and 37% of older workers.

29. One limitation of these comparisons for assessing trends is that the two years available relate to somewhat different cyclical positions: 1989 was near a cyclical peak in most of these countries, while 1997 was a mid-expansion year.

30. A similar trend is observed in Australia, where the annual Morgan Poll asks employees whether they think their job is safe. In 1989, 82% believed their job was safe, compared with 77% in 1997 and 75% in 2002.

31. Campbell et al. (2001) show that high fear of unemployment is associated with significantly lower wage levels, in Britain.

32. Increased perceptions of insecurity could, instead, increase productivity, if an increased fear of loosing one's job increases work effort. However, the hypothesis of a negative relationship has received more empirical support (see, for example, Buchele and Christiansen, 1999).

33. See OECD (1997) for a somewhat dated analysis. A partial updating of that study confirmed this finding (data not shown).

34. The two groups are distinct, but not mutually exclusive: individuals who are dismissed may or may not experience unemployment before becoming re-employed; while individuals who experience some unemployed when moving between two jobs may or may not have been dismissed.

35. The pooled model contains fixed country effects, while all of the models include individual fixed effects to control for unobserved (and time-invariant) characteristics affecting earnings potential. These earnings regressions were estimated over the 1994-99 period covered by the ECHP. Unfortunately, the short length of the panel does not allow to check for changes over time in the effect of job loss (or unemployment) on earnings.

36. Nickell et al. (2002) and Nicoletti et al. (2001) argue that a comprehensive measure of insecurity should reflect both the probability of job loss and the resulting costs. The index used here omits wage losses once re-employed. However, it may provide a reasonable proxy for a comprehensive measure of insecurity, if long spells of unemployment following dismissal are be associated with higher wage losses once re-employed (e.g. due to greater skill deterioration), in addition to reflecting foregone earnings while jobless.

37. Some partially discrepant evidence should be noted. First, the subjective data on job security indicate lower perceived insecurity for women than for men (Table 1.5), but confirm higher insecurity for youth than for their older counterparts (data not shown). Wage regressions of the type reported in Table 1.6 suggest that women, youth and low-educated workers experience wage losses following dismissal that are similar to (or a little lower than) those experienced by other groups, provided they become re-employed relatively quickly. However, individuals in these groups are less likely to find a new job quickly.

ANNEX 1

Supplementary Evidence

1. MORE AND BETTER JOBS? AGGREGATE PERFORMANCE DURING THE PAST DECADE

Table 1.A1.1. **Productivity and real wage growth and wage share in OECD countries, 1970-2002**

Percentage growth

	Labour productivity growth in the business sector				Real wage growth in the business sector				Wage share of the business sector[a]				
	1970-80	1980-90	1990-95	1995-02	1970-80	1980-90	1990-95	1995-02	1970	1980	1990	1995	2002
Australia	2.1	1.1	2.1	2.0	-1.1	0.2	0.1	1.3	..	52.5	49.6	45.2	44.0
Austria	3.1	2.2	1.8	1.9	4.0	1.5	1.1	0.8	49.9	59.6	56.4	56.1	53.9
Belgium	3.1	2.0	1.3	1.1	4.6	0.8	1.8	0.6	51.2	59.5	52.7	53.0	52.5
Canada	1.3	1.2	1.3	1.4	1.6	0.8	0.2	1.5	55.9	59.3	55.8	51.4	52.8
Czech Republic	..	..	..	2.1	..	..	..	2.5	..	..	..	43.3	43.7
Denmark	2.5	1.3	2.8	1.7	1.8	1.2	0.8	1.3	..	59.6	59.8	54.8	55.0
Finland	3.4	3.2	3.6	2.1	4.0	3.1	-0.4	1.3	50.1	55.4	59.0	48.4	47.0
France	3.1	2.4	1.3	1.1	3.2	0.7	0.0	0.7	59.7	64.7	57.5	54.5	54.6
Germany	2.9	1.2	-0.2	0.8	3.2	0.7	-0.5	-0.1	53.6	59.5	58.7	58.0	54.2
Greece	4.5	-0.2	0.5	3.1	5.5	0.1	-1.9	2.1	..	..	..	..	..
Hungary	..	..	..	2.6	..	..	..	1.6	..	..	..	28.4	27.9
Iceland	3.9	1.1	-1.9	2.2	2.6	1.0	-1.3	2.6	80.4	69.1	64.1	67.7	72.7
Ireland	4.1	3.8	1.9	3.4	3.9	1.2	1.4	1.1	..	63.9	48.1	46.4	41.5
Italy	2.9	1.8	1.7	0.5	3.6	0.9	0.1	-0.2	48.1	50.6	45.9	40.7	39.8
Japan	3.5	2.6	0.5	1.0	3.9	1.3	0.3	0.3	51.4	57.5	54.2	56.9	56.1
Korea	5.0	6.1	4.0	3.5	5.7	5.4	2.4	1.0	..	41.0	51.6	50.3	40.7
Luxembourg	..	..	1.6	0.8	..	0.7	1.4	1.3	..	..	56.2	56.9	60.5
Mexico	..	-0.2	0.1	1.5	..	-3.7	4.0	0.0	..	67.3	44.1	45.7	42.5
Netherlands	3.0	1.4	1.2	0.6	3.3	0.2	0.6	0.7	58.9	61.9	55.1	52.6	54.2
New Zealand	0.5	1.7	0.6	1.0	1.0	0.2	0.0	0.2	..	55.9	46.0	43.7	41.8
Norway	3.1	0.6	2.9	1.1	-0.1	0.7	1.4	2.4	..	68.1	68.7	66.1	76.7
Poland	..	..	..	4.9	..	..	4.1	3.4	..	..	..	43.0	38.7
Portugal	3.0	1.9	0.0	1.5	5.6	-0.6	2.5	1.8	52.6	55.7	47.0	47.4	49.2
Slovak Republic	..	..	..	3.8	..	..	..	2.8	..	..	..	40.7	37.2
Spain	3.7	2.1	2.0	0.7	4.5	0.8	1.8	0.8	45.2	52.8	49.6	48.5	50.9
Sweden	1.7	1.8	3.2	1.5	2.0	0.7	0.5	2.3	66.2	70.1	64.2	53.0	57.9
Switzerland	1.0	0.3	0.0	0.7	1.3	1.2	0.2	1.4	..	63.8	70.0	68.9	72.6
Turkey	..	2.9	0.9	1.8	..	..	..	-5.4	..	..	..	..	..
United Kingdom	2.5	2.0	1.9	1.0	2.4	1.4	0.8	2.1	66.6	67.5	61.3	57.9	65.4
United States	1.3	1.3	1.2	1.8	1.0	0.6	0.7	1.6	65.0	63.4	59.3	57.4	57.3
Euro zone[b]	**3.0**	**1.7**	**1.0**	**1.1**	**3.5**	**0.8**	**0.2**	**0.4**	**55.5**	**59.7**	**55.3**	**52.8**	**53.3**
OECD[b]	**2.0**	**1.6**	**1.1**	**1.7**	**2.1**	**0.8**	**0.4**	**1.3**	**58.7**	**60.8**	**56.8**	**55.4**	**55.5**

a) The wage share of the business sector is defined as the business wage rate times total business sector employment over business sector output at factor cost.
b) GDP-weighted average for countries with data for all years shown.

Source: OECD Economic Outlook, No. 72, June 2002.

Table 1.A1.2. **Growth in real labour costs in excess of productivity growth[a] in OECD countries, 1970-2001[b]**

Percentage change (annual)

	Annual average growth in the 1970s	Annual average growth in the 1980s	Annual average growth in 1990-95	Annual average growth in 1995-2001
Australia	0.3	−0.9	−1.1	−0.8
Austria	0.7	−0.8	−0.6	−1.4
Belgium	1.2	−1.5	0.7	−1.0
Canada	0.9	−0.5	−1.1	−0.2
Czech Republic	..	..	..	0.3
Denmark	..	..	−1.5	−0.4
Finland	0.8	0.8	−3.4	−1.3
France	0.6	−1.5	−1.0	−0.2
Germany	0.4	−1.1	1.8	−1.0
Greece	1.1	0.8	−2.9	−0.9
Hungary	..	..	−4.9	−1.6
Iceland	−0.4	−0.1	−1.6	1.1
Ireland	0.0	−2.3	−0.9	−2.7
Italy	0.7	−0.4	−2.2	−0.9
Japan	0.4	−1.4	−0.5	−0.8
Korea	2.0	−0.5	−2.4	−3.4
Luxembourg	2.3	−1.7	−1.4	−0.5
Mexico	..	..	5.6	−1.6
Netherlands	0.9	−1.8	−0.6	−0.1
New Zealand	0.7	−1.2	−0.5	−0.7
Norway	−2.8	−1.3	−2.4	1.2
Poland	..	..	..	−1.6
Portugal	..	..	..	0.4
Slovak Republic	..	..	..	−1.9
Spain	..	−1.1	−0.2	−0.3
Sweden	..	..	−3.1	0.8
Switzerland	..	..	0.5	0.1
Turkey	0.4	−1.7	1.5	−4.3
United Kingdom	0.4	0.1	−2.0	0.7
United States	0.0	−0.5	−0.5	−0.3
Euro zone[c]	0.4	−1.7	−0.4	−0.5
OECD[c]	0.0	−1.7	−1.0	−0.5

.. Data not available.
a) Difference between the growth rate of real labour costs (defined as the ratio of gross nominal compensation per employee to the GDP deflator) and the growth rate of real output per worker.
b) Annual average growth in 1970 refers to 1971-1980 for Ireland; to 1972-1980 for the Netherlands and Turkey; and to 1975-1980 for Korea and Norway.
c) Employment-weighted average.

Source: OECD Economic Outlook, No. 72, June 2002.

Table 1.A1.3. **Growth in multi-factor productivity and the employment to population ratio in selected countries, 1980-1990 and 1990-2000**

	1980-1990		1990-2000	
	Multi-factor productivity[a]	Employment to population ratio[b]	Multi-factor productivity[a]	Employment to population ratio[b]
Australia	0.57	2.7	1.31	3.9
Austria	1.82	..	1.56	−0.4
Belgium	1.72	1.2	1.24	5.2
Canada	0.63	4.3	1.30	2.8
Denmark	1.00	5.3	1.45	0.8
Finland	2.38	2.9	3.16	−3.1
France	1.86	−4.8	1.00	1.0
Germany[c]	1.49	−1.5	0.94	−0.5
Ireland	3.60	−0.3	4.41	13.0
Italy	1.55	−1.6	1.03	1.4
Japan	2.15	2.4	1.02	0.8
Netherlands	2.26	7.5	1.58	9.3
New Zealand	0.20	−5.0	0.76	5.4
Norway	1.19	0.1	1.74	4.9
Spain	2.06	−2.1	0.72	5.5
Sweden	1.03	3.2	1.42	−6.9
United States	0.92	5.0	1.13	3.4

.. Data not available.

a) Annual growth rate in the business sector based on cyclically-adjusted series, 1980s and 1990s. 1983-1990 for Belgium, Denmark and Ireland; 1985-1990 for Austria and New Zealand; 1990-1996 for Ireland and Sweden; 1990-1997 for Austria, Belgium and New Zealand; 1990-1998 for the Netherlands; 1990-1999 for Australia, Denmark, France, Italy, Japan; and 1991-2000 for Germany.
b) Percentage-point change. 1983-1990 for Belgium, Denmark and Ireland; 1986-1990 for New Zealand.
c) Western Germany before 1991.

Source: OECD (2003), The Sources of Economic Growth in OECD countries, Paris.

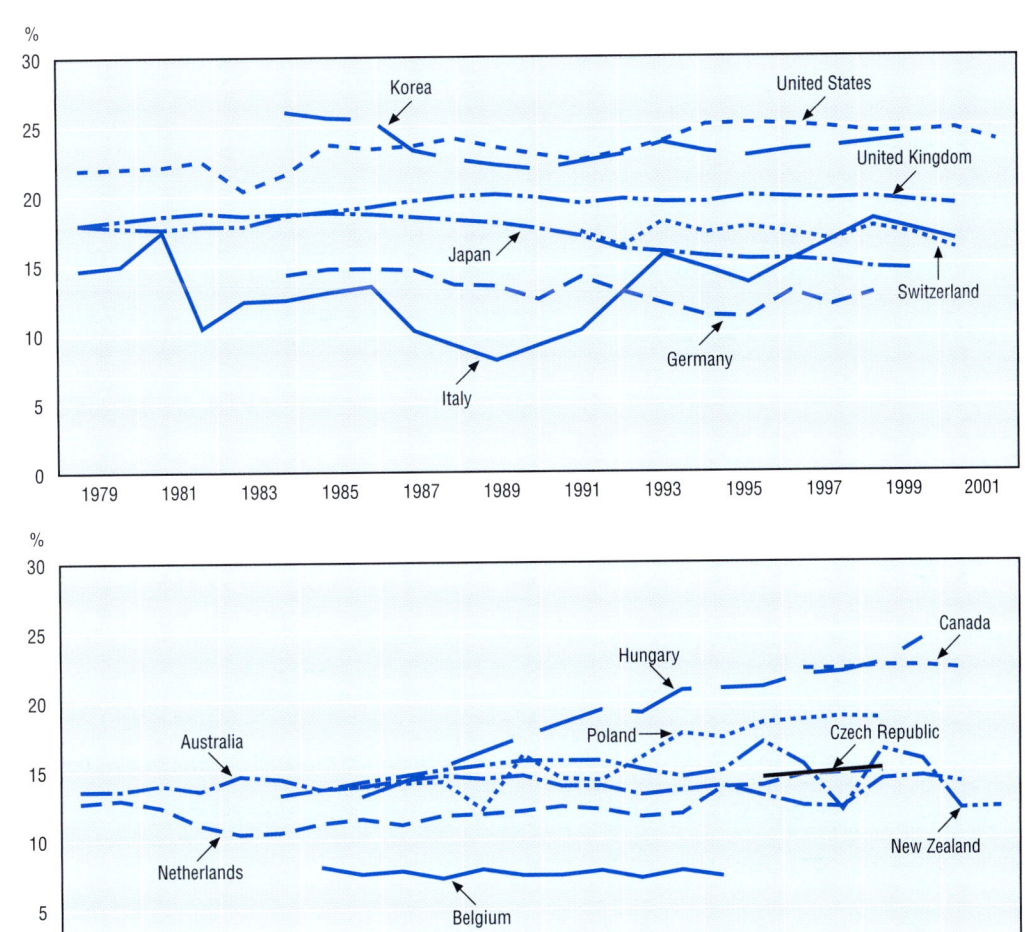

Chart 1.A1.1. **Trends in the incidence of low pay,**[a, b] **1979-2001**

a) Percentage of full-time workers receiving less than two-thirds of median gross earnings.
b) Data for Italy refer to net earnings.
Source: OECD database on earnings.

Bibliography

ARULAMPALAM, W. (2001), "Is Unemployment Really Scarring? Effects of Unemployment Experiences on Wages", *Economic Journal*, Vol. 111, No. 475, November, pp. F585-606.

BEAN, C., R. LAYARD and S. NICKELL (1986), "The Rise in Unemployment: A Multi-Country study", in C. Bean, R. Layard and S. Nickell (eds.), *The Rise in Unemployment*, Blackwell, Oxford.

BELOT, M. and J. VAN OURS (2000), "Does the Recent Success of Some OECD Countries in Lowering Their Unemployment Rates Lie in the Clever Design of their Labour Market Reforms", *IZA Discussion paper*, No. 147, April.

BENTOLILLA, S. and G. BERTOLA (1990), "Firing Costs and Labour Demand: How Bad is Eurosclerosis?", *Review of Economic Studies*, No. 57, pp. 381-402.

BENTOLILLA, S. and G. SAINT-PAUL (1992), "The Macroeconomic Impact of Flexible Labour Contracts, with and Application to Spain", *European Economic Review*, No. 36, pp. 1013-1047.

BLANCHARD, O. and P. DIAMOND (1989), "The Beveridge Curve", *Brookings Paper on Economic Activity*, No. 1, pp. 1-60.

BLANCHARD, O. and F. GIAVAZZI (2000) "Macroeconomic Effects of Regulation and Deregulation in Goods and Labor Markets", Massachusetts Institute of Technology, *Department of Economics Working Paper* 01/02.

BLANCHARD, O. and L. KATZ (1997), "What We Know and Do Not Know about the Natural Rate of Unemployment", *Journal of Economic Perspectives*, Winter, No. 11-1, pp. 51-73.

BLANCHARD, O. and J. WOLFERS (2002) "The Role of Shocks and Institutions in the Rise of European Unemployment: The Aggregate Evidence", *Economic Journal*, Vol. 110, No. 462, pp. C1-33.

BOERI, T., G. NICOLETTI and S. SCARPETTA (2000), "Regulation and Labour Market Performance", *CEPR Discussion Paper*, No. 2420.

BOHLE, P., M. QUINLAN and C. MAYHEW (2001), "The Health and Safety Effects of Job Insecurity: An Evaluation of the Evidence", *Economic and Labour Relations Review*, Vol. 12, No. 1, June, pp. 32-60.

BUCHELE, R. and J. CHRISTIANSEN (1999), "Employment and productivity growth in Europe and North America: the impact of labour market institutions", *International Review of Applied Economic*, Vol. 13, No. 3, pp. 312-332.

CAMPBELL, D., A. CARRUTH, A. DICKERSON and F. GREEN (2001), "Job Insecurity and Wage Outcomes in Britain", mimeo, University of Kent, Canterbury.

COMMONWEALTH (2002), *Safety Net Review – Wages: 2001-2002*, Australia.

DAVERI, F. and G. TABELLINI (2000), "Unemployment, Growth and Taxation in Industrial Countries", *Economic Policy*, April, pp. 49-90.

DOLADO, J., F. KRAMARZ, S. MACHIN, A. MANNING, D. MARGOLIS and C. TEULINGS (1996), "The Economic Impact of the Minimum Wage in Europe", *Economic Policy*, No. 23, pp. 317-372.

ELMESKOV, J., J. MARTIN and S. SCARPETTA (1998), "Key Lessons for Labour Market Reforms: Evidence from OECD Countries' Experiences", *Swedish Economic Policy Review*, Vol. 5, pp. 205-252.

ESTEVÃO, M. and N. NARGIS (2002), "Wage Moderation in France", *IMF Working Paper*, No. 151.

EUROPEAN COMMISSION (2001), *The EU Economy 2001 Review, Investing in the Future*, European Economy 2001, No. 73, DG Economic and Financial Affairs, Brussels.

EUROPEAN COMMISSION (2002), *Employment in Europe: Recent Trends and Prospects*, Brussels.

FARBER, H. (2003), "Job Loss in the United States, 1981-2001", *NBER Working Paper*, No. 9707.

GREEN, F. (2002), "Work Intensification, Discretion and the Decline in Well-Being at Work", mimeo, University of Kent, Canterbury.

GREEN, F. and D. GALLIE (2002), "High Skills and High Anxiety: Skills, Hard Work and Mental Well-Being", mimeo, University of Kent, Canterbury.

GREGG, P. and J. WADSWORTH (2000), "Mind the Gap, Please: The Changing Nature of Entry Jobs in Britain", *Economica*, No. 67, pp. 499-524.

GREGORY, M. and R. JUKES (2001), "Unemployment and Subsequent Earnings: Estimating Scarring among British Men 1984-94", *Economic Journal,* Vol. 111, No. 475, November, pp. F607-625.

INTERNATIONAL MONETARY FUND (2001), "Selected Euro-Area Countries: Rules-Based Fiscal Policy and Job Rich Growth in France, Germany, Italy, and Spain – Report with Supplementary Information", Country Report No. 01/203.

KEATING, M. (2003), "Earnings and Inequality", Centre for Economic Policy Research, *Australian National University Discussion Papers,* No. 460.

LALIVE, R., J. VAN OURS and J. ZWEIMULLER (2002), "The Effect of Benefit Sanctions on the Duration of Unemployment", IZA Discussion Paper No. 69.

LAYARD, R., S. NICKELL and R. JACKMAN (1991), "*Unemployment: Macroeconomics Performance and the Labour Market*", Oxford University Press, Oxford.

MISHEL, L., J. BERNSTEIN and H. BOUSHEY (2003), "*The State of Working America*", Cornell University Press, Ithaca.

MORTENSEN, D. and C. PISSARIDES (1999), "New Developments in Models of Search in the Labour Market", in O. Ashenfelter and D. Card (eds.), *Handbook of Labour Economics,* North Holland, Amsterdam.

NICKELL, S. (1997), "Unemployment and Labor Market Rigidities: Europe *versus* North America", *Journal of Economic Perspectives,* No. 3, pp. 55-74.

NICKELL, S. (2002), "A Picture of European Unemployment: Success and Failure", paper prepared for the conference *Unemployment in Europe: Reasons and Remedies,* Yrjö Jahnsson organizer, Munich.

NICKELL, S. and R. LAYARD (1997b), "Labour Market Institutions and Economic Performance", Centre for Economic Performance, London School of Economics, *Discussion Paper*, No. 23.

NICKELL, S. and J. VAN OURS (2000), "The Netherlands and the United Kingdom: A European Unemployment Miracle?", *Economic Policy: A European Forum*, No. 30, pp. 135-175.

NICKELL, S., P. JONES, and G. QUINTINI (2002), "A Picture of Job Insecurity Facing British Men", *The Economic Journal,* Vol. 112, No. 476, pp. 1-27.

NICKELL, S., L. NUNZIATA, W. OCHEL and G. QUINTINI (2003), "The Beveridge Curve, Unemployment and Wages in the OECD", in P. Aghion, R. Frydman, J. Stiglitz and M. Woodford (eds.), *Knowledge, Information and Expectations in Modern Macroeconomics: in Honour of Edmund S. Phelps*, Princeton University Press.

NICOLETTI, G., S. SCARPETTA and O. BAYLAUD (1999), "Summary Indicators of Product Market Regulation with an Extension to Employment Protection Legislation", *OECD Economics Department Working Paper*, No. 226, OECD, Paris.

NICOLETTI, G., A. BASSANINI, E. ERNST, S. JEAN, P. SANTIAGO and P. SWAIM (2001), "Product and Labour Markets Interactions in OECD Countries", *OECD Economics Department Working Paper*, No. 312, OECD, Paris.

OCHEL, W. (2000), "Collective Bargaining (Centralization and Co-ordination)", Ifo Institute for Economic Research, Munich.

OECD (1994a), *The Outlook Jobs Study: Facts, Analysis, Strategies*, Paris.

OECD (1994b), *The Outlook Jobs Study: Evidence and Explanations Part 1 – Labour Market Trends and Underlying Forces of Change*, Paris.

OECD (1996), *Employment Outlook*, Paris.

OECD (1997), *Employment Outlook*, Paris.

OECD (1998a), *Employment Outlook*, Paris.

OECD (1998a), *Employment Outlook*, Paris.

OECD (1998b), *Maintaining Prosperity in an Ageing Society*, Paris.

OECD (1999a), *Employment Outlook*, Paris.

OECD (1999b), *Implementing the OECD Jobs Strategy: Assessing Performance and Policy*, Paris.

OECD (1999c), *OECD Economic Surveys: Sweden*, Paris.

OECD (2001a), *Employment Outlook*, Paris.

OECD (2001b), *Economic Outlook*, No. 71, Paris.

OECD (2002a), *Employment Outlook*, Paris.

OECD (2002b), *An Update of the OECD Composite Leading Indicators*, Paris.

OECD (2003), *The Sources of Economic Growth in OECD countries*, Paris.

OSWALD, A. (1997), "The Missing Piece of the Unemployment Puzzle", Inaugural Lecture, University of Warwick.

PEHKONEN, J. (2000) "Employment, Unemployment and Output Growth in Booms and Recessions: Time Series Evidence from Finland, 1970-1996", *Applied Economics*, No. 32, pp. 885-900.

RICHARDSON, P., L. BOONE, C. GIORNO, M. MEACCI, D. RAE and D. TURNER (2000), "The Concept, Policy Use and Measurement of Structural Unemployment: Estimating a Time Varying NAIRU Across 21 OECD countries", *OECD Economics Department Working Paper*, No. 250, OECD, Paris.

SAINT-PAUL, G. (1999), "The Political Economy of Employment Protection", Universitat Pompeu Fabra, *Economics and Business Working Paper*, No. 355.

STEPHENS, M. (2003), "Job Loss Expectations, Realizations, and Household Consumption Behaviour", *NBER Working Paper*, No. 9508.

ISBN 92-64-10061-X
OECD Employment Outlook: 2003
Towards More and Better Jobs
© OECD 2003

Chapter 2

The Labour Mobilisation Challenge: Combating Inactivity Traps and Barriers to Moving Up Job Ladders

> *This chapter analyses the scope for policies to raise aggregate employment rates by fostering greater labour market participation among population groups that tend to be under-represented in employment. Under-represented groups are diverse and their relative numerical importance differs from country to country. Nonetheless, women, older workers and less educated workers represent the largest reservoirs of underutilised labour potential in most OECD countries. To what extent are certain population groups, such as women, older workers and less educated workers, trapped in situations of labour market inactivity? Once in employment, do they have career prospects or is there a risk that they will become trapped in low-quality jobs? How would a better mobilisation of these groups help respond to the challenges of population ageing?*

Introduction 68
Main findings 69
1. Raising employment by mobilising potential labour supply 70
2. The many faces of non-employment 81
3. Getting into work, staying there and moving up job ladders 90
Conclusions.. 102

Annex 1. Supplementary evidence 107

Bibliography 111

Introduction

The previous chapter documented encouraging signs of structural improvements in aggregate labour market performance in a number of OECD countries. However, it still remains the case that important groups in the working-age population continue to experience low employment rates or are disadvantaged in terms of the quality of the jobs that they hold. This chapter analyses population groups which represent important reservoirs of underutilised labour potential: women, older workers and less educated workers, bearing in mind that there are overlaps between all such groups. Youths, lone parents, immigrants and persons with disabilities also receive some attention. In all cases, the intent is to identify the population groups with the greatest unrealised potential in the labour market and to describe their situations.

This chapter's focus is motivated by the increased prominence – among the objectives of employment and social policy – given to raising the *aggregate* employment rate (see, *e.g.* European Commission, 2003a). This policy orientation combines the conventional concern to lower unemployment with a more novel concern to increase participation. The latter objective is receiving increased emphasis in the context of population ageing and also because of widespread interest in the possibility that benefit dependency could be reduced among persons of working age. The main purpose of this chapter is to provide a factual baseline for assessing the labour mobilisation challenge facing OECD economies. Estimates of the quantity of underutilised labour potential are presented and the labour market situation of the population groups representing the largest pockets of inactivity or under-employment described. This analysis is intended to clarify which groups should receive particular attention from policies aimed at raising participation and employment. A second aim of the chapter is to provide an initial indication of the types of barriers to fuller integration into employment (or into more productive forms of employment) that need to be addressed for a mobilisation strategy to succeed. Chapters 3 to 5 analyse a number of such barriers in greater detail, as well as policies for overcoming them.

The chapter is organised as follows: Section 1 assesses the scope for policies to raise the overall employment rate. After summarising possible rationales for adopting increased employment rates as a policy objective, several estimates of potential labour supply and employment are presented. Detailed comparisons of the labour force status of different population groups are presented in Section 2, so as to provide a fuller picture of which groups have low participation rates or are at a high risk of unemployment, and how these patterns vary across OECD countries. The labour market experience of these groups is analysed using longitudinal data in Section 3, in order to characterise more fully the difficulties they often encounter in entering employment, staying in employment and moving up job ladders. The evidence for inactivity and low-pay traps is considered, as well as the relationship between labour market status and poverty among persons of working age.

Main findings

- Three rationales can be offered for policies to foster higher participation rates in OECD countries. First, participation rates may be inefficiently low due to disincentives to employment created by policies, such as high marginal effective tax rates. Second, low participation rates can create fiscal stress to the extent that non-participation involves the receipt of social benefits. Finally, higher participation can further social inclusion and equity goals. These rationales take on added urgency in the context of population ageing, which will place great pressure on living standards and the fiscal sustainability of important social programmes if participation rates do not rise, particularly among older persons.

- If supply- and demand-side barriers to employment are not addressed, population ageing will imply a sharp deceleration of labour force growth during the next three decades – including absolute declines in nearly one-half of the OECD countries. The ratio of persons aged 65 years and older to the labour force would also rise from 27% in 2000 to 47% in 2030, while the share of workers aged 50 years and older in the labour force would rise from 23% to 31%.

- Estimates of *potential* labour supply based on, alternatively, self-response data (*i.e.* inactive persons saying they want to work) and international benchmarks indicate that policies to expand participation could plausibly increase employment by between 7% and 12% of the working-age population (OECD average values). Juxtaposing the self-response and benchmark estimates indicates that many persons "distant" from the labour market would need to be mobilised to bring low-participation countries up towards the levels of high-participation countries, but also that a significant share of inactive persons are potentially interested in employment in all countries, even those in which employment rates are already high. These potential labour supply estimates also highlight the heterogeneity of the population groups under-represented in the labour market.

- Women, older and less skilled workers represent the largest pools of underutilised labour potential in most OECD countries. The social returns to increased employment among lone parents and persons with partial handicaps also appear to be high, despite these groups having less numerical weight as regards to raising aggregate employment rates. Barriers to employment for youths and immigrants also raise special social concerns, but the application of the labour mobilisation orientation to these groups is complex. Youth non-participation frequently takes the form of full-time schooling which adds to the human capital stock, thereby supporting future growth, and ensuring a smooth transition from schooling to working appears to be the key issue. As for the latter group, the employment gap for (male) immigrants is relatively small in most OECD countries (and negative in a few countries) and diminishing inactivity traps appears to be of less concern than ensuring adequate earnings and career prospects.

- There is considerable overlap across the different population groups that are under-represented in employment. This overlap is a reminder that some individuals face multiple barriers to participating in the labour market and that an integrated package of policy interventions may be necessary to allow them to participate fully in the labour market. For example, employment rates are particularly low for women and older persons with low educational attainment. Similarly, the strong geographic concentration of non-employment in many OECD countries means that barriers to employment due to individual factors are often combined with the disadvantages resulting from a depressed local labour market.

- Persons of working age who were non-employed in the mid-1990s spent an average of 4 ¼ of the next five years outside employment in Europe compared with 3½ years in the United States. Relatively high persistence in non-employment, especially in Europe, suggests that many of these non-employed persons may be difficult to "activate". Unless, of course, there should be a major change in their time-use preferences towards participating in employment, or substantial improvements in their employment opportunities and economic returns to working. However, the short duration of many "escapes" from non-employment suggests that employment instability is also an important factor depressing participation rates, especially in the United States.

- Persistence in non-employment is particularly strong for women, less educated adults, and, especially, older persons describing themselves as retired. These patterns hold in all of the countries considered, but gender and age differences in persistence are particularly strong in the United States. Unemployed persons move into employment at much higher rates than persons who are outside of the labour force, confirming that the statistical distinction between these two categories of non-employed persons is of practical importance for labour market programmes. Increased emphasis on policies to foster higher participation is an important complement to the conventional focus on helping unemployed persons into jobs, but it is no substitute for it.

- There is considerable evidence for the existence of so-called "low-pay traps", particularly when persons cycling between low-paid jobs and non-employment are considered. In both Europe and the United States, persons who were low paid in an initial year spent nearly four of the next five years in either low-paid employment or non-employment on average. This fraction is even higher for women, less educated workers (especially in the United States) and older workers (especially in Europe). However, persistence in low pay for some co-exists with upward earnings mobility for others, especially youths and persons with advanced educational qualifications. Policies broadening the access of low-paid workers to job ladders appear to be an important complement to measures that help place non-employed persons into jobs.

- Most often, joblessness and low-paid employment do not result in poverty-level household incomes, due to the presence of other earners in the family or alternative sources of income (including social benefits). However, the risk of chronic poverty is substantially higher for persons who are either prone to be jobless or in low-paid jobs, particularly in the United States. Whereas fewer than 3% of working-age persons continuously employed during a five year period are long-term poor in Europe, the risk of long-term poverty rises to 13% for persons who are never employed (5 and 32%, respectively, in the United States). Similarly, the risk of long-term poverty is 13% in Europe for workers who are continuously low paid over five years (41% in the United States). The association between both non-employment and low-paid employment, and an elevated risk of poverty, is particularly strong for low-educated persons and immigrants.

1. Raising employment by mobilising potential labour supply

A. Why increase aggregate labour supply and employment?

While the policy rationale for lowering unemployment is evident, that for raising participation rates and employment is much less so, since there is no presumption that all persons of working age should work.[1] Nonetheless, three arguments can be made for concluding that policies to foster higher participation rates could be welfare-enhancing: i) participation rates may be inefficiently low due to disincentives to employment created by certain policies; ii) higher participation rates could reduce the fiscal stress associated with high rates of benefit recipiency among working-age persons; and iii) higher participation might further social inclusion and equity goals. Each of these rationales is briefly summarised below. Sub-section B shows that these rationales take on added force in the context of population ageing.

Demand- and supply-side barriers may hinder employment of under-represented groups

A first rationale stresses economic efficiency considerations. It calls for the removal of existing disincentives to employment and labour force participation. Minimum wages and regulations setting minimum quality thresholds for jobs have the potential to limit employment opportunities and the disincentives to hiring created by these regulations frequently have a disproportionate effect on certain work-force groups.[2] The tax/transfer system may also create disincentives to labour supply that can be especially large for certain population groups. For example, the labour market participation of married women may be discouraged by the high marginal tax rates that second earners face in joint taxation systems (OECD, 2002d). Similarly, the marginal effective tax rate on earned income may be extremely high for persons receiving public transfers, with the combined impact of benefit claw-backs and taxes creating so-called "inactivity traps" (OECD, 2000b). A final example is that many public pension systems and early retirement schemes create strong financial disincentives to continued employment beyond the age of entitlement to begin receiving benefits (Gruber and Wise, 2002; OECD, 2002e; and Chapter 3 of this publication).

Higher employment of under-represented groups would reduce fiscal stress

Income transfer programmes which discourage socially productive employment also imply public spending that may create fiscal stress. Chapter 4 shows that a considerable share of the working-age population receives income-replacement benefits in the 16 OECD countries for which the necessary data could be assembled, with this share ranging up to 38% in the Slovak Republic and exceeding 20% in six EU countries in 1999. In all of the countries considered, a strong majority of benefit recipients of working age (more than three-quarters on average) were receiving social benefits other than unemployment benefits and were unlikely to be labour market participants. Although many of these persons either cannot work or should not be expected to do so, that is not the case for other benefit recipients (particularly in the countries with the highest recipiency rates). If greater participation can be fostered among the latter group, the tax-financing required to meet society's social insurance and equity goals could be lessened.

Promoting employment of under-represented groups would also serve social objectives

A third rationale for considering policies to foster higher participation is that they could advance social integration and equity goals in some cases. The shift towards an employment-oriented social policy reflects the judgement that many working-age recipients of social benefits could work, with the proper encouragement and assistance, and that both they and society would benefit from their greater integration into the labour market (see Chapter 4). One of the factors motivating the increased priority placed on "activating" benefit recipients is a growing appreciation of the long-term disadvantages (social, as well as fiscal) of allowing significant numbers of working-age persons to fall into benefit traps. As shown in Chapter 3, many recipients of lone parent benefits would like to have greater employment opportunities. Also, in the presence of firms' financial difficulties, older workers are sometimes forced into early retirement. These individuals constitute a form of hidden unemployment and there may be a high social cost to providing them assistance in a form that discourages reintegration into employment.

Taken together, these three rationales suggest that policies to encourage greater participation merit serious consideration, even if it is not easy to justify a specific target rate for participation or employment. Indeed, the case for fostering greater participation takes on added urgency in the context of population ageing.

B. The demographic challenge: adapting to population ageing

As is well-known, declining fertility and increasing longevity imply a dramatic ageing of the population in OECD countries in the coming decades, posing a major challenge to economic and social policy. As is shown in Chart 2.1, Panel A, national population projections[3] imply that the old-age dependency ratio will rise by 14 percentage points during the next three decades for the OECD as a whole (from 20% to 34%). Some countries will be affected sooner or more strongly than others, but all OECD countries will need to adapt to a significantly older population.

The implications of population ageing for labour markets depend on participation patterns by age and how they evolve. As can be seen in Chart 2.1, Panel B, age-participation profiles were affected by three major shifts during 1970-2000: i) a shift towards longer schooling and later labour force entry that affected both women and men; ii) a trend towards earlier retirement that was especially pronounced for men aged over 50; and iii) an upward trend in participation rates for each succeeding cohort of women. The first two trends magnified the tendency of population ageing to lower the number of working persons in the total population, while a continuing trend towards earlier retirement ages would result in an accelerating fall in the number of producers relative to consumers with adverse consequences for living standards (OECD, 1998b). However, the secular increase in the share of women in the labour force has tended to offset the potential drag of the first two trends on per-capita income and may continue to play this role in the future, particularly in OECD countries where the gender gap in participation is still very large (*e.g.* Southern Europe, Mexico and OECD Asia).

Unless action is taken, population ageing will entail a major slowdown in labour force growth...

A simple, demographic-driven scenario is useful for assessing the potential impact of population ageing on the labour force during the coming decades. This scenario is purely demographic in the sense that it combines population projections with the assumption that age and gender-specific participation rates remain unchanged at their 2000 values through to 2030, except that participation rates are adjusted for cohort effects.[4] These calculations show that the demographic developments associated with population ageing have strong implications for the growth of the labour force and its age composition in all OECD regions.

2. THE LABOUR MOBILISATION CHALLENGE: COMBATING INACTIVITY TRAPS AND BARRIERS TO MOVING UP JOB LADDERS

Chart 2.1. **The ageing challenge**

A. **The ratio of older to working-age persons will rise dramatically...**
Old-age dependency ratios[a] in selected OECD areas,[b] 1970 to 2030[c]

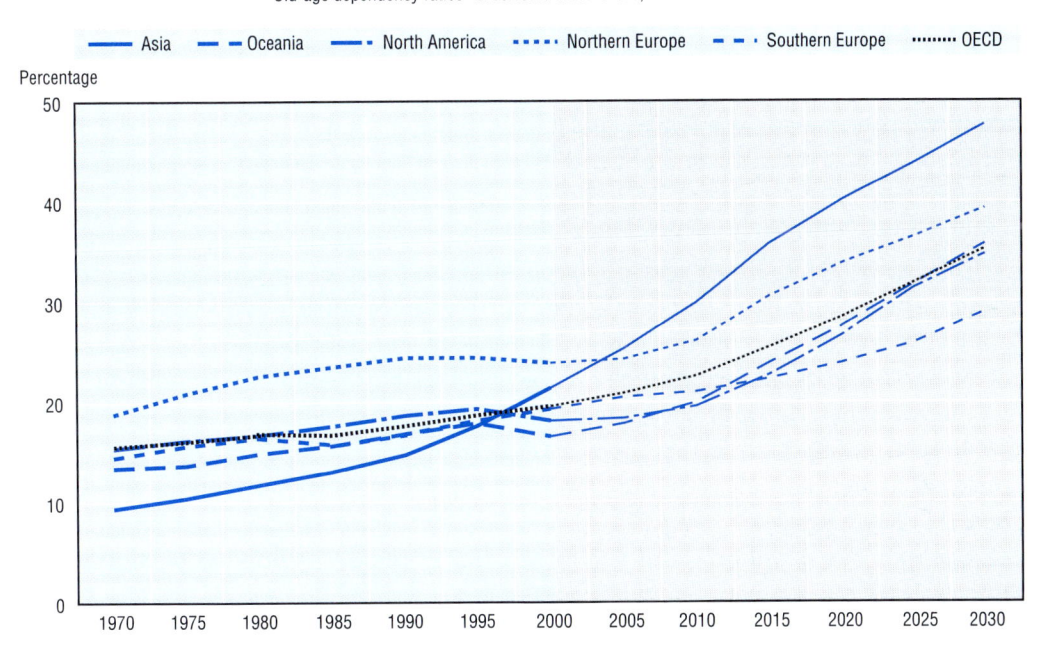

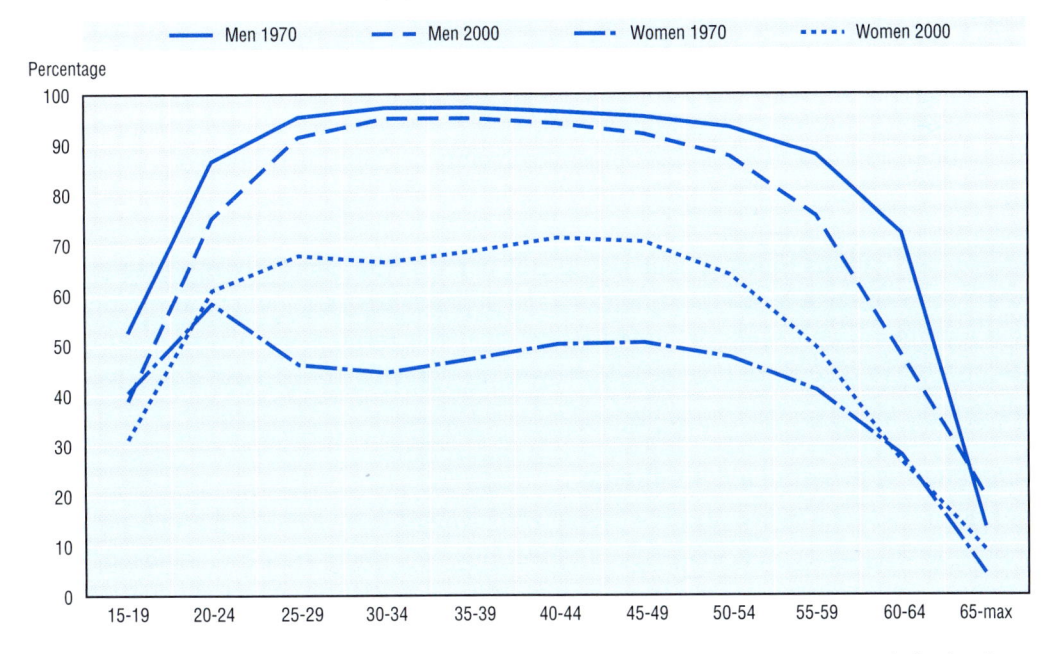

B. **...while the trend has been toward earlier retirement for men**
Age-participation profiles[d] 1970 and 2000

a) Old-age dependency ratio is the population aged 65 years or older divided by the working-age population (aged 15 to 64 years).
b) Population-weighted averages for the following regional groupings: Asia (Japan and Korea); Oceania (Australia and New Zealand); North America (Canada and the United States); Northern Europe (Denmark, Finland, Norway and Sweden); Southern Europe (Greece, Italy, Portugal, Spain and Turkey); OECD (all 30 member countries).
c) Values for 2001-2030 are projections.
d) Population-weighted average for OECD countries.

Source: Secretariat calculations using national population estimates and projections (medium variant) and OECD database on Labour Force Statistics.

The demographic-driven scenario implies a sharp deceleration in the rate of growth of the labour force to 2030 (Chart 2.2, Panel A). If participation patterns remain unchanged, the annual growth rate of the OECD labour force will slow from 1.3% during the past 30 years to below 0.3% over the next 30 years. The labour force will actually decline compared with its 2000 level in 14 OECD countries, with the decrease being at least 0.5% annually in Austria, the Czech Republic, Hungary, Italy, Japan and Poland. Only Mexico and Turkey will continue to experience rapid (albeit, slowing) growth in the number of persons in the labour force (country data not shown).

... and a sharp increase in dependency rates

The demographic-driven scenario implies that the ratio of persons aged 65 years and older to the total labour force will rise more rapidly during 2000-2030 than it did during 1970-2000 in all countries (Chart 2.2, Panel B). For the OECD area as a whole, this "modified old-age dependency ratio" rose by 0.2 percentage points per annum during the past three decades, but is projected to rise at 0.7 percentage points per annum, from 27% in 2000 to 47% in 2030. It is this increase that threatens the solvency of pay-as-you-go pension schemes, as well as living standards more generally, particularly in countries where this rise is especially steep (*e.g.* Austria, Finland, Germany, Italy, Japan and Korea). In this context, the economic and social returns to fostering greater participation – particularly, later retirement – could be very high.[5]

A "greying" workforce

Another implication of population ageing for the labour market is that the workforce will become older. Under the demographic-driven scenario, the share of workers aged 50 and older in the total labour force rises between 2000 and 2030 in every OECD country and work-force "greying" accelerates markedly in most countries (Chart 2.2, Panel C). In the OECD area as a whole, the older-worker share of the labour force was constant during 1970-2000, but is projected to rise by 2.6 percentage points per annum, from 23% in 2000 to 31% in 2030. The rising share of older persons in the workforce may require important adjustments in employment and training practices, and employer personnel policies.[6] Simple calculations indicate that significant parts of the deceleration of labour force growth and the rise in the modified old-age dependency ratio, which are implied the demographic-driven scenario, could be offset if the trend toward earlier retirement during 1970 to 2000 were reversed. However, the "greying" of the workforce would be reinforced.

C. Estimating potential labour supply

How large of an increase in the overall employment rate would be feasible and which groups, among non-employed persons of working age, might best be mobilised? These questions defy precise answers because it is difficult to identify which groups represent potential labour supply that could be unlocked by appropriate policies. This sub-section uses two different methodologies to estimate potential labour supply. Both methodologies have important limitations. Nonetheless, they help to clarify the potential magnitudes involved, the population groups that are numerically most important to efforts to increase overall employment and the international variation in the size and demographic profile of mobilisable labour.

2. THE LABOUR MOBILISATION CHALLENGE: COMBATING INACTIVITY TRAPS AND BARRIERS TO MOVING UP JOB LADDERS

Chart 2.2. **Population ageing and the labour force: recent experience and a demographic-driven scenario**[a] **in selected OECD areas**

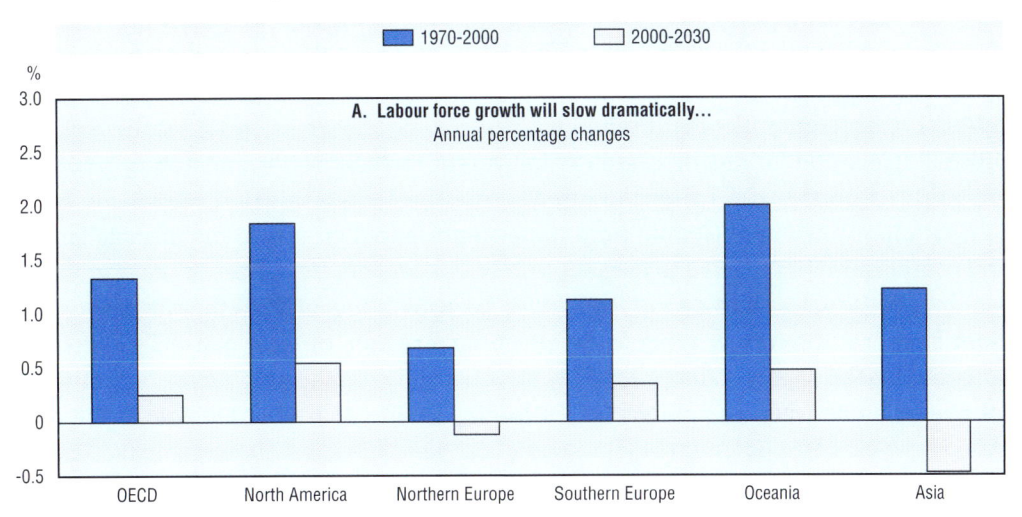

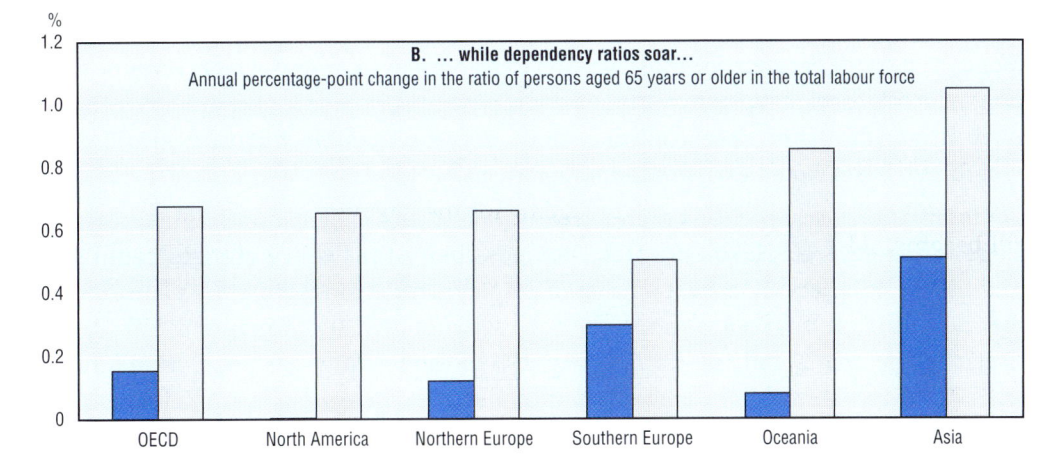

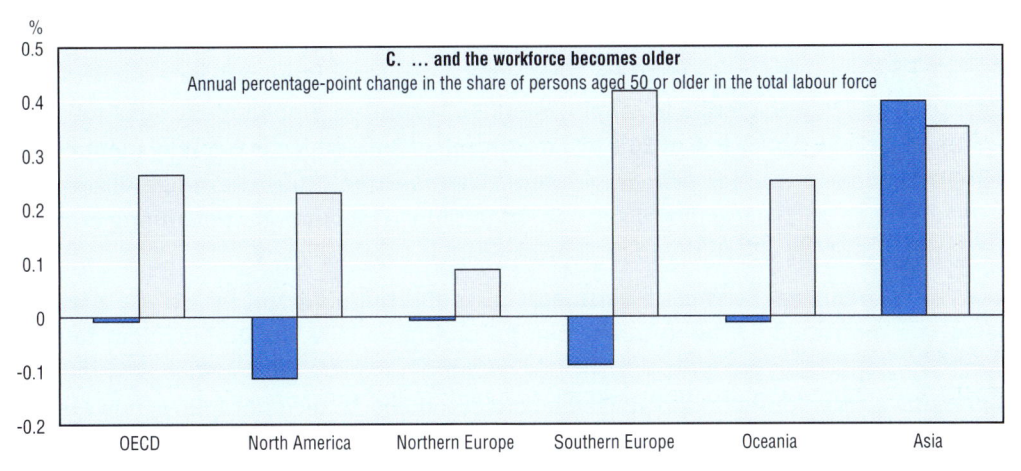

■ 1970-2000   □ 2000-2030

A. Labour force growth will slow dramatically...
Annual percentage changes

B. ... while dependency ratios soar...
Annual percentage-point change in the ratio of persons aged 65 years or older in the total labour force

C. ... and the workforce becomes older
Annual percentage-point change in the share of persons aged 50 or older in the total labour force

a) The demographic-driven scenario assumes that age and gender-specific participation rates remain unchanged at their 2000 values during 2000-2030, except that participation rates are adjusted for cross-cohort differences in participation rates (see text).
b) See Chart 2.1 note b) for definitions of the regional groupings displayed.
Source: Secretariat calculations using national population estimates and projections (medium variant), and historic participation data from the OECD database on Labour Force Statistics and ILO (1996).

Large differences in employment rates suggest room for raising employment of certain groups

As is shown in Chart 2.3, Panel A, employment rates for prime-age men are substantially higher than those for many other groups in the working-age population, including prime-age women, older and younger age groups, immigrants and persons with low educational attainment or disabilities. These comparisons suggest that there might be considerable scope for raising overall employment rates by better integrating groups that are under-represented in employment into the labour market. However several complications arise in reasoning from under-represented groups to mobilisable labour. A first complication is the need to take account of the very different sizes of these groups. For example, the employment rate of low-skilled persons is higher than that for persons with disabilities, yet the former represent a much larger share of total non-employment and potential labour supply (Chart 2.3, Panel B). A second complicating factor is that there is some overlap between the groups.[7] This overlap means that summing all of the groups would over-estimate potential labour supply, but also that some individuals face multiple barriers to participating in the labour market (Berthoud, 2003). A final complication lies in the difficulty of determining how much of the employment gap between prime-age men and the various under-represented groups can or should be closed. In many cases, there appear to be good reasons for these groups to be employed at lower rates than prime-age men: in some cases, employment may be simply impossible (*e.g.* for persons with severe disabilities); in other cases, employment may be feasible but undesirable, since opportunity costs would exceed economic returns.[8]

International comparisons represent a second source of benchmarks for assessing the scope to increase employment rates. The possibility that policy choices could have a quantitatively important impact on overall employment is rendered more plausible by the observation that aggregate employment rates for OECD countries differ by up to 40 percentage points, ranging from 45% to 85% of the working-age population (Chart 2.3, Panel A). Moreover, most of the cross-country variation in aggregate employment rates is due to international differences in the employment rates of different population groups, rather than to differences in population mix.[9] International variations in employment rates are greatest for under-represented groups, suggesting that a key determinant of overall employment rates may be how well national labour markets facilitate the participation of these groups in employment. For example, employment rates for prime-age women range from a low of 26% to a maximum of 86% (which is virtually identical with the OECD average rate for prime-age men). This is three times the range observed for prime-age men and suggestive of substantial untapped labour potential among prime-age women in countries where their employment rate is especially low.

The *international benchmark* estimates of mobilisable labour, which are presented below, are motivated by the intuition that an internationally low employment rate for a particular population group in a particular country is *prima facia* evidence that the group represents a reservoir of under-utilised labour resources. It need not follow, however, that the potential labour supply identified in this manner should be mobilised or, in any case, could be easily mobilised. Accordingly, an alternative, *self-response* estimate of potential labour supply is also presented, based on non-employed persons who state that they would like to work.

Chart 2.3. **Some groups are significantly under-represented in employment**

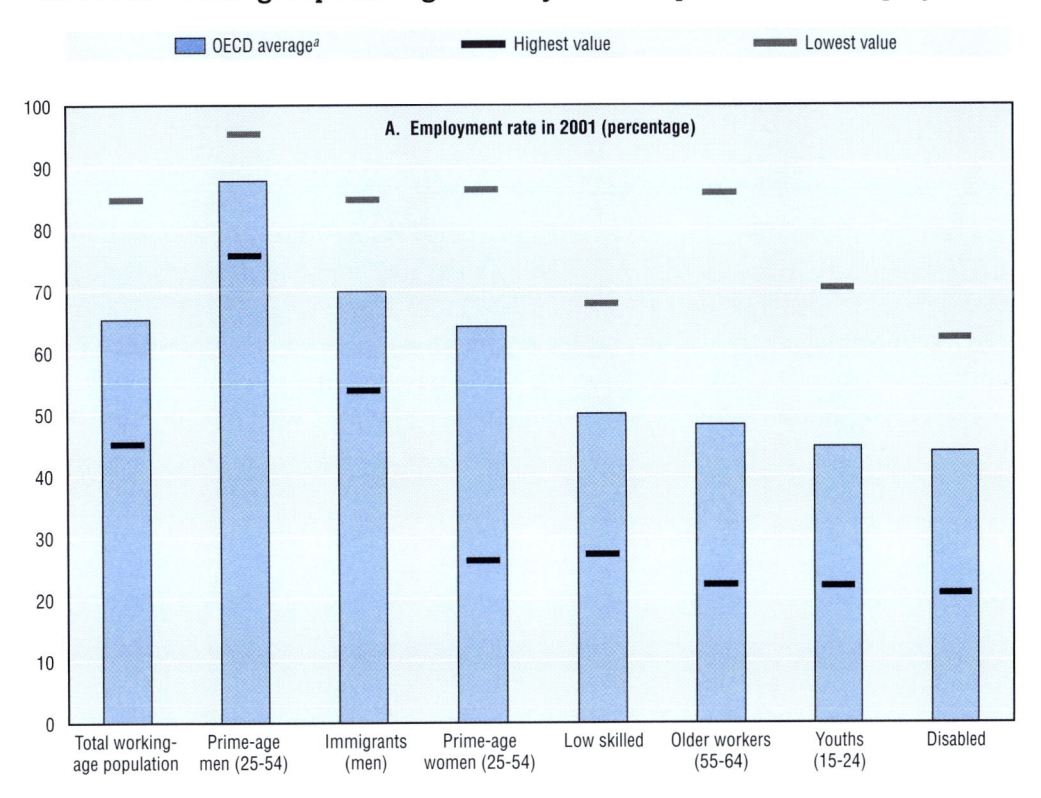

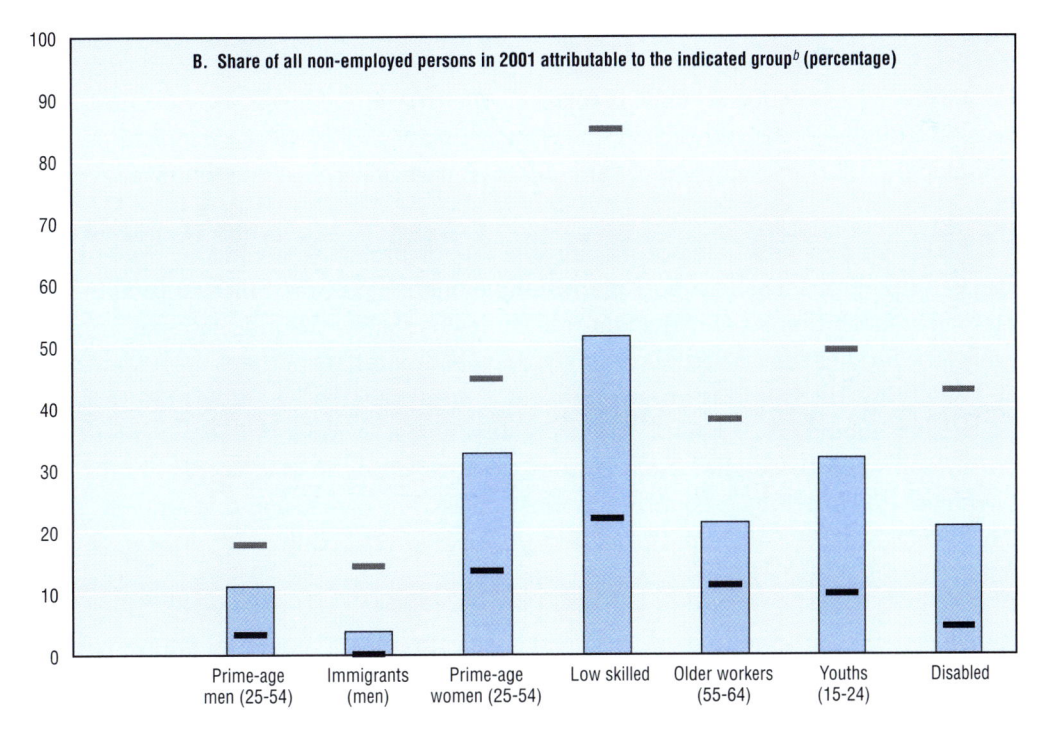

□ OECD average[a]   ▬ Highest value   ▬ Lowest value

A. Employment rate in 2001 (percentage)

B. Share of all non-employed persons in 2001 attributable to the indicated group[b] (percentage)

a) Population-weighted averages for, respectively, all OECD countries (prime-age men, prime-age women, low skilled, older workers, youth), the 23 countries shown in Chart 2.9 (male migrants) and the 19 countries shown in Chart 2.10 (disabled).
b) The immigrant, low-skilled and disabled groups overlap with the four age-gender groups.
Source: See Charts 2.6-2.10.

International-benchmarking estimates of potential labour supply

The international benchmark estimates were computed as follows:

- The working-age population in each country was divided into six sub-groups defined by gender and the three age ranges, under 25, 25-54, and 55-64.

- An international-benchmark participation rate for each sub-group was selected as the third highest value observed in the OECD in 2001.[10]

- "Excess inactivity" was then defined as any (positive) excess of inactivity above the population share implied by the benchmark participation rate (this was calculated separately for each sub-group and then summed to yield total excess inactivity).

- "Excess unemployment" was defined as any (positive) excess of unemployment in 2001 above 5%[11] (this was first calculated for the total working-age population and then "allocated" across the sub-groups according to their shares of total unemployment).

- Total mobilisable labour resources are calculated as the sum of excess inactivity and excess unemployment.[12]

Chart 2.4 presents the international-benchmark estimates of mobilisable labour resources (*i.e.* the potential increase in employment that could be achieved by mobilisation policies) for the 28 OECD countries for which the necessary data could be assembled. By construction, the benchmark estimates of mobilisable labour resources produce strong international convergence in employment rates.[13] The estimated potential for raising employment rates averages 12% and ranges from 35% in Turkey (where the current employment to population ratio is 45%) to zero in Iceland (current employment to population ratio of 88%). Excess inactivity accounts for 92% of mobilisable labour resources and unemployment for just 8% (OECD averages, see Chart 2.4, Panel A). Women of all ages contribute 71% of the total and persons aged 55-64 contribute 29%, for a combined contribution of 83% (once account is taken of the overlap between the two groups). As discussed in the previous sub-section, the relative importance of older persons to potential labour supply will rise strongly in coming decades, particularly if retirement ages continue to fall.

The benchmark estimates of mobilisable labour probably provide an upper-bound estimate of potential labour supply in low-employment countries, since cultural or other factors may mean that an employment rate somewhat below the international frontier is appropriate for these countries. Accordingly, these estimates are perhaps most informative for identifying the population groups that would have to be integrated into paid employment should OECD countries with relatively low or moderate employment rates wish to approach the higher employment rates recorded in the Nordic countries or Switzerland (the benchmark countries in most cases). The conclusion that emerges is that such countries generally should place top priority on attracting more women into the labour force and inducing older workers to delay retirement.

Inactive persons wanting to work: self-response estimates of potential labour supply

A second approach to estimating potential labour supply among persons outside of the labour force is to identify the subset of inactive persons who would be predisposed to respond to improved employment opportunities by entering the labour force. This is a hypothetical criterion that cannot be directly implemented using standard labour force survey (LFS) data. However, LFS data provide indirect indicators which suggest that a

2. THE LABOUR MOBILISATION CHALLENGE: COMBATING INACTIVITY TRAPS AND BARRIERS TO MOVING UP JOB LADDERS

Chart 2.4. Raising participation among women and older persons is key
International-benchmark estimates of mobilisable labour resources,[a, b] 2001

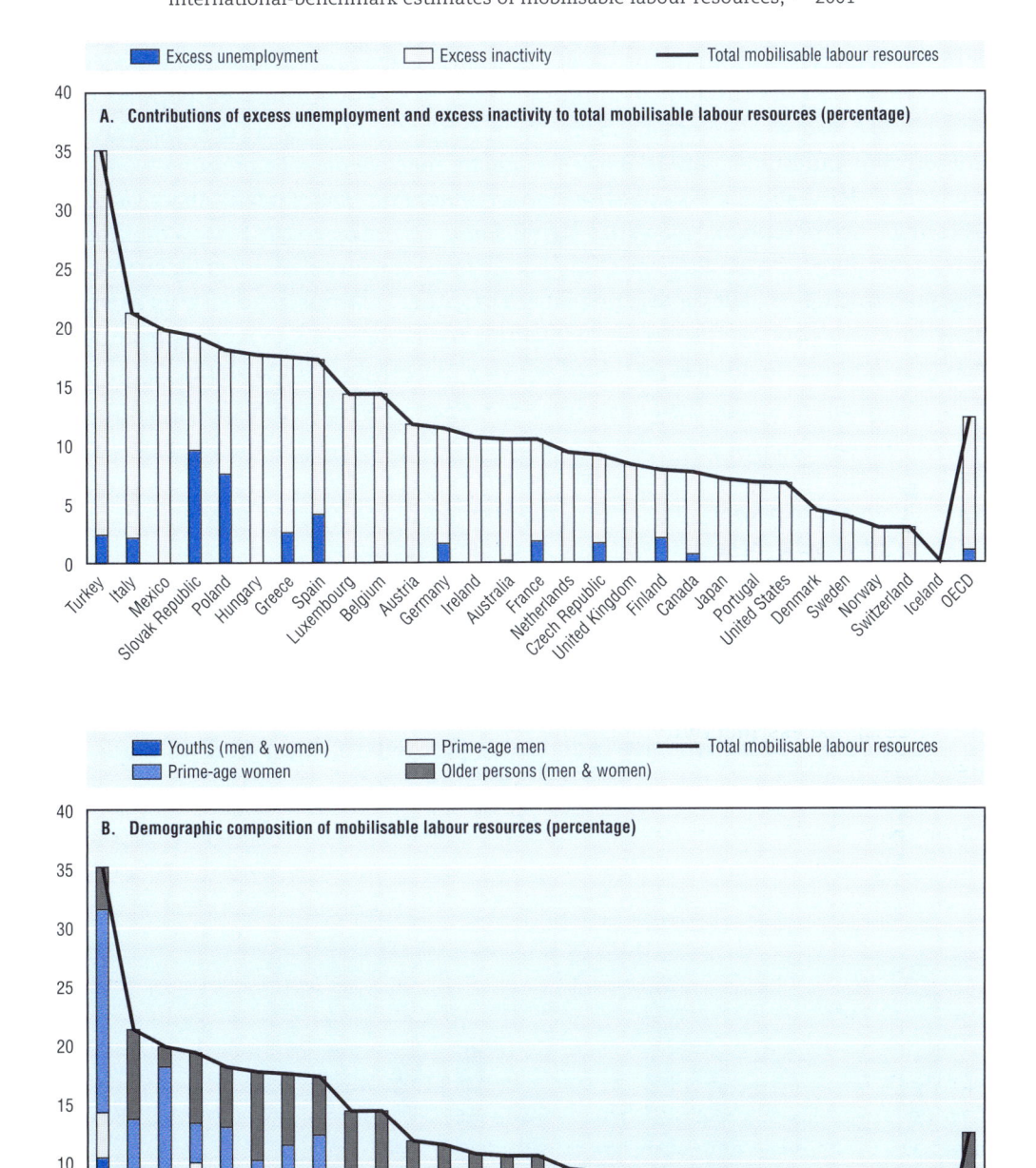

A. Contributions of excess unemployment and excess inactivity to total mobilisable labour resources (percentage)

Legend: Excess unemployment | Excess inactivity | Total mobilisable labour resources

B. Demographic composition of mobilisable labour resources (percentage)

Legend: Youths (men & women) | Prime-age men | Total mobilisable labour resources | Prime-age women | Older persons (men & women)

Note: OECD: Population-weighted average for the 28 countries shown.

a) Mobilisable labour resources are shown as the vertical sum of excess unemployment and excess inactivity. Excess unemployment is defined as unemployment above 5% of the labour force (if any). Excess inactivity is based on comparisons between actual participation rates for cells defined by age and gender, and international benchmark rates (see text for details).

b) Countries are shown from left to right in descending order of mobilisable labour resources.

Source: Secretariat calculations based on OECD database on Labour Force Statistics and OECD database on Labour Market Status by educational participation.

significant share of inactive persons would enter the labour market under the right conditions. In particular, the number of inactive persons of working age saying that they would like to work provides a *self-response* estimate of potential labour supply. On average for the 19 countries covered by the European Labour Force Survey, this criterion identifies 12% of inactive persons (corresponding to 7% of the working-age population) as constituting a reserve of potential labour supply (Chart 2.5). This share does not vary much between men and women, but is above average for inactive persons of prime-working age or having at least completed upper secondary schooling. The share of inactive persons indicating a desire to work also varies significantly, according to the reason that they cite for not searching for a job. Persons citing family responsibilities are most likely to express a desire to work (22%), but those citing illness or "other" reasons are nearly as likely to do so. By contrast, only one in ten persons citing education want to work (currently) and persons describing themselves as retired are very unlikely to want to work.

It is difficult to assess the behavioural significance of the self-response estimates of potential labour supply. *A priori*, the self-response data will tend to over-estimate potential labour supply to the extent that inactive persons saying that they want to work exaggerate their willingness to accept a job, taking full account of the reasons they are not, in fact, working. Conversely, these data will tend to under-estimate potential labour supply in the long run, to the extent that they reflect preferences under existing conditions and, hence, miss some of the additional labour supply that would emerge should policy reforms render work more attractive in a way that is sustained. Table 2.A1.1 (in Annex 1) shows that this

Chart 2.5. **Many inactive individuals (but few retirees) want to work**

Self-response estimates of potential labour supply in Europe by gender, age, educational attainment[a] and reason for inactivity, 2001

Share of inactive persons of working age wanting to work (percentage)[b]

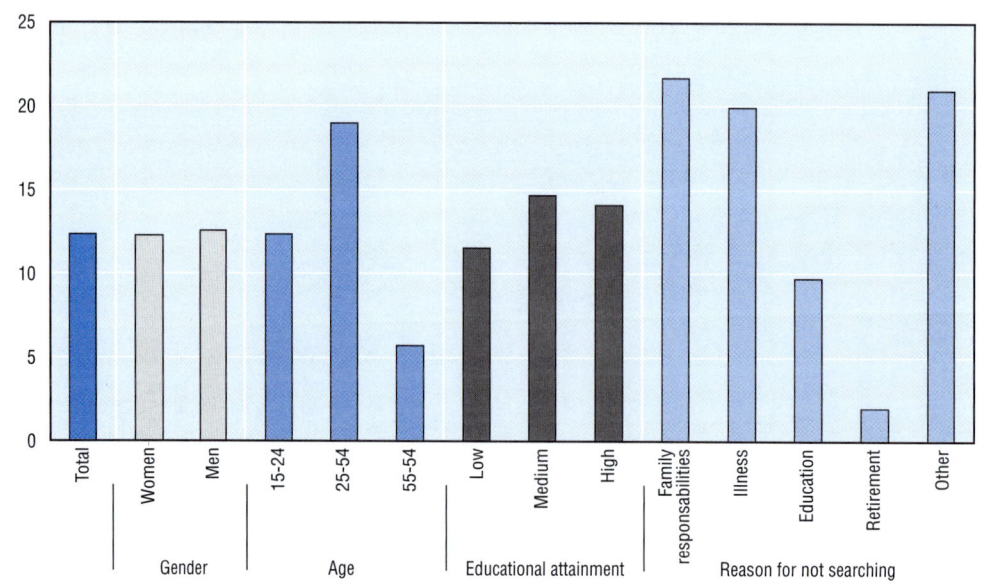

a) Low educational attainment corresponds to not having completed upper secondary schooling and high educational attainment to having completed a university or tertiary degree.
b) Population-weighted averages for Austria, Belgium, the Czech Republic, Denmark, Finland, France, Gremany, Hungary, Iceland, Ireland, Italy, Luxembourg, the Netherlands, Poland, Portugal, the Slovak Republic, Spain, Sweden and the United Kingdom.

Source: Secretariat calculations based on the European Labour Force Survey, data provided by Eurostat.

second bias is potentially large. Survey questions inquiring about respondent's desire to work, either currently or in the future, generate significantly higher estimates of potential labour supply, averaging 64% of inactive persons of working age across the countries analysed.[14] Despite these caveats, the self-response estimates should give some indication of the share of persons outside of the labour force who would be receptive to working, if policy initiatives should increase their access to employment or made it easier for them to reconcile work with their other obligations and activities.[15]

Comparing the benchmark and self-response estimates of potential labour supply

The benchmark estimate of potential labour supply is higher than the self-response estimate for the OECD as a whole and this difference is especially pronounced in low-employment countries.[16] This difference suggests that a substantial share of the existing gaps in employment rates across OECD countries can only be closed by attracting inactive persons into the labour force who are "distant" from the labour market, in that sense that they are not currently predisposed to respond to improved employment opportunities by entering the labour market. Within countries, the benchmark estimates of potential labour supply are more strongly concentrated among women and, especially, older persons than are the self-response estimates. The fact that the potential labour supply identified using self-response data includes many fewer older persons probably indicates that it would be difficult to reverse retirement decisions, once taken. However, it may be easier to encourage future cohorts of workers to delay or phase in their retirement.[17]

2. The many faces of non-employment

This section provides a descriptive overview of groups in the working-age population that are under-represented in employment. In addition to women and older workers – groups that were highlighted in the analysis of potential labour supply in Section 1 – other groups potentially on the margins of the labour market are considered, including youths, low-skilled persons, persons with disabilities and immigrants.[18] The intent is to provide a more detailed portrait of the *diversity* of non-employment and to bring out international differences, or other patterns, that shed some light on the causes of low employment rates that might be amenable to policy interventions. The considerable overlap across these groups means that they should not be summed to arrive at an overall estimate of persons at risk of exclusion from the labour market, but also that some individuals confront multiple barriers to participating in the labour market. Although not analysed here, it also should be borne in mind that non-employment is strongly concentrated in lagging regions and localities in many OECD countries (OECD, 2000a). Accordingly, policies addressing employment barriers which are associated with the individual characteristics analysed here should be combined with economic development strategies for increasing employment opportunities in the local labour market.

A. *Women are still significantly under-represented in the labour market*

The secular increase in female participation continued in almost all countries over the past decade, accompanied by a decline in unemployment in countries where aggregate labour market conditions improved (Chapter 1). However, despite these positive developments, the labour market position of women is still lagging behind that of men: inactivity rates were on average 21 percentage points higher in 2001, translating into a gender employment gap of 20 percentage points and women accounting for nearly two-thirds of all non-employment in the working-age population (Chart 2.6). However, these OECD averages hide very large differences across countries, with the inactive share of working-age women ranging from 17% in Iceland to 73% in Turkey. Cultural differences may account for an important share of these differences, but the large increases in female participation that have occurred in many OECD countries during the past several decades indicate that economic and institutional factors also play an important role and can be influenced by policy choices.[19]

The tendency for women to be under-represented in employment is also particularly strong for the least educated women and mothers with young children (OECD, 2002a).[20] Non-employment among mothers is of particular concern when they are lone parents. Non-employment rates actually tend to be slightly lower for the 3% of women who are lone parents than for other women (43% *versus* 45%, according to 2001 data from the European Labour Force Survey for 14 EU countries). However, lone mothers are much more likely than other women to be in a jobless household, since they are the only potential earners in their households. Whereas 15% of women of working age who are not lone parents live in a jobless household, this rate rises to 43% for lone mothers.[21]

B. About 15% of youths are neither working nor studying in the OECD as a whole

Employment rates are substantially higher and more uniform internationally for the prime-age population (*i.e.* persons aged 25 to 54) than for their younger and older counterparts (compare Panel B of Chart 2.7 with Panels A and C). The non-employment rate for youths (persons aged 15 to 24) is 32 percentage points higher than for prime-age workers for the OECD as a whole, but the majority of non-employed youths are enrolled in education and this throws a different light on the low youth employment rate.[22] The proportion of youths neither employed nor studying averaged 15% for the OECD as a whole. This is below the non-employment rate of prime-age persons (24%) and such youths represent less than 5% of total non-employment (not associated with schooling) in the working-age population. However, this group is quite large in a few countries, representing approximately 20% of youths in Italy and Mexico, 31% in the Slovak Republic and 40% in Turkey. Furthermore, out-of-school youths who are not working raise particular social concerns, since their long-run career prospects could be compromised by early difficulties in the labour market. Research results have been mixed concerning these so-called "scarring" effects, but nearly unanimous that early school leavers lacking a solid base of cognitive and vocational skills fare poorly in the labour market (Burgess *et al.*, 2003; Neumark, 1998).

C. Withdrawal from the labour market starts well before the official retirement age

For the OECD as a whole in 2001, the non-employment rate of older individuals – defined here as those aged 55 to 64 – averaged just over 50%, as compared with a little under 25% for prime-age individuals (Chart 2.7). As a result, the older age group accounts for a third of total non-employment in the (non-student) working-age population. The decline in employment for persons nearing the conventional retirement age of 65 is entirely due to an increase in the inactivity rate (50% for older persons *versus* 20% for persons of prime working age), since unemployment rates (as a share of population) are considerably lower for the older group (2% *versus* 4%).[23] The patterns of labour force withdrawal with age are very diverse across OECD countries (OECD, 2002e). Inactivity rates for older persons are highest in Central and East European countries (especially, Hungary

2. THE LABOUR MOBILISATION CHALLENGE: COMBATING INACTIVITY TRAPS AND BARRIERS TO MOVING UP JOB LADDERS

Chart 2.6. **Women's participation rates vary widely across OECD countries**
Decomposition of the working-age population between employment, unemployment and inactivity by gender, 2001
Percentages of the indicated groups[a]

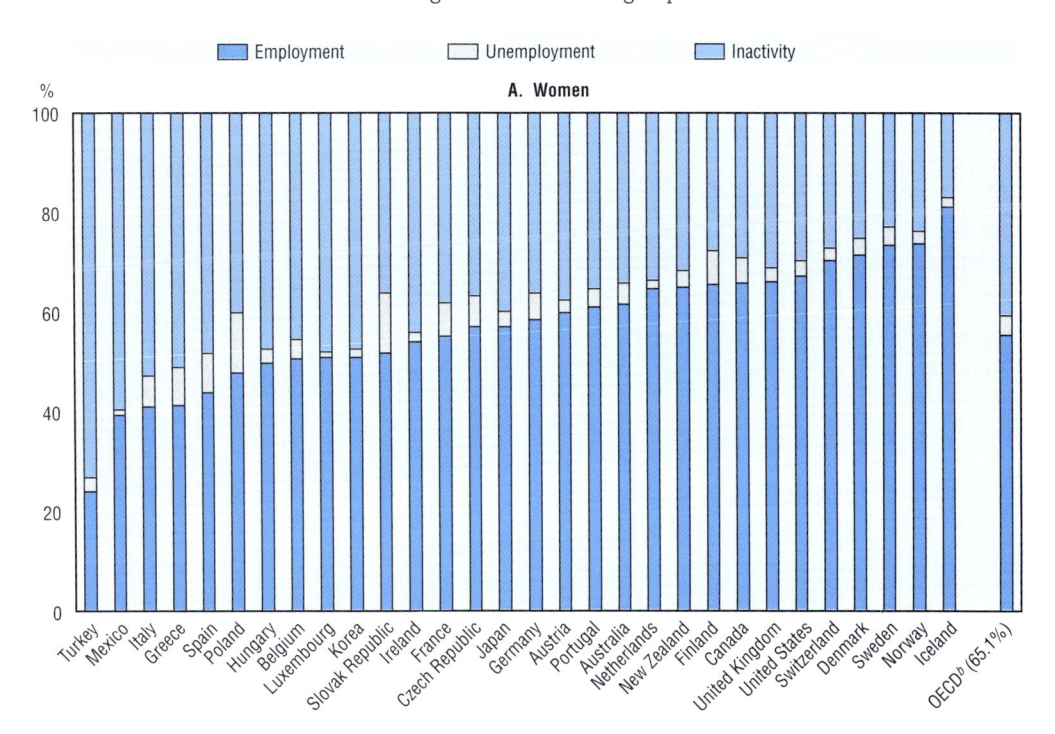

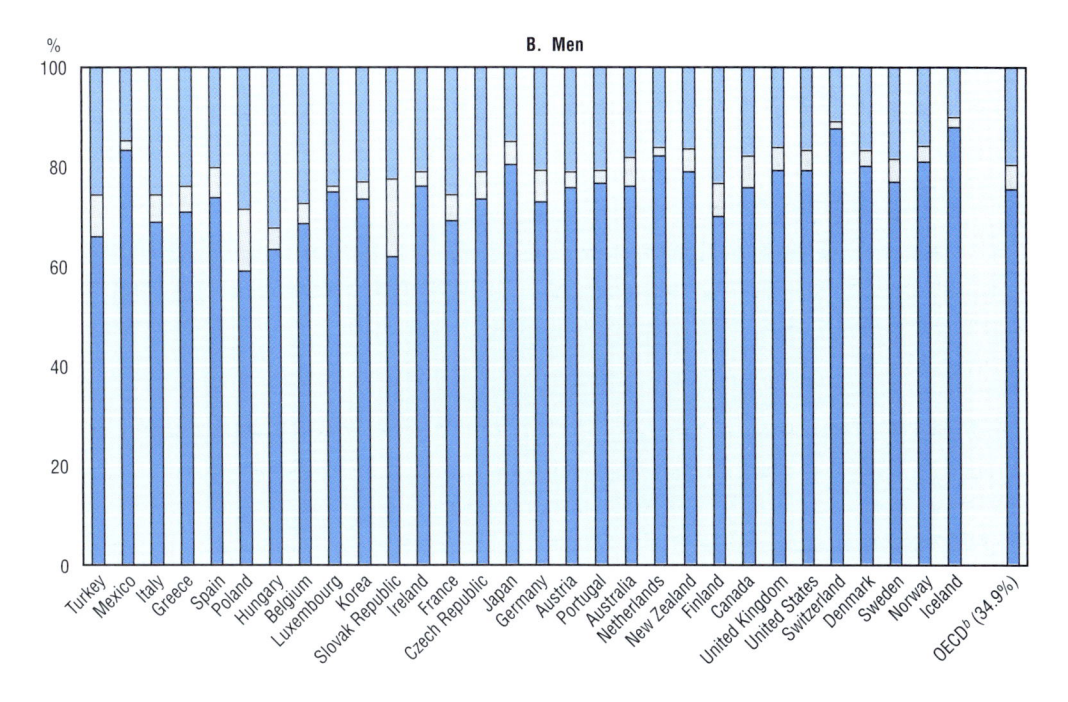

A. Women

B. Men

a) Countries ordered from left to right by increasing employment to population ratio for women.
b) Population-weighted average for the countries shown (value in parenthesis is group's share of total non-employment).

Source: OECD database on Labour Force Statistics.

2. THE LABOUR MOBILISATION CHALLENGE: COMBATING INACTIVITY TRAPS AND BARRIERS TO MOVING UP JOB LADDERS

Chart 2.7. **Withdrawal from work starts well in advance of age 65 in most OECD countries**
Decomposition of the working-age population between employment, unemployment and inactivity by age, 2001
Percentages of the indicated groups[a]

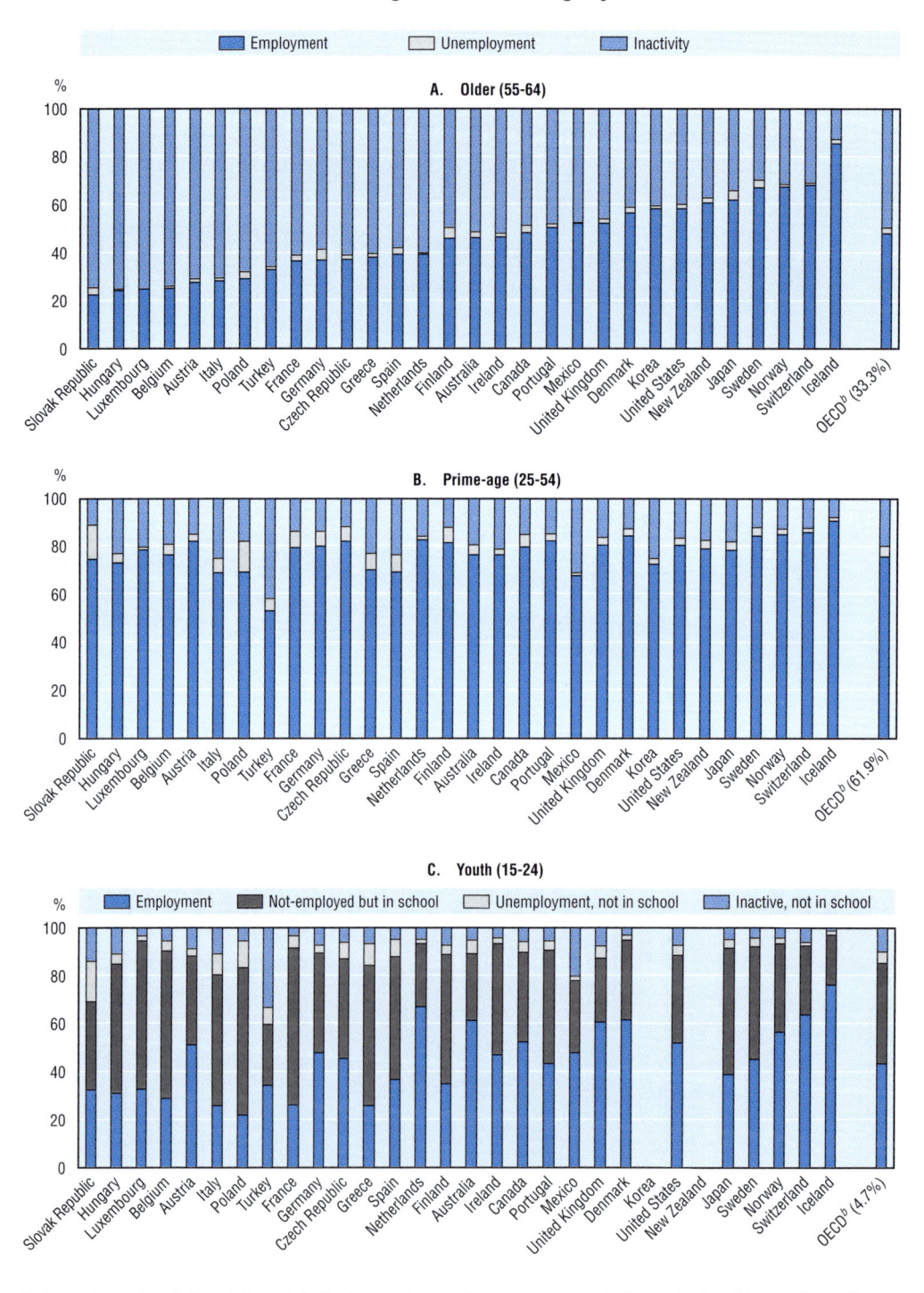

a) Countries ordered from left to right by increasing employment to population ratio for older workers. Korea and New Zealand do not appear in Panel C because the necessary data on school enrolment are not available.
b) Population-weighted average for the countries shown (value in parenthesis is group's share of total non-employment).
Source: OECD database on Labour Force Statistics and OECD database on Labour Market Status by Educational Participation.

84　　　OECD EMPLOYMENT OUTLOOK – ISBN 92-64-10061-X – © OECD 2003

and the Slovak Republic), where the transition from centrally-planned to market-based economies was accompanied by large reductions in participation among older workers, and in some EU countries (especially, Austria, Belgium, France, Italy and Luxembourg), where extensive use has been made of early-retirement and other benefit schemes to encourage older workers to withdraw from the labour market (OECD, 2002e). At the other end of the spectrum, only 13% of older individuals are outside the labour force in Iceland and only approximately one-third in Japan, Norway, Sweden and Switzerland.

There are various pathways out of the labour market and reasons for non-participation, and these differ in importance across countries (Table 2.1). A large share of persons aged 50 to 64 describe themselves as "retired" in countries that have had broad recourse to early retirement programmes as a way to deal with mass layoffs or persistently high unemployment.[24] However, the proportion of this age group citing either illness or disability as the reason for inactivity is quite high in several countries, exceeding one in five in Poland and being near 15% in Denmark, Finland, the Netherlands and the United Kingdom. In some of these countries, there are no or fewer "formal" early retirement schemes than in countries such as Belgium (OECD, 2003b), so disability benefits may be

Table 2.1. **Older workers follow multiple pathways out of the labour market**
Labour force status of persons aged 50 to 64 years and reasons for being inactive, 2000
Percentages

	Active			Inactive					
	Employed	Unemployed	Total	No work available	Retired	Illness or disability	Family duties	Other	Total
Austria	44.1	3.1	47.2	0.3	38.2	2.4	7.6	4.3	52.8
Belgium (2001)	40.9	1.2	42.1	28.4	28.3	0.3	0.1	0.8	57.9
Czech Republic	54.8	3.6	58.4	0.3	31.5	8.7	0.6	0.6	41.6
Denmark	65.3	2.6	67.9	0.6	13.8	13.8	2.2	1.8	32.1
Finland	58.4	5.0	63.4	2.0	12.3	15.9	1.3	5.1	36.6
France	48.7	4.0	52.7	..	..	..	..	..	47.3
Germany	48.6	6.0	54.6	0.4	28.7	4.1	5.0	7.1	45.4
Greece	47.1	2.2	49.2	0.2	21.2	2.3	12.5	14.6	50.8
Hungary	39.1	1.6	40.6	1.8	47.2	6.5	0.8	3.2	59.4
Iceland	89.3	0.6	89.9	0.6	0.0	6.6	1.3	1.7	10.1
Ireland	53.0	1.7	54.8	..	..	..	..	..	45.2
Italy	38.4	1.8	40.2	1.9	28.9	4.2	18.4	6.3	59.8
Korea[a]	62.6	1.8	64.3	..	2.4	1.6	25.5	6.1	35.7
Luxembourg	42.3	0.7	43.0	0.0	20.2	7.9	25.2	3.7	57.0
Netherlands	52.0	1.1	53.1	1.2	11.0	13.3	7.3	14.0	46.9
Norway	72.8	0.9	73.7	..	..	..	..	..	26.3
Poland	43.3	4.6	48.0	2.5	15.7	22.3	4.8	6.7	52.0
Portugal	59.0	2.1	61.1	0.1	16.0	7.0	9.5	6.3	38.9
Slovak Republic	40.5	6.1	46.6	0.3	50.4	1.5	0.8	0.3	53.4
Spain	44.6	4.6	49.2	0.9	10.3	7.1	12.7	19.8	50.8
Sweden	72.0	4.1	76.1	..	..	..	..	..	23.9
Switzerland	71.0	1.5	72.5	0.3	11.9	4.3	9.5	1.4	27.5
United Kingdom	60.7	2.8	63.4	0.5	12.8	14.2	5.1	3.9	36.6
OECD[b]	**50.6**	**3.4**	**54.1**	**1.3**	**16.9**	**6.6**	**8.5**	**6.2**	**45.9**

.. Data not available.
a) The category "other" includes the reason "no work available".
b) Population-weighted average for countries shown.
Source: European Union Labour Force Survey 2000 and 2001; Korean Survey of the economically active population.

serving as an alternative route to early retirement. Indeed, the receipt of disability benefits rises strongly with age, particularly in Austria, the Netherlands, Norway, Poland, Portugal and Sweden (OECD, 2003a and Chapter 4 of this publication). In Korea and Luxembourg, over 25% of those aged 50 to 64 cite family duties, which probably reflects caring for older relatives, as the reason for being inactive.

D. Fewer than one-half of the less educated are employed in the OECD as a whole

Employment rates are significantly lower for less educated persons than for their more educated counterparts,[25] and persons not having finished upper secondary schooling account for over half of non-employment (Chart 2.8). In 2001, the employment rate for persons not having completed upper secondary schooling was a little below 50% for the OECD area as a whole, as compared with over 80% for working-age persons with a university or tertiary degree. Fully 45% of working-age persons in the low-education group were neither working nor looking for a job in 2001, as compared to 24% of their medium-educated counterparts and 15% of high-educated individuals. These large differences in participation suggest that the more limited labour market opportunities available to workers not having completed secondary schooling have a strong discouraging effect on participation, a pattern which appears to have become more pronounced in recent decades (Gregg and Manning, 1996; Juhn, 1992). When in the labour force, this group also tends to experience higher unemployment than the high-educated group, but similar unemployment to the medium-educated group (an OECD average of 5% for low and medium-educated workers *versus* 3% for high-educated workers).

There are major differences across OECD countries in the extent to which low education is associated with low participation and employment rates. The proportion of low-educated individuals who are inactive is over 50% in Central and Eastern European member countries, Belgium, Italy and Turkey. At the other extreme, it is under 20% in Iceland, and also relatively low in Japan and Portugal (28 and 29%, respectively). Participation rates are more uniform internationally for medium and, especially, high-educated individuals. There is also significant cross-country variation in unemployment rates for low-educated persons, which tends to reinforce the differences in participation. The unemployment to population ratios for less educated workers are highest, at between 8 and 13%, in the Czech Republic, the Slovak Republic, and Poland – bringing non-employment for low-educated individuals above 70% in these three countries.

E. Immigrants: a very heterogeneous group

Immigrants are another group that sometimes occupies a disadvantaged position in the labour market and whose economic (and social) integration raises particular concerns (Borjas, 1999; Coppel *et al.*, 2001; OECD, 2001). However, this is a very heterogeneous group, as the country of origin and the reason for and timing of immigration may all affect labour market outcomes in the host country (OECD, 2001 and 2002g). Immigrants are also very diverse as concerns educational qualifications: in the majority of OECD countries in Europe and North America, foreigners are over-represented in both the low and high-education groups, as compared to nationals.

In 1999-2000, the employment rates of foreigners were lower than those of nationals in the majority of OECD countries for which data are available (Chart 2.9). However, the average difference was small, particularly for men (70% *versus* 74%). Foreign men actually had a higher employment rate than their native counterparts in some countries, including

2. THE LABOUR MOBILISATION CHALLENGE: COMBATING INACTIVITY TRAPS AND BARRIERS TO MOVING UP JOB LADDERS

Chart 2.8. **Low skilled account for half of total non-employment in the OECD area**
Decomposition of the working-age population between employment, unemployment and inactivity by educational attainment,[a] 2001
Percentages of indicated groups[b]

A. Low skilled

B. Medium skilled

C. High skilled

a) Low educational attainment corresponds to not having completed upper secondary schooling and high educational attainment to having completed a university or tertiary degree.
b) Countries ordered from left to right by increasing employment to population ratio for low skilled persons.
c) Population-weighted average for the countries shown (value in parenthesis is group's share of total non-employment).

Source: OECD (2003), Education at a Glance.

Chart 2.9. **Employment gap is small for immigrant men in all but a few countries**

Employment rates of working-age nationals and foreigners[a] by gender in selected OECD countries, 1999-2000 averages[b, c]

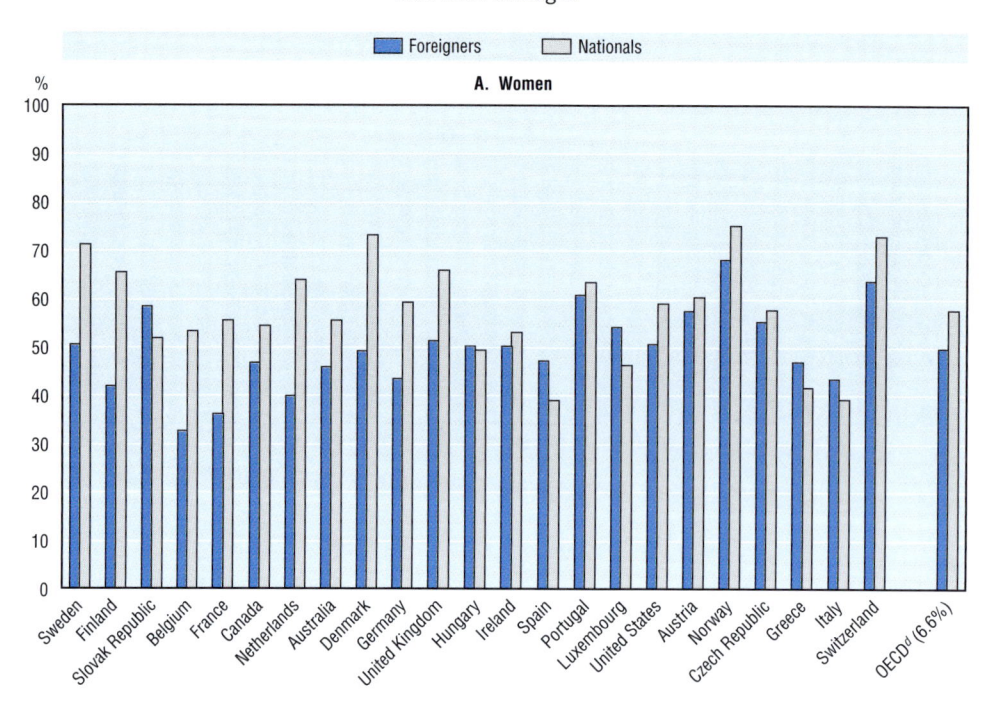

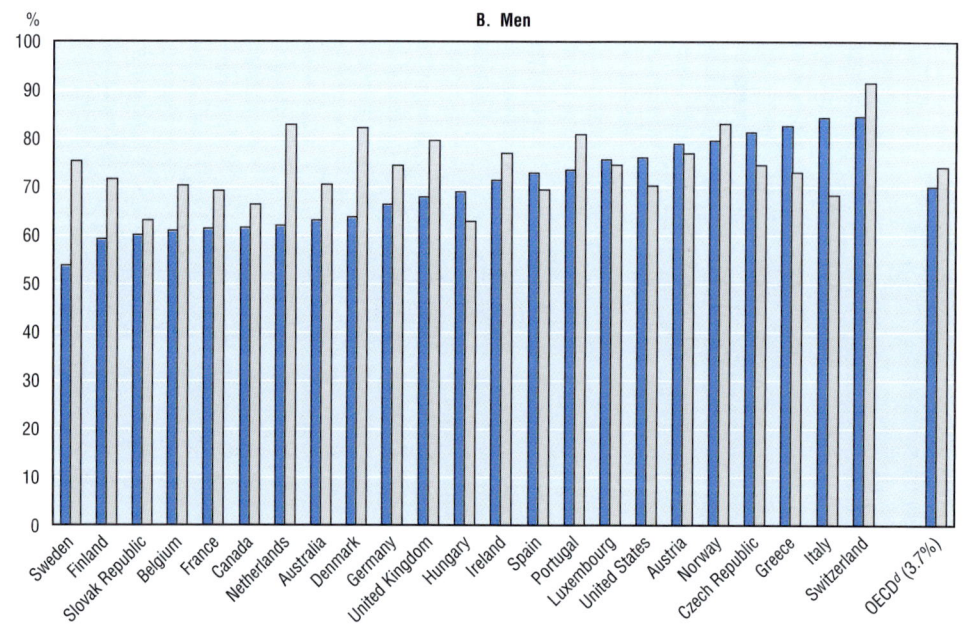

A. Women

B. Men

Countries (left to right): Sweden, Finland, Slovak Republic, Belgium, France, Canada, Netherlands, Australia, Denmark, Germany, United Kingdom, Hungary, Ireland, Spain, Portugal, Luxembourg, United States, Austria, Norway, Czech Republic, Greece, Italy, Switzerland, OECD[d] (6.6% for women, 3.7% for men)

a) Nationals and foreigners refer to persons born in the host country and born abroad, respectively, for Australia, Canada, Hungary and the United States.
b) Countries ordered from left to right by increasing employment to population ratio for foreign men.
c) August 2000 for Australia; 1996 for Canada and March 2000 for the United States.
d) Population-weighted average for the countries shown (value in parenthesis is the share of total non-employment attributable to foreigners of the indicated gender).

Source: Labour Force Survey, data provided by Eurostat and by the Australian Bureau of Statistics; 1996 census, Statistics Canada; *Current Population Survey*, US Bureau of the Census.

Central, Eastern and Southern European countries and the United States. The average employment gap for foreigners is twice as large for women as it is for men (8 as compared with 4 percentage points). Employment rates for foreign women lagged those for their national counterparts most strongly in Denmark, Finland and the Netherlands, while the employment rates of foreign women were lowest in Belgium and Spain. In general, differences between foreigners and nationals in employment are relatively small compared with the differences analysed above between men and women, age groups and educational groups. Foreigners represented just 10% of total non-employment on average in 2001, but this share was significantly higher in a few high-immigration countries.

F. Few persons with disabilities are in work

Employment rates for working-age disabled people are significantly lower than for non-disabled (Chart 2.10). For the 19 countries for which data are available, the

Chart 2.10. **Employment rate of disabled persons varies widely across OECD countries**

Employment rates of disabled and non-disabled persons aged 20-64 in selected OECD countries,[a,b] late 1990s

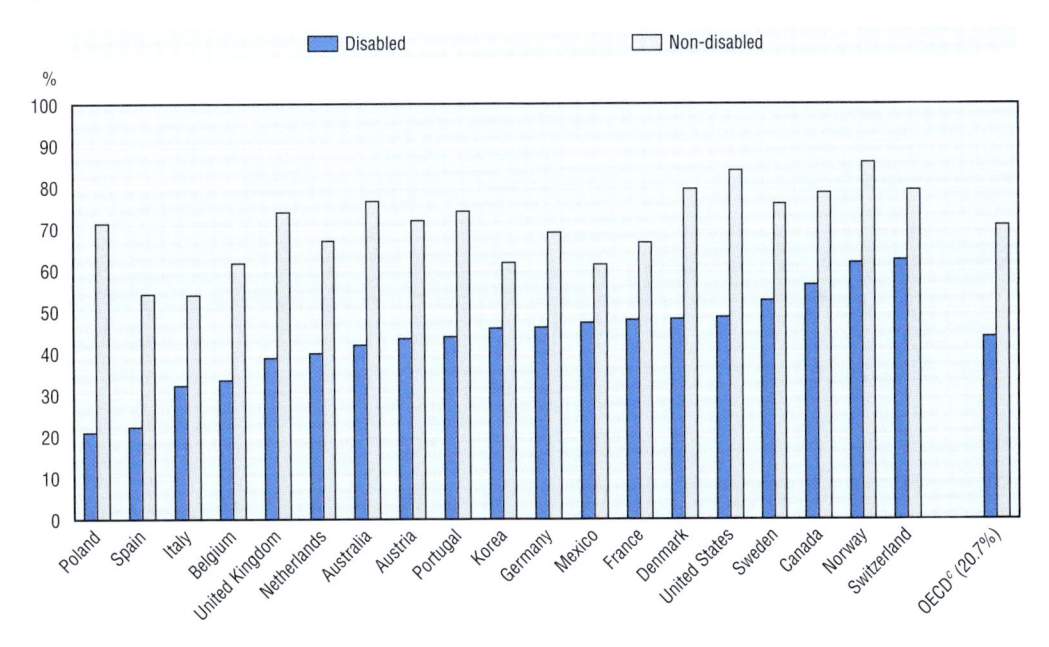

a) Disability status based on self-assessment of survey respondents.
b) Countries are ordered from left to right by increasing employment to population ratio for disabled persons.
c) Unweighted average of the 19 countries shown (value in parenthesis is disabled persons' share of total non-employment).

Source: OECD (2002), Society at a Glance.

employment rate for persons who assess themselves as having a disability was 27 percentage points lower than for persons saying that they were not disabled (employment to population ratios of 44% and 71%, respectively). In more than half of the OECD countries analysed, the employment rate of disabled people varies between 40 and 50%. However, employment rates of the disabled vary widely in other countries. In Switzerland and Norway, the rate is over 60%, while relatively few working-age people with disabilities are in work in Poland and Spain (21% and 22%, respectively). On average, the disabled account for 21% of non-employment in the working-age population, but there is a large overlap between the disabled and older groups because disability incidence rises strongly with age (OECD, 2003a).

A study conducted by the OECD (2003a) looks at the labour market situation of disabled persons in detail and concludes that more should be done to integrate them into employment (see also Chapter 3 of this publication). Employment rates for *severely* disabled people are only about one third of those of the non-disabled population, with little variation across countries, consistent with many such individuals not being capable of participating in the labour market. However, employment rates for *moderately* disabled individuals are much higher, averaging around 70% of those of non-disabled people, and cross-country variation is much greater for this group, suggesting a considerable scope for policies to foster employment for this group. It also appears that encouraging employment among disabled persons able to work can result in important welfare gains related to improved social and economic outcomes. Thus, persons with disabilities appear to be an appropriate target group for policies to foster participation and employment, especially in countries with a high incidence of non-employment among moderately disabled individuals. However, this group often has specific needs that must be addressed (*e.g.* medical and vocational rehabilitation, reorientation or training if the disability is such as to require a change of occupation, and special equipment or structures to facilitate their access to work).

3. Getting into work, staying there and moving up job ladders

Sections 1 and 2 suggest that there may be considerable scope to increase employment rates, provided that policies to lower unemployment are complemented with measures to foster greater labour force participation. The evidence presented also points to the highly diverse nature of the non-employed population of working age, suggesting that successful policy initiatives need to be clear about the groups to be mobilised and the barriers currently limiting their participation in employment. This section uses longitudinal data for 11 European countries and the United States to shed some further light on these barriers. Many of the under-represented groups highlighted in Sections 1 and 2 above are considered, but a longer-run view of their situation is provided by following individuals over a five year period and analysing how frequently inactive persons enter the labour market and how they fare.[26] Among the questions posed are: *i)* what share of persons not working in any specific year is at high risk of getting locked into inactivity; *ii)* among persons finding employment, how great is the risk of employment instability; *iii)* how great is the risk of being trapped in low-paid jobs; *iv)* how frequently do non-employment and low-paid employment result in poverty; and *v)* do these patterns differ across demographic groups and OECD countries?

A. *Inactivity traps from a multi-year perspective*

Table 2.2 provides a first look at non-employment dynamics and how they vary across groups in the working-age population. This transition matrix presents probabilities of moving between different main activity statuses, which were calculated for working-age persons in Europe during 1997-98.[27] The values on the main diagonal of this matrix indicate a high degree of persistence in many of these states, particularly in employment of 15 or more hours per week (93%), and in the homemaker (85%) and retired (93%) categories of inactive persons. Nonetheless, some non-employed groups move into employment in considerable numbers: 36% of the persons classified as unemployed in 1997 were employed the following year, compared with 15% to 20% for discouraged workers or persons in education or training. However, the corresponding rates are much lower for most other groups outside of the labour force (the only exception being the small number of persons in military/community service), especially for retirees. Clearly, the unemployed and persons nearing the end of their formal schooling (or military/community service) are much "closer" to the labour market than are most persons classified as being outside of the labour force. In particular, the low transition rates into employment of homemakers and retirees – two groups which received much attention in Sections 1 and 2 – confirm that the benchmark estimates of potential labour supply include many persons showing only a weak tendency to move into employment.[28]

Table 2.2. **Big differences in how easily non-employed groups move into employment**

Movements between main activity status for working-age persons in Europe, 1997-1998
One-year transitions probability (percentages)[a]

	Main status in 1998								
	Employed (at least 15 hours per week)	Employed (less than 15 hours per week)	Unemployed	Discouraged workers	In education or training	Military or community service	Homemaker	Retired	Other inactive
Main status in 1997									
Employed (at least 15 hours per week)	**92.8**	1.6	2.7	0.1	0.3	0.1	0.9	1.2	0.3
Employed (less than 15 hours per week)	31.7	**43.8**	4.7	0.1	6.2	1.0	8.1	3.7	0.8
Unemployed	32.1	3.8	**46.3**	3.2	3.7	0.5	6.6	3.1	0.7
Discouraged workers	13.9	1.6	32.2	**20.4**	2.8	0.2	24.0	2.1	2.8
In education or training	14.2	5.6	8.8	0.2	**68.4**	1.5	0.7	0.0	0.6
Military/community service	45.8	6.9	25.5	1.0	11.8	**8.8**	0.1	0.0	0.2
Homemaker	4.7	2.8	3.2	0.9	0.2	0.0	**84.7**	2.1	1.3
Retired	0.6	1.8	0.6	0.1	0.0	0.0	2.4	**93.1**	1.3
Other inactive	6.9	2.6	4.8	1.1	1.6	0.6	13.2	8.0	**61.1**
Total sample	63.2	3.8	6.4	0.5	5.6	0.3	11.8	7.1	1.3

a) Population-weighted averages for 12 European countries (Austria and the 11 EU countries reported in Chart 2.11.).
Source: Secretariat calculations based on the European Community Household Panel, waves 4 and 5 (1997 and 1998).

A richer picture of the importance and nature of inactivity traps emerges when non-employment dynamics are analysed over a five year period. Chart 2.11 provides a comparison of the *annual* rate of non-employment (i.e. non-employment rates in a cross-section, such as were analysed in Sections 1 and 2 above) with two measures of non-employment incidence over five years: the larger share of persons *ever* non-employed during the five year period and the smaller share of *always* non-employed. If there were no turnover in non-employment, the ever, annual and always non-employed incidence rates would be equal. In fact, 2.2 times as many working-age persons in Europe were non-employed at some point during the five year period as were continuously non-employed during that period, implying considerable movement into

Chart 2.11. **Considerable turnover in non-employment**
Alternative incidence measures of non-employment over five years in Europe and the United States

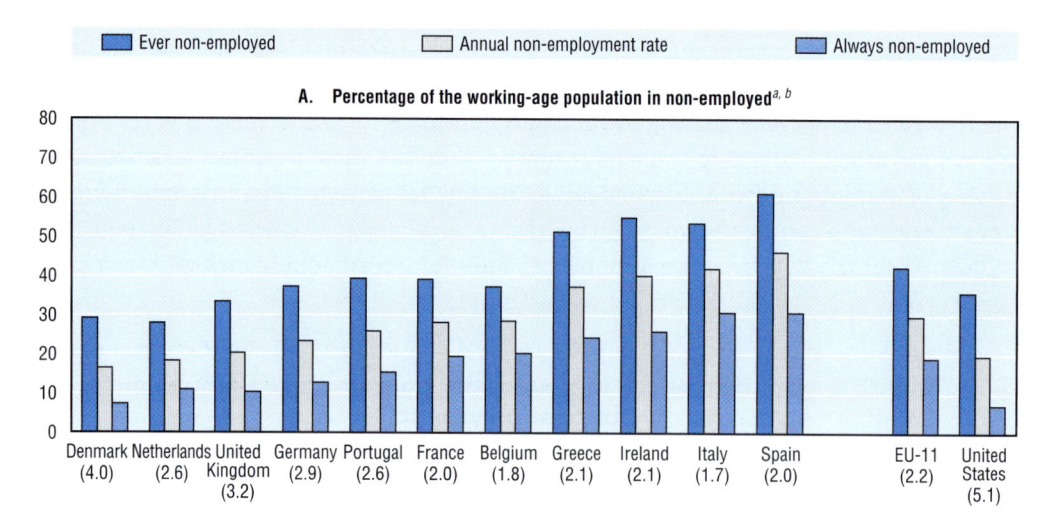

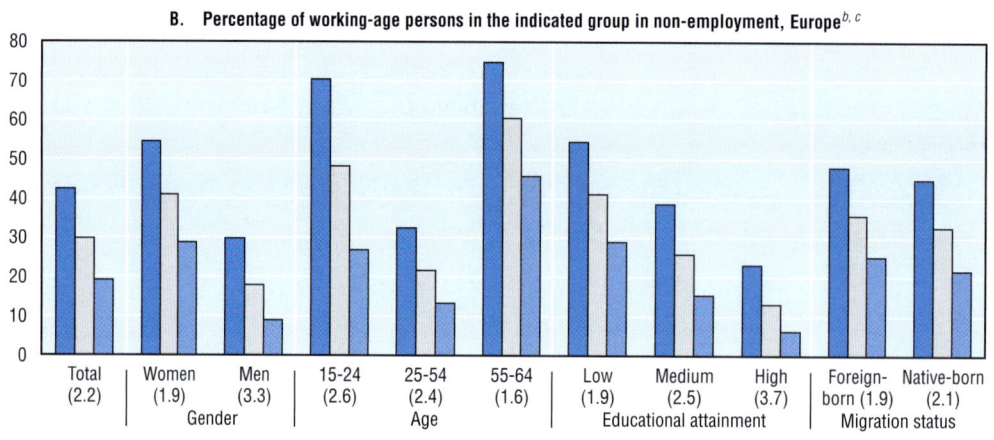

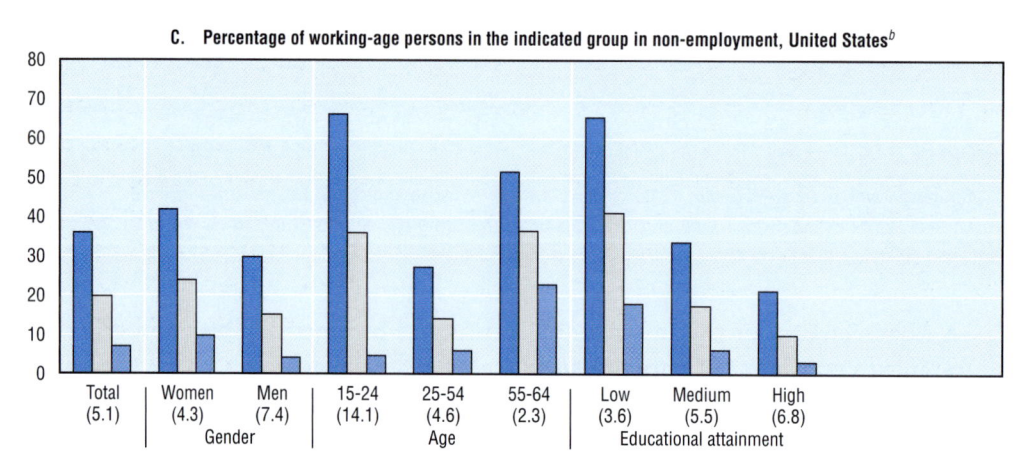

Legend: Ever non-employed | Annual non-employment rate | Always non-employed

A. Percentage of the working-age population in non-employed[a, b]

Country	Ever	Annual	Always	Ratio
Denmark	29	17	7	(4.0)
Netherlands	28	18	11	(2.6)
United Kingdom	33	20	10	(3.2)
Germany	37	23	13	(2.9)
Portugal	39	26	15	(2.6)
France	39	28	19	(2.0)
Belgium	37	28	20	(1.8)
Greece	51	37	24	(2.1)
Ireland	55	40	26	(2.1)
Italy	53	41	30	(1.7)
Spain	60	45	30	(2.0)
EU-11	41	29	18	(2.2)
United States	35	19	7	(5.1)

B. Percentage of working-age persons in the indicated group in non-employment, Europe[b, c]

Total (2.2); Gender: Women (1.9), Men (3.3); Age: 15-24 (2.6), 25-54 (2.4), 55-64 (1.6); Educational attainment: Low (1.9), Medium (2.5), High (3.7); Migration status: Foreign-born (1.9), Native-born (2.1)

C. Percentage of working-age persons in the indicated group in non-employment, United States[b]

Total (5.1); Gender: Women (4.3), Men (7.4); Age: 15-24 (14.1), 25-54 (4.6), 55-64 (2.3); Educational attainment: Low (3.6), Medium (5.5), High (6.8)

Note: EU-11: Population-weighted average for the European countries shown.
a) European countries shown in ascending order of single-year rates of non-employment.
b) Values within parenthesis below the country and group labels are the ratio of the ever to the always non-employed rates (an index of turnover).
c) Population-weighted averages for the 11 European countries reported in Panel A.

Source: Secretariat calculations based on the European Community Household Panel, waves 1 to 5 (1994-1998) for the European countries and Secretariat calculations based on the PSID from the Cross-National Equivalent Files, 1993-1997 for the United States.

and out of non-employment (Chart 2.11, Panel A). Turnover in non-employment – as indicated by the ratio of ever jobless to always jobless – is considerably higher in the United States, where five times as many persons were ever jobless during the five year period, as were always jobless. However, there is considerable diversity within Europe, with non-employment incidence and turnover in Denmark, the Netherlands and the United Kingdom close to that observed in the United States. Both the comparison of the United States with the European average and cross-country comparisons among EU countries suggest that non-employment turnover is lower in countries where the annual non-employment rate is higher. This suggests that labour market institutions that facilitate movements into (and out of) jobs may help to raise overall employment rates.[29]

Demographic differences in the dynamics of non-employment are also apparent (Chart 2.11, Panels B and C). The qualitative patterns are similar in Europe and the United States, with turnover being lowest for the 55 to 64 age group and highest for youths. Turnover in non-employment is also lower for women than for men. As for international comparisons, demographic groups with higher single-year incidences of non-employment tend to have lower turnover.[30] Consequently, the under-represented groups identified as being at a relatively high risk of non-employment using cross-sectional data (*e.g.* in the analysis of Sections 1 and 2), tend to have a risk of being always non-employed that is even further above the average value for the working-age population.

Of particular importance for labour mobilisation policy, the considerable turnover in non-employment co-exists with a strong concentration of non-employment on persons who rarely work.[31] Chart 2.12 provides data on cumulative time in non-employment over five years, as well as on the rate at which individuals exit and re-enter non-employment. On average for the 11 EU countries, persons non-employed in 1994 were non-employed during 4.2 of the five years from 1994 to 1998. The corresponding figure for the United States is nearly as high, with persons non-employed in 1993 averaging 3.6 years outside of employment during 1993-1997. Time non-employed accumulates strongly for two reasons. First, the flow rate into employment is relatively low for this sample (see note 31). Among persons non-employed in the first of the five years considered, the proportion becoming employed in the following year was 14% in the EU countries and 25% in the United States. A second reason non-employment time accumulates strongly is that many persons finding employment soon experience a repeat spell of non-employment. Cumulative time in non-employment over five years is particularly high for women, older persons of working age and less educated persons. Although these data do not allow a precise diagnosis of the underlying causes, they suggest that many of the persons non-employed in a cross-section are either indisposed to work (or to work steadily) or face significant barriers to finding or keeping jobs, and might be characterised as being in inactivity traps.

B. *Low-pay traps and unstable employment*

Low pay may represent an important disincentive to participation in the labour market (or to stable participation) for certain under-represented groups. Whether or not that is so, the prevalence of low-pay traps is of considerable interest, as is clarifying which labour-force groups have the greatest difficulty moving up job ladders.[32] Consequently, this section analyses the incidence and dynamics of low-paid employment.

2. THE LABOUR MOBILISATION CHALLENGE: COMBATING INACTIVITY TRAPS AND BARRIERS TO MOVING UP JOB LADDERS

Chart 2.12. **Time in non-employment accumulates strongly**
Five-year dynamics of non-employment in Europe and the United States

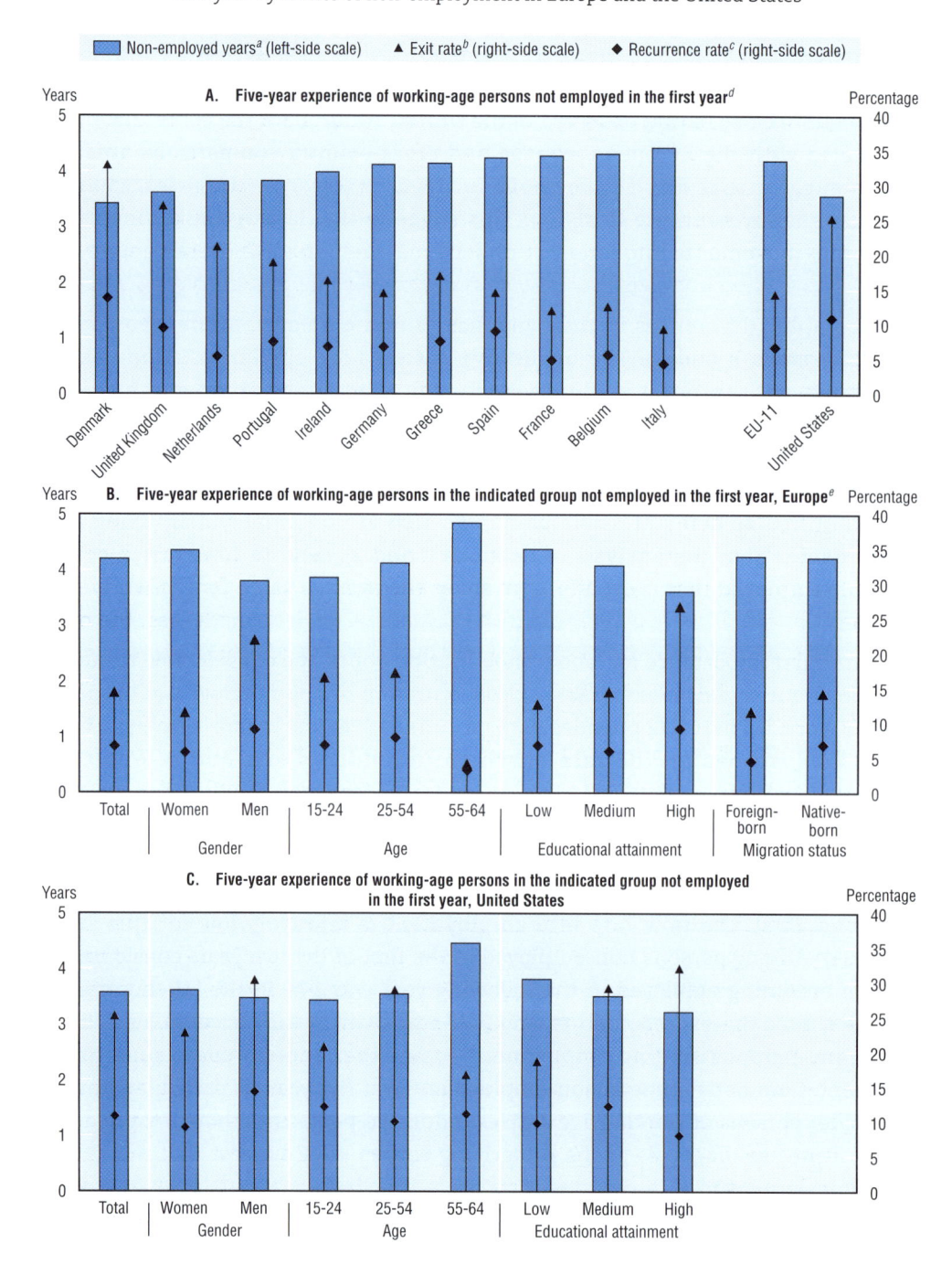

■ Non-employed years[a] (left-side scale)   ▲ Exit rate[b] (right-side scale)   ◆ Recurrence rate[c] (right-side scale)

A. Five-year experience of working-age persons not employed in the first year[d]

B. Five-year experience of working-age persons in the indicated group not employed in the first year, Europe[e]

C. Five-year experience of working-age persons in the indicated group not employed in the first year, United States

Note: EU-11: Population-weighted average for the European countries shown.
a) Average years.
b) Share of 1994 (1993) non-employed persons who were employed in 1995 (1994) in Europe (the United States).
c) Share of 1994 (1993) non-employed persons exiting non-employment in 1995 (1994) but experiencing a repeat spell of non-employment during 1996-1998 (1995-1997) in Europe (in the United States).
d) European countries shown in ascending order of average years of non-employment.
e) Population-weighted averages for the 11 European countries reported in Panel A.

Source: Secretariat calculations based on the European Community Household Panel, waves 1 to 5 (1994-1998) for the European countries and Secretariat calculations based on the PSID from the Cross-National Equivalent Files, 1993-1997 for the United States.

The annual, low-pay rate is substantially higher in the United States than in all of the European countries, except Greece, while turnover in low-paid employment in the United States is moderately higher than the average for these EU countries (Chart 2.13).[33] In both Europe and the United States, the relative incidence of low pay is much higher for youths than for older groups, for women than for men and for the least educated than for persons with more education (Chart 2.13, Panels B and C). Immigrants in Europe are significantly more likely to experience low pay at some point than are natives, but also have higher turnover. Turnover in low-paid employment tends to be significantly higher than in non-employment, as can be seen by comparing Charts 2.11 and 2.13. For example, five times as many European workers ever held a low-paid job during 1994-1998 as were always low paid, while the ever non-employed were only about twice as numerous as the always non-employed.[34]

There is considerable evidence for the existence of low-pay traps, with persons low-paid in the first year (and working all five years) averaging 3.1 years of low-paid employment in Europe and 3.6 years in the United States (Chart 2.14, Panel A). These are somewhat lower than the values for cumulative time in non-employment, due to the exit rate out of low pay into higher pay (36% for both the European average and the United States) being substantially higher than the transition rate from non-employment to employment. However, repeat spells of low-paid employment are common, suggesting that some "escapes" from low pay represent small and transitory fluctuations in earnings, rather than sustainable upward earnings mobility (OECD, 1997). Nonetheless, the overall picture is one of great heterogeneity, and significant upward mobility into higher pay does occur. Over a quarter of low-paid workers in 1994 earned at least 80% of the median wage 4 years later (annex Chart 2.A1.1). This share rises to near 40% for men, youths, workers with a university or other tertiary degree and foreign workers (who show more upward wage mobility than native workers). However, the upward mobility prospects of women, the least educated workers and, especially, older workers (73% of which are still low paid four years later) are less good.

The mobility prospects of low-paid workers look less reassuring when intermittent workers are incorporated into the analysis (Chart 2.15). In both Europe and the United States, workers low paid in the first year averaged nearly four of the next five years in either non-employment or low-paid employment (with non-employment accounting for more than a year of that total). This share was especially high for older workers in Europe (4.6 years) and the least educated workers in the United States (4.2 years). Similarly, more than one in five of European workers low-paid in the first year were not employed in the fifth year. This share rises above 50% for the older group, for whom low pay frequently is a prelude to labour force withdrawal (Chart 2.A1.1). Movements from low-paid employment into non-employment are also relatively frequent for women and immigrants. These results suggest that relatively few workers are persistently trapped in low-paid jobs, but a substantially greater number cycle between low pay and non-employment, with or without transitory spells of higher pay, and for some workers low-paid employment is a prelude to a permanent departure from the labour market.

C. The intertwined risks of non-employment, low pay and poverty

Do non-employment and low-paid employment have an important effect on the risk of poverty? Annual poverty rates for the total working-age population are 9.3% on average

Chart 2.13. **Low-pay incidence highest for youths and less educated workers**
Alternative incidence measures of low-paid employment[a] over five years in Europe and the United States[b]

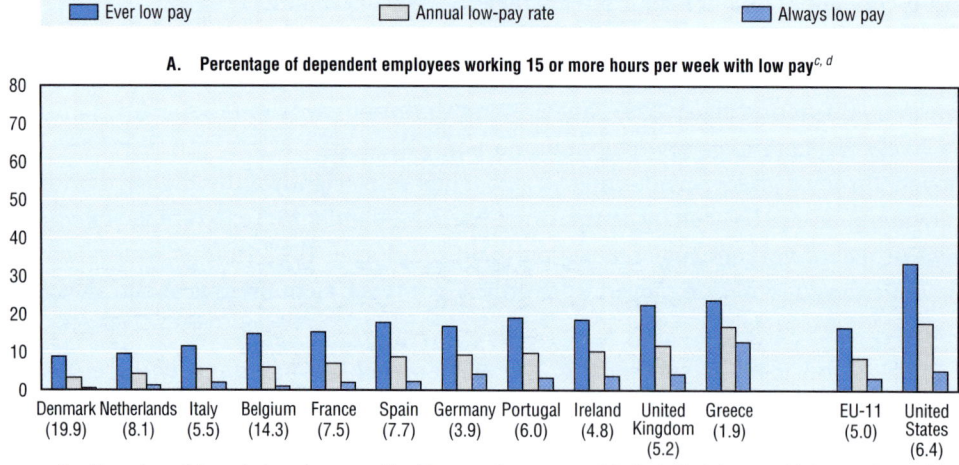

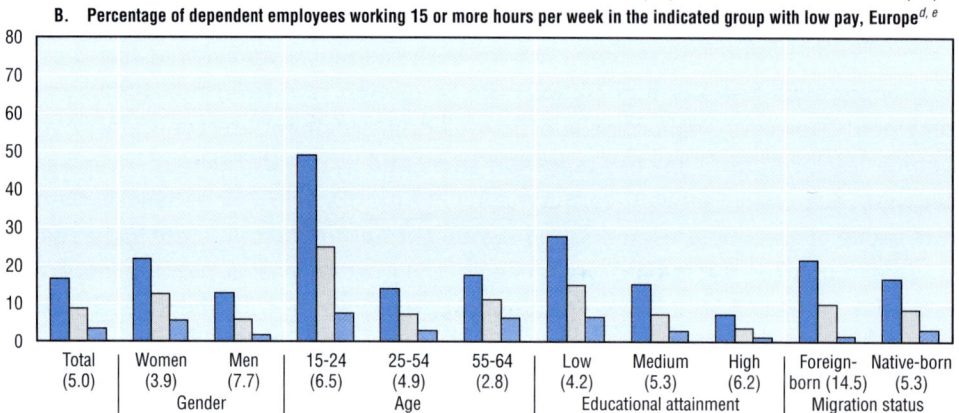

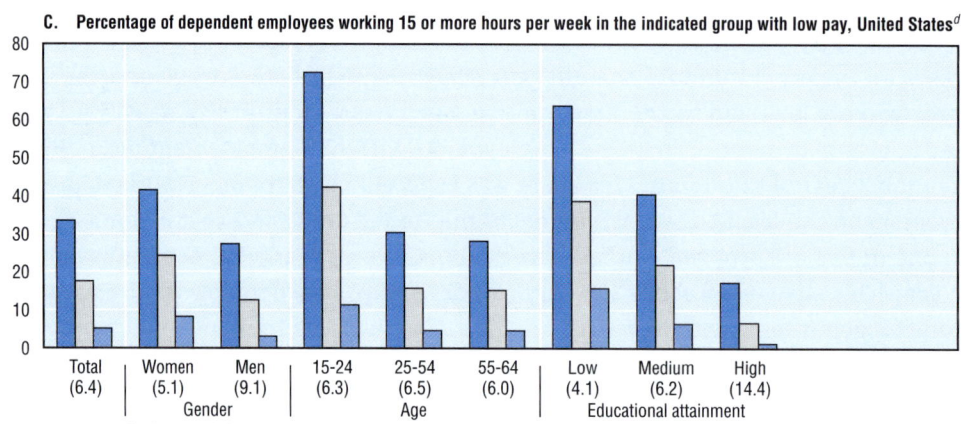

Legend: Ever low pay · Annual low-pay rate · Always low pay

A. Percentage of dependent employees working 15 or more hours per week with low pay[c, d]

Countries (with ratio of ever to always low paid in parenthesis):
Denmark (19.9), Netherlands (8.1), Italy (5.5), Belgium (14.3), France (7.5), Spain (7.7), Germany (3.9), Portugal (6.0), Ireland (4.8), United Kingdom (5.2), Greece (1.9), EU-11 (5.0), United States (6.4)

B. Percentage of dependent employees working 15 or more hours per week in the indicated group with low pay, Europe[d, e]

Total (5.0) | Gender: Women (3.9), Men (7.7) | Age: 15-24 (6.5), 25-54 (4.9), 55-64 (2.8) | Educational attainment: Low (4.2), Medium (5.3), High (6.2) | Migration status: Foreign-born (14.5), Native-born (5.3)

C. Percentage of dependent employees working 15 or more hours per week in the indicated group with low pay, United States[d]

Total (6.4) | Gender: Women (5.1), Men (9.1) | Age: 15-24 (6.3), 25-54 (6.5), 55-64 (6.0) | Educational attainment: Low (4.1), Medium (6.2), High (14.4)

Note: EU-11: Population-weighted average for the 11 European countries shown.
a) Workers are considered to be in low-paid employment if they work at least 15 hours per week and receive an hourly wage of less than two-thirds the median value in that country and year.
b) Sample for calculations restricted to persons who were continuously employed as dependent employees working at least 15 hours per week during all five years analysed.
c) European countries shown in ascending order of single-year rates of low-paid employment.
d) Values within parenthesis below the country and group labels are the ratio of the ever to the always low paid (an index of turnover).
e) Population-weighted averages for the 11 European countries reported in Panel A.

Source: Secretariat calculations based on the European Community Household Panel, waves 1 to 5 (1994-1998) for the European countries and Secretariat calculations based on the PSID from the Cross-National Equivalent Files, 1993-1997 for the United States.

2. THE LABOUR MOBILISATION CHALLENGE: COMBATING INACTIVITY TRAPS AND BARRIERS TO MOVING UP JOB LADDERS

Chart 2.14. **Low pay harder to escape for women, older workers (in Europe) and less educated workers (in the United States)**
Five-year dynamics of low-paid employment[a] in Europe and in the United States

Low-paid employment years[b] (left-side scale) ▲ Exit rate[c] (right-side scale) ◆ Recurrence rate[d] (right-side scale)

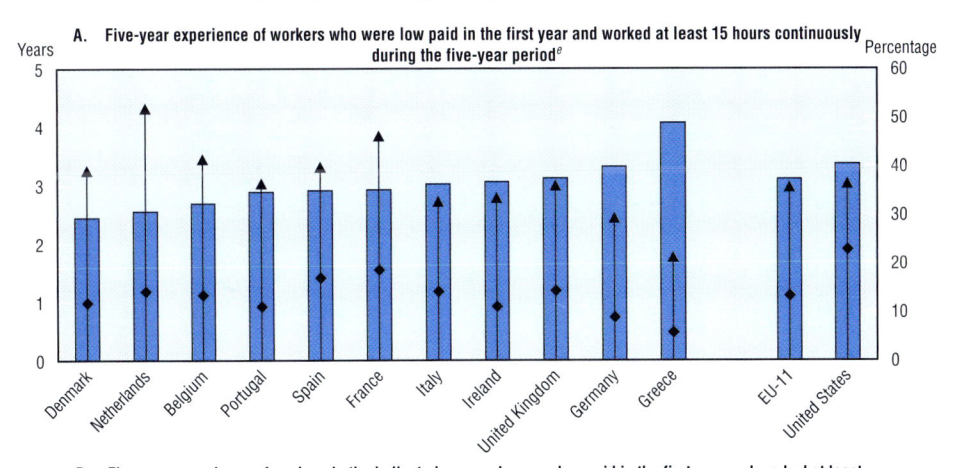

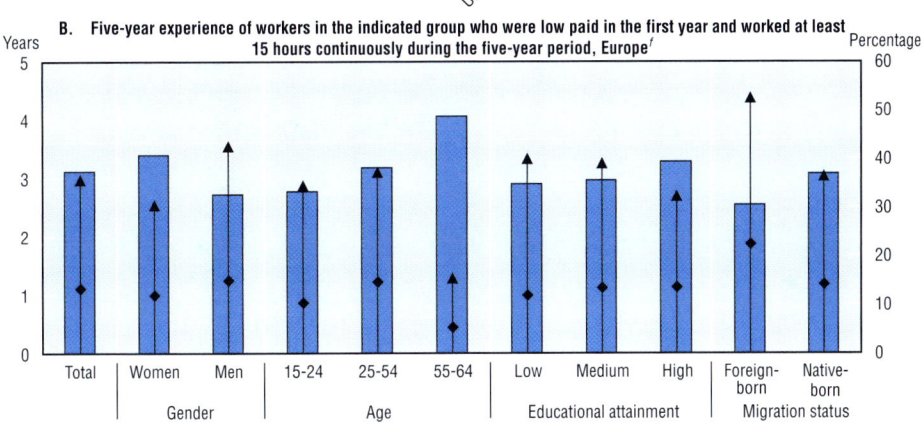

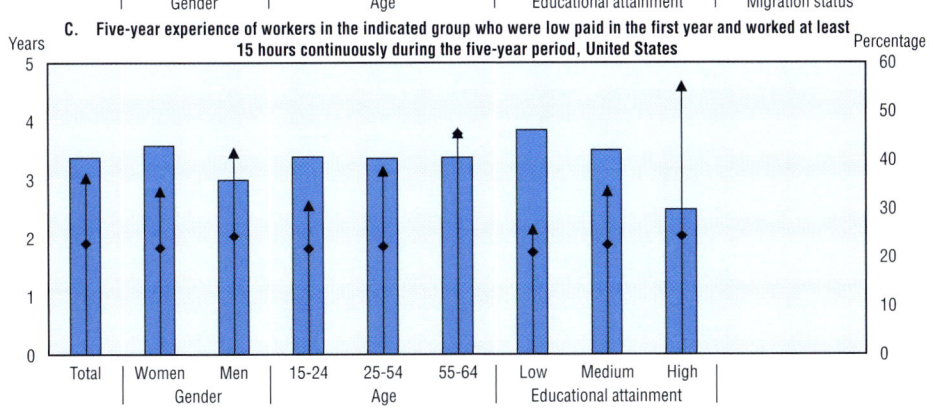

A. Five-year experience of workers who were low paid in the first year and worked at least 15 hours continuously during the five-year period[e]

B. Five-year experience of workers in the indicated group who were low paid in the first year and worked at least 15 hours continuously during the five-year period, Europe[f]

C. Five-year experience of workers in the indicated group who were low paid in the first year and worked at least 15 hours continuously during the five-year period, United States

Note: EU-11: Population-weighted average for the 11 European countries shown.
a) Workers are considered to be in low-paid employment if they work at least 15 hours per week and receive an hourly wage less than two-thirds the median wage in their country of residence.
b) Average years.
c) Share of 1994 (1993) low-paid persons who were high-paid in 1995 (1994) in Europe (in the United States).
d) Share of 1994 (1993) low-paid persons exiting low pay in 1995 (1994) but experiencing a repeat spell of low pay during 1996-1998 (1993-1997) in Europe (in the United States).
e) European countries shown in ascending order of average years of low-paid employment.
f) Population-weighted averages for the 11 European countries reported in Panel A.

Source: Secretariat calculations based on the European Community Household Panel, waves 1 to 5 (1994-1998) for the European countries and Secretariat calculations based on the PSID from the Cross-National Equivalent Files, 1993-1997 for the United States.

2. THE LABOUR MOBILISATION CHALLENGE: COMBATING INACTIVITY TRAPS AND BARRIERS TO MOVING UP JOB LADDERS

Chart 2.15. **Low-paid employment often alternates with non-employment**
Cumulative years of no pay, low pay and high pay[a] over five years, in Europe and the United States

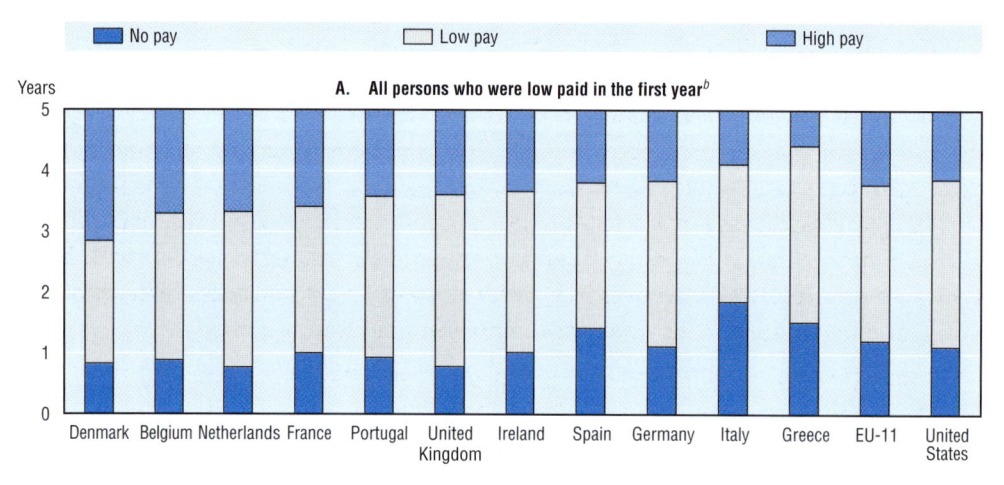

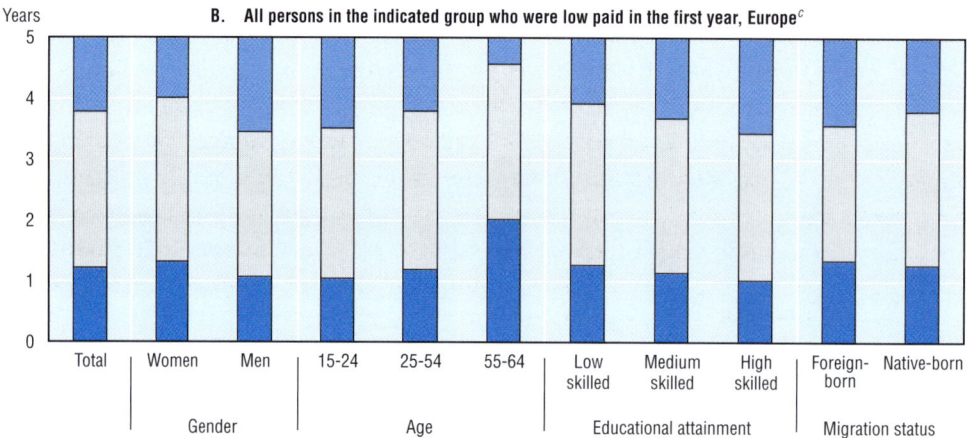

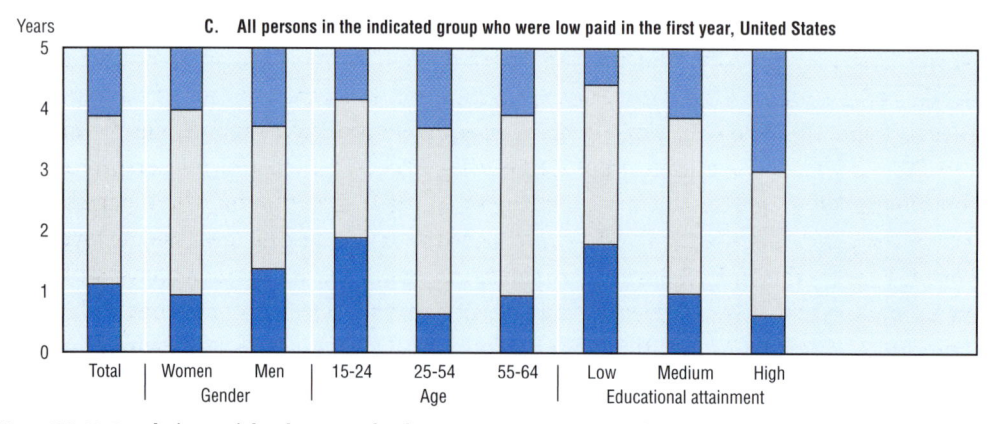

■ No pay   □ Low pay   ■ High pay

A. All persons who were low paid in the first year[b]

Denmark, Belgium, Netherlands, France, Portugal, United Kingdom, Ireland, Spain, Germany, Italy, Greece, EU-11, United States

B. All persons in the indicated group who were low paid in the first year, Europe[c]

Total | Women, Men (Gender) | 15-24, 25-54, 55-64 (Age) | Low skilled, Medium skilled, High skilled (Educational attainment) | Foreign-born, Native-born (Migration status)

C. All persons in the indicated group who were low paid in the first year, United States

Total | Women, Men (Gender) | 15-24, 25-54, 55-64 (Age) | Low, Medium, High (Educational attainment)

Note: EU-11: Population-weighted average for the 11 European countries shown.
a) Each year, working-age persons are classified across the three earnings statuses as follows: non-employed persons and employed persons working fewer than 15 hours per week are classified as "no pay"; employed persons working at least 15 hours per week and receiving an hourly wage less than two-thirds the median wage in their country of residence are classified as "low pay"; and employed persons working at least 15 hours per week and receiving an hourly wage of at least two-thirds the median wage are classified as "high pay".
b) European countries shown in ascending order of years spent in either no pay or low pay.
c) Population-weighted averages for the 11 European countries reported in Panel A.

Source: Secretariat calculations based on the European Community Household Panel, waves 1 to 5 (1994-1998) for the European countries and Secretariat calculations based on the PSID from the Cross-National Equivalent Files, 1993-1997 for the United States.

for the 11 EU countries and 17% in the United States (Chart 2.16).[35] Persistence in poverty is also somewhat higher in the United States than in Europe. Of particular relevance for this chapter's analysis, the risk of poverty is significantly higher for individuals who are non-employed than for their employed counterparts. The one year poverty incidence for an employed individual is 4% in Europe (average value for persons working 10 or more months in the year) and 13% in the United States, while the corresponding rates for jobless individuals are 18 and 36%, respectively. Low-paid employment is also an important risk factor for poverty, even if a strong majority of low-paid workers are not poor (Brandolini *et al.*, 2002). The single-year poverty rates of low-paid workers are 15 and 28% in Europe and the United States, respectively, as compared to much lower rates for workers with higher hourly wages (Chart 2.16).[36] Turnover in poverty is lower (and persistence higher) for non-employed and low-paid persons, than for their better paid counterparts.

Even though non-employment and low-paid employment are important risk factors for poverty, it is still true that the majority of individuals with no or low earnings are not poor, due to their families having other income sources (*e.g.* the earnings of other workers in the household or social benefits). A confirmation of the importance of other earners in the family is that household joblessness is more strongly associated with poverty than is individual joblessness (Chart 2.16). This is particularly true in the United States, were public transfer payments to jobless families are less often sufficient to raise their incomes above the poverty threshold used here (OECD, 2001).[37] Family structure also has a major impact on poverty risk. Most notably, lone parents are at a substantially greater risk of poverty in any given year (26% in Europe and 44% in the United States) than are working-age persons who either live with another adult or are without children. Lone parents also show greater persistence in poverty, representing a significantly higher share of persons always poor during the five year period, than of the ever poor.

The association between individual non-employment and poverty is stronger when chronic joblessness is analysed as a risk factor for chronic poverty. Chart 2.17 shows the relationship between income averaged over five years (which provides a proxy measure of household living standards over the medium-term) and non-employment experience over the same five year period. Working-age persons in Europe who were continuously employed had less than a 3% risk of being "permanent-income poor" (*i.e.* of having a five year average income below 50% of the median equivalent disposable income).[38] This risk rises to 11% for persons ever non-employed during 1994-98 and to 13% for persons always non-employed. This association is even stronger in the United States, where permanent-income poverty incidence is 5, 25 and 41%, respectively, for the never, ever and always non-employed. Even in the United States, a majority of non-employed persons have sufficient access to income over a multi-year period to avoid chronic poverty, consistent with much inactivity reflecting a voluntary time-use choice. Nonetheless, stable employment greatly reduces the risk of chronic poverty.

The risk of poverty among non-employed persons of working age in Europe is quite similar for most demographic groups (data not shown). However, immigrants who are non-employed have a risk of being poor which is about double that of the groups with the lowest poverty rates (persons aged 55-64 and medium and high educated persons). Demographic differences are more pronounced in the United States, where family incomes tend to be low for non-employed persons of prime working age or with a low level of education.

2. THE LABOUR MOBILISATION CHALLENGE: COMBATING INACTIVITY TRAPS AND BARRIERS TO MOVING UP JOB LADDERS

Chart 2.16. **Poverty risk is high for lone-parent families and jobless households**
Alternative incidence measures of working-age poverty[a] over five years by employment and pay status, and family structure[b]

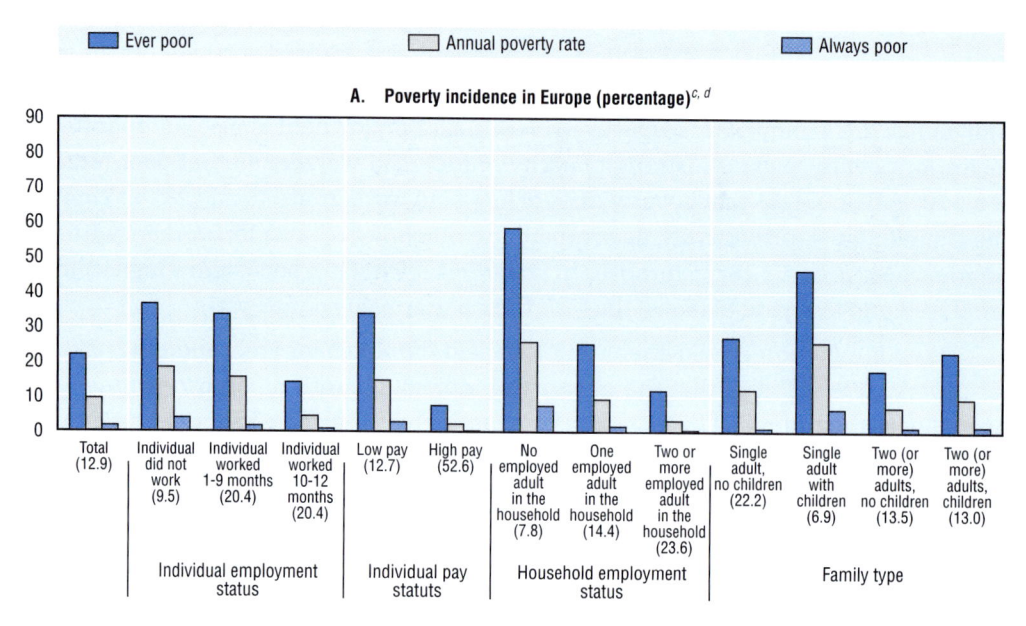

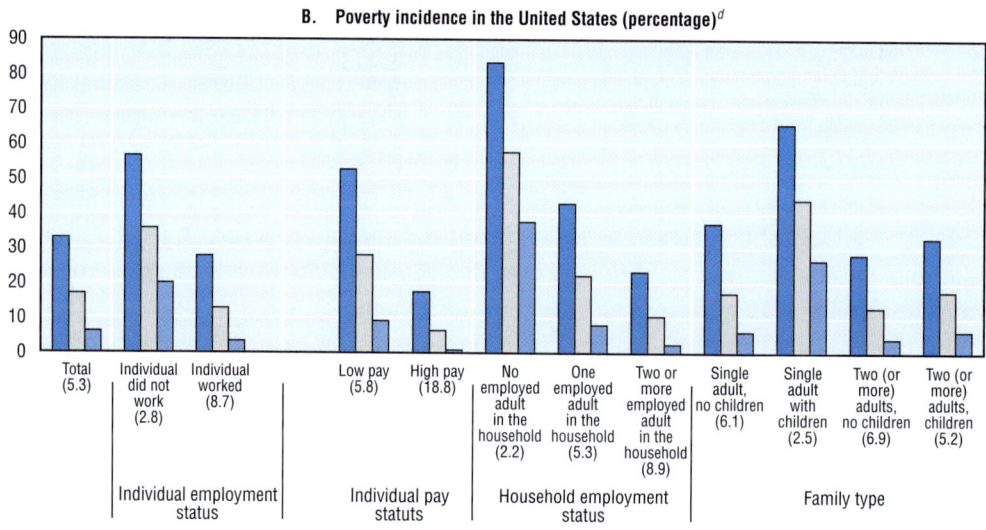

■ Ever poor   □ Annual poverty rate   ■ Always poor

A. Poverty incidence in Europe (percentage)[c, d]

B. Poverty incidence in the United States (percentage)[d]

a) Persons between the ages of 15 and 60 years in 1994 (1993) are considered to be of working-age throughout 1994-1998 (1993-1997) in Europe (the United States). They are considered to be poor if their equivalent disposable income in the previous year is less than 50% of the median value in their country of residence. Single-year poor refers to the poverty rate in the first year.
b) Family structure and employment and pay status measured in the first of the five years. See note a of Chart 2.13 for the definitions of low and high pay.
c) Population-weighted averages for the 11 European countries shown in Chart 2.15, Panel A.
d) Values within parenthesis below the country and group labels are the ratio of the ever to the always poor (an index of turnover).

Source: Secretariat calculations based on the European Community Household Panel, waves 1 to 5 (1994-1998) for the European countries and Secretariat calculations based on the PSID from the Cross-National Equivalent Files, 1993-1997 for the United States.

Chart 2.17. Chronic poverty is closely linked to persistence in non-employment and low-paid employment

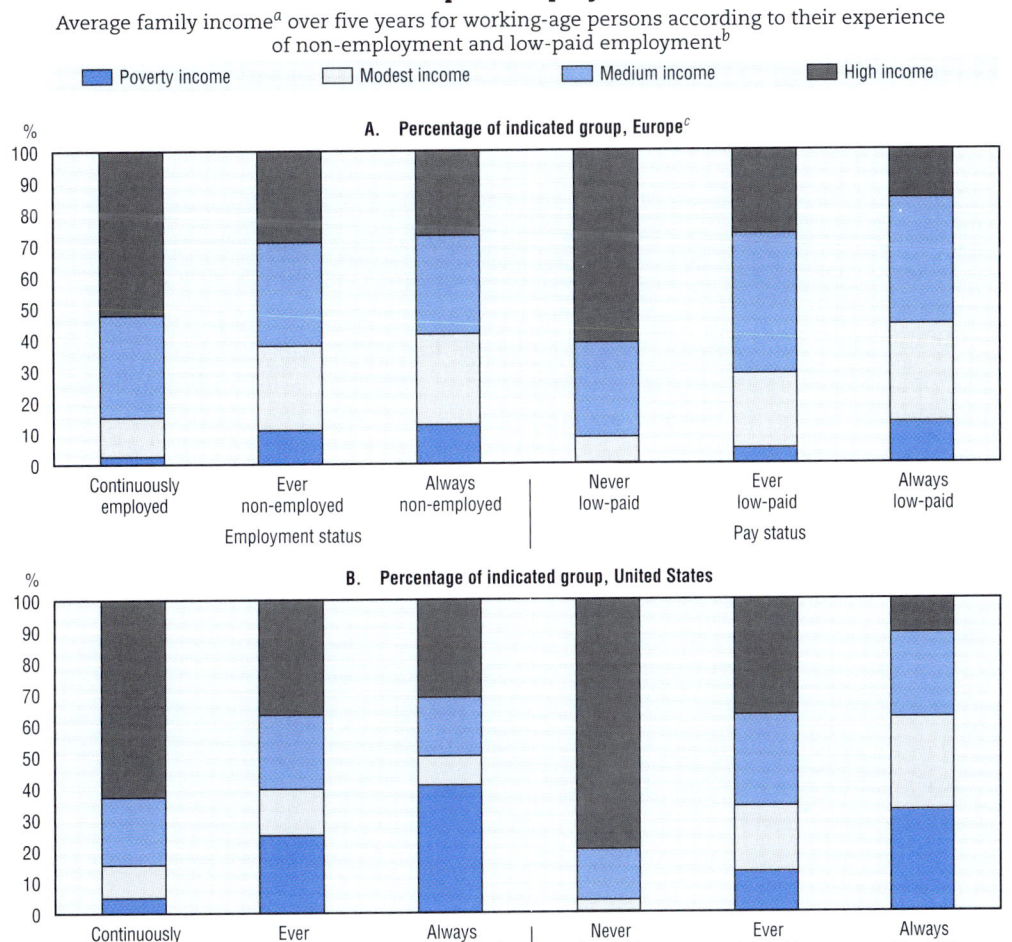

Average family income[a] over five years for working-age persons according to their experience of non-employment and low-paid employment[b]

Legend: Poverty income | Modest income | Medium income | High income

A. Percentage of indicated group, Europe[c]

Employment status: Continuously employed | Ever non-employed | Always non-employed
Pay status: Never low-paid | Ever low-paid | Always low-paid

B. Percentage of indicated group, United States

Employment status: Continuously employed | Ever non-employed | Always non-employed
Pay status: Never low-paid | Ever low-paid | Always low-paid

a) Equivalent disposable household income is classified into four ranges: "poverty" (less than 50% of the median value in the country of residence); "modest" (at least 50% but less than 80% of the national median); "medium" (at least 80% but less than 120% of the national median); "high" (at least 120% of the national median).
b) Workers are considered to be in low-paid employment if they work at least 15 hours per week and receive an hourly wage less than two-thirds of the median wage in their country of residence. When identifying the "never", "ever" and "always" low-paid groupings, only persons continuously working at least 15 hours in dependent employment during the five-year period analysed are considered.
c) Population-weighted averages for 11 European countries shown in Chart 2.15, Panel A.

Source: Secretariat calculations based on the European Community Household Panel, waves 1 to 5 (1994-1998) for the European countries and Secretariat calculations based on the PSID from the Cross-National Equivalent Files, 1993-1997 for the United States.

As with non-employment, the link between chronic low-paid employment and permanent-income poverty is much stronger than the association between low pay and poverty in a single year (Chart 2.17). European workers who are continuously employed at an hourly wage of at least two-thirds the median value are essentially exempt from poverty, whereas the poverty rate is 5% for ever low-paid workers and 13% for the always low-paid workers. The corresponding values for the United States are nil, 13, and 32%. Among low-paid workers in Europe in 1998, family incomes are lowest for immigrants, who have only about a 1 in 3 chance of obtaining an income level equal to 80% of the national median in their country of residence. Among American workers, low-paid employment is most strongly associated with low family incomes for prime-age and low-skilled workers.

Conclusions

This chapter highlights a tension that is likely to play a central role in the shaping of employment policies in the coming decade. Labour markets need to be *dynamic* if they are to perform well in the context of rapid demographic and technical changes, and intense international competition. They also need to be *inclusive*, enabling a wide cross-section of the community, and not just those who are the most able-bodied or best educated, to participate in the world of work. One lesson learnt from the experience of the past 30 years is that policies that discourage labour force participation (*e.g.* early retirement or disability schemes that make little effort to support reintegration into work) are ultimately unsustainable and may end up promoting rather than alleviating social exclusion. Accordingly, the increased interest being given to policies intended to foster, rather than to discourage, participation in the labour market it is a very welcome development. However, translating a broad intention to mobilise underutilised labour potential into a workable strategy for realising this aspiration is a major challenge. This is especially true since some of the dynamic adjustments occurring in labour markets (*e.g.* rising skill requirements resulting from the application of new technologies and forms of work organisation) may tend to exclude certain work-force groups (*e.g.* less educated, partially disabled or older workers).

The analysis presented in this chapter provides some signposts for mapping out such a policy strategy. A first message is that there appears to be considerable scope to increase employment by mobilising potential labour supply, particularly among women, less educated persons and older persons of working age. Smaller groups, such as lone parents, early school leavers and immigrants, also appear to merit particular attention, since social integration and equity goals could be furthered by increasing their participation. The great diversity of non-employed persons of working age is a second lesson. As exemplified by the policy analysis in this publication, an effective mobilisation strategy needs to confront the specific barriers to fuller participation in employment that affect the different groups. These include the unintended consequences of other policies (*e.g.* labour supply disincentives created by public pensions or income replacement benefits, as is discussed in Chapters 3 and 4). Also needed are policies that encourage innovative employment practices that better accommodate the particular needs or preferences of specific populations groups (*e.g.* work-family reconciliation measures for mothers with caring responsibilities, or improved access to vocational training for less educated and older workers, as discussed in Chapters 3 and 5, respectively).

Policies that encourage jobless individuals to look for work and help them to find entry-level jobs quickly are an essential component of a strategy aimed at raising participation and employment (Chapter 4). However, the longitudinal analysis in this chapter suggests that many of the individuals "activated" by such policies will have difficulty remaining in employment and moving up job ladders. Relatively little is known about how best to foster employment stability and upward career mobility, and further research – including rigorous programme evaluations – are particularly needed in this area. Nonetheless, several tentative lessons can be drawn from what is already known. First, activation *per se* may improve longer-term opportunities for some, since there is considerable upward mobility from low-paid jobs. Others will remain trapped in low-paid and unstable jobs, but certain policies may be able to reduce the size of this latter group. For example, Chapter 5 identifies a number of policy approaches to broadening access to employer-sponsored training. Finally, the link between low-paid employment and family poverty suggests that in-work benefits have an important role to play in insuring adequate incomes for working families, in addition to their role in reinforcing the economic incentive to work (Chapter 3).

This analysis highlights the potential contribution of a mix of policies that are tailored to the specific situations of diverse population groups. However, further development of such policies should not be allowed to replace continued efforts to enact structural reforms with the aim of improving the *overall* functioning of the labour market. In particular, good framework conditions are required to further lower equilibrium unemployment and to support overall job creation (see Chapter 1 and the references cited there). In the absence of such efforts, policies seeking to facilitate the integration of specific groups into employment are likely to take on a zero-sum character that would do little to enhance overall welfare and much to erode political support for inclusive employment policies.

Notes

1. Unemployment represents a thwarted desire to work that is often associated with economic hardship. It is also unproductive, above the minimum level of frictional unemployment required to match workers to jobs efficiently. By contrast, inactivity reflects time-allocation choices that are for the most part voluntary. Accordingly, a general presumption that paid employment would represent a more productive time use than the non-market activities it would displace would not be justified.

2. While empirical work suggests that minimum wages do not have a significant effect on overall employment rates (OECD, 1998a; Dolado *et al.*, 1996), there is considerable evidence that excessively high minimum wages may negatively affect the availability of employment to low-productivity groups, including youths and low-skill workers (Neumark and Washer, 1999; Kramarz and Philippon, 2001; Laroque and Salanié, 2000). Bertola *et al.* (2002) analyse labour market regulations more broadly and conclude that "labor market institutions meant to improve workers' income share imply larger disemployment effects for groups whose labour supply is more elastic" (*e.g.* women, youth, and older workers).

3. The medium or central variant is chosen for countries producing a range of population projections.

4. Inter-cohort shifts in participation behaviour are estimated by assuming that: i) the age-participation profile for all cohorts has the shape implied by the five year changes in participation rates observed for synthetic cohorts between 1995 and 2000; and ii) new cohorts reaching working age after 2000 follow the same profile as the cohort entering in 2000. The labour force projections, including the novel cohort adjustment, are documented in Burniaux *et al.* (2003).

5. Although population ageing can be considered as providing an independent rationale for labour mobilisation policy, it is perhaps best understood as increasing the urgency of the three rationales for enacting policies to foster increased participation that were discussed above. Gruber and Wise (2002) show that the disincentives to labour supply created by public pensions have been a major factor in the declining participation of older persons in employment (first rationale), while Dang *et al.* (2001) show that a continuation of these trends would create enormous fiscal strain (second rationale). The combination of increasing longevity and earlier retirement means that it has become common to concentrate several decades of full-time leisure at the end of the life cycle. Hicks (2002) argues that this is an undesirable time-use pattern that isolates and demoralises many seniors (third rationale).

6. Chapter 5 discusses the specific issue of training access for older workers, while Chapter 3 discusses expanding employment opportunities for older workers more broadly. These issues are also being examined in detail as part of the OECD Thematic Review of policies to improve employment prospects of older workers (OECD, 2003b and c).

7. The immigrant, low-skilled and disabled groups partially overlap with each other and completely overlap with the 4 (non-overlapping) groups defined by age and gender.

8. For example, the opportunity costs of employment could be particularly high for some youths (foregone study) and mothers with young children (foregone parenting activities), and economic returns particularly low for some low-skilled or partially disabled workers.

9. A shift-share analysis of international differences in the aggregate employment rate indicates that differences in population structure explain very little of the cross-country variation for OECD countries, which is dominated by differences in employment rates for population cells defined by gender and age.

10. The choice of the *third* highest value in the OECD as a benchmark represents a pragmatic adjustment for outliers. The very high participation rates sometimes observed for demographic groups in one or two OECD member countries, which have small populations and are geographically compact, probably are not realistic benchmarks for more populous and geographically dispersed countries.

11. Excess unemployment equals zero when the unemployment rate is 5% or less. The 5% ceiling for unemployment rates is somewhat arbitrary and significantly higher that the lowest unemployment rates observed within the OECD area. However, it is intended to approximate the equilibrium unemployment rate that structural reforms might reasonably obtain in the long run in countries where unemployment is currently above that level.

12. The youngest age group was treated differently due to the importance of schooling for this age group and the judgement that international benchmarks based on low educational attainment would not reflect a reasonable policy objective. Before applying the benchmark methodology to persons under the age of 25, the "employed" group was redefined to include all youths either employed or in school. Accordingly, the benchmarking estimates of excess inactivity and excess unemployment for this age group refer exclusively to non-students. This adjustment requires data cross-classifying youths by school enrolment status and labour force status. New Zealand and Korea had to be dropped from the analysis because the necessary data were not available.

13. The benchmark estimates do not imply complete convergence for two reasons. First, it was judged more realistic to set the benchmarks for both inactivity and unemployment somewhat above the minimum values observed among OECD countries (see notes 10 and 11.) A second reason for incomplete convergence is that the international benchmarks for participation rates are defined separately for age-gender cells, causing the implied benchmark values for the aggregate participation rate in different countries to vary with the age and gender structure of the population.

14. Consistent with labour supply responses being greater over longer time horizons, Chapter 4 shows that the full impact of social benefits on labour supply can take several decades to unfold.

15. A further indication that a significant share of inactive persons represent potential labour supply is that approximately two-thirds of them – and substantially higher shares of those aged 25 and older – have previously worked (see annex Table 2.A1.2). Their decision to withdraw from the labour force might be reversible, depending on the reason why they stopped working and how their situation and employment opportunities evolve. Burniaux *et al.* (2003) use econometric techniques to study how much future labour supply can be increased in OECD labour markets, by implementing specific examples of policies intended to encourage greater participation of women and older workers.

16. The more long-run character of the benchmark estimates of potential labour supply is one factor explaining why they tend to be larger than the self-response estimates. This difference is largest in countries with relatively low employment rates because the self-response estimates of potential labour supply are only modestly higher in countries where the employment-to-population ratio is lower (correlation coefficient of –0.32), whereas this association is much stronger for the benchmark estimates (correlation coefficient of –0.83). As a consequence, the self-response estimates imply much less potential for closing the employment gap between low and high employment rate countries, than the benchmark estimates.

17. Chapter 1 showed that participation rates of older persons increased in a considerable number of OECD countries during the past decade, where labour market conditions improved and pension reforms were introduced. See Chapter 3 for a discussion of policies to encourage later retirement.

18. Some under-represented groups are not treated here despite raising important social concerns and representing a significant share of mobilisable labour resources in certain OECD countries. Examples include ethnic minorities (Altonji and Blank, 1999; Berthoud, 2003) and residents in

lagging regions (OECD, 2000a). However, these groups overlap with the groups that are analysed (*e.g.* with the low skilled and immigrants).

19. Chapter 3 discusses different policies and institutional factors, such as the availability of child care, that can help mothers reconcile work with family life.

20. The gender gap in employment for persons with a tertiary degree averages 13%, whereas it is more than twice as large for women not finishing upper secondary schooling, at 28 percentage points. Even when working, less educated women have relatively poor access to upgrade training (Chapter 5), suggesting that their prospects for career advancement may tend to be limited.

21. Jobless households containing working-age persons may be at a high risk of economic deprivation and social isolation (OECD, 1998a). These concerns are particularly strong when children are present in the household, whose developmental prospects could be compromised.

22. Typically, schooling represents a productive investment in skills that will enhance future earnings potential. However, school enrolment sometimes reflects a constrained choice, even a form of disguised unemployment, particularly in the context of depressed labour markets.

23. Although the proportion of older individuals who are unemployed is rather low, even in high-unemployment countries, unemployment durations tend to be longer for older workers (OECD, 2002a). The high incidence of long-duration unemployment in this age group reflects both the reluctance of employers to hire older job seekers (OECD, 1998a) and a tendency for governments to place a low priority on activating jobless persons receiving unemployment (or other) benefits, who are nearing retirement age (Chapter 4).

24. Workers aged 50 to 54 are included in these tabulations, because, the withdrawal from the labour force associated with ageing begins before age 55 in many OECD countries. However, most of the analysis in this publication defines older working ages as 55-64 years, since international data are more generally available for that age grouping.

25. The one exception is Portugal, where low-educated persons of working age have a higher employment rate than their medium-educated counterparts (68 versus 63%), but a far lower employment rate than high-educated persons (90%).

26. 1994-1998 data from the December 2001 version of the European Community Household Panel (ECHP) users' database are used to analyse five year labour market dynamics in Belgium, Denmark, France, Germany, Greece, Ireland, Italy, the Netherlands, Portugal, Spain and the United Kingdom, while 1993-1997 data from the Panel Study of Income Dynamics (PSID), as reported in the 1980-2001 Cross National Equivalent File (CNEF), are used for the United States. (These are the most recent five year periods for which data were available at the time the analysis was performed.) Austrian data from the 1997-1998 waves of the ECHP are also reported in Table 2.2. Sample size constraints in the ECHP preclude analysing persons with disabilities, while the limited range of PSID variables included in the CNEF preclude analysing either persons with disabilities or immigrants. OECD, 2001 provides an overview of these data sources (see also European Commission, 2003b; Burkhauser *et al.*, 2001).

27. Although not presented here, two, three and four year transition matrices showed qualitatively similar patterns of mobility, although there is some tendency for mobility rates to increase as the period of time considered lengthens. Unfortunately, the CNEF data for the United States do not allow analogous transition probabilities to be calculated.

28. This result also suggests that the desire to work, which is expressed by many non-employed mothers, is not easily realised, perhaps, due to the difficulty of reconciling their role in their families with employment.

29. The cross-country correlation between the annual rate of non-employment and the ever/always ratio (an index of turnover in joblessness) is –0.78 for the 12 countries analysed. A consequence of this correlation is that country rankings are very similar for the 3 non-employment incidence measures, but international differences are most pronounced for comparisons of the share of the working-age population always non-employed over the five year period (*i.e.* for the risk of durable non-employment traps).

30. Correlation coefficients of –0.80 based on data in, respectively, Panels B and C of Chart 2.11.

31. This apparent paradox is often observed in data on labour market dynamics and is easily resolved. A significant share of persons ever experiencing non-employment over a five year period typically work, but experience a single, brief interruption in their employment history. Consequently, many non-employment spells are short. However, persons who are typically employed represent a much smaller share of all persons non-employed at a specific time, since chronically non-employed

persons are more likely to be outside of employment on any given date. In fact, most persons non-employed in a given year show quite high persistence or experience repeat spells of non-employment. Chronically non-employed persons account for an even larger share of the total time spent in non-employment over a multi-year period. OECD (1996, 1997) explain these relationships in greater detail, in the context of an analysis low-pay dynamics.

32. Workers are considered to be in low-paid employment if they work at least 15 hours per week in dependent employment and receive an hourly wage less than two-thirds of the median wage in their country of residence.

33. Whereas higher single-year incidence of non-employment is associated with lower turnover, no consistent relationship between low-pay incidence and turnover is evident.

34. Since these calculations of low-pay incidence refer to the sample of persons working in all five years, turnover refers exclusively to movements between low- and better-paying jobs. Persons moving between low-paid employment and non-employment are incorporated into the analysis in Chart 2.15 (below).

35. An individual is classified as being poor if their equivalent disposable household income is below 50% of the median value in their country of residence. See OECD (2001) for a discussion of this relative poverty criterion and its use in an extensive analysis of poverty incidence and dynamics.

36. Employment, earnings and poverty status are all measured in the first year. In a more elaborate analysis, OECD (2001) shows that many of the entries into and exits out of poverty that occur in a multi-year period coincide with *changes* in employment, earnings or household structure.

37. As shown in Chart 2.16, the annual poverty rate is 58% for a working-age person in the United States who is a member of a jobless household and 83% of such persons were poor at least once during the five year period. The corresponding values for Europe are lower, but still quite high, at 26 and 58%, respectively.

38. See OECD, (2001), for a justification for using a permanent-income poverty criteria based on averaging income over multiple years.

ANNEX 1

Supplementary Evidence

Tables 2.A1.1–2.A1.2 provide supplementary evidence supporting the analysis of potential labour supply in Section 1 of the main text, while Chart 2.A1.1 provides supplementary evidence supporting the analysis of low-pay dynamics presented in Section 3 of the main text.

2. THE LABOUR MOBILISATION CHALLENGE: COMBATING INACTIVITY TRAPS AND BARRIERS TO MOVING UP JOB LADDERS

Table 2.A1.1. **Inactive persons of working age who would like to work (now or at some time in the future), 1997**

Persons aged 15 to 64 years (percentages)

	\multicolumn{8}{c	}{Share of inactive persons who would like to work[a]}	\multicolumn{4}{c}{Share of inactive persons having previously worked, who would like to return to work, by reason why they stopped working}
	All	Women	Men	15-24 years	25-54 years	55-64 years	Low skilled	Medium skilled	High skilled	Retirement	Health problems	End of contract[b]	Family responsabilities
Canada	77.8	76.4	79.8	98.4	87.1	35.6	69.9	77.1	82.2	48.5	38.2	91.0	95.8
Czech Republic	57.4	56.5	59.4	93.8	81.1	27.1	50.0	71.1	86.7	26.4	68.3	80.0	96.2
Denmark	50.5	54.0	44.8	100.0	70.5	15.4	31.0	71.6	67.1	26.6	51.3	60.2	–
France	61.1	71.3	36.4	98.1	86.5	14.6	32.9	66.5	68.9	17.2	–	83.7	63.5
Germany, western Länder	63.0	65.3	57.9	94.3	80.4	23.9	53.0	91.5	80.0	10.5	50.0	85.7	74.0
Germany, eastern Länder	69.3	62.2	80.0	100.0	87.5	38.2	63.8	–	–	26.7	81.3	–	–
Hungary	30.6	31.0	29.8	95.9	43.4	13.8	26.3	45.7	43.1	15.4	15.8	79.9	69.2
Italy	74.0	73.3	76.1	98.3	82.1	45.3	68.9	80.3	81.1	40.8	–	88.2	66.5
Japan	61.0	57.0	73.2	86.7	68.7	27.5	57.6	55.6	72.6	45.8	66.7	–	53.6
Netherlands	55.1	55.7	53.6	96.4	64.0	16.4	52.4	50.0	67.7	1.6	58.7	80.4	62.1
New Zealand	73.7	75.6	67.6	100.0	85.1	46.2	67.4	65.8	80.6	39.3	84.6	88.9	85.1
Norway	72.6	71.4	75.0	95.7	84.5	34.1	62.5	88.9	80.4	53.8	57.1	80.0	82.1
Poland	65.8	61.0	74.4	95.9	76.0	37.7	57.6	74.3	93.1	39.3	70.8	70.4	79.9
Portugal	63.7	67.1	55.3	92.9	75.2	41.1	61.8	96.7	78.4	25.0	52.2	72.4	63.4
Spain	65.5	67.4	60.4	94.6	72.5	32.5	59.8	77.3	84.5	19.5	48.5	78.9	63.4
Sweden	77.5	75.6	79.2	91.7	94.3	20.6	..	..	..	21.1	48.3	96.4	92.8
Switzerland	62.8	64.9	53.7	95.1	77.5	22.0	65.8	60.8	68.8	16.8	45.5	74.7	77.0
United Kingdom	65.6	65.5	65.7	100.0	82.0	20.7	60.0	81.1	70.9	15.7	70.0	88.1	76.6
OECD average[c]	64.4	64.3	64.6	94.5	77.3	28.3	55.3	68.7	73.1	29.2	47.4	61.8	66.1
For comparison: European averages[d]													
Source ISSP	64.5	65.9	60.6	96.8	79.1	27.7	53.4	72.3	72.1	..	..	..	..
Source EULFS[e]	11.8	11.7	12.2	11.5	18.3	5.4	10.9	14.0	14.0	..	..	..	..

.. Data not available.
– Values not reported because of the small number of observations.
a) Question V66 : "Would you like to have a paid job, now or in the future?".
b) Includes job displacement, dismissal and end of job contract.
c) Population-weighted average for countries shown with valid data.
d) Population-weighted average calculated for countries with data for both surveys: Denmark, France, Germany, Hungary, Italy, Netherlands, Poland, Portugal, Spain, Sweden, Switzerland and the United Kingdom.
e) Among non-active persons who are not seeking employment, share of those who would nevertheless like to have work (now). Data for 2001.

Source: International Social Survey Programme (ISSP), 1997; European Union Labour Force Survey (EULFS), 2001.

Table 2.A1.2. **Inactive persons of working age who have worked previously and the reasons why they stopped working, 1997**

Persons aged 15 to 64 years (percentages)

	Share of inactive persons who have previously worked for one year or more	Retirement	Health problems	End of contract[b]	Family responsibilities	Other
Canada	72.0	32.9	12.1	30.4	20.3	4.3
Czech Republic	84.3	51.5	24.0	8.8	15.2	0.6
Denmark	82.3	37.4	43.4	14.5	3.5	1.2
France	67.8	46.9	7.6	15.6	24.7	5.2
Germany, western Länder	77.0	20.9	14.1	7.3	40.8	16.8
Germany, eastern Länder	65.8	32.0	36.0	20.0	8.0	4.0
Hungary	82.7	35.4	38.9	10.8	9.8	5.2
Italy	44.6	30.2	1.6	12.8	22.0	33.3
Japan	52.5	19.7	17.2	8.2	23.8	31.1
Netherlands	74.2	13.8	20.0	12.0	31.4	22.8
New Zealand	86.3	21.2	9.8	20.5	35.6	12.9
Norway	70.4	10.3	51.6	11.9	22.2	4.0
Poland	67.2	47.1	30.6	8.0	13.8	0.5
Portugal	52.2	21.5	37.6	15.6	22.0	3.2
Spain	58.7	15.4	14.1	26.2	21.9	22.4
Sweden	51.1	33.4	15.0	33.6	16.7	1.2
Switzerland	87.3	17.5	6.0	10.8	37.5	28.2
United Kingdom	85.1	24.7	10.6	20.3	40.3	4.0
United States	76.0	21.4	15.4	19.7	35.9	7.7
OECD averages[c]						
Total	68.4	25.7	15.9	16.2	29.8	12.4
Women	69.5	18.7	12.4	15.1	39.0	14.8
Men	64.8	46.4	25.2	19.5	3.6	5.4
15-24	28.0	6.6	1.1	48.1	33.9	10.3
25-54	77.6	8.2	17.6	17.8	41.4	15.0
55-64	84.6	51.6	17.4	7.6	12.7	10.7
Low skilled	66.8	28.9	18.1	15.3	26.2	11.5
Medium skilled	68.0	23.6	14.6	18.1	32.9	10.7
High skilled	64.9	28.5	13.9	16.5	27.5	13.6

a) Percentage share of inactive persons who have previously worked for one year or more.
b) Includes job displacement, dismissal and end of job contract.
c) Population-weighted averages for countries shown.
Source: International Social Survey Programme (ISSP), 1997.

2. THE LABOUR MOBILISATION CHALLENGE: COMBATING INACTIVITY TRAPS AND BARRIERS TO MOVING UP JOB LADDERS

Chart 2.A1.1. **Four-year earnings mobility of low-paid workers[a] in Europe and the United States**

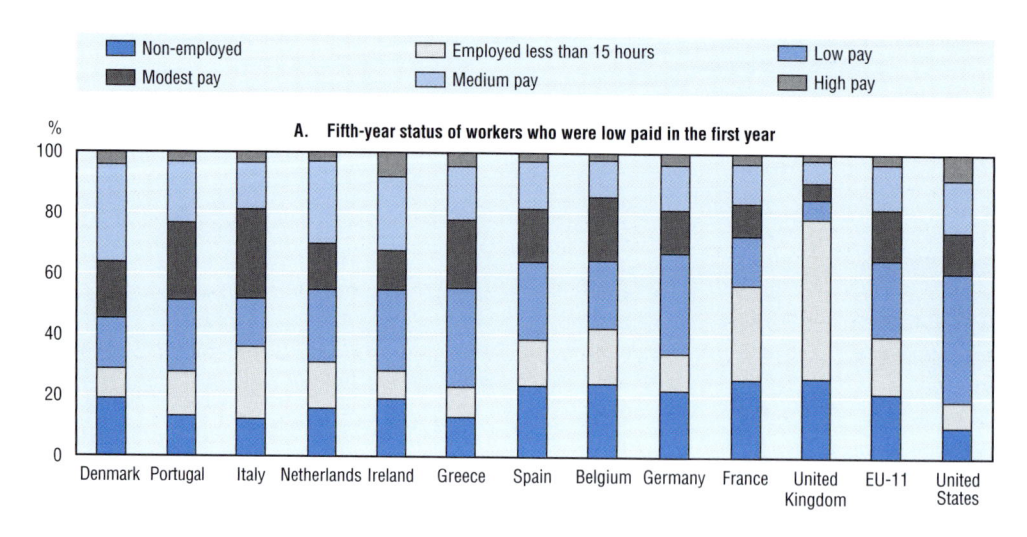

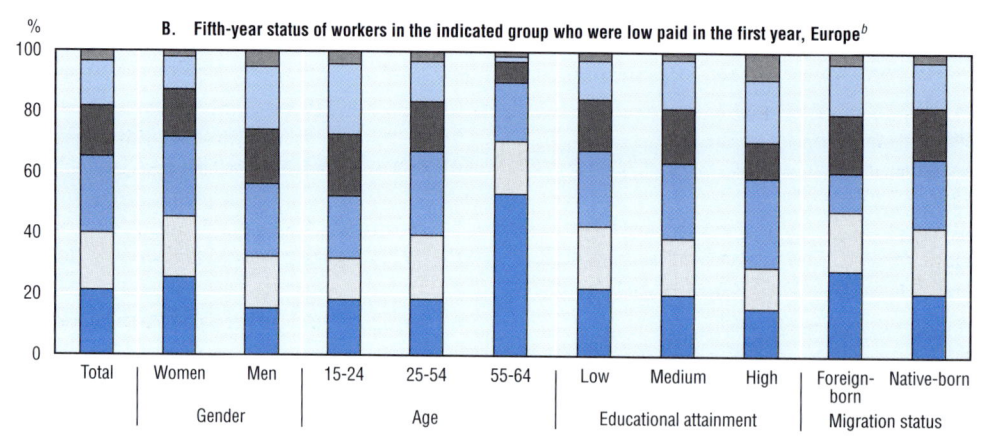

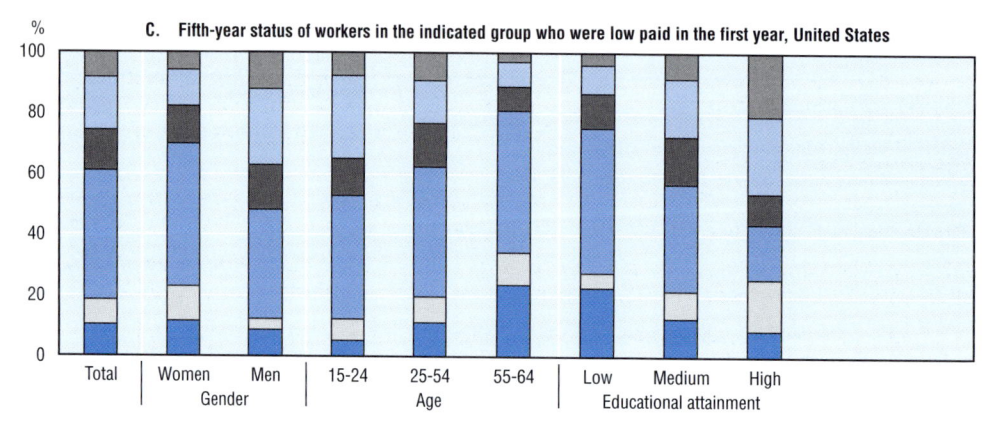

A. Fifth-year status of workers who were low paid in the first year

B. Fifth-year status of workers in the indicated group who were low paid in the first year, Europe[b]

C. Fifth-year status of workers in the indicated group who were low paid in the first year, United States

Note: EU-11: Population-weighted average for the 11 European countries shown.
a) Persons working at least 15 hours per week are considered to be low paid if their hourly wage is less than two-thirds the median wage in their country of residence; modestly paid if their wage is at least two-thirds but less than 80% of the median wage; moderately paid if their wage is at least 80% but less than 120% of the median wage; and highly paid if the wage is at least 120% of the median wage.
b) Population-weighted average for the 11 European countries shown in Panel A.
Source: Secretariat calculations based on the European Community Household Panel, waves 1 to 5 (1994-1998) for the European countries and Secretariat calculations based on the PSID from the Cross-National Equivalent Files, 1993-1997 for the United States.

Bibliography

ALTONJI, J. and R. BLANK (1999), "Race and Gender in the Labor Market", in O. Ashenfelter and D. Card (eds.), *Handbook of Labor Economics*, North-Holland Press, Amsterdam.

BERTHOUD, R. (2003), "Multiple Disadvantage in Employment: A quantitative analysis", Joseph Rowntree Foundation, York.

BLAU, F., G. ERTOLA and L. KAHN (2002), "Labor Market Institutions and Demographic Employment Patterns", *NBER Working Paper*, No. 9043.

BORJAS, G. (1999), "The Economic Analysis of Immigration", in O. Aschenfelter and D. Card (eds.), *Handbook of Labour Economics*, Vol. 3, North-Holland Press, Amsterdam.

BRANDOLINI, A., P. CIPOLLONE and P. SESTITO (2002), "Earnings Dispersion, Low Pay and Household Poverty in Italy, 1977-98", in D. Cohen, T. Piketty and G. Saint-Paul (eds.), *The Economics of Rising Inequalities*, Oxford University Press, London.

BURGESS, S., C. PROPPER, H. REES and A. SHEARER (2003), "The Class of 1981: the effects of early career unemployment on subsequent unemployment experiences", *Labour Economics*, Vol. 10, No. 3, June.

BURKHAUSER, R., B. BUTRICIA, M. DALY and D. LILLIARD (2001), "The Cross-National Equivalent File: A product of cross-national research", in I. Becker, N. Ott and G. Rolf (eds.), *Social Sicherung in einer dynamischen Gesellschaft*, Festschrift für Richard Hauser zum 65. Geburtstag, Campus Verlag, Frankfurt am Main.

BURNIAUX, J.-M., R. DUVAL and F. JAUMOTTE (2003), "Coping with Ageing: a dynamic approach to quantify the impact of future labour supply on alternative policy options," OECD Economics Department Working Paper, Paris (forthcoming).

COPPEL, J., J-C. DUMONT and I. VISCO (2001), "Trends in Immigration and Economic Consequences", OECD Economics Department Working Paper No. 284, Paris.

DANG, T., P. ANTOLIN and H. OXLEY (2001), "Fiscal Implications of Ageing: Projections of Age-Related Spending", OECD Economics Department Working Paper No. 305, Paris.

DOLADO J., F. KRAMARZ, S. MACHIN, A. MANNING, D. MARGOLIS and C. TEULINGS (1996), "The Economic Impact of the Minimum Wage in Europe", *Economic Policy*, Vol. 23, pp. 317-372.

EUROPEAN COMMISSION (2003a), *The Future of the European Employment Strategy (EES): A Strategy for Full Employment and Better Jobs for All*, Communication from the Commission to the Council, the European Parliament, the Economic and Social Committee and the Committee of the Regions, COM(2003) 6 final, Brussels.

EUROPEAN COMMISSION (2003b), *ECHP UDB manual: European Community Household Panel Longitudinal Users' Database, Waves 1 to 7, Survey Years 1994 to 2000*, Eurostat, Doc. PAN 168/2003-6, Luxembourg.

GRUBER, J. and D. WISE (2002), "Social Security Programs and Retirement around the World: Micro Estimation", Working Paper No. 9407, National Bureau of Economic Research, Cambridge.

GREGG, P. and A. MANNING (1996), "Labour Market Regulation and Unemployment", in D. Snower and G. de la Dehesa (eds.), *Unemployment Policy: How Should Governments Respond to Unemployment?*, Cambridge University Press, Cambridge.

HICKS, P. (2002), "Preparing for Tomorrow's Social Policy Agenda", *SRDC Working Paper*, No. 02-04.

ILO (1996), *Economically Active Population Estimates and Projections: 1950-2010*, www.ilo.org/public/english/bureau/stat/child/actrep/ecacpop.htm.

JUHN, C. (1992), "Decline of Male Labor Market Participations: The Role of Declining Market Opportunities", *Quarterly Journal of Economics*, Vol. 107, pp. 79-121.

KRAMARTZ F. and T. PHILIPPON (2001), "The Impact of Differential Payroll Tax Subsidies on Minimum Wage Employment", *Journal of Publics Economics*, Vol. 82-1, pp. 115-146.

LAROQUE G. and B. SALANIÉ (2000), "Une décomposition du non-emploi en France", *Économie et Statistique*, No. 331, pp. 47-66.

NEUMARK D. (1998), "Youth Labor Markets in the US: Shopping Around vs. Staying Put", *NBER Working Paper*, No. 6581.

NEUMARK D. and W. WASHER (1999), "A Cross National Analysis of the Effects of Minimum Wages on Youth Employment", *NBER Working Paper*, No. 7299.

OECD (1996), *Employment Outlook*, Paris.

OECD (1997), *Employment Outlook*, Paris.

OECD (1998a), *Employment Outlook*, Paris.

OECD (1998b), *Maintaining Prosperity in an Ageing Society*, Paris.

OECD (2000a), *Employment Outlook*, Paris.

OECD (2000b), *OECD Economic Studies*, 31, Paris.

OECD (2001), *Employment Outlook*, Paris.

OECD (2002a), *Employment Outlook*, Paris.

OECD (2002b), *An Update of the OECD Composite Leading Indicators*, Paris.

OECD (2002c), *Society at a Glance: OECD Social Indicators*, Paris.

OECD (2002d), *Babies and Bosses: Reconciling Work and Family Life*, Paris.

OECD (2002e), *Economic Outlook*, 72, Paris.

OECD (2002f), *Labour Force Statistics: 1981-2001*, Paris.

OECD (2002g), "The Economic Impact of International Migration: A Framework for EDRC Country Reviews", DEELSA/ELSA(2002)4, Paris.

OECD (2003a), *Transforming Disability into Ability: Policies to Promote Work and Income Security for Disabled People*, Paris.

OECD (2003b), *Vieillissement et politiques de l'emploi – Belgique*, Paris.

OECD (2003c), *Ageing and Employment Policies – Sweden*, Paris.

ISBN 92-64-10061-X
OECD Employment Outlook: 2003
Towards More and Better Jobs
© OECD 2003

Chapter 3

Making Work Pay Making Work Possible

> *Pay is a major determinant of the employment of under-represented groups. Sometimes, work is not financially rewarding for would-be workers. On the other hand, if pay is too high vis-à-vis market realities, it will act as a demand barrier to employment. And non-financial factors, such as the possibility for women to reconcile work and family life, also matter. How can "make work pay" policies help improve the employment prospects of under-represented groups? To what extent can family-friendly policies and flexible work arrangements, such as part-time jobs, facilitate access to employment for these groups?*

Introduction 114
Main findings 115
1. Financial incentive schemes: making work pay and facilitating access to employment 116
2. Promoting employment while taking specific situations into account.... 131
Concluding remarks 152
Annex 1. Tables 3.A1.1 to 3.A1.4 157
Bibliography 166

Introduction

Both participation and employment remain unequally distributed across work-force groups in virtually all OECD countries. In particular, as documented in Chapter 2, women, lone parents, older workers and disabled persons are under-represented in the labour market. Whether under-representation in employment is a problem is a question that encompasses fundamental issues of a social, cultural and economic nature that differ both within and across countries, and from one population category to the next. Nevertheless, lack of training or occupational skills are factors common to a large proportion of those outside the labour market. Among young women, older workers and disabled persons, non-employed persons are much more frequently less-educated than those who are employed (see Table 3.A1.1 in the annex). In addition to specific barriers to employment, there is the broader issue of the insecure employment status of low-skilled workers.

For groups with an insecure employment status to return to employment, it must *pay* for them to work. Part of the problem lies in the fact that the market wage available to these groups is sometimes too low compared with welfare benefits to encourage labour supply. This explains why many poorer households often move between work and welfare without always managing to escape the poverty trap (OECD, 2001a, Chapter 2). So for governments, one problem is how best to make work pay by modifying taxes, benefits and minimum wages.

But attention should also be devoted to the demand-side. Employment should be financially rewarding for workers, but it also needs to be *affordable* for employers. High non-wage labour costs can reduce demand for low-skilled workers. Hence, various employment subsidies can be an important link between work that "pays" and is "affordable" for the low-skilled, at least in the short run. These measures should ensure that every individual receives a decent income, sufficient to avoid poverty, without imposing excessive labour costs on employers. They play an important distributional role, but also shape labour market behaviour.

Work must also be *accessible*. Parents in particular will seek to balance the competing demands of work and family life. Lone parents may experience specific difficulties in participating in the labour market arising from inflexible working-time arrangements. Perceptions and expectations may also play an important role. For example, disabled persons, in addition to possibly being affected by a non-work oriented design of existing benefit schemes and the lack of appropriate activation policies, may have to face attitudinal and organisational hurdles keeping them outside of the labour market, even if they are only slightly disabled. Examining these non-financial factors and taking them into account through integrated and multi-dimensional policy approaches may help encourage these different groups to return to work.

The purpose of this chapter is to discuss these specific issues. The related issues of activation strategies and training policies are discussed in Chapters 4 and 5, respectively. The first part of this chapter addresses the question of pay. It reviews measures aimed at making work pay, in particular assessing their capacity to promote both participation and employment. The second part addresses more specific supply- and demand-side barriers to employment, by looking in turn at the participation/employment choices of women, lone parents, the working-age disabled and older workers. It gives particular attention to the ways in which policies can respond to the specific needs of these groups without weakening their attachment to the labour market.

Main findings

- Making work pay policies can provide effective incentives to find a job, while being an important redistributive tool. For instance, the United States and the United Kingdom have longstanding experience of employment-conditional benefits. While being both a pillar of their redistribution systems and accounting for substantial transfers, evaluations have shown them to provide effective incentives to return to employment, particularly for lone parents.

- Several factors influence the ability of employment-conditional benefits to promote employment. If they are not closely targeted, their effects on employment appear limited, compared to what may be a prohibitive cost for every job created. Restricting such benefits to groups well outside the labour market (with little incentive to work otherwise) and time-limiting payments to encourage genuine self-sufficiency in the labour market appear to be the keys to success.

- For disadvantaged groups, a minimum wage often plays a key role in making work pay. But it is a doubled-edge one. When the statutory minimum wage is high relative to the average or median wage, it usually pays to work but labour demand is likely to be reduced; and very broad measures directed at encouraging labour supply, like employment-conditional benefits, are in this case ineffective, since the priority is to enhance labour demand. Conversely, broad measures such as those introduced in the United States and the United Kingdom (or countries moving towards more flexible wage structures) need to be backed up with a moderate minimum wage to act as a floor below which wages cannot fall.

- Subsidies aimed at reducing labour costs can enhance labour demand for disadvantaged groups, where the common characteristic is low education attainment or low skills. In countries such as Belgium, France and the Netherlands that have implemented such schemes, evaluations show positive impacts on unskilled employment. But the windfall effects are likely to be substantial, at least in the short run. Moreover, employment subsidies are more effective in facilitating access to work for disadvantaged groups when closely targeted. In addition, interventions that support employment in the private sector lead to better integration into the world of work than direct job creation in the public sector.

- Striking a better work/life balance is vital, particularly since a fairly high number of women who have left work to care for their families appear to miss the workplace. The opportunity to take paid maternity leave may increase women's attachment to the labour market. But extended leave is likely to make more difficult and uncertain the return to employment, especially for women with insecure employment status. Female labour supply is relatively sensitive to childcare costs, particularly for women with low skills and low pay. Thus, providing subsidies to reduce the costs of child-care services can help young mothers return to work. Finally, the expansion of part-time work has been instrumental in countries with high female participation rates. Measures aimed at facilitating access to part-time jobs or flexible working-time arrangements are one way of preventing young mothers from leaving work.

- Lone parents are among the groups with the highest level of joblessness in many OECD countries. Addressing the disadvantages of this group is very important in the context of reducing child poverty and social exclusion. This implies that welfare support for this group should be made more work-oriented. It is important to recognize that long-term or indefinite receipt of benefits is only likely to deepen and prolong poverty. The components of such a work-oriented safety net will vary across countries, depending on existing institutional features (child care, education, family benefits, health care and labour market programmes). Preferences for working part-time and for reconciling work and family life also need to be taken into account. But in the context of a comprehensive approach, better outcomes can be achieved.

- Health problems are one of the main reasons for withdrawing from the labour market. Here too, a considerable proportion of those no longer in work for health reasons would like to return to work. Yet employment rates among disability benefit recipients are relatively low. Early intervention may often be the best way of preventing long-term benefit dependency. As soon as the disability is recognised, it should immediately trigger an individually-tailored intervention process. The package of arrangements should also include job rehabilitation and training, job-search assistance, choice among a wide range of different forms of work (normal, part-time, subsidised or sheltered employment) and benefits in-cash or in-kind based on the person's ability to work.

- Improving the employment prospects of older workers is especially important in the face of population ageing. This will require a comprehensive range of coordinated measures to influence both labour supply and demand: raising the normal age of retirement as life expectancy improves and reducing incentives to early retirement; reforming income support programmes that offer alternative pathways to early retirement, particularly disability programmes, long-term sick leave and unemployment benefits; providing effective active labour market programmes and training schemes to assist older workers to stay in employment or re-enter employment; promoting flexible working arrangements, including consideration of flexible retirement, and improving working conditions to make them appropriate to older workers; and addressing age discrimination in employment.

1. Financial incentive schemes: making work pay and facilitating access to employment

In assessing programmes to make work pay, it is important to recognize that specific programmes will reflect the institutional environment of each country. Thus, the type of support for low-income working individuals and their families that will be appropriate in different countries will depend on the level of the minimum wage, the level and composition of taxation, the nature of the social insurance and social assistance schemes operating in each country, the degree of reliance on social assistance compared to insurance, the nature and level of family payments, and other forms of support, for example for child care or for health care costs.

To take a simple example, reductions in employer social security contributions will be a more relevant option to consider in countries where these taxes are high. Countries that rely to a greater extent on income-tested payments than on social insurance or universal payments may have overall lower levels of social expenditure, and therefore aggregate tax levels will tend to be lower. However, income-testing will increase effective marginal tax rates over the range of income in which benefits are withdrawn. While the overall tax wedge may be lower in these countries, the distribution of effective tax rates will differ, and there may be groups, presumably in the lower half of the income distribution, who would receive lower returns from additional work effort than corresponding income groups in countries with higher aggregate levels of taxation.

The level of provision and the costs of child care, the age at which children start school and the availability of pre-school care will also impact on the design of programmes to make work pay. Even in countries that appear to be similar, there are important differences in the design of benefit systems, which complicate the lessons that can be drawn. For example, receipt of income support in the United Kingdom requires social assistance recipients to be working less than 16 hours per week. In contrast, in Australia and New Zealand there are no such hours rules and the income tests use much lower withdrawal rates than in the United Kingdom or many other OECD countries. This means that in Australia and New Zealand social assistance itself can help subsidize low-paid work. This does not mean that lessons cannot be learned from the experiences of different countries, but it is important to bear in mind these and other relevant differences in drawing conclusions from these differing experiences.

It is also important to recognize that programmes to make work pay may have a number of *competing* objectives, and thus their effectiveness cannot be judged solely on the basis of their effects on employment. In particular, some programmes of benefits for working families with children are also designed to alleviate child poverty, or have broader distributional goals. As a result, such programmes may be much more expensive than targeted employment subsidies, for example. These multiple objectives may further complicate comparisons across countries.

A. *Encouraging labour supply by making work pay: employment-conditional benefits*

The United States and the United Kingdom have longstanding experience of employment-conditional benefits. *They are one of the pillars of their redistribution systems.* Initiated in the 1970s, these make-work-pay schemes gradually increased in scale and are now widely used in both countries. The experiment has spread, and a large number of OECD countries are making such benefits a feature of their redistribution and/or employment policies (OECD, 2002c).

Different forms of employment-conditional benefits

In both countries, these benefits are directed at families with low earned incomes, particularly those with children. The amounts actually paid are relatively high. In the United Kingdom, the benefits are conditional upon a minimum number of hours of work and are highest for households with the lowest earned incomes. In the United States, the benefit is phased in as earnings rise up to a threshold. In both cases, the benefit is not time-limited but depends on household income, with a very simple exit arrangement: benefits are gradually reduced over a set income level. People targeted by such policies should be able to rely upon *sustained* support, reflecting the fact that their difficulties in entering the labour market are in no way cyclical (Blundell and Meghir, 2002).

There are some variants on this basic structure (see also Table 3.A1.2 in annex):

- Some benefits are *individually based*, no longer targeting the family as a whole but individual family members. This is the case in a number of countries (including Australia, Canada, Belgium, France and the Netherlands) and it shifts the thrust slightly away from redistribution and towards a work-incentive policy.[1] The reason is that basing the benefit on overall household income may reduce the incentive for the spouse to work and such a risk may be crucial in those countries where non-employment is concentrated among spouses. However, this perverse effect may be attenuated when eligibility requirements are individually based.

- The *generosity* of these benefits varies substantially across countries, and necessarily depends on other components of redistribution policy and on institutional features of the social welfare system (*e.g.* the minimum wage, whether or not there are universal payments, family or housing benefits, etc.).
- *Eligibility* for benefits may depend on the recipient's prior status, rather than just being income-tested. More precisely, in a number of countries only people leaving welfare or the long-term unemployed have access to benefits such as tax credits or employment-conditional benefits. Household composition may also be a criterion.
- The benefit may be *time-limited*. The argument in favour of time limits is that it strengthens incentives. Limiting the payment of benefits over time may encourage recipients to progress more rapidly in their jobs, for instance through training, and eventually achieve real self-sufficiency in the labour market (Blundell, 2002). How long it takes to eliminate job insecurity and, consequently, how long a programme should be remains an open question.

In some countries, tax policy has been used to make work more attractive to individuals. For instance, the Belgian in-work tax credit (currently being introduced) can be seen as a component of a more comprehensive tax reform aimed at promoting employment. In the context of this reform, employee social security contributions have been cut for low-wage workers, leading to a substantial increase in the lowest net earnings. In Germany, the tax and transfer system in the low-wage sector has been recognized to be an impediment to employment. The Federal Government has therefore undertaken a phased reduction of the burden imposed by taxation and other charges on labour, as part of the "employment-friendly reforms" (European Commission, 2002). Among other things, the objective of this reform is to increase disposable income after tax and social security contributions, especially for low-wage workers.[2] The reduction in taxes on low income people recently enacted in Italy provides another case in point. This reform is part of a more ambitious programme of across the board tax cuts, while also raising incentives to start participating in the labour market, particularly for spouses.

Employment-conditional benefits can provide effective incentives to work, under certain conditions

The impact of make-work-pay policies depends on a number of features, including eligibility criteria and the generosity of benefits.

First, in both the United Kingdom and the United States, tax credits appear to be an effective means of encouraging entry or a return to employment by lone-parent families and households where no-one works (Table 3.1). But there is also evidence of the perverse effect that is to be expected among two-earner households with regard to the labour supply of spouses. Income-tested tax credits make it less worthwhile for the second family member to earn additional income, particularly if they move the household into the withdrawal phase of the tax credit scheme where effective marginal tax rates are very high. In this case, some people will find it worthwhile to stop working or reduce their hours of work. The same conclusions are reached by a large number of evaluations, regardless of the methodological approach (controlled experiments, natural experiments or micro-simulations). Both the

Earned Income Tax Credit in the United States (EITC) and the Working Family Tax Credit in the United Kingdom (WFTC), for instance, are reported to have lowered the employment rate of married women with working spouses (Table 3.1). Therefore, the employment effects of this type of measure, which targets household income, differ across groups and may, overall, be relatively modest. And from a purely employment point of view, it may be preferable to have individually-based eligibility criteria, or to differentiate the intervention according to the target group, lone parents and other people.

Table 3.1. **In-work benefits and their effects on labour-market participation and employment: lone parents, a highly receptive group**

	Working Family Tax Credit (UK)	Earned Income Tax Credit (US)
Costs	GBP 5 billion (0.6% of GDP)	USD 32 billion (0.33% of GDP)
Number of recipients	1.3 million households (1 household in 20)	20 million households (1 household in 5)
Employment effects	Effects of the 1999 reform which increased the generosity of benefits (corresponding to a GBP 1.5 billion increase in public spending)	Effects of the 1987 expansion of the EITC, passed as part of the Tax Reform Act of 1986 and representing the first major expansion of the EITC (the maximum credit increased from USD 550 to USD 851)
	Percentage points change in transitions from non-employment to employment (evaluation based on simulations)[a]	Percentage points change in participation rates (evaluation based on natural experiments)
	Lone parents 2.20	Single mothers[b] (1985-1991) 2.4
	Married women with:	Married women[c] (1986-1994) −2.4
	– a non-working spouse 1.32	
	– a working spouse −0.57	
	Married men with:	Married men[c] (1986-1994) 0.2
	– a non-working spouse 0.37	
	– a working spouse 0.30	
	Number of additional jobs 27 500	

a) Blundell and Hoynes (2001), Table 5.2.
b) Eissa and Liebman (1996).
c) Eissa and Hoynes (1998), Table 7.

Second, in terms of eligibility criteria, another question is whether income-testing is sufficient in itself or whether a more selective approach is better, for example, restricting eligibility for benefits to the most disadvantaged categories of recipients (*e.g.* long-term unemployed, long-term welfare recipients, lone parents). This solution has been recommended by various authors (Blundell, 2002), but it has certain risks. First, narrower targeting may increase the stigma attached to the measure, which can undermine the recipient's labour-market integration. Second, confining eligibility to welfare recipients alone may alter welfare-claiming behaviour, with longer and more frequent periods on welfare that offers entitlement to tax credits or similar benefits. Third, restricting generous measures to a small sub-set of the population may raise concerns about equity – former welfare recipients may receive higher disposable incomes than people doing otherwise similar jobs. In turn, this may have undesirable incentive effects. Nevertheless, there is some evidence that this sort of targeting can be effective. Canada's experience with the Self-Sufficiency Project, targeted at single parents who have been welfare recipients for a year, suggests that this group is particularly receptive to make-work-pay policies (Box 3.1).

Third, imposing a minimum-hours requirement for eligibility for payments may have ambiguous effects on labour supply. On the one hand, it may be ineffective in helping those with young children take a job that involves too many hours of work. But on the other, the prospects for career development and wage progression are often better in full-time employment (Corcoran and Loeb, 1999). And a minimum-hours requirement reduces the

3. MAKING WORK PAY – MAKING WORK POSSIBLE

> **Box 3.1. Canada's Self-Sufficiency Project (SSP): promoting employment and reducing poverty among lone parents**
>
> The Self-Sufficiency Project (SSP) was launched in Canada in the mid-1990s. The scheme was a large-scale "controlled experiment", which ran for five years and is now concluded. Enrolees (i.e. persons offered the supplement) were assigned on a random basis, and their behaviour was compared with persons not offered the supplement. The SSP paid an earnings supplement targeted at single parents who had been welfare recipients for at least a year. The supplement was paid for up to three years and equalled half the difference between a participant's earnings from employment and an "earnings benchmark", provided that the recipient worked for at least 30 hours per week. The supplement roughly doubled the earnings of many low-wage workers (before taxes and work-related expenses). Recipients of this earnings supplement were not entitled to receive welfare but were eligible for other cash transfer payments such as employment insurance and child benefit. However, the SSP was a voluntary scheme and enrolees could at any time opt out of the programme and return to welfare.
>
> **SSP impacts on employment and earnings**
>
> | Year | 1 | 2 | 3 end of programme | 4 | 5 1st quarter | 5 2nd quarter |
> |---|---|---|---|---|---|---|
> | **Monthly employment rate (%)** | | | | | | |
> | Programme group | 29.7 | 40.6 | 39.9 | 41.2 | 42.1 | 41.8 |
> | Control group | 25.4 | 30.1 | 32.6 | 36.8 | 39.8 | 41.9 |
> | Difference (Impact) | 4.3 | 10.5 | 7.3 | 4.4 | 2.3 | n.s. |
> | **Monthly full-time employment rate (%)** | | | | | | |
> | Programme group | 18.0 | 28.5 | 27.7 | 28.5 | 28.3 | 28.0 |
> | Control group | 11.6 | 16.0 | 18.4 | 22.3 | 25.0 | 26.5 |
> | Difference (Impact) | 6.4 | 12.5 | 9.3 | 6.2 | 3.3 | n.s. |
> | **Average monthly earnings (CAD)** | | | | | | |
> | Programme group | 233 | 370 | 387 | 476 | 499 | 496 |
> | Control group | 186 | 269 | 317 | 424 | 462 | 488 |
> | Difference (Impact) | 47 | 101 | 70 | 52 | n.s. | n.s. |
>
> n.s.: not statistically significant.
> The same individuals have been followed during five years. Persons offered the supplement (the programme group) had one year to take advantage of the offer. They could sign up for the supplement if they found a full-time job within the year after random assignment. If they did not sign during that year, they could never receive the supplement. Overall, about 36% of the programme group received at least one supplement payment, but the number receiving supplement payments in any given month was never that large, peaking at 25% of the programme group near the beginning of the second year.
> *Source:* Michalopoulos et al. (2002), Table ES.1.

The findings of SSP evaluations are encouraging.[a] The scheme brought a large number of people back into work, a feature noticeable throughout the period of eligibility for the earnings supplement (the first three to four years). As the SSP promoted a return to full-time work, it also had substantial effects on wages and hence on income and poverty, reducing the proportion of families with incomes below Statistics Canada's low-income cut-offs by up to 12.4 percentage points (among the programme group by comparison to the control group). The effect of the supplement offer was mostly to speed up by two or three years the entry into employment of lone parents who had been on welfare at least one year prior to random assignment. Indeed, the impact on employment and earnings gradually wore off once payment of the earnings supplement ceased. This was mainly due to the fact that the employment rate of the control group gradually caught up to that of the programme group.

Box 3.1. **Canada's Self-Sufficiency Project (SSP): Promoting employment and reducing poverty among lone parents** (cont.)

To a lesser extent, the SPP effects on employment fell over time because some people in the programme group who went to work lost their job. The supplement might have been more effective and might have produced a longer-lasting effect if it had been combined with job-retention or reemployment services (Michalopoulos et al., 2002; see also Box 3.3). In addition, it appears that when the programme was offered to *new* entrants to welfare, the positive employment and earnings effects were especially large and long-lasting.[b] This suggests that the effectiveness of SSP would increase over time if it was operated as a programme (Ford et al. 2003).

a) See also Box 3.2 for the financial aspects.
b) A sub-experiment which offered the financial incentive to lone parents who had been on welfare *exactly* one year produced longer-lasting positive effects on full-time employment and larger effects on earnings while participants received less overall in supplements payment.

scope for the main household earner to use earnings supplements to cut down on hours of work or to manipulate hours to become eligible for payments. In any case, this type of requirement definitely has an impact on labour supply behaviour. In the United Kingdom, for instance, there is a very clear "spike" in the number of hours worked by single mothers, a spike that corresponds exactly to the number of hours required to become eligible for the WFTC and is not found among single women without children who are not eligible (Blundell, 2002).

Fourth, the fact that the benefit is paid as long as wages remain below a given threshold does not encourage recipients to develop their skills and competences. A recent study by Heckman et al. (2002) suggests that EITC recipients may have cut down on their training effort, since their wage profiles remained relatively flat (owing to their participation in the scheme). Nevertheless, entitlement to benefits should last for a sufficiently long period because career prospects and wage progression among the low-skilled and/or low-paid are both limited and slow. For instance, although the Canadian SSP increased the number of people who experienced high wage growth over a three-year period (10.9% of the programme group saw their wages increase by 20% or more between the end of the first year and the end of the fourth year of the experiment, compared to 7% of the control group), average wages were still fairly low for many workers at the end of the period (Michalopoulos et al., 2002).

Fifth, the impact of employment-conditional benefits on labour supply behaviour is highly contingent on the generosity of the benefits and their ability to raise earned income above the level of welfare. In many cases, the benefits provide only small financial gains (Table 3.A1.2 in the annex). The avowed success of the EITC in the United States, particularly among single mothers, stems partly from the fact that the scheme provides relatively strong financial incentives[3] (Blundell and Hoynes, 2001), particularly at a time when access to welfare benefits was being restricted. The generosity of the earnings supplement awarded under Canada's SSP also partly explains the scale of the employment effects observed among programme members[4] (Blank et al., 1999). Conversely, *ex-ante* evaluations of France's *Prime pour l'emploi* (PPE) are pessimistic. Financial support for recipients is very low, accounting at most for 4.7% of declared income[5] (compared with 40% on average for the EITC). The anticipated effect on employment is fairly marginal, particularly as the scheme partly excludes from the target group those with the lowest earned incomes, *i.e.* those for whom there may be a real trade-off between welfare and work (Cahuc, 2001; and Box 3.2).[6]

Box 3.2. **Making work pay policies: different costs for different goals**

It is hard to generalise about the costs associated with tax credit schemes and speak of their economic efficiency without placing them in their context. Such schemes fulfil different functions depending on the country and, while their stated goal – regardless of country – is to promote employment, their role with regard to the welfare system and redistributive issues may differ substantially.

The EITC and the WFTC are expensive schemes (Table 3.1),[a] but they also redistribute resources to a *significant* proportion of low-income families with children, who are making an effort to support themselves through work. For instance, Liebman (1998) suggests that the EITC would have offset 23% of the decline in income between 1976 and 1996 for households in the lowest fifth of the income distribution, and offset 10% of the decline for households in the second fifth. To some extent, the EITC acts as a welfare benefit for low-wage earners. According to estimates by Grogger (2003), the increased generosity of the scheme during the 1990s helped reduce the number of entrants into the welfare system over the same period: "each percentage-point increase in the credit rate reduces initial entry by 3.2%. Thus the increase in the mean credit rate for multiple-child families between 1993 and 1999 would have decreased initial entry by more than a half." Some potential welfare recipients are said to have operated a trade-off and opted for the EITC, and hence for work. Reducing poverty, in particular among children, was also one of the key goals of the UK Government in its 1999 and subsequent reforms which featured the WFTC and made the tax credit system more generous (HM Treasury, 2000). The reforms have also increased family payments for jobless parents, without undermining financial incentives to return to employment.

In this particular context, when employment-conditional benefits are intended to substitute for income-support expenditures, they cannot be expected to be financially neutral. Duncan and MacCrae (1999) estimate, for instance, that labour supply behaviour induced by the expansion of the WFTC resulted in a cut of some 14% in the *ex-ante* cost of the measure. Apparently, then, the reform costs less in terms of public expenditure than straightforward welfare payments with no requirement to work. If one were to assess this programme solely on the basis of the employment goal, however, the outcome would appear to be extremely inefficient, with 86% of the very significant cost shouldered by the public purse. Clearly, this is not the appropriate way to assess such programmes, given their important distributional objectives. In order to assess their economic efficiency it is necessary to make a comparison of their cost with that of social transfers, which may provide significant disincentives to work. Moreover, this means that it may not be meaningful to compare the costs and apparent outcomes from such programmes with more selective measures focussing purely on encouraging the transition from welfare to the world of work.

Canada's SSP, for instance, maximises employment impacts by targeting single-parent families only, but also limits costs by targeting welfare recipients who must give up income assistance in order to receive the SSP earnings supplement. Thus, this scheme does not involve very significant redistribution since it covers a small group, but it provides large financial incentives to those who are entitled. As the scheme also promotes full-time employment, the earned income of those on the project is relatively high, as are the taxes they pay. Overall, the net cost per person has been low, since benefits (in terms of higher taxes collected on re-employed individuals and lower welfare payments) have been relatively high.[b] These results have been contested, however. The conclusions derive from a controlled experiment and are based on partial equilibrium results. A general equilibrium analysis, namely one that analyses the results of a broad programme available

> Box 3.2. **Making work pay policies: different costs for different goals** (cont.)
>
> to all welfare recipients and takes into account displacement effects and entry effects,[c] has been estimated to lead to significantly less positive outcomes (Lise *et al.*, 2003). However, even this model is limited as it does not apply to a fully national programme. The conclusion appears to be that a scheme like the SSP may be effective if limited to a small subset of the population, where it would not be expected to have large equilibrium impacts. Conversely, France's PPE has very little targeting and the financial gains for beneficiaries are relatively small. The stated goal of this scheme was to promote employment and payments are effectively too low to have a significant distributional effect. But PPE generates far too high a cost per job creation, since the financial incentives are too small for there to be any substantial effects on employment (Laroque and Salanié, 2002).
>
> a) However, they are also part of the overall system of other OECD social protection, which in the case of the United States has significantly lower budgetary costs than in many European countries.
> b) SSP cost the government only about CAD 2 700 more than income assistance for each program member over a five-year period. The bulk of the cost of SSP came in the form of supplement payments. However, the financial gains to the government from increased income taxes made up for most of the losses in increased transfer payments (Michalopoulos *et al.*, 2002, Chapter 7).
> c) Welfare recipients as well as unemployed persons may delay their return to employment in order to become eligible for the supplement.

B. *Supporting labour demand by lowering labour costs*

Employment-conditional benefits may encourage disadvantaged groups to (re)enter the labour market. But there is also a labour demand issue: the cost of labour may effectively limit a firm's ability to hire low-skilled individuals. The idea of lowering labour costs to promote the employment of under-represented groups has shaped employment policies in some OECD countries, particularly in those European countries where social security contributions are high relative to average earnings. Measures to reduce labour costs can take a variety of forms, but fall into two main categories: broad measures covering all those in low-paid work, and schemes more closely targeted at those who are jobless and not easily employable.

Reducing labour costs at the bottom of the wage ladder: substantial effect on unskilled employment, but high deadweight costs

Support to the demand for low-paid jobs can take the form of a reduction in employers' social security contributions. As the wage level is the only qualifying condition, the reduction applies to both new recruits and longstanding members of the workforce. The reduction in contributions remains in effect as long as the monthly wage remains below a pre-defined ceiling, with no other limit as to duration. When the reduction is based on the monthly wage alone and not on the number of hours worked, this type of measure leads to substantially more part-time work at what may be relatively high hourly rates. If low-skilled, low-paid jobs are the real target, the reduction in employers' contributions should be proportional to the hourly wage.

In countries that have implemented this type of measure (mainly Belgium, France and the Netherlands), most available macroeconomic evaluations report significant effects on employment, in particular for low-skilled labour (Table 3.2). Broad measures to reduce employers' social security contributions for low-paid jobs pose, however, a major funding

Table 3.2. **Examples of broad reductions in social insurance contributions for low-paid jobs**

Description of measure	Evaluations
Belgium Sliding-scale reduction for low wages, decreasing with relevant pay ceiling and ranging from 50% to 10% of overall amount due in employers' contributions. Measure abolished on 1 April 1999. Measure introduced on 1 January 2000. Reduction in employers' social insurance contributions that declines as the gross wage increases. The largest reduction, for the EUR 2 565 to EUR 3 333 wage bracket, is EUR 736 (a reduction of between 28.7 and 22% of the gross wage). In the upper wage bracket, there is a sliding-scale reduction limited to EUR 246 as from EUR 4 614 (or at most 5.3% of the gross wage). For part-time workers, the reduction is commensurate with the number of hours worked, providing they exceed ⅓ of full-time work. From ⅘ of full-time work, the reduction in contributions is at its highest.	The measure abolished on 1 April 1999 has been evaluated by Sneessens and Shadman (2000). These authors used a general equilibrium model calibrated on the Belgian economy, with two categories of labour (skilled and unskilled), to simulate a 21% cut in employers' contributions for unskilled jobs. The result was an increase of 6.7% in low-skilled employment and 3.2% in total employment (market sector), for an overall cost amounting to 1% of GDP (the funding effects were not taken into account[b]).
France Measure initially introduced in 1993 in a slightly different form.[a] Reductions in employers' social security contributions on low wages. Sliding-scale reduction, which may exceed 18.2% of gross salary at the SMIC (minimum wage) level and stops at or over 1.3 SMIC. For part-time workers, the cut in contributions is commensurate with the hours worked.	This measure has given rise to numerous evaluations based on macroeconomic models calibrated on French data. For instance, Laffargue (2000) and Audric et al. (2000) reach a figure of between 110 000 and 440 000 jobs created (or between about 0.7 and 2.9% of employment in the business sector), for a total annual cost of 0.5% of GDP (with various funding hypotheses). On the basis of econometric estimates using individual data on firms, Crépon and Déplatz (2001) put the number of jobs created at between 255 000 and 670 000 (orders of magnitude similar to those found by Sneessens and Shadman, 2000). However, the funding effects of these reductions are not taken into account.[b]
Netherlands SPAK: Introduced in 1996: reduction in employers' contributions on low wages. The reduction declines as the wage rises and ceases when the wage reaches 115% of the statutory minimum wage. The reduction is highest at the level of the statutory minimum wage, and cuts employers' contributions by around 60%, or 13% of gross pay (or just over 10% of all wage costs). Below 36 hours per week, the reduction is commensurate with the number of hours worked (thereby excluding part-time workers earning high hourly rates). T-SPAK (Transitional SPAK): measure introduced in 1997 to cushion the increase in the tax burden of employers who raise the pay of workers receiving SPAK benefits. For workers earning over 115% but less than 130% of the minimum wage, employers may apply for half of the normal SPAK. This measure is only granted for workers who have received the SPAK. The T-SPAK is awarded for two years from the date on which entitlement to SPAK ceased. SPAK and T-SPAK have been abolished over a period of four year as from 1 January 2003.	Evaluations were based on a general equilibrium model of the Dutch economy (MIMIC: Bovenberg et al., 1998; European Commission, 1999). The simulations predicted a total increase in employment of almost 1%, with an increase of over 5% in less-skilled employment, for an overall cost of 0.5% of GDP, funded by a cut in public spending. A recent evaluation based on a comparison between firms applying for the wage subsidy and non-applying firms suggests that the effect of SPAK on employment would have been very low or even zero (Mühlau and Salverda, 2000). But the study covers the period 1996-1998, where the subsidy was about EUR 500. In 1998, the SPAK was increased to EUR 1 800.

a) The reductions introduced more recently under legislation on the 35-hour week cannot be equated to measures to cut labour costs. They were introduced to maintain monthly wages following the reduction in working hours, without increasing hourly labour costs for employers.
b) For instance, such schemes can be funded by lowering public expenditures or increasing other taxes, and the evaluated employment effects depend on the funding source which is chosen.

Source: OECD (2002b); SPF (2001, Belgium); DARES (1999, France); European Commission (1999, Netherlands).

issue. The deadweight effects are likely to be substantial as a broad group of workers is covered and with fast-expanding companies receiving the same subsidy as those in decline. This is the main criticism levelled at this kind of policy, which also subsidises existing jobs that are not under threat and job creation that might have occurred anyway.

For instance, according to employer surveys in the Netherlands, between 20 to 60% of *new* recruits would have been hired without the financial support.[7] These views may also reflect the fact that, in the short term, companies basically tailor employment to demand for their goods or services. The longer-term impacts to be expected from these measures are probably underestimated in employer surveys, since lower labour costs may give companies a financial boost and enhance their capacity for job creation.

From the recipients' standpoint, there is also a risk of seeing low-pay traps emerge. This is because payroll tax reductions for low-paid jobs make the tax system more progressive (or at least less regressive), and make it more expensive for companies to award wage increases at the bottom end of the wage ladder. To address this problem, the Netherlands has launched an interesting initiative. It has introduced a complementary measure (T-SPAK), which temporarily subsidies wage increases that would otherwise cause employers to lose their entitlement to the broader reduction in contributions (Table 3.2).[8]

Closely targeted hiring subsidies effectively help under-represented groups

One obvious way of reducing the "pure" windfall effects of measures designed to lower labour costs is to introduce tighter targeting. The target groups may range from the long-term unemployed to welfare recipients or low-skilled single parents. Their common characteristic is the problems they tend to face in finding work. Targeted employment subsidies are found throughout the OECD area and account for a significant share of expenditure on active labour-market policies (Table 3.3).

Under certain conditions, these special measures may prove useful in improving the employment prospects of target groups:

- First, these schemes produce better outcomes when programme participants are allowed to do more *regular* work. In this regard, the evaluation evidence suggests that private sector wage subsidies are more effective than direct-job creation in the public sector in helping unemployed people return to employment in the open labour market (Martin and Grubb, 2001). Most jobs provided through direct job creation do not offer opportunities to gain work experience that could be transferable to "normal" jobs in the private sector (Table 3.4). The risk is that recipients may become marginalised, and for this reason, it is important for such policies to be targeted at highly disadvantaged groups with little prospect of entering the "normal" labour market, helping them to maintain contact with the labour market.

- Targeted employment subsidies may help people in the targeted groups in finding a job, but this can happen largely at the expense of other groups. If deadweight and substitution effects cannot be eliminated, the evaluation evidence suggests that it may be possible to raise *net* employment gains associated with private sector wage subsidies to 20-30% or more through effective targeting of the measures to specific groups (*e.g.* the long-term unemployed) and close monitoring of employer behaviour in order to curb abuses (Martin and Grubb, 2001). However, such measures may have the drawback of stigmatising the group in question, and this may undermine the chances of people in the group of finding work. It is therefore preferable to restrict eligibility to those having significant difficulties in the labour market.

- Many of the highly targeted schemes have a low take-up rate among employers, who may be unaware of their existence or put off by the restrictions imposed. Moreover, most

Table 3.3. **Targeted employment subsidies account for a significant share of expenditure on active labour market programmes**
Subsidies to regular employment in the private sector and direct job creation (public or non-profit), 2001

	Employment subsidies		Distribution of employment subsidies	
	As a percentage of total public spending on active labour market programmes	As a percentage of GDP	Subsidies to regular employment in the private sector	Direct job creation in the public sector
			(% of total employment subsidies)	
Australia	18.6	0.08	8.0	92.0
Austria	18.0	0.09	63.6	36.4
Belgium	53.8	0.69	41.1	58.9
Canada	6.0	0.03	15.5	84.5
Czech Republic	39.9	0.08	49.3	50.7
Denmark (2000)	10.7	0.17	11.6	88.4
Finland	27.7	0.26	55.4	44.6
France	26.2	0.34	46.9	53.1
Germany	17.8	0.21	13.5	86.5
Greece (1998)	10.5	0.06	100.0	–
Hungary	58.6	0.28	32.3	67.7
Ireland	47.0	0.53	32.4	67.6
Italy	..	0.29	82.0	18.0
Korea	44.1	0.14	10.5	89.5
Luxembourg (1997)	23.3	0.06	96.7	3.3
Mexico	39.3	0.02	–	100.0
Netherlands	24.0	0.38	12.6	87.4
New Zealand (2000)	11.6	0.06	81.2	18.8
Norway	0.6	0.01	100.0	–
Poland	..	0.04	60.1	39.9
Portugal (2000)	9.7	0.06	18.6	81.4
Spain	39.3	0.33	74.8	25.2
Sweden	13.3	0.19	98.4	1.6
Switzerland	23.1	0.10	36.8	63.2
United Kingdom	7.3	0.03	63.2	36.8
United States	8.1	0.01	37.7	62.3
OECD unweighted average[a]	**24.1**	**0.18**	**47.8**	**52.2**

.. Data not available.
– Nil or less than half of the last digit used.
a) For above countries only.
Source: OECD database on labour market programmes.

of the subsidised contracts are with major companies (which are often more aware of the schemes than small and medium-sized firms). It might be worthwhile to promote such measures among smaller firms, many of which are unaware that the support is available and yet would stand to gain relatively more from it than large firms. The visibility of these measures for employers could be enhanced by not having a host of different schemes, many of them based on the same rationale and competing with one another, rather than being complementary.

- The measures should be designed to ensure that labour market integration is as *sustained* as possible. The temporary nature of the subsidy may increase labour turnover, if employers continue to fill the same post using workers recruited on subsidised contracts. Some measures contain clauses aimed at employers who may, for instance,

Table 3.4. Targeted employment subsidies: recipient outcomes and employers' views (examples drawn from recent evaluations)

Description of measure	Available evaluations
A. Effects of employment subsidies on recipient outcomes	
Germany, eastern Länder (Sachsen-Anhalt) Subsidised jobs in public institutions, a private non-profit organisation or a firm. The job subsidised must not replace an existing job and the work done must be useful for the public. This scheme is targeted at the unemployed for at least six months, with priority going to the unemployed aged 50 years and over, the long-term unemployed, unskilled youth, the disabled. The duration of the programme is around one year at most.	Eichler and Lechner (2002) One to two years after having been in the programme, participants have a higher employment probability compared with non-participants having the same observable individual characteristics (e.g. age, gender, education).
France Subsidised jobs in the non-market sector, targeted at individuals with serious difficulties on the labour market (very long-term unemployed, long-term unemployed aged 50 and over, welfare recipients, the disabled). The duration of the programme is five years at most.	Bardaji (2001) While subsidised employment contracts help to maintain the worker in the non-market institution, it is highly detrimental when people do not stay: very few subsequently find work. Thus, experience gained in a subsidised job does not appear to be highly valued (no adjustment for selection bias).
Slovak Republic Subsidised private-sector jobs, targeted at unemployed and school-leavers aged under 18. The duration of the programme is two years minimum. Subsidised public-sector jobs targeted at low-skilled. The duration of the programme is nine months maximum.	van Ours (2002) Employment subsidies may increase unemployment exit rates, provided the programme is not too long. Very long programmes may have adverse effects on the rate of return to unsubsidised employment.
Sweden Six main types of Swedish programmes that were available to adult unemployed workers entitled to unemployment benefits in the 1990s: labour market training, workplace introduction, work experience placement, relief work, trainee replacement and employment subsidies.	Sianesi (2002) Employment subsidies for private companies are by far the most effective type of programme to help bring people back into work (notably in terms of sustained employment).
Eight active measures available for unemployed persons. These programmes can be classified in four categories: self-employment services, subsidised on the job training, wage and employment subsidies and, classroom training services.	Carling and Richardson (2001) Programmes in which the participants obtain subsidised work experience and training provided by firms have better outcomes than programmes providing classroom vocational training. Further, the more regular work the participants are allowed to do, the better the programme is relative to other ones.

B. Private-sector subsidies and their impact on hiring decisions: employers' views

	Percentage of subsidised hiring that can be considered as…		Total
	Deadweight[b]	Substitution effect[c]	
Belgium, van der Linden (1997)[a] Reduction in employers' contributions for a period of eight months (*Voordeelbanen*), targeted at young, jobless and other disadvantaged groups.	53	36	> 89
France, Belleville (2001) Reduction in employers' contributions (CIE), targeted at long-term unemployed, young people with no skills, jobless aged 50 and over, welfare recipients, the disabled.	19-39	45	64-84
Netherlands, van Polanen Petel et al. (1999)[a] Reduction in employers' contributions (VLW), target at long-term unemployed.	27-60	37-63	57-87

a) In Marx (2001).
b) Employer states that the worker would have been hired without the financial support, and the same person would have been hired.
c) Employer states that recruitment would have occurred without the financial support, but the support influenced the profile of the person hired.

lose the right to benefit from the subsidy if they refuse to extend the contract of a worker hired in this way. Another solution is to make payment subject to a training requirement, thereby strengthening the ties between the person hired and the employer investing in the training. The Job Training Partnership Act (United States, 1983-2000) included such measures, offering employers temporary subsidies while promoting the training of new recruits and monitoring employer behaviour (see also Box 3.3).[9]

By and large, employment subsidies can be effective provided they are carefully targeted at groups experiencing serious difficulties in the labour market. In fact there are two possible interpretations of the evaluation evidence (Table 3.4). On the one hand, employer surveys report major deadweight effects. On the other, studies on recipient outcomes are more optimistic. This suggests that targeted subsidies do redistribute employment opportunities to the more disadvantaged, without necessarily creating many more jobs. Moreover, such schemes may also prevent the long-term unemployed from becoming discouraged and quitting the labour market, so they can also help to mobilise labour resources. Finally, such measures can only lead to sustained integration in the labour market if the jobs enable people to develop their human capital. But career progression is very slow among those with few skills, which is a common feature in the groups targeted by these schemes. This raises the issue of tying the subsidy to a training requirement. A few experiments along this line have been tried with promising results and further experimentation would be desirable.

C. Subsidising workers or employers? Relevance and drawbacks of each option

Tax-credit schemes and employer subsidies have both been the subject of an extensive literature. But seldom have the two options been addressed on a comparative basis, and the issue of when one is preferable to the other remains open.[10] Moreover, tax-credit schemes and employer subsidies pose questions about the minimum wage and the level at which it should be set.

The role of the minimum wage

The minimum wage is an important element in the making-work-pay-policy toolbox. By setting a wage floor below which employers cannot legally pay, a statutory minimum wage aims to reduce wage inequality and to reduce poverty among working households (OECD, 1998). But while the minimum wage can make work pay, it also makes work less accessible for some groups of workers and may thus be an inappropriate tool for helping the most disadvantaged groups. To the extent that the minimum wage has undesirable effects on the level of unemployment, then its redistributive impact will be reduced. Overall, a high minimum wage (compared to the average or median wage) might have only a limited effect on poverty, with the risk of excluding from the labour market those on the borderline between employment and unemployment (Neumark and Wascher, 1997, 1998).

Indeed, while available cross-country evidence suggests that statutory minimum wages, at the levels at which they are currently set in OECD countries, do not have major perverse effects on aggregate employment (OECD, 1998; Dolado *et al.*, 1996), a high statutory minimum wage undermines the employment prospects of disadvantaged groups (Neumark and Wascher, 1999; Kramarz and Philippon, 2001; Laroque and Salanié, 2000). For these groups, the most effective solution in terms of employability would therefore be to lower the minimum wage. But this could reduce the attractiveness of work compared to welfare receipt for some groups (for example, young people). A second-best solution would be to offer employers a reduction in non-wage labour costs for those employed at or around the minimum wage. That is, a high minimum wage appears to call for policies that support labour demand.

Moreover, since employment-conditional benefits are mainly directed at enhancing labour supply, a high minimum wage makes it more difficult to justify the introduction of such schemes. Unless these benefits are closely targeted at individuals who experience difficulties in moving from welfare to work, for instance, they will mainly support those who are already in jobs or are likely to find work. And they will overlook those outside the core labour market, with weak employment prospects. In addition, a high minimum wage compresses the wage distribution at the bottom of the wage ladder, which makes it very expensive to introduce broad in-work benefits since targeting low wage earners may, in fact, represent a relatively large proportion of those in employment (Bassanini *et al.*, 1999). In terms of both equity and economic efficiency, employment-conditional benefits therefore appear to be inappropriate in the presence of relatively high minimum wages. However, it is possible that tax-credits or in-work benefits could lead to lower increases in minimum wages if seen as a package.[11] Nevertheless, earnings supplements are not perfectly substitutable with wages, since the latter have broader implications for unemployment insurance benefits, the level of future pensions, and related entitlements, which in-work benefits generally do not have.

Finally, while the introduction of tax credits may be theoretically ineffective in the presence of a *high* minimum wage, this does not rule out keeping a moderate minimum wage. The introduction of employment-conditional benefits should increase labour supply which, in turn, is likely to put downward pressure on wages. Some of the positive repercussions expected from these benefits might thus be cancelled out by the drop in wages at the bottom of the wage ladder. Hence, it may be desirable to set a wage floor below which employers cannot go. This is in fact the option chosen by the United Kingdom, which introduced a minimum wage just as its tax-credit policy was being extended (European Commission, 2000). Various evaluations consider this to be a sound option, stressing its beneficial impact on low wages with no apparent repercussions on employment (UK Low Pay Commission, 2001).

Common disadvantages: towards more comprehensive schemes for sustained returns to employment

Policies targeting groups experiencing the greatest difficulty in the labour market are shifting to more comprehensive schemes, which pay specific attention to the career development of disadvantaged groups. The Joint Report on Social Inclusion by the Council of the European Union (2001), for instance, advocates an "integrated and multi-dimensional approach to policy development" which may include individually-tailored benefits. In the United States and the United Kingdom, there are numerous debates on the services to be provided for people moving from welfare to work, to give them optimal support and improve their chances of sustained employment (Karen *et al.*, 2002; Bloom *et al.*, 2002). Certain experiments combining financial incentives, job-search assistance and training are already showing how worthwhile it is to have schemes that provide more than just financial support (Box 3.3).

Employment-conditional benefits also raise the issue of the *quality* of the jobs available to disadvantaged groups. The chance of an earnings supplement may prompt some to accept poorly paid, temporary work with weak career prospects. In the United

> **Box 3.3. Combining training, job-search assistance and financial incentives to strengthen job attachment**
>
> Supplementing financial incentives with training provision and/or job-search assistance is one path taken in some countries. Two interesting experiments have been conducted in the United States and Canada. One is the Minnesota Family Investment Program (MFIP) which offers an income supplement and job-search assistance. The other is Canada's SSP (see Box 3.1 above). Some people on the MFIP received only financial support while, in the Canadian project, those on "SSP Plus" benefited from additional employment services such as low-cost job search and job counselling services (help writing résumés, job-finding clubs, etc.). In both cases, those on the fuller programmes obtained higher wages, possibly indicating better jobs. The observed effects of the MFIP have been substantial and sustained, while those of SSP Plus are slightly more mixed as many programme members lost their jobs fairly soon (Bloom and Michalopoulos, 2001). However, when jobs were kept in the short term, they proved more stable than those taken by enrolees on the ordinary SSP project, with fewer people exiting once payment of the earnings supplement ceased (Michalopoulos et al., 2002). This suggests that those on SSP Plus managed to become more self-sufficient with regard to welfare than those on the ordinary SSP programme.
>
> Combining hiring subsidies for the employer with job-search assistance and training can also be effective. Following a detailed review of the leading wage subsidy programmes in the United States, Katz (1998) was somewhat sceptical as to the scope for increasing labour demand for highly disadvantaged groups using subsidies alone. But he concluded that this kind of policy, backed up with training or job-search assistance, could be quite effective, based on evaluations of the temporary (6-month) subsidy programme set up by the Job Training Partnership Act (United States, 1983-2000). Thirty months after the programme was launched, there were still beneficial impacts on employment and wages, whereas evaluations of programmes confined to subsidies alone showed fairly disappointing outcomes. Likewise, Cockx et al. (1998) present evaluations of various subsidy programmes in Belgium. They draw a distinction between pure wage subsidies and subsidies combined with training, and look explicitly at the impact of each programme on the length of job tenure. Only measures combining subsidies and training have a positive, statistically significant effect on the length of job tenure.

States, the majority of those moving from welfare to work are subject to great insecurity, with regular spells of unemployment and very low wages (Campbell et al., 2002). Very few manage to find stable employment. While a rapid return to employment remains a priority, it should be tempered by the fact that the quality of the jobs people accept is likely to play a key role in determining how long their return to the world of work will last. This highlights the need for a balanced approach in which make work pay policies are complemented by other measures which, through both demand and supply channels, improve career prospects.

In terms of good-quality, sustained returns to employment, various studies refer to the Portland JOBS programme, which has had encouraging results (Campbell et al., 2002; Bloom and Michalopoulos, 2001). Programme members are given a short training course and assistance with their job search. Although the aim is to promote a rapid return to employment, members are encouraged to keep searching until they find a "good" job, i.e. full-time positions, paying above the minimum wage and offering a range of other advantages (in particular, employer-provided health benefits). Bloom and Michalopoulos

(2001) have surveyed the evaluations of some thirty schemes for welfare recipients, and in their review the advantages of the JOBS programme stand out quite clearly. Training provision, combined with job-search assistance, is an important key to success here (overall, programmes combining these two services stand out from those focusing on only one of them, which are less successful). But emphasis on the need to accept good jobs may also be important and further experimentation would be desirable.

2. Promoting employment while taking specific situations into account

Making work pay is a fundamental and necessary step towards motivating and helping under-represented groups enter the labour market. But as has been seen, this is not enough. For instance, even if the incidence of low-paid employment is slightly higher among older workers (see Chapter 2), it is not sufficient to explain their low participation in the labour market. Factors, such as working conditions and employer behaviour, as well as pension schemes, are likely to play a more important role. In addition, family responsibilities and health problems explain a significant share of labour market outflows (see Chapter 2). This involves considerations which go beyond the question of pay. And although a certain pessimism is sometimes perceptible in debates about the employment prospects of non-active persons, a significant proportion of these persons state that they would like to have a job, not only for financial reasons, suggesting the existence of other barriers to work. For instance, a recent French survey shows that, apart from financial considerations, one of the important reasons given by interviewed women for leaving the labour market is that they were unable to find working-time arrangements that would have made it possible for them to combine work and family-life (DARES, 2003). Moreover, child-care costs loomed large among the financial considerations in question.

A. Mothers with young children

The differences in overall labour market participation rates between countries are to a significant extent due to differences in women's participation behaviour (see Chapter 2). Female participation rates are influenced by whether they have children; maternity is one of the main reasons why some women leave the labour market (OECD, 2002f, Chapter 2). The idea that young children may suffer if their mother works is relatively widespread in all countries and has an impact on the labour force participation of women of child-bearing age (Chart 3.1). Although opinions vary considerably across countries, the countries in which young women's participation rates are lowest are also those in which there is relatively wide agreement among the population that it is detrimental to family life and to young children for their mothers to work. This suggests that policies which would help to reconcile work and family life would likely have positive effects on employment among mothers of young children. In this regard, the experience of the Nordic countries is enlightening. Their family policies have a long tradition of offering facilities and subsidies to encourage mothers to combine family and work. And studies on female labour supply show that, contrary to most other countries where young children have a large negative impact on mothers' labour supply, this effect is much smaller or non-existent in the Nordic countries. Thus, the positive effects on the labour market tend to outweigh the costs of implementing such policies (Pylkkänen and Smith, 2003).

3. MAKING WORK PAY – MAKING WORK POSSIBLE

Chart 3.1. **Women working and family life: differing opinions**
Percentages

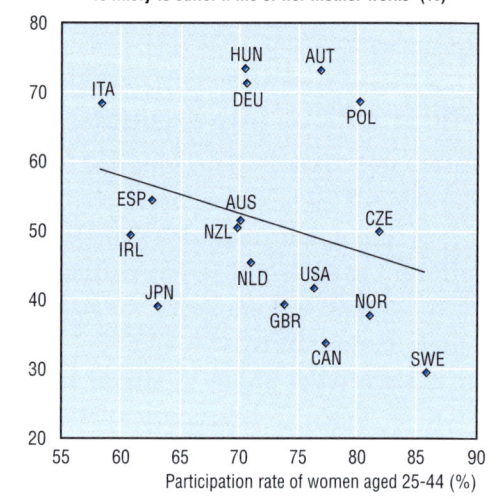

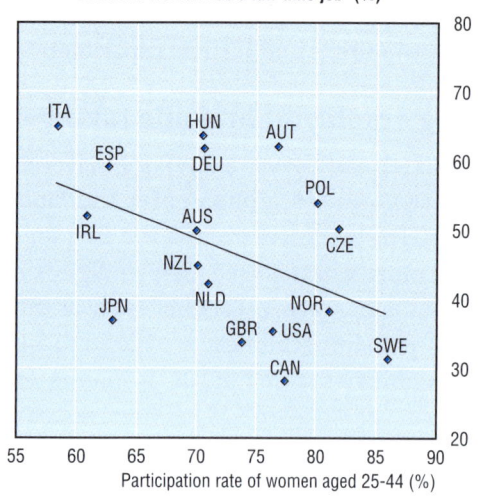

Note: Data for Germany only concern the western Länder.
a) Question V5: "A pre-school child is likely to suffer if his or her mother works." Strongly agree or agree. The regression line is: $y = -0.54x + 90.26$ ($R^2 = 0.09$, $t = -1.19$) and without Austria, Germany, Hungary and Poland, the line would be: $y = -0.82x + 103.78$ ($R^2 = 0.50$, $t = -3.25$).
b) Question V6: "All in all, family life suffers when the woman has a full-time job." Strongly agree or agree. The regression line is: $y = -0.68x + 96.61$ ($R^2 = 0.20$, $t = -1.91$).
Source: International Social Survey Programme (ISSP), 1994; OECD database on Labour Force Statistics.

Maternity leave may increase women's attachment to the labour market, under certain conditions

Maternity leave is a partial and temporary response to the problems of reconciling family life and work. Nevertheless, when people are surveyed, the right to paid maternity leave receives over 80% support in all countries (except for Australia, the Netherlands and New Zealand, see Table 3.5). The availability of this leave can also have an impact on the patterns of women's labour force participation.

Table 3.5. **Near unanimous support for the right to paid maternity leave**
Percentages[a]

Australia	41.7	Japan	96.1
Austria	83.3	Netherlands	69.8
Canada	82.6	New Zealand	50.7
Czech Republic	96.8	Norway	90.9
Germany, western Länder	93.9	Poland	94.7
Germany, eastern Länder	99.1	Spain	93.9
Hungary	98.1	Sweden	90.4
Ireland	95.1	United Kingdom	83.8
Italy	91.2	United States	75.8
		OECD unweighted average[b]	**84.9**

a) Share of persons answering "strongly agree" or "agree" to "working women should receive paid maternity leave when they have a baby" (question V42).
b) For above countries only.
Source: International Social Survey Programme (ISSP), 1994.

Paid maternity leave with a job guarantee makes work more attractive for young women, as it enables them to care for their children on a full-time basis while maintaining their labour market attachment. Consequently, this kind of leave can raise women's participation rates, since the prospect of benefiting from it may stimulate young women without children to enter the labour market, while it encourages young mothers to return to work on the termination of the leave. The length of this leave is an important factor in this regard, for very long leave may in the medium term cut women off from the labour market, leading to a decline in their future employment rate and earnings (Box 3.4). Moreover, employers may be discouraged from hiring female workers of child-bearing age. However, it is difficult to assess a "reasonable" length for maternity or parental leave, which would not be damaging for career prospects and labour market participation. For instance, employment rates of Danish or Swedish women are amongst the highest of OECD countries, while they are entitled to relatively generous leave schemes (both in terms of duration and compensation). But these systems are part of a comprehensive family-friendly policy that helps mothers to combine family and work (Pylkkänen and Smith, 2003).[12]

Finally, it is important to determine which women leave employment most readily after having a child. Various studies have shown that education and the type and quality of the job held before going on maternity leave play a key role here. Having a low level of education and having held a precarious or unstable job seem to lower the chances of returning to work.[13] However, the possibility of taking relatively long parental leave, especially when it is combined with financial benefits, is particularly attractive to women in precarious job situations,[14] *i.e.* precisely those women who subsequently find it most difficult to return to work. There are many inequalities related to education and training in the female labour market – even more than for the male population (see Chapter 2) – and policies should take this specific characteristic into account.

Child-care services and working-time facilities for better reconciliation between work and family life

Child-care services, their costs and their ability to give mothers time to work, can also play an important role. Child-care costs may be a barrier to employment, particularly at the lower end of the wage scale, among women with the lowest education levels. Studies that distinguish between various individual characteristics such as education and income show that the lower the income or the education level, the higher the sensitivity of labour supply to child-care costs (see Anderson and Levine, 1999, for a review of US studies). Even though these costs are generally covered, at least partially, subsidies are often employment-conditional. And the fact is that unemployed young mothers are often in a less favourable situation regarding access to child care. Except for certain activation programmes targeting specific groups (lone mothers and mothers receiving subsistence benefits), the presence of young children can make it very costly to look for a job because of the lack of resources available to young unemployed mothers. It would be preferable for subsidies to be conditional on a genuine job-search requirement (as in Denmark), rather than only on employment.

In addition to the problem of costs, there is the issue of the availability of different types of child-care and the number of places that they can provide. Although there is a positive relationship between women's participation rates and the availability of formal

Box 3.4. **The impact of the length of maternity/parental leave on wages and employment: some recent studies**

Rhum (1998) considers that the introduction of job-protected paid maternity leave has made it possible to increase the employment rate of women significantly without having a major impact on wages, when this leave has been relatively short (approximately three months). Longer leave (around nine months) seems to produce comparable results in regard to employment rates, but leads to a decline in relative wages (the study covered nine OECD countries: Denmark, Finland, France, Germany, Greece, Ireland, Italy, Norway and Sweden, during the 1969-93 period). Gupta and Smith (2002) have re-examined the case of Denmark using individual data that enable them to take into account experience acquired in the labour market. Although maternity leave does have the effect of lowering wages, this is only temporary. This is due to the fact that there is no human capital accumulated during the period when the career is interrupted, and consequently no potential wage progression. However, this does not rule out the possibility of a progressive recovery of lost ground, which will be longer the more protracted the length of leave.

Ronsen and Sundstöm (2002) have compared the patterns of women returning to work in Finland, Norway and Sweden (over the 1972-92 period). During the three years following the child birth, women who are entitled to paid leave have a higher employment rate than women who are not entitled (*i.e.* working women who did not have enough work experience before their child was born to entitle them to this type of leave). As the women who take this leave tend to use the totality of their entitlement, the higher employment rates are concentrated in the period following the end of their leave (except in Sweden, where they are higher during the entire leave period). In all countries, the lengthening of maternity leave causes the mothers concerned to return to work later. Lastly, according to German experience, giving women the opportunity to take *very* long parental leave (three years) may make it difficult for them to return to work, even though employers are required to reinstate them. Faced with such requirement, companies may also become reluctant to hire young women of child-bearing age. Some studies do show that return-to-work rates are lower after protracted parental leave and that when women return, their chances of wage increases are far poorer (results for the western Länder, Ondrich *et al.*, 1999; and Ondrich *et al.*, 2002). A recent survey (conducted by IAB, see European Foundation, 2001) also shows that 41% of women who had stopped working when they had a child had still not returned to work after an interruption of three years (16% of them were registered as unemployed).

Allowances that enable mothers to stop work for a considerable time without job protection may have an even more marked impact on the employment trajectory of recipients. For example, Ronsen and Sundström (2002) consider that the Finnish system of allowances for mothers at home reduces the likelihood of their returning to work. In France, the Parental Education Allowance (APE) enabling women with at least two children to interrupt their work until the youngest child reaches the age of three has had a considerable influence on the pattern of labour force participation of the women concerned. After rising slowly for several years, the participation rate of mothers with a second child under the age of three fell from 69% in 1994 (the year when this group became eligible for the APE) to 53% in 1997 (Afsa, 1998). This downturn was especially sharp for women with low skills, for whom the APE had two advantages: it was attractive financially and could be used as a stop-gap measure if they were in a difficult job situation (between 1994 and 2002, employment rates of mothers with a second child under the age of three, decreased by 25% for the low-skilled, compared to 16% for skilled

> Box 3.4. **The impact of the length of maternity/parental leave
> on wages and employment: some recent studies** *(cont.)*
>
> women). In 1999, a survey was taken of women who had been without employment for three years and in receipt of the APE for the second child. Half of the women who had held a job before they stopped working had not returned to work during the period of six months to one year after they had exhausted their APE entitlement, and 20% of women saw their situation deteriorate, going from a stable job to a precarious job or unemployment (Simon, 1999).

child-care arrangements (Chart 3.2), the direction of causality is unclear. In Denmark, for example, child-care capacity was not developed prior to the high level of women's labour force participation, but was a response aimed at meeting the expectations of women who had already a job (OECD, 2002d). Nevertheless, surveys in the United States and the United Kingdom show that a far from negligible number of young mothers remain outside employment because they do not have access to a satisfactory child-care system. Chevalier and Viitanen (2002) focused explicitly on direction of causality between the participation rate and child-care possibilities (in the United Kingdom). It appears that an extension of child-care support might increase women's labour force participation.

Chart 3.2. **Female labour force participation and child care**
Late 1990s, percentages

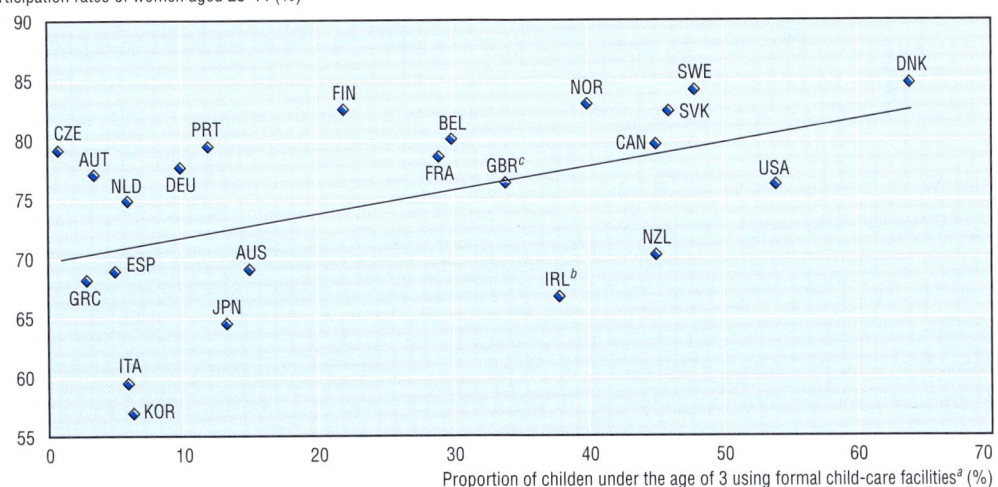

Note: The regression line is: $y = 0.20x + 69.69$ ($R^2 = 0.25$, $t = 2.62$).
a) The data include both public and private provision, and cover the following types of formal child-care facilities:
   - Group-care in child-care centres (nurseries, kindergarten, play-schools), sometimes organised within the educational system.
   - Residential care, including specialist services such as care for disabled children.
   - Childminders, based in their own home, looking after one or more children.
   - Care provided by a carer who is not a family-member but frequently lives in with the family.
b) Proportion of children under five.
c) England only.
Source: OECD (2001a), Table 4.7; OECD database on Labour Force Statistics.

The number of places available to care for children whose mothers are working is not the only consideration. The hours available must also be compatible with working hours. In Italy, for example, child-care systems do not allow mothers to work on a full-time basis, even though part-time work opportunities are very limited. Together with the limited number of child-care places, this is one of the reasons for the low participation rate of Italian women (Del Boca, 2002). In the Netherlands, the child-care system mainly provides part-time care but, as part-time employment is very widespread, this does not raise any particular problems (since women often wish to work on a part-time basis), and the female participation rate remains high (OECD, 2002d).[15]

For mothers, working time is a key aspect of working and employment conditions. A recent study by the European Foundation for the Improvement of Living and Working Conditions stresses that long and atypical working hours are the factor most detrimental to family life in the opinion of households (Fagan and Burchell, 2002). In this regard, part-time work can be a good compromise between non-participation and full-time work, facilitating the reconciliation between work and family life. The criticism often levelled at part-time employment is that it does not provide women with the same career prospects as men. Although there is truth in this argument, it fails to consider the fact that, without part-time employment, some women would involuntarily remain outside the labour market and the gap between men's and women's personal income might be even greater.

As part-time work can be a means of entering employment or obtaining permanent status, the possibilities of access to part-time jobs influence the patterns of women's labour force participation. In this regard, Euwals (2001) has examined the relationship in the United Kingdom between satisfaction with working hours and the likelihood of going from employment to non-employment. Women who say that they wish to reduce their working time significantly are more likely to leave employment. Along similar lines, Gutiérrez-Domenech (2003) considers that the employment rates of young mothers in Germany, Italy and Spain might be higher if access to part-time work was facilitated, and Germany has taken steps in this direction.[16] To illustrate this, Chart 3.3 shows the relationship between the participation rates of young women in various European countries and a crude indicator showing the "mismatch" between demand and availability of part-time employment.[17] The lower this indicator, the better is the match between the wishes of those looking for a job and the type of job that they may be offered. And there is an inverse relation between the value of this indicator and female participation rates, showing that some women seem to give up employment altogether if they cannot work part-time. This decision may be more or less imposed by outside circumstances, and this is probably more often the case when the types of child care available are not compatible with full-time work. Lastly, this type of relation is not characteristic of the male labour market, where part-time employment is generally involuntary.

However, the solution of part-time work entails certain risks and should be backed up by appropriate policies, for part-time employment is often confined to a limited number of jobs and offers fewer career prospects (OECD, 2002f, Chapter 2). In addition, it does not always enable working women to achieve real financial independence from their spouses or the social assistance system. The specific institutional arrangements governing part-time work are important. For example, since July 2000, many Dutch employees have had the *right* to change their working hours to part-time or full-time

Chart 3.3. **Part-time work: a bridge to female labour market participation**

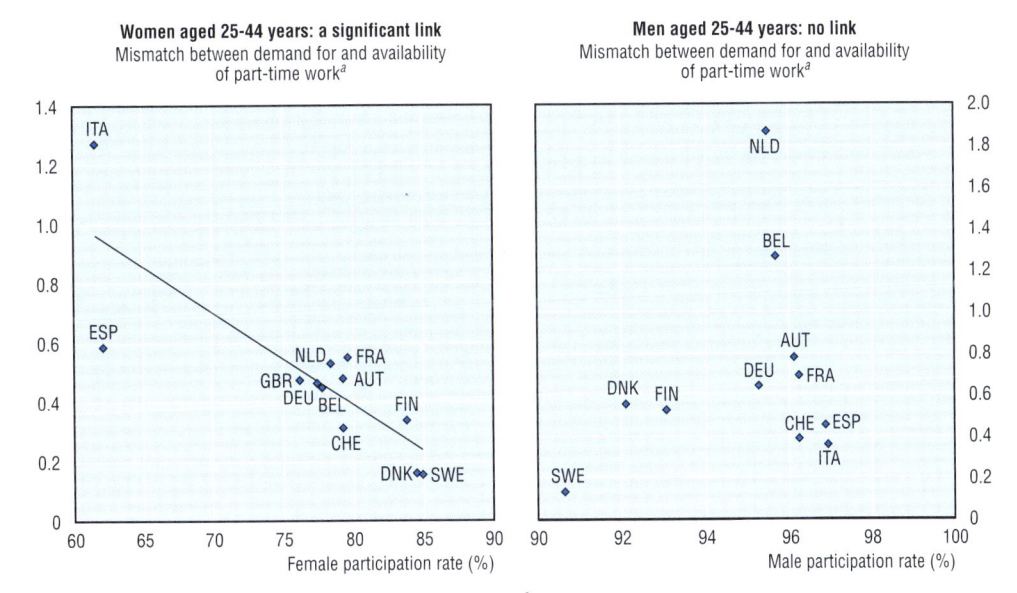

Women aged 25-44 years: a significant link
Mismatch between demand for and availability of part-time work[d]

Men aged 25-44 years: no link
Mismatch between demand for and availability of part-time work[d]

Note: For women, the regression line is: y = –0.03x + 2.86 (R² = 0.68, t = –4.6).
d) This is measured as the rate of "demand" for part-time jobs to the observed rate of part-time jobs. The rate of "demand" for part-time jobs is defined as the ratio of the sum of the number of unemployed persons looking for a part-time job and of employed persons looking for a job with fewer hours, to the sum of the total number of unemployed and employed persons looking for another job.
Source: European Union Labour Force Survey, Eurostat, 2001.

work, although employers can refuse to allow them to do so if it is impossible (in which case they must justify their refusal) or if it threatens the company's financial stability (OECD, 2002d, Chapter 6). In Germany, the "Part-Time and Fixed-Term Employment Act" has introduced, since 2001, rules for entitlement to part-time employment similar to those in the Netherlands. In particular, the Act gives employees greater control over working hours. However, there is no entitlement for workers in part-time work to a full-time job. They merely have an entitlement to preferential consideration.

Lone parents and employment

Lone parents face particular labour market and social problems in most OECD countries. Despite improvements in employment rates among lone-parent families in many – but not all – OECD countries, non-employment remains high and many lone-parents tend to remain in receipt of benefits for long periods. The high incidence of joblessness among lone parents raises significant policy concerns. In particular, child poverty is much higher in families where the lone parent is not working – and indeed the employment status of parents appears to be the most important determinant of whether children are poor or not (Table 3.6).

Most lone parents are women, but their age and the age and numbers of their children vary significantly. Generally, it is younger, less qualified and never-married mothers with young children who have the lowest rates of employment. In contrast, lone fathers tend to be older than lone mothers, have fewer children, have higher educational qualifications and they are more likely to be widowed or divorced (Bradshaw et al., 1996). As a result, they are more likely to be employed than lone mothers. In some countries, there are higher

Table 3.6. **Non-employment among lone-parents: a factor behind child poverty**
Percentages

	Lone-parent non-employment rates, 2001[a]	Poverty rates,[b] 1993-95	
		Non-working single parents	Working single parents
Australia	57	57.1	9.3
Austria	17	20.8	8.9
Canada	49	72.5	26.5
Denmark	26	34.2	10.0
France	35	45.1	13.3
Germany	34	61.8	32.5
Greece	34	36.8	16.3
Italy	26	78.7	24.9
Mexico	34	31.0	27.2
Netherlands	40	41.3	17.0
Norway	39	29.6	4.6
Sweden	13	24.2	3.8
Turkey	55	39.9	16.3
United Kingdom	51	65.0	22.7
United States	23	93.4	38.6

a) Data refer to 1996 for Australia, Canada and Mexico, 1995 for Norway and Sweden, 1994 for Denmark and Turkey.
b) Percentage of persons living in households with incomes below 50% of the median adjusted disposable income of the entire population.

Source: For non-employment rates, OECD (2001b); for poverty rates, Förster (2000).

rates of lone parenthood in ethnic minority groups, who may face additional barriers to employment.

The absence of a partner's income should provide a significant incentive for lone mothers to seek employment, and in a number of OECD countries employment is higher among lone mothers than among married/partnered mothers. However, such incentives are not enough, particularly when confronted with generous benefits. Policies are needed to support the labour market participation of lone parents, while also providing adequate income support (see Box 3.5). Social attitudes to the employment of mothers more generally are also likely to be influential. In most countries, it is still the case that most lone-mother families are formed out of separation, divorce or widowhood. Expecting lone mothers to seek employment may be less effective where it was not expected before lone parenthood.

B. Working-age disabled persons

The disabled are a highly diverse population that is not easily defined. Among non-active persons who have a disability or at least are classified as having one, some could work and would like to do so. As has been seen, a significant proportion of non-active persons who have left employment for health reasons would like to work again,[18] even though this does not prompt them to look actively for a job (see Chapter 2). This situation points to a contradiction that social policy and employment measures must seek to resolve.

Employment, a real asset for economic integration of disabled persons

The OECD recently carried out an in-depth study of the situation of the working-age disabled in 20 member countries (OECD, 2003a). The report emphasises repeatedly the difficulty of defining the concept of disability. Although the term is naturally thought of as

> Box 3.5. **Lone parents and employment: towards a work-oriented safety net**
>
> There is considerable debate about how to provide adequate income support to lone parents, while enhancing their incentive to participate in the labour market. This is an important issue since, as stressed in Chapter 4, benefit systems can affect employment rates.
>
> In this regard, the conditions under which benefits are granted may play a key role. Non-employment is particularly high in countries where lone-parent benefits are effectively available on an indefinite basis until the youngest child reaches school-leaving age. In contrast, in countries where benefits are restricted to those with younger children, or where duration is limited, or where there are work tests or similar obligations, benefit receipt is lower and employment tends to be higher. Rules regarding requirements to work for lone parents are changing in many countries, and lone mothers are now very likely to be expected to be available to seek work once their children reach school or nursery school age. Thus, in the countries with the lowest employment rates among lone parents there does seem to be a more common acceptance of the idea that it is appropriate to support lone parents of pre-school children to provide full-time care, but once children reach school-age then employment expectations should be imposed (Millar, 2001). Some countries also use a "stepping-stones" type model, in which work requirements become more stringent as children get older. However, there is need for flexibility to ensure that people with younger children can also participate in labour market programmes if they wish to do so.
>
> Other policies can improve incentives to work for lone parents, while maintaining social objectives to reduce poverty. Receipt of child support from the absent parent can provide an important addition to the income of lone parents, and substitute for income-related benefits, reducing problems with high effective marginal tax rates. There may be incentive implications for the parent paying maintenance, however.
>
> A fundamental issue is the acceptance of the expectation that for most lone parents employment should be regarded as the basis of a sustainable safety net. As noted by Waldfogel *et al.* (2001) "(…) following this path requires a range of policy and services (…) that would more completely transform a cash-based safety net into a work-based safety net". The components of such a work-based safety net will vary across countries depending on already existing services (child care, education arrangements, general family benefits, health care and labour market programmes). But in the context of a *complete* package, good results can be obtained. Chapter 4 examines the role of activation strategies in supporting the employment of lone parents.

referring to severe, lifelong disabilities, in many countries the real situation of the disabled is far removed from this image. Although countries tend to have their own definitions of what constitutes a disability, the general conclusion to emerge is that the disabled population is highly diverse, and that a large proportion of the disabled have disabilities that are fairly minor, and may even be curable. A growing proportion of them suffer from mental illness and psychological problems. Given this diversity, the first major difficulty is to identify disabilities correctly, distinguishing between minor and major disabilities. This entails two major risks. The first is that of excluding some disabled by failing to include within the social protection system persons whose health condition should be partially or fully covered by disability benefits. The second risk is that of mistakenly including persons in the disability benefits system, thereby limiting their possibility of entering the labour market for no real reason.

No country can avoid these two major difficulties. This is borne out by the very imperfect correlation between the fact that people are receiving disability benefits and whether they actually consider themselves to be disabled (Table 3.7). One out of three recipients does not acknowledge the disabled "status" that he or she has nevertheless been granted, and a considerable proportion of those who do state that they have a disability receive neither income from work nor disability benefits. Obviously, there is reason to be

Table 3.7. **Disability benefits: some disabled who are excluded, some recipients who do not acknowledge that they have any disabilities and very low exit rates**
Late 1990s, percentages

	Proportion of disability benefit recipients declaring that they are not disabled	Proportion of disabled persons aged 20-64 years with neither income from work nor income from benefits	Annual rates of outflow from disability benefits
Australia	15.2	15.7	0.49
Austria	27.7	14.2	1.04
Belgium	43.4	16.2	..
Canada	..	..	0.85
Denmark	26.2	6.3	..
France	33.3	11.7	..
Germany	..	11.9	1.25
Italy	43.9	28.8	..
Korea	0.0	49.5	0.05
Mexico	91.4[a]	52.5	..
Netherlands	30.6	19.5	3.34
Norway	28.4	12.2	..
Portugal	28.6	20.9	0.97
Spain	18.3	28.0	0.57
Sweden	48.9	1.1	..
Switzerland	29.8	14.2	..
United Kingdom	43.3	9.1	5.64
United States	46.7	18.8	1.16
OECD unweighted average[b]	**34.7**	**19.4**	**1.5**

.. Data not available.
a) In 1999, the disability benefit recipiency rate was 0.6% in Mexico, compared with 5 to 9% in the other OECD countries (with the exception of Korea, where the proportion of persons receiving disability benefit was 0.3%; OECD, 2003a, administrative data). Thus, the extremely high proportion of Mexican disability benefit recipients declaring that they are not disabled represents, in fact, a relatively small number.
b) Average for countries having non-missing data for the reported indicator.
Source: OECD (2003a).

wary of data based on such statements, particularly when the question being asked is relatively subjective – i.e. questions on whether or not a person has a health problem that is limiting activities of daily living. Moreover, self-assessed disability prevalence derived from a national survey is related to receipt of disability benefit, which is based on a quite different definition of disability. However, these data suggest that there is a real problem in identifying disabilities, and this constitutes a major policy challenge. There can be no simple solution to this problem, for there is a continuous range of situations between being disabled and not disabled and between being able and unable to work. For example, although making access to disability benefits more difficult makes it possible to reduce errors of inclusion, it also increases the risk of exclusion. Employment policies also have a role to play in "activating" those with disabilities. The term "disabled" should no longer be equated with being unable to work. However, the outflow from disability benefit systems is extremely low in most countries, despite the fact that one-third of recipients do not consider that they have any disability at all.

Even among those who say that they have minor or moderate disabilities, employment rates rarely exceed 70% of those of the non-disabled population. Nevertheless, employment is the best guarantee against poverty and social exclusion even though, on the whole, the situation of the disabled with regard to poverty does not give particular cause for concern. In most of the countries studied, the incomes of households with a disabled person are very close to those of households in which no one has a disability. However, the *personal* income of the disabled depends greatly on their employment status and the unemployed disabled have much lower incomes than those who work (Table 3.8). On average, the total personal income of an unemployed disabled person comes to barely half of the income received by a disabled person who is working. At the same time, there is little difference in earnings between disabled and non-disabled persons. In most countries, the work incomes of the disabled are on average scarcely lower than those of other wage-earners, with the gap in earnings between the two categories ranging between 5 and 15%. Consequently, in many cases, the disabled who work appear to be successfully integrated into the labour market.

Table 3.8. **Employment, a real asset for the economic integration of disabled persons**

Late 1990s, percentages

	Relative employment rate of disabled persons aged 20-64 compared with the non-disabled aged 20-64	Relative income from work of disabled over non-disabled persons[a]	Relative average personal income of disabled persons working over disabled persons not working
Australia	0.55	0.93	..
Austria	0.60	0.97	1.96
Belgium	0.54	0.90	1.91
Canada	0.72	..	..
Denmark	0.61	0.88	1.38
France	0.72	..	1.83
Germany	0.67	0.92	1.79
Italy	0.60	0.94	1.94
Korea	0.74	..	..
Mexico	0.77	..	9.76
Netherlands	0.60	0.87	1.45
Norway	0.72	0.88	1.71
Poland	0.29	0.91	..
Portugal	0.59	..	1.81
Spain	0.41	0.86	2.07
Sweden	0.69	0.70	1.37
Switzerland	0.79	0.98	..
United Kingdom	0.53	0.84	1.61
United States	0.58	0.71	2.84
OECD unweighted average[b]	**0.62**	**0.88**	**2.39**

.. Data not available.
a) Relative average personal income from work of disabled over non-disabled persons who work. Median income for Australia and equivalised household income for Poland and Switzerland.
b) Average for countries having non-missing data for the reported indicator.
Source: OECD (2003a).

3. MAKING WORK PAY – MAKING WORK POSSIBLE

Managing work-limited capacity with vocational rehabilitation and training

In many cases, receiving disability benefits goes along with a quasi-permanent exit from the labour market. These benefits should not be used to offset a difficult labour market situation and many disability benefit recipients who have the potential to work should not be encouraged to settle permanently into the status of non-active disabled persons. In this regard, disability benefit systems all too often still generate a certain inertia and "activation" policies could help move people out of benefit dependency (see Chapter 4 for a discussion).

Vocational rehabilitation and training can be critical to achieve or secure employment. A person becoming disabled may, even after completion of the medical rehabilitation process, not be able to continue to work in his or her previous occupation. Similarly, a disabled person trying to enter the labour market for the first time may need additional vocational training at an adult age. Participation in such programmes may be compulsory before a disability benefit is granted or entirely voluntary (see Chapter 4). In all countries, eligibility is bound to the expected returns to the programme, usually defined as the prospect that another job can be carried out by the applicant. In mandatory rehabilitation schemes, this prospect may be restricted to jobs commensurate with the person's qualifications (as in Austria, Spain and to some extent also in Switzerland), or could include "inferior" jobs (Denmark, Sweden).

Too few resources are generally devoted to vocational training and rehabilitation. Only in Denmark and Norway do more people go through vocational rehabilitation and training each year than are granted a disability benefit, the ratio being only slightly lower in Korea – though the data do not tell what proportion of those ultimately being granted a benefit have received vocational measures beforehand (Chart 3.4). The per capita expenses for people in rehabilitation services are as relevant for the programme assessment as the

Chart 3.4. **Too few resources devoted to vocational rehabilitation**
Number of persons in vocational rehabilitation schemes as a proportion of disability benefit inflows,[a] percentages, 1999

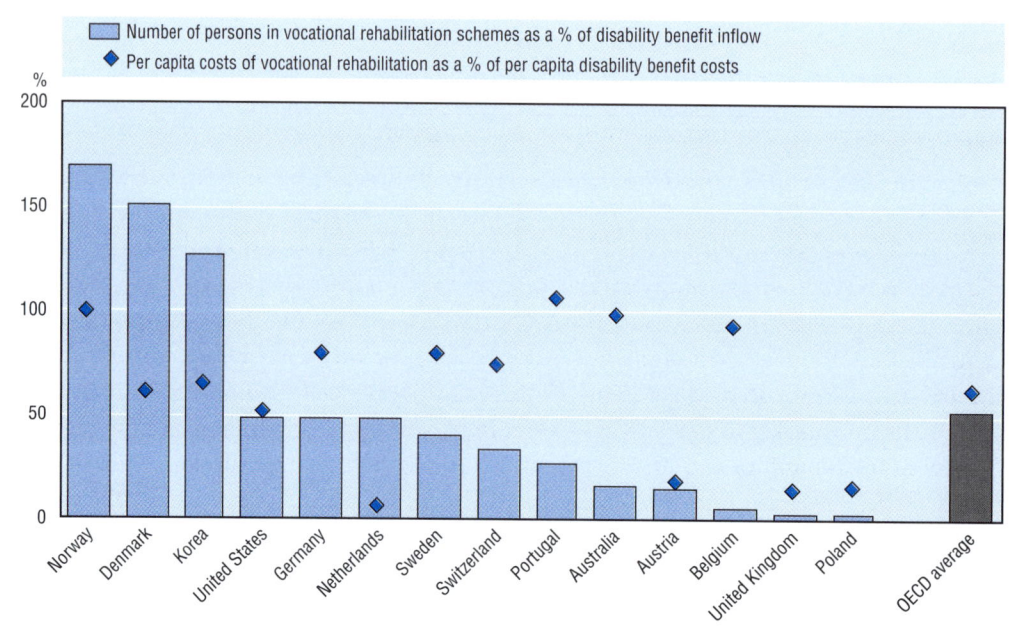

Note: Countries are ranked in decreasing order of the ratio of people in vocational rehabilitation over benefit inflows.
a) Contributory disability benefits, except non-contributory disability scheme for Australia and Denmark.
Source: OECD (2003a).

number receiving the services. Two groups of countries can be identified (Chart 3.4): those in which expenditures per rehabilitee are small compared with the per capita cost of a disability benefit (the Netherlands, Poland, the United Kingdom and Austria) and those in which rehabilitation costs on average are between 60 and 100% of an average disability benefit. Some countries appear to have high relative rehabilitation expenses mainly because they have relatively low disability benefits (Australia and Portugal).

Vocational training and rehabilitation are often made available too late, since *early intervention* can play a decisive role, the chances of reintegration into employment declining with the time that the disabled person spends outside employment. Often, participation in vocational rehabilitation plans is only considered after the individual's health condition has stabilised, and it can take months (and often a year or more) before the person concerned comes into contact with the rehabilitation assistance services. Very few countries react at a sufficiently early stage to effectively prevent the risk of the disabled exiting employment on a long-term or permanent basis. Incentives to promote an early return to work are used in Germany and Sweden, where rehabilitation programmes are explicitly designed to be made available during the first stages of an illness. In Germany, the authorities responsible for rehabilitation (Federal Institute for Employment, pension insurance funds, welfare offices, etc.) decide whether a vocational rehabilitation procedure is required before, during and after medical rehabilitation. In the case of progressive diseases, for example, this system enables the persons concerned to reorient their career at a very early stage towards activities compatible with their state of health and work capacities. In Sweden, employers are directly involved in the rehabilitation process, which can begin while the persons are still employed, on a preventive basis, before the post that they hold becomes unsuited to their work capacities.

Although all countries provide vocational training and rehabilitation measures that specifically target the disabled, the approaches differ sharply across countries and relatively little is known about the impact of these measures on the future work history and well-being of recipients. However, the data suggest that even the highest average per-capita costs will pay off in the medium run should the vocational intervention result in successful and durable labour market re-integration.

Supporting employment with individual work/ benefit packages

Of the 20 countries covered in the OECD report (2003a), none can be considered as having a really satisfactory policy for reintegrating the disabled into work. Nevertheless, there are differences in results in this respect. These differences are linked to the choices made by countries and can provide some lessons as to the best-practice policies. The report strongly emphasises the need to provide each disabled person with a "participation package" adapted to individual needs and capacities. Merely looking after the financial needs of disabled people through cash benefits is insufficient; this would still leave many excluded from the labour market and sometimes even from society more generally. These packages could contain rehabilitation and vocational training, job-search support, choices from among a wide range of forms of employment (regular, part-time, subsidised, sheltered) and benefits in-cash or in-kind. In practice, four categories of employment assistance schemes are available to the disabled (in addition to vocational rehabilitation and training measures):

- Employment subsidies.
- Supported jobs, the term "supported" referring to any type of individual employment assistance granted to employers or employees (guidance or training).

- Continuing assistance with disability aids and related costs once a person makes the transition from benefits to paid employment.
- Sheltered jobs, i.e. which are carried out in a separate environment, such as a special workshop or social enterprise or a sector (or job) that is sheltered from the labour market.

Subsidised jobs and protected jobs specifically targeting the disabled have their equivalents in the more general active policy measures mentioned in the first part of this chapter (Section 1.B), and lessons from the evaluations of such policies are largely applicable to the situation of people with disabilities. Some of the critique, e.g. regarding deadweight or substitution effects, is less relevant, because of the permanent productivity loss of some groups of disabled people.

While sheltered employment is increasingly seen as inappropriate and in need of being replaced by supported employment-type initiatives, it still continues to be the dominant mode of employment for disabled persons on special employment support schemes (Table 3.9). For the disabled, this type of scheme provides the possibility of returning to work but not of real reintegration into the labour market. Sheltered jobs

Table 3.9. **Sheltered employment remains the most common employment assistance scheme for disabled persons**
Participation rate and per capita costs of various employment assistance schemes, 1999

	Persons in special employment programmes for disabled persons per 1 000 of the total population of working age				Per capita employment programme expenditure in percentage of per capita disability benefits			
	Subsidised employment[a]	Supported employment[a]	Sheltered employment[a]	All	Subsidised employment[a]	Supported employment[a]	Sheltered employment[a]	All
Australia	0.2	1.6	1.5	3.4	43	58	73	63
Austria	3.6	0.7	2.7	7.0	26	9	24	24
Belgium	0.7	0.0	2.9	3.6	90	..	146	135
Denmark	3.0	0.6	2.4	5.9	62	98	44	58
France	6.3	[b]	3.2	9.5	23	..	102	49
Germany	0.2	0.6	3.3	4.1	128	54	78	78
Italy	0.3	[b]	0.6	0.8	39	..	..	39
Korea	0.1	0.0	0.2	0.3	57	42	57	57
Netherlands	[b]	[c]	9.2	9.2	..	..	184	184
Norway	2.4	0.5	4.3	7.2	139	66	67	91
Poland	2.0	x	10.1	12.1	153	..	37	56
Portugal	0.1	x	0.1	0.2	185	..	78	133
Spain	0.6	x	0.6	1.2	23	..	72	49
Sweden	10.8	0.2	5.2	16.2	120	..	164	135
Switzerland	x	x	5.6	5.6	..	..	42	42
United Kingdom	0.5	0.7	[c]	1.2	24	150	..	93
United States	[b]	1.1	[c]	1.1	..	41	..	41
OECD unweighted average[d]	..	..	..	5.2	80	65	83	78

.. Data not available.
x No such programme up to the present.
a) Three major categories of employment assistance schemes are available to the disabled: employment subsidies; supported jobs, the term "supported" referring to any type of individual employment assistance granted to employers or employees (guidance or training); sheltered jobs, i.e. that are carried out in a separate environment, such as a special workshop or social enterprise or a sector (or job) that is sheltered from the labour market.
b) Minor programme, no data available.
c) Significant programme, no data available.
d) For above countries only.
Source: OECD (2003a).

generally have characteristics that are too specific for the work experience acquired to be easily transferable, and the "normal" or "competitive" labour market becomes increasingly less accessible. Consequently, sheltered jobs must be carefully targeted at persons whose work capacity is very limited on a permanent basis, and for whom it would be very difficult to attain the "productivity norm" required in the competitive sector, even if they receive assistance in performing in their work.

Employment subsidies must be adapted to the public that they target. This implies an individually-based approach and stringent medical monitoring. Some countries already have experience with this type of measure (Table 3.10) and first evaluations are promising. In Denmark, a qualitative study on *flexjobs* (see European Commission, 2001) shows that the scheme appears to satisfy both employees and employers. However, the study does point out one negative aspect in this positive assessment, mentioning possible stigmatisation effects. The *flexjob* is half way between social protection and employment, and some people seem to have difficulty in accepting assisted-person status and prefer not to declare their disability. In this regard, supported jobs can be an effective compromise,

Table 3.10. **Subsidised and supported jobs: examples of good practice**

	Employment subsidies: adjustable subsidies, *i.e.* tailored to a person's ability to work
Belgium	Firms employing disabled workers are eligible for subsidies to offset the reduced productivity of disabled workers. They are granted through collective agreements (CCT 26, 50% of labour costs) or regional agreements. Most of these subsidies are renewable and can become permanent. Disabled claimants must enrol with the regional disability agency. Their ability to work is assessed by a doctor, and external multidisciplinary teams make recommendations to the responsible authority (the federal inspectorate of labour for CCT 26, or regional administration for other subsidies).
Denmark	*Flexjobs*: subsidised jobs for the long-term disabled (permanent disability). Depending on the seriousness of the disability and the person's ability to work, the subsidy may cover one-third, one-half or two-thirds of the minimum wage, for an unlimited duration. The disabled persons assisted must necessarily have completed vocational rehabilitation and are eligible if the competent authorities decide they cannot occupy "normal" or make-work jobs. *Flexjobs* are necessarily full-time positions and cannot be combined with receipt of disability benefits. In the future, *flexjob* availability is expected to increase considerably (from 9 000 in 2002 to some 40 000), gradually replacing partial-disability benefits (the ability to handle a *flexjob* will become the determining factor when awarding disability benefits).
Korea	Employment subsidies for any disabled worker for a period of three years (with declining subsidy rate) were abolished in 1999 and replaced by far more generous subsidies, of unlimited duration, only for employment in excess of the mandatory employment quota; the new subsidy varies with the degree of disability and gender – the basic rate is 100% of the minimum wage, topped up by another 50% if severely disabled and another 25% if female.
Sweden	Flexible wage-subsidy scheme to promote recruitment of the disabled: subsidy covers up to 80% of wage costs (and on average 60%). The subsidy can also vary over time, depending on changes in health status. Eligibility is assessed on the basis on a medical certificate and the type of work that the person is to carry out. The subsidy is awarded for up to four years and is regularly re-adjusted. It can be resumed after three years in non-subsidised work.
	Job support: individually tailored for better labour-market integration
Austria	Vocational counselling (*Arbeitsassistenz*) is aimed at facilitating access for the disabled in the open labour market, and making their career paths more secure; it is provided by non-profit organisations and qualified social workers, psychologists or other specialists. Financed by the rehabilitation authorities, it consists of five phases: *i)* contact with the disabled person, *ii)* preparation of an occupational or training plan, *iii)* information and entrance phase (reconciling employer and employee needs), *iv)* follow-up assistance (a few weeks or months) and *v)* intervention whenever needed. *Arbeitsassistenz* involves: developing skill profiles, identifying and minimising obstacles to employment, finding the right job for the person concerned, introduction to the workplace, psychological and social assistance in the workplace, developing personal working methods and organisational structures, installation of working aids, establishing communication, exchange of information between the disabled, their colleagues and supervisors, conflict management, and crisis management in the event of pending dismissal.
Denmark	Personal assistant can be hired to assist with practical occupational functions arising from specific employment; this type of assistance is of unlimited duration, and for up to 20 hours per week for a full-time job of 37 hours a week. The subsidy is given to the employer (or the self-employed disabled person), because the assistant is a regular employee. The assistant must be approved by the disabled person. Similar assistance can be granted in work-related education and during vocational rehabilitation.
Germany	Severely disabled people can be granted additional support to make full use of their skills and capabilities and secure full integration (this assistance is also provided for temporary jobs or part-time employment of at least 15 hours per week).

Source: OECD (2003a), Tables A4.5 and A4.6.

since they offer a broad array of different types of support, ranging from the psychological to the vocational. As a result, they have a greater chance of ensuring real acceptance of the disability in the work environment – by fellow-workers and disabled persons alike. Unfortunately, as Table 3.9 shows, supported jobs are still not very widespread and are available to too few disabled persons in too few countries.

Finally, no matter how good the policy framework in place is, promoting more access to employment for the disabled requires profound changes in behaviour, especially on the part of employers (see Box 3.6). But policies can help change negative attitudes to the

> ### Box 3.6. **Promoting employment among disabled persons: involving employers in the process**
>
> Existing employer-employee relationships should be utilised as much as possible – both through positive incentives and through mandated obligations. Many countries have regulations which legally oblige the employer to make an effort for disabled employees. In Italy, employers have recently been required to assign the disabled person equivalent tasks or, if not possible, lower-graded tasks but with the same remuneration. Similarly, Swedish employers must equip the workplace appropriately for their disabled workers or, if possible, provide them a different job in the company. In Germany, employers have a general obligation to promote permanent employment of severely disabled employees – via provision of adequate workplaces according to skills and capabilities, preferential selection for in-house training and support for external training measures. In practice, however, many of these regulations are difficult to enforce, despite the possibility of imposing sanctions for non-compliance. The same holds true for anti-discrimination legislation, which is often undermined by the undue hardship clause. Even in those countries that have mandatory quotas for employment of disabled persons, fines for non-compliance are often so low that employers may find it easier to pay than comply.
>
> Apart from legal loopholes, another reason for ineffectiveness appears to be that employers need help to fulfil their obligations. Workplace and job adjustments generally require small financial investments. More crucial are technical assistance and guidance, including assessment of the problem and development of an intervention strategy for the participation plan. Recent disability management service pilots in the Netherlands, which aim to match job requirements with the disabled person's possibilities, are a good example to follow. Employers who make an effort to (re)employ disabled persons should not be penalised financially compared with employers who fail to make an effort. In some cases, compensation payments for the higher cost of employment of disabled persons may therefore be appropriate. The justification, however, would depend on the system in the individual country. If quotas or strong anti-discrimination legislation exist, for example, compensation payments would theoretically be unnecessary and could even be inconsistent with legal obligations. Special employment protection for disabled people per se, on the other hand, will only help people to stay in work or go back to their workplace if accompanied by individual assistance. The Netherlands had a negative experience with a regulation forbidding employers to dismiss an employee because of sickness for a period of two years. In the absence of measures to promote re-entry into the labour market, the regulation proved ineffective, merely shifted costs and delayed the transfer of the beneficiary to a long-term disability benefit. People often waited on sickness benefits without any intervention until applying for a disability benefit – a problem that Dutch policy makers have been addressing with several reforms since the mid-1990s.

disabled in the workplace by launching information campaigns, providing incentives and even imposing requirements (see also Chapter 4).

C. Improving employment prospects of older workers[19]

Developing policies to improve the labour market situation of older workers is important from a number of perspectives. First, as noted in Chapter 2, unless the participation rate of older workers is increased, population ageing will strongly affect the availability of labour resources, economic growth and the sustainability of social protection systems. Second, ensuring a smooth work-retirement transition is also important from the point of view of individual well-being. In some firms, there is considerable pressure on older workers to accept early retirement packages. And, more generally, older workers suffer from negative perceptions regarding their employability.

A mix of policies that would successfully increase employment at older ages, and thereby increase the *effective age of retirement* could help to alleviate the economic and social effects of ageing populations. Eliminating incentives for early retirement would help raise participation of older workers in the labour market. But this is obviously not enough: demand would have to rise to match the higher supply, otherwise unemployment would rise among older workers.

Enhancing labour supply through pension reform is an important medium-term requirement...

To encourage later retirement in line with improvements in longevity, some countries are considering the possibility of extending the official retirement age. The standard official retirement age to qualify for a public pension is currently 65 in most OECD countries. The chief exceptions to this are France and Korea, where it is 60, and Norway, where it is 67. Increases in the standard retirement age of women to match that of men are being phased-in in Australia and Germany. Such initiatives may affect both male and female retirement ages, since the retirement decision is often made jointly by the members of the household rather than by each member separately. In other countries (*e.g.* Hungary, Italy, Japan, Korea, the United States), increases in the standard retirement age are being phased-in for both men and women. Another approach, as in France and Hungary, is to prolong the contribution period needed to qualify for a full pension.

... and phasing out subsidies to early retirement is needed urgently

Nevertheless, the effectiveness of pension reforms will crucially depend on whether or not incentives to early retirement have been tackled.[20] It is indeed important to note that, on average, people retire three to five years earlier than the standard official age (Chart 3.5).[21] And there is a weak correlation between the effective retirement age and the official age, suggesting that raising the effective age to match the official age should be a high priority.

Several countries offer early retirement pensions allowing people to retire two to five years before the standard age. In many cases, these schemes were introduced in a context of prolonged recessions and mass lay-offs. Early retirement was expected to reduce unemployment, especially among younger workers. But studies have shown that such solutions are counter-productive and costly (OECD, 2003c) and have fostered an early retirement culture in many countries. Reversing this trend, therefore, constitutes a major policy challenge in a number of OECD countries. In Belgium, for example, retirement is

Chart 3.5. **Effective age of retirement: lower than the official age in many OECD countries**[a]

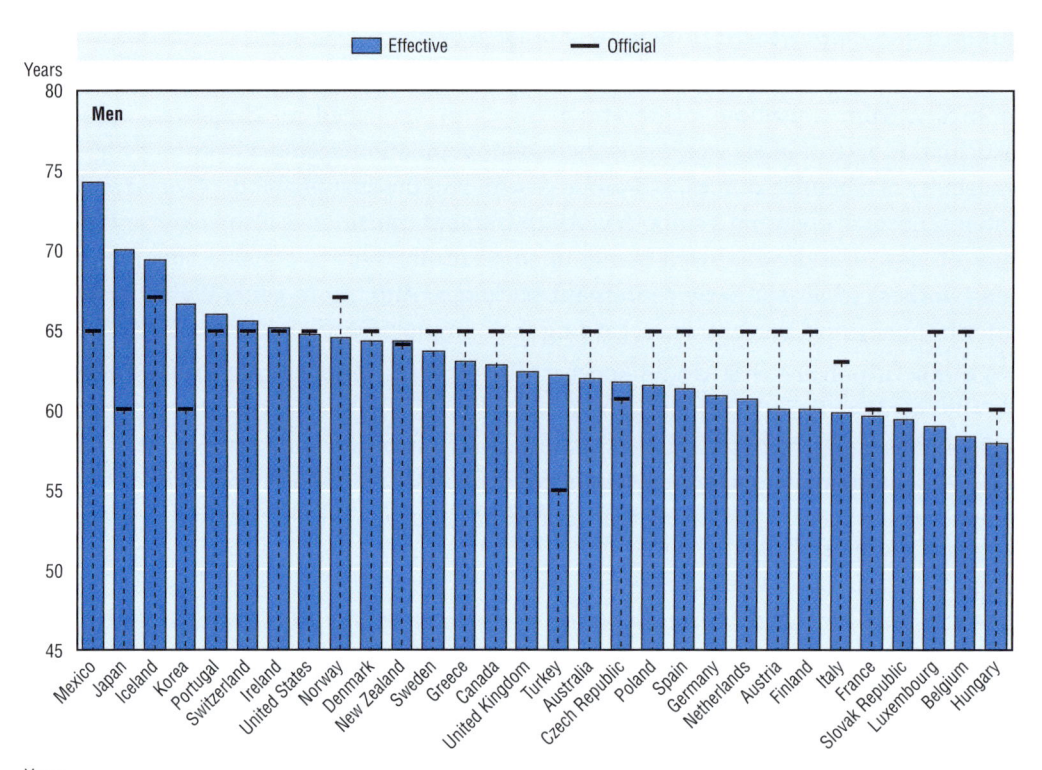

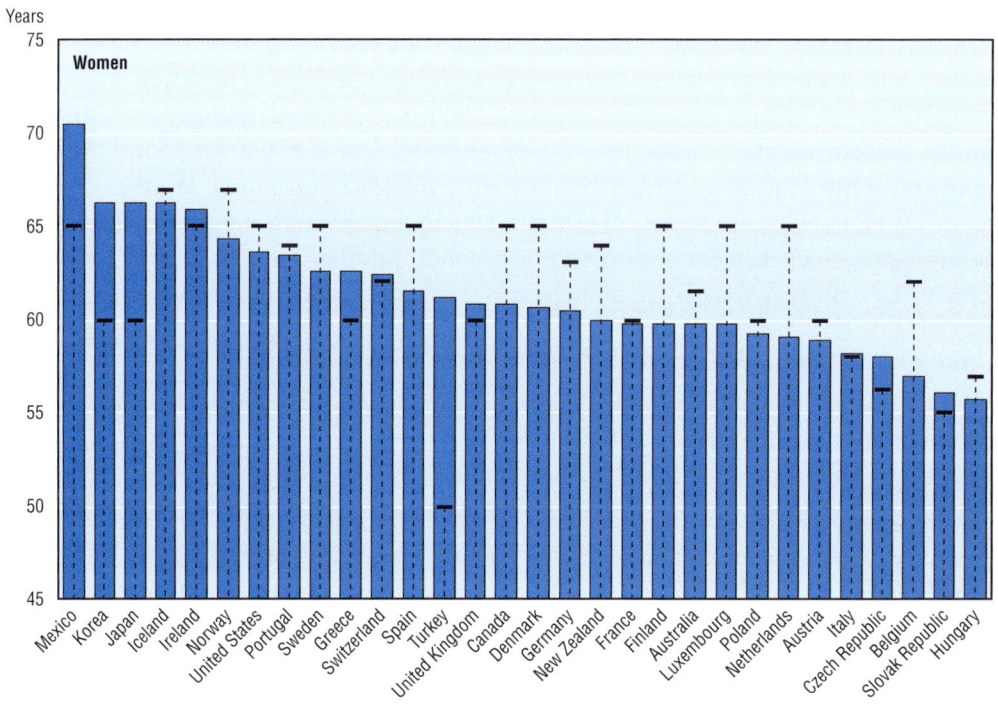

a) The effective age of retirement refers to the average age at which persons aged 40 and over left the labour force during the period 1995-2000. The official age of retirement refers to the earliest age at which workers are entitled to a full old-age public pension.

Source: OECD estimates.

stated as the reason for inactivity by almost 29% of those aged 50 to 64, which is a much higher proportion than in other countries for which data are available, and the attachment to the labour market has become very weak after 50 (see OECD, 2003d).

Other avenues to early exit from the labour market need to be addressed too. As underlined in Chapter 2, in a number of countries, disability pensions, long-term sickness benefits and unemployment benefits have been used as an early retirement device. Thus, restraining the availability of early retirement programmes may lead to an increase in other forms of benefit receipt (see the discussion on benefit substitution in Chapter 4). A comprehensive approach is therefore needed.

More flexible work-retirement transitions may also help

While raising the average effective age of retirement is a desirable objective, it is also important to recognize that older workers are a very heterogeneous group. In all countries, depending on skill, work experience, geographical location and a range of other personal factors, there is a wide variation in labour force status, in pay and working conditions for those in employment, and in the timing of retirement. There is also wide variation in the household situation of older people within countries, which will also affect their work and retirement choices. Thus, it is desirable that older workers should have more choice about when they retire and whether this is done abruptly or progressively. But one crucial issue is how to build more flexible pathways to retirement without actually decreasing labour supply in terms of aggregate hours worked by older people.

More choice in the timing of the retirement decision has been introduced in Spain, Sweden and Switzerland by allowing both early and later retirement, but with a corresponding adjustment in the old-age pension (although not always strictly on an actuarially-neutral basis). This reduces pressure on pension funding by ensuring that benefits are more in line with contributions. Finland, Germany, Iceland, Italy, Netherlands, Norway, Sweden and the United States are all moving in this direction. In contrast, Australia has introduced a pension bonus scheme to encourage people to postpone taking a pension until after the official retirement age. One important characteristic of these reforms is that they provide financial incentives to stay longer in the labour force.

Creating greater opportunities for working-time reductions is often mentioned as another way of encouraging older people to postpone retirement. Progressive retirement schemes have been introduced in many European Union countries (see Table 3.A1.3 in the annex for details). These allow older workers nearing retirement to reduce their working hours and to receive some form of income support to compensate for the loss in wages. It should be noted, however, that the take-up of these schemes is very variable.[22] In addition, the net effect on hours worked is unclear, while the financing of the subsidy entails a deadweight loss: on the one hand, a subsidy may raise the participation and number of hours worked of individuals who would have retired otherwise, but on the other hand it may induce others to reduce their working hours. Thus, progressive retirement schemes should be carefully targeted and limited, for example, to workers experiencing difficult working conditions or suffering from health problems. Spain and Sweden abolished their partial pension schemes as part of recent reforms to their old-age pension systems. Instead, under their new systems, there is considerable flexibility in combining full- or part-time work with an old-age pension (either in full or in part) but with no implicit subsidy of part-time work. In Japan, workers aged 60 and over are entitled to a full pension (but at a reduced rate compared with the rate at age 65) if they work part-time but not if they work full-time.[23]

But policies also need to tackle the demand-side of the equation, first by reducing obstacles to firms' retention of older workers...

The above-mentioned policies will undoubtedly help reduce disincentives to early retirement. However, demand-side barriers to the retention or hiring of older workers need to be addressed as well. There are concerns that older workers bear the brunt of layoffs as a result of company restructuring and bankruptcies and yet face the biggest hurdles in terms of finding new jobs. This has prompted the Belgian government to introduce a measure requiring firms laying-off older workers to pay the costs of outplacement services to help find new jobs for these workers. Likewise, in Spain, firms that lay-off older workers have to compensate the social security system for the shortfall in social security contributions entailed by the lay-off. However, a policy that increases the effective costs of firing older workers is likely to lead to lower hiring rates of older workers and thus could make it harder for older job seekers to find jobs. Thus, one issue to be resolved is how best to protect older workers from job loss and its consequences without lowering the incentives of employers to hire older job seekers.

Age discrimination is another factor affecting retention of older workers. For instance, setting a mandatory retirement age well below the official age for receiving the full old-age pension is standard firm practice in both Japan and Korea. And many older workers face a substantial cut in wages once they reach their firm's mandatory retirement age and have to switch to a new job, whether within or outside of the firm. It is now forbidden in Japan to set it below 60 years of age, but there is no such compulsory rule in Korea.[24] In both countries, there is an active debate about whether firms should be obliged to raise their mandatory age of retirement or abolish it altogether.[25] In contrast, in the United States, firms are prohibited from setting a mandatory retirement age. Within the European Union, the United Kingdom has taken the most comprehensive approach to tackling age discrimination but one that is based on a voluntary code of practice rather than legislation. However, all EU countries will be required to comply with the EU Employment Directive on Equal Treatment (2000/78/EC) to introduce by 2003 legislation prohibiting direct and indirect discrimination at work on the grounds of sexual orientation, religion and belief, and by 2006 on the grounds of age and disability.

In many countries, wages tend to increase with age. This may reflect the increasing productivity of workers as they gain more experience. However, the age-profile of earnings may also be the result of an implicit contract between the employer and the employee. Accordingly, wages would grow with seniority in order to enhance employee's commitment to the firm and work effort, especially when it is difficult for firms to monitor work effort (Lazear, 1979). Moreover, in a number of OECD countries, wage determination is strongly influenced by collective agreements and seniority wages may also be present in wage-setting practices. In Spain, for instance, although seniority has been playing a less important role over the past few years, about 80% of collective agreements still include seniority clauses. In countries such as Korea and Japan, seniority wages are a deeply embedded part of their national wage practices, and this means that setting a mandatory age of retirement lower than the official age is also a standard firm practice in these countries. Beyond a certain age, the wage may exceed the employee's marginal productivity, which would explain employer's incentive to encourage early retirement.

... second, by facilitating hiring of older workers

There are considerable differences across countries in the risk of unemployment and in the incidence of long-term unemployment for older people. In general, the unemployment rate for those aged 50 to 64 is either the same or somewhat lower than for those aged 25 to 49, while the opposite is true in terms of the incidence of long-term unemployment. It is not clear how country differences in these unemployment patterns should be interpreted. In some countries, early retirement schemes are much more pervasive than in others and thus a higher proportion of older job losers may move out of the labour market altogether before experiencing either a short or long spell of unemployment. In addition, in countries where older persons are not obliged to register as actively looking for work, their unemployment rate may be artificially lowered. However, one stylised fact is common across all countries: once they lose their job, it is especially difficult for older workers to find a new one.

Employment subsidy schemes are often used to promote the labour force participation of older workers. Policies to provide subsidized employment for older workers in both the private and public sectors have been developed in many countries (see Table 3.A1.4, in the annex for details). As discussed above, the results of evaluations in a number of OECD countries indicate that there are likely to be large deadweight and displacement effects associated with wage subsidy programmes. In Korea, the employment promotion subsidy for older workers is also reported to have a large deadweight effect (Jang, 2000). A further problem is that subsidies for older workers as a group may lead to stigmatisation and reinforce negative attitudes to hiring and retaining older workers on the part of employers. A wage subsidy that is granted solely on the basis of age may not be a very effective measure as opposed to a subsidy targeted at older, low-paid workers only or at long-term unemployed job seekers. For example, for the "New Deal 50 plus" in the United Kingdom, while there are a number of positive reports on this programme, some job centres also report cases of negative experiences for older workers (Joseph et al., 2002). Moreover, the fact that older workers are a very heterogeneous group also suggests that policies which are targeted on age alone risk being quite blunt instruments.

It is also necessary to consider other aspects of active labour market policies. While older workers do not always face a higher risk of becoming unemployed than younger workers (partly because they may leave the labour force altogether), they generally face a higher incidence of long-term unemployment. While age discrimination and a general lack of job opportunities may account for some of the difficulties that older unemployed people face in finding work, there is room to improve the employment services that are offered to them (see also Chapter 4). In some countries, eligibility rules for unemployment benefits that require active job search on the part of the benefit recipient are either explicitly or implicitly waived for older job seekers, and thus the incentives and help given for job search are minimal or non-existent. "Activation" policies that have tied the continuation of unemployment benefits to either the acceptance of a job offer or participation in active labour market programmes have often been directed at younger people. In Spain, recent active measures have also been introduced for older unemployed people. There may also be a need to tailor active labour market programmes to the individual needs of older workers. For example, older job seekers can and do participate in Sweden's extensive range of programmes, but they do not appear to rate these programmes as being very effective in terms of improving their employment chances, which is partly borne out by the relatively high incidence of long-term unemployment among the older unemployed in Sweden.

Towards a life-cycle approach to preserve employability and attachment to the labour market

While raising the average age of retirement is a desirable objective, especially in those countries where it is currently very low, it is important to consider the quality of the jobs that older people would be able to obtain if they remain longer in the labour market. Since the incidence of health problems rises strongly with age, adapting the working environment and working arrangements may play a key role in retaining older workers in the labour force. Moreover, as has been seen (see Table 3.A1.1 in the annex), non-employed older workers are much more frequently low-educated than those who are employed. In many OECD countries, more than the half of the non-employed persons aged 55 to 64 are low-educated. Insuring that skill and competencies match firms' productivity requirement throughout the working life is crucial to maintain the employability of older workers.

Providing greater training opportunities for older people is an important issue. However, relatively few significant initiatives have been put in place targeted specifically at older workers. But, providing training opportunities to older workers without any provision of vocational training at an earlier stage of their working-life is unlikely to be very effective. Employers may be reluctant to give training to older workers because they do not expect these workers to remain long enough with the firm to gain a sufficient return on their training investment. Older workers may be reluctant to invest in training themselves because existing training programmes are not well adapted to their needs or because the opportunity costs of investing in further training are too high *versus* the expected financial returns (see Chapter 5). Thus, a life-cycle perspective suggests that it is necessary to promote greater training opportunities for workers at earlier stages in their careers and not just after they reach the age of 50.

Improving working conditions in order to reduce health-related problems may have a positive effect in delaying exit from the labour market and extending the work life of older workers. In this area, there have been only a few initiatives taken in some OECD countries. In 2001, the Swedish Government introduced the *11-point programme for better health in working life* (Ministry of Health and Social Affairs, 2001). This focuses on measures for a better working environment and clearer employer responsibilities, as well as measures for an early return to work after illness. It provides a framework rather than a ready-made package of specific measures to be implemented immediately. The programme will be carried out in close liaison with the social partners. At this stage, nothing has so far been implemented. In Japan, employers who improve workplace facilities and equipment to facilitate employment of workers aged 60-64 years, and actually increase the number of such employees, or those who open new plants where they have many older employees, can receive benefits of JPY 250 000 to JPY 20 million for three to five years. In addition, since 2000, employers can also receive two-thirds of the cost if they create barrier-free workplaces for older workers. A loan programme with special interest rates is also available for investments such as remodelling the workplace. In Korea, according to the proposed "Aged Employment Promotion Act", the government will be able to provide financial support to those companies improving working conditions for older workers, with financial resources coming from either the general budget or the EIS fund.

Conclusions

Across OECD countries, work is unequally distributed, with the main groups under-represented in the labour market including women in general, and mothers and lone mothers in particular, older workers and people with disabilities. To assist these groups to enter or return to the labour market, work should pay and be accessible, but work also needs to be affordable for employers. Governments that wish to make work pay need to consider the possible financial incentives and subsidies that are most appropriate and most likely to be effective in the specific circumstances of their countries. Employment-conditional benefits such as tax credits can in the right circumstances provide effective incentives for increased labour supply and enhance employment, but it is also necessary to bear in mind their broader distributional objectives and their institutional context. Interactions with the minimum wage are important, also in regard to subsidies aimed at reducing labour costs for employers. Appropriate targeting of either form of assistance is important, and appropriate time limits should be considered. The labour supply of older workers can be increased if existing incentives to early retirement in pension systems are removed, and other benefits are also reformed so that they do not offer alternative paths to early retirement. Similarly, disability benefit schemes should be reformed in order to prevent long-term dependency and encourage work.

Such reforms also need to be accompanied by effective initiatives to increase demand for these groups. Enhancing accessibility requires consideration of different issues for different groups. Striking a better balance between work and family life is vital for parents, in particular, while for people with disabilities, there should be individually-tailored interventions, including rehabilitation and training. Older workers may also need retraining and flexible working arrangements. Effective policies to combat discrimination in the workplace are also important. Most importantly, particularly for a wide range of beneficiary groups it is necessary to recognise that employment is the most sustainable and secure foundation for effective social protection. Building this more effective system of social protection requires a comprehensive policy approach.

Notes

1. A stated aim of the UK initiative, for instance, is to tackle the adverse effects of poverty on children (Brewer, 2000). This objective is less relevant when the eligibility requirements are based on individual criteria, regardless of whether or not there are children in the household unit.

2. The basic rate of income tax will be reduced to 15% by 2005 (starting from 25.9% in 1998) and the top tax rate to 42% (from 53% in 1998). In addition, households in the lowest income tax bracket benefit from a substantial increase in the basic tax-free allowance. Moreover, in the context of a special labour policy programme, tests of the so-called Mainz Model have been extended to Germany as a whole on 1 March 2002: upon taking up employment, low-income workers receive a sliding-scale subsidy towards their social security contributions. Overall, low-wage workers will see their disposable income (after tax and social security contributions) increase by a significant amount, which should encourage them to enter regular employment.

3. The employment effects of the WFTC scheme in the United Kingdom are not as positive. One explanation might be the differential nature of the WFTC, since entitlement to these payments means the partial loss of other welfare benefits.

4. Visibility can play an important role when it comes to benefits. Individuals cannot be expected to react well to a policy if they are unable to evaluate with accuracy how much they stand to gain from it. The publicity given to Canada's SSP probably contributed to its success (Greenwood and Voyer, 2000). Enrolees were given clear, detailed information on its content and main goal, which was to make work pay. This aspect is sometimes overlooked. US taxpayers, for instance have only a very vague idea how much tax credits can help to increase their incomes (Hotz and Sholz, 2000). The British experiment, when reforming the WFTC, of delegating to employers the responsibility for paying the benefit along with wages, is an interesting recent innovation in this respect.

5. In 2004, the generosity of the PPE should be increased. It would then account at most for 7% of declared income.

6. Workers earning less than 30% of the monthly minimum wage are not eligible for the PPE, while the welfare benefit (RMI) is higher than this threshold.

7. A survey reported in van Polanen Petel *et al.* (1999) indicates even larger deadweight losses, accounting for over 90% of new recruits.

8. This complementary measure was not based on any evidence of a decline in wage mobility at the bottom of the wage ladder (European Commission, 1999). More generally, there is as yet no evidence of low-pay traps emerging once employers have benefited from payroll tax reductions, but this is because most of the evaluation work to-date has focused mainly on the employment effects of such measures.

9. Companies were supposed to provide workers hired in this way with genuine employment prospects, and would not be eligible for further subsidies if they shed them too rapidly. Evaluations of this scheme have highlighted its sustained impact on employment and on the wages of those concerned (with the exception of young people; see Katz, 1998).

10. Employment-conditional benefits or tax-credit schemes and employer subsidies targeted at the low end of wage distribution or to the hiring of disadvantaged groups are in principle equivalent when wages are fully flexible. In practice, they may be not equivalent, as wages are not fully flexible, so that the presence of a wage floor would suggest acting through employers if the goal is to maximise employment gains. Moreover, specific aspects of the wage determination process may be relevant, as stigmatization issues may become relevant.

11. In this respect, the introduction of employment-conditional benefits may ease the transition to a more flexible wage structure, with more decentralised wage bargaining institutions.

12. Among other things, this includes: a legal framework which guarantees the same or a comparable position upon the parent's return from leave and the possibility to work shorter hours for parents with young children (in both the private and public sector in Sweden, but only for publicly employed parents in Denmark), access to highly subsidised, publicly provided childcare services, etc.

13. In the case of Germany, various measures have been taken to facilitate access to long-term maternity leave. Ondrich *et al.* (1996) show that women are much more likely to return to work when they previously had a strong job attachment (significant work experience and a full-time job). Similarly, studies that make it possible to distinguish patterns of participation on the basis of the level of education show that women with higher education more frequently return to work (for example, see Dex *et al.*, 1996, for the United Kingdom; Gutiérrez-Domenech, 2002, for Spain; and Bratti, 2001, for Italy).

14. In France, for example, women who use the APE to stop all paid activity for three years have very specific characteristics: "Two types of women use the APE: those with high job security and those with a history of very precarious jobs" (Simon, 1999). Consequently, this type of measure might further widen the employment gap between the skilled and less skilled that is observed more generally.

15. The *quality* of child-care services provided is also a key aspect that experts on the development of very young children have emphasised when seeking to determine whether it is detrimental to children's development for mothers to work. Relatively little is known about the relationship between the quality of child-care services and whether women work, partly because it is difficult to measure the quality of these services. In practice, this issue is often raised last, after the problems of availability and cost of child care have been solved or at least addressed (OECD, 2002d). For example, Denmark has a very extensive child-care system that provides full-time, institutionalised care starting at the youngest ages. It has become standard practice for parents to use it, and the vast majority of women return to work after having a child, often on a full-time basis. As a result, the focus is now mainly on the quality of the various types of child care provided.

16. Since 1992, combining part-time work with raising children (until the 10th year for the youngest child) has been 50 % better valued in terms of the subsequent pension entitlement. Moreover, the "Part-Time and Fixed-Term Employment Act", introduced in 2001, aims at facilitating access to part-time work in all occupations, for both men and women. The key elements of the act are the improvement of protection against discrimination for part-time employees, greater transparency about part-time work opportunities, and the promotion of part-time work by extending employees' rights.

17. The indicator proposed is imperfect, for it does not permit to distinguish between a relative shortage of part-time jobs and a poor distribution of part-time jobs (since involuntary part-time employment can coexist with unsatisfied demand for part-time jobs).

18. The match between non-active persons who state that they stopped working for health reasons and non-active persons who state that they have a disability is obviously imperfect, but it is reasonable to believe that these two groups overlap significantly.

19. For the purpose of this discussion, and as far as available data permit, older workers are defined as workers aged 50 and over. This age is not meant to be a watershed in itself in terms of defining who is "older" and who is not. However, in many countries, the age of 50 marks the beginning of a decline in participation rates.

20. The OECD has calculated two measures of early retirement incentives in public pension schemes. The first is the replacement rate – a person's pension as a percentage of his or her working income prior to retirement: the higher the replacement rate, the higher the incentive to retire. The second measure is the change in net pension wealth from working an additional year; the principle here is that the incentive to retire early would rise if working an extra year implied paying additional contributions with little or no increase in future pension gains. Using this measure for 15 countries, it is clear that there are incentives to retire early in the regular old-age pension system, though not before the age of 60. The exceptions are Italy (where the earliest retirement age is 57 and the replacement rate of pension income is above 50% of previous earnings) and Australia (where individuals can draw on their mandatory savings from 55). In the United Kingdom and Canada, complementary occupational pension schemes also provide incentives for early retirement – the retirement age in some UK companies that have their own private pension schemes is 60, and not the UK standard of 65.

21. Only in the United States does the effective retirement age correspond to the current official age (65). Even so, the United States is gradually raising the retirement age to 67, and is debating the merits of later retirement. The average worker in Japan and Korea retires at 69 and 67, respectively four and seven years later than the official age. But these are the exceptions.

22. In Belgium, for instance, only just over 1 000 persons in 2001 opted for early retirement on half normal working hours. This measure is quite complex and needs the cooperation of several actors (the unemployment benefit institution, the employer, the pension institution). In contrast, around 37 000 persons aged 50 and over chose a career-break in 2001. Similarly, the scheme in Luxembourg is very complex and has very low take-up.

23. Another concern is whether older workers or all workers more generally, should be given the right to work part-time and what impact this would have on firms' performance. In Belgium, for example, under the "*crédit temps*" scheme introduced in January 2002, employers with ten or more employees are obliged to allow workers to switch to part-time work, if they so wish, within a limit of 5% of their total workforce.

24. In Korea, the mandatory retirement age was set at 56 years of age or less in half of medium-to-large firms in 2001.

25. The Korean Government has urged firms to raise their mandatory age of retirement to 60, but only on a voluntary basis. Similarly, in Japan, firms have been urged to raise it to 65.

ANNEX 1

Tables 3.A1.1 to 3.A1.4

3. MAKING WORK PAY – MAKING WORK POSSIBLE

Table 3.A1.1. **Non-employment among young women, older workers and disabled persons: a low level of education as a common factor**

Percentages

	Women aged 25 to 44, 2001			All persons aged 55 to 64, 2001			Disabled persons aged 25 to 64, 1997		
	Share of low educated in total non-employed[a]	Share of low educated in total employed[a]	Ratio	Share of low educated in total non-employed[a]	Share of low educated in total employed[a]	Ratio	Share of low educated in total non-employed[a]	Share of low educated in total employed[a]	Ratio
Australia	52.6	32.6	1.6	66.9	44.5	1.5	..	..	..
Austria	32.1	17.5	1.8	39.8	23.5	1.7	43.9	20.9	2.1
Belgium	50.6	19.9	2.5	67.4	40.7	1.7	59.8	32.2	1.9
Canada	22.1	8.3	2.7	40.9	25.3	1.6	..	..	..
Czech Republic	16.6	7.9	2.1	31.3	10.8	2.9	..	..	..
Denmark	32.7	13.2	2.5	38.9	19.9	2.0	52.2	23.9	2.2
Finland	18.9	8.9	2.1	57.5	39.2	1.5	55.0	29.6	1.9
France	44.1	21.4	2.1	59.2	44.4	1.3	69.9	39.2	1.8
Germany	27.9	12.3	2.3	28.9	16.8	1.7	34.6	21.2	1.6
Greece	43.8	25.0	1.7	71.5	73.9	1.0	80.1	63.9	1.3
Hungary	35.7	15.3	2.3	64.0	30.4	2.1	..	..	..
Iceland	46.8	37.1	1.3	52.0	43.1	1.2	..	..	..
Ireland	47.8	20.5	2.3	72.8	55.5	1.3	76.0	53.6	1.4
Italy	57.6	30.2	1.9	82.5	61.3	1.3	89.1	52.7	1.7
Japan	5.7	4.1	1.4	39.8	35.7	1.1	..	..	..
Korea	14.4	22.1	0.7	68.7	71.1	1.0	..	..	..
Luxembourg	48.9	34.9	1.4	60.6	26.7	2.3	..	..	..
Mexico	83.0	63.7	1.3	90.3	87.6	1.0	..	..	..
Netherlands	48.1	21.3	2.3	57.5	37.2	1.5	41.1	26.3	1.6
New Zealand	30.0	14.9	2.0	51.7	32.4	1.6	..	..	..
Norway	14.0	5.4	2.6	43.0	22.0	2.0	..	..	..
Poland	18.1	7.4	2.4	44.8	33.4	1.3	..	..	..
Portugal	84.3	66.5	1.3	92.8	90.2	1.0	96.4	88.9	1.1
Slovak Republic	18.6	6.0	3.1	40.9	10.1	4.0	..	..	..
Spain	61.1	35.9	1.7	88.6	73.8	1.2	89.8	78.1	1.1
Sweden	18.7	8.3	2.2	44.3	30.3	1.5	36.9	27.0	1.4
Switzerland	13.9	9.5	1.5	28.1	15.0	1.9	..	..	..
Turkey	83.9	62.7	1.3	85.0	90.0	0.9	..	..	..
United Kingdom	27.3	8.0	3.4	39.6	22.6	1.8	..	..	..
United States[b]	20.5	7.9	2.6	24.9	12.1	2.1	39.8	16.1	2.5
Unweighted OECD average	37.3	21.6	2.0	55.8	40.7	1.6	61.7	41.0	1.7
Standard deviation	21.7	17.4	0.6	19.7	24.2	0.6	21.6	22.9	0.4

.. Data not available.
a) Low educational attainment corresponds to less than upper secondary degree.
b) For disabled, data refer to persons aged 20 to 64.
Source: OECD (2002g); OECD (2003a).

3. MAKING WORK PAY – MAKING WORK POSSIBLE

Table 3.A1.2. Examples of employment-conditional benefits[a]

	Name	Type of recipient	Maximum benefit (% of full-time median wage)[b]	Minimum hours worked	Description of benefit	Unit
Australia	Employment Entry Payment	Lone parents and long-term income support recipients (12 months or more)	AUD 104/year (0.3%)	–	Lump sum paid when entering employment (eligible only every 12 months)	Both individual and household criteria
Belgium	Refundable tax credit (being introduced)	Wage earners or self-employed with an earned income of between EUR 3 260 and EUR 14 140 per year	EUR 440/year in 2004 (1.3%)	None	Lump sum	Individual
Canada[c]	Individual provinces provide employment-conditional benefits: *e.g.* Ontario's Start Up Benefit	Social assistance recipients	CAD 253/year (0.8%)	None	Lump-sum paid to social assistance recipients who begin/change employment or join training programme (once every 12 months only)	Individual
France[d]	Employment allowance: *Prime pour l'emploi*	Individual with an earned income of between EUR 3 265 and EUR 15 235 per year (or EUR 23 207 for a married person with an unemployed spouse)	EUR 720/year in 2004 (3.3%)	None	Entry phase: benefit increases with income. Exit phase: benefit decreases with income. Supplement for dependants	Individual
Ireland[e]	Family Income Supplement	Families with children and low wages (threshold from EUR 362 to 539 per week depending on number of children)		19 hours per week	Amounts to 60% of the difference between effective income and eligible income	Families with children
	Back-to-Work Allowance	Long-term unemployed (min. 12 months) and welfare recipients	75% of previous allowance	20 hours per week	Limited to three years, decreasing over time (50% then 25% of previous allowance in 2nd and 3rd years)	Individual
Netherlands[f]	Employment-conditional tax credit	Wage-earners or self-employed	EUR 920/year (3.4%)	None	Entry phase: benefit increases with income	Individual
New Zealand	Family Tax Credit	Families with children and low earned income (under NZD 18 368 before tax, per year)		30 hours per week for a couple, 20 hours for a single parent	Provides a minimum income of NZD 18 368 per year, or NZD 286 after tax per week	Families with children
United Kingdom[g]	Working Family Tax Credit	Working parents with low income (threshold depends on household composition)	GBP 88.95/week (one-child family) (10.3%)	16 hours per week (supple-ment for 30 hours or more)	Exit phase: benefit decreases with income (depends on hourly wage). Supplements for extra dependent children	Families with children
United States[h]	Earned Income Tax Credit	Working families with children and individuals with low salaries	USD 2 428/year (8.1%) USD 4 008/year (13.4%) USD 364/year (1.2%)	None	Entry phase: benefit increases with income. Exit phase: benefit decreases with income	Families with children/individual

a) The benefits presented here fall into two categories: tax credits for earned income or cash supplements to offset benefits foregone upon return to employment. Other countries (*e.g.* Spain, Finland and Japan) grant wage-earners tax relief, which amounts to exempting a share of their earned income (the relief is usually higher for low incomes). Such exemptions are not included here (for more details, see OECD, 2002b).

b) The figure in brackets refers to the percentage of full-time median earnings in 1998 for Belgium, 1999 for France and the Netherlands, 2000 for others countries.

Table 3.A1.2. **Examples of employment-conditional benefits**[a] (cont.)

c) The previous Working Income supplement has been replaced by the National Child Benefit (NCB) supplement. This is a nationwide measure targeted at all low-income families; it does not really constitute an employment-conditional benefit. However, each Canadian province has special benefits for welfare recipients who enter or re-enter employment.
d) In 2003, the maximum benefit was EUR 479.
e) Ireland has other employment-conditional subsidies, including an allowance for returning to part-time work (fewer than 24 hours per week) after a long period of unemployment (at least 15 months).
f) In 2001, the Netherlands tax system underwent radical change, including the introduction of a variety of tax credits. Some families, for instance, can deduct some of their childcare costs from taxes. Welfare recipients are also eligible, under certain conditions, for a back-to-work allowance.
g) As from April 2003, this tax credit for working families is being replaced by two separate benefits, one being employment-conditional and the other covering childcare costs.
h) The first figure applies to one-child families, the second to families with two children or more, and the third to families with no children.

Source: OECD (2002a), Department of Family and Community Services (Australia), Ministry of Finance (Belgium), Internal Revenue Service (United States), Cahuc (2002 – for France), Department of Social and Family Affairs (Ireland), Inland Revenue (New Zealand), Gradus and Julsing (2001 – for the Netherlands), Inland Revenue (United Kingdom); OECD database on earnings.

3. MAKING WORK PAY – MAKING WORK POSSIBLE

Table 3.A1.3. **Main features of progressive retirement schemes**

Country and year of introduction	Scheme and hours reduction	Minimum age and career requirements	End of the scheme	Income and incentives (besides part-time pay)	Compensatory recruitments
Austria 2000	Part-time work for older workers. Full-timers can work up to 28 hours per week and part-timers up to 70% of previous hours.	55 for men, 50 for women. Unemployment insurance contributions for at least 15 years in the last 25 years.	Early retirement age (61.5 for men and 56.5 for women).	Worker: at least 50% of the pay reduction. Employer: the Labour Market Service pays 25% of gross pay and covers social contributions exceeding actual working hours.	Repealed in 2000. No longer required.
Austria 1993	Partial pension. Hours reduction of 40%–60%.	61.5 for men, 56.5 for women (new limits progressively implemented up to October 2002). Pension contributions for at least 450 months.	Retirement age (65).	Worker: proportionate "partial pension".	None.
Belgium 2002	Time credits. 1) Right to a time credit for a maximum of one year, employees can interrupt work or reduce it to half-time without breaking contract of employment or losing social security rights. Can be extended to maximum of five years by agreement at sectoral or company level. 2) During their career, for a maximum of five years, an employee has a right to reduce working hours by one-fifth, generally four-day working week instead of five. Workers over 50 entitled to reduce working hours indefinitely by either 20% or 50%.	All, but special conditions for 50 and over. For over-50s, 20 years' employment and five years' service with current employer.	Indefinite for those 50 and over.	Worker: career break benefit of around EUR 500 per month.	None
Belgium 1994	Early retirement on half working hours. Hours reduction of 50%.	55 a) Full-time employment in same enterprise for at least 12 months prior to reduction of working hours; b) entitled to unemployment benefits; c) 25 years of working life.	Retirement age.	Worker: half-time salary, unemployment benefit and supplementary compensation from employer.	Obligation to replace employee with unemployed worker (some exceptions).
Belgium 1985 until 2001	Career break. Hours reduction of 20% or 50%.	None. For over-50s, 20 years' employment and five years' service with current employer.	For over-50s, the career break will be re-examined every six months.	Worker: career break benefit of around EUR 300 per month.	Employer must hire an unemployed worker (some exceptions).
Denmark 1998	Flexible early retirement. Variable hours reduction.	60. Eligibility for early retirement, i.e. membership of unemployment fund for 25 years.	Retirement age (65), or early retirement.	Worker: a) proportionate partial early retirement pay; b) a tax-free payment if worker postpones full early retirement.	None.
Denmark 1990	Working hours reduction and part-time work (as part of older workers policies). Variable hours reduction.	Usually 60 but 55 in the public sector. Varies by sector and firm.	Retirement age (65).	Varies according to collective agreements and usually includes provision of a partial pension.	None.

OECD EMPLOYMENT OUTLOOK – ISBN 92-64-10061-X – © OECD 2003

161

Table 3.A1.3. Main features of progressive retirement schemes (cont.)

Country and year of introduction	Scheme and hours reduction	Minimum age and career requirements	End of the scheme	Income and incentives (besides part-time pay)	Compensatory recruitments
Denmark 1986	Partial pension. Hours reduction of at least seven hours or 25%, part-time hours of 12-30 hours per week.	60. Full pension contributions for ten years during last 20 years.	Retirement age (65).	Worker: partial pension.	None.
Finland 1987, 1989	Progressive retirement. Weekly working time must be reduced to 16-28 hours.	58 (56 on an experimental basis until 2002). Private sector: a) full-time employment for 12 months during last 18 months; b) five years of pensionable employment during the last 15 years. Public sector: full-time employment for three years during previous five, of which six months just before starting part-time work.	Retirement age (65).	Worker: a) part-time pension of 50% of difference between full-time and part-time earnings; b) no significant reduction in old-age pension entitlement.	None.
France 1998	Gradual retirement. Variable hours reduction.	60. a) Enough pension contributions to qualify for full pension; b) only one part-time activity.	"Late" retirement after the age of 60 (or return to full-time job or second part-time job).	Worker: partial pension proportionate to percentage of full-time hours worked.	None.
France 1996	Progressive early retirement. Average hours reduction of 50%.	55. a) Service in firm for at least one year; b) affiliation to a social security scheme for ten years; c) in full-time work. Workers over 60 must have fewer pension contributions than needed to qualify for full pension.	Retirement age (60). Scheme continues after 60 only if worker cannot qualify for full pension.	Worker: a) benefit of c.30% of previous basic wage; b) social contribution reductions; c) company agreements may grant special bonus. Employer: contribution to financial costs of scheme – contribution level depends on compensatory recruitment.	Employers' financial contribution depends on level of compensatory hiring and proportion of recruits from priority groups: contribution lower for more compensatory recruitment.
France 1992	Phased-in retirement (for public sector employees only). Hours reduction of 50%.	55. a) Full-time job; b) 25 years' service as state employee.	Retirement age (60). Scheme continues after 60 only if worker cannot qualify for full pension.	Worker: 30% of basic wage.	None.
Germany 1996	Progressive retirement. Hours reduction of 50%.	55 (possible to enter programme until 2009). a) Unemployment contributions for 36 months during last five years; b) not entitled to full pension.	Retirement age (65)	Worker: at least 70% of former net full-time income. Employer: if employers hire new workers, they receive payments to compensate the difference between actual working hours (50%) and wage (at least 70%) and 90% of full-time worker's pension contributions; incentives may last up to six years.	Needed in order for employers to benefit from economic incentives.
Netherlands 1980	Progressive retirement (part of pre-pension schemes). Variable hours reduction.	60. Varies according to collective agreements	Retirement age (65).	Varies according to collective agreements.	None.

3. MAKING WORK PAY – MAKING WORK POSSIBLE

Table 3.A1.3. **Main features of progressive retirement schemes** (cont.)

Country and year of introduction	Scheme and hours reduction	Minimum age and career requirements	End of the scheme	Income and incentives (besides part-time pay)	Compensatory recruitments
Norway 1988, 1997	Partial pension. Variable hours reduction.	62. a) Employed in company for three years, or covered by agreement on early retirement for five years; b) ten years of pension contributions since age of 50.	Retirement age (67).	Worker: partial pension.	None.
Spain 1997	Deferred retirement (still awaiting implementation). Variable hours reduction.	61. 35 years' pension contributions in order to benefit from incentives.	"Late" retirement after age of 65.	Worker: a) a higher pension on retirement; b) reduction of social contributions. Employer: social contribution reductions.	None.
Spain 1984	Early retirement through hand-over contracts. Hours reduction of 50%.	60. Eligibility for early retirement, i.e. 30 years of pension contributions.	Retirement age (65).	Worker: partial pension proportionate to working hours reduction.	Obligation to recruit replacement.

Source: European Industrial Relations Observatory (2001), Table 5.

Table 3.A1.4. **Employment subsidy schemes for older workers in selected OECD countries**

	Description of measure
Austria	There are employment subsidies for older workers that are large (100%) and available for up to two years. From 1996, the employer's share in unemployment insurance contributions could be halved, if over 50-year-olds were recruited, and completely dropped for workers over 55. Since 2000, the employer's share in unemployment insurance contributions can be dropped completely for those hiring workers aged over 50. This "bonus" is the first half of Austria's Bonus-Malus system, where the "malus" is a penalty payment for dismissing workers over the age of 50. In addition, the Austrian government has been implementing a progressive retirement programme, under which it compensates at least 50% of the lost income due to the shorter working hours.
Belgium	Since 1996, employers who hire job seekers aged 50 or over, who had been unemployed at least six months, can claim a 50% reduction in their social security contributions, for the first year following recruitment, and thereafter employers can get a 25% reduction for an unlimited period.
Denmark	Early retirement rules have been tightened and a pilot scheme has been introduced between 2000 and 2001 by the Ministry of Labour to subsidise public sector employment of long-term unemployed people aged over 48. The subsidy of DKK 100 000 is paid to the employer as long as the older workers remain with the organisation.
Finland	Private firms and municipalities can claim subsidies for six months if they employ people aged 55-59 who have recently become unemployed.
France	*Contract to promote employment – Contrat Initiative Emploi (CIE)*. The target group for subsidy is unemployed persons aged 50 and over. Other individuals are also eligible, including the long-term unemployed, recipients of social assistance benefits, disabled workers, single parents, low-skilled, unemployed youth, and former prisoners. The firm must not have laid-off workers in the preceding six months for economic reasons, and must not dismiss a previous employee on a permanent contract or make someone redundant in order to take on a subsidized employee. The subsidy provides an exemption from employer social security contributions (including for work accidents) for the part of wages corresponding to the level of the minimum wage, *i.e.* around 40% of gross minimum wages. The subsidy is normally for 24 months for a permanent employment contract or for the length of a fixed-term contract. The subsidy is Indefinite in the case of an older person (aged 50-64) who has been either unemployed or on social assistance for more than one year or is disabled
Germany	In keeping with the goals of the European employment strategy, older workers are an explicit target group of the Act for Modern Services on the Labour Market (1 January 2003). A number of measures are being taken with this special group in mind. On the supply side, the so-called wage safeguard for older workers has been introduced for workers 50 years of age and older. The wage supplements, to which there is a legal right, consist of two elements. On the one hand, there is a grant of 50% of the "net difference" between the wages earned before and after the unemployment phase. This wage supplement is tax-free and not subject to social contributions. In addition, the reduction in old-age security resulting from the lower wage level is partially offset by increasing coverage in the statutory pension insurance. The insurance contributions are boosted to 90% of those paid in the previous job. The benefits of the wage safeguards are granted exclusively to older jobless persons who have a (residual) claim to at least 180 days of unemployment benefit or, in the case of workers threatened by unemployment, have a corresponding potential claim. The wage safeguards are granted for the maximum period for which there is a claim to unemployment benefit. To prevent free-riders from cashing in on the benefits, their granting is prohibited in various situations. The last possibility of eligibility for this support is 31 December 2005; benefits may be paid out until 31 August 2008 at the latest. On the demand side, employers are given incentives to hire older workers. Employers who hire jobless persons who have reached the age of 55 are exempt from paying their share (3.25 %) of unemployment insurance. The measures to provide more flexibility in employing older workers have also been extended to cover the field of labour law. The age limit that is laid down in the Part-Time and Fixed-Term Employment Act and that defines the age from which fixed-term employment contracts may be concluded without citing any objective ground and without setting a maximum time period is being lowered, initially for a period of four years, from the age of 58 to that of 52. This provision is aimed at improving older jobless persons' chances of re-integration in the labour market. The Job-AQTIV Act (1 January 2002) has also improved incentives for the further training of employees aged over 50. The costs of their further training can be assumed by the Federal Institute for Employment. To be entitled to this, they must at least be employed in a small or medium-sized firm with up to 100 employees and be entitled to pay during the further training.
Greece	Under a scheme operated by the Manpower Employment Organisation, companies hiring workers aged 55 and over can receive subsidies for 12 months.
Italy	Employers hiring older workers are exempt from paying social insurance contributions for one year.
Japan	The Japanese government provides various subsidy programs for older workers based on the "Law for Employment Stabilisation for Older People". A subsidy can be given to employers who either continue employment of existing older workers or who hire older persons. The amount of subsidy for continuing employment ranges from JPY 500 000 to JPY 250 000. Employers who raise the mandatory retirement age or introduce a continued employment system can receive a subsidy of JPY 500 000 to JPY 3 000 000, up to maximum of five years. Employers employing more than 15% of 60-64 years old among their total employees can be given benefits of JPY 15 000 per month. For small and medium-sized enterprises, additional 60-64 year old employees exceeding the 15% can be given JPY 20 000 up to maximum of five years.

Table 3.A1.4. **Employment subsidy schemes for older workers in selected OECD countries** (cont.)

	Description of measure
Korea	*1) Bounty to Promote Employment for Many Aged Workers.* To be eligible the number of older workers (aged 55 and over) should exceed 6% of a firm's workforce. The number of part-time workers working fewer than 13 days per month or less than 15 hours per week is excluded from both the denominator and numerator when calculating the employment share of older workers. The subsidy is KRW 150 000 per quarter for every older worker exceeding the 6% requirement, *i.e.* around 2% of average wages per month, and is available indefinitely, as long as the 6% requirement is met.
	2) Bounty to Promote New Employment of Aged Workers. In order to access this subsidy, the firm must hire an older worker (aged 55 and over) who has been registered as looking for work with the Public Employment Service for at least three months. The firm must not lay-off any older workers during the period of three months prior to, or six months after, applying for the subsidy. The subsidy is KRW 250 000 per worker per month, *i.e.* 13.9% of average wages for six months
	3) Bounty to Promote Re-employment of Aged Workers. A firm is eligible for the subsidy for all retired workers (aged between 45 and 60) that it re-hires within a period of between three months and two years after they originally retired from the firm. However, as with the New Employment Bounty, it must not lay-off any older workers either during the period of three months prior to and six months after applying for the subsidy. The subsidy is KRW 300 000 per worker per month, *i.e.* 16.7% of average wages, for a maximum duration of six months.
	In addition to the existing subsidy programmes in Korea, the government is planning to introduce a further subsidy programme to boost the re-employment of retired workers through the revision of the "Aged Employment Promotion Act", which authorizes subsidies to employers. The government plans to provide subsidies from the EIS Fund to employers when they re-hire older workers after their retirement, with the subsidy planned to be about KRW 300 000 for six months.[a]
Luxembourg	Financial incentives are provided for employers to take on unemployed workers aged over 50.
Spain	Measures were introduced in 1997 in the form of lower social security contributions for companies for hiring workers aged over 45.
Sweden	"*Special Employment Subsidies*". This subsidy introduced in November 2000 is also intended to encourage employers to recruit at an earlier stage. The target group is persons over 57 years, and unemployed for two years or more. The subsidy is paid to employers for a maximum period of 24 months and covers up to 75% of the wage costs to a maximum of SEK 525 per day, *i.e.* SEK 10 500 per month (roughly half of the average salary for a full-time worker). In 2001, only around 1 900 persons participated in the programme.
United Kingdom	*New Deal 50+.* Persons aged 50 and over who have been on benefits for six months or more are assisted. Financial help also includes a tax-free Employment Credit. This Employment Credit is paid on top of an individual's wages when they go back to work, and can be paid for up to 52 weeks. "New Deal" programmes are also available for other target groups, including youth and long-term unemployed, disabled people, and lone parents. A New Deal Employer Agreement must be signed by the firm with the local labour office, and the firm is required to retain New Deal employees at the end of the six-month period provided they show aptitude and commitment. If not, this must be agreed in advance with the local labour office. The firm must pay New Deal employees the going rate for the job, which must be at least as much as the subsidy received, and must not dismiss a previous employee or make someone redundant in order to take on a New Deal employee. The subsidy is GBP 75 per week for each New Deal employee working full-time (at least 30 hours per week) and GBP 50 for those working part-time (16-29 hours a week), for six months.

a) In addition, large-scale public work programmes used after the financial crisis in 1997 absorbed significant numbers of older workers, with data (in 1999) showing that more than one-third of participants were aged over 50 (OECD, 2000).

Bibliography

AFSA, C. (1998), "L'allocation parentale d'éducation: entre politique familiale et politique pour l'emploi", *INSEE Première*, No. 569, February.

ANDERSON, P. and P. LEVINE (1999), "Child Care and Mother's Employment Decisions", *NBER Working Paper*, No. 7058.

AUDRIC, S., P. GIVORD and C. PROST (2000), "Estimation de l'impact sur l'emploi non qualifié des mesures de baisse de charges", *Revue Économique*, Vol. 51, No. 3, pp. 513-522.

BARDAJI, J. (2001), "Un an après la sortie d'un contrat emploi consolidé : près de six chances sur dix d'avoir un emploi", *Premières Synthèses*, No. 43.3, DARES, Ministère de l'Emploi et de la Solidarité, France.

BASSANINI, A., J. RASMUSSEN and S. SCARPETTA (1999), "The Economic Effects of Employment-Conditional Income Support Schemes for the Low-Paid: An Illustration from A CGE Model Applied to Four OECD Countries", *Economics Department Working Paper*, No. 224, OECD, Paris.

BELLEVILLE, A. (2001), "L'utilisation des aides à l'emploi par les entreprises: permanence ou logique conjoncturelle ?", *Premières Synthèses*, No. 25.1, DARES, Ministère de l'Emploi et de la Solidarité, France.

BLANK, R., D. CARD and P. ROBINS (1999), "Financial Incentives for Increasing Work and Income Among Low-Income Families", *NBER Working Paper*, No. 6998.

BLOOM, D. and C. MICHALOPOULOS (2001), "How Welfare and Work Policies Affect Employment and Income: A Synthesis of Research", Manpower Demonstration Research Corporation.

BLOOM, D., J. ANDERSON, M. WAVELET, K. GARDINER and M. FISHMAN (2002), "New Strategies to Promote Stable Employment and Career Progression: An Introduction to the Employment Retention and Advancement Project", Manpower Demonstration Research Corporation.

BLUNDELL, R. (2002), "Welfare-to-Work: Which Policies Work and Why?", *Keynes Lectures in Economics: 2001*, www.britac.ac.uk/pubs/src/keynes01/index.html

BLUNDELL, R. and H. HOYNES (2001), "Has In-Work Benefit Reform Helped the Labour Market?", *NBER Working Paper*, No. 8546.

BLUNDELL, R. and C. MEGHIR (2002), "Active Labor Market Policy Versus Employment Tax Credit: Lessons from Recent UK Reforms", *IFAU Working Paper*, No. 2002:1.

BONNET, C. and M. LABBE (1999), "L'activité professionnelle des femmes après la naissance de leurs deux premiers enfants, l'impact de l'allocation parentale d'éducation", *Études et Résultats*, No. 37, DREES, Ministère de l'Emploi et de la Solidarité, France.

BOVENBERG, L., J. GRAAFLAND and R. de MOOIJ (1998), "Tax Reform and the Dutch Labor Market: an Applied General Equilibrium Approach", *NBER Working Paper*, No. 6693.

BRADSHAW, J., S. KENNEDY, M. KILKEY, S. HUTTON, A. CORDEN, T. EARDLEY, H. HOLMES and J. NEALE (1996), *The Employment of Lone Parents: A Comparison of Policy in 20 Countries*, Family Policy Studies Centre, London.

BRATTI, M. (2001), "Labour Force Participation and Marital Fertility of Italian Women: The Role of Education", Royal Economic Society Annual Conference 2002, No. 34, Royal Economic Society.

BREWER, M. (2000), "Comparing In-Work Benefits and Financial Work Incentives for Low-Income Families in the US and UK", *Working Paper* WP 00/16, Institute for Fiscal Studies, London.

BREWER, M. and T. CLARK (2002), "The Impact on Incentives of Five Years of Social Security Reforms in the UK", *Working Paper*, WP 02/14, Institute of Fiscal Studies, London.

CAHUC, P. (2002), "A quoi sert la prime pour l'emploi?" (The Prime Pour l'Emploi: What to Do with It? With English summary), *Revue Française d'Économie*, Vol. 16, No. 3, pp. 3-61.

CAMPBELL, N., J. MANIHA and H. ROLSTON (2002), "Job Retention and Advancement in Welfare Reform", *Policy Brief*, 18 March, Brookings Institution.

CARLING, K. and K. RICHARDSON (2001), "The Relative Efficiency of Labor Market Programs: Swedish Experience From the 1990's", *IFAU Working Paper*, No. 2001:2.

CHEVALIER, A. and T. VIITANEN (2002), "The Causality Between Female Labour Force Participation and the Availability of Childcare", *Applied Economics Letters*, Vol. 9, No. 14, pp. 915-918.

COCKX, B., B. van der LINDEN and A. KARAA (1998), "Active Labour Market Policies and Job Tenure", *Oxford Economic Papers*, Vol. 50, No. 4, pp. 685-708.

CONCIALDI, P. and S. PONTHIEUX (2000), "Salariés à bas salaire et travailleurs pauvres : une comparaison France États-Unis", *Premières Synthèses*, No. 02.1, DARES, Ministère de l'Emploi et de la Solidarité, France.

CORCORAN, M. and S. LOEB (1999), "Will Wages Grow with Experience for Welfare Mothers?", *Focus*, Vol. 20, No.2, pp. 20-21.

COUNCIL OF THE EUROPEAN UNION (2001), "Joint Report on Social Inclusion", *europa.eu.int/comm/employment_social/soc-prot/soc-incl/joint_rep_en.htm*

CREPON, B. and R. DEPLATZ (2001), "Une nouvelle évaluation des effets des allégements de charges sociales sur les bas salaires", *Économie et Statistique*, Vol. 348, No. 8.

DARES (1999), *Bilan de la politique de l'emploi 1998*, Ministère de l'Emploi et de la Solidarité, France.

DARES (2003), *Note sur les facteurs expliquant l'arrêt d'activité des femmes mères de jeunes enfants*, Ministère des Affaires sociales, du Travail et de la Solidarité, France.

DEL BOCA, D. (2002), "Low Fertility and Labour Force Participation of Italian Women: Evidence and Interpretations", *Labour Market and Social Policy Occasional Papers*, No. 61, OECD, Paris.

DEPARTMENT OF FAMILY AND COMMUNITY SERVICES, Social Security Act 1991, Part 2.13 – Employment Entry Payment,

DEPARTMENT OF SOCIAL AND FAMILY AFFAIRS, "Family Income Supplement", *portal.Welfare.ie/publications/allpubs/sw22.pdf*, and "Back To Work Allowance", *education.welfare.ie/publications/sw93.pdf*, Ireland.

DEX, S., H. JOSHI, A. MCCULLOCH and S. MACRAN (1996), "Women's Employment Transitions Around Childbearing", *CEPR Working Paper*, No. 1408.

DOLADO, J., F. KRAMARZ, S. MACHIN, A. MANNING, D. MARGOLIS and C. TEULINGS (1996), "The Economic Impact of the Minimum Wage in Europe", *Economic Policy: A European Forum*, No. 23, pp. 317-357.

DSS (1998), *New Ambitions for Our Country: A New Contract for Welfare*, Cm 3805, The Stationery Office, London.

DUNCAN, A. and J. McCRAE (1999), "Household Labour Supply, Childcare Costs and In-Work Benefits: Modelling the Impact of the Working Families Tax Credit in the UK", paper presented to the Econometric Society European Meetings, Santiago de Compostela, September, *www.nottingham.ac.uk/~lezad/downloads/adjm.pdf*

EICHLER, M. and M. LECHNER (2002), "An Evaluation of Public Employment Programmes in the East German State of Sachsen-Anhalt", *Labour Economics: An International Journal*, Vol. 9, No. 2, pp. 143-186.

EISSA, N. and H. HOYNES (1998), "The Earned Income Tax Credit and the Labor Supply of Married Couples", *NBER Working Paper*, No. 6856.

EISSA, N. and J. LIEBMAN (1996), "Labour Supply Responses to the Earned Income Tax Credit", *Quarterly Journal of Economics*, Vol. 112, No. 2, pp. 605-637.

EUROPEAN COMMISSION (1999), "Reduction of Non Wage Labour Costs, Particularly for Low Paid Labour: Dutch Review", Peer Review, *peerreview.almp.org/en/9901.html*

EUROPEAN COMMISSION (2000), "Making Work Pay: Tax and Benefit Reform in the UK", Peer Review, *peerreview.almp.org/en/UKnov00.htm*

EUROPEAN COMMISSION (2001), "Social Responsibility of Enterprises: Denmark", Peer Review, *peerreview.almp.org/en/DKSept01.htm*

EUROPEAN COMMISSION (2002), *National Action Plan For Policy on Employment 2002*, Federal Republic of Germany.

EUROPEAN FOUNDATION FOR THE IMPROVEMENT OF LIVING AND WORKING CONDITIONS (2001), "Study Examines Employment Situation of Women after Taking Parental Leave", *www.eiro.eurofund.ie/print/2001/feature/de0108240f.html*

EUROPEAN INDUSTRIAL RELATIONS OBSERVATORY (2001), "Progressive Retirement in Europe", September, *www.eiro.eurofound.ie/2001/09/study/TN0109184S.html*

EUWALS, R. (2001), "Female Labour Supply, Flexibility of Working Hours, and Job Mobility", *The Economic Journal*, Vol. 111, No. 471, pp. 120-134.

FAGAN, C. and B. BURCHELL (2002), "Gender, Job and Working Conditions in the European Union", European Foundation for the Improvement of Living and Working Conditions.

FORD, R., D. GYARMATI, K. FOLEY and D. TATTRIE with, L. JIMENEZ (2003), *Can Work Incentives Pay for Themselves? – Final Report on the Self-Sufficiency Project for Welfare Applicants*, SRDC, September.

FÖRSTER, M. (assisted by M. PELLIZZARI) (2000), "Trends and Driving Factors in Income Distribution and Poverty in the OECD Area", *Labour Market and Social Policy Occasional Papers*, No. 42, OECD, Paris.

GRADUS, R.H. and J.M. JULSING (2001), "Comparing Different European Income Tax Policies: Making Work Pay", OCFEB *Research Memorandum* 0101, Erasmus University.

GREENWOOD, J. and J.-P. VOYER (2000), "Experimental Evidence of the Use of Earnings Supplements as a Strategy of Make Work Pay", *OECD Economic Studies*, Vol. 31, No. 2, pp. 43-68, OECD, Paris.

GROGGER, J. (2003), "Welfare Transitions in the 1900s: the Economy, Welfare Policy, and the EITC", *NBER Working Paper*, No. 9472.

GUPTA, N. and N. SMITH (2002), "Children and Career Interruptions: The Family Gap in Denmark", *Economica*, Vol. 69, No. 276, November, pp. 609-629.

GUTIERREZ-DOMENECH, M. (2002), "Employment Penalty after Motherhood in Spain", *Discussion Paper*, No. 546, Centre of Economic Performance, London.

GUTIERREZ-DOMENECH, M. (2003), "Employment after motherhood: a European Comparison", *Working Paper*, WP1177, Centre of Economic Performance, London, *econ.lse.ac.uk/phdc/0203/papers/MariaGutierrezDomenechJMP.pdf*

HECKMAN, J., L. LOCHNER and R. COSSA (2002), "Learning-by-Doing vs. On-the-Job Training: Using Variation Induced by the EITC to Distinguish Between Models of Skill Formation", *NBER Working Paper*, No. 9083.

HM TREASURY (2000), "Tackling Poverty and Making Work Pay: Tax Credits for the 21st Century", *The Modernisation of Britain's Tax and Benefit System*, No. 6, HM Treasury, March, London.

HOTZ, V. and J. SCHOLZ (2000), "Not Perfect, but Still Pretty Good: The EITC and Other Policies to Support the US Low-Wage Labour Market", *OECD Economic Studies*, Vol. 31, No. 2, pp. 25-42, OECD, Paris.

INLAND REVENUE (New Zealand), "Family Tax Credit", *swww.ird.govt.nz/familyassistance/famtaxcredit*

INLAND REVENUE (United Kingdom), "Your guide to Working Families' Tax Credit", *www.inlandrevenue.gov.uk/pdfs/wftc_bk1.pdf*

INTERNAL REVENUE SERVICE, *Department of the Treasury, Earned Income Credit (EIC): Are you Eligible?*, Publication No. 596, *www.irs.gov/pub/irs-pdf/p596.pdf*

JANG (2000), "Characteristics of Older Workers' Labor Market and Employment Policies in Korea", Korea Labor Institute, Seoul.

JOSEPH, M., D. FODEN and M. HUTSEBAUT (2002), "Active Strategies for Older Workers in the European Union", ETUI (European Trade Union Institute), Brussels.

KAREN, K, L. ADELMAN, A. CEBULLA and C. HEAVER (2002), *From Job Seekers to Job Keepers: Job Retention, Advancement and the Role of In-Work Support Programmes*, Research Report No. 170, Department for Work and Pensions, London.

KATZ, L. (1998), "Wages Subsidies for the Disadvantaged", in R. Freeman and P. Gottschalk (eds.), *Generating Jobs: How to Increase Demand for Less-Skilled Workers*, Russell Sage, New York.

KRAMARTZ, F. and T. PHILIPPON (2001), "The Impact of Differential Payroll Tax Subsidies on Minimum Wage Employment", *Journal of Publics Economics*, Vol. 82, No. 1, pp. 115-146.

LAFFARGUE, J-P (2000), "Effets et financements d'une réduction des charges sur les bas salaires", *Revue Économique*, Vol. 51, No. 3, pp.489-498.

LAROQUE, G. and B. SALANIE (2000), "Une décomposition du non-emploi en France", *Économie et Statistique*, Vol. 331, pp. 47-66.

LAROQUE, G. and B. SALANIE (2002), "Institution et emploi, les femmes et le marché du travail en France", Octobre, *www.crest.fr/pageperso/lma/laroque/mono01a.pdf*

LAZEAR, E. (1979), "Why Is There Mandatory Retirement?", *Journal of Political Economy*, Vol. 87, No. 6, pp. 1261-1284.

LIEBMAN, J. (1998), "The Impact of the Earned Income Tax Credit on Incentives and Income Distribution", *Tax Policy and the Economy*, Vol. 12, pp. 83-119.

van der LINDEN, B. (1997), "Effets des formations professionnelles et des aides à l'embauche : exploitation d'une enquête auprès d'employeurs belges", *Économie et Prévision*, Vol. 131, pp. 113-130.

LISE, J., S. SEITZ and J. SMITH (2003), "Equilibrium Policy Experiments and the Evaluation of Social Programs", IFAU Discussion Paper series, No. 758.

MARTIN, J.P and D. GRUBB (2001), "What Works and for Whom: a Review of OECD Countries' Experiences with Active Labour Market Policies", *Swedish Economic Policy Review*, Vol. 8, No. 2, pp. 9-56.

MARX I. (2001), "Job Subsidies and Cuts in Employers' Social Security Contributions: The Verdict of Empirical Evaluation Studies", *International Labour Review*, Vol. 140, No. 1, pp. 69-83.

MICHALOPOULOS, C., D. TATTRIE, C. MILLER, P.K. ROBINS, P. MORRIS, D. GYARMATI, C. REDCROSS, K. FOLEY and R. FORD (2002), *Making Work Pay: Final Report on the Self-Sufficiency Project for Long-Term Welfare Recipients*, SRDC, July.

MILLAR, J. (2001), "Work-related Activity Requirements and Labour Market Programmes for Lone Parents", in J. Millar and K. Rowlingson (eds.), *Lone Parents, Employment and Social Policy: Cross-National Comparisons*, The Policy Press, Bristol.

MINISTRY OF FINANCE, Belgium (2002), "Réforme fiscale: l'impôt des personnes physiques – Loi du 10 août 2001".

MINISTRY OF HEALTH AND SOCIAL AFFAIRS, Sweden (2001), "The Government's 11-point Programme for Better Health in Working Life", Fact Sheet on the Swedish Government's Budget Bill for 2002, Stockholm.

MÜHLAU, P. and W. SALVERDA (2000), "Effects of low-wage subsidies: the example of 'SPAK' in the Netherlands", in W. Salverda, B. Nolan and C. Lucifora (eds.), *Policy Measures for Low-Wage Employment in Europe*, Edward Elgar.

NEUMARK, D. and W. WASCHER (1997), "Do Minimum Wages Fight Poverty?", *NBER Working Paper*, No. 6127.

NEUMARK, D. and W. WASCHER (1998), "The Effect of Minimum Wages on the Distribution of Family Income: a Non-Parametric Analysis", *NBER Working Paper*, No. 6536.

NEUMARK, D. and W. WASCHER (1999), "A Cross National Analysis of The Effects of Minimum Wages on Youth Employment?", *NBER Working Paper*, No. 7299.

NEUMARK, D. and W. WASCHER (2000), "Using the EITC to Help Poor Families: New Evidence and a Comparison with the Minimum Wage", *NBER Working Paper*, No. 7599.

OECD (1998), *OECD Employment Outlook*, Paris.

OECD (2000), *Pushing Ahead with Reforms in Korea: Labour Market Policies and Safety Nets*, Paris.

OECD (2001a), *OECD Employment Outlook*, Paris.

OECD (2001b), *Society at a Glance: OECD Social Indicators*, Paris.

OECD (2002a), *Benefits and Wage: OECD Indicators*, Paris

OECD (2002b), *Taxing Wages*, Paris.

OECD (2002c), "Latest Developments in Making Work Pay Policies", Joint policy forum with the working party on tax policy analysis and tax statistic, October, Paris.

OECD (2002d), *Babies and Bosses – Reconciling Work and Family Life (Vol. 1): Australia, Denmark and the Netherlands*, Paris.

OECD (2002e), "Participative Disability Policies for the Working-age Population: Toward a Coherent Policy Mix", Working Party on Social Policy, DEELSA/ELSA/WP1(2002)1, April, Paris.

OECD (2002f), *OECD Employment Outlook*, Paris.

OECD (2002g), *Society at a Glance: OECD Social Indicators*, Paris.

OECD (2003a), *Transforming Disability into Ability: Policies to Promote Work and Income Security for Disabled People*, Paris.

OECD (2003b), *Society at a Glance: OECD Social Indicators*, Paris.

OECD (2003c), "Policies for an Ageing Society: Recent Measures and Areas for Further Reform", *Economics Department Working Paper*, Paris, forthcoming.

OECD (2003d), *Ageing and Employment Policies, Belgium*, OECD, Paris.

ONDRICH, J., C.K. SPEISS and Q.YANG (1996), "Barefoot and in a German Kitchen: Federal Parental Leave and Benefit Policy and the Return to Work after Childbirth in Germany", *Journal of Population Economics*, Vol. 9, No. 3, pp. 247-266.

ONDRICH J., C.K. SPEISS and Q.YANG (2002), "The Effect of Maternity Leave on Women's Pay in Germany 1984-1994", *DIW Discussion Papers*, No. 298, Berlin.

ONDRICH, J., R. PISCHNER, C.K. SPEISS and G. WAGNER (1999), "Labor Force Status Before and After Childbirth in Germany 1984-1996", *faculty.maxwell.syr.edu/jondrich/Papers%20OnLine/lablorce.pdf*

van OURS, J. (2002), "The Locking-in Effect of Subsidized Jobs", *IZA Discussion Paper*, No. 527, Germany.

van POLANEN PETEL, V., T. HU, J. de KONING and C. van der VEEN (1999), *Werkgelegenheidseffecten van de SPAK en VLW*.

PYLKKÄNEN, E. and N. SMITH (2003), "Career Interruptions due to Parental Leave: A Comparative Study of Denmark and Sweden", *Social, Employment and Migration Working Papers*, No.1, OECD, Paris.

RHUM, C. (1998), "The Economic Consequences of Parental Leaves Mandates: Lessons From Europe", *The Quarterly Journal of Economics*, Vol. 113, No. 1, pp. 285-317.

RONSEN, M. and M. SUNDSTÖM (2002), "Family Policy and After-birth Employment among New Mothers – a comparison of Finland, Norway and Sweden", *European Journal of Population*, Vol. 18, No. 2, pp. 121-152.

SIANESI, B. (2002), "Differential Effects of Swedish Active Labour Market Programmes for Unemployed Adults During the 1900s", *IFAU Working Paper*, No. 2002:5.

SIMON, M.-O. (1999), "L'allocation parentale d'éducation, Une parenthèse de trois ans... ou plus", CREDOC *Consommation et Modes de Vie*, No. 136, June.

SNEESSENS, H. and F. SHADMAN (2000), "Analyse macroéconomique des effets des réductions ciblées des charges sociales", *Revue Belge de Sécurité Sociale*, Vol. 3, pp. 613-630.

SPF (2001) – Service Public Fédéral Sécurité Sociale, "Extrait de l'aperçu de la sécurité sociale en Belgique, titre II. Le régime des travailleurs salariés", *http://socialsecurity.fgov.be/apercu/2001/partiel-t2.pdf*

TAYLOR, P. (2001), "Analysis of Ways to Improve Employment Opportunities for Older Workers: Report to the European Commission", University of Cambridge, United Kingdom.

UK LOW PAY COMMISSION (2001), *The National Minimum Wage, Making a Difference*, Third Report (Vol. 1 & 2) of the Low Pay Commission, Report Summary.

WALDFOGEL, J., S. DANZIGER, S. DANZIGER and K. SEEFELDT (2001), "Welfare Reform and Lone Mother's Employment in the US", in J. Millar and K. Rowlingson (eds.), *Lone Parents, Employment and Social Policy: Cross-National Comparisons*, The Policy Press, Bristol.

Chapter 4

Benefits and Employment, Friend or Foe? Interactions Between Passive and Active Social Programmes

> *In many countries, the share of the working-age population receiving income-replacement benefits continued to increase in the 1990s, particularly as regards old-age, disability, lone-parent and social assistance benefits. In some countries, most of the people who are neither employed nor studying receive an income-replacement benefit. To what extent can "activation" strategies help reduce benefit dependency? How can key elements of these strategies, such as intensive job counselling and benefit sanctions for refusal of a suitable job, be applied to groups traditionally on the margins of the labour market? And when reliance on one benefit is reduced, do people transfer to other types of benefits or do they really find jobs?*

Introduction	172
Main findings	172
1. Trends in benefit dependency	174
2. The meaning and measurement of the "active" content of policy	192
3. Outcomes from "active" policies	201
Concluding remarks	214
Annex 1. Definition and measurement of benefit recipiency rates	221
Annex 2. How long adjustment lags arise from interaction and feedback	230
Bibliography	232

Introduction

While Chapter 3 focuses mainly on financial incentives to find work or stay in employment, this chapter examines a complementary approach involving job-search requirements and other "activation" policies. Many countries expect the short-term unemployed to re-enter work mainly through self-directed job search, but other activation strategies are particularly important for the disadvantaged job-seekers identified in Chapter 1.

The focus of activation strategies has traditionally been on unemployment beneficiaries. However, in view of the trend rise in the number of recipients of other social security benefits, many countries have tried to extend activation strategies to population groups which traditionally had not been considered unemployed. Activation measures increasingly require lone-parent and social assistance beneficiaries to be available for work.[1] Countries with large numbers of disability beneficiaries have tried using active labour market policies to get some of them into work as well.

This chapter focuses particular attention on the concept of benefit dependency rates, i.e. the proportion of people receiving an income-replacement benefit,[2] and measures that attempt to get benefit recipients into work. The main questions examined are:

- How have patterns of benefit dependency varied across countries and over time? (Section 1).
- What are "activation" strategies? (Section 2).
- To what extent do activation strategies move people out of benefit dependency into market work? Are reduced numbers in the target group (mainly unemployment, lone parent and social assistance beneficiaries) offset by increases in the numbers on other benefits (e.g. early retirement or disability benefits)? How do these strategies influence future employment and earnings? (Section 3).

Main findings

- *In some countries, most non-employed people of working age receive an income-replacement benefit.* Some countries have now reached a position where most of the working-age population that is neither employed nor participating in education has an income-replacement benefit. In this situation, it will be difficult to increase employment greatly without also reducing benefit dependency.

- *An upward trend in benefit dependency has been recorded in most countries.* On average, among the OECD countries for which data are available, the proportion of people of working age receiving a social protection benefit rose quite sharply in the 1980s, and more slowly in the 1990s. Experiences remain varied, with little sign of convergence in benefit dependency rates within Europe or across OECD countries.

- *Activation policies can move people out of benefit dependency.* Activation strategies that require beneficiaries to make intensive efforts to prepare and search for work can forestall and reverse growth in benefit dependency rates. In the 1990s, several countries experienced declines in the number of recipients of benefits targeted by activation policies. These declines seem to be mainly structural, rather than limited to the period of cyclical upswing.

- *Benefit eligibility criteria are important for activation.* Early retirement benefits, and often disability benefits and sometimes lone-parent benefits, do not require beneficiaries to be available for work as a condition for benefit receipt. In this case it is still possible to provide a range of employment services, and require participation in some work-related activities such as interviews where job opportunities are discussed and employment services offered. However, extensive requirements to participate in work-related activities, without requirements to take up work when it is available, would be incoherent. As a rule, claimants who are thought to be able to work should be subject to a clear availability-for-work requirement.

- *Workfare and "training-fare" matter.* Compulsory participation in employment and training programmes is often an important feature in activation strategies, especially in countries where benefit replacement rates are high. It can limit the maximum duration of "passive" benefit receipt, while maintaining the income of individuals and families that comply with the conditions.

- *There is a risk of substitution between benefits.* Declines in the number of recipients of benefits targeted by an activation strategy may be offset by increases in the number of recipients of other benefits. While many examples of such substitution exist, there are also mechanisms that work in the other direction. For example, success in reducing unemployment makes it easier to tighten entry criteria for early-retirement and disability benefits. Although declines in the number of recipients of benefits targeted by activation strategies have been offset by higher recipiency of other, inactive, benefits in specific cases, there is no clear evidence that this occurs systematically.

- *Activation policies may have an impact on employment.* Policies which tighten benefit eligibility while also applying activation principles may help to reduce beneficiary numbers and raise employment. However, some people who move off benefits do not enter work. This highlights the importance of the focus on employment and raising worker productivity, and keeping benefits generous enough to discourage labour market withdrawal as a response to activation measures. The Nordic countries, with a strong emphasis on active policy, have relatively high employment rates as well as generous benefits.

- *Activation strategies can reduce poverty rates.* In some cases, policies which accelerate exit from unemployment also result in lower average earnings on entry to employment. However, even weak earnings and career prospects may remain preferable to the erosion of work skills that arises from prolonged non-employment, and high employment rates reduce poverty. Moreover, evaluations also suggest that intensive employment counselling can increase earnings. Experience in some European countries suggests that activation strategies are consistent with low poverty rates, and in the United States, poverty indicators and other indicators of well-being for lone parents and their children have tended to improve during the process of welfare reform.

- *Benefit entitlements have a long-lasting impact, and activation strategies need to recognise this.* According to historical examples, growth in the number of beneficiaries, following the creation of new or significantly more generous benefits, is a relatively long-lasting process. The full impact of activation strategies in reversing beneficiary growth probably develops on a similar long time-scale.

● *Activation policies cannot solve all labour market problems.* The impact of activation strategies is greatest where labour markets function well. Without some favourable background conditions that help in obtaining a significant impact, activation strategies may lose political support.

1. Trends in benefit dependency

Not all people who receive social protection benefits can or should work. Benefit recipients are a very heterogeneous group. Some of them may want to work, or can be "activated", and others are likely to stay out of the labour market. In order to gauge the potential labour supply which might be mobilised through benefit entitlement and activation policies, this section examines patterns in the dependency rate, *i.e.* the proportion of people of working-age who receive a public income-replacement benefit. Eight main categories of social protection benefits are distinguished, namely old-age, survivors (widows and orphans), sickness, disability, maternity and home parenting, care (a benefit paid to people who care for another invalid person) and labour market leave (sabbatical leave from work for a limited time but without other conditions), unemployment, and lone-parent and non-categorical social assistance. The data on benefit dependency presented here are further described in Annex 1.

The primary objective of these benefits is to safeguard the welfare of people who are temporarily or permanently unable to work. However, objectives often go beyond the provision of a minimum income. They include the provision of benefits related to former earnings; compensation for employer liability, in the case of industrial injury benefits; allowing people to withdraw from the labour market in order to care for children or other dependants, in the case of parental benefits; and facilitating better job matches and macroeconomic stabilisation in the case of short-term unemployment insurance (UI) benefits. Promotion of part-time, temporary or seasonal work on a salaried basis rather than an informal basis may be an additional objective.

A. Analysis of benefit recipiency rates

Benefit dependency varies significantly across countries

As shown in Table 4.1, there is considerable cross-country variation in benefit dependency rates among the working-age population (defined as the population aged from 15 to 64) across the 16 countries for which estimates have been made. In 1999, this benefit dependency rate ranged from 11% in Japan and Spain to 23% or 24% in Belgium and France, and 38% in Slovak Republic. Table 4.A1.1 shows the breakdown of these figures by benefit category. The largest categories in 1999 were disability (4.6% of the population of working age), unemployment (4.1%), and old age (3.6%, referring to benefits paid to people aged under 65). Lone-parent and non-categorical social assistance (2.4%), sickness (2.0%), and survivors (1.3%) each had half or a third as many beneficiaries as the first three large categories. The population shares relying on maternity and parental benefits (0.8%), and care and labour market leave benefits (0.2%) were much smaller. Although the proportions receiving unemployment and disability benefits vary considerably, all countries have significant numbers in these categories, confirming that these are two core types of benefit. The distribution of the remaining benefit dependency across benefit categories varies greatly from one country to another. In recent years, old-age benefits have been the most variable category, with recipiency rates below 1% in three countries and above 7% in

Table 4.1 **Employment rates and benefit dependency rates in the working-age population,**[a] **1980 to 1999**

Percentages

	Employment rates (full-time equivalent)[b]			Benefit dependency rates[c]			No benefit, no work		
	1980	1990	1999	1980	1990	1999	1980	1990	1999
Australia	57.5	57.9	56.4	13.0	13.7	17.5	29.5	28.4	26.1
Austria	60.2	61.8	64.0	15.5	18.0	21.5	24.3	20.2	14.5
Belgium	53.8	50.7	52.9	17.4	24.4	23.6	28.8	24.9	23.5
Canada	60.2	63.2	62.6	13.4	19.9	18.0	26.4	16.9	19.3
Denmark	65.7	67.3	69.7	20.1	23.2	23.1	14.1	9.5	7.2
France	60.8	56.3	55.5	13.9	20.2	24.2	25.3	23.5	20.4
Germany	59.7	59.5	58.9	15.2	18.1	22.4	25.0	22.4	18.8
Ireland	52.4	49.3	56.3	12.4	18.9	19.3	35.2	31.8	24.4
Japan	61.6	62.0	60.6	8.8	10.0	11.4	29.6	28.0	28.0
Netherlands	48.5	51.1	58.2	15.9	19.9	17.8	35.6	29.0	24.0
New Zealand	57.9	58.9	59.9	6.6	15.6	16.8	35.5	25.4	23.2
Slovak Republic	. .	. .	57.7	19.6	24.8	38.2	. .	. .	4.2
Spain	49.4	48.5	51.7	8.3	12.3	11.2	42.3	39.2	37.1
Sweden	68.7	72.0	66.2	16.1	17.0	20.0	15.2	11.0	13.8
United Kingdom	62.2	62.4	60.7	15.2	18.5	18.9	22.7	19.1	20.4
United States	60.0	65.2	67.0	16.8	15.6	13.7	23.2	19.2	19.3
Averages for:									
EU countries above	58.1	57.9	59.4	15.0	19.1	20.2	26.9	23.1	20.4
All countries above[d]	**58.6**	**59.1**	**60.0**	**13.9**	**17.7**	**18.6**	**27.5**	**23.2**	**21.3**

a) Population aged 15 to 64. Includes estimates for age 15 in countries where the labour force survey relates to ages 16 to 64.
b) Employment is measured in full-time equivalents. The distribution of hours worked for all employed persons is used to estimate the ratio of the average weekly hours of part-time workers, defined as those working less than 30 usual hours per week, and full-time workers. This ratio is applied to convert part-time employment to a full-time equivalent basis. In Austria and Sweden, the part-time employment share based on the national definition is used for 1980 and 1990. In Belgium, Denmark, France, Germany, Netherlands, Spain and the United Kingdom, the part-time employment share in 1980 is assumed to be the same as in 1983. For Austria, Belgium, Denmark and the United Kingdom, employment among persons of working age in 1980 (and also 1990 for Austria) was estimated by splicing with data for employment of all ages.
c) See text and Annex 1 for definitions.
d) Except Slovak Republic.
Source: For benefit dependency rates, NEI-SZW database (see Annex 1 for details), partially revised and augmented by OECD; for employment, OECD database on Labour Force Statistics. .

four others, reflecting large variations in the provision of early retirement benefits as well as a standard retirement age below 65 in some countries.

These aggregate benefit dependency rates may be compared with rates of employment and participation in education, also measured on a full-time equivalent basis (Chart 4.1) (see Box 4.1 for a discussion of technical issues involved in this comparison). In the EU countries for which data are available, except the Netherlands and Spain, the majority of people of working age who are not employed (net of sickness and related absence from work), and are not participating in education, are receiving a benefit. Benefit dependency among people of working age is about one-third of employment (net of sickness and related absence) in six EU countries, but higher in Belgium, France, Germany and Slovak Republic. This ratio is about one-fifth in Spain, Japan and the United States, and is at intermediate levels in Australia, Canada and New Zealand.

Chart 4.2 shows, on the one hand, full-time equivalent rates of participation in either employment or education, and, on the other hand, rates of benefit dependency. There is

4. BENEFITS AND EMPLOYMENT, FRIEND OR FOE? INTERACTIONS BETWEEN PASSIVE AND ACTIVE SOCIAL PROGRAMMES

Chart 4.1. **In some countries, most non-employed adults receive a benefit**
Percentages of working-age population,[a] 1999

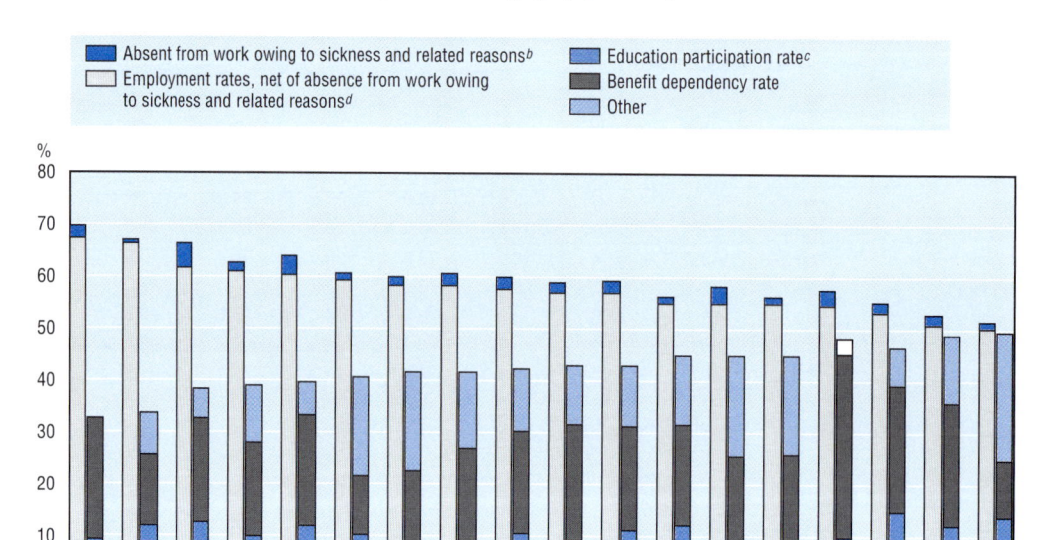

Legend:
- Absent from work owing to sickness and related reasons[b]
- Employment rates, net of absence from work owing to sickness and related reasons[d]
- Education participation rate[c]
- Benefit dependency rate
- Other

Note: Countries are ordered by decreasing employment rate net of absence from work owing to sickness and related reasons. All variables are measured in full-time equivalents. Full-time employed students are counted as employed, not students.

a) Population aged 15 to 64. Includes estimates for age 15 in countries where the labour force survey relates to ages 16 to 64. Armed forces and the institutional population are excluded from both employment and population in certain countries.

b) For EU countries, share of the working-age population that is employed, but absent from work because of sickness/disablility, maternity, short-time working (slack work) and bad weather reasons during the survey reference week, with part-week absences are converted to full-time equivalents using a weight of 0.5. For Australia, data based on average daily absence from work on sick leave in September 1999 (ABS data cited at www.injurynet.com.au/resource/Article_Absence.pdf). For Canada, data based on total workdays lost in 2000 (Labour Force Survey data cited at www.hrmguide.net/canada/general.absences_2001.htm). For Japan, Secretariat estimate based on comparative recipiency of public sickness benefits. For the United States, data based on absence from work because of illlness/iInjury/medical problems, maternity/paternity leave or bad weather reasons (Secretariat estimates based on CPS data).

c) The incidence of student status within the working-age population is calculated on a full-time equivalent basis, using a weight of one for students who are inactive in the labour market, 0.5 for those who are unemployed or working part-time, and zero for those who are working full-time. 15-year-olds are assumed to be students where relevant (see note a).

d) The distribution of hours worked for all employed persons is used to estimate the ratio of the average weekly hours of part-time workers, defined as those working less than 30 usual hours per week, to those of full-time workers. This ratio is applied to convert part-time employment to a full-time equivalent basis.

e) For Slovak Republic, "other" is negative (shown in white) and this part of the bar represents benefit dependency double-counted with one of the other variables.

Source: For benefit dependency rates, NEI-SZW database, partially revised and augmented by OECD (see text for details); for employment and population, OECD database on Labour Force Statistics; for data on absence for sickness and other reasons, European Community Labour Force Survey data and sources as cited in note b); for education participation rates, Secretariat database on labour market status by educational participation (*Employment Outlook 2002*, Chapter 1, provides some further tabulations from this database).

not a simple correlation between employment and student participation rates and benefit dependency rates, but rather two relationships. The sum of employment, student participation and benefit dependency rates as measured here lies below 100%, except in the Slovak Republic.[3] Unless income-replacement benefits are often paid to those who are

Chart 4.2. **Employment and benefit dependency: a complex link**
Percentages of working-age population, 1999

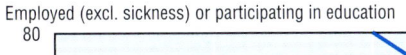

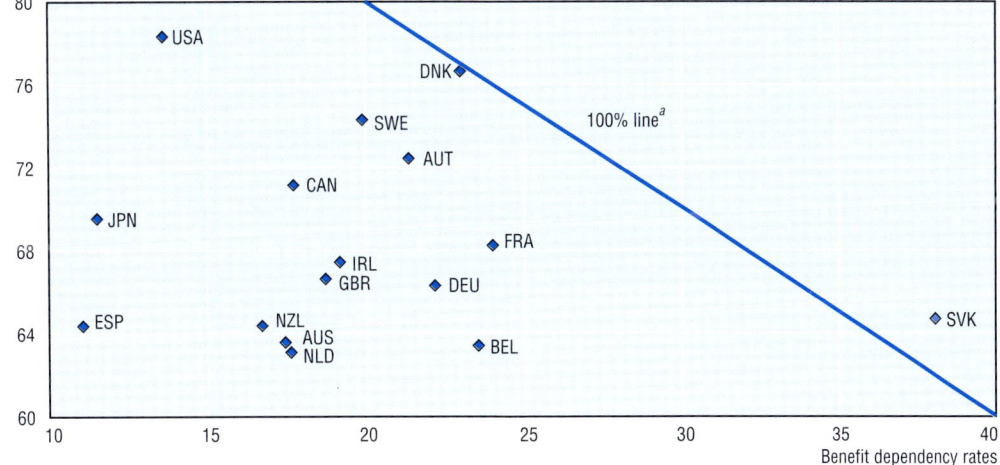

a) The 100% line shows points where employment (excluding absences due to sickness, maternity and slack work), student participation, and benefit dependency on a full-time equivalent basis sum to 100% of the working-age population.

Source: See Chart 4.1.

studying or in employment, the countries where the total is close to 100% – such as Austria, Denmark, France, Sweden and the United States – will tend to face a negative trade-off between employment rates and levels of benefit dependency. On the other hand, if we look at countries with varying levels of the "residual" category not in employment, education or benefit receipt – comparing Spain or the Netherlands with France or Sweden, for example – there is no negative relationship between employment and benefit dependency.

Though data are not available, it is likely that patterns in the other Nordic countries (Finland and Norway) are similar to those in Denmark and Sweden. Likewise, patterns in Greece and Italy are likely to be similar to those in Spain (this is less true for Portugal which has a relatively high employment rate). Turkey, Korea and Mexico no doubt have low benefit dependency rates, which are combined with low employment rates in Turkey and intermediate rates in Korea and Mexico.

The residual category mainly represents people who depend on the income of a spouse or other family members, *i.e.* housewives and young adults. In Japan, the Netherlands and the United Kingdom, female part-time employment is particularly common, and insofar as this is rarely combined with any benefit, this contributes to a relatively high level of the residual. In Spain and probably some other Southern European countries, the residual is particularly large. This may partly reflect underreporting of employment.[4] However, the most important factor is probably a pattern of high and prolonged dependency on the incomes of other family or household members.[5]

This cross-country comparison suggests that policies to increase employment rates can consist of attempts at both i) bringing those adults who can work, but do not receive benefits, into salaried employment – implying a move towards the top right in Chart 4.2 – and ii) shifting benefit dependants into employment – implying a move towards the top left. The mix between these two policy thrusts needs to vary between countries depending on the starting position.

Box 4.1. **Aggregate benefit dependency rates compared with employment and education participation**

Charts 4.1 and 4.2 compare 1999 rates of employment and education participation with rates of benefit dependency. Several definitional features in these charts merit attention:

First, the employment rates relate to ages 15 to 64 and do not include 7.5% of total employment in Japan and 3% in the United States, which are accounted for by people aged 65 and over.

Second, the data are on a full-time equivalent basis. Average hours usually worked by part-time workers are relatively low (0.40 to 0.42 of full-time hours) in Denmark, the Netherlands and the United Kingdom and relatively high (0.50) in Austria and France.

Third, an attempt has been made to avoid double-counting of employees who are temporarily absent from work. To ensure that these employees are not counted in both the employment total as well as the beneficiary total, employment is calculated net of people who were absent from work owing to sickness, maternity and slack work (those absent for other reasons, e.g. holiday, are still included). This deduction ranges from 1% of employment in the United States up to nearly 6% in Sweden, reflecting the high sickness rates in the latter country.

Fourth, labour force surveys provide information on student status, but do not directly record whether individuals are studying full-time or part-time (e.g. apprentices). To reduce double-counting, students who are also unemployed or part-time employed are given a weight of 0.5, and students who are working full-time are given a weight of zero.

Fifth, the definition of benefit dependency excludes people with student grants, participants in full-time active labour market (training and employment) programmes, and benefits designed to supplement income from full-time work.

Together, these measurement principles should help prevent individuals being counted more than once among the three main categories, i.e. employment, education and benefit dependency. However, some exceptions are possible. In particular, individuals with benefit only count for less than one full-time equivalent in the total for benefit dependency if their benefit is paid at less than the normal rate. Certain benefits – widows' pensions, workers' injury pensions (which are often paid for partial disability), and even ordinary retirement pensions (which are included in this database when paid to people aged under 65) – may not be reduced when the beneficiary works. Most other benefits, such as ordinary disability and unemployment benefits, are not affected by part-time work when earnings and hours remain below some threshold. Therefore, people who are counted as a full-time beneficiary may also be working part-time, and in some cases even full-time. This type of double counting may explain the low level of the residual shown in Charts 4.1 and 4.2 for Denmark (0.3%).

More generally, the measurement instruments used for Charts 4.1 and 4.2 are subject to error. For example in labour force surveys, people with income-replacement benefits may describe themselves as students, and in the administrative data for benefit dependency some benefits may be accidentally omitted, or people receiving two benefits may be counted twice because there are no data to indicate that such double-counting is present. Little evidence about the size of these potential errors is available.

4. BENEFITS AND EMPLOYMENT, FRIEND OR FOE? INTERACTIONS BETWEEN PASSIVE AND ACTIVE SOCIAL PROGRAMMES

Benefit dependency has followed an upward trend

Chart 4.3 shows a near-universal rise in the aggregate benefit dependency rate among the population of working age between 1980 and 1990, with Japan and the United States being the only exceptions.[6] In the 1990s, growth in average benefit dependency rates nearly ceased. However, the standard deviation of benefit dependency rates across countries increased slightly, as dependency rates in Slovak Republic increased while those in Spain and the United States, two of the countries with lowest rates in 1990, decreased. Thus, there is little evidence of international convergence in patterns either across the OECD as a whole or within Europe.

Some countries show little cyclical movement in aggregate benefit dependency rates while in others cyclical movements are more pronounced – although more in the 1990s than in the 1980s. Most of the cyclical movement is accounted for by unemployment benefits. Cyclical movements in recipiency of lone-parent and non-categorical social assistance benefits are large in only a few countries. Average disability benefit recipiency rose relatively rapidly from 1990 to 1994 and then stabilised, suggesting a degree of cyclicality in these benefits, although this is not very prominent in Chart 4.3. Despite some cyclical movements in some of the components, the variation in aggregate recipiency rates which can be seen when comparing two "peak" years (*e.g.* 1990 with 1980, or 1999 with 1990) seems to be relatively long-term in nature. Recent trends do not suggest any particular tendency for countries that experienced reductions in benefit recipiency in the 1990s to experience greater increases in the current slowdown.

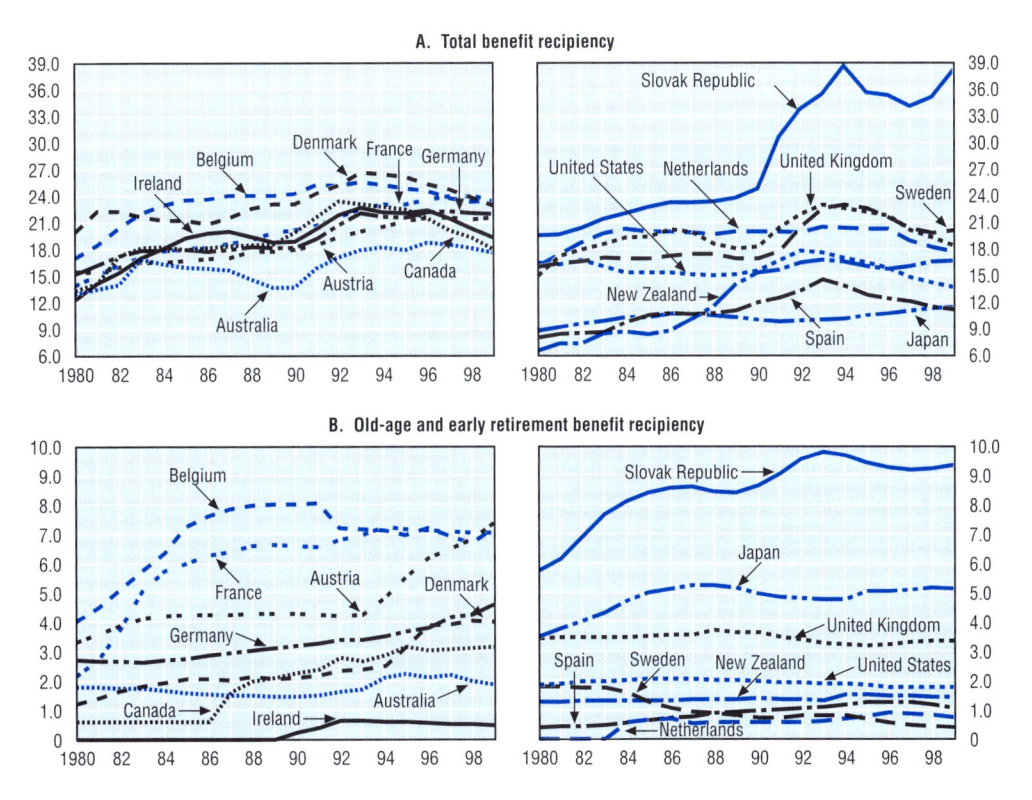

Chart 4.3. **Trends in benefit recipiency**
Percentage of the working-age population, 1980-1999

A. Total benefit recipiency

B. Old-age and early retirement benefit recipiency

Chart 4.3. **Trends in benefit recipiency** *(cont.)*
Percentage of the working-age population, 1980-1999

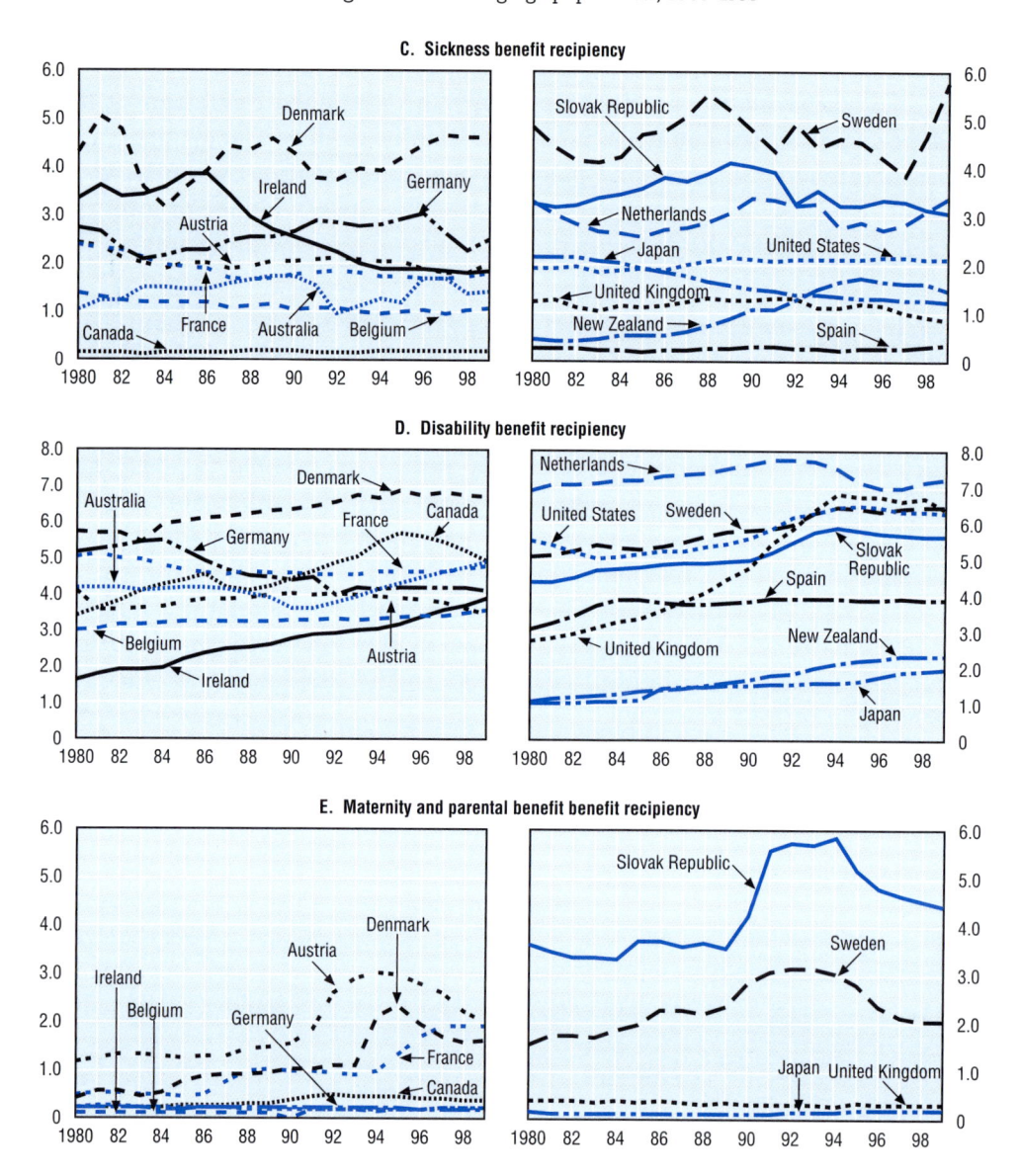

C. Sickness benefit recipiency

D. Disability benefit recipiency

E. Maternity and parental benefit benefit recipiency

Average recipiency of most types of benefit included in this database increased between 1980 and 1999 – the exceptions are survivors' benefits (for widows and orphans) where recipiency declined quite significantly and sickness benefits where there was no average change. It also seems that in the 1990s, the trend rise for unemployment benefits may have been stopped or reversed:

- Recipiency of *old-age* benefits in the working-age population has increased since 1980 in many countries. In the deep recession of the early 1980s a number of countries greatly expanded formal early retirement arrangements. In the 1990s, despite another recession, the use of formal early retirement benefits declined in some countries.[7]

Chart 4.3. **Trends in benefit recipiency** (cont.)
Percentage of the working-age population, 1980-1999

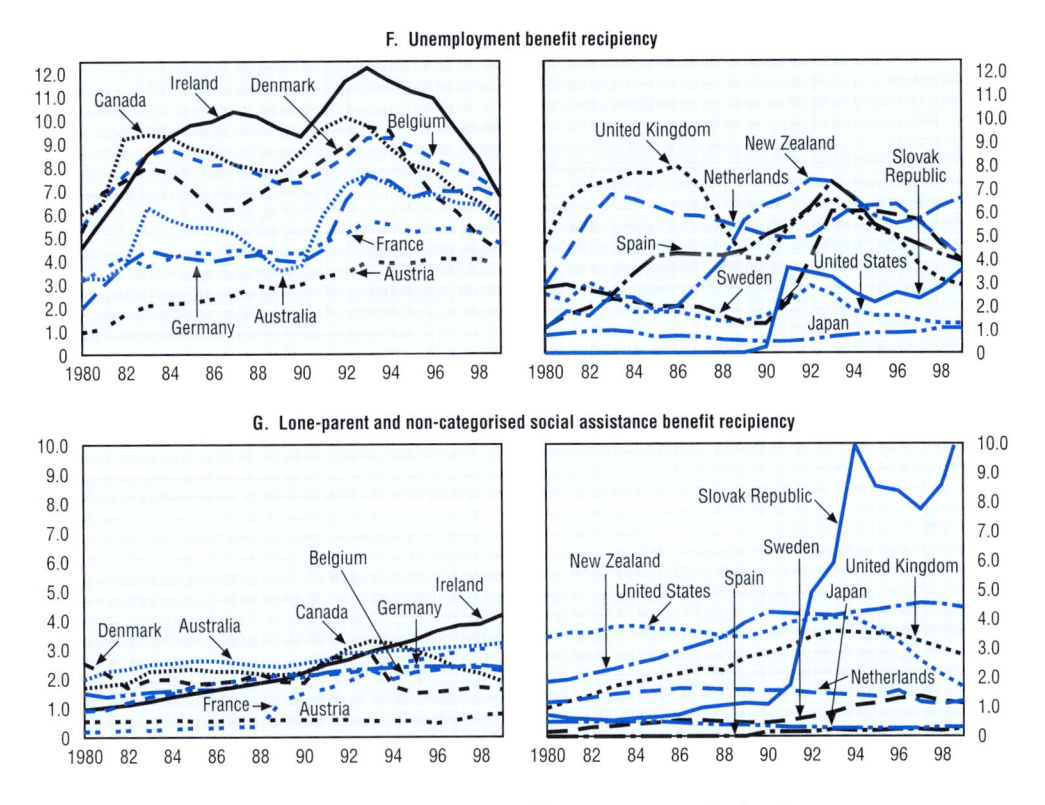

F. Unemployment benefit recipiency

G. Lone-parent and non-categorised social assistance benefit recipiency

Source: NEI-SZW database, partially revised and augmented by OECD. See text for details.

- Recipiency of *survivors'* benefits declined in most countries. Probable reasons are: *a)* trends to later marriage and increased life expectancy, which reduce the incidence of widowhood among the population of working age; *b)* increasing employment rates among widows which reduced the demand for assistance-type widows' benefits; *c)* in some OECD countries where female employment is considered the norm, entitlements to a pension on grounds of widowhood have almost been eliminated; and *d)* with growing benefit dependency rates, the proportion of widow pensioners that are also receiving a disability or old-age pension has increased in some countries, and these pensioners have been allocated to the latter category of benefit (see Annex 1).

- Recipiency of *sickness* benefits was on average unchanged over the period. A number of countries sharply increased incentives for employers to monitor sickness absence, by obliging employers to pay benefits for the first three weeks to six months of a spell.[8]

- There was often some upwards trend in *disability* benefit recipiency, with relatively large rises in Canada, Ireland, Sweden and the United Kingdom.[9] Numbers with war disability pensions and pensions from workers' injury insurance often declined, so the aggregates shown here partly mask the extent of the rise in recipiency of the main contributory and non-contributory disability benefits.

- Average recipiency rates for *maternity and parental* benefits increased greatly, although from a low base except in the case of Slovak Republic. This increase mainly reflects entitlements to relatively long-term parental benefits in Austria, Denmark, France and Sweden. In the three countries with *care* benefits, recipiency has risen sharply, recently reaching 1% of the working-age population in the United Kingdom. *Labour market leave* benefits have existed only in Belgium, where they have declined in recent years, and Denmark where they were nearly eliminated by 1999.[10]

- Recipiency rates for *unemployment* benefits, in this sample of countries, increased sharply in the 1980s. Recessionary rises in unemployment benefit recipiency in the early 1990s were as sharp as in the early 1980s, but falls during latter 1990s were often far stronger. Over the last cycle from 1990 to 1999, national experiences were very variable. Declines in some countries (Canada, Denmark, Ireland, Netherlands, Spain, and the United Kingdom) were at least as large as rises in others (Australia, Austria, France, Germany, Japan, Slovak Republic and Sweden), so that by 2000 and 2001 average recipiency in this category was probably at its lowest level since 1982.

- Recipiency rates for *lone-parent and non-categorical social assistance* benefits on average have more than doubled since 1980, but in 1999 they remained lower than rates for disability and unemployment benefits. Growth in lone-parent populations has been a major cause of the increase. The highest rates arise where lone-parent recipiency is high (*e.g.* in Ireland and New Zealand) and/or where disabled and unemployed assistance beneficiaries were not statistically identified and reallocated to those social risk categories (*e.g.* France and Slovak Republic).

Over the longer run, benefit dependency has been shaped by changes in benefit entitlements on the one hand, and the adoption of activation strategies on the other.[11] Although stabilisation or retrenchment in benefit systems became a common objective as from the 1980s, direct cuts in replacement rates and benefit duration have been few and limited (see Box 4.2).[12] In relation to disability benefits, many countries made administration stricter and this has been accompanied by a fall in inflows to disability benefit schemes since 1990 in the majority of countries for which data are available (OECD, 2003), although recipiency rates themselves have not so often fallen.[13] Activation strategies, which in relation to unemployment and social assistance benefits were widely adopted at least in mild forms in the 1990s, are discussed further in Section 2 below.

B. Long adjustment lags to policy changes

Major changes in beneficiary numbers involve long-term and interlinked changes in the expectations and behaviour of recipients, benefit administrations and in some cases, employers. An examination of adjustment processes for beneficiary numbers (Boxes 4.3 to 4.5) shows long lags which suggests that much of the growth in beneficiary numbers has been due to induced growth in the eligible population rather than growth in the "take-up" of the benefit among people already qualified for it – insofar as such a distinction can be made – or external macroeconomic factors. This has important implications for analysis and policy:

- Methods commonly used for estimating the impact of policies, based mainly upon short-run changes observed in microeconomic data or the outcome of an experiment that affects only a small "treatment" group of workers, do not tell the full story. Such microeconomic estimates of policy impact provide some insights, but they cannot reliably capture the mechanisms of learning,[14] investments in different lifestyles, and

Box 4.2. **Trends in entitlements for unemployment and disability benefits**

The OECD's summary measure of unemployment benefit entitlements (Chart 4.4) suggests that most OECD countries increased unemployment benefit entitlements between 1961 and 1981. After this, through to 1991, there was a tendency towards stabilisation of entitlements. Chart 4.4 shows some further rises in entitlements since 1991 in a few countries. Some factors involved were:

First, in three cases (Greece, Italy and Portugal), unemployment benefits were relatively little developed until the late 1980s (early 1980s, in the case of Portugal), and the increases in entitlements can be interpreted in terms of convergence towards the norms for other EU countries.[a]

Second, in Denmark, maximum UI duration increased from 2.5 years to seven years starting in 1994: it was then reduced in stages to reach four years in 2000. However, in 1994 the possibility of renewing benefit entitlement through six months' participation in a labour market programme was abolished and benefit in the last three years of the entitlement period (as from 2000, this starts at the end of the first year of benefit) was made conditional on continuous participation in work and/or training programmes. If only the "passive" period of unemployment benefit receipt were taken into account, Denmark's benefit system, where the maximum duration of passive benefits is one year would appear less generous than Sweden's (see Box 4.7 for recent developments in Sweden), in contrast with the outcome shown in Chart 4.4.

Third, in Switzerland, legislation after 1991 to increase the maximum UI duration was a response to a very sharp rise in the actual duration of unemployment. Towards the end of the decade, unemployment fell back sharply and in 2001 (not shown in the chart) maximum UI duration for most workers was cut from 24 to 18 months.

Although high unemployment rates in the 1980s and early 1990s sometimes encouraged increases in entitlements to unemployment and early retirement benefits, it seems unlikely that rising recipiency rates have motivated increases in disability benefit replacement rates (benefit durations in this case have always been indefinite). Relatively little summary evidence is available on this point. Blondal and Pearson (1995) estimated that between 1974 and 1993 the simple EC average of replacement rates in disability benefit programmes increased slightly, from the mid-40s to the upper 40s in percentage terms, but also estimated that the 1981 rate for the Scandinavian countries, Austria and Switzerland was 66% and by 1993 this had fallen to 61%.[b] OECD (2003) notes that few countries have changed the disability benefit entitlement formula since about 1990. Therefore, it seems that increases in replacement rates for disability benefits had mainly stopped as early as 1980, but relatively few large decreases have been implemented subsequently.

a) In Portugal, due to increases in UI entitlements and the recent introduction of a minimum income scheme, the index shown in Chart 4.4 has risen above the OECD average level.
b) Also, in the Netherlands, one of the first OECD countries to experience substantial growth in disability benefit recipiency rates, net replacement rates were reduced on two occasions (see note 24 below). Many countries did take restrictive measures in relation to disability benefits in terms of the type of work which the person can do, medical assessment procedures, and making benefit entitlement in principle temporary (OECD, 2003, p. 72).

feedbacks between different actors (see Annex 2) that seem to be important in determining long-run outcomes.

- Initial rises in the number of recipients of a new benefit reflect its effectiveness in covering the population that was originally targeted by the benefit. However, as rises continue, they

4. BENEFITS AND EMPLOYMENT, FRIEND OR FOE? INTERACTIONS BETWEEN PASSIVE AND ACTIVE SOCIAL PROGRAMMES

Chart 4.4. Index of unemployment benefit entitlements[a]

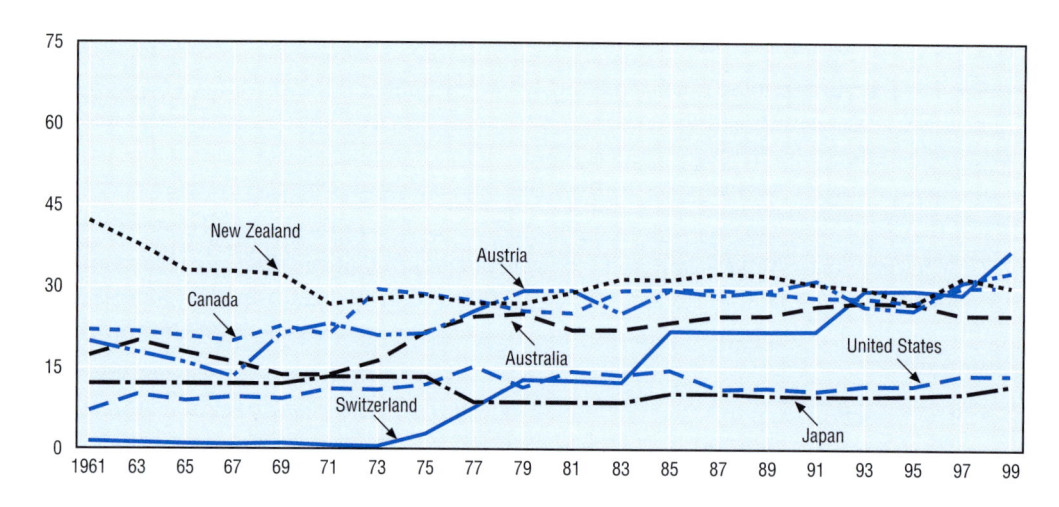

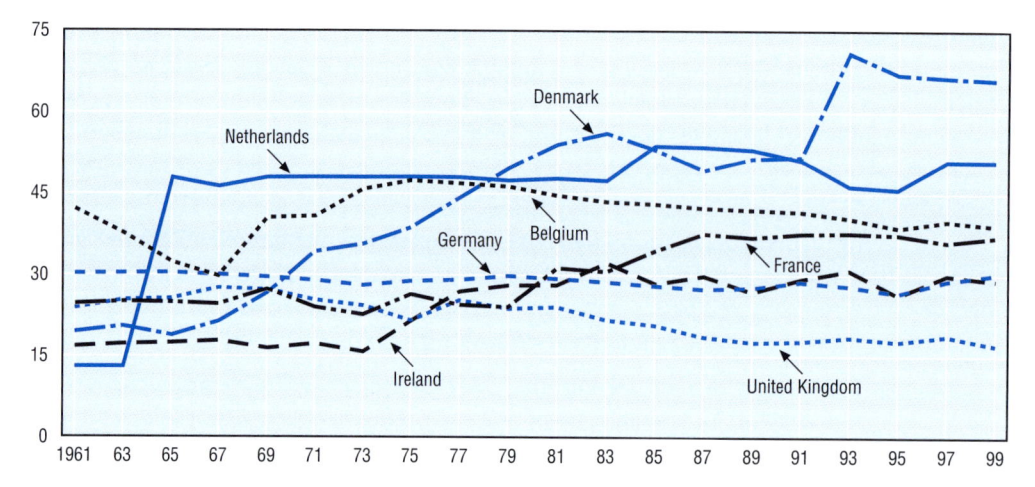

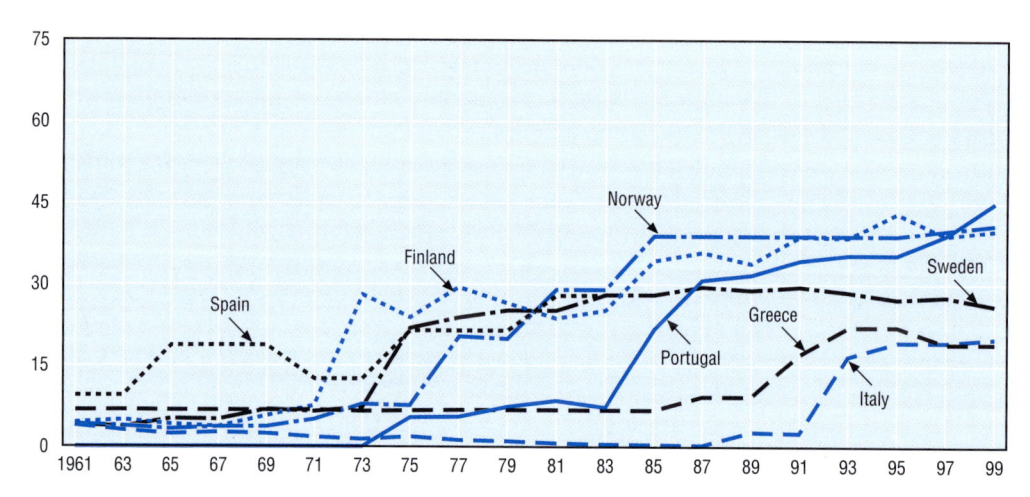

a) This OECD summary measure is defined as the average of the gross unemployment benefit replacement rates for a worker with a full record of employment at two earnings levels (APW and two-thirds of APW), three family situations (single, married with dependent spouse, married with spouse in work) and three unemployment spell durations (first year; second and third year; fourth and fifth year).

Source: See OECD (2002), Benefits and Wages, Figure 3.4.

increasingly reflect growth, induced by the existence of the benefit itself, in the size of population that meets the eligibility conditions. This further growth is usually unintended and often is undesirable. Induced growth in the population that is eligible for assistance benefits is particularly problematic because it involves higher poverty rates.[15]

- Active policies, which ensure that employment is taken up whenever possible, can plausibly reverse much of the historical growth in benefit recipiency.[16] But the impact of active policies is likely to involve similarly long-term mechanisms.

Three special unemployment benefits: adjustment lags of seven to ten years

Available examples suggest that increased benefit entitlements or relaxed eligibility conditions can exert upwards pressure on the number of beneficiaries over a long period. The minimum period in the examples cited here is about seven years, in the case of special types of UI benefit (Box 4.3). The levelling off of growth in these cases was attributable to restrictive changes to entitlement criteria (and, in some cases, benefit rates), relative to the

---

Box 4.3. Adjustment lags for three European unemployment benefit schemes

It is difficult to distinguish the impact of changed benefit entitlements from that of macroeconomic labour market conditions in the case of a country's main UI or unemployment assistance benefits. It is easier to disentangle these factors in the case of specialised benefits.

Chart 4.5 shows trends in beneficiary numbers for three special unemployment benefit schemes with unusually generous entitlement conditions.[a] These are Belgium's part-time unemployment benefit, Spain's benefit scheme for casual agricultural workers in Andalucia and Extremadura, and Italy's ordinary unemployment benefit with reduced requirements. The scheme in Belgium and Spain have accounted for a significant proportion of the unemployment beneficiary total, and the reduced-requirements scheme in Italy accounts for about half of spending on ordinary unemployment benefits (MLPS, 2000).

In Belgium, an important change took place in 1983 when it became possible for unemployed people to receive benefit in respect of days worked part-time (previously, benefit could be received only in respect of entire days not worked).[b] After the 1983 change, the number of persons receiving a part-time unemployment benefit in Belgium rose rapidly to reach a peak around 1990, *i.e.* six or seven years after the relaxation of conditions. By that time, about half of all part-time workers in the economy were receiving a benefit for involuntary part-time work. In 1992, some restrictions were introduced (OECD, 1994b): unemployment benefits for involuntary part-time work were refused for three months to an employee taking up work with the same employer who had previously laid him or her off from a full-time job, an employer tax on the employment of part-time workers receiving unemployment benefits was introduced, part-time benefits were limited to the equivalent of 13 days per month, and – to limit the form of fraud in which workers are in fact working full-time but are declared to be working part-time – a *carte de contrôle* was introduced on which the part-time worker must mark in advance the hours he or she will work (making it possible for anomalies to be detected through surprise inspections at the workplace). This policy change was followed by a fall of about 60% in the number of part-time beneficiaries, taking place over a period of five years (see ONEM, 1999 for a comprehensive study of the beneficiary numbers and changing benefit entitlements).[c]

In Andalucia and Extremadura, two high-unemployment regions of Spain, a new kind of benefit was created for casual agricultural workers in 1984. This benefit, despite its limited

Box 4.3. **Adjustment lags for three European unemployment benefit schemes** (cont.)

regional and occupational scope, has in many years accounted for around 20% of all unemployment beneficiaries in Spain. It required the payment of a minimum 60 days of contributions within a 180-day period in order to qualify for a benefit at 75% of the minimum wage for 100 to 180 days (maximum in any 12-month period). In 1986, the minimum conditions were relaxed by allowing limited benefits following 20 days of contributions, and allowing a certain number of days worked in a public works scheme (*Plan de Empleo Rural*) to qualify as contributions. Currently, 35 days are required to qualify for a benefit duration of 120 to 180 days. The number of male recipients of this special scheme has approximately followed the decline in agricultural employment.[d] However, the number of female beneficiaries grew fivefold between 1984 and 1992 (although the female share in agricultural employment in Spain has changed little) and has stabilised since then. Therefore, this benefit apparently had a large incentive effect in terms of bringing women into the temporary agricultural labour force (possibly in the sense that the work of female family members is now declared rather than being done on an informal basis) for just long enough each year to qualify.

In Italy's system of ordinary unemployment benefits with reduced requirements, a minimum of 78 days of work in a year entitles a person to the same number of days of benefit in the following year. Following legislation in 1988 and a reform that increased the benefit level in 1990, claims grew from about 150 000 in 1991 to over 350 000 in 1998, even though aggregate unemployment in Italy was almost unchanged. Growing recourse to temporary labour, creating a continuous flow of persons who have acquired the right to benefits, probably contributed to this development (MLPS, 2000). In the 1990s, over 50% of individuals who claimed this benefit in one year claimed it the next year, suggesting that learning following a first claim could be an important factor in growth. Here, the growth in beneficiary numbers continued for at least ten years after the benefit's introduction.

a) These three country cases are prominent examples of specialised unemployment benefits (distinct from the main unemployment benefit) that eventually reached high levels of recipiency.
b) In most countries, when a wholly unemployed person with an unemployment insurance benefit starts a part-time job, earnings from it beyond a certain "disregard" level are deducted one-for-one from benefits. However, some countries reduce benefits not in line with earnings but in proportion to weekly hours worked, *i.e.* benefit is halved when the unemployed person finds work in a job with half normal weekly working hours. This increases the incentive to work part-time, as compared to working not at all or full-time.
c) In Belgium the number of part-time unemployment beneficiaries had already fallen slightly by the time the policy changes occurred in 1992. This pattern seems to be fairly common, perhaps because the broad lines of policy changes are debated and partly known by labour market actors well before the date of any formal legislation or decree and its application. Similarly, Carling et al. (1999) estimate that a 5 percentage point cut in the UI replacement rate in Sweden taking effect on 1 January 1996 increased the transition rate out of unemployment by about 10%, and they note "evidence of anticipatory behavior among the unemployed; the effects of the reform seem to operate several months before its actual implementation in January 1996". Annex 2 explains in general terms why the impact of reforms often appears to be immediate.
d) In 1990, the benefit scheme for casual agricultural workers was restricted by making entitlements conditional on the claimant's age and his/her family size and income (*www.inem.es/legis/desempleo/rd5_97.htm*). This reform no doubt accounts for the stabilisation of the beneficiary rate as from 1990. In 2002, a one-day national general strike, the first since 1994, was held in protest at a package of labour reforms, with proposed further reforms to this special agricultural scheme being one of main issues. For a description of developments up to early 2003, see *http://217.141.24.196/2003/02/InBrief/ES0302201N.html*.

Chart 4.5. **Long adjustment lags for special unemployment benefit schemes in Belgium, Italy and Spain, 1979-2002**
Percentages of population aged 15-64

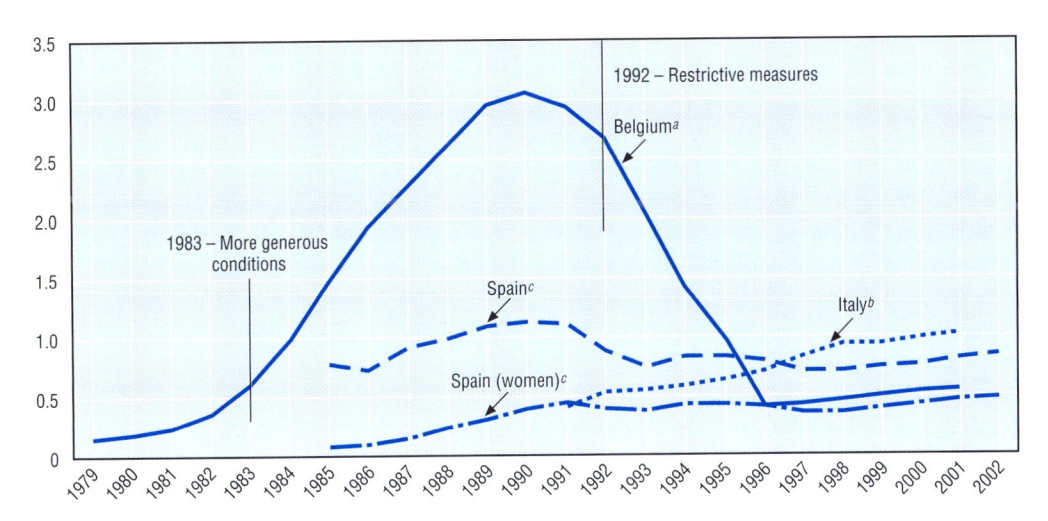

a) Beneficiaries of part-time unemployment benefits.
b) Beneficiaries of ordinary unemployment benefit with reduced requirements.
c) Beneficiaries of special benefit for casual agricultural workers in Andalucia and Extremadura.
Source: NEI-SZW database and for Belgium, *Chômage en Belgique – Werkloosheid in België*, monthly averages and ONEM, *Rapport Annuel 2001* (www.onem.be – publications); for Spain, www.mtas.es/estadisticas/BEL/PRD/Index.html with breakdown by sex 1984-1987 from MTSS (1989), *Mercado de trabajo en España durante 1987* (1988 to 1991 estimated by interpolation); for Italy, *Synthesis of the Monitoring Report on the Employment and Labor Policies No. 2/2000, Rapporto di monitoraggio 2/2001 and Monitoraggio delle politiche occupazionale e del lavoro 2003* (www.minlavoro.it). For population, United Nations (2001), *World Population Prospects 1950-2050 (The 2000 Revision)*, mid-year estimates and medium variant population projections.

initial pattern. Without these, the growth in beneficiary numbers might well have continued to some extent.

Longer adjustment lags for lone-parent and social assistance programmes

In the case of lone-parent and unemployment assistance programmes, the period of growth in beneficiary numbers has usually been 15 years or longer (Boxes 4.4 and 4.5). External macroeconomic conditions were clearly driving factors in some large short-term movements, but there are also reasons for thinking that longer-term benefit dynamics largely determined long-run outcomes:

- Growth rates of beneficiary numbers averaged close to 10% per year or more, over a decade or more (i.e. beneficiary numbers grew by a factor of at least 2.5 over a full cycle).[17, 18]

- In some cases, the number of recipients of social assistance benefits and long-term UI benefits (in the countries which have these, such as Denmark) has evolved in ways that have had only a tenuous relationship to general macroeconomic conditions. In the United Kingdom, starting from a low base in 1949, social assistance beneficiaries as a proportion of the working-age population grew rapidly during years of prosperity and full employment, as well as years of worldwide slow growth and rising unemployment. In France, between 1993 and 2000 the number of beneficiaries of RMI (social assistance system introduced in 1989) grew by 45% – even though this was a period of cyclical upswing.[19] More generally, although recessions greatly influence recipiency of UI and

> **Box 4.4. Adjustment lags for the main unemployment assistance and social assistance schemes in four countries**
>
> The OECD *Jobs Study* (1994b) documented the long-term growth in beneficiary numbers for indefinite-duration unemployment assistance or social assistance benefits following their date of introduction in four European countries (United Kingdom in 1948, Netherlands in 1963, Finland in 1971 and France in 1988). Chart 4.6.A shows these data updated to a recent year. For the United Kingdom, Netherlands and France, series are shown both for the assistance benefit relating specifically to unemployment and for the total of this with broader social assistance (in the United Kingdom, lone-parent) benefits (but not including disability or other benefits). Growth in beneficiary numbers, abstracting from slight cyclical downturns, continued for about 45 years in the case of the United Kingdom,[a] 15 years in the Netherlands, 25 years in Finland, and ten years in France (if years are counted from the introduction of the general social assistance benefit RMI in 1989, which rapidly came to outweigh quantitatively the unemployment assistance benefit). In two of these cases, the Netherlands and the United Kingdom, the falls in beneficiary totals following the introduction of activation policies have been fairly large (see Section 3.A below for further discussion).
>
> a) However, the 45 years of growth in the United Kingdom reflect changes in administration as well as the 1948 legislation. The Ministry of Labour lost policy responsibility for unemployment benefit in 1945 and this change "had over the succeeding 20 years gradually eliminated interest in benefit control among senior officers in the ministry, even if the controls continued to apply at local office level" (Price, 2000, p. 129). A strategy document in 1968 omitted benefit control from the list of objectives (*ibid*, p. 138), and the beneficiary growth after this continued for about 20 years, more in line with experience elsewhere.

some assistance benefits, widely varying changes in recipiency rates remain after a recession has passed.[20]

In sum, when a new benefit has been created and a large increase in the eligible population has resulted, this always occurs over a fairly long period. Commonly, the numbers have stopped rising at a time when entitlements were restricted or activation measures were introduced.[21]

Adjustment lags for disability benefits

The Netherlands experienced rapid growth in disability benefit recipiency earlier than most other countries did, and this led to intensive study of the links between recipiency and new entitlements to disability benefit and their subsequent reform. The disability insurance law (WAO) of 1967 stipulated that adjudicators, in their assessment of the degree of disability, should take account of the difficulties partially disabled persons might experience in finding commensurate employment, but "an explicit application of this provision turned out to be impossible (…). As from 1973, this administrative problem was solved by coarsely assuming that poor employment opportunities result from discriminatory behaviour, unless the contrary can be proven. (…) Partially disabled applicants were treated as if they were fully disabled" (Aarts and de Jong, 1990). Thus, the relaxation of eligibility criteria for entry to disability benefits occurred mainly in 1967 and 1973.[22] Chart 4.7 shows the timing of the increase in the numbers receiving disability benefits (both insurance and assistance-based).[23] The main period of growth occurred from about 1971 (when the recipiency rate was 3.3%) to 1981 (when it reached 7.7%), *i.e.* over a period of 10 years. Starting in 1981, successive restrictive measures were

4. BENEFITS AND EMPLOYMENT, FRIEND OR FOE? INTERACTIONS BETWEEN PASSIVE AND ACTIVE SOCIAL PROGRAMMES

Chart 4.6. **Long adjustement lags for assistance benefits**
Percentages of population aged 15-64

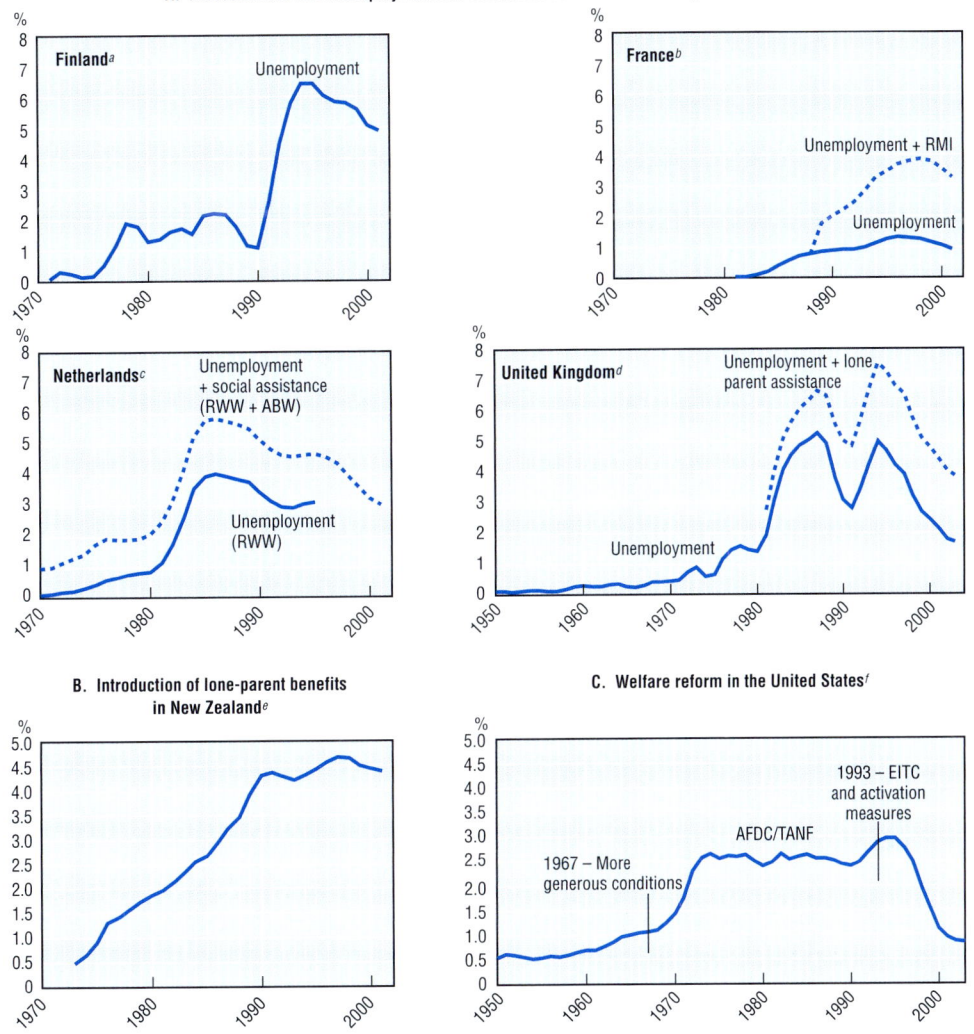

A. Introduction of new unemployment and assistance benefits in four European countries

B. Introduction of lone-parent benefits in New Zealand[e]

C. Welfare reform in the United States[f]

a) State unemployment assistance, created in 1971, and labour market support.
b) Allocation de Solidarité Spécifique, created in 1984, and RMI created in 1988. For RMI, beneficiaries in Métropole (excluding DOM) on 31st December.
c) RWW was created in 1963 and abolished in 1996, with transfer of beneficiaries to the general social assistance benefit.
d) Unemployment assistance benefit named National Assistance (from 1949), Supplementary Benefit (from 1966), Income Support (from 1988) and Jobseekers Allowance (income-based) from 1996. Lone-parent data refer to data published under the heading "One-parent families not included in other groups" or "Lone parent premium: not in other groups" for years up to 1990, and to "Statistical group: lone parents" in recent years. Data relate to a specific week of the year (a week in May as from 1987). Data do not include people also receiving a UI benefit.
e) Refers to Domestic Purposes Benefit, introduced in 1973, June figures from 1990 onwards. A relatively small number of beneficiaries of Widows' Benefit who are lone parents are not included. Unemployment assistance (not shown) also grew sharply over these years.
f) AFTC / TANF rates for adult beneficiaries only (not including caretaker recipients)

Source: NEI-SZW database; OECD (1994); for Finland, Finnish Labour Review 3/2002, Table 23; for France, www.unedic.fr/unistatis/index.php – données détaillées and "Légère hausse des bénéficiaires du RMI au 03 juin 2002" (www.caf.fr/CoupDOeil.htm – publications); for the Netherlands, www.cpb.nl/eng/data/mev2003/a10.xls; for United Kingdom, Work and Pensions Statistics (www.dwp.gov.uk/asd/wandp.html); for New Zealand, "Historical Summary – Number of People Receiving Income Services, 1940-2000", in Social Services Sector Statistical report for the year ending 2000 (www.msp.govt.nz/publications/statistics.html); Quarterly Client Profile (www.workandincome.govt.nz – statistics). Data for 1973-74 and 1976-79 are estimates (growth is described at www.radstats.org.uk/no069/article5.htm); for the United States, 1965-2000: Indicators of Welfare Dependence: Annual Report to the Congress 2002 (aspe.hhs.gov/hsp/indicators02/appa-tanf.htm); 1950, 1955, 1955, 1960-1964: Social Security Statistics Annual Statistical Supplement (www.ssa.gov/statistics/Supplement). Data refer to total recipients less child recipients. Other years estimated by interpolation/extrapolation based on Schafer and Clemens (2002) and www.ncsl.org/statefed/welfare/welfare.htm. For population, as for Chart 4.5.

> Box 4.5. **Lone-parent benefits in two countries**
>
> **"Welfare" in the United States**
>
> Adult recipiency rates for the US "welfare" benefit for lone parents, AFDC/TANF, rose only slightly from 1950 to 1960, then rose rapidly to reach a peak first in 1973 (equalled in 1981) and then in 1993 at nearly 3% of the working-age population (Chart 4.6.C). Growth in recipiency was driven largely by growth in the number of lone-parent families. The particularly sharp rise from 1967 to 1971 was related to changes in benefit rates and eligibility rules.[a] The lack of any strong upwards trend after this through to 1990, despite a continuing increase in the number of lone-parent families, could be related to declines in the real value of AFDC benefits.[b] From the point of view of timing, the most interesting period is the fall in recipiency after 1993. This probably reflects successive increases from 1987 onwards in the return to working for lone parents[c] and activation measures introduced in the 1990s (see Section 3.A below for further discussion).
>
> **Lone-parent benefit in New Zealand**
>
> The most important benefit to be introduced in New Zealand over the last 50 years has been the Domestic Purposes Benefit (DPB). For some years prior to its introduction, there existed an emergency benefit for sole parents, but it was temporary in nature with a low benefit level (Liebschutz, 1999). The DPB was established in 1973 to allow sole parents to provide full-time care for children with adequate income support (Goodger and Larose, 1998). The ratio of benefit to the average weekly wage for females was cut from 59% to 50% in 1991, but Bradshaw et al. (2000) regard this as remaining (comparatively) high. Following introduction of the DPB, growth in the number of beneficiaries was very rapid through to 1976 and then continued at an average of about 9% per year through to 1991 (Chart 4.6.B), i.e. 18 years after the introduction of the benefit. The first slight reduction in beneficiary numbers was related to a sharp cut in benefit rates in 1991 (MacKay, 1998), but growth in recipiency resumed three years later. In 1997, a requirement on the lone parent to be available for part-time work when the youngest child was aged 14 or more was introduced and this limit was reduced to aged 6 or more as from 1999 (see Ministry of Social Development, 2001, for further details). This is likely to be a factor in the renewed downward trend since 1997. Requirements have now been relaxed again, but this occurred too recently to have any impact on the data shown here.
>
> a) Stephens (2002), citing Fraker and Moffitt (1988) and Garfinkel and McLanahan (1986), explains that "When the increased real effective benefit level [due to the introduction of Medicaid and expansion of Food Stamps] combined with a legal ruling that AFDC was available to cohabiting single mothers provided that the father was not the biological parent, caseload numbers increased from 67% of eligible families in 1967 to nearly 90% in 1971."
> b) See http://aspe.hhs.gov/hsp/indicators01/apa-TANF.htm for data showing the decline in the real value of AFDC/TANF benefits from 1978 to 1998.
> c) According to calculations by Elwood (1999), the earnings of a single parent who moved from AFDC to a minimum wage job were subject to an effective tax rate (including child-care costs) of about 80% in 1986 and 30% in 1997. More than half of the 50 percentage point fall in the effective tax rate between these years was due to the increased rate of the Earned Income Tax Credit (EITC). The lower real level of TANF benefits out of work and the increased availability of child-care subsidies in work each contributed about 10 points. The maximum annual level of the federal EITC for a family with one child increased from about USD 500 to USD 900 in 1987, USD 1 200 in 1991 and USD 2 000 in 1994.

introduced, but recipiency rates nevertheless drifted up by another percentage point through to 1991.[24]

Data on the distribution of invalidity benefit stocks and inflows by five types of medical condition (mental, muscular-skeletal, cardiovascular, injuries, other diseases) for

Chart 4.7. **Recipiency rate for disability insurance and assistance benefits**[a] **in the Netherlands, 1969-2001**

Percentages of population aged 15-64

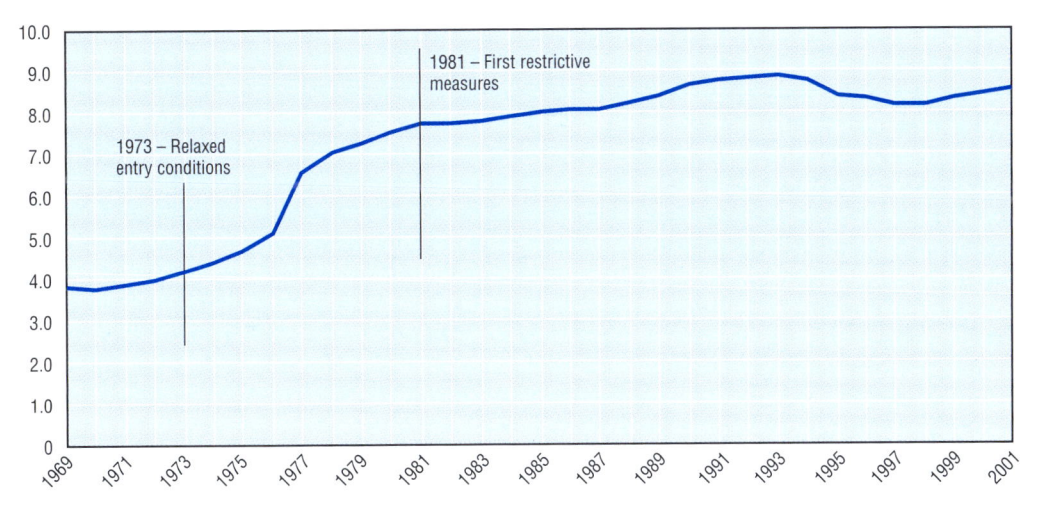

1973 – Relaxed entry conditions

1981 – First restrictive measures

a) Beneficiaries of the Invaliditeitswet, part of the Invalidity and Age Act 1919 (whose numbers had declined to a low level by 1981 and to zero by 1991), invalidity insurance (WAO) introduced in 1967 and invalidity assistance (AAW) introduced in 1976.

Source: CPB (2002), *Macroeconomic Outlook 2003* (www.cpb.nl/eng/data/), Appendix 7. For population, as for Chart 4.5.

a number of countries give an insight into one way that benefit recipiency has increased. The shares of the first two categories (mental and muscular-skeletal conditions) have generally increased between 1980 and 1999. While the trends are often slow, they have a cumulative impact: inflows or stocks in a recent year were on average 20% to 25% higher than they would have been, if the first two medical conditions had grown only in line with the other categories. Applications for benefits on such grounds, and the success rate of these applications, may have grown as precedents accumulate.

Cross-country data provide another insight into how disability benefits may encourage growth in the population that is eligible for them. Chart 4.8 compares measures of *disability prevalence*, based upon perceptions of disability as self-reported in population surveys with *disability benefit recipiency* rates, as recorded in administrative statistics. The two rates are correlated, not only for the full data set but also among the 11 EU countries where (subject to issues of translation) the same questions (from the European Community Household Panel, ECHP) are used in determining disability prevalence, and income levels and health outcomes are relatively uniform.[25] Although correlation does not prove causation, a common interpretation is that disability benefit systems differ across countries and they influence recipiency outcomes more than differences in true health status do.[26] Chart 4.8 thus illustrates how the availability or attractiveness of a benefit might tend to increase the population eligible for that benefit. This type of feedback can generate long lags in the impact of benefit system parameters on recipiency (Annex 2).

Some large falls in recipiency occur

The examples given in Boxes 4.3 to 4.5 include four cases where beneficiary numbers have fallen sharply: the special benefit for involuntary part-time unemployment in

Chart 4.8. **Disability prevalence and disability benefit recipiency rates in the late 1990s**

Percentage of population aged 20-64

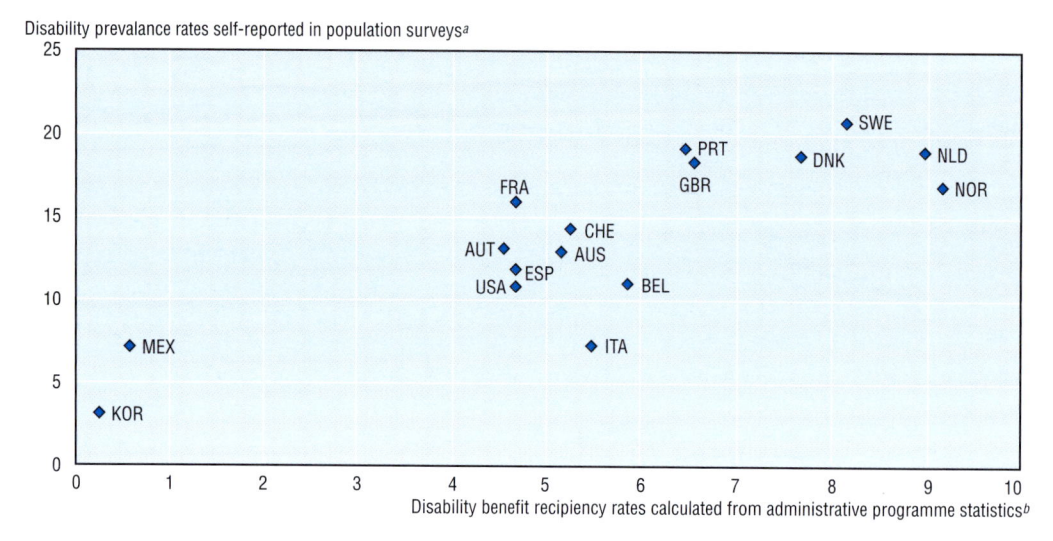

Note: Disability prevalence rates are always higher than recipiency rates, the scales for each axis are therefore different.

a) In the analysis of population survey data, people in EU countries are classified as disabled if i) to the question "Do you have any chronic physical or mental health problem, illness or disability" they responded "yes" and ii) to the question "Are you hampered in your daily activities by this chronic physical or mental health problem, illness or disability" they responded "moderately" or "severely". For non-EU countries, surveys using questions that resemble these as closely as possible were used. See OECD (2003), Annex 1, for details.

b) Contributory and non-contributory benefits only, not including war disability pensions or work injury benefits.

Source: OECD (2003), Tables 3.1 and 3.7.

Belgium, unemployment assistance benefits in the Netherlands[27] and the United Kingdom, and lone-parent benefits in the United States. These outcomes suggest that it is quite possible for beneficiary numbers to fall to a half or a third of their previous level following changes in passive and/or active policies. In the case of Belgium's part-time unemployment benefit, beneficiary numbers fell primarily in response to passive policies (reducing the compensation rate, and restricting access). An active policy approach – i.e. assisting and monitoring the search for full-time work by part-time unemployed people – would have placed unrealistic demands on the capacities of the Belgian PES, and would probably not have worked. Similarly in the case of the special unemployment benefits in Italy and Spain, the short-term nature of the benefits would make it difficult for the PES to do much through active policies. In the case of unemployment assistance and lone-parent benefits, the potential for activation strategies to succeed seems greater, as will be discussed further below.

2. The meaning and measurement of the "active" content of policy

Activation strategies in relation to unemployment and social assistance benefits have had a large impact in reducing benefit recipiency in some countries and plausibly, a more modest impact in most other countries. Activation policies can be understood in the narrow sense of compulsory training or employment measures for the unemployed (Andersen *et al.*, 2002). However, active labour market policies include a much wider range of approaches. The purpose of this section is to review the different approaches that national authorities can consider in order to increase the active content of their policies with the aim of reducing benefit dependency. It draws upon experience with reviews of the Public Employment Service (PES) and labour market policies and findings from microeconomic evaluation studies (see for example OECD, 2001a; 2001b; Martin and Grubb, 2001). Activation policies typically apply to unemployment and (if different) employable social assistance beneficiaries, but similar principles are increasingly being applied to lone-parent and disability beneficiaries (see Subsection F below).

A. *Spending on "active" vs. "passive" labour market programmes*

Total spending on active labour market programmes can be expressed in different ways, for example: *a)* as a percentage of GDP; *b)* as active spending per person unemployed relative to GDP per person employed; or *c)* as active spending as a percentage of active and passive spending on labour market programmes combined. Table 4.2 shows these measures for 25 OECD countries. *A priori b)* is a good measure: an "active" policy is one

Table 4.2 **Indicators for spending on active labour market programmes**

		Spending on active labour market programmes[a]		
		As a percentage of GDP	Ratio of spending as a percentage of GDP to the unemployment rate[b]	As a percentage of total spending (active and passive) on labour market programmes[c]
Australia	2000-01	0.46	0.07	32.0
Austria	2001	0.53	0.15	33.1
Belgium	2000	1.32	0.19	37.6
Canada	2000-01	0.41	0.06	36.4
Czech Republic	2001	0.21	0.03	46.6
Denmark	2000	1.58	0.36	34.3
Finland	2001	0.94	0.10	32.0
France	2000	1.32	0.14	44.4
Germany	2001	1.21	0.16	38.6
Greece	1998	0.46	0.04	49.8
Hungary	2001	0.47	0.08	55.4
Ireland	2001	1.14	0.29	61.9
Japan	2000-01	0.28	0.06	34.2
Korea	2001	0.31	0.08	66.9
Luxembourg	1997	0.24	0.09	28.3
Mexico[b]	2001	0.06	0.02	100.0
Netherlands	2001	1.74	0.67	48.0
New Zealand	2000-01	0.57	0.10	28.9
Norway	2001	0.79	0.22	63.9
Portugal	2000	0.61	0.15	40.5
Spain	2001	0.84	0.08	38.9
Sweden	2001	1.39	0.29	59.2
Switzerland	2001	0.45	0.18	48.0
United Kingdom	2000-01	0.37	0.07	40.0
United States	2000-01	0.15	0.03	32.9
Averages for:				
EU countries above		0.98	0.20	41.9
All countries above		0.71	0.15	45.3

a) Active measures are public employment services and administration, labour market training, youth measures, subsidised employment and measures for the disabled.
b) OECD standardised unemployment rate, except for Mexico (national definition).
c) Passive measures are unemployment compensation and early retirement for labour market reasons.
Source: OECD database on Labour Market Programmes; OECD database on Main Economic Indicators.

where a relatively large amount is spent per unemployed person. However, countries that score high on this measure often also have high levels of passive spending (on unemployment benefits). Arguably an "active" orientation arises only when indicator c) is high as well. Among the countries where indicators a) and b) are above average, only in three (Ireland, Norway and Sweden) is indicator c) also much above average. In two more countries (France and the Netherlands), indicators a), b) and c) are all near or above average level. One more country (Switzerland) has a high level of spending according to indicators b) and c) while indicator a) remains relatively low, thanks to a low unemployment rate.

A fundamental question for these statistics is what spending should be counted as "active". OECD analyses suggest that the PES is the key actor in activation strategies for the unemployed.[28] Spending on the PES may represent a relatively small proportion of total spending, but a large proportion of the spending on other programmes is delivered through the PES. Spending on these other programmes consists to a considerable extent of income support payments to programme participants, and transfers to employers in the form of hiring subsidies. As a result, the "active" nature of this spending is not assured: it depends on how referrals and programme content are managed. Within the area of PES functions, the distinction between job-search assistance and benefit administration is not always clear: some of the main activities such as interviewing job-seekers and maintaining the PES register contribute to both. These factors mean that labour market spending data provide at best highly approximate measures for the "active" content of policy. The remaining sections look at further key factors that shape the "active" character of policies.

B. PES interventions in the unemployment spell

The concept of "interventions in the unemployment spell" refers to arrangements where the unemployed person has compulsory contacts with PES, or other obligations to engage in job-search activities. While applications for job vacancies registered by the PES are mainly voluntary (*i.e.* the unemployed person selects the vacancy from a notice board or electronic database), various other types of contact with the PES (signing-on, interviews with PES officers, setting up an individual action plan) occur mainly on a compulsory basis, and participation in longer-term programmes may be mainly voluntary or compulsory. In some countries, after initial contacts which establish the person's rights to benefit and provide basic information about PES services, during the next few months of an unemployment spell the unemployed person is expected to search independently for work and the PES intervenes very little.

Scheduled interventions in the unemployment spell can be of four different types, in terms of the time within the unemployment spell at which they apply:

- First month of the spell: often a lengthy initial registration interview is conducted and some countries also require participation in collective information sessions.

- Ongoing contacts: regular contacts for job-search reporting; direct referrals to a vacant job (requirement to attend a job interview); occasional intensive interviews with PES staff; and less intensive but more frequent signing-on procedures.

- Individual action plans: these usually involve an additional intensive interview at a defined month of the unemployment spell (although in some countries, at initial registration) and follow-up interviews. In some cases, a high proportion of participants in an action plan are referred to a labour market programme.

- "Active period of benefits": at some duration of unemployment, continued payment of unemployment benefit becomes conditional on ongoing participation in an active labour market programme, while other interventions (interviews and job-search monitoring) continue according to a modified schedule. (This type of intervention can be an enhanced type of individual action plan.)

Results from a questionnaire addressed to OECD countries in 1999, concerning arrangements for interventions in the unemployment spell, were reported in OECD (2001a, pp. 41-48). Initial registration procedures that establish jobseeker details appear to demand a significant proportion of PES resources. This is because many unemployment spells are short, and terminate before much further intervention has occurred. Patterns of intervention vary widely: for example, in some countries direct referrals to vacant jobs are an important type of intervention, while in others they are not often made, and job-search reporting requirements are more important.

C. Benefit eligibility criteria and benefit sanctions

Strict eligibility criteria for the receipt of unemployment benefit, which have to be met on pain of benefit sanctions, provide another tool for "activation" – so as to reduce the risk of benefit traps, where beneficiaries have little incentive to look for a job. Activation policies in such countries as Denmark, the Netherlands and the United Kingdom have involved increased attention to questions of benefit eligibility:

- *Legislation:* in Denmark, legislation introduced the "active period of benefits" in 1994, with further revisions in 1999; in the Netherlands, new guidelines concerning "suitable work" were issued several times (1992, 1994 and 1996) and a new law on sanctions (*Wet Boeten en Maatregelen*) was adopted in 1996 (see Engelfriet, n.d.); and in the United Kingdom entirely new benefit legislation (Jobseekers' Allowance) was developed and effective as from 1996. These changes arguably involved some increase in strictness, but this is not always clear (*e.g.* Denmark still has mild sanctions for a first refusal of suitable work, and the UK definition of suitable work is not particularly strict). The main thrust was towards clarification – often including a more rather than a less detailed specification of eligibility criteria.

- *Administration:* in Denmark, there was a major administrative drive in 1994 and 1995 (new computer systems and creation of an "availability inspection unit") to permit effective supervision of, and communication with, the benefit funds, which are run by unions. In the Netherlands, the institutions managing benefits were completely reformed in the 1990s, and were given funds allowing them to purchase employment services from the PES and, increasingly, through competitive tendering.

- *Sanctions:* in the Netherlands and the United Kingdom, a sharp increase in the incidence of benefit sanctions occurred at some early stages of the activation strategy.[29] However, it is not clear that the enforcement of eligibility criteria needs to involve particularly high sanction rates on a long-term basis.[30]

Sanctions are needed as a last-resort measure to enforce requirements. In theory, social welfare is maximised by a policy where sanctions are very harsh but – because compliance is complete – they never need to be applied. In practice, the severity of sanctions is limited (the maximum sanction is exclusion from unemployment benefit, except in cases of fraud), compliance is not complete, and some sanctions are necessary to enforce requirements. If the outcome that most jobseekers comply with requirements is achieved, the detailed method of enforcement is not so important: the most important issue is the nature of the requirements (*e.g.* reporting of job search, attendance at fortnightly interviews, participation in training) and the effectiveness of the services that are delivered within this framework.

D. Compulsory vs. voluntary participation in labour market programmes

One important feature of "activation" policies for unemployment and social assistance benefits has been to make participation in labour market programmes compulsory (as a condition for receipt of benefits) rather than voluntary.

In a number of countries, actual rates of participation in obligatory labour market programmes are low. For the Netherlands, Van Oorschot (2002) remarks that the participation rate in full-time programmes relative to the total target group of activation policies has been very small (*e.g.* "In 1988 (…) about 7 000 young unemployed participated in the TW-GWJ [youth guarantee], while nationally about 45 000 met the criteria"). Similarly, in the United States, in 1999 about 3.3% of TANF families were participating in work experience programmes (Strawn *et al.*, 2001).[31] In the United Kingdom, obligatory participation in longer-term employment and training programmes hardly existed before the short-lived 1997 Project Work scheme, and remains low. In Canada's "Ontario Works" programme (described by Morel, 2002, as "hard-core" workfare, although this may be exaggerated), only 2 to 5% of social assistance recipients have been on workfare assignments (Mulvale, 2002). However, these low percentages remain consistent with the idea that an obligation applying under specific conditions (*e.g.* when the spell of benefit recipiency has been uninterrupted for over a year) can have a large impact in motivating people to avoid the obligation.

In some other countries, rates of compulsory participation in labour market programmes have become rather high. This outcome may arise where replacement rates or compensation for participants come close to market wages.[32] In recent years, Denmark and Sweden have had high participation rates, with a significant percentage of the labour force in labour market programmes. These countries try to make good use of the time participants spend in programmes by strengthening training and education content. Nevertheless, the programmes are expensive and participants' time is often not so productively used as it would be in unsubsidised work.

The effectiveness of compulsory participation strategies is likely to depend strongly on how effectively people are helped in searching for market work alternatives. Individual action plans, PES assistance in between assignments to programmes, and counselling during the lengthy "gateway" period of the UK New Deal should promote this objective. The "active" nature of actual participation in programmes, when this occurs, is not clear. During participation, "lock-in" effects arise (*i.e.* during participation in a programme, job-search intensity and rates of entry to unsubsidised work tend to be lower than they are in open unemployment). After participation, according to evaluation findings, prospects for unsubsidised employment are not necessarily improved, especially in the case of public sector job creation schemes.

The OECD's reviews of social assistance (OECD, 1998a; 1998b; 1999) identify several other considerations that have encouraged the adoption of this type of welfare-to-work strategy: *a)* fraud control; *b)* a perception that long-term benefit recipients do not realise that participation in programmes is in their own best interest; *c)* political considerations, in particular public willingness to finance programmes, may be greater when assistance is within a mutual obligations framework; and *d)* these strategies often force government bureaucracies to pay attention to disadvantaged groups.[33]

E. Institutional arrangements

The *OECD Jobs Study* (OECD, 1994a) recommended that the three PES functions of placement and counselling, the payment of unemployment benefits and the management of labour market programmes, should be integrated. The degree of *functional integration* is an important dimension of the "active" orientation of policy. Functional integration can be partly a matter of institutional arrangements, but it also involves what Clasen and van Oorschot (2002) describe as "blurring of the traditional division between the policy areas of social protection and labour market policy".

In Ireland, until 1996 there was no obligation on unemployment beneficiaries to register with the placement service (implying that the placement service did not monitor or enforce availability for work, job-search or acceptance of suitable work) and the introduction of an obligation to register for placement clearly increased the level of functional integration. In the Netherlands, government funding of benefit institutions to allow them to purchase placement services for their clients began in 1996, and this might also be regarded as a measure of integration between the benefit and placement functions. In the UK reforms of the late 1980s, integration was pursued by merging the previously-separate local offices that handled benefit processing and placement, but with the benefit and placement staff remaining employees of different ministries. In some other countries (*e.g.* Greece and Spain), the benefit administration and placement functions are both responsibilities of a quasi-independent Public Employment Service body (OAED, INEM), but staff working on these functions are to varying extents separated at local office level. In Germany's PES (the BA) these functions have been reunited since 2000, with most client needs being handled by staff teams in a single local office.

One factor that is liable to influence the degree of effective integration is whether the same bodies finance unemployment benefits and active labour market programmes. Many European countries and Canada have a nationally-financed UI system alongside a municipally-financed (provincial, in the case of Canada) system of social assistance, and municipal social services which also do some placement work. Under this arrangement, municipalities are often willing to create jobs for the long-term unemployed on a large scale: in many countries this attracts central government subsidies for job-creation programmes targeted on UI recipients, and reduces the number of UI exhaustees transferring to social assistance. Often, although the national PES in principle services the whole population, municipalities find that "their" clients do not get sufficient attention from it and their social services develop a placement function. A further complication is that in at least four OECD countries (Belgium, Canada, Spain and Switzerland), the network of local placement offices is managed by regional governments, creating a risk that links with the federal UI system will be lost. Among these countries, Switzerland has set up a federal system evaluating the performance of individual placement offices (OECD, 2001a), and Canada has set up a system of federal-provincial agreements and performance evaluation (Box 4.6).

Box 4.6. **National *versus* regional financing and management of insurance and assistance benefits in Canada**

During the 1980s, the Canadian federal government made massive fiscal transfers between provinces in terms of UI benefits (a federal responsibility), regional development programmes, and fiscal equalization payments, which under the Canada Assistance Plan (CAP) financed 50% of the provinces' social assistance costs. By the early 1990s, the federal government was seeking to reduce its direct expenditure on UI benefits and its social assistance expenditures under the CAP. The near-doubling of social assistance caseloads between 1982 and 1992 had also become a factor contributing to provincial budgetary difficulties.

In the mid-1990s, payments under the CAP were replaced by block grants under the Canadian Health and Social Transfer (CHST). Soon afterwards, the federal government also entered into a series of Labour Market Development Agreements (LMDAs) that transferred funding and management responsibility for employment service staff and active labour market measures (called Employment Benefit and Support Measures, EBSMs) to the provinces of Quebec, Alberta, Manitoba, Saskatchewan, and New Brunswick.[a] Quebec joined with a number of other provinces in claiming that this would bring about greater accountability, reduce conflicting interventions and duplication between services for UI and social assistance clients, and improve the matching of labour supply and demand at local level.

Following the 1994 and 1996 changes to UI programme parameters, the proportion of unemployed entitled to benefits (now renamed as Employment Insurance, EI) declined substantially. Fortin and Cremieux (1998) estimate that the EI changes increased social assistance caseloads by 10% to 25%, depending on the province. However, research also attributed a large part of the decline in EI coverage to a change in composition of the unemployed population, with relatively fewer workers having a high degree of labour force attachment and awaiting recall, and relatively more workers having precarious employment histories with little recent work experience. Consistent with this development, there was a large increase in the share of social assistance beneficiaries that were considered to be employable (estimated to have risen from 38% to 64% over 1980-92 in British Columbia).

Since provinces only bear the costs of the social assistance programmes, they have an incentive to shift workers at the margins of the labour force between programmes to minimise programme outlays. There are some well-known cases of job-creation schemes for social assistance clients implemented by local governments that were designed mostly to entitle the participants for EI benefits. However, these are mostly dated: blatant cost-shifting of this kind would be embarrassing for both levels of government, which want the "flexible federalism" principle of LMDAs to succeed.

In managing the EI system, the "results-based accountability" criteria[b] used to evaluate performance under the LMDAs create incentives to recruit claimants with high EI entitlements into the EBSMs, since placements in this case result in greater savings to the EI account. However, EBSM participation is sometimes followed by relatively precarious employment and a return to EI: preliminary evidence suggests that this has happened to perhaps 25% of participants. The legislation that created the LMDAs calls for sophisticated summative evaluations of the longer-term impacts of the EBSMs on outcomes such as EI receipt, earnings, and unemployment spells. This work in progress should provide further insights into patterns of savings to the social assistance and EI accounts.

Box 4.6. **National *versus* regional financing and management of insurance and assistance benefits in Canada** (cont.)

Provinces, now responsible for the full cost of social assistance benefit payments, have adopted a variety of welfare-to-work strategies, which Morel (2002) has described as "soft-core" workfare in Quebec and "hard-core" workfare in Ontario. Despite the EI cutbacks, social assistance recipiency rates fell by a third between 1994 and 2000.[c]

a) Other provinces entered into a different form of LMDA whose scope was not "full devolution", but rather limited to a "co-management" arrangement. See OECD (2001a) for a more detailed description.
b) The three criteria are: savings to the EI account stemming from the placement of a current EI claimant, the number of EI clients served, and the number of clients returned to work. At the current stage, there are no medium-term, not to mention long-term, accountability indicators.
c) Earlier cyclical movements in social assistance caseloads in Canada were small: the recipiency rate fell by less than 10% in the late 1980s upswing, and hardly at all in the late 1970s upswing.

Source: As cited, and Gray (forthcoming).

F. Activating "inactive" benefits and gatekeeping in inactive programmes

"Activation" measures are mainly targeted on recipients of unemployment benefits and, in certain cases, recipients of social assistance benefits. In the latter case, the application of an activation strategy to some extent converts the social assistance benefit into an unemployment benefit under another name. However, to the extent that social assistance clients need social worker assistance with problems such as housing, debt, and drugs, there may be a case for keeping benefit and administrative arrangements for these clients separate from those for the short-term unemployed. Other possible target groups for activation measures are recipients of earmarked lone-parent benefits, where these exist, and disability benefits.

In many countries, lone parents on assistance benefits must, if there are no other impediments, be available for work in order to qualify for assistance. In the mid-1990s, this applied when the youngest child reached six months to 12 years (depending on province) in Canada, three years in Austria, Finland, France and Sweden, five years in the Czech Republic and the Netherlands, six years in Luxembourg and (for part-time work) in New Zealand, and eight years in Norway (Eardley *et al.*, 1996; OECD, 1998a; Goodger and Larose, 1998; *www.childpolicyintl.org/childsupport.html*; Millar and Rowlingson, 2001).[34] In Norway, since 1998 assistance without an availability requirement is usually limited to three years. In Germany, social workers try to ensure that lone parents have priority access to institutional child care, and availability for work is expected insofar as child care is available. Ireland and the United Kingdom still pay lone-parent benefits without an availability-for-work requirement while the youngest child is under 16, and attempts at reforming similar arrangements in Australia and New Zealand have encountered strong political opposition. In most countries with tight age limits (France is an exception), lone parents with children above these age limits receive social assistance benefits that are financed and managed at local (in Canada, provincial) level. Thus, it may be quite difficult to implement availability-for-work requirements on lone parents within a framework of entitlements to a nationally-managed benefit. Nevertheless, international experience suggests that it can be reasonable to require availability for work and apply activation policies as a general rule where the youngest child is in school, and at a lower age when child-care provision is adequate.

Strategies for the activation of the disabled face a number of difficulties: the heterogeneity of the disabled population; the complexity of assessing work capacity and its evolution through time; and the long-term nature of the assistance needed to get some people into work and maintain them in work. However, disability benefits are in some cases subject to work-related requirements (see also the discussion in Chapter 3, Section 2.B). OECD (2003) scores countries for various indicators of the "integration" dimension of disability policy, in particular the obligation to participate in a rehabilitation programme, the timing of the obligation (with a high score if it applies early, *e.g.* while still at work), and the duration of the possible benefit suspension. Scores above 1 on the first indicator mean that rehabilitation is not entirely voluntary, and scores above 1 on the third indicator indicate that benefit suspension of some kind is possible (for disability beneficiaries). Belgium, Denmark, Germany, Netherlands, Norway and Sweden (among 21 OECD countries) score above 1 on both indicators around 2000 (only in the Netherlands does this represent a change of policy, as compared to 1985), and thus might be said to have some practice of obliging people who have already been granted a disability benefit to be available for work, at least in the sense of participating in rehabilitation activities that are supposed to help prepare them for work. Belgium, Denmark, Norway and Sweden are also scored as having strong programmes of subsidised employment for the disabled. Together these conditions create a possibility for public authorities to place a person who is already on a disability benefit, or who will otherwise qualify for a disability benefit, into a market job albeit a subsidised one. However with the possible exceptions of Belgium and Germany, these countries have above-average disability benefit recipiency rates. Plausibly, countries where disability benefits are in principle granted only in cases of permanent and near-complete loss of work capacity do less to promote employment after benefits have been granted.

There are some examples of "activation" methods being applied to people for whom benefit entitlement is not conditional on availability for work. For example, Australia has a specialised employment service (Jobs, Education and Training) for lone-parent beneficiaries who are not required to be available for work, as well as a service (Return to Work) for mothers who need to transfer from parental to unemployment benefits, but lack recent labour market experience (OECD, 2001b). Non-compulsory employment services are generally considered useful and successful for those who use them, but their aggregate impact is limited by low take-up rates. One recent development in Australia, New Zealand and the United Kingdom has been to require people on lone-parent benefits to attend interviews, where the possibilities of entering work are discussed but without an obligation to take up job offers.[35] However, there is a risk that broad-brush attempts at applying "activation" strategies to "inactive" benefits will divert the energies and resources of the PES – which are limited, both in terms of staff and in terms of job vacancies – away from openly unemployed clients. This may account for disappointing results from pilot studies of the UK's "One" approach, which extends the principle of integration of unemployment benefit administration with employment service offices at local level to other types of benefits.[36]

If beneficiaries of disability or lone-parent benefits are considered able to work, an alternative to applying activation strategies directly to their beneficiaries is to restrict access to these benefits, so that a larger proportion of potential claimants must instead claim general unemployment or social assistance benefits where the availability-for-work requirement applies. Thus, the *Allocation de Parent Isolé* in France and the

Transitional Allowance in Norway do not require availability for work, but the low age and duration limits on these benefits mean that lone parents who are not in work must transfer to general social assistance benefits while their children are still quite young. Benefit eligibility criteria for unemployment benefits can make explicit allowance for child-care responsibilities or partial disability by providing for advance notification of referrals to a job interview, or specifying that only part-time jobs are regarded as suitable work.

In cases where a person with a work handicap cannot continue in the current job, or his/her productivity has fallen well below wage costs, it may be possible to prevent entry to passive disability benefits by offering rehabilitation and subsidised employment instead. Denmark's "Flexible Working Arrangements" (see Chapter 3, Table 3.10) is a recent development in this field. OECD (2003) describes a reform strategy in Luxembourg with similar features. When recognition of a work handicap is followed by placement into more suitable employment with a subsidy paid to the employer, the risk that the person can transfer to benefit on a passive basis in the following years is reduced. Generalisation of such arrangements might effectively dissuade employee misuse of disability as a route for early exit from the labour market, although it might also give employers incentives to encourage applications for the subsidy. Currently, in cases where the employee and employer agree that the person can no longer do their job (*e.g.* owing to a stress-related mental condition or back pain), often the only options open to the authorities are to reject this assessment, or to accept a permanent transition to a passive disability beneficiary status.

In the 1980s, many countries provided early retirement benefits for older workers who were laid off, removed job-search requirements for older unemployed people, and excluded older unemployed from employment measures. Already by the early 1990s, some countries had begun to reverse this tendency. In France, 700 000 people were on early retirement pensions paid through the UI system by 1983, but little new inflow was allowed in the 1990s. In Finland, the lower age limit for "Unemployment Pension" was increased from 55 to 60 years between 1986 and 1990. Belgium and the Netherlands recently started phasing out exemption from job-search requirements (formerly applying from age 50 and 57.5, respectively) for older workers, and Australia is closing its Mature Age Allowance to new entrants from 2003.[37] Spain recently created an "Active Insertion Income" benefit for unemployed workers aged over 45 which requires beneficiaries to have an individual action plan, and Denmark in 1999 increased the lower age limit for relaxation of availability rules from 50 to 55.

Measures that restrict access to early retirement or disability benefits will often increase inflows to unemployment benefit. When the PES and other labour market policies are functioning well – placing unemployed people in jobs quickly and implementing benefit eligibility conditions effectively – even the more disadvantaged unemployed are often placed in jobs within a year or two. In this way, success in reducing unemployment can in the longer term contribute to reducing dependency on other "inactive" benefits.

3. Outcomes from "active" policies

This section considers the impact of "active" policies on beneficiary numbers,[38] employment and earnings. This approach is appropriate for most OECD countries, where the majority of participants in active labour market programmes are drawn from the stock of people on unemployment, social assistance or disability benefits. Possible substitution between different social protection benefits is also examined.

A. The role of activation strategies in reducing benefit dependency

Employment rates and active policies in cross-country comparison

Activation policies can help reconcile a relatively generous level of benefits with high employment rates, as in Sweden.[39] The Swedish system includes effective availability-for-work requirements. Sweden had the second highest score (after Luxembourg) in the Danish Ministry of Finance's index of the strictness of availability criteria for receipt of unemployment benefits (MoF, 1998). Here, the "duty to work" has always been a core element in social and labour market policy (Andersen, 2002) and the principle of a jobseeker obligation to participate in labour market programmes has not been questioned, although choice is possible in respect of the timing and type of programme, which are to a considerable extent also determined by the unemployed person's caseworker.[40] As regards unemployment,[41] the main weakness in the range of active measures was the so-called "carousel" effect which allowed unemployed people to cycle repeatedly between unemployment benefit receipt and programme participation without entering unsubsidised work. Sweden has recently moved to curb the "carousel" effect by introducing an "activity guarantee" (see Box 4.7). Norway has also managed to keep its employment rate high. Here, unemployment benefit eligibility criteria are strict, benefit sanction rates are high, and according to Halvorsen (2002), social assistance is stigmatising and there is no sign of a "culture of dependency" among long-term unemployed or recipients of social assistance. Lower replacement rates as compared to Sweden may reduce incentives for unemployed people to cycle between employment and benefit receipt, or between benefit receipt and programme participation. One problem, however, is the relatively high number of recipients of disability benefits.

Activation strategies have helped reduce benefit recipiency in some countries

A move towards more "active" employment policy has occurred in most OECD countries. Major policy changes can be dated from 1994 (but arguably a little earlier) in Denmark, from 1996 in Ireland, from the early 1990s in the Netherlands and from 1986 in the United Kingdom, where the process was however relatively drawn-out (Table 4.3). Studies in these countries have reported microeconomic evidence of impact from certain types of activation measures, or certain stages in the activation process, that points to these measures as a likely reason for reductions in aggregate unemployment beneficiary numbers. Box 4.8 discusses this for Ireland.

In the United States, alongside a large increase in the financial return from working (see Chapter 3), the more "active" employment strategy for lone parents involved active measures such as the integration of placement and benefit administration, individual action plans, frequent meetings with clients, job-search requirements, etc. Restrictions on entitlement to benefit (in terms of time limits and general administrative discretion over granting benefit), and restrictions on practical access to benefit (in terms of "diversion" strategies) have also been important (see Box 4.9).[42] Differences between US welfare reform

> Box 4.7. **Sweden's Activity Guarantee and the "carousel" effect**
>
> Concern has often been expressed about the risk of "carousel" effects, which arise when a period of open unemployment is broken by a spell of programme participation, but this leads into another period of open unemployment with continued benefit receipt. In Sweden, the introduction of the "Activity Guarantee" has limited this risk. The maximum duration of UI has been doubled (from 60 weeks to 120 weeks).[a] The possibility of renewing benefit entitlement through programme participation has been eliminated, and the possibility of participating in the "Activity Guarantee" indefinitely, until the person leaves unemployment, has been created. The activity guarantee is a framework within which all regular labour market measures can be used. The participant is supposed to be engaged in job search, a labour market programme or in studies. The activities are supposed to be full-time.[b]
>
> Local employment offices retain considerable flexibility over the implementation of the activity guarantee. It is typically offered near the time of termination of the benefit period. Towards the end of the first 60-week period of UI, caseworkers assess which job-seekers are likely to find a job on their own and can be granted a second 60-week period of UI benefits. Referrals to the activity guarantee frequently occur either then or towards the end of the second period.
>
> The content of the activities is developed by local PES offices in cooperation, so far as possible, with local government and other local labour market actors: 68% of local PES offices have signed an agreement with a municipality. Mainly in metropolitan areas, some PES offices have agreements with private firms. Information from central authorities stressed the importance of *full-time* and *organised* job-search and other activities. The government bill anticipated activities in groups of 10-15 persons, while the Labour Market Board subsequently recommended 25-30 persons. In addition to group activities, participants in the activity guarantee can take part in all other Swedish active labour market programmes. However, in survey responses, 58% of programme supervisors considered that information about the activity guarantee was insufficient. Almost a quarter of the PES offices reported that participants were not offered a full-time activity, owing to lack of staff.
>
> Participant survey responses indicate that a common way of working has been to initially offer job-seeking activities in groups and later to offer a slot on a labour market programme. Two-thirds of participants surveyed said that they had been "activated" full-time during their time in the programme. However, almost half met their supervisor less than once a month. Participants on average had applied for two jobs during the four-week period preceding the telephone interview, but 60% of them had not applied for any job. Three out of four were very or fairly content with the programme, but almost half were critical due to a lack of individual adjustment and meaningfulness, and the majority did not think that participating had had any effect on their chances of getting a job.
>
> a) The maximum is not an entitlement, but the UI fund may decide on one extension of the 300-day benefit period, making a total 600 days (SO, 2002).
> b) According to desired labour supply. This means that, for example, an individual whose desired labour supply is stated to be 100 %, but who is on part-time sick leave, is supposed to participate full time minus the percentage of time on sick leave.
>
> *Source:* Forslund *et al.* (forthcoming).

and European activation strategies should not be exaggerated. For example, until recently, relatively few US clients had lost a full benefit owing to the operation of time limits.[43]

In Denmark, Ireland, the Netherlands, the United Kingdom and the United States, sharp declines in beneficiary totals followed the introduction of activation policies. In Denmark and

Table 4.3 **Elements in the activation strategies of Denmark, Ireland, the Netherlands and the United Kingdom**

	Denmark
1989	First in a series of tighter definitions of the obligation to accept "suitable work".
1992	Job offers, previously made after 2 ½ years of unemployment, are brought forward for young people.
1994	"Active period of benefits" which starts after four years of unemployment. Individual action plans introduced. New government information systems to track communications between the PES and benefit institutions.
1995	Creation of a central government "availability inspection unit" to supervise the implementation of benefit eligibility criteria.
1996	"Active period of benefits" applies after two years of unemployment.
1999	The unemployed must be registered with the PES from the first day of unemployment. The relaxation of availability rules for 50-59-year-olds is limited to 55-59-year-olds.
2000	"Active period of benefits" applies after one year of unemployment.
	Ireland
1996	Labour force survey finds that 25% of a sample of individuals on the Live Register (unemployment benefit register) are not reported to be a usual resident at the address given: only 25% are confirmed to be ILO unemployed. A questionnaire is mailed to all beneficiaries and an anti-fraud drive initiated. Beneficiaries aged 18 and 19 and unemployed for more than six months are required to register with the placement service FÁS.
1998	Beneficiaries aged under 25 and crossing the six-month threshold of benefit receipt enter processes under Ireland's Employment Action Plan (EAP – part of the European Employment Strategy). These processes require attendance at an interview.
1999	25-34-year-olds crossing a 12-month threshold enter EAP processes.
2000	20-54-year-olds crossing a 9-month threshold enter EAP processes.
	Netherlands
Late 1980s	A "change in focus" which results in sanctions for UI benefits increasing from 27 000 in 1987 to 140 000 in 1994.
1991	Introduction of the Youth Work Guarantee.
1992	Guidelines as regards "suitable work" are defined. Sanction frequency for assistance beneficiaries increases sharply.
1995	Radical reforms to the institutional structure of benefit administration. "Melkert" jobs are introduced (the stocks of participants in job creation schemes rose from about 20 000 in 1994 to 80 000 by 1999).
1996	New legislation concerning benefit sanctions. Sharply increased attention is given to the long-term unemployed: part of the direct grant to the PES is earmarked for the reintegration programmes for disadvantaged jobseekers, and another part is diverted to the benefit institutions for them to purchase such programmes.
	United Kingdom
1986	Programme of Restart interviews introduced. In later years many different types and schedules of interviews are tested and successful models are applied nationwide.
1989	"Actively seeking work" becomes a condition for benefit eligibility. Benefit administration and placement offices are united at local level (over several years).
1991	Participation in a one-week job-search course is made obligatory for those who have been unemployed for over two years.
Early 1990s	"Stricter benefit regime" leads to a doubling of benefit sanctions.
1996	Benefit legislation overhauled with the introduction of the Jobseekers Allowance.
1998	New Deal for Young People makes participation in a 6-month labour market programme obligatory for all youth remaining unemployed after six months plus an additional four-month "Gateway" period of intensive counselling.
2000	New Deal for Adults applies after 18 months unemployed.

Source: OECD (1993, 1998, 2000, 2001); AM (2000); Corcoran (2002); OECD database on Labour Market Programmes.

the United Kingdom, the unemployment beneficiary total by 2001 was one and a half to two times lower than the trough levels of the late 1980s (two to three times lower than in the mid-1990s).[44] In the United States, the number of adults on welfare by 2001 was two and a half times lower than the trough of the late 1980s (three times lower than in 1993).[45] Large falls that are seen when comparing two peak years in the economic cycle, and which contrast with the absence of such falls in other OECD countries, are not easily explained by cyclical factors. Although other factors were involved in individual cases, activation

Box 4.8. **The impact of activation measures in Ireland**

Ireland was the country with the highest ratio of beneficiary to labour force survey unemployment by 1995 (Belgium held this position in 1991: see OECD, 1994b; 1997). This is partly because the beneficiary concept used, the "Live Register", is unusually comprehensive (it includes claims awaiting decision, persons paid for only part of the week, and "credits only" cases – people for whom only social insurance contributions are paid but cash benefit is not payable under means-testing rules), and only about three-quarters of cases are in receipt of a full payment. From 1975 to 1985 beneficiary and labour force survey measures of unemployment tracked each other very closely (Chart 4.9). After this, a gap emerged and steadily widened as labour force survey (LFS) unemployment fell sharply, yet beneficiary unemployment did not.

This could be related to the fact that there was very little activation in Ireland before 1996: there was no requirement on benefit claimants to register with the employment service for placement and the benefit administration did little to enforce job-search criteria, although it carried out anti-fraud activity to detect claims by people in work. After 1996, the beneficiary total fell sharply – in line with the timing of the activation measures listed in Table 4.3 – and microeconomic evidence suggests that the activation measures had a large impact on beneficiary unemployment.

However, LFS unemployment fell after 1996 even more rapidly (see Walsh, 2003, for an analysis of these trends by age and sex). One possible explanation is that the activation measures were targeted on those more likely to find work – who tend to be recorded as unemployed in the LFS – and relatively inactive older workers, very long-term unemployed or "credits only" cases were not so often targeted. Overall, in Ireland it seems that beneficiary and labour force survey measures did move together for many years, but after they diverged, the relationship between the two became quite complex.

Corcoran (2002) presents data for outflows from the Live Register (unemployment benefit register) among people referred to Ireland's Employment Action Plan (EAP) between June 1999 and September 2000. These were persons aged under 25 who crossed the threshold of six months unemployment and persons aged 25 to 54 who crossed the threshold of nine months unemployment. On average, nearly 35% of those referred did not actually attend an interview within three months, but those who did attend an interview had on average five contacts with their case officer in the period after referral. Overall, 64% of those referred left the register within three months and 93% left within 12 months: these proportions vary little by age or gender: the proportions leaving were slightly higher among those who did not attend the interview. Of those who left the register, 85% were still off the register at the end of the 12 months. Although this study did not have a control group, the rates of leaving cited appear to be much higher than usual in Ireland. The distribution of the Live Register by unemployment duration suggests that the usual rate of exit from unemployment is about 30% per quarter.[*]

In two areas, Kilkenny and Ballyfermot, under a pilot programme all persons who had been unemployed for more than six months (rather than only those who cross the threshold of six months unemployment if aged under 25 and 9 months if aged 25 to 54) were referred to EAP. Corcoran (2002) presents graphs to show that the fall in the total Live Register (from October 1999 to June 2001) in each of these areas was about 20 percentage points greater than for the surrounding region as a whole.

[*] The number of persons on the Live Register with an unemployment duration of 9-12 months is about half the number with an unemployment duration of 3-6 months, implying a "survival" rate of about 70% per quarter. The study cited also provides information about rates of entry to employment among those referred to EAP, but it is not clear what these imply in terms of impact.

Chart 4.9. **Unemployment beneficiaries and LFS unemployment[a] have tended to diverge in Ireland since 1986**
Percentages of population aged 15-64

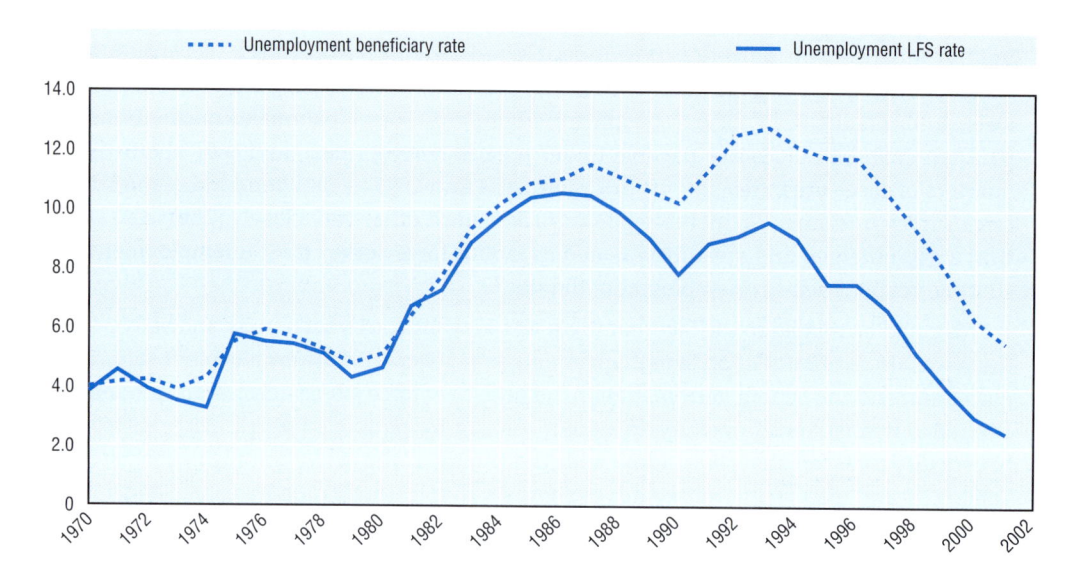

a) Live Register, annual average: estimates based on December data for 1970 to 1979; labour force statistics, April.
Source: CSO, Statistical Abstract, various years; www.irlgov.ie/daff/publicat/1996comp/etable17.xls; eirestat.cso.ie/LRAMvarlist.html. For unemployment, OECD Labour Force Statistics database (Quarterly Labour Force Statistics for 2002). For population, as for Chart 4.5.

strategies seem to be the main common policy development across these five countries, so there is a case that their influence has been particularly important.

This does not necessarily mean that such policies will always be effective. Two reasons for caution can be advanced:

- The above-mentioned activation strategies started from a position where the administration had few compulsory contacts with beneficiaries to promote work.[46] This made it easy for the first activation measures to have an impact. Outcomes from further intensification of activation measures may face declining returns.

- The number of available jobs and, in general, labour demand matters. The five countries each had some feature that could facilitate a reasonable flow of job vacancies arising in the labour market. In Ireland and the Netherlands, restrictive national wage agreements had improved competitiveness and economic growth prior to the introduction of "activation" strategies. The other three countries have high rates of job turnover. Regardless of any direct impact of turnover on aggregate employment, a higher flow of job openings makes it easier to assess jobseeker availability for unsubsidised work through tracking the outcome of job interviews, reasons for job loss, etc., and thus enforce this criterion. Where there are very few job openings, it may be difficult to get a large employment impact from activation strategies. Activation strategies have substantial costs, and may not be politically sustainable if their impact is limited.

Box 4.9. **The content of welfare reform in the United States**

The US assistance benefit "Aid to Families with Dependent Children" (AFDC) was introduced in 1937. The system has generally been restricted to lone-parent families. For a long time, efforts to reduce welfare use and promote self-sufficiency met with little success. In 1996, as part of a major reform effort, AFDC was replaced by Temporary Assistance for Needy Families (TANF), with encouraging results.

Prior to welfare reform, states administered AFDC and established maximum benefit levels. However, federal funds paid half the cost of the benefit payments and federal legislation determined how benefits should change when the individual had earnings, and required states to aid all families eligible under their rules. Beneficiaries were required to be available for work in principle, but this was not always enforced. TANF combined federal funding for AFDC benefits and administration and two related programs – Emergency Assistance to Needy Families (EA) and the Job Opportunities and Basic Skills Training Program (JOBS) – into fixed block grants, while also imposing a Maintenance of Effort rule that requires states not to reduce their own spending by more than 20 to 25% below its pre-TANF level. TANF also: *a)* allows states to decide whether to disregard some earnings as a work incentive, and, if so, how much *b)* expressly denies entitlement to individuals; *c)* sets a five-year limit on federally-funded aid for a given claimant, with some exemptions; and *d)* requires claimants to work (as defined by the State) after a maximum of two years of benefits, and requires states to engage a rising percentage of their total caseload in work activities (Committee on Ways and Means, 2000).

Some of the provisions of the 1996 law are complicated.* Despite this complexity, some reports have given a fairly clear picture of its implementation (Gallagher *et al.*, 1998; GAO, 1998). Nathan and Gais (1999), in research based on 19 state reports, emphasise that changes in state administrative practices were rapid and profound, and had quite broad support. Employment, labour, or workforce development agencies became closely involved, although some states had been developing links between welfare and employment programs for some time. Large urban offices tend to rely on specialists – sometimes working as teams – while offices with smaller caseloads consolidate eligibility and employment functions in one position. About half the sites require new applicants to conduct some sort of initial and often independent search for work. Two-thirds review families for "diversion" assistance. This can be a lump-sum cash payment or loan in exchange for waiving eligibility for cash benefits for some time, such as six months. The term "diversion" can also refer to activities such as eligibility screening, when carried out in ways that discourage pursuit of the claim. Other important developments include the use of "personal responsibility agreements", which vary greatly but may be specific and individualised, and may involve frequent meetings with clients to track compliance. States are likely to impose "graduated, calibrated, or even 'vanishing' sanctions" (sanctions that are notified but later withdrawn) to get parents to pay attention to programme requirements. "Case workers can act very selectively."

States have also increased their support for work. Many states expanded eligibility higher up the income scale for a variety of benefits, including child-care assistance, state earned income tax credits, transportation services, health care, help in emergencies, and child support enforcement. In 1999 a federal regulation in 1999 exempted spending that helps employed families to keep their jobs and advance in the workforce from time limits (Gais and Nathan, 2001). To some extent, there has also been a shift away from a strictly "Work First" approach towards tackling barriers faced by the hard-to-employ (Holcomb and Martinson, 2002).

* Welfare reform legislation set strict federal requirements, but at the same time encouraged states to develop their own welfare reforms. It is difficult to provide a sense of how the policies are implemented: "for example, how the state's work requirement works in practice, what happens when an applicant walks in the door, what services go to which families, who gets sanctioned and why. And in states that have devolved further to counties or localities, it is sometimes not even meaningful to talk of a state policy. (...) We can look at state data about caseload declines, but in the absence of common eligibility rules across states, one cannot readily tell to what extent a decline in a state reflects reduced need or contracted eligibility (Greenberg, 2001)".

B. Substitution between benefits

It is sometimes claimed that tightening eligibility criteria for one benefit may lead some recipients to move onto other benefits. Such substitution effects would reduce the *net* impact of policy changes on total benefit recipiency. Where activation strategies are plausibly doing much to reduce dependency on the "active" benefits, success may seem to be undermined or threatened by increased dependency on early retirement, disability, lone-parent benefits (when these are inactive) or even (in the case of Sweden) sickness benefits. And if reductions in unemployment have been achieved only through transfers of beneficiaries from unemployment to early retirement and disability schemes, the improvement is illusory.

Existing evidence on substitution effects of this kind is mixed:

- In some cases, substitution effects dominate. Very large international differences in rates of inflow to disability benefits in the 60-64 age group reflect differences in the statutory age of regular retirement and the availability of early retirement programmes. In Australia, declining access to alternative payments such as Wife Pension and Widow Pension partly explains recent increases in disability benefit recipiency (OECD, 2003, pp. 81 and 99).

- However, in behavioural terms disability and early retirement schemes can also be complements, rather than substitutes.[47]

- There also seems to be some evidence that tighter eligibility criteria for disability benefits result in somewhat higher unemployment levels. However, the opposite is not necessarily true: "there is little evidence that high or increasing unemployment leads to high or increasing levels of disability benefit recipiency" (OECD, 2003, p. 10).

- OECD (2002a, Chapter 4) identified Belgium, Ireland and Italy as the only EU countries where 2% or more of the working-age population were unemployed for nearly every month in a four-year observation window (1994-97). These countries had the highest rates of continuing unemployment among the long-term unemployed, but other countries had higher rates of transition from long-term unemployment into inactivity. This suggests substitution between very-long-term unemployment and some forms of inactivity.

To check the importance of these phenomena further, Chart 4.10 shows changes in recipiency of "active" and "inactive" benefits between 1990 and 1999. These years are chosen to minimise the impact of cyclical factors, since 1990 and 1999 were both peak years in most countries. Charts 4.10.A and 4.10.B treat unemployment as the only "active" benefit category and all other benefits as inactive. Charts 4.10.C and 4.10.D treat lone-parent and non-categorical social assistance benefits also as "active". On the latter basis, a fall in the unemployment plus social assistance benefit total occurred in Denmark, Great Britain, the Netherlands and the United States – countries where, according to the analysis here, activation policies were probably an influence – as well as in Canada and Spain. In Denmark and Great Britain, declines in unemployment and social assistance recipiency from 1990 to 1999 were in fact mainly offset by increased recipiency of other benefits. The increases were mainly in old-age and general (not lone-parent) parental benefits in Denmark, and disability and care benefits in Great Britain.

Overall there is a weak (statistically insignificant) tendency in Charts 4.10.B and 4.10.D for a fall in recipiency of "active" benefits to be accompanied by an increase in recipiency of other "inactive" benefits. However, this tendency is too weak to make much difference to the final result: there is a strong positive correlation between changes in recipiency rates

4. BENEFITS AND EMPLOYMENT, FRIEND OR FOE? INTERACTIONS BETWEEN PASSIVE AND ACTIVE SOCIAL PROGRAMMES

Chart 4.10. **Is there substitution between active and inactive benefits?**
Percentage points change in recipiency rates, 1990 to 1999

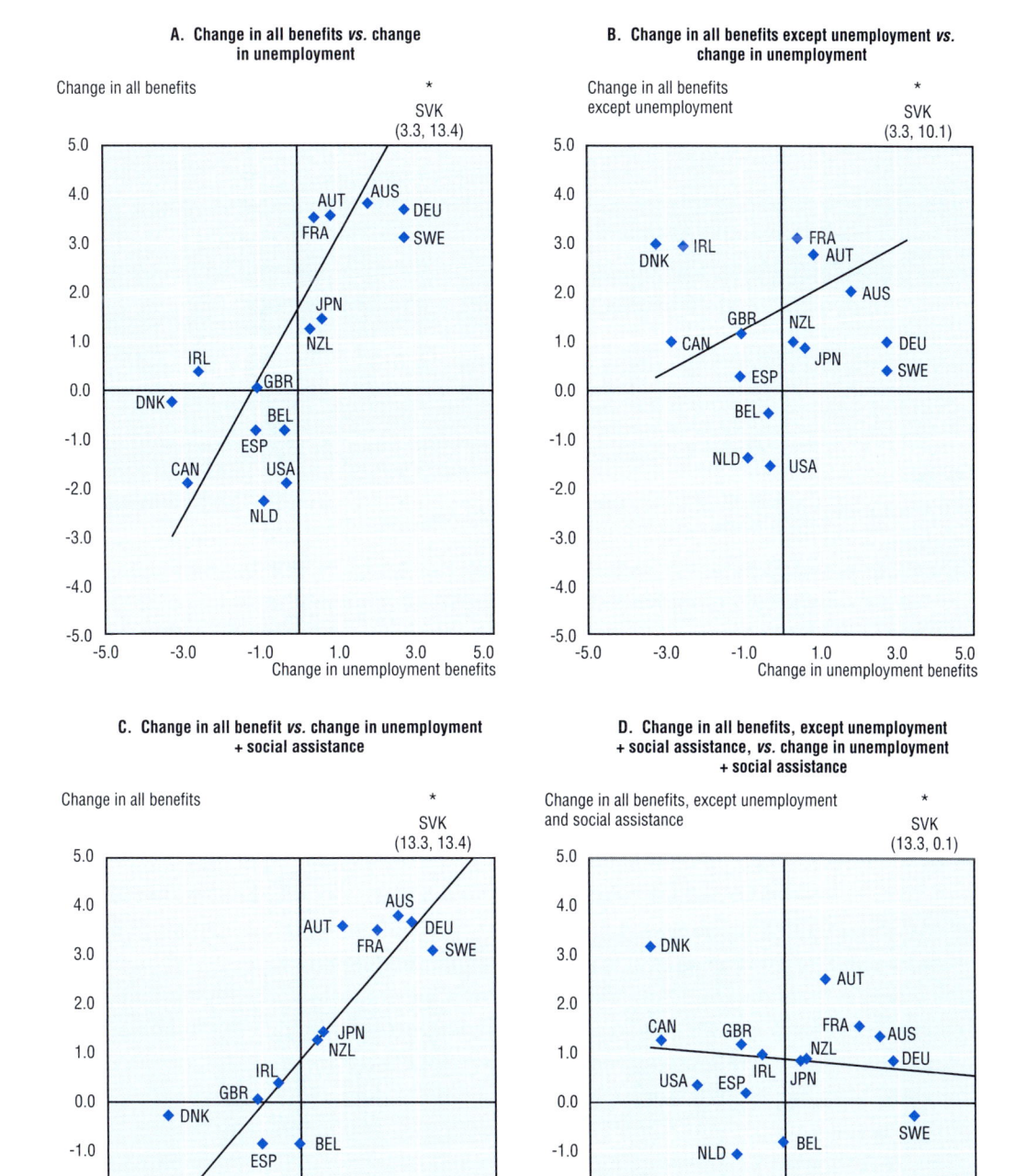

A. Change in all benefits *vs.* change in unemployment

B. Change in all benefits except unemployment *vs.* change in unemployment

C. Change in all benefit *vs.* change in unemployment + social assistance

D. Change in all benefits, except unemployment + social assistance, *vs.* change in unemployment + social assistance

* Point outside the axes. This is included in the calculation of the regression lines.
Source: See Chart 4.3.

for the "active" benefits and changes in overall benefit dependency, *i.e.* relatively larger declines in the "active" benefits were not significantly offset by relatively larger increases in other benefits. Substitution across large benefit categories is unlikely to be complete – there are unemployed workers who cannot easily qualify for disability benefits, and disability beneficiaries who cannot qualify for early retirement benefits, etc. – and it may not require a specific policy response, beyond paying specific attention to the issues of administering each benefit correctly according to its own eligibility criteria.

C. *The effect on employment, earnings and career prospects*

Evaluations suggest that activation strategies, combined with tight eligibility criteria, can help raise employment prospects of benefit recipients. However, there is also a risk that some individuals end up neither with benefits nor in employment.

Benefits with tight eligibility criteria can enhance the incentive to look for a job…

On the basis of international comparisons, an important distinction can be made between older workers and younger workers. Among older workers, aggregate data, if available, would probably show a strong negative relationship between benefit dependency (summing across regular old-age pensions, early retirement pensions, and disability and unemployment benefits) and employment rates. Among younger workers, such a relationship probably does not exist. The countries of Southern Europe, except Portugal, have low rates of youth employment and at the same time low rates of youth benefit dependency owing to the absence of a general minimum income or social assistance benefit. Dependency on parental support rather than on a public benefit is common, and participation in initial education may also be relatively prolonged. In this case, the non-availability of benefits is not successful in promoting employment, and a combination of benefits with activation measures might be more successful.

… together with activation strategies, this may result in higher employment, but also sometimes more people with neither jobs nor benefits.

There is some evidence that when new income-replacement benefits are introduced without job requirements, some reduction in employment results. The lone-parent benefit of New Zealand (see Box 4.5 above) is a case in point. Goodger and Larose (1998) note that employment rates of divorced and separated women were substantially higher than those of married women in the 1971 Census, and there was little difference in the labour force participation rates of lone compared to partnered mothers in the 1976 Census. Then, through to 1981, the employment rates of lone parents declined. Bradshaw *et al.* (2000) report that the employment rate of lone mothers was 27% in 1991, increasing to 36% in 1996, but this was still the lowest rate among the six countries in this comparative study, and 29 percentage points lower than for married mothers. This gap in employment rates between lone mothers and married mothers thus developed in New Zealand after the introduction of the lone-parent benefit, whereas the employment rate gap is small in other countries where work requirements are present (*e.g.* the United States after welfare reform, or Denmark and Sweden). However, the total shortfall of lone-parent employment that might be attributed to the Domestic Purposes Benefit (DPB) seems to be less than half of the total number of DPB recipients.[48]

Conversely, the total number of single mothers in the United States was about the same in 2001 as in 1993, at 8.9 million (Table 4.4).[49] Between these two dates, the number

Table 4.4. Decline in welfare recipiency and increase in employment for single mothers in the United States

Source	Adult AFDC/TANF beneficiaries (Administrative data)		Single mothers[b] (Current Population Survey)			Percentages[c] of single mothers aged 16-45, excluding disabled and students, who had nonzero annual income from: (Current Population Survey, March supplement)				Total adults with income during the year from AFDC/TANF[d]
	Total	Of which: single mothers[a]	Total	Of which: employed	Employment rate	Work, not welfare	Work and welfare	Welfare, not work	Neither work nor welfare	
	000s	000s	000s	000s	%	%	%	%	%	000s
	(1)	(2)	(3)	(4)	(5)	(6)	(7)	(8)	(9)	(10)
1984	3 713	3 024	7 027	3 910	55.6	62.9	9.7	20.8	6.6	..
1985	3 648	3 019	7 161	4 059	56.7	61.9	11.5	20.1	6.6	..
1986	3 695	3 082	7 288	4 249	58.3	61.0	11.8	20.4	6.9	..
1987	3 684	3 113	7 604	4 432	58.3	61.6	12.2	18.9	7.3	3 611
1988	3 595	3 084	7 570	4 386	57.9	62.7	11.6	19.4	6.4	3 639
1989	3 565	3 094	7 769	4 549	58.6	65.3	10.5	17.7	6.4	3 518
1990	3 705	3 208	7 789	4 744	60.9	62.8	13.1	17.9	6.3	3 951
1991	4 079	3 431	8 221	4 818	58.6	61.4	12.6	19.4	6.6	4 327
1992	4 399	3 624	8 566	4 917	57.4	60.9	12.8	19.3	6.9	4 337
1993	4 583	3 721	8 905	5 169	58.0	61.2	14.2	18.0	6.6	4 649
1994	4 615	3 744	9 378	5 512	58.8	64.5	14.6	14.3	6.6	4 224
1995	4 379	3 574	9 375	5 773	61.6	67.2	13.3	12.4	7.1	3 806
1996	3 974	3 250	9 435	6 002	63.6	68.6	13.5	10.8	7.1	3 634
1997	3 154	2 496	9 598	6 349	66.1	71.7	12.5	8.3	7.5	2 914
1998	2 523	2 092	9 378	6 484	69.1	75.0	11.6	5.6	7.8	2 329
1999	1 869	1 587	9 433	6 741	71.5	79.9	9.6	3.8	6.7	1 924
2000	1 576	1 370	9 266	6 810	73.5	82.0	7.2	3.6	7.1	1 686
2001	1 478	1 284	8 899	6 515	73.2	81.9	5.9	3.2	8.9	1 600
Change from 1993 to 2001	–3 105	–2 437	–6	1 346	15.2	20.7	–8.3	–14.8	2.3	–3 049.0

AFDC: Aid to Families with Dependant Children.
TANF: Temporary Assistance for Needy Families.

a) Single mother recipients are estimated as total recipients, less child recipients, less the percentage of adult recipients who are married or widowed (estimated for years prior to 1998 using data for unemployed parent beneficiaries).
b) Excludes widowed mothers.
c) Includes widowed mothers. "Welfare" refers to income from AFDC/TANF.
d) Includes adult caretakers in child-only AFDC/TANF cases, who are not beneficiaries.

Source: Columns 1 and 2: US Department of Health and Human Services, Indicators of Welfare Dependence (aspe.hhs.gov/hsp/indicators02/appa-tanf.htm); Columns 3 and 4: unpublished tabulations by the Bureau of Labour Statistics, provided by Gary Burtless; Columns 6 to 9, calculations from Current Population Survey, March supplements, provided by Jeffrey Liebman; Column 10: CPS March supplements at www.census.gov/hhes/income/dinctabs.html and Richard Bavier.

of single mothers receiving AFDC/TANF on the basis of administrative statistics fell by about 2.4 million, and the number in employment rose by 1.35 million, only slightly more than half the fall in recipient numbers.[50] The number of single mothers reporting no income from either employment or welfare at any time during the year rose slightly, by about 0.2 million. Data for the number that are neither in employment nor receiving welfare in the average month are not available, but the change measured on this basis could have been somewhat greater. However the proportion of those without any work income who had some benefit income (i.e. column 8, as a proportion of the sum of columns 8 and 9), which was consistently about three-quarters up to 1993, fell to about one-quarter by 2001. This suggests that access to benefits has become much more difficult for those who are not in work at all. In the United States, as in New Zealand, interpretation is made more difficult by evidence that surveys are not identifying all the people who are receive benefits according to administrative data.[51] Thus part of the fall in recipiency that is seen in administrative data may relate to single mothers who are omitted from survey data, and under-sampling of particular categories (e.g. mothers with no income from either work or welfare) may have increased.

Random-assignment evaluations of labour market programmes at the 11 sites of the US National Evaluation of Welfare-to-Work Strategies (NEWWS) are among the most informative such evaluations ever conducted. In particular, they provide data on employment and earnings for five years after participation (or selection into the control group) in a programme. The programmes involved in the experiments can be roughly categorised into human capital development, i.e. mainly training, and labour force attachment, i.e. mainly job-search assistance (Grogger et al., 2002). All programmes reduced benefit receipt. On average, among programme participants, benefit receipt declined by about five percentage points,[52] the percentage employed grew by about 3.5 points and total annual earnings by about USD 350, which can be interpreted as 3% of year-round full-time earnings in a low-wage job. Putting these numbers together suggests that participation in a NEWWS programme had an impact on employment that was about 60% or 70% of the impact on welfare recipiency. Overall, several types of evidence[53] point to the conclusion that the proportion of welfare leavers (or divertees) who are employed is about 60% and is similar to the proportion of all lone parents or indeed all mothers in general that work in the United States. Such results suggest that the beneficiary population, in the years of high recipiency rates, did consist to a large extent of people who were employable and able to actually (perhaps with help from employment services) find work after a change in the passive and active policy environment.

Activation strategies which include job-search assistance and skill formation can also enhance job stability

US and UK evaluations of activation strategies have found some evidence that additional pressure on unemployed people to take up jobs results in them entering work at lower wages on average:

- In Maryland job-search experiments, reported by Benus et al. (1997), one of the experimental treatment groups was released from the usual requirement to report work search contacts each week (although these claimants were still informed that they must search for work). This treatment increased the average duration of UI payments, relative to the control group, by 0.4 weeks, but it also increased total annual earnings by USD 347, or 4.1%). Possible explanations are that jobseekers when freed from job-search constraints waited longer for recall by the previous employer or for a better-paid job, or searched more efficiently, or had a stronger bargaining position with potential employers (OECD, 2000, p. 141).

- In the UK evaluation of the Jobseekers' Allowance, which was introduced in 1996, it emerges that after the change in benefit legislation, larger proportions of jobseekers re-entered work rapidly, but among them mean re-employment earnings (at constant prices) were lower by 21% for males and by 3% for females. This was due in particular to a large fall in the proportion of re-entrants who obtained jobs in the highest pay band. It seems that potentially high-paid workers are relatively well able to respond to pressure to re-enter work more quickly, but at the cost of accepting lower pay (Martin and Grubb, 2001).

However evaluations of two other UK measures – Restart interviews (introduced in 1986) and the New Deal for Young People (introduced in 1998) – have reported no evidence that higher rates of return to work are accompanied by lower job quality in terms of wages or job duration (van Reenen, 2003).

NEWWS findings suggest that impacts of US welfare-to-work programmes on earnings often stayed positive for five years when, in some cases, impacts on employment were fading. Programmes providing intensive job matching and skill development assistance gave relatively positive results. The large impact of one programme in Portland supports the idea that skilled and intensive case management, and selectivity in making referrals to training and employment programmes, can significantly improve long-term outcomes. This is further supported by findings from Canada's SSP Plus programme, where impact of financial incentives on employment and earnings faded away after the three years of in-work benefits had ended (see Box 3.1 in Chapter 3), but additional employment services had an impact that increased over time, becoming highest in these years (Michalopoulos *et al.*, 2002, Table ES.7).

Grogger *et al.* (2002) examine the effects of in-work benefits, which are discussed in more detail in Chapter 3. Two of the three random-assignment studies examined show no effect on earnings, which the authors consider is consistent with the idea that the income effect which arises from the financial incentive dominates the substitution effect. Other programmes which combined mandatory work requirements with financial work incentives did generally increase both employment and earnings. Earlier research (Berlin, 2000) similarly concluded that for these programmes "(…) employment and earnings gains among long-term welfare recipients were among the largest found in any previously evaluated welfare-to-work programs, and the income gains and accompanying poverty reductions were unprecedented". Overall, the evidence seems consistent with the idea that imposing job-search requirements without at the same time offering job-search assistance can result in entry to lower-paid jobs, but job-search requirements with intensive employment counselling and additional assistance can improve employment stability and earnings.

The more expensive labour market strategies, with a strong emphasis on training to improve jobseeker productivity, may narrow the earnings distribution by gradually raising skill levels among the population of low-paid workers. Denmark and the Netherlands, among European countries that had significant success in cutting benefit recipiency in the 1990s, have a relatively equal distribution of earnings and low incidence of poverty (Andersen and Jensen, 2002). These observations suggest that the reduction of beneficiary totals through activation policies can be compatible with good poverty outcomes, although the latter are influenced by a range of factors other than activation.

The impact of activation strategies on income distribution could be quite different from their impact on earnings distribution. Given that unemployment is a major factor in poverty and inequality and that employment pays more than benefits, higher employment rates reduce income inequality. At the same time, tight eligibility conditions and work requirements for benefits could reduce the benefit coverage of the population that is not in employment. However as long as the tightening of eligibility conditions has a substantial impact on employment, it seems plausible that the former effect could dominate. In the United States, despite evidence that job entry under welfare reform occurred at relatively low earnings and that benefit coverage of single mothers who are not in work has fallen sharply, poverty rates for children in female-headed families moved favourably through to 2000, even as compared to earlier periods of cyclical upswing in the economy (Brookings Institution, 2002).[54]

Conclusions

There is scope for much further research into benefit recipiency, and its determinants and consequences. It will be useful to improve the cross-country availability of well-documented data on benefit recipiency, with parallel information about benefit entitlements and other measures that may influence recipiency. This can help expand the range of national experiences in terms of the activation measures experimented in different countries, and provide evidence on which types of policies seem to have an impact and how key labour market outcomes such as unemployment, employment rates and poverty rates are affected by policies that are administratively targeted on beneficiaries.

Some other questions warrant answers:

- Are increased unemployment and social assistance benefit entitlements, when associated with effective activation measures, able to pull people into the labour force and retain them in employment?
- Decentralisation of employment programmes needs to be combined with strategies for sharing information (*e.g.* using common reporting standards and computing systems) and ensuring that objectives do not diverge excessively (*e.g.* whether through continuous discussion to ensure political consensus, or through performance measurement). Does the financing and political governance of unemployment benefits and active policy measures at different levels of government (*e.g.* national, regional and local) have any systematic impact?
- A more systematic analysis of the links between active programme participation, job stability and career advancement is needed. For example, would a combination of in-work benefits and occasional contacts with beneficiaries provide a route to greater job stability and higher earnings?
- The more general issue of how activation principles can be applied to benefits that traditionally have been regarded as non-employment benefits (*e.g.* lone-parent and disability benefits) deserves further scrutiny. For instance, how essential is it to have requirements of availability for work similar to those applying for unemployment benefits? What are the consequences of changing the administrative borderlines so that people are reallocated, at the margin, between benefits such as disability and

unemployment, or lone-parent and social assistance? Should activation measures for beneficiaries of non-employment benefits have their own administrative structure, or should the Public Employment Service always have the main responsibility?

- Finally, despite widespread agreement on the importance of programme evaluation, the situation leaves much to be desired in practice. To what extent do microeconomic impact studies capture long-run or aggregate impacts? What should be done to take system organisational issues and components of activation strategies other than formal labour market programmes into account?

Notes

1. In Ireland, the United Kingdom, Australia and New Zealand, social assistance benefits subject to an availability-for-work condition have traditionally been called "unemployment" benefits (although more recently renamed "jobseeker", "newstart" or "community wage" allowances, in the last three countries). In other countries the last-resort form of assistance benefit has often been considered as something very different from unemployment insurance, but to the extent that availability for work is an eligibility condition, these too can be regarded as unemployment benefits.

2. "Income-replacement" benefits refer to benefits which compensate for the absence of another main source of income, usually earnings from work.

3. In the Slovak Republic, complete data on receipt of social assistance together with another benefit were not available, so some double counting arises within the benefit dependency estimates. Also, social assistance can be paid to students and old age pensioners can work while receiving pension for one year and often do so: these two factors can account for 2%, possibly more, of the working-age population being employed or studying while also being included in the benefit dependency estimates. Also, it may be noted that the share of non-observed activities in GDP is over 20% (much higher than in Belgium or Italy, which themselves are among the OECD countries with a relatively large shadow economy: see Blades and Roberts, 2002). In a survey conducted in 2000, 15% of respondents reported being engaged in the undeclared sector often or occasionally, working about four hours a day on average (Hanousek and Palda, 2002, Tables 2 and 5). Undeclared work by recipients of income-replacement benefits could cause rates of employment, education participation and benefit dependency as measured here to total more than 100%.

4. Underreporting of employment in the labour force survey might arise when earnings are not declared for tax and social security purposes: see for example *www.eurofound.eu.int/emire/SPAIN/UNDECLAREDEMPLOYMENT-ES.html*

5. One-person households are 15% to 24% of all households in Nordic countries, but only 4% to 8% of all households in the countries of Southern Europe. Divorce rates are well above average in the Nordic countries, except Denmark, and well below average in Greece, Italy, Spain and Portugal (OECD, 2001c). In the latter countries, youths tend to live longer with their parents: according to 1987 data cited by Fernandez Cordón (2001), about 75% of 20 to 24 year-olds in Portugal and over 80% in Italy and Spain were living with their parents: these countries also had the highest rates (out of eleven EU countries covered in the data set) for 25 to 29 years olds.

6. Although the data available in the format used here do not go back before 1980, it seems likely that these rates in Europe rose even more rapidly in the two decades preceding 1980, due to legislative activity to improve benefit levels and coverage and economic recession following the first oil shock. In Denmark, Finland, Norway and Sweden, social security expenditure as a percentage of GDP increased from an average 10% in 1962 to 16% in 1970 and 25% in 1980 (statistics from the 1980 and 1986 *Yearbook of Nordic Statistics*). Thus, growth in social spending in the 1980s was much slower than in either the 1970s or the 1960s. According to official statistics (see recent issues of *Statistisk Tiarsoversigt*) the number of full-year recipients of income-replacing benefits in Denmark doubled between 1970 and 1980.

7. Falls in older-worker participation rates, as recorded in labour force statistics, sometimes continued in the 1990s through entry to disability and unemployment benefits, with informal relaxation of access to disability benefits and job-search monitoring for older unemployed persons, and through private and government-sector employer-funded pension and early retirement benefits.

8. Employer-paid sickness benefits, when legally obligatory, are included in the data presented here (although often on an estimated basis, when official statistics are lacking).

9. All UK data for benefit recipiency presented here in fact relate to Great Britain, which has about 97.3% of the UK population.

10. Note that, in contrast to Danish terminology, only sabbatical leave is classified here as a form of labour market leave (parental leave is classed as a parental benefit, and educational leave is excluded).

11. Demographic factors are a further significant influence on benefit recipiency rates, which are cited here as a percentage of the working-age population. The share of 20 to 39 year olds in the working-age population, which influences lone-parent numbers, rose from 1970 to 1990 by about 20% (not 20 percentage points) in the United States and about 10% in other English-speaking OECD countries, and then fell. The actual population of lone parents has often grown more rapidly, but this is not necessarily exogenous with respect to benefit entitlements. Until 1995, population age structures did not drive up disability prevalence (OECD, 2003, Box 3.2) but by the year 2000 the share of 50 to 64 year olds in the working-age population, an influence on disability numbers, was increasing in many countries.

12. Two major cases of reductions in benefit entitlements were the erosion during the 1980s of replacement rates for unemployment benefits in the United Kingdom (shown in Chart 4.4) and replacement rates for AFDC/TANF in the United States (discussed further below).

13. A relaxation of the eligibility criteria for a benefit will lead to surge in inflows as those newly eligible get the benefit. Inflows subsequently slow even if there is no later tightening of eligibility criteria.

14. Lemieux and Macleod (2000) find that the 1971 change in UI parameters in Canada did not immediately lead individuals to use UI repeatedly. The typical pattern of repeat use started only after an individual experienced unemployment for the first time due to an "external" cause – natural turn-over or recession. In the authors' view, this learning mechanism explains why the 1971 UI legislation can plausibly be seen as the main cause of the gap between Canadian and US unemployment rates which emerged in the 1980s and peaked in the mid-1990s (when the Canadian rate was about 4 points higher than the US rate).

15. Individuals and households usually qualify for assistance benefits only if their incomes are close to the poverty line. Long-term growth in the population that is eligible for insurance benefits is often undesirable because it involves growing distortion of behaviour (e.g. employment in spells just long enough to maximise UI benefit payouts relative to contributions) and transfers which are costly, but not well targeted on need.

16. Reversing of beneficiary growth through active policies – rather than cuts in benefit entitlements – helps to preserve positive consequences that can arise when benefits allow young people to reduce their reliance on the income of other family members. These may include greater geographical mobility, easier formation of new families and increased contact with placement, training and activation measures.

17. Beneficiary numbers grew, in the ten years prior to the global peak year, by a factor of 3.8 for Great Britain (peak in 1986), 7.9 in the Netherlands (peak also in 1986), 3.1 in Finland (peak in 1996), and 2.5 for New Zealand's lone-parent benefit (peak in 1991), even though the start date of such calculations are eight years and more after the benefit was introduced. In these cases, although in some sense the beneficiary growth was caused, or partly caused, by recession, the growth cited does represent change between two dates at a comparable point in the economic cycle. 1977 in Great Britain and 1986 in Finland were local peak years in these beneficiary series, and in the other two countries growth was uninterrupted up to the global peak year.

18. The patterns of beneficiary growth shown above are partly influenced by factors such as changes in replacement rates or variations in the conditions for other benefits (e.g. UI and disability assistance), but these are relatively minor influences. In the United Kingdom, the duration of the UI benefit was increased from 30 weeks to 52 weeks in 1967, but the assistance beneficiary total reached new peaks after this: the duration was cut back again to 26 weeks in 1996, but the assistance beneficiary total nevertheless kept falling.

19. Some of the growth in RMI beneficiary numbers in the 1990s reflects specific factors, such as reforms to "*intéressement*" arrangements which from 1998 allowed full or partial benefit to be paid during the first 750 hours or first 12 months of work in a new job. Cornilleau et al. (2000) estimate the impact of several factors but they nevertheless attribute most of the growth to an underlying trend (+69 000 per year until 1994, +39 000 per year thereafter). The number of beneficiaries of the

unemployment assistance benefit (*Allocation de Solidarité Spécifique*, created in 1984) also grew over the period, so growth in RMI numbers cannot easily be explained by substitution between benefits.

20. For example, in Finland specific macroeconomic factors (a collapse of asset markets and of trade with the former Soviet Union) were the immediate cause of the huge rise in numbers on unemployment assistance in the early 1990s that is seen in Chart 4.6. By 2003 those specific factors were history, yet much of the rise in beneficiary numbers remained. The long-term rise would no doubt have been smaller if the pre-1971 system of social assistance at the discretion of municipal authorities had been retained.

21. As illustrated in Annex 2, a change in benefit entitlements can have an immediate impact on the trend in beneficiary numbers, even though the impact on the level of beneficiary numbers is subject to long lags. Lemieux and Macleod (2000) in their concluding remarks also suggest the response to subsequent reforms is rapid, in contrast to the long-lagged nature of responses to an initial large increase in benefit entitlements, but they propose a different explanation for this.

22. For uninsured persons in the Netherlands, the relaxation of disability benefit eligibility criteria occurred later, in 1976, when the disability assistance law (AAW) aligned the assessment criteria with those for insured persons. This concerns a relatively small proportion (about a quarter, at most times) of total beneficiaries.

23. The data series used here includes beneficiaries under the former Invaliditeitswet (part of the 1919 Invalidity and Age Act), which was replaced by WAO and AAW.

24. In 1981 the net replacement rate for the Dutch disability insurance benefit was reduced by making insurance contributions deductible from disability insurance benefits. In 1985 measures to tackle abuse were introduced, and in 1989 the gross replacement rate was reduced from 80% to 70% (Anderson, 2002). Further measures in the 1990s also helped reverse beneficiary growth slightly, but only temporarily. Growth in the 50 to 64 year old share in the population has become another factor putting upwards pressure on the beneficiary numbers.

25. The EU countries are also more comparable in terms of their demographic structures. The non-EU countries shown (Korea, Mexico and the United States) have younger populations. If Europe had unchanged age-specific disability prevalence rates but the population age structure of Mexico, the youngest country, its average prevalence rate would be 25% lower (OECD, 2003, Box 3.2).

26. National differences in the intensity of work might also generate the type of correlation shown in Chart 4.8, but there is no evidence for this. OECD (2003) observes that all countries with high disability benefit recipiency rates have high income-replacement levels (p. 65) and that rates of application for disability benefits are more similar across countries than effective benefit inflow rates because rejection rates vary considerably (pp. 87-88).

27. From 1995, unemployment assistance benefits in the Netherlands have not been distinguished from other social assistance benefits in official statistics. But it seems likely that social assistance for reasons of unemployment fell rapidly, because registered unemployment and unemployment as measured by the labour force survey both fell sharply within a few years (from above 6% of the labour force in 1995 to below 3%).

28. The key role played by the national placement service however is sometimes limited to the beneficiaries of nationally-financed benefits. Local social services may have similar or greater relevance for the beneficiaries of locally-financed benefits, where these exist.

29. Engelfriet (n.d.) claims that the benefit eligibility rules are now very strictly enforced in the Netherlands.

30. Denmark's activation measures have been backed up by tough sanction provisions of last resort, but actual rates of sanction are not very high in international terms (6th out of 14 countries in Grubb, 2001, Table 2) and do not seem to have in themselves to have become a topic of much political controversy.

31. Wiseman (2001) concludes: "The basic message is that, aside from Wisconsin, there is not much work in American workfare (…), the core of American workfare is the message that work, even at low wages, is better than welfare, and welfare without work will be a hassle. It's not the 'job you can't refuse'; it's the 'appointment you can't refuse'".

32. In most employment programmes, benefits or earnings per hour of work are close to the minimum wage: hours of work are, if necessary, adjusted to ensure this outcome. The OECD countries where the initial *net* replacement rates, at $\frac{2}{3}$ of an average production worker (APW) earnings level, exceed 80% for three or four family types are Belgium, Denmark, Luxembourg, the Netherlands, Portugal, Sweden and Switzerland (OECD, 2002b, Table 3.2). This correlates fairly well with the list

of countries that spent more than 1% of GDP on active labour market measures in 2000 and 2001 (Belgium, Denmark, France, the Netherlands and Sweden).

33. Activation strategies that force the administration to interact with difficult-to-place clients include Denmark's scheduling of programme participation after one year of unemployment; the Dutch earmarking of part of PES finance specifically for long-term unemployed; scheduling of regular intensive interviews in the United Kingdom; and changes in local-level administrative practice in the United States which made benefit administrators responsible for promoting work and other alternatives to benefit (see Box 4.9).

34. National reports in Millar and Rowlingson (2001) provide detailed descriptions of arrangements for lone parents in five countries. In the Netherlands, where the obligation to seek work when children are aged over five was introduced in 1996, in practice the municipalities exempt about half of the lone mothers concerned.

35. Participation in the UK's New Deal for Lone Parents is not compulsory, but attendance at a work-focused interview was made obligatory for all benefit claimants in the "ONE" pilots. These provide a single point of entry for unemployment and other benefits, bringing together the Employment Service, local authorities and Benefits Agency staff to offer advice in one place. Within the ONE programme, interviews are now scheduled to take place annually. In New Zealand, in 1999 lone parents with children under the age of 6 were expected to attend a compulsory interview once a year (see Ministry of Social Development, 2001, for a description and evaluation of these policies), although this obligation was later dropped. In Australia, an annual interview for lone parents with children below the age of 13, and an actual obligation to participate in some activity for six hours a week where children are aged over 13, will be introduced from September 2003. One argument for compulsory work-focused interviews in the case of lone-parent beneficiaries is that most of them do enter work, often before any requirement to do so, and information about employment and employment services is likely to help this process. This consideration is less relevant for disability beneficiaries, many of whom never restart work.

36. Although incapacity and lone-parent beneficiaries in the ONE pilot areas were more likely to have received advice and information about jobs and training in the early months of their claim than similar beneficiaries in control areas, they did not generally receive more services, and were not significantly more likely to leave benefit. Another econometric estimation method, focusing on the new claimants in the ONE areas, found a statistically insignificant increase in hazard rates off benefit among people claiming incapacity benefits, accompanied by a weakly significant fall in male hazard rates off unemployment benefit (DWP, 2003): this might reflect the diversion of employment service resources away from the latter group.

37. Although reforms are occurring, many early retirement provisions still remain in place: in France unemployment assistance beneficiaries can request exemption from job-search requirements from the age of 55, and the United Kingdom allows males aged 60-64 to claim Income Support without showing availability for work.

38. Activation strategies such as interventions in the unemployment spell or stricter benefit eligibility criteria apply to beneficiaries. The main exceptions are probably labour market training programmes in Mexico and the United States, and to a limited extent in other countries, where participants often get a training or subsistence allowance that is unrelated to any UI or other entitlement. Also, all countries provide labour market information services including job matching (less frequently extending to personalised services such as career counselling) which are open to all jobseekers. But in general activation strategies are not likely to have a direct effect on unemployed people who are not claiming benefit (such as student unemployed).

39. The Swedish social protection system is generous mainly in the sense that replacement rates for those on labour market measures, unemployment benefits or other benefits are relatively high, and these measures have high coverage. However, the duration of unemployment benefits is limited.

40. Sianesi (2001), describing the institutional background to programme participation by unemployed people in Sweden, explains that "(…) even when focusing on individuals having just entered unemployment, it can in general be claimed that they will join a programme at some future point in time, provided that they remain unemployed 'long enough'" and "when considering the decision to choose one specific programme among those available, Harkman (2000) has found the caseworker to be the relevant decision-maker".

41. Like other countries Sweden has increasingly experienced problems with the management of "non-employment" benefits: from 1997 the number of employed people absent from work on sickness benefit – which has tended to be higher in Sweden than any other country analysed here

– more than doubled (see *www.rfv.se/english/stat/sick/sjukp.htm* for recent statistics and *www.eiro.eurofound.ie/2003/01/InBrief/SE0301103N.html* for some recent policy developments).

42. Moffitt (2002) notes that "More than thirty states have either diversion policies or have imposed work requirements that must be fulfilled prior to eligibility for benefits. (…) In some states, the decline in entry onto welfare has been more important quantitatively than the increase in exit rates in accounting for the caseload decline." Grogger and Michapoulos (2003) and Grogger (forthcoming) cite differential responses to welfare reform by age of children as evidence of an anticipatory response to time limits (mothers with children aged over 13 would not be expected to change behaviour in response to the federal 5-year time limit).

43. By end 2001 or early 2002, about 231 000 families (5% of the 1996 stock of AFDC/TANF families) had reached either the Federal time limit (5 years) or a shorter state time limit. However, owing to exemption and extension provisions, the number of "cases closed" was lower (around 2%). Most of this total was in five states and in several of these a large proportion of cases closed were already employed (that is, were mixing work and welfare) before they reached the state time limits. Also, many states allow families whose cases are closed to return to welfare under certain conditions (Bloom et al., 2002). See also Wilkins (2002).

44. Falls in the number of unemployment beneficiaries were also large in Ireland (see Box 4.8), and probably large in the Netherlands, although fully consistent statistics are not available (see note 27).

45. US analysts have often referred to a halving of caseloads, but in terms of adult AFDC/TANF beneficiaries the fall was about two-thirds between 1993 and 2001. The AFDC/TANF caseload in terms of families fell less, by about 55%. Some recipient families (when the child is cared for by a relative) have no adult beneficiary.

46. In Ireland and the United Kingdom, prior to the current activation strategies, there was no requirement on unemployed people to contact or use the employment service, so there was little possibility of enforcing work-related benefit eligibility criteria. The PES in Netherlands in the 1980s suffered from "file pollution": when unemployed people found work, the PES was often unaware of this for months afterwards, and registered unemployment data came to be regarded as almost meaningless.

47. "Somewhat unexpectedly, those countries in which (early) retirement seems to play a very important role for people with disabilities as an alternative route for labour force exit (…) are also countries in which disability benefit recipients are overwhelmingly aged 45 and over (…). There appears to be a correlation between generous early retirement and (de facto) age profiling in the disability benefit regulations (…). This creates an early exit culture, which increases the burden on both the retirement and the disability schemes (…). Norway is a particularly telling example in this context, because the introduction of an early retirement programme in 1989 and the gradual broadening of this programme ever since has led to a rapid increase in the influx into this programme in parallel to a rise in the influx into disability benefits" (OECD, 2003, p. 97).

48. Around 1992, the shortfall in the employment rates of lone mothers possibly caused by DPB was 29 percentage points, but the DPB coverage of lone mothers was 84%: the first percentage is about a third of the second. Although 20% of lone parents are reported to be working full-time, Stephens (2002) also reports that the total of lone parents receiving benefits (DPB or other benefits) in administrative statistics is high relative to the census population count of lone parents. Probably some of those who have benefits reported in administrative statistics are not identified as lone parents in the survey statistics.

49. Moffitt (2002) writes: "The overriding single piece of evidence showing that progress has been made on the agenda of helping mothers on welfare work is the dramatic increase in employment rates among single mothers in the last decade. Employment rates among single mothers, the group most affected by welfare reform, have been slowly increasing for over 15 years, but have jumped markedly since 1994 (…). Employment rates rose from 60% in 1994 to 72% in 1999, a very large increase by historical standards. Among single mothers who have never been married (the group with the lowest levels of education and some of the highest rates of welfare receipt) employment rates rose even more, from 47% to 65% over the same period… despite other factors [Earned Income Tax Credit and some others] there is no question that welfare reform has played a significant role (…)."

50. One complication is that some single mothers who received AFDC/TANF before welfare reform may now be employed, but no longer be single mothers: as shown in Table 4.4, the longstanding trend rise in the number of single mothers has been reversed since 1997. Bitler et al. (2003) find that

welfare reform has led to an increase in the number of black inner-city children who live with neither parent, and a decline in the divorce rate among Hispanic women.

51. Table 4.4 shows that administrative data reported a monthly average of 4.6 million adult AFDC/TANF recipients in 1994, while survey data reported 4.2 million adults with any receipt of AFDC at any time during the year. However, it should be noted that the monthly average number of recipients is about 20% lower than the number of persons with any receipt during the year (this can be estimated from the distribution of spells by duration, as reported in *aspe.hhs.gov/hsp/indicators02/ch2.htm*. Also, within the survey data reported average months of receipt per year have varied from about 10 in 1993 to little over 9 in 2001). In addition, administrative data for "recipients" exclude the caretaker parents in cases where AFDC/TANF is paid only for the child (who might be described as recipients because they receive the money, but not beneficiaries), whereas survey data for "people 15 years old and over – number with income" include them. Calculations allowing for these factors suggest that underreporting in survey data was about 20% in the early 1990s, increasing to 40% by 2000 (unpublished estimates by Richard Bavier).

52. Programme impacts on welfare receipt tend to decline in later years, related to the fact that levels of welfare receipt decline for both the control and the treatment groups. Strawn *et al.* (2001) claim on the basis of NEWWS findings that impacts in job-search-focused programmes, but not training programmes, often fade entirely within five years. However, is hard to see much systematic difference of this kind in the data presented by Grogger *et al.* (2002).

53. Moffitt (2002) cites a review of follow-up surveys which reports that the employment rate of women just after leaving welfare is about 60%. About 75% of them work at some point in the year after leaving, but "only a little over a third work four quarters in a row, signalling a potential problem with employment retention and stability (…). After a year or two off the rolls, earnings gains slightly exceed the losses in TANF benefits. When EITC income is added in, the gains are slightly higher. However, the major change in income after leaving welfare comes from increased income from other family members (…)." This suggests that welfare leavers who do not enter work often become dependent on other family members.

54. Declines in poverty among the children of single mothers reflect higher income from in-work benefits, as well as increased employment rates. It remains to be seen how robust the improvement has been during the current slowdown.

ANNEX 1

Definition and Measurement of Benefit Recipiency Rates

Background

A definitional and conceptual framework for reporting and classifying social protection expenditure and receipts called ESSPROS was developed by Eurostat from 1971, with major revisions of the classification manuals in 1981 and 1996. Relatively complete data according to the ESSPROS system are available for many EU countries for years back to 1980 (although often with a statistical break in data series in 1990). The concept of "social protection expenditure" that is currently implemented includes not only public expenditure but also mandatory private expenditure and voluntary private expenditure (although not all countries supply data for the last two components) and, in principle, both cash expenditure (income transfers to beneficiaries) and in-kind benefits.[1] More recently, data going back to 1980 for 29 OECD countries has been assembled in OECD's SOCX database (see *www.oecd.org/social*: this is based mainly on ESSPROS data as regards EU countries).

There are no equally comprehensive data sets relating to the number of beneficiaries of social protection spending. This has for many years been an important barrier to analytical understanding of the labour market implications of social protection benefits, and *vice versa*. Most labour market data refer to persons, so that the social protection data and labour market data available for cross-national analysis have used different units. Moreover, some information on the characteristics of beneficiaries is needed in order to achieve substantive comparability of the data on benefit spending. For example, in some countries 30% or more of disability beneficiaries are aged 65 and over while in other countries this percentage is close to zero because disability pensions are systematically replaced by old-age pensions at retirement age. Therefore, spending data are not comparable in the absence of additional data on the age distribution of disability benefit recipients.

In some countries, survey data on benefit recipiency are available, and these typically provide more information about demographic characteristics of recipients than administrative data. However, there are several reasons for preferring administrative data sources when assessing overall levels and trends of benefit dependency:

- In many countries comprehensive information about benefit recipiency is not available from surveys, especially on a comparable basis through time.
- Survey data, when available, are affected by underreporting and misclassification.[2]
- In countries with high levels of benefit recipiency, many policy measures – including benefit eligibility criteria, benefit replacement rates, and most spending on active labour market programmes – are targeted on recipients of specific benefits identified through

administrative records, rather than broad demographic groups or categories such as lone parents, the disabled or the unemployed in general.

Relatively intractable problems arise in trying to define a fully satisfactory conceptual framework for measuring the number of beneficiaries of social protection schemes. In particular, the *gross recipiency rate* for social protection benefits (*i.e.* the number of benefit recipients as a proportion of the population) is likely to be high in a country with a universal child benefit, and low in a country where there is no such benefit but children are taken into account in the personal income tax system. Gross recipiency rates can be very different as between situations which in substantive terms are actually fairly similar.[3]

The Dutch Ministry of Social Affairs has recently published studies entitled *Benefit dependency ratios: an analysis of nine European countries, Japan and the US* (Arents et al., 2000) and *Benefit dependency ratios by gender: an international comparison* (Moor et al., 2002) which estimate *inter alia* the full-time equivalent number of working-age (15 to 64-year-old) recipients of earnings- and income-replacement benefits each year from 1980 to 1999.[4] In this approach to measuring beneficiary numbers:

- The limitation of scope to income-replacement benefits rather than all benefits *a)* makes the data more potentially relevant for explaining labour market outcomes such as employment rates; and *b)* avoids problems that arise due to benefits that are delivered in some countries as cash benefits and in others through tax credits and tax schedules, because income-replacement benefits always have a cash-benefit component.
- The measurement of beneficiary numbers in full-time equivalent terms reduces the weight on individuals whose benefit-dependency status is not clear-cut (*e.g.* who are both employed part-time and receiving a part-time unemployment benefit). It also facilitates links between beneficiary and spending data.[5]

This chapter therefore adopts the main lines of the NEI-SZW[6] definitions and presents a revised version of the NEI-SZW estimates. The revision is based on an examination of the detailed spreadsheet files supplied by the Dutch authorities to identify the most significant areas where approximate estimation methods were used, and cross-checks against national statistical publications, other Secretariat databases and general knowledge of national social protection systems in order to identify possible discrepancies, omissions and misclassifications. It should be kept in mind that the estimates remain approximate, because it is likely that some significant issues of data quality have not yet been identified, and because in some areas the use of approximate estimation methods remains unavoidable (because appropriate data have never been published, or never collected).[7]

Definitions

Definitions are important when interpreting these data or using them for analytical purposes. To the extent that different statistical definitions might reasonably have been used and would have generated different figures, the substantive comparability and accuracy of aggregate statistics is limited. In this sense, the definitional issues are a prime determinant of the degree of approximation and uncertainty in the data that are presented.

The main principles used here, in reporting the number of beneficiaries, have been carried over from those used for the NEI/SZW estimates (Arents et al., 2000):

- "The number of persons dependent on some kind of social benefit was expressed in full-time equivalents, referred to as benefit-years." This applies, for example, to benefits for partial unemployment or compensation for partial disability due to work injuries.[8]

- "When the number of beneficiaries is aggregated over several categories (like unemployment benefit and disability pension) some persons will be counted twice as dependent persons (…). Information on the number of persons receiving two or more benefits at the same time (…) was used to reduce double-counting." This means that in principle one person counts for no more than one full-time equivalent benefit dependent even if they receive two benefits at the full normal rate.[9] The elimination of double counts is sometimes achieved by allocating people 100% to their "main" benefit category, resulting in an understatement of benefit recipiency in the secondary benefit category.[10]

- "(…) in some countries, the old age pension and social assistance are expected to replace family income instead of individual income (…). For reasons of comparability, it is necessary to 'individualise' the figures on the number of pensions paid." This means that when an old-age pension or social assistance is paid to a couple, both partners are counted as beneficiaries. However, the OECD revision presented here tends to minimise the scope and impact of the application of this principle.[11]

As regards the types of benefit covered:

- "Only periodic benefits that are paid in the event of a loss of earnings are included, which are referred to as earnings or income replacing benefits. This means that lump sum cash benefits that are paid for the purchase of specific goods or services, like funeral grants to widows, are not included."

- "Only social security benefits that are regulated by law are included, regardless of the way in which they are administered and financed."[12]

Benefits are classified first into seven categories based on the individual's "social risk" category, according to administrative records (which may differ from his or her status as reported in household surveys):

- *Old age*. This includes early retirement benefits, *i.e.* benefits that are restricted to persons above a certain age, and are not conditional on any of the other social risks listed below. Benefits which are conditional on having been disabled or unemployed in the past are included, if current age is a condition for eligibility but current disability or unemployment status is not.

- *Survivors (widows and orphans)*. This includes payments from old-age and disability insurance schemes when they are not conditional on the survivor himself/herself being old aged or disabled. In order to minimise double-counting with students, where data allowed only orphans in the age range 20 to 64 were included.

- *Sickness*. Beneficiaries include persons receiving sick pay from employers, when employers are legally required to make these payments.

- *Disability*. This includes contributory and non-contributory disability benefits, periodic cash payments of industrial injury benefits (but not lump-sum or in-kind benefits) and war disability pensions.

- *Maternity and parental*. Parental benefits are those which can replace the earnings of one of two parents: by contrast, means-tested lone-parent benefits are included with non-categorical social assistance (see below).[13] General child benefits which only compensate the direct costs of children, and child-care benefits which finance the purchase of child care, are not included.

- *Care and labour market leave*. Care benefits replace the earnings of a person who works full time caring (on an otherwise unpaid basis) for a disabled relative.[14] Labour market leave

4. BENEFITS AND EMPLOYMENT, FRIEND OR FOE? INTERACTIONS BETWEEN PASSIVE AND ACTIVE SOCIAL PROGRAMMES

Table 4.A1.1. **Recipiency rates by type of benefit in the population of working age: average, trends and standard deviation, 1980 to 1999**[a]

Percentages

		Australia	Austria	Belgium	Canada	Denmark	France	Germany	Ireland	Japan	Netherlands	New Zealand	Slovak Republic	Spain	Sweden	United Kingdom	United States	Mean	Standard deviation
Old age	1980	1.79	3.34	4.00	0.62	1.21	2.15	2.72	0.00	3.47	0.00	1.25	5.73	0.41	1.81	3.45	1.84	2.03	1.67
	1990	1.45	4.27	8.02	2.25	2.09	6.59	3.20	0.25	4.95	0.59	1.38	8.63	0.99	0.75	3.64	1.98	3.10	2.73
	1999	1.87	7.41	7.21	3.14	4.00	7.03	4.63	0.49	5.14	0.76	1.44	9.35	1.07	0.42	3.38	1.76	3.60	2.94
	Average	1.75	4.74	6.85	1.92	2.45	6.05	3.28	0.26	4.78	0.54	1.37	8.50	0.89	1.01	3.45	1.92	3.03	2.53
	Trend (percentage points per year)	0.02	0.16	0.11	0.17	0.14	0.21	0.09	0.04	0.06	0.04	0.01	0.16	0.05	-0.08	-0.01	-0.01	0.07	0.08
	Standard deviation (percentage points)	0.25	1.13	1.17	1.08	0.87	1.49	0.58	0.28	0.51	0.30	0.08	1.13	0.30	0.48	0.15	0.10	0.61	0.46
Survivors	1980	0.80	3.01	1.57	1.27	0.49	0.46	1.57	1.54	0.78	1.78	0.81	1.84	1.55	1.53	1.62	1.28	1.66	1.60
	1990	0.57	2.56	1.52	1.87	0.00	0.39	1.73	1.60	1.10	1.80	0.57	1.54	1.76	1.12	1.15	0.71	1.53	1.54
	1999	0.29	2.14	1.14	1.73	0.00	0.35	1.67	1.43	1.57	1.02	0.37	1.08	1.80	0.34	0.86	0.58	1.32	1.50
	Average	0.56	2.56	1.48	1.72	0.09	0.39	1.69	1.58	1.11	1.67	0.54	1.47	1.74	1.10	1.21	0.80	1.52	1.54
	Trend (percentage points per year)	-0.03	-0.05	-0.03	0.02	-0.02	-0.01	0.00	-0.01	0.04	-0.02	-0.02	-0.04	0.01	-0.06	-0.04	-0.03	-0.02	0.03
	Standard deviation (percentage points)	0.19	0.27	0.18	0.21	0.19	0.03	0.07	0.09	0.24	0.22	0.15	0.24	0.06	0.36	0.23	0.19	0.18	0.10
Sickness	1980	1.03	2.42	1.38	0.15	4.32	2.39	2.72	3.35	2.17	3.29	0.46	3.28	0.26	4.84	1.24	1.93	2.17	1.45
	1990	1.71	2.05	1.03	0.17	4.27	1.77	2.66	2.55	1.50	3.37	1.08	4.05	0.31	4.76	1.26	2.11	2.10	1.45
	1999	1.44	1.99	1.06	0.20	4.61	1.82	2.51	1.86	1.24	3.39	1.46	3.07	0.36	5.76	0.84	2.13	2.02	1.58
	Average	1.42	2.03	1.11	0.17	4.20	1.88	2.56	2.72	1.64	2.98	1.02	3.49	0.27	4.65	1.16	2.03	2.02	1.37
	Trend (percentage points per year)	0.01	-0.01	-0.02	0.00	0.01	-0.03	0.02	-0.12	-0.06	0.01	0.08	-0.01	0.00	0.01	-0.01	0.02	-0.01	0.03
	Standard deviation (percentage points)	0.23	0.15	0.12	0.02	0.48	0.22	0.27	0.77	0.35	0.27	0.50	0.32	0.04	0.49	0.13	0.11	0.25	0.20
Disability	1980	4.18	4.11	3.00	3.42	5.74	5.04	5.15	1.61	1.01	6.90	1.06	4.35	3.04	5.07	2.72	5.50	3.80	1.85
	1990	3.62	4.00	3.27	4.42	6.35	4.60	4.38	2.77	1.52	7.64	1.69	4.99	3.85	5.79	4.78	5.58	4.22	1.83
	1999	4.90	3.46	3.58	4.91	6.70	4.79	4.08	3.88	1.94	7.21	2.31	5.63	3.86	6.46	6.38	6.30	4.63	1.90
	Average	4.16	3.82	3.28	4.59	6.29	4.71	4.61	2.68	1.45	7.29	1.70	5.14	3.76	5.80	4.82	5.73	4.26	1.81
	Trend (percentage points per year)	0.02	0.00	0.02	0.10	0.07	-0.02	-0.08	0.11	0.05	0.01	0.08	0.08	0.03	0.08	0.26	0.08	0.05	0.07
	Standard deviation (percentage points)	0.34	0.18	0.14	0.66	0.44	0.18	0.51	0.67	0.31	0.27	0.45	0.51	0.25	0.51	1.57	0.55	0.44	0.36

Table 4.A1.1. Recipiency rates by type of benefit in the population of working age: average, trends and standard deviation, 1980 to 1999[a] (cont.)

Percentages

		Australia	Austria	Belgium	Canada	Denmark	France	Germany	Ireland	Japan	Netherlands	New Zealand	Slovak Republic	Spain	Sweden	United Kingdom	United States	Mean	Standard deviation
Maternity and parental leave	1980	0.00	1.16	0.11	0.21	0.43	0.49	0.23	0.24	0.10	0.00	0.00	3.62	0.00	1.55	0.34	0.00	0.53	0.93
	1990	0.00	1.54	0.00	0.36	1.00	0.99	0.22	0.19	0.08	0.00	0.00	4.22	0.00	2.82	0.27	0.00	0.73	1.21
	1999	0.00	1.99	0.23	0.39	1.61	1.93	0.18	0.24	0.16	0.00	0.00	4.41	0.00	2.03	0.27	0.00	0.84	1.24
	Average	0.00	1.88	0.14	0.34	1.12	0.99	0.22	0.21	0.11	0.00	0.00	4.30	0.00	2.31	0.29	0.00	0.74	1.18
	Trend (percentage points per year)	0.00	0.09	0.01	0.01	0.08	0.08	0.00	0.00	0.00	0.00	0.00	0.11	0.00	0.05	0.00	0.00	0.03	0.04
	Standard deviation (percentage points)	0.00	0.69	0.06	0.10	0.57	0.52	0.02	0.03	0.03	0.00	0.00	0.90	0.00	0.51	0.04	0.00	0.22	0.31
Care and labour market leave	1980	0.00	0.00	0.00	0.00	0.00	0.00	0.00	0.14	0.00	0.00	0.00	0.00	0.00	0.00	0.01	0.00	0.01	0.03
	1990	0.08	0.00	1.07	0.00	0.00	0.00	0.00	0.06	0.00	0.00	0.00	0.00	0.00	0.00	0.37	0.00	0.10	0.28
	1999	0.31	0.00	0.92	0.00	0.00	0.00	0.00	0.52	0.00	0.00	0.00	0.00	0.00	0.00	0.98	0.00	0.17	0.34
	Average	0.10	0.00	0.54	0.00	0.02	0.00	0.00	0.19	0.00	0.00	0.00	0.00	0.00	0.00	0.43	0.00	0.08	0.17
	Trend (percentage points per year)	0.02	0.00	0.06	0.00	0.00	0.00	0.00	0.02	0.00	0.00	0.00	0.00	0.00	0.00	0.06	0.00	0.01	0.02
	Standard deviation (percentage points)	0.09	0.00	0.45	0.00	0.05	0.00	0.00	0.13	0.00	0.00	0.00	0.00	0.00	0.00	0.38	0.00	0.07	0.14
Unemployment	1980	3.25	0.94	5.43	6.00	5.22	3.13	1.95	4.52	0.77	2.92	1.05	0.00	2.80	1.12	4.67	2.52	2.83	1.94
	1990	3.75	2.96	7.31	8.64	7.60	4.29	3.92	9.29	0.49	5.01	6.32	0.23	5.02	1.25	3.96	1.59	4.08	2.97
	1999	5.56	3.79	6.94	5.76	4.35	4.70	6.64	6.72	1.07	4.10	6.61	3.55	3.91	3.96	2.88	1.25	4.07	2.05
	Average	5.48	2.91	7.90	8.17	7.15	4.57	5.10	9.34	0.77	5.45	4.50	1.33	4.46	3.19	5.70	1.89	4.59	2.76
	Trend (percentage points per year)	0.15	0.16	0.05	−0.03	−0.01	0.10	0.25	0.16	0.00	0.01	0.33	0.21	0.14	0.25	−0.17	−0.05	0.08	0.12
	Standard deviation (percentage points)	1.41	1.00	0.91	1.28	1.41	0.67	1.68	2.03	0.18	0.95	2.24	1.52	1.30	1.87	1.59	0.54	1.15	0.58
Assistance	1980	1.98	0.57	1.48	1.71	2.50	0.19	0.90	0.96	0.50	1.16	1.87	0.75	0.00	0.17	0.99	3.42	1.08	0.95
	1990	2.50	0.58	2.05	2.20	1.83	1.48	2.12	2.21	0.34	1.55	4.29	1.09	0.16	0.48	2.88	3.61	1.57	1.05
	1999	3.17	0.80	2.37	1.88	1.62	3.04	2.24	4.17	0.32	1.22	4.42	11.07	0.26	1.14	2.80	1.68	2.36	2.59
	Average	2.67	0.58	1.97	2.36	1.99	1.39	1.89	2.32	0.39	1.43	3.52	3.81	0.10	0.69	2.57	3.45	1.72	1.15
	Trend (percentage points per year)	0.05	0.00	0.06	0.04	−0.02	0.18	0.07	0.17	−0.01	−0.01	0.16	0.58	0.02	0.06	0.12	−0.05	0.08	0.15
	Standard deviation (percentage points)	0.33	0.07	0.39	0.45	0.41	1.13	0.47	1.04	0.09	0.18	0.97	3.88	0.11	0.38	0.83	0.62	0.65	0.92

Table 4.A1.1. **Recipiency rates by type of benefit in the population of working age: average, trends and standard deviation, 1980 to 1999**[a] (cont.)

Percentages

		Australia	Austria	Belgium	Canada	Denmark	France	Germany	Ireland	Japan	Netherlands	New Zealand	Slovak Republic	Spain	Sweden	United Kingdom	United States	Mean	Standard deviation
Total	1980	13.02	15.54	16.97	13.38	19.90	13.85	15.24	12.36	8.79	16.05	6.50	19.57	8.07	16.09	15.04	16.49	14.12	5.29
	1990	13.69	17.96	24.27	19.91	23.15	20.11	18.23	18.91	9.99	19.95	15.33	24.75	12.08	16.97	18.32	15.58	17.44	6.63
	1999	17.54	21.57	23.45	18.02	22.91	23.65	21.96	19.31	11.44	17.69	16.61	38.16	11.26	20.11	18.39	13.70	19.02	8.26
	Average	16.15	18.51	23.27	19.27	23.30	19.98	19.35	19.31	10.25	19.37	12.65	28.03	11.22	18.74	19.63	15.82	17.96	6.79
	Trend (percentage points per year)	0.24	0.36	0.26	0.32	0.25	0.52	0.36	0.38	0.08	0.05	0.62	1.10	0.25	0.31	0.20	–0.04	0.29	0.26
	Standard deviation (percentage points)	1.86	2.20	2.26	2.70	2.00	3.12	2.25	2.79	0.66	1.19	3.96	6.93	1.85	2.33	2.00	1.07	2.19	1.50

a) Average, trend and standard deviation are calculated from data for the 20 years. Trend refers to the coefficient in a regression.
Source: NEI-SZW database, partially revised and augmented by OECD. See text for details.

benefits allow persons to take sabbatical leave from the labour market for a limited time but without restrictions on the beneficiary's condition or behaviour during the period of benefit receipt.

- *Unemployment.* This refers to benefits – except for those which are primarily disability or lone-parent benefits – that are paid conditional upon the person being available for work.

The eighth category is:

- *Lone-parent and non-categorical social assistance.* This includes beneficiaries of means-tested benefits, including lone-parent benefits,[15] who cannot be allocated to any of the risk categories above.[16] It excludes individuals in study or full-time employment.[17]

Two other types of "beneficiary" who have a kind of income-replacement benefit, but are not included, are full-time participants in education (who may receive scholarship incomes or student grants), and full-time participants in active labour market programmes.[18] The main social risk categories that appear in standard classifications of social protection spending (ESSPROS and SOCX), but are not included, are certain family benefits (notably child allowances), housing benefits, payments that reimburse health care costs, and in-kind services (*e.g.* health services, family services, services for the disabled and employment services).

Notes

1. Although the ESSPROS data include in-kind benefits, only the data for cash benefits are relatively complete. Countries report data by "scheme" and this concept in many countries is used to refer to institutions, or budget lines. In general, schemes which provide significant amounts of cash benefits are included in ESSPROS (usually together with the in-kind spending under these schemes) but schemes which provide only in-kind benefits – such as the PES in countries where this organisation does not manage unemployment benefits – are often omitted. As a result, only the cash benefit data are really comparable.

2. Comparisons between benefit payouts and income surveys suggest that unemployment and disability/invalidity benefit incomes are 30% underreported in the Australian Income Survey; UI benefits are underreported by 25% in Canada's SCF, unemployment benefit income is overreported by 15% but Disability Benefit income is underrported by 28% in Ireland's main survey; and UI and AFDC income are both underreported by about 25% in the US CPS (Atkinson *et al.*, 1995, Tables A6.3, A6.5, A6.10, A.6.13). Income Distribution Survey data for Australia from 1982 to 1996, as compared to administrative data, understate recipiency rates for lone-parent, disability and unemployment benefits although they overstate recipiency for partners, carers and parental benefits (Landt and Pech, 2000). In the mid-1990s, according to the European Community Labour Force Survey (ECLFS) only 6% of unemployed people in Greece and 25% in Portugal had benefits, whereas administrative data suggested that proportions were 30% in Greece and 50% in Portugal (OECD, 1998b, Table 4.3).

3. Eurostat (ESSPROS) and OECD (SOCX) data for spending on social protection are on a pre-tax basis. Adema (2001) provides estimates for social protection spending in 18 countries net of tax and social security contributions, adding in the value of tax breaks granted for social purposes.

4. The Dutch administration has been motivated to research benefit dependency abroad by the Dutch Act on Linkage with Conditional Suspension (WKA) which specified that the minimum wage should be updated in line with a composite index of contractual wage increases in the market and government sector unless the ratio between the number of people claiming social benefits and the number of people working (called the I/A-ratio: inactive/active ratio) exceeds 82.6% (in which case the government may decide not to link).

5. When the number of beneficiaries is estimated by dividing total spending by the rate of the benefit at a full or normal rate, the result is an estimate of the full-time equivalent number of beneficiaries.

6. The research was carried out by consultants (NEI Labour and Social Policy, Rotterdam) on behalf of the Dutch Ministry of Social Affairs and Employment (SZW).

7. Data from household income surveys (or labour force surveys) might be used to estimate the age distribution of beneficiaries, when no administrative data on this point are available. However,

household income surveys often do not identify the exact official name of benefits received, and underreporting of benefit receipt is also a problem.

8. Food Stamps in the United States, in cases where they are paid to people with no other income, were treated as a partially replacing income by reference to payment rates for other assistance (SSI) benefit.

9. The fact that double-counting within the total of benefit dependency is eliminated, in principle, will not always prevent double-counting between benefit dependency and employment. Some benefits, *e.g.* industrial injury and war disability pensions, widows' contributory pensions and certain old-age pensions, may not be reduced at all when the beneficiary has earnings from full-time work. Other benefits, *e.g.* unemployment and ordinary disability benefits, are usually paid at a full rate when the beneficiary works in a job with earnings and hours below certain thresholds. In these situations, some overlap between full-time equivalent measures of benefit dependency and employment will arise.

10. For example in Austria, the level of widows' benefit is relatively low and beneficiaries receiving this and another benefit have been allocated to the category of the other benefit. As a rule, double benefit recipients are allocated to the old age category with priority over disability which in turn has priority over survivors pension status. Also, individuals who receive a social assistance top-up to their insurance benefit are allocated to their insurance benefit status. Individuals were not split across categories (*e.g.* part-disabled, part-social assistance), unless the original data give this result (*e.g.* if the administrative data for unemployment and disability benefits are in full-time equivalent terms, an individual who has a part-rate unemployment and part-rate disability payment is split pro rata between these categories).

11. In the OECD revision the impact of "individualisation" is minimised by *a)* counting only the beneficiary whose social risk (*e.g.* unemployment or disability) generates the entitlement to benefit, even if the person has a dependent spouse; *b)* reallocating social assistance beneficiaries from the category "social assistance" to their category of social risk (*e.g.* unemployment or disability) whenever possible; and *c)* focusing attention on the working-age population. This means that "individualisation" affects the working-age beneficiary total only for social assistance beneficiaries who could not be allocated to a social risk category, and for persons aged under 65 who are in receipt of an ordinary retirement pension.

12. The meaning of "regulated by law" can be unclear, *e.g.* in cases of *a)* collective agreements which are negotiated by industry-level representatives but are legal enforced on all employers and/or employees in the industry; *b)* public sector and nationalised industry bodies that are authorised to operate their own old-age, disability, maternity or other benefits; *c)* benefit spending by UI funds in Denmark or Sweden that are legally autonomous, but whose spending is financed primarily by government subsidies that themselves are regulated by law; and *d)* sickness absence, when employment protection legislation constrains the employer's ability to dismiss sick workers.

13. Parenting Payment (Partnered) and some related benefits (which were introduced in 1995) have been excluded from the count of benefit dependency in Australia. This improves time-series comparability of the data. This benefit is usually payable only when the person's spouse qualifies for a different benefit, and is usually not payable when he/she has full-time work. In other countries, the partner who is unemployed or disabled is counted while the parent who looks after children is not.

14. The Australian and UK care benefits seem likely to result in the carer being recorded as inactive in labour force statistics. Other countries pay benefits to disabled people to cover the cost of personal care when this is needed.

15. Lone-parent assistance benefits provide income for the whole family the same way as a social assistance benefit does for a two-parent family. The allocation of the means-tested benefits for lone parents to the "social assistance" category is common practice in the sense that *a)* "welfare" in the United States refers mainly to lone-parent benefits and *b)* in many other countries, lone parents receive non-categorical social assistance benefits (rather than a lone-parent benefit with a distinct name, administrative structure or statistical existence).

16. In principle, social assistance beneficiaries who are disabled or are lone parents should be classified to these categories, and others who are required to be available for work or to seek work (*e.g.* register for employment) should be classified as unemployed (see the definition of unemployment). In practice, suitable data are often not available. In Canada, a fixed proportion of social assistance beneficiaries was allocated to the categories unemployment and disability. The proportion of provincial social assistance beneficiaries that is considered employable has sharply increased with welfare reform (see OECD, 1999, Table 3.11). However, McIntosh and Boychuk (2000)

argue that this is because several provincial social assistance regimes now define a greater proportion of their beneficiary population (*e.g.* lone parents) as employable, and the nature of the caseload has not changed dramatically. The Netherlands had a distinct administrative category (RWW benefit) for beneficiaries receiving social assistance for reasons for unemployment until 1995: the statistics shown here extrapolate this distinction to 1999 assuming that the unemployed share in the social assistance total remained at its 1995 level. In the United Kingdom, official statistics allocate most social assistance beneficiaries to a particular social risk category, but information about numbers receiving benefit for reasons of sickness was incomplete, so these beneficiaries were left in "non-categorical social assistance".

17. Not counting social assistance payments to people in study or full-time employment as income-replacement benefits helps to minimise double-counting (*i.e.* it ensures that a given individual is not counted for more than one person in full-time-equivalent terms when summing data for benefit dependency and employment). But it also improves substantive data comparability since reductions in tax and employee social security contributions for low-paid workers and subsidies to employers for hiring low-paid workers have comparable economic effects, and are not covered. A consistent framework, accounting for tax progressivity and other transfers, would need to be developed to compare levels of "in-work" benefits across countries or through time.

18. There is a case for regarding full-time participants in active labour market programmes as benefit dependants when they receive unemployment benefits. However, participants may also receive training grants outside the contributory or non-contributory social security systems. Also, their training may be regarded a social investment similar to general education, and participants on employment programmes may be counted as employed in labour force statistics. Therefore, counting programme participants as benefit dependants would quite often lead to double-counting with employment and student participation statuses. Sweden regularly distinguishes between "open" unemployment and "total" unemployment which includes participants in labour market programmes: the difference between the two rose to about 4% of the labour force in the early 1990s.

ANNEX 2

How Long Adjustment Lags Arise from Interaction and Feedback

When different actors or different factors in the economy interact, economic aggregates change on a much longer time-scale than individual behaviour does. Suppose that disability prevalence (the percentage of the population that consider themselves to suffer from a disability) is related to benefit recipiency (the percentage receiving a benefit) as shown in Chart 4.8 but with a one-year lag:

$$P = 4 + 1.6\ B(-1)$$

Suppose also that half of all persons who consider that they suffer from a disability apply for benefit, and start receiving benefit a year later:

$$B = c.P(-1)$$

where c, the rate of coverage, is a policy parameter for the strictness of benefit administration. Different values of the parameter c result in different equilibrium values of B and P, consistent with the first equation. The growth of benefit prevalence and recipiency when a benefit is created with $c = 0.5$ (equivalently, when c is raised from 0 to 0.5) in year zero is shown below:

Year	0	1	2	3	4	6	8	10	15	20	Long run equilibrium
B	0.00	2.00	2.00	3.60	3.60	4.88	5.90	6.72	8.32	8.93	10
P	4.00	4.00	7.20	7.20	9.76	11.81	13.45	14.76	16.64	18.28	20

In this example, even though adjustment of disability prevalence to recipiency or *vice versa* takes just one year, the *levels* of benefit recipiency and prevalence both more than double between years 3 and 10, and then rise further by between a quarter and a third through to the 20th year after creation of the benefit. Interaction and feedback between two variables generates long lags in adjustment, similar to those which are observed empirically for several important types of benefit. The long-run solution value of this equation system is sensitive to small changes in the policy parameter c. Thus, in the example above, although c is set to give a benefit coverage rate B that is only 0.5 of P in the long run, after a few years B overtakes the value of P that prevailed prior to introduction of the benefit. Another point worth noting is that year-on-year *changes* in benefit recipiency are greatest in the years immediately after a policy reform. This distinction can explain why, in the examples shown in Charts 4.5 to 4.7, reforms to the parameters of an existing benefit have influenced *trends* in beneficiary totals immediately.

This model is just one example of an interaction and feedback mechanism. Any mechanism whereby individual benefit recipiency is influenced, with a slight lag, by population-average levels of benefit recipiency will give similar results. Such an influence could involve the behaviour of employers (*e.g.* if employers' offer of seasonal work in one year is influenced by the supply of seasonal workers the previous year), or the behaviour of the benefit administration (*e.g.* if actual job-search intensity is influenced by both financial incentives and the job-search intensity that the benefit administration expects, and the latter is influenced by actual job-search intensity).

In some cases, following the introduction of a new benefit, the initial phase of growth in beneficiary numbers has been exponential from a low base, so that growth in terms of absolute numbers at first accelerates. This pattern can persist as long as learning from peers is the main factor involved (*e.g.* each person who has successfully applied for benefit helps two more eligible people to apply for it, some time later).

Bibliography

AARTS, L. and P. de JONG (1990), *Economic Aspects of Disability Behaviour* (thesis, published in 1992 by Elsevier Science).

ADEMA, W. (2001), *Net Social Expenditure: 2nd Edition*, OECD Labour Market and Social Policy Occasional Papers No. 52, Paris (www.oecd.org/els/social – working papers).

ANDERSEN, J. (2002), "Denmark: From the Edge of the Abyss to a Sustainable Welfare State", in Andersen et al., pp. 143-162.

ANDERSEN, J. and J. JENSEN (2002), "Changing Labour Markets, Unemployment and Unemployment Policies in a Citizenship Perspective", in Andersen et al. (eds.), pp. 1-57.

ANDERSEN, J., J. CLASEN, W. VAN OORSCHOT and K. HALVORSEN (eds.) (2002), *Europe's New State of Welfare: Unemployment, Employment policies and Citizenship*, The Policy Press, Bristol.

ANDERSON, K. (2002), "Welfare State Adjustment in Sweden and the Netherlands" (www.europanet.org/conference2002/papers/b2_anderson.doc).

ARENTS, M., M. CLUITMANS and M. VAN DER ENDE (2000), *Benefit Dependency Ratios: An Analysis of nine European Countries, Japan and the US: Final Report*, SZW (Dutch Ministry of Social Affairs) No. 16.153/2000, Elsevier's Gravenhage.

ATKINSON, A., L. RAINWATER and T. SMEEDING (1995), *Income Distribution in OECD Countries: Evidence from the Luxembourg Income Study*, OECD, Paris.

BENUS, J., J. JOESCH, T. JOHNSON and D. KLEPINGER (1997), *Evaluation of the Maryland Unemployment Insurance Work Search Demonstration: Final Report*, Batelle Memorial Institute in association with Abt Associates Inc. (http://wdr.doleta.gov/owsdrr).

BERLIN, G. (2000), *Encouraging Work Reducing Poverty: The Impact of Work Incentive Programs*, MDRC (www.mdrc.org/Reports2000/ework-rpoverty.pdf).

BITLER, M., G. GELBACH and H. HOYNES (2003), "The Impact of Welfare Reform on Living Arrangements", mimeo (www.glue.umd.edu/~mbitler).

BLADES, D. and D. ROBERTS (2002), "Measuring the Non-observed Economy", OECD Statistics Brief No. 5, Paris (www.oecd.org/statistics – documentation – newsletters).

BLONDAL, S. and M. PEARSON (1995), "Unemployment and other Non-Employment Benefits", *Oxford Review of Economic Policy*, Vol. 11, No. 1, pp. 136-169.

BLOOM, D., M. FARRELL, and B. FINK with D. ADAMS-CIARDULLO (2002), *Welfare Time Limits: State Policies, Implementation and Effects on Families*, MDRC report submitted to the Department of Health and Human Services (www.mdrc.org/Reports2002/welfaretimelimits/wtl_exsummary.htm).

BRADSHAW, J., L. TERUM and A. SKEVIK (2000), "Lone Parenthood in the 1990s: New Challenges, New Responses?", paper for the year 2000 ISSA conference, Helsinki (www.issa.int/engl/publ/2conthelsinki.htm).

BROOKINGS INSTITUTION (2002), "Welfare Reform and Beyond: PowerPoint Presentation" (www.brook.edu/dybdocroot/wrb/facts/).

CARLING, K, B. HOLMLUND and A. VEJSIU (1999), "Do Benefit Cuts Boost Job-findings? Swedish evidence from the 1990s", IFAU working paper 1999:8.

CLASEN, J. and W. VAN OORSCHOT (2002), "Work, Welfare and Citizenship: diversity and variation within European (un)employment policy", in Andersen et al. (eds.).

COMMITTEE ON WAYS AND MEANS (2000), *2000 Green Book: Background material and data on programs within the jurisdiction of the Committee on Ways and Means*, US Government Printing Office, Washington (downloadable at www.utdallas.edu/~jargo/).

CORCORAN, T. (2002), "Retrospective Analysis of Referral under the Employment Action Plan (EAP)", FÁS (cited at: *www.fas.ie/FAS_Review/SF.html*).

CORNILLEAU, G., D. DEMAILLY, C. GILLES and J-P PAPIN (2000), "Les évolutions récentes du RMI : un effet perceptible de la conjoncture économique", DREES Études et résultats, No. 86 (*www.sante.gouv.fr/drees/etude-resultat/*).

DANZIGER, S. (1999), "What Are the Early Lessons?", in S. Danziger (ed.), *Economic Conditions and Welfare Reform*, W.E.Upjohn Institute, Kalamazoo.

DWP – Department of Work and Pensions (2003), "The Final Effects of ONE", DWP Research Report No. 183 (*www.dwp.gov.uk/asd/asd5/rrs2003.html*).

EARDLEY, T., J. BRADSHAW, J. DITCH, I. GOUGH and P. WHITEFORD (1996), *Social Assistance in OECD Countries: Synthesis Report*, Department of Social Security Research, Report No. 46, HMSO, London.

ELWOOD, D. (1999), "The Plight of the Working Poor", Brookings Childrens Roundtable Policy Brief No. 2 (*www.brookings.edu/comm/childrensroundtable/issue2.pdf*).

ENGELFRIET, R. (no date), "The Changing Definition of Suitable Work" (*members.lycos.nl/richieboy/pasarbeid.html*).

FERNANDEZ CORDÓN, J. (2001), "Youth as a Transition to Full Autonomy", *Family Observer*, No. 3 (*europa.eu.int/comm/employment_social/eoss/publications_en.html*).

FORSLUND, A., D. FRÖBERG and L. LINDQVIST (forthcoming), "The Swedish Activity Guarantee", OECD Working Paper, Paris.

FORTIN, P. and P. CREMIEUX (1998), "The Determinants of Social Assistance Rates: Evidence from a Panel of Canadian Provinces 1977-1996", Department of Economics working paper, University of Quebec at Montreal.

FRAKER, T. and R. MOFFITT (1988), "The Effects of Food Stamps on Labor Supply: A Bivariate Selection Model", *Journal of Public Economics*, Vol. 35, No. 2, pp. 25-56.

GAIS, T. and R. NATHAN (2001), Status report on the Occasion of the 5th Anniversary of the 1996 Personal Responsibility Welfare-Reform Act (*www.rockinst.org*).

GALLAGHER, J., M. GALLAGHER, K. PERESE, S. SCHREIBER and K. WATSON (1998), "One Year after Federal Welfare Reform: a Description of State Temporary Assistance for Needy Families (TANF) Decisions as of October 1997" (*newfederalism.urban.org/html/occas6.htm*).

GAO – United States General Accounting Office (1998), *Welfare Reform: States are Restructuring Programs to Reduce Welfare Dependence* (*www.gao.gov/archive/1998/he98109.pdf*).

GARFINKEL, I. and S. McLANAHAN (1986), *Single Mothers and their Children: a New American Dilemma*, Urban Institute, Washington.

GOODGER, K. and P. LAROSE (1998), "Changing Expectations: Sole Parents and Employment in New Zealand", paper for the 6th Australian Institution of Family Studies Conference (*www.aifs.org.au*).

GRAY, D. (forthcoming), "National *versus* Regional Financing and Management of Unemployment and Related Benefits: the case of Canada", OECD Working Paper, Paris.

GREENBERG, M. (2001), "Welfare Reform and Devolution: Looking Back and Forward", *Brookings Review*, Vol. 19, No. 3, Summer.

GROGGER, J. (forthcoming), "The Effects of Time Limits, EITC and other Policy Changes on Welfare Use, Work, and Income among Female-Headed Families", *Review of Economics and Statistics*.

GROGGER, J. and C. MICHAPOULOS (2003), "Welfare dynamics under time limits", *Journal of Political Economy*, Vol. 111, No. 3.

GROGGER, J., L. KAROLY and J. KLERMAN (2002), *Consequences of Welfare Reform: A Research Synthesis*, Rand Corporation (*www.rand.org/child/bib/26.html* .

GRUBB, D. (2001), "Eligibility Criteria for Unemployment Benefits", in OECD (2001a).

HALVORSEN, K. (2002), "Unemployment and (un)Employment Policies in Norway: the case of an affluent but oil-dependent economy: the paradox of plenty?", in Andersen et al. (eds.).

HANOUSEK, J. and F. PALDA (2002), "Why People Evade Taxes in the Czech and Slovak Republics: A Tale of Twins", CERGE-EI Discussion Paper Series No. 85 (*home.cerge-ei.cz/hanousek/*).

HARKMAN, A. (2000), "Vem placeras i åtgard?", mimeo, Office of Labour Market Policy Evaluation, Uppsala.

HOLCOMB, P. and K. MARTINSON (2002), "Implementing Welfare Reform Across the Nation", Urban Institute (www.urban.org – research – welfare to work programs).

HRDC – Human Resources Development Canada (1998), *An Analysis of Employment Insurance Benefit Coverage*, Applied Research Branch (www.hrdc-drhc.gc.ca/sp-ps/arb-dgra/publications/research/abw-98-35e.shtml).

LANDT, J. and PECH, J. (2000), "Work and Welfare in Australia: the Changing Role of Income Support", paper for the 7th Australian Institute of Family Studies Conference, Sydney, July (www.aifs.org.au).

LEMIEUX, T. and B. MACLEOD (2000), "Supply Side Hysteresis: the Case of Unemployment Insurance in Canada", *Journal of Public Economics*, Vol. 78, Nos. 1-2, October, pp. 139-170.

LIEBSCHUTZ, D. (1999), "Taxes and Poverty in New Zealand: the impact of the tax and benefit systems on low-income New Zealanders", Ian Axford Fellowships Office, Wellington, (www.fulbright.org.nz/voices/axford/docs/liebschutzd.pdf)

LODEMEL, I. and H. TRICKEY (eds.) (2001), *"An Offer You Can't Refuse": Workfare in International Perspective*, The Policy Press, Bristol.

MACKAY, R. (1998), "Targeting Social Security: the New Zealand Experience", paper presented at the 2nd International Research Conference on Social Security, Jerusalem (www.issa.int/engl/publ/2contjeru.htm).

MARTIN, J. and D. GRUBB (2001), "What Works and for Whom: A Review of OECD Countries' Experiences with Active Labour Market Policies", *Swedish Economic Policy Review*, Vol. 8, No. 2, Fall, pp. 9-56.

MCINTOSH, T. and G. BOYCHUK (2000), "Dis-covered: EI, Social Assistance and the Growing Gap in Income Support for Unemployed Canadians", in T. McIntosh (ed.), *Federalism, Democracy and Labour Market Policy in Canada: 2000*, Institute of Intergovernmental Relations (www.iigr.ca/pdf/publications/197_Federalism_Democracy_and.pdf).

MICHALOPOULOS, C., D. TATTRIE, C. MILLER, P.K. ROBINS, P. MORRIS, D. GYARMATI, C. REDCROSS, K. FOLEY and R. FORD (2002), *Making Work Pay: Final Report on the Self-Sufficiency Project for Long-Term Welfare Recipients*, Social Research and Demonstration Corporation (SRDC) (www.srdc.org/english/publications/SSP54.htm)

MILLAR, J. and K. ROWLINGSON (eds.) (2001), *Lone Parents, Employment and Social Policy: Cross-National Comparison*, The Policy Press, Bristol.

MINISTRY OF SOCIAL DEVELOPMENT – New Zealand (2001), "Evaluating the February 1999 Domestic Purposes Benefit and Widows Benefit Reforms: summary of key findings" (www.dol.govt.nz/PDFs/DPBreform.pdf)

MLPS – Ministerio del Lavoro e della Previdenza Sociale (2000), Rapport di monitoraggio sulle politiche occupazionali e del lavoro, No. 2.

MOF – DANISH MINISTRY OF FINANCE (1998), *Availability Criteria in Selected OECD Countries*, Working Paper No.6, Ministry of Finance, Copenhagen (www.fm.dk – udgivelser)

MOFFITT, R. (2002), "From Welfare to Work: What the Evidence Shows" (www.brook.edu/dybdocroot/wrb/publications/pb/pb13.htm).

MOOR, I., I. VOSSEN and M. ARENTS (2002), *Benefit Dependency Ratios by Gender: An International Comparison: Final Report*, SZW (Dutch Ministry of Social Affairs) No. 16.317/02, Elsevier, 's-Gravenhage.

MOREL, S. (2002), "The Insertion Model or the Workfare Model? The Transformation of Social Assistance within Quebec and Canada" (www.swc-cfc.gc.ca/pubs/0662323467/200209_0662323467_6_e.html).

MULVALE, J. (2002), "Jamie Peck. Workfare States", *Canadian Journal of Sociology Online* (www.arts.ualberta.ca/cjscopy/reviews/workfare.html).

NATHAN, R. and T. GAIS (1999), "Implementing the Personal Responsibility Act of 1996: A First Look", Rockefeller Institute of Government, State University of New York (www.rockinst.org).

OECD (1994a), *The Jobs Study: Facts, Analysis, Strategies*, Paris.

OECD (1994b), *The Jobs Study: Evidence and Explanations, Part II: the Adjustment Potential of the Labour Market*, Paris.

OECD (1997), *Economic Survey of Ireland*, Paris.

OECD (1998a), *The Battle Against Exclusion: Social Assistance in Belgium, the Czech Republic, the Netherlands and Norway*, Paris.

OECD (1998b), *The Public Employment Service: Greece, Ireland, Portugal*, Paris

OECD (1999), *The Battle Against Exclusion: Social Assistance in Canada and Switzerland*, Paris.

OECD (2000), "Eligibility Criteria for Unemployment Benefits", *Employment Outlook*, Chapter 4, Paris.

OECD (2001a), *Labour Market Policies and the Public Employment Service*, Paris.

OECD (2001b), *Innovations in Labour Market Policy: the Australian Way*, Paris.

OECD (2001c), *Society at a Glance*, Paris.

OECD (2002a), *Employment Outlook*, Paris.

OECD (2002b), *Benefits and Wages: OECD Indicators*, Paris

OECD (2003), *Transforming Disability into Ability: Policies to Promote Work and Income Security for Disabled People*, Paris.

ONEM (1999), *Les statuts à temps partiel dans l'assurance-chômage* (www.onem.fgov.be – études).

PRICE, D. (2000), *Office of Hope: a History of the Employment Service*, Policy Studies Institute, London.

SIANESI, B. (2001), "The Swedish Active Labour Market Programmes in the 1990s: Overall Effectiveness and Differential Performance", *Swedish Economic Policy Review*, Vol. 8, No. 2, pp. 133-169.

SO – Arbetslöshetskassornas Samorganisation (2002), "What You Need to Know about Unemployment Insurance" (www.alfakassan.com).

STEPHENS, R. (2002), "Poverty and Employment: A Comparison of Policy and Outcomes for Single Mothers between the United States and New Zealand", mimeo, Victoria University of Wellington.

STRAWN, J., M. GREENBERG and S. SAVNER (2001), "Improving Employment Outcomes Under TANF", Centre for Law and Social Policy (www.clasp.org/DMS/Documents/997391689.65/view_html).

VAN OORSCHOT, W. (2002), "Labour Market Participation in the Netherlands: trends, policies and outcomes", in Andersen *et al.* (eds).

VAN REENEN, J. (2003), "Active Labour Market Policies and the British New Deal for the Young Unemployed in Context", NBER Working Paper 9576 (www.nber.org).

WALSH, B. (2003), "How 'Live' is the Live Register and other Puzzles in the Measurement of Unemployment", University College Dublin Centre for Economic Research, Working Paper 03/07 (www.ucd.ie/~economic/workingpapers/WP03.07.pdf).

WILKINS, A. "Time-Limited TANF Recipients", NCSL Documents, National Conference of State Legislatures (www.ncsl.org/statefed/welfare/timelimitbrief.pdf).

WISEMAN, M. (2001), "Making Work for Welfare in the United States", in I. Lodemel and H. Trickey, pp. 215-247.

ISBN 92-64-10061-X
OECD Employment Outlook: 2003
Towards More and Better Jobs
© OECD 2003

Chapter 5

Upgrading Workers' Skills and Competencies

Upgrading skills is an essential component of any comprehensive lifelong learning strategy; it is particularly important to improve the employment prospects of under-represented groups. Yet, in all OECD countries, these groups receive much less training than those who are already highly skilled or have a good job. What explains the relatively low training incidence among the less educated, older workers, women, immigrants, part-timers and temporary workers? How can training policies effectively reduce these inequalities and what is the role of co-financing arrangements in such a strategy?

Introduction 238
Main findings 239
1. Continuous vocational training: a glance at the data 240
2. Not enough and not equal? A closer look at the determinants of training patterns 245
3. Policy approaches to improve training outcomes 256
Conclusions 275
Annex 1. Data Description and Detailed Estimation Results 280
Annex 2. Identification and Estimation of Training Demand and Supply 290
Bibliography 293

Introduction

While Chapters 3 and 4 focus on policies to mobilise underutilised labour resources by improving their employment and wage prospects, this chapter looks at human capital policies to improve the career prospects of those that are already in employment. Education and training have in fact a significant impact on output growth as well as on individual wages and employability (OECD, 1994, 1999a, 2001a). Although initial education must remain a priority to foster growth in the long-run, policy strategies to increase human capital should also focus on adult learning. In 10-15 years from now, the bulk of the labour force will still be composed of individuals who are currently in the labour market. Furthermore, due to population ageing and the effect of policies aimed at prolonging working life, most of these individuals will have completed their initial schooling many years before, and rapid technological change will have made part of their competencies obsolete. The education and training they receive after having started their working life is therefore crucial for both output growth and individual career prospects.

There is a lively debate, however, concerning whether the current level of investment in training is adequate. Furthermore, past research has shown that training activities are unequally distributed, with workers who are already in a better position in the labour market having more opportunities and incentives to acquire new skills. To remedy these problems, policy innovations – intended to increase investment in and equal access to adult education and training – have been experimented in OECD countries in recent years. Nevertheless, implementation problems have sometimes accompanied the introduction of these innovations, usually because the factors behind inadequate training outcomes have not been addressed properly. The purpose of this chapter is therefore twofold: *a)* to identify the reasons behind possible under-provision of training and inequality of outcomes; and *b)* to discuss policy approaches, by mapping each policy instrument into the potential problems it can address.

The empirical analysis of this chapter focuses on formal continuous vocational training (CVT). This is done for three reasons. First, there are no cross-country comparable data on informal training. This is an important limitation, since research conducted in Australia and the United States has shown that informal training represents at least one half of total training and it is conceivable that inequality patterns in the provision of informal training might differ from those associated with formal training (Australian Bureau of Statistics, 1990; Barron *et al.*, 1997; and Loewenstein and Spletzer, 1999a). Second, formal CVT accounts for the largest share of formal education and training of the adult workforce in almost all OECD countries. Third, CVT is closely related to the labour market and therefore must be analysed separately from the market for formal education.

The first section of the chapter quantifies the relative weight of training and education in adult learning and provides further evidence of inequality in training participation and intensity across the different labour market groups identified in Chapters 1 and 2. The second section looks at the evidence of under-provision of training, as well as at the determinants of uneven training incidence. It also presents econometric evidence of training supply and demand effects for different groups. In the light of the empirical results, different policy instruments are reviewed in the third section, with particular attention devoted to co-financing schemes. Good practices are discussed, although little empirical evaluation exists for most schemes. The final section draws some conclusions.

Main findings

- There is large cross-country variation in the incidence and intensity of CVT. In practically all countries, CVT is unequally distributed across individuals and firms, with women, older workers, low-skilled workers, immigrants as well as workers in small firms receiving less training. For example, the probability of receiving employer-sponsored training is estimated to be on average 9 percentage points smaller for workers with less than upper secondary education than for individuals with a tertiary qualification, and 6 percentage points smaller for immigrants than for natives.

- There is some evidence of under-provision of formal training, although the extent of the problem is difficult to quantify and its implications may be somehow softened by the presence of informal training. Pay scales do not reflect productivity closely; in most cases, therefore, employees cannot fully reap the benefits from training, which reduces their incentives to invest in human capital. As a result, most of the training is entirely funded by employers. However, employers themselves might be investing less than is optimal, since a significant share of employer-sponsored formal training appears to concern skills that are transferable across firms. Although there is some evidence that employers may have some market power over their pool of trained workers, thereby being able to appropriate part of the benefits from training in transferable skills, current employers are unlikely to be able to internalise the benefits that will accrue to other employers, when a trained worker switches firm.

- There is also some empirical evidence of other market failures in the market for training – such as individual borrowing constraints for training purposes and lack of contractibility of training content and quality. These failures prevent an efficient sharing of the costs of, and benefits from, training between employers and employees, thereby reducing the incentives to invest in workers' human capital.

- Disentangling employers' supply – training opportunities employers offer to their employees – from workers' demand of training is a difficult exercise. Even more complex is to identify the supply or demand channel through which the above mentioned market failures may affect training outcomes. Nonetheless, the empirical analysis suggests that low training is mostly due to the workers' demand side in the case of low-educated and older workers. Conversely, for women, immigrants, workers with low literacy, involuntary part-time and temporary workers and employees in small firms, employers' supply seems to fall short of employees' demand, sometimes dramatically.

- The above findings suggest that public policy may have a role to play to improve individuals' and employers' incentives to invest in human capital. Appropriate policy schemes may enhance efficiency – by tackling market failures – and increase equity. In order to do this it is important that policy schemes identify the appropriate channel, *i.e.* the choices and the behaviour of employers or employees. Moreover policy schemes should take into account the risk of inefficient substitution between formal and informal training and the links between adult training activities and the education system through which they had earlier passed.

- Co-financing strategies involving employers, including corporate tax deductions (*e.g.* as in Austria, Luxembourg and the Netherlands) and pay-back clauses, can help raise overall training provision. Insofar as low-educated and older workers are not disfavoured by employers, providing incentives to the latter may also boost the relative position of these groups.

- However, in order to reduce inequality of access for those groups which have a relatively high demand for training but nevertheless receive little employer-sponsored training (*e.g.* women, immigrants, temporary workers), raising individual incentives is likely to yield a better outcome than channelling co-financing through employers. This can be done through individual subsidy schemes, such as individual learning accounts (*e.g.* as in the United States) and/or provisions for training leave (*e.g.* as in Sweden) or part-time study (*e.g.* as in Australia).

- In any case, due to the heterogeneity of workers' needs, a comprehensive policy strategy is required in order to reduce both under-investment in training and inequality. However, due to the methodological complexity of *ex-post* assessment in this area, evaluation mechanisms should be included into policy design to ensure timely corrections of policy mistakes.

1. Continuous vocational training: a glance at the data

Vocational training accounts for two thirds of adult learning...

In almost all the OECD countries participating in the International Adult Literacy Survey (IALS),[1] CVT accounts for at least 60% of adult education and training,[2] with the only exception of Australia (Chart 5.1). Furthermore, on average, two-thirds of total CVT is employer-sponsored – that is provided or paid for by the employer, at least partially.

... but training participation and intensity vary considerably across countries...

There is substantial cross-country variation in the incidence and intensity of employer-sponsored CVT courses. On average, 26% of employed persons participate in employer-sponsored CVT each year with an annual training volume of 18 hours per employed person, *i.e.* equivalent to two and a half working days (Table 5.1). These figures imply that each participant receives on average about 68 hours of training per year – that is slightly less than nine working days. The country with the highest CVT volume (as well as the highest participation rate) is Denmark where workers receive on average 36 hours per year of employer-sponsored CVT, which translates into 81 hours per participant per year or about two working weeks.

... and across groups

Despite the fact that the intensity of CVT is relatively low on average, CVT appears to have a key role in improving career prospects, in terms of better earning profiles and

Chart 5.1. **CVT courses account for more than two thirds of formal adult learning**

Decomposition of the volume[a] of formal education and training[b, c]

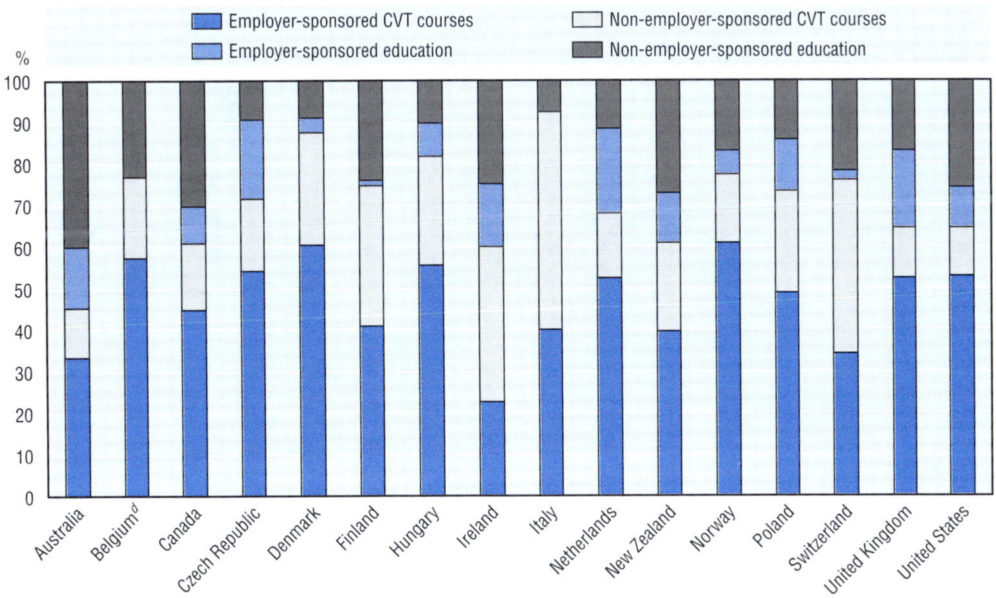

a) Hours spent in CVT courses undertaken for job or career-related purposes.
b) Data refer to employed persons aged 26 to 65 years.
c) Data refer to 1994 for Canada, Ireland, the Netherlands, Poland, Switzerland (German and French-speaking regions) and the United States, to 1996 for Australia, Belgium, New Zealand and the United Kingdom, and to 1998 for the Czech Republic, Denmark, Finland, Hungary, Italy, Norway and the Italian-speaking regions of Switzerland.
d) Flanders only.

Source: IALS.

employment security (Box 5.1). Therefore, if those already having greater earnings or employment security receive more training, CVT may increase inequalities between different worker groups. Chart 5.2 shows the incidence and volume of employer-sponsored CVT by gender and age. There does not appear to be any significant difference in participation rates by gender. Nevertheless there is a clear gender-training gap in terms of volume, with female workers receiving on average 17% fewer hours of training than male.

The incidence of training tends to decline with age. In particular, the average training participation rate of workers aged 56 to 65 years is about three-quarters of that of prime-age workers (aged 36 to 45 years). The participation profile is flatter at younger ages. However, the inverse correlation between age and training is more clear-cut when measured in terms of training volume. On average, workers aged 56 to 65 years receive 12 hours of CVT courses per year, against 18 hours for workers aged 36 to 45 years and 21 hours for workers aged 26 to 35 years.

Likewise, training participation and intensity differ considerably across educational and occupational groups (Chart 5.3). Participation in low-skilled occupations (13%) is about one-third of participation in high-skilled occupations (38%). A similar pattern is found between different educational groups (16% for workers with less than upper secondary education against 35% for those having a tertiary degree).

The worker's position in the hierarchical ladder has an impact on his/her training opportunities. Chart 5.3 also shows that employees with a high degree of supervisory

5. UPGRADING WORKERS' SKILLS AND COMPETENCIES

Table 5.1. **Cross-country variation of training outcomes is large**
Employer-sponsored education and training[a]

	Participation rate[b]			Annual volume (hours per employed person)		
	Total job-related education and training	of which: CVT[c] courses	of which: Formal education	Total job-related education and training	of which: CVT[c] courses	of which: Formal education
Australia	27	24	5	22	15	7
Belgium[d]	13	13	0	10	10	0
Canada	31	28	3	21	17	3
Czech Republic	20	16	5	18	13	5
Denmark	45	45	1	39	36	2
Finland	42	42	1	23	23	1
Hungary	15	14	2	15	13	2
Ireland	12	10	2	14	9	6
Italy	14	14	0	8	8	0
Netherlands	27	24	3	30	21	8
New Zealand	36	34	4	30	23	7
Norway	46	45	1	38	35	3
Poland	12	11	2	10	8	2
Switzerland	15	14	0	9	9	1
United Kingdom	45	44	3	30	22	8
United States	35	33	3	22	18	3
Unweighted average	**27**	**26**	**2**	**21**	**18**	**4**

a) Data refer to job-related education and training that employers provided (or partially paid) to their workers aged 26 to 65 years in 1994 for Canada, Ireland, the Netherlands, Poland, Switzerland (German and French-speaking regions) and the United States, in 1996 for Australia, Belgium (Flanders only), New Zealand and the United Kingdom, and in 1998 for the Czech Republic, Denmark, Finland, Hungary, Italy, Norway and the Italian-speaking regions of Switzerland.
b) Ratio of employed persons participating in training to total employment (in per cent).
c) Continuous vocational training.
d) Flanders only.
Source: IALS.

Box 5.1. **The impact of CVT on earnings and employment security**

Most studies find a positive and persistent effect of training on earnings (see e.g. Bishop, 1997; OECD, 1999b; Ok and Tergeist, 2003). However, the majority of them use only dichotomous explanatory variables (such as training participation dummies), making it difficult to assess precisely the impact on earnings of short training spells. Recent studies, however, use the volume of training as an explanatory variable and permit a sharper evaluation. For instance, Loewenstein and Spletzer (1999b) estimate for the United States that one week of employer-paid training of newly hired workers leads to 1.4 percentage point higher wage growth in the two years after hiring and that 17% of the average wage growth in the same period can be explained by CVT (whose average length in the sample is of about one and a half weeks per year). Similarly, Booth and Bryan (2002) estimate for the United Kingdom that one week of accredited formal training leads to about 1% greater wages at subsequent employers. The effect of CVT on employment security is less well established in the literature. Yet, certain analyses point to a greater probability of rapid re-employment in the case of involuntary job loss if the worker has previously received training (see Bishop, 1997; and Ok and Tergeist, 2003).

Chart 5.2. **Older workers and women receive less training**
Employer-sponsored CVT courses by gender and age[a, b]

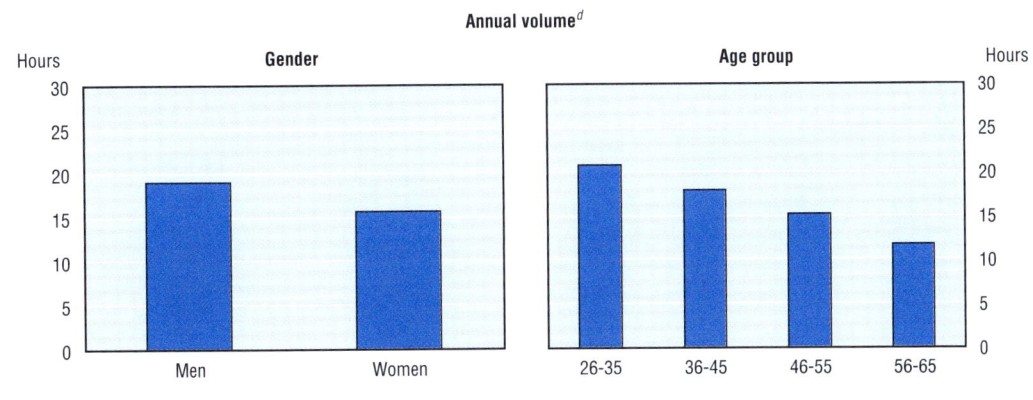

Participation rate[c]

Annual volume[d]

a) Data refer to employed persons aged 26 to 65 years.
b) Unweighted average of Australia, Belgium (Flanders only), Canada, the Czech Republic, Denmark, Finland, Hungary, Ireland, Italy, the Netherlands, New Zealand, Norway, Poland, Switzerland, the United Kingdom and the United States.
c) Ratio of employed persons participating in training to total employment (in per cent).
d) Volume of hours spent in CVT courses per employed person.
Source: IALS.

responsibility are twice as likely to participate in employer-sponsored training as are employees without any supervisory role. This pattern is more pronounced in terms of hours of training: on average, employees performing non-supervisory functions spend less than one-third as much time on training as employees with a strong supervisory role. Training incidence is also particularly low in the case of the self-employed.

Immigrants are somewhat less likely to participate in employer-sponsored CVT than natives, but the difference is not large (about 5 percentage points).[3] Immigrants also receive fewer hours of training on average (16 hours per employed person per year, *i.e.* about three hours less than their native peers). However, immigrants receive more employer-sponsored training than natives in Canada and Italy, as well as in the Netherlands (participation rates only) and Australia (training volume only).

Finally, data on training rates in large and small firms from the European Continuing Vocational Training Survey (CVTS) show that workers in small firms receive less employer-sponsored training than workers in large firms (Table 5.2).[4] Except in a few countries (*e.g.* Ireland and the United Kingdom), this gap is even greater when training is measured in volume terms: workers in large firms receive almost twice as many hours of employer-sponsored training as workers in small firms.

5. UPGRADING WORKERS' SKILLS AND COMPETENCIES

Chart 5.3. **Native and skilled workers receive more training**
Employer-sponsored CVT courses by socio-economic characteristics[a, b]

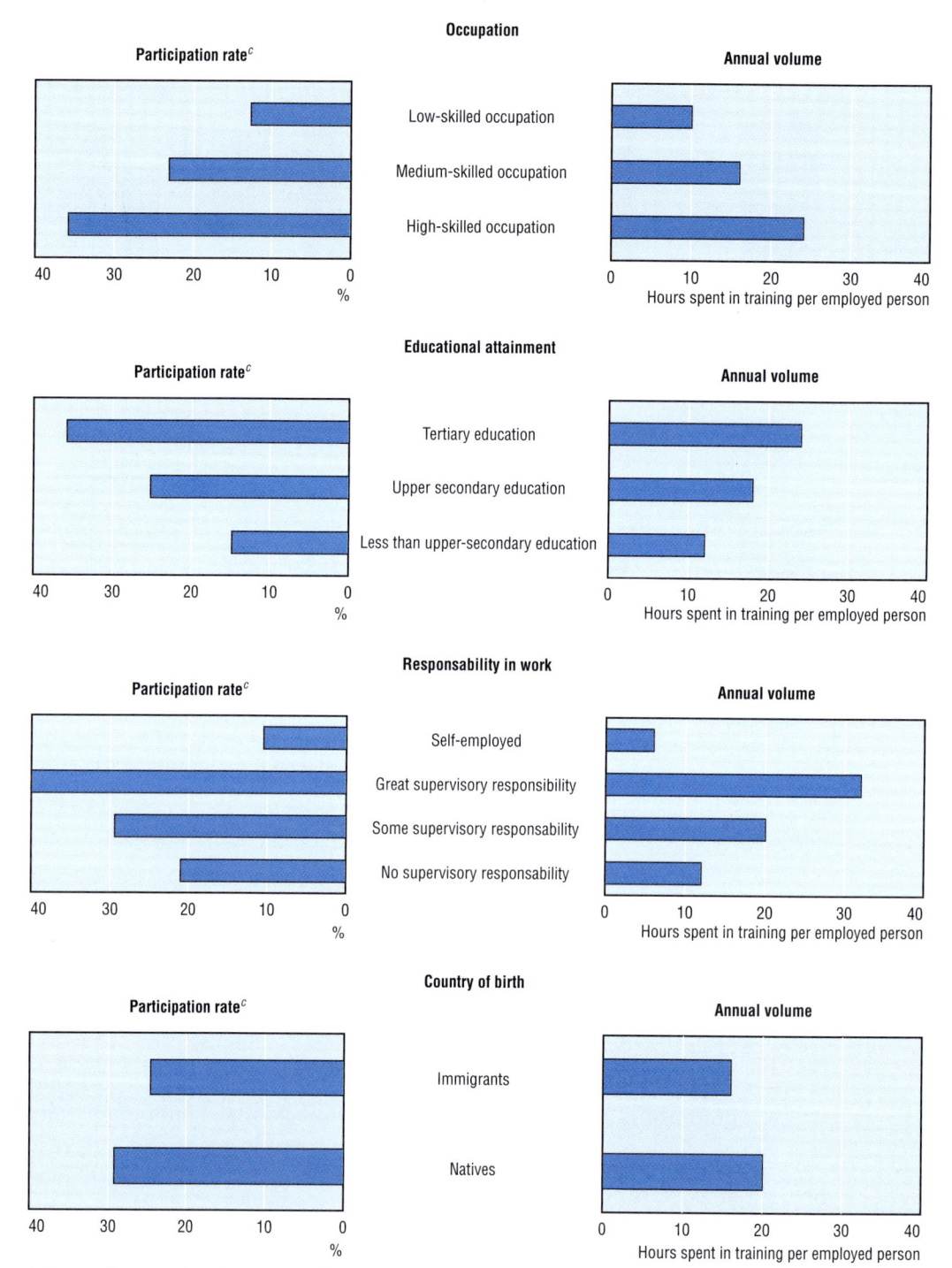

Occupation

Participation rate[c] — Low-skilled occupation, Medium-skilled occupation, High-skilled occupation (% scale 0–40)

Annual volume — Hours spent in training per employed person (scale 0–40)

Educational attainment

Participation rate[c] — Tertiary education, Upper secondary education, Less than upper-secondary education (% scale 0–40)

Annual volume — Hours spent in training per employed person (scale 0–40)

Responsability in work

Participation rate[c] — Self-employed, Great supervisory responsibility, Some supervisory responsability, No supervisory responsability (% scale 0–40)

Annual volume — Hours spent in training per employed person (scale 0–40)

Country of birth

Participation rate[c] — Immigrants, Natives (% scale 0–40)

Annual volume — Hours spent in training per employed person (scale 0–40)

a) Data refer to employed persons aged 26 to 65 years.
b) Unweighted average of Australia, Belgium (Flanders only), Canada, the Czech Republic, Denmark, Finland, Hungary, Ireland, Italy, the Netherlands, New Zealand, Norway, Poland, Switzerland, the United Kingdom and the United States. Due to missing data, Belgium is excluded from "Occupation"; Australia, Denmark, Ireland, New Zealand and Norway are excluded from "Responsibility in work"; Belgium, the Czech Republic, Finland, Hungary and Poland are excluded from "Country of birth".
c) Ratio of employed persons participating in training to total employment (in per cent).
Source: IALS.

Table 5.2. **Workers in small firms receive relatively little training**
Employer-sponsored CVT courses by firm size, 1999[a]

Number of employees in the firm	Participation rate[b] 10-49	>1 000	All[c]	Annual volume (hours per employee) 10-49	>1 000	All[c]
Austria	24	43	31	7	14	9
Belgium	20	66	41	7	21	13
Czech Republic	24	55	42	6	12	10
Denmark	48	56	53	18	24	22
Finland	38	62	50	16	20	18
France	23	62	46	8	25	17
Germany	25	38	32	6	10	9
Greece	3	33	15	1	12	6
Hungary	7	26	12	3	10	5
Ireland	28	52	41	13	14	17
Italy	11	52	26	4	16	8
Luxembourg	19	59	36	8	20	14
Netherlands	36	42	41	11	19	15
Norway	..	..	..	12	22	16
Poland	8	46	16	3	11	4
Portugal	4	43	17	2	14	7
Spain	10	46	25	6	18	11
Sweden	51	68	61	15	22	18
United Kingdom	35	52	49	12	10	13
Unweighted average	**23**	**50**	**35**	**8**	**17**	**12**

CVT = Continuous vocational training.
a) Initial vocational training is not included.
b) Ratio of employees participating in training to total employees (in per cent).
c) All firms with at least ten employees.
Source: CVTS2, New Cronos.

Bivariate correlations can however be misleading, to the extent that certain characteristics are correlated (for instance, occupation, education and supervisory role). In order to correct for such a bias, a multivariate analysis has been carried out. The resulting estimates (see Annex 1) seem to broadly confirm the qualitative patterns of training inequality discussed above. For example, the probability of receiving employer-sponsored training is estimated to be on average 6 percentage points smaller for immigrants than for natives, and 9 percentage points smaller for workers with less than upper secondary education than for individuals with a tertiary qualification. Furthermore, the gender training gap, in terms of training volume, remains significant even after controlling for part-time status. Finally, the overall conclusion remains that important differences in training participation and intensity exist between OECD countries, even after adjusting for a considerable number of characteristics of both workers and their employers.

2. Not enough and not equal? A closer look at the determinants of training patterns

The above section identifies patterns of unequal training provision across different worker groups. This section examines the source of the inequalities and assesses whether the observed patterns are optimal in terms of economic efficiency. More specifically, Section 2.A reviews the empirical evidence on the existence of various market failures affecting training outcomes. However, although their impact may differ across worker groups, these market failures do not explain training gaps entirely. For instance, training provision might increase with educational attainment simply because it is more profitable for a firm to train high-educated workers or because high-educated workers are more eager to participate in training courses, due to greater rates of return. In general, it is important for policy to understand the source of training inequalities, and in particular, whether training gaps are due to either employers' or employees' behaviours. For this reason, Sections 2.B and 2.C examine how employers' supply and employees' demand vary across worker groups. Implications for policy-making are then derived in Section 3.

A. Market failures affecting training outcomes

In order to understand the incentives of individual workers and employers to invest in human capital, it is important to make a distinction between firm-specific and general training:

- In principle, the optimal amount of investment in *firm-specific* human capital – *i.e.* those skills that are valuable only at the firm providing them – can be obtained only if costs and returns can be shared by the worker and the firm (Becker, 1975; Hashimoto, 1981). Sharing is required for two reasons: *i)* this investment creates rents to continuing a relationship, which the parties can bargain over; and *ii)* once training expenditures have been made, the firm incurs a greater loss if the worker quits. As a consequence, there is an incentive for the employer to increase post-training wages to prevent voluntary quits (see *e.g.* Parsons, 1986).

- By contrast, only the worker will pay for *general* training – that is training that raises productivity at other employers to the same extent as at the employer who provides it – under perfect competition in the labour market. This occurs because only the worker can reap the benefits from this type of training, since any alternative wage offer rises proportionately with his/her productivity. However, imperfections in other markets (*e.g.* the capital market) may prevent workers from choosing the optimal amount of human capital investment (Becker, 1975).

Most employer-paid training courses provide skills that are transferable across firms

Chart 5.4 shows that most CVT courses are entirely paid by employers. With the exception of three countries (Ireland, Italy and Switzerland) where about one-half of CVT courses are paid by employers, firms fully pay for more than 70% of CVT courses.[5] Does this mean that most of the recorded training is firm-specific? In fact, empirical evidence suggests that purely firm-specific skills are relatively rare (see *e.g.* Neal, 1995). Stevens (1994, 1999) argues that, in practice, most skills provided through training are likely to be neither fully general nor fully firm-specific and uses the term "transferable skills" for skills that are valuable at more than one firm but nonetheless are not valuable at all firms.

Few national surveys contain explicit information about the generality of skills provided through formal training. From those that do, it appears that most formal training is quite general and almost all is transferable.[6] Furthermore, it seems that off-site CVT courses (*i.e.* courses occurring outside the workplace) impart essentially general skills. By contrast, it is more difficult to establish the generality of workplace training (Loewenstein and Spletzer, 1999b). When the analysis is restricted to CVT fully paid by the employer, it emerges that only 35% of the formal courses take place at work (Chart 5.5). Even in the United Kingdom, the country for which the greatest share of workplace training is

5. UPGRADING WORKERS' SKILLS AND COMPETENCIES

Chart 5.4. **Most training is entirely paid by employers**
Percentage of CVT courses entirely paid by employers[a]

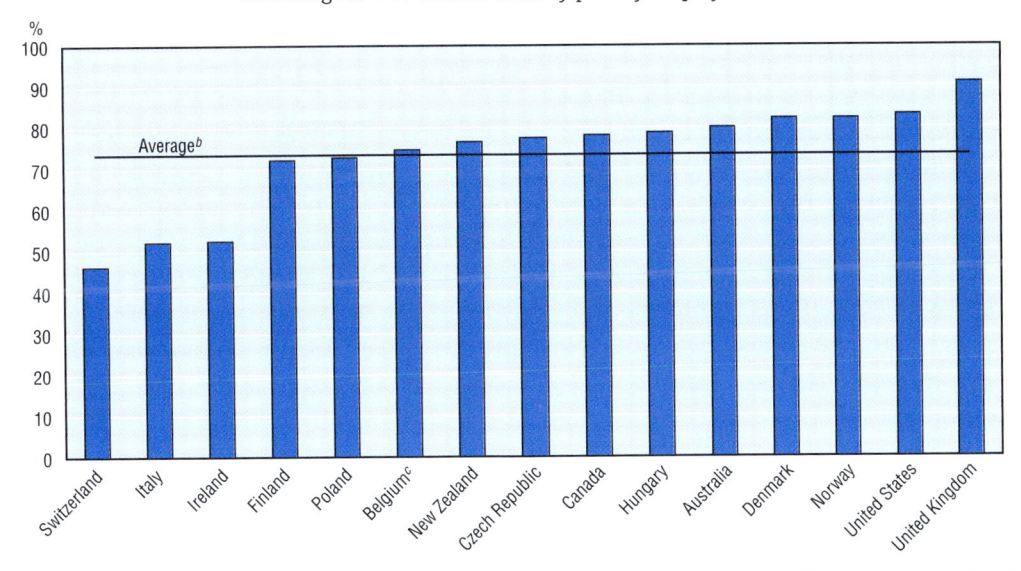

[Bar chart showing percentages by country, ranked in ascending order: Switzerland (~47), Italy (~53), Ireland (~54), Finland (~73), Poland (~74), Belgium[c] (~76), New Zealand (~78), Czech Republic (~79), Canada (~80), Hungary (~81), Australia (~82), Denmark (~84), Norway (~84), United States (~85), United Kingdom (~93). Average[b] line at ~75%.]

a) Data refer to all CVT courses (both employer-sponsored and non-employer-sponsored) received by employed persons aged 26 to 65 years and to 1994 for Canada, Ireland, Poland, Switzerland (German and French-speaking regions) and the United States, to 1996 for Australia, Belgium (Flanders only), New Zealand and the United Kingdom, and to 1998 for the Czech Republic, Denmark, Finland, Hungary, Italy, Norway and the Italian-speaking regions of Switzerland. Countries are ranked from left to right in ascending order.
b) Unweighted average of countries shown.
c) Flanders only.
Source: IALS.

Chart 5.5. **Employer-paid CVT less frequently imparts firm-specific skills**
Percentage of employer-paid CVT courses taking place at work[a]

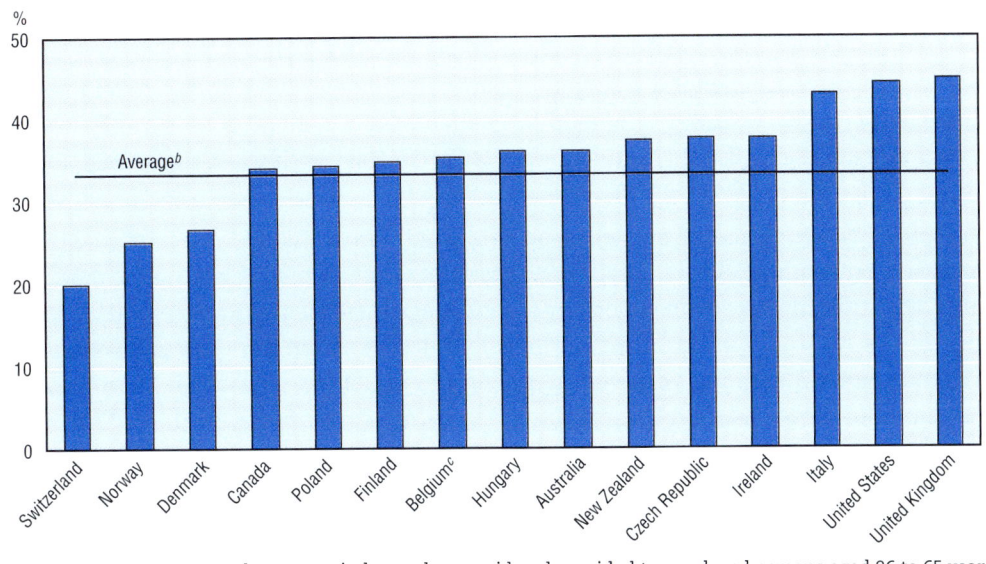

[Bar chart showing percentages by country, ranked in ascending order: Switzerland (~20), Norway (~25), Denmark (~27), Canada (~34), Poland (~35), Finland (~35), Belgium[c] (~36), Hungary (~36), Australia (~37), New Zealand (~38), Czech Republic (~38), Ireland (~38), Italy (~44), United States (~45), United Kingdom (~46). Average[b] line at ~34%.]

a) Data refer to CVT courses that are entirely employer-paid and provided to employed persons aged 26 to 65 years. Also, they refer to 1994 for Canada, Ireland, Poland, Switzerland (German and French-speaking regions) and the United States, to 1996 for Australia, Belgium (Flanders only), New Zealand and the United Kingdom, and to 1998 for the Czech Republic, Denmark, Finland, Hungary, Italy, Norway and the Italian-speaking regions of Switzerland. Countries are ranked from left to right in ascending order.
b) Unweighted average of countries shown.
c) Flanders only.
Source: IALS.

reported, more than 50% of reported training occurs outside the workplace. In other words, most of the employer-paid training reported in available cross-country data seems to be transferable. This finding runs counter to the theory whereby employers should not fully pay for courses that provide transferable skills.

Labour market imperfections explain why employers invest in transferable skills...

This inconsistency between theory and evidence suggests that, in fact, labour markets are not perfectly competitive. This would explain why firms have an incentive to pay for a significant share of training courses, which are in fact general or transferable. For example, if firms have some degree of monopsony power over their trained personnel, employers may be able to recoup training costs by paying a trained worker less than his/her post-training marginal product, while still retaining the worker (see *e.g.* Acemoglu and Pischke, 1999a; Stevens, 1999). Stevens (1994, 2001) argues that these conditions are particularly likely to prevail for skills that cannot be useful at many other employers. But this also applies in the case of fully general training in the presence of a wide range of imperfections such as asymmetric information and lack of certification (or lack of recognition of qualifications), frictions and search costs, wage-bargaining institutions, adverse selection affecting quits and lay-offs, or complementarity with specific investments (Acemoglu and Pischke, 1999b).

... but these imperfections may also reduce training participation

Imperfect competition in the labour market is likely to result in under-provision of training. Employers' monopsony power, by compressing the wage distribution, creates the conditions under which a significant share of general training costs is borne by the firm – since, under these conditions, firms are more able to reap the benefits of training. But under-investment is nevertheless likely to occur, because current employers cannot internalise the benefits from training that will accrue to future employers.[7]

Labour market imperfections, such as those described above, also reduce workers' incentives to invest in general training. In particular, if pay scales do not reflect marginal productivity, workers cannot fully reap the benefits from general training and, therefore, are not able to internalise its lifetime benefits (in contrast with what they could do under perfect competition; Becker, 1975).

Empirical evidence shows that under-provision is likely to occur in all OECD countries. For example, Barron *et al.* (1999a) estimate that, in the United States, productivity gains after training are seven times larger than wage increases, suggesting that firms reap most of the returns from training. Furthermore, Loewenstein and Spletzer (1998, 1999b) find that general training received at previous employers, at least if certified, has a greater effect on wages than training provided by the current employer, who can exploit its market power to recoup the costs of training – at least partially. From a longer term perspective, Lengermann (1999) finds that the effect of general training received at current employers increases over time. Empirical studies for a number of European countries have obtained similar results (see *e.g.* Booth and Bryan, 2002; Ok and Tergeist, 2003; and Fougère *et al.*, 2001).

Other market failures also affect training outcomes (see Box 5.2). Combined with labour market imperfections, capital and training market failures might reduce disproportionately the training opportunities for low-educated workers. In fact, recent empirical studies suggest that credit constraints may create a barrier to training for

> Box 5.2. **Non-labour market sources of market failures: theoretical aspects**
>
> There are several sources of non-labour market failures that may affect training outcomes. The most frequently considered in the literature on general training are:
>
> *Training market imperfections:* First, workers and employers may lack information on teaching quality and be unable to distinguish between different providers of educational services. Second, and perhaps more importantly, training might not be fully contractible: while the amount of training can be written down in a contract, its type and quality are less likely to be specified in a manner that is verifiable by third parties such as tribunals (Malcomson, 1997, 1999; Gibbons and Waldman, 1999). This may induce both the employee and the employer to behave non-co-operatively and invest in training separately without bargaining, leading to sub-optimal outcomes (Acemoglu and Pischke, 1999a). The non-contractibility of training might also exacerbate possible conflicts between employers and employees – the former preferring providing specific training and the latter receiving general skills that can be re-sold in the labour market (Stevens, 1994; Barron et al., 1999b).
>
> *Capital market imperfections:* Unlike physical capital, human capital cannot be used as collateral for borrowing (Becker, 1975). Moreover, individual human capital investment is often indivisible so that the risk associated to it cannot be diversified. Furthermore this risk can be insured only partially, if at all: in practice, private insurance markets are unlikely to work in a proper way, due to the unobservability of the trainee's effort and the size of human capital investments (the level of individual liability required to avoid adverse selection would be too high, see e.g. Stevens, 1999). The employer can partially relax the employee's credit constraint to the extent that the employee accepts a lower wage during the training period. However, in order to smooth consumption over time the employee may not accept large wage cuts and there is a limit to the extent to which small firms can borrow to finance training expenditures using physical capital as collateral.
>
> *Co-ordination failures:* When returns to training are interdependent, both employers and workers may decide not to invest if each side expects low returns. A bad co-ordination equilibrium may therefore arise, leading to sub-optimal investment in training (Redding, 1996). The same argument can be applied to specialisation in high-tech industries. Workers and firms in low-tech industries have little incentive to invest in further training since the "upskilled" worker would not perform an "upskilled" activity in the same firm and industry, while opportunities for the worker in other (high-tech) industries are small if the share of the latter in national output is small (Crouch et al., 1999).

low-educated (low-income/low-wealth) workers or, alternatively, that these workers find it difficult to negotiate with their employers about the content and quality of training programmes.[8] In such a situation, co-financing policies that increase incentives for firms to invest in training (such as corporate tax deductions, see Section 3) are likely to have a positive impact also on the amount of training received by low-educated workers.

B. Disentangling employers' supply from employees' demand

The findings of Section 2.A suggest that market failures might have an impact on the level of training. Some evidence also suggests that these imperfections might lie behind training inequalities, although the magnitude of their impact has not been established yet. Beyond market failures, training outcomes will depend on the extent to which employers and employees will have an incentive to invest in human capital. From the point of view of policy making it is essential to understand whether possible under-investment and inequalities are mainly due to either employers' or employees' behaviour, and this is the task of this section.

The market for CVT can be broken into *two sub-markets*: an upstream market, in which employers buy training services from a training provider; and a downstream market, in which employers re-sell these training services to their employees, with the price for training hidden in wages.[9] In the downstream training market, one can in principle distinguish between supply (by the employer) and demand (by the employee). Training outcomes represent the resulting equilibrium between supply and demand.

While the amount of employer-sponsored training supplied by employers and demanded by workers at the equilibrium price in the downstream market can be observed, demand and supply curves cannot. However, the IALS contains information on CVT courses that workers would have liked to have taken but could not because they could not afford (or did not want) to pay for the implicit or explicit price required. This information is used in this section to identify supply and demand factors underlying equilibrium outcomes (see Annex 2).[10] For different groups of workers, Table 5.3 shows relative patterns of demand (by employees) and supply (by employers), derived from the estimation of bivariate probit models of the probability of demanding training at zero cost for the employee and receiving employer-sponsored training in equilibrium.[11]

Women and immigrants are less likely to be included in employer-paid training.

Female workers have greater demand but lower supply than their male peers. Supply is also smaller for immigrants with respect to natives. These results possibly reflect lower expected benefits – in the case of women, due to career breaks, maternity leave, etc. – or higher expected costs – in the case of immigrants, due to the need of providing complementary language courses – for the employer.

Older workers and the low-educated have low demand for training...

Training supply for young workers (aged 16 to 25 years) appears to be smaller than that of prime-age employees, while the opposite occurs for older workers who, by contrast, have a lower demand for training.[12] Age might in part capture the effect of tenure, for which there are insufficient controls in the equation due to data limitations. However, the result for older workers might reflect possible differences in pay-back periods between employers and employees.[13] In equilibrium, pay-back periods for general training are likely to be longer for the employee than for the employer.[14] As a consequence, the age above which it is no longer profitable to pay for training (because the pay-back period is longer than the remaining number of years before retirement) is likely to be lower for the employee than for his/her employer.

Demand for training is estimated to be greater the higher the level of educational attainment, but this is not the case for supply.[15] These results might arise because of non-economic factors affecting demand (such as access to information, motivational aspects, and lack of appropriate pedagogy; see OECD, 2003a) or as a result of employers' monopsony power, credit constraints and training market imperfections – *e.g.* imperfect information or contractibility – that appear to be greater the lower the level of educational attainment (see Section 2.A).

Table 5.3. **Training supply and demand vary across firms and individuals**
Estimated changes in the demand and supply of training associated with each factor[a]

	Demand	Supply
Gender		
(reference: men)		
Women	+	–
Country of birth		
(reference: born in country of interview)		
Immigrants	0	–
Age groups		
(reference: aged 36-45)		
Aged 16-25	0	–
Aged 26-35	0	0
Aged 46-55	–	+
Aged 56-65	–	+
Educational attainment		
(reference: upper secondary)		
Less than upper secondary	–	0(?)
Tertiary	+	0(?)
Literacy		
(reference: average literacy score)		
Greater literacy score	0	+
Part-time		
(reference: full-time)		
Family and health problems	0	–
Still in education	–	–
Voluntary part-time for other reasons	–	?
Involuntary part-time	+	–
Temporary contract		
(reference: permanent)		
Temporary contract	+	–
Occupation		
(reference: clerks)		
Managers	0	+
Professionals	+	?
Technicians and associate professionals	+	?
Service workers and shop and market sales workers	0	–
Craft and related trades workers	0	–
Plant and machine operators and assemblers	0	–
Elementary occupations	–	–
Supervisory role		
(reference: some supervisory role)		
No supervisory	–	?
Great supervisory	0	+
Firm size		
(reference: 100 to 199 employees)		
20 to 99 employees	0	–
200 to 499 employees	0	+
500 and more employees	0	+

a) Estimated shift in the demand and supply of training with respect to the reference individual, who is indicated in the table. Estimates are obtained subject to the assumption that, by threatening lay-offs and/or offering monetary compensation, an employer can always convince a worker to be trained. +, – and 0 mean that, with respect to the reference individual, a given characteristic is estimated to increase demand (supply), reduce demand (supply), leave demand (supply) unchanged. The sign ? implies that nothing can be said on the supply shift. See Annex 1 for detailed estimation results and Annex 2 for the description of the estimation method.

Source: OECD estimates based on IALS.

... while training supply by firms is affected by workers' basic competencies.

Demand and supply of training are likely to be influenced by individual histories preceding current job experience and entry in the labour market. These histories are not fully captured by educational attainment. For instance, literacy scores of those participating in employer-sponsored training are greater than those of non-participants at any level of education (Chart 5.6). The average literacy score of participants is 4% greater for

Chart 5.6. **Workers with better literacy skills receive more training**
Average IALS literacy scores, by participation in employer-sponsored CVT and educational attainment[a, b]

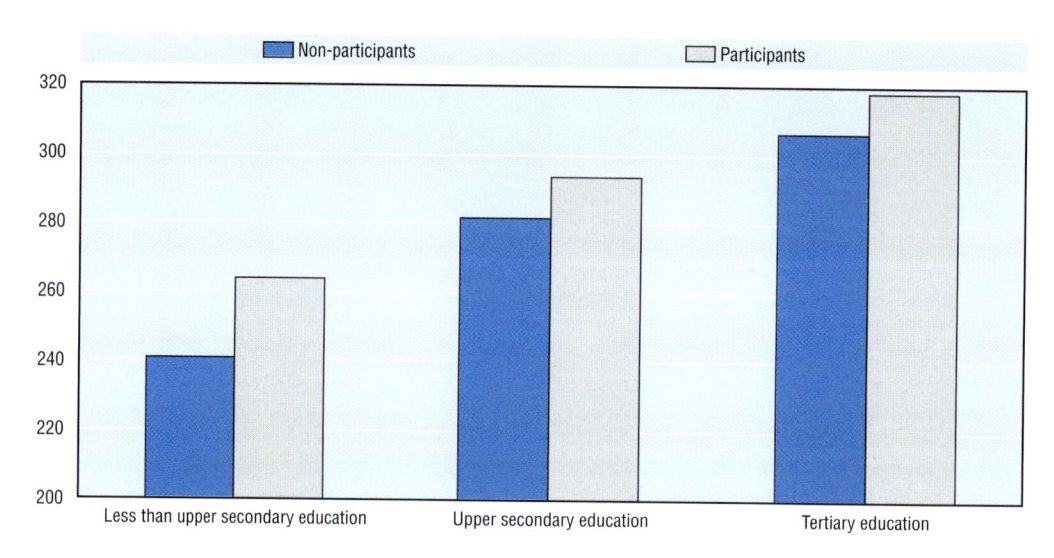

a) Data refer to employed persons aged 26 to 65 years.
b) Unweighted average of Australia, Belgium (Flanders only), Canada, the Czech Republic, Denmark, Finland, Hungary, Ireland, Italy, the Netherlands, New Zealand, Norway, Poland, Switzerland, the United Kingdom and the United States. The literacy levels are calculated as an average over the three types of literacy skills reported in the IALS, namely prose, documentation and quantitative skills.
Source: IALS.

workers with a tertiary qualification and 9% greater in the case of those with less than upper secondary education. Although the direction of causality is not clear-cut, there is some evidence that most literacy skills are developed by individuals at relatively young ages, typically before joining the labour market,[16] and that subsequent education or CVT spells do not modify the level of literacy in a significant way. Thus, Chart 5.6 suggests a causal relationship between literacy and training participation.

Instrumental variable (IV) techniques have to be used to confirm this statement.[17] The derived effect of literacy on training supply and demand based on IV estimates is shown in Table 5.3 (detailed estimation results are presented in Table 5.A1.3 in Annex 1). The table shows that, while training demand is not significantly affected by literacy, training supply is increasing with the level of literacy, suggesting that employers believe that learning ability increases (and therefore training costs decrease) with basic general skills, including literacy.

There are few employer-paid training opportunities for most part-time and temporary workers...

There is some evidence in the literature that in many OECD countries the incidence of employer-sponsored training is lower for part-time (Leuven and Oosterbeek, 1999) and temporary workers (OECD, 2002a). As shown in Table 5.3, with respect to full-time employees, there is strong evidence that training supply for involuntary part-time workers is much lower than for full-time workers, while demand is not significantly lower. The same applies to workers with temporary contracts compared to those with permanent contracts. Statistical discrimination, tenure effects and higher probability of quitting (voluntarily) can plausibly explain these findings. Similarly, employees working part-time for family or health reasons tend to be confronted with lower supply than full-time workers, although estimates are not always significant.[18]

... as well as for workers in low-skilled occupations or tasks...

The estimates also indicate that the type of occupation has little influence on the demand for training, while supply is estimated to increase with the degree of skill-intensity (see also Table 5.A1.2). Similarly, training supply is unambiguously greater for individuals with a great supervisory role compared with individuals with some or no supervisory responsibility, while demand is not significantly different. These findings may suggest that employers tend to sort more able employees into better career and training opportunities simultaneously.

... and in small firms

Finally, training supply is estimated to be increasing with firm size while training demand is not. This pattern is consistent with the hypothesis that larger internal labour markets present greater opportunities to reap the benefits from training through internal promotion or re-assignment of trained workers. Large firms may also have lower unit costs of training and greater access to credit and information.

C. The impact of workers' opportunity costs on training participation

There are two reasons why the amount of training employers pay for or provide at the equilibrium and the amount of training workers' demand at zero cost may differ. First, the employer might not have been ready to share the cost of a given training course, but the worker might have borne all the direct and opportunity costs – such as foregone income and time. In this case, in the IALS questionnaire, this worker will report having participated in non-employer-sponsored training. Second, for a given desired training course, the worker may perceive either the direct or the opportunity costs involved as being excessively high. In this case, it can be expected that the worker will report that there is additional training he/she would have liked to take but could not. On average, in the OECD countries participating in the IALS, about one-fourth of employed workers did not take all the training they wanted (Table 5.4). In all countries except Finland, this condition is more frequent in the case of workers who participated in training than for non-participants (31.5% *versus* 23%). Amongst training participants, on average, almost 37% of workers who did not receive support from their employer would have liked to receive more training.

Lack of time is a serious obstacle to training participation...

The relative importance of different cost items on the gap between potential demand and actual equilibrium might have a bearing on the effectiveness of possible policy measures. For example, policy schemes allowing only relaxation of financial constraints (such as loan schemes or individual subsidies) will not help much when time-related

5. UPGRADING WORKERS' SKILLS AND COMPETENCIES

Table 5.4. **A quarter of all workers would like to take more training**
Percentage of workers reporting that they wanted to take further training, but did not[a]

	All	Not trained[b]	Trained[c] All trained	Of which: Not employer-sponsored	Of which: Employer-sponsored
Australia	26.9	25.2	31.2	34.5	30.3
Belgium[d]	19.2	17.2	30.8	38.9	28.9
Canada	33.6	30.2	41.4	64.3	37.4
Czech Republic	15.4	14.7	19.1	26.1	18.5
Denmark	33.3	31.1	35.4	39.1	34.6
Finland	38.1	38.9	37.2	38.6	37.0
Hungary	15.4	14.5	20.0	24.9	18.7
Ireland	19.2	17.5	29.0	29.2	29.0
Italy	24.1	21.1	34.0	36.4	32.2
Netherlands	22.5	21.7	24.6	23.9	24.7
New Zealand	33.0	28.2	40.3	48.6	38.5
Norway	34.4	29.4	39.9	30.6	41.0
Poland	16.0	14.6	25.5	36.8	22.8
Switzerland	27.2	26.6	29.7	25.3	31.4
United Kingdom	25.4	20.1	31.2	47.1	29.3
United States	26.1	21.9	34.6	43.1	33.6
Unweighted average	**25.6**	**23.3**	**31.5**	**36.7**	**30.5**

a) Data refer to employed persons aged 26 to 65 years, and to 1994 for Canada, Ireland, the Netherlands, Poland, Switzerland (German and French-speaking regions) and the United States, to 1996 for Australia, Belgium (Flanders only), New Zealand and the United Kingdom, and to 1998 for the Czech Republic, Denmark, Finland, Hungary, Italy, Norway and the Italian-speaking regions of Switzerland.
b) Employed persons who did not receive training for professional or career-related purposes.
c) Employed persons who received training for professional or career-related purposes.
d) Flanders only.
Source: IALS.

opportunity costs are the main obstacle to training participation. In the latter case, more effective policy instruments might be provisions for training leaves, part-time study or time accounts (see Section 3). As shown in Chart 5.7, around 15% of trained workers and 10% of non-trained workers claim that they could not take the desired additional training due to lack of time. Furthermore, a significant number of workers declare that they could not take all the training they wanted either because they were too busy at work, because the time schedule was inappropriate or because of family responsibilities. Since multiple answers are allowed in the survey, these figures are not additive. Nevertheless, taking multiple answers into account, time is an issue for more than 60% of the workers who could not take the training they wanted.

... but financial factors play a role for the low-skilled

Though less important than time-related costs, many employees also report that they could not afford or did not want to pay for the full cost of the training courses they wanted to take (about 7% of trained workers and 5% of non-trained workers).[19]

The incidence of each constraint varies significantly across groups. In particular, the probability of reporting financial reasons is 4 percentage points lower for managers than for clerical workers, while it is 7 percentage points higher for workers in elementary occupations (Chart 5.8). Conversely, among workers who did not take all the training they

5. UPGRADING WORKERS' SKILLS AND COMPETENCIES

Chart 5.7. **Time is the most frequently reported reason for which training costs may be too high for the workers**

Percentage of workers who could not take the additional course they wanted, by reason[a, b]

Trained[c] / Not trained[d]

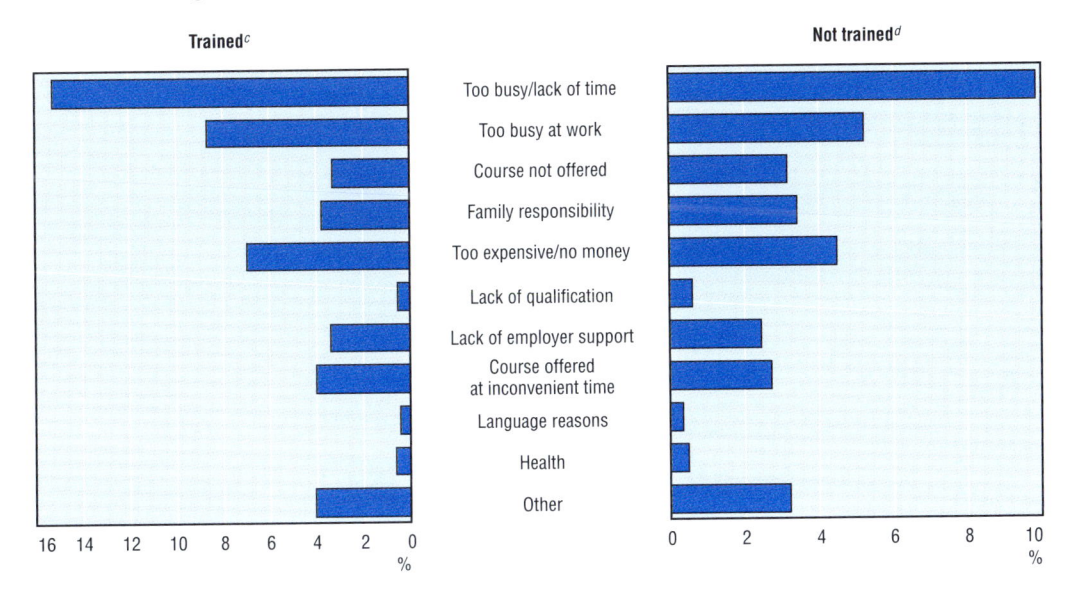

Categories: Too busy/lack of time; Too busy at work; Course not offered; Family responsibility; Too expensive/no money; Lack of qualification; Lack of employer support; Course offered at inconvenient time; Language reasons; Health; Other.

a) Employed persons aged 26 to 65 years.
b) Unweighted average of Australia, Belgium (Flanders only), Canada, the Czech Republic, Denmark, Finland, Hungary, Ireland, Italy, the Netherlands, New Zealand, Norway, Poland, Switzerland, the United Kingdom and the United States.
c) Individuals who received training for professional or career-related purposes.
d) Individuals who did not receive training for professional or career-related purposes.

Source: IALS.

wanted, the probability of being "time-constrained" is estimated to be, *ceteris paribus*, 9 percentage points greater for managers and 10 percentage points lower for workers in elementary occupations than for clerks. In other words, policy measures affecting direct costs (*e.g.* individual subsidies) may increase training participation of workers in low-skilled occupations even when they do not increase workers' time availability (*i.e.* even in the absence of schemes such as time accounts or training leave).

Family responsibilities are important constraints for women

Amongst those women working full-time who did not take all the training they wanted, the estimated probability of reporting either financial reasons or family responsibilities is 7 and 8 percentage points higher, respectively, than for men (Chart 5.8). This might be explained by two factors. On the one hand, women are less likely to be offered employer-sponsored training (see Section 2.B) and earn on average less than men – so that they might find training courses less affordable. On the other hand, women are less likely to exploit training opportunities available outside normal working hours, since these would make them stay away from home for even longer hours. The same argument applies to individuals working part-time because of health or family reasons. In particular, amongst women working part-time who did not take all the training they wanted, the estimated probabilities of reporting financial reasons or family constraints are 13 and 31 percentage points higher, respectively, than in the case of men working full-time.

5. UPGRADING WORKERS' SKILLS AND COMPETENCIES

Chart 5.8. Cost factors vary across worker groups
Probability of reporting a specific reason for not taking the desired additional course, conditional to reporting at least one reason[a]

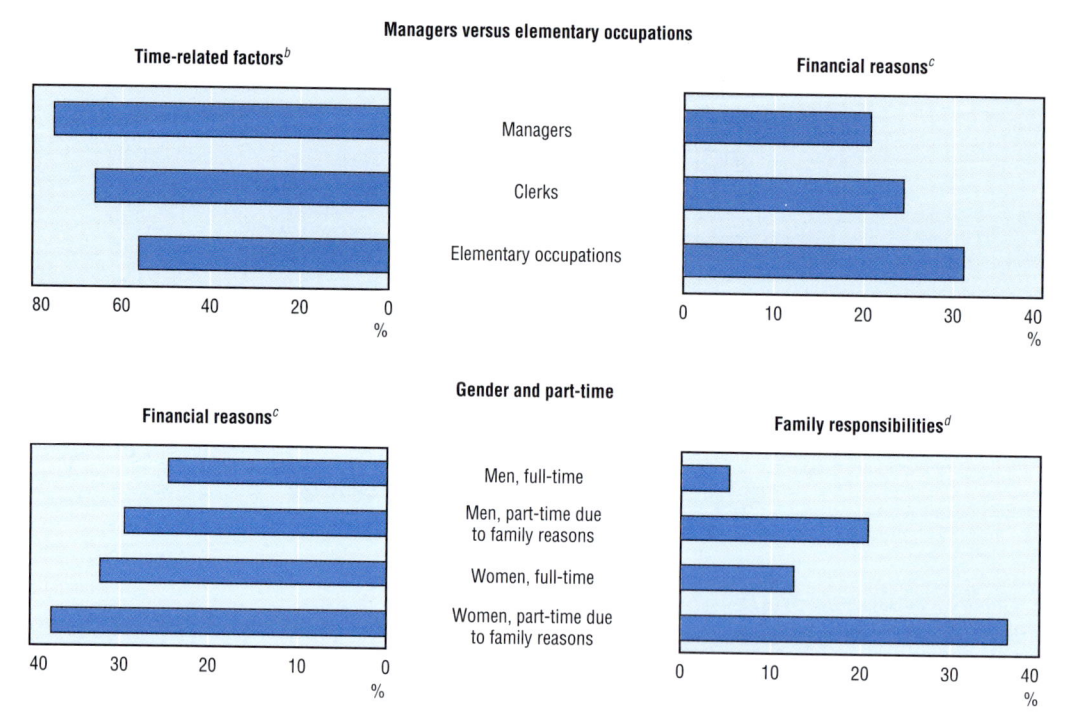

Managers versus elementary occupations

Time-related factors[b] — Managers, Clerks, Elementary occupations

Financial reasons[c] — Managers, Clerks, Elementary occupations

Gender and part-time

Financial reasons[c] — Men, full-time; Men, part-time due to family reasons; Women, full-time; Women, part-time due to family reasons

Family responsibilities[d] — Men, full-time; Men, part-time due to family reasons; Women, full-time; Women, part-time due to family reasons

a) Estimated on the basis of a probit model, in which the dependent variable takes value 1 if the individual reported a given specific reason and 0 otherwise. The sample refers to employed persons who reported at least one reason of firms with more than 20 employees, with at least some education, aged 16 to 65 years and not working in the agricultural sector. All equations include dummies for gender, educational attainment, age classes, community size, part-time status, country of birth, number of employers (last 12 months), firm size classes, industries, occupations and countries, and are estimated only for those countries where sample size is greater than 200 observations (Australia, Canada, Denmark, Finland, Italy, New Zealand, Norway, Switzerland, the United Kingdom and the United States).
b) Too busy/lack of time, too busy at work, family responsibilities, and course offered at inconvenient time were reported as reasons for not taking the desired additional training.
c) Course too expensive/no money was reported as reason for not taking the desired additional training.
d) Family responsibilities were reported as reasons for not taking the desired additional training.

Source: OECD estimates based on IALS.

3. Policy approaches to improve training outcomes

As shown above, training opportunities are unevenly distributed across workers, and there is some evidence that the incidence of formal training falls short of socially desirable levels. Factors that affect the costs and benefits of CVT appear to contribute to both uneven distribution and under-investment in formal training. The purpose of this section is i) to shed light on how policy can address some of the factors behind training inequalities and under-provision, and ii) to document policy initiatives in this area.

A. From diagnosis to remedies

Section 2 has identified several sources of market failures (including labour, capital and training market imperfections) leading to under-investment in formal training, although more research is needed to quantify the impact of these failures on observed outcomes. Furthermore, it has decomposed the downstream training market in order to trace the extent to which differences in the provision of employer-sponsored training across groups of workers are due to demand (by employees) or supply (by employers). The empirical results suggest that employers are less likely to include women, immigrants, young employees, involuntary part-time and temporary workers, workers in low-skilled occupations and workers with low literacy, when selecting which employees to train (Table 5.5). By contrast, lower demand appears to account for lower training participation

Table 5.5. **From evidence to policy**
Co-financing policy options likely to raise training participation of specific groups

Disadvantaged group	Main barrier to training[a]		Co-financing schemes
Older workers, low-educated workers	Weak demand with equal or higher employers' supply		– Incentives for employers (corporate tax deductions, pay-back clauses)
			– Low-educated/low income workers only: fostering demand by relaxing individual credit constraints (loan schemes, ILAs, pay-back clauses)
Women, immigrants, workers with low literacy, involuntary part-time workers, temporary workers, non-supervisory workers	Low employers' supply with equal or higher demand	Low supply due to individual characteristics	– Relaxing individual credit constraints (loan schemes, ILAs, pay-back clauses)
			– Relaxing individual time constraints (time accounts, training leave)
			– Improving cost-sharing (pay-back clauses)
Workers in small firms, workers in low-tech industries and/or industries with many firms		Low supply due to firm characteristics	– Relaxing individual credit constraints (loan schemes, ILAs, pay-back clauses)
			– Incentives for employers (targeted tax deductions, pay-back clauses)
Low literacy workers with low qualifications	Low demand and low employers' supply		– "Empowering" schemes (ILAs)

ILA: Individual learning accounts.
a) Barriers to training refer to the main reasons for the weak participation in employer-sponsored training of a particular worker group relative to the reference group, namely native, high-skilled, full-time, prime-age male employees in large high-tech firms.
Source: OECD estimates based on IALS.

of older and less educated workers. In the case of older workers, labour market imperfections affecting the distribution of training benefits and the length of employers' and employees' pay-back periods are perhaps behind this pattern. In the case of less educated workers, credit constraints and/or training market imperfections – due to lack of training information and contractibility between employers and employees – might partially explain this finding. However, non-economic factors, such as lack of motivation or bad pedagogical experiences, must also be taken into account. Finally, demand does not appear to vary with firm size. However, supply rises with firm size, perhaps due to lower unit costs of training, larger benefits, and greater access to credit and information for large firms.

Policies must address the causes of training inequalities as well as under-investment

Insofar as market failures are responsible for training inequalitites, a first-best approach would be to overcome them through structural reforms. However, some of these failures are due to "natural" imperfections of certain markets[20] and effective reforms to overcome them have not been proposed yet. Furthermore, other imperfections are induced by institutions and policies that do not concern primarily training outcomes (*e.g.* those affecting the wedge between wages and productivity such as minimum wages;

see Acemoglu and Pischke, 2003), whose reform cannot be undertaken without a careful evaluation of other relevant trade-offs. A second-best approach is to increase the economic incentives to invest in education and training, through fiscal policy and institutional arrangements favouring cost-sharing among private parties. This second-best approach can also target disadvantaged groups more easily, given that training gaps are due to market failures only partially (as discussed in Section 2.B). However, policy design is crucial, since some of the identified sources of market failure (e.g. lack of contractibility of training quality) can equally lead to policy failures, with the risk of large deadweight losses and heavy burdens for the public budget.

This section reviews the experience of OECD member countries with various second-best approaches to surmount financial and economic barriers to the provision of and participation in adult education and training. However, great care must be exerted when drawing general conclusions from this type of exercise for three reasons. First, in most cases, public policies focus on formal education and training. This entails a risk of inefficient substitution between formal and informal training. This risk must be taken into account in the case of policies affecting employers' incentives to provide formal training, to the extent that informal training is more likely to be employer-paid, since it imparts competencies that are less easily signalled to the external labour market (making informal training, *de facto*, firm-specific, see Acemoglu and Pischke, 1999b; and Barron et al., 1999b). Second, policies are discussed here in a partial equilibrium framework – that is, without considering the effect of the distortions induced by fund-raising schemes required to finance training policies. Third, and perhaps more importantly, the analysis is essentially based on deductive arguments derived from the empirical results of the previous sections. In fact, there are only few empirical evaluations of existing schemes and, with few exceptions, those available are limited to descriptive statistics and do not build up counterfactuals against which a rigorous assessment could be made. The lack of evaluations can partly be ascribed to the novelty of the policy initiatives. However, in principle, well-designed policies should include evaluation mechanisms in their design to ensure timely corrections of policy mistakes.[21] For these reasons, it is only possible to discuss the problem each specific policy can try to address and, to a limited extent, whether it has been implemented in a consistent way. But, at this stage, it is not possible to make a more general assessment of whether each intervention has been excessive, insufficient or just right *vis-à-vis* the target.

Co-financing arrangements lie at the heart of a comprehensive strategy to foster training

Since the 1960s, policies were formulated to address, first and foremost, perceived rigidities on the supply side that interfered with adult education. The underlying assumption was one of substantial economic and social demand for adults to return to formal education. Thus, the objective of *recurrent education* was to improve learning opportunities for individuals by enhancing the capacity of the formal education sector to accommodate those wishing to return to education. However, recurrent education never emerged as an enduring widespread practice, in part because its associated costs were never adequately funded.

More recently, greater emphasis has been devoted to the demand-side. This new emphasis has entailed a shift in the target of public policy from providers and systems geared to provision of education and training with relatively homogeneous content to the demand of individuals and employers for more heterogeneous learning outcomes. In other words, in contrast to children in initial education, learning objectives of individual adults are ever-changing and very heterogeneous so that such needs can best be met through a more differentiated arrangement of providers and courses than the delivery mode characterising initial education. As a consequence, policy strategies to increase human capital accumulation of adults have shifted from direct subsidisation of external (public or private) providers of training services to co-financing schemes intended to increase incentives for employers and/or individuals to invest in more specific education and training. The shift towards this policy approach is based on three general principles:

- in most societies, because of budget constraints, public authorities alone cannot provide the necessary financial resources for lifelong learning;
- as lifelong learning generates considerable private returns, employers and employees should finance most of its costs; and
- greater reliance on market forces could strengthen the incentives both for learners to seek more efficient learning options and for providers to achieve higher levels of efficiency.

Co-financing mechanisms – *i.e.* schemes that channel resources from at least two parties among employers, employees and governments – can be designed so as to increase incentives to invest in human capital for employers, for individuals or for both.

Since the primary reason for which employers may invest in training less than the socially optimal amount is that current employers cannot internalise benefits from training that will accrue to future employers (as discussed in Section 2.A), *tax arrangements* or *grant schemes* for enterprises can be used to tackle aggregate under-investment. By modifying the marginal cost of training, these schemes may raise employers' supply towards the socially optimal level. These schemes can also be complemented by policies favouring cost-sharing between employers and employees, such as regulatory provisions for *pay-back clauses* and *time accounts*, to the extent that training market imperfections are not too strong. In fact, cost-sharing is unlikely to occur if the content and quality of training are not contractible (see Box 5.2). Moreover, transparent accounting and disclosure practices can have an important role in channelling resources from the stock market towards training firms, thereby increasing their incentives to train (OECD and Ernst & Young, 1997).

It can be inferred from the analysis of Section 2 that co-financing incentives directed to employers (such as tax arrangements and grant schemes) might help to foster training participation of prime-age skilled men and of those with little demand, whose training is nonetheless profitable for firms, such as older workers and the low educated (see Table 5.5).[22] For the same reason, this kind of policies is also likely to benefit workers in large firms, high-tech industries and industries where the number of competitors is relatively small. If targeted, these policies might improve the position also of other groups, particularly workers in small firms, but the risk of inefficient substitution between targeted and untargeted workers is high.

For workers who have less frequent opportunities to receive employer-sponsored training – namely women, immigrants, involuntary part-time and temporary workers, workers in small firms, in low-skilled occupations, in low-tech industries and/or workers with low literacy within each educational attainment class – it is likely to be difficult to target policies focussing on employers' incentives in an efficient way (Table 5.5). Individual-based demand-side policies (such as *loan* and *subsidy schemes*), by relaxing individual borrowing constraints and increasing expected rates of return, can thus play a role. Furthermore, some of these policies (*e.g.* subsidy schemes such as *individual learning accounts*) address both economic and non-economic barriers to adult learning. However, they require information that workers often do not have. In addition, portability of skills must be assured, particularly in the case of CVT not delivering formal diplomas. As a consequence, financial incentives must be accompanied by adequate framework conditions. Even in this case it might be difficult to target with precision certain workers (such as workers with poor literacy skills among the group of low-educated workers). Strengthening delivery of initial education emerges therefore as a necessary complementary policy instrument (see OECD, 2002b).

On the basis of OECD member countries' experience, the next two subsections describe co-financing strategies to overcome the economic and financial barriers to invest in adult learning as well as framework conditions necessary to make these strategies effective. With few exceptions (for example in the case of issues of "portability" and "signalling" of skills), most of the co-financing schemes and framework conditions that are discussed therein concern both adult education and CVT.

B. Strategies for addressing economic and financial barriers

Tax arrangements for enterprises

Tax-based schemes have the advantage of building on existing institutional arrangements for taxation, allowing them to be generally and immediately applied with limited implementation costs; for the same reason they have the disadvantage of being difficult to target precisely. When these schemes are targeted, they may induce inefficient substitution across groups (see below). In fact, tax-based schemes typically leave total freedom to choose training content and participants to firms, and must be seen mainly as instruments to reduce aggregate under-provision.

"Train or pay" schemes, which establish training levies to be paid by employers who do not train, are a route to tackling free-riding and under-provision that was popular in the 1970s. France first adopted this approach with the *Loi du 16 juillet 1971*, which introduced a minimum training expenditure and required that each firm pays as a levy an amount equal to the difference between this legal minimum and its actual training expenditure. The law initially required employers to invest an amount equal to 0.8% of total payroll. That requirement has risen gradually to 1.5% in recent years, being even higher for temporary work agencies and workers with fixed-term contracts. A number of other countries including Australia, the Quebec province of Canada, Korea and the United Kingdom adopted similar provisions in subsequent years, but abandoned them later. Today, only Quebec is still following the French model.

Up to the legal minimum, train-or-pay schemes confront employers with a financially neutral choice between training (and not paying the tax), or not training (and paying the tax). Strictly speaking firms receive no automatic subsidy since grants are not necessarily awarded (grant schemes are discussed separately, below). "Train or pay" levies, however, are equivalent to schemes where there is an additional tax of a given percentage of payroll independent of training expenditures and a 100% subsidy of training expenditures up to that percentage of payroll. For this reason, dead-weight is large in the case of employers that would have spent more than the legal minimum anyway.[23] Moreover, the scheme is likely to be quite burdensome for those companies for which returns to training are small[24] and/or might induce them to target expenditure with little attention to quality and effective needs. Finally, to the extent that payroll taxes can be shifted onto wages, training levies based on payroll act more as a device to reduce under-investment by employees due to credit market imperfections than as a policy instrument to reduce under-investment by employers, at least insofar as transferable training is concerned. In fact, if payroll taxes can be shifted onto wages, the training levy induces an implicit transfer from workers who do not receive training to those who do, but leaves incentives for employers unchanged (except that they can choose the recipients of the transfer, that is the workers to be trained). Conversely, tax incentives targeting profits are likely to be more effective to address under-provision of employer-sponsored training caused by externalities due to labour market imperfections (Stevens, 2001).

Public authorities in certain countries – including Austria (in 2000), Italy (in 2001), Luxembourg (in 1999) and the Netherlands (in 1998) – have attempted to address this issue by allowing employers to deduct more than 100% of the cost of CVT from turnover when determining taxable income (Table 5.6).[25] The extra-deduction amounts to 10% of training expenditures in Luxembourg, 20% in Austria and the Netherlands and up to 50% in Italy.

Table 5.6. **Corporate tax deductions for training expenditures in selected OECD countries**

	Main provisions	Restrictions
Austria	Deduction of 120% of CVT cost from turnover. Alternatively, deduction of 6% from previous or subsequent year's tax liability (since 2002).	For externally provided CVT that is relevant to company interests (since 2000); for internal CVT organised by a separate in-company training unit (since 2003).
France	Training expenditure tax credit of 35% applying to expenditure in excess of that made in the previous year (since 1988).	In 2002, restricted to SMEs with turnover of less than EUR 7.63 million and for which at least 75% of the capital is owned by physical persons.
Italy	Deduction of 150% of CVT cost from turnover (since 2001). If no taxable income in a given year, deduction can be postponed for up to four years.	150% deduction only for expenditures normally counted as operating costs (such as trainees' and trainers' wages). Deduction may include up to 20% of payroll.
Luxembourg	Deduction of up to 110% of CVT cost from turnover (since 1999). If no taxable income in a given year, deduction can be postponed for up to ten years.	
Netherlands	Deduction of 120% of CVT cost from turnover (since 1998). More generous schemes for small firms and low-educated workers.	Only for training that is relevant to current functions of trainee. In the case of internal training, only cost of time spent by trainer can be deducted, with the exception of training for previously unemployed workers (aged 23 years or older) that are trained to basic qualification level, for which employers can deduct also workers' wages and indirect training costs such as those due to extra supervision and modification of production plans (since 2002).

CVT: Continuous vocational training.
Source: OECD Secretariat on the basis of information supplied by the countries in question.

The main differences across countries concern the type of expenditures that are eligible for deduction. In fact, although internal training expenditures are more difficult to define in a clear and transparent way, covering only external expenditures might lead to inefficient substitution of external for internal training, with little or no impact on the overall volume. While in the Netherlands and Luxembourg both external and internal training are covered by these schemes, in Austria internal training expenditures are eligible for deduction only if provided by an in-company training institution (or separate legal entity; see Box 5.3).[26] Another key issue is whether only direct costs are eligible for the extra tax deduction or if trainees' wages are also considered. For instance, in the Italian

> **Box 5.3. Corporate tax deductions training expenditures in Austria**
>
> Since 2000, Austrian employers can claim a special tax allowance for investment in training. This training incentive is regulated by federal tax law. Initially, the tax allowance was 9% of the expenses on external training only. From 2003 onwards, the allowance has been increased to 20% and extended to training measures organised internally. The incentive allows companies not only to deduct the actual cost of training as a business expense from their taxable income but also an additional "virtual expense" of 20%. Thus, the tax base is diminished by 120% of the actual expense. Companies that do not make enough profit in a given year to benefit from this tax deduction can, as an alternative, claim a credit for training expenses of 6% of the actual expense which is deducted from the tax liability or paid out to the firm.
>
> Criteria for the tax allowance for external training measures:
>
> - The training must be provided by a training organisation different and independent from the company claiming the tax allowance.
> - The recipients of the training measure must be employees of the company.
> - The training has to be in the interest of the company and has to be fully paid for by the employer claiming the tax allowance.
>
> Criteria for the tax allowance for internal training measures:
>
> - Only expenses resulting from training organised and offered by the company itself for its employees can be deducted.
> - The department (or subsidiary) providing the training must have a degree of independence and organisational autonomy (*e.g.* own accounting system).
> - Training must be formal (*e.g.* a course, a seminar) and must be verifiable (*e.g.* proof of attendance lists, curricula, etc.).
> - The maximum amount per day to serve as a basis for the tax allowance is EUR 2 000, irrespective of the number of participants.
>
> Note that the training tax credit of 6% is subject to the same criteria as the tax allowance for external training. Employers can only receive the credit if they have not already claimed the tax allowance.
>
> As these measures have been introduced relatively recently, no evaluations are available as yet. After the most recent changes, it has been estimated that the loss of tax revenue due to them is about EUR 60 million annually.

scheme the latter are included up to 20% of payroll, while in the Dutch scheme they are generally excluded. When trainees' wages are excluded, it can be expected that these types of incentives tend not to be neutral with respect to trainees' characteristics and favour those for whom employers' opportunity cost of training (in terms of wage plus foregone productivity) is lower, such as inexperienced newly-hired workers. Nevertheless, most of these schemes are very recent and therefore there are no rigorous evaluations of their impacts.

Tax deductions provide no incentive to increase training if employers do not expect positive profits in a given fiscal year. This is particularly undesirable insofar as it is precisely during slack periods that the economic cost of foregoing production during training is lowest. To address this issue, Austrian law provides that 6% of all training expenditures incurred in a given year, which cannot be deducted in that year, can be either paid out to the firm or subtracted from the firm's tax liability in the previous or subsequent year. Similarly, deductions of training expenditures can be postponed for up to four and ten years in Italy and Luxembourg, respectively, if taxable income is negative. A Swedish survey reports that employers would expect to increase training expenditures significantly if similar arrangements were introduced in their country (Håkanson et al., 2002).

While targeting certain types of firms whose training supply is particularly low (such as small firms) through additional corporate tax deductions is feasible – at least in principle, targeting specific worker groups may involve undesirable *substitution* effects. For example, Leuven and Oosterbeek (2003) show that the 40% extra-deduction to train workers aged 40 years or older, introduced in the Netherlands in 1998 and recently abolished, induced significant substitution between training workers above the age threshold and training workers immediately below it. Once the substitution effect is taken into account, the overall effectiveness of the scheme becomes questionable.

Summarising, it can be tentatively concluded that an effective use of tax incentives to reduce firms' *under-investment* in training requires extra-deductions of training expenditures rather than deductions from payroll taxes. This is particularly likely to be the case if the latter are envisaged in the framework of "train or pay" schemes, which involve a large deadweight cost. It is also desirable that these deductions can be postponed for several years if companies have no positive profits in the year they make the expenditure.

Grant schemes and special funds for enterprises

In "train or pay" schemes, the levy is payable only if the firm's own training effort falls short of a legal minimum. By contrast, other *levy/grant schemes* imply that all companies pay a training levy independently of their training expenditure – normally as a percentage of payroll – after which they can try to recover (part of) their payment through applications for grants to fund training. Grants do not tend to reflect company payments and therefore allow redistribution of funds towards predefined priorities.

Prime examples of this kind of levy/grant schemes at national level are found in Belgium and Spain. In Belgium, a nation-wide collective agreement, which was later converted into a law, requires employers to pay 0.25% of payroll into a training fund, a sum that can be topped up by branch-level collective agreements. In Spain, employers pay 0.7% of payroll into a training fund administered by the Tripartite Training Foundation, where sectoral commissions staffed by employer and trade union representatives decide and manage training grants.

In addition to systems established by nation-wide legislation, a number of countries have sectoral training levies established through branch-level collective agreements. For example, the Netherlands and Denmark have followed this route, with half of the Dutch and one-third of the Danish workforce currently covered by sectoral levies and training funds (Gasskov, 2001). The average contribution rate in the Netherlands is 0.5%, but with considerable variation across branches. Other countries, such as Belgium and France, have set up many sectoral funds on top of their national levy regulation. Similarly, the United States has compulsory schemes for making contributions to training funds in a few sectors or companies with high trade union density, such as the automotive industry. Typically, there is a bipartite or tripartite joint governance of the training funds financed through levy schemes (see Ok and Tergeist, 2003, for detailed examples), but there are some exceptions (notably Korea, where the public employment service administers the respective fund).

Apart from programmes financed through specific levies, most OECD countries (*e.g.* European Union countries, the Czech Republic, Japan, Korea, Mexico, Poland, and the United States) have some programmes for subsidising company training expenditures that are financed out of the central government budget. EU countries have often integrated their respective subsidies with resources from the European Social Fund (ESF) in this area. ESF support is designed to contribute to projects undertaken by member states in a complementary fashion; matching funds comes from central and local governments. Nevertheless, countries freely determine the type of expenditure (*e.g.* participant salaries and/or overhead costs), the share of expenditure (up to 50%, *e.g.* in the case of Finland), and the type of firms that can be subsidised (often special provisions apply to small firms). Similar variation can be found in non-EU countries. Internal guidelines and/or laws usually specify which preconditions must be fulfilled for an application for subsidies to be accepted, such as choice of recipients (with a view to equity of access) or a proof of participation by workers' representatives in the set-up of the training plan.

Grant schemes, whether financed through a special levy or out of the normal budget, have the drawback of high administrative costs. Also, there is a trade-off between allowing flexibility to accommodate demand-driven needs and constraining the scheme via rigid eligibility criteria to ensure transparency and minimise abuse (see also Section 3.C). Furthermore, it has been argued that small firms may find comparatively more costly to meet all the conditions required to file grant applications (Gasskov, 1998).

Pay-back clauses and apprenticeships

In principle, statutory or contractual pay-back clauses can specify that a worker leaving the firm within a specified period after an education or training spell has to agree to reimburse at least part of the training costs incurred by the employer. Pay-back clauses are intended to mitigate two of the market failures potentially affecting education and training. On the one hand, they limit the extent to which future employers can appropriate the benefits from current employers' investments in training through the poaching of trained employees, thereby allowing current employers to recoup the cost of training by setting wages below productivity after the training spell. On the other hand, they permit workers to share the costs of training even in the presence of serious individual credit constraints, by *de facto* borrowing from their employers with low default risk.

In Luxembourg, if no collective agreement specifies differently, the *Loi cadre 22 juin 1999* establishes a pay-back clause covering part of the expenses paid by the employer in the three years preceding a voluntary quit, except when the latter is due to the employer's misconduct. Similar provisions apply also in the case of lay-offs for serious fault by the employee. In many countries (*e.g.* Austria, the Czech Republic, Germany, Italy, Korea, the Netherlands, Norway, Switzerland, and the United States), pay-back clauses are not established by law but are permitted within certain limits in individual contracts or collective agreements. Finally, the United Kingdom is planning to introduce legal provisions allowing employers to sign contracts with their employees whereby the employer finances training costs through loans but, if the worker quits for another job after the training spell, the responsibility for remaining payments shifts to the new employer.

Even where pay-back clauses are legal, their application might be limited due to problems of contractibility of training contents that discourage an effective sharing of training costs (see Section 2.A). Pay-back clauses may be well suited for formal education or external training programmes, leading to certification, since training-related expenditures, training content and quality as well as the value of being trained for the employee (i.e. the market price for the skills acquired through education or training) can be easily assessed. However, this is not the case for many other types of training.[27] For instance in Italy, pay-back clauses have been used particularly for newly hired managers enrolling in MBA programs. Similarly, statutory provisions in Luxembourg apply only to training leading to certification and in the context of an agreed firm training plan, while in Germany courts have found contractual pay-back clauses admissible only if the quitting employee can benefit from the content of training in other jobs. Nonetheless, Bellmann and Düll (2001) report that about 15% of German enterprises apply pay-back clauses.[28]

Apprenticeships are another type of contract that allows sharing the cost of training in a similar way to pay-back clauses. In many countries, apprenticeships represent a longstanding system of combining training and employment so that people entering an occupation can receive instruction in the specific skills needed while working in that particular occupation. Common features of apprentice contracts are that they last for a duration specified at the start, apprentices are paid less than their productivity during most of the period covered by the contract, and a recognised qualification is delivered at the end, with the apprentice receiving a substantial wage increase if he/she stays with the same firm. These features make apprentice contracts a valid option even for non-contractible training (Malcomson et al., 2003). Similarly to contracts involving pay-back clauses, employers can recoup the cost of training by paying workers less than their marginal product in the final stage of the apprenticeship. But contrary to pay-back clauses workers can quit before the end of the contract without penalty except that, if they do, they do not receive the final certification. For this reason, workers have an interest to stay at least until the end of the apprenticeship, but firms have an interest to provide good-quality training to minimise quits. To the extent that there are no age limits, apprentice contracts can be successful also within groups of low-qualified mature workers. For instance, in Australia, since all age restrictions were removed from apprenticeships and traineeships in 1992, the number of apprentices and trainees aged 25 years and over has grown enormously, but this strong growth has not come at the expense of younger apprentices whose number also rose (OECD, 2003b).

Working-time and training-time accounts

In many OECD countries, increased flexibility of working-time arrangements, featuring *inter alia* the annualisation of working hours or long hours-averaging periods, has led to the creation of working-time accounts for individual employees. The basic idea behind working-time accounts is that over a certain period of time an employee is able to work longer or shorter hours than the standard working time established by the employment contract, and thereby accumulate working-time credits or debits in an individual account, which are later compensated for by additional free time or work. As a result, they can be used to share training costs in a similar way to pay-back clauses, except that with working-time accounts workers *de facto* anticipate their share of the cost. Additionally, they may facilitate overcoming those constraints posed by time constraints, which are one of the most important factors preventing workers from taking the desired amount of training (see Section 2.C).

Already in 1994, France adopted a law introducing a "time-saving account" for employees (*compte épargne-temps*). This account allowed workers to accumulate time credits over a number of years – using, for example, overtime hours or reduced working hours in the framework of the move towards the 35-hour week – and subsequently decide whether to make use of this "time capital" for, inter alia, early or gradual retirement, the take up of part-time work, or training leave. So far, the use of the account for training has occurred only in a small minority of cases. However, the social partners are currently negotiating about how to stimulate the use of working-time accounts for training purposes, for example by introducing the separate category of a "training-savings account" (*compte épargne formation*; MEDEF, 2001).

In the Netherlands, about one-fourth of large collective agreements establish the possibility of saving spare time for educational purposes. Compensating accumulated overtime hours in the form of extended leave at a later date is a very common practice in Denmark (EIRO, 2001). In a recent employer survey in western Germany (excluding Berlin), 11% of all companies that offer training – primarily the larger ones – and that operate working-time accounts offer the option of using the accumulated working-time capital for training purposes (Dobischat and Seifert, 2001). Such "training time accounts" can be fed through accumulated overtime hours or through special employer bonuses. As in the case of other instruments that facilitate a sharing of training costs between employers and employees, time accounts are likely to be effective only to the extent that training is contractible. As such, their use is likely to be limited when training opportunities must be chosen by the employee within the training plan of the company, except when the latter has resulted from an effective negotiation among social partners (see Section 3.C).

Loan schemes

As discussed in Section 2.A, one of the main sources of market failures affecting CVT stems from the difficulty for employees of financing training through borrowing. Public authorities can put in place schemes – such as loan guarantees, subsidisation of interest payments and/or lending by public bodies – to address the reluctance of private financial institutions to make loans for education or training purposes.

Two problems have arisen in connection with loan schemes for tertiary education. One is the general issue of levels of *student indebtedness*. In New Zealand, for example, much of the recent expansion of tertiary education was made possible by a student loan scheme introduced in 1992. However, this success has also raised concerns that the resulting debt levels for students pursuing higher education would seriously depress consumption, delay child-bearing, impinge on future credit-worthiness and stimulate a "brain drain" among graduates who may leave the country to avoid repayment or in search of higher salaries to facilitate repayment (Tertiary Education Advisory Committee, 2001; also see Callender, 2002). A second issue concerns *risk* – uncertainty over whether an individual will be able to earn enough to pay off a loan, which can discourage individuals from financing human capital investment through borrowing. As more countries have introduced or raised student fees, authorities have attempted to address this issue by implementing loan schemes that include provisions for income-contingent repayment. Experience in countries with long histories of reliance on student loans, such as the United States, however, suggests that default rates among student borrowers are quite high; therefore schemes involving income-contingent repayments can be quite expensive for the public budget.

These issues appear to be relevant also for the feasibility of loans for financing individual costs of any type of adult learning. A few countries (*e.g.* the United Kingdom and the United States) have established loan schemes that are available also for CVT and are intended to provide adults with financial resources to cover cost of living as well as direct costs. For example, Career Development Loans were launched in the United Kingdom in 1988. They allow adults (18 and over) to borrow from GBP 300 to GBP 8 000 to pay for vocational education or training while public authorities subsidise interest repayments for the duration of training. In the first 13 years of operation, more than 150 000 individuals have taken loans averaging around GBP 3 700. Though more than 80% of borrowers reported that they would not have taken the training if it had not been for the loans, the overall number approved has fallen far short of what was expected. Furthermore, loan recipients have been mostly males (who have been twice as likely as females to receive loans; see Quarrie, 2002). This experience suggests that loan schemes may have only limited appeal because adults tend to be more reluctant than younger persons to finance learning through loans, perhaps, due to existing debts (*e.g.* home mortgages), family responsibilities, or shorter payback periods (Callender, 2002).

Tax incentives for individuals

While loan schemes try to address capital market failures only, most other individual-based demand-side schemes try to address simultaneously individual borrowing constraints and low or uncertain rates of return for specific groups who typically do not receive employer-sponsored training (see Section 3.A above). The main rationale for individual-based demand-side schemes is that they can be more precisely targeted than financial incentives for employers (or training institutions), while providing the individual with a greater range of training choices.

While expenditures for formal education usually can be deducted from personal income taxes, tax systems are typically more restrictive in their treatment of CVT expenditure by *individuals*. Generally, such expenditure cannot be deducted from the taxable income of individuals, except under circumstances in which such CVT is required for the job they currently hold. Moreover, when employers provide financial support for training that leads to recognised qualifications, the expenditure by the employer may be treated as taxable income to the learners.

However, some initiatives have been taken to relax these restrictions. For instance, starting in 2003, Austrian legislation will allow individuals to deduct costs related, not only to training required for their current job, but also for training that equips them to change jobs or enter a new profession. However, tax deductions of current individual expenses for education and training are likely to be more effective for short and/or part-time training as well as for high-wage employees, since individuals can only make use of these deductions if they earn enough in a fiscal year to be liable to pay taxes. There is no such limitation only when tax deductions apply to saving schemes to finance future learning activities (*e.g.* individual learning accounts and leave-saving schemes, see below).

Subsidies to individuals

Most countries have schemes to subsidise directly individuals enrolling in training courses. Subsidies are flexible instruments that can target specific groups. However, they often require careful attention to framework conditions in order to work properly (see also Section 3.C below). Three issues are key in the economic analysis of subsidies to individuals: i) what the subsidy covers (fees and/or living expenses and/or foregone income); ii) what requirements individuals must satisfy to qualify for the subsidy; and iii) to what extent individuals are free to choose the type and timing of training as well as the training provider.

There is an evident tension between, on the one hand, increasing training demand and individual choice without boosting costs and, on the other hand, conveying adequate information about training quality to individuals and preventing possible abuses. In principle, the former objective would require allowing the supply of training services to respond freely to demand through free entry and course innovations. However, a certain amount of time-consuming screening, monitoring and control is called for by the second objective (see also Section 3.C). In practice, subsidy schemes that give total freedom of choice to individuals are rare. In most cases governments compromise between these conflicting objectives by constraining training choices within a more or less wide menu and adjusting the subsidy rate accordingly.[29] For instance, training vouchers (used, for example, in certain regions of Austria, Italy and Switzerland) typically leave free individual choice within courses offered by accredited training providers (see Box 5.4).

Box 5.4. **The Geneva Training Voucher**

The May 2000 Act on Continuing Training for Adults in the Swiss canton of Geneva contains the feature of an annual training voucher, up to a value of CHF 750, available for all adults residing in the canton. The voucher is a response to a survey conducted in 1996 by the Swiss Statistical Office, which expressed concern over the low participation of the lower-skilled in CVT.

The voucher can be used for basic training, training in professional skills, or the acquisition of new skills. The amount of CHF 750 is equivalent to 40 hours of continuing training courses. The voucher can be carried over from one year to the next for a maximum of three years. It entitles trainees to attend courses offered by public or community training institutions, but also by certain accredited private establishments.

Currently about 400 courses offered by 62 institutions are accessible via the training voucher. Applicants usually submit their request for a voucher in one of the vocational training offices of the canton, after having identified a particular training course. In 2001, five out of six such applications (out of a total of 1 240) were granted. 61% of beneficiaries were women and 44% were foreign residents (Broyon et al., 2002). However, the share of low-skilled applicants has remained low (persons with no more than compulsory schooling were only 16% of applicants in 2001).

In some cases, subsidies target explicitly specific segments of the population. For instance, in Germany, the government subsidises training expenditures of workers aged over 50 and workers with no vocational qualification (or those with vocational qualifications but who have been in semi-skilled or unskilled occupations for more than four years). In Korea, subsidies are provided by the Employment Insurance Fund for government-designated training courses taken by workers at risk of redundancy and workers aged 50 years or older. Even when not targeted, however, subsidy schemes might be effective in reaching groups that participate in training less frequently. For example, many of the beneficiaries of the Geneva Canton voucher scheme in 2001 were foreign citizens (see Box 5.4). This is particularly true for schemes that are available only for workers taking training leaves as well as those that combine tax arrangements and/or loans together with subsidies and/or cost-sharing arrangements (such as individual learning accounts).

Individual learning accounts (ILAs)

ILAs emerged in the late 1990s as an alternative to traditional subsidy and loan schemes. ILAs are savings accounts that can be opened by individuals for the purpose of funding future learning activities. Third parties (employers and government) may also contribute to the account while individuals generally retain freedom of choice concerning the type and timing of training, training provider and amount invested. The philosophy underlying these initiatives is to "empower" individuals in education and training markets by encouraging them to take responsibility in an asset-building process.

In a review of recent experience with ILAs, the OECD and the European Learning Account Network identified ILA initiatives in five OECD countries (Canada, the Netherlands, the Basque region of Spain, the United Kingdom and the United States; see OECD, 2003b). Another special scheme has been established in Sweden by Skandia, a private insurance company. Most of these schemes have been set up on a trial basis to test the feasibility of a savings-based approach to increase training. They differ significantly with respect to their purposes and the details of their structure and administration, but conform to the broad framework described above (Table 5.7).

The main differences between such schemes are the objectives and, as a consequence, their financial scale. The approach adopted most often is to establish accounts to help defray the direct costs of education and training, including course fees, instructional materials, and transportation. In this case, contributions by third parties are relatively low. Only few cases of ILA initiatives are intended to replace income for individuals who pursue full-time learning activities.

In the case of ILAs, accountability issues have been problematic, due to pressure to put large innovations into place quickly and the concern of ensuring their "user-friendliness", since the aim of these schemes is to reach persons who do not typically participate in learning activities. Where direct contributions have been involved, the most common approach to preserve accountability has been for the co-financing partner (government or employer) to match individual contributions at the time of a transaction to purchase education or training services. However, this has not always prevented that either individual's or co-finance partners' funds were spent on activities that were not allowable.[30]

Unfortunately, despite this recent burst of interest in ILAs, there is little evidence on their impact on learning behaviour and subsequent labour market outcomes. Estimating impacts is made difficult by the newness of most of the initiatives and the fact that most of them (with the exception of the British national ILA schemes) are small-scale initiatives. However the available evidence suggests that ILA schemes have been popular among individuals, even those who usually do not participate in training. In most cases they have managed to reach middle-aged poorly qualified people of both genders, although young and older workers have been under-represented (Owens, 2001; CINOP, 2002; York Consulting, 2002). Evidence from evaluations of the US Individual Development Accounts

5. UPGRADING WORKERS' SKILLS AND COMPETENCIES

Table 5.7. Individual learning accounts in OECD countries

Country	Targeted worker groups	Funding shares	Use of funds	Other conditions
Canada *Learn$ave* (pilot project)	Eligibility conditions: *i)* adults aged 21 to 65 years or 18 to 21 years who have been out of school for at least two years; *ii)* adults who are not full-time student; *iii)* households with pre-tax income below a specified threshold (*e.g.* CAD 19 390 for one-person families); *iv)* adults who have liquid savings less than 10% of their annual income	– The fund contributes CAD 3 for every CAD 1 saved by the participants – Participants have up to three years to save a maximum of CAD 1 500 – *i.e.* the maximum value of the financial asset at the end of the period is CAD 6 000	– Purchase of education or training services – Setting up own business	– Participants should save at least 12 months before they can withdraw matched saving credits (up to three years) – The matched contributions are never paid directly to the participant but instead are paid directly to the supplier of the good or service being purchased
Netherlands (eight pilot projects)	Low-educated workers	– The government contributes up to EUR 454 – In two projects, participants are asked for a contribution – In seven projects, the government contribution is supplemented by contributions by the employer or by sectoral training funds	Only direct costs of training in most of cases	..
Spain (the Basque region) IKASTXEKIN (pilot projects)	Vocational training teachers	Credit accounts cover 75% of the direct learning expenses, while the remaining 25% is borne by individuals.	Direct learning expenses	– The beneficiaries must take training courses provided by officially approved training centres – The credit accounts must be used in a given period which cannot exceed two years
Sweden (Skandia)	Company-based schemes (with priority given to low-skilled workers)	– Both the employee and the employer pay one half – The contribution share is ¼ and ¾, respectively, for the low-paid employees – Up to 10% of annual salary per year (20% for low-skilled and low-paid employees)	– Direct training costs – Living expenses during the training	..
United Kingdom Nation-wide programmes (suspended)	– Any individual older than 19 can open an ILA – Public contribution is allowed only to workers who are not enrolled in full-time training or education that is already publicly supported	– Public contribution of GBP 150 against individuals' contribution of at least GBP 25 for the first million ILA holders – 20% discount on standard rate courses (up to GBP 100 per year) – 80% discount on higher rate courses (up to GBP 200 per year) – Employers' contributions are voluntary and subject to tax relief	Direct training costs or some associated costs (*e.g.* assessment fees)	The balance in the account should be used during the first year
United States[a] (Arkansas)	Employed persons who have a household income less than 180% of the poverty line and no more than USD 10 000 assets other than a house and a car are eligible	The government pays USD 3 for every USD 1 saved by the individual	Home-ownership, post-secondary education, starting-up a small business	Account holder must take six classes in economic literacy

.. Information not available.

a) For the United States, ILAs exist under various forms depending on the state. The case of Arkansas is taken only as an example.

Source: OECD Secretariat on the basis of information supplied by the countries in question.

suggests that such schemes may have a positive impact on economic self-sufficiency, self-esteem, credit-worthiness, and savings behaviour, as well as the likelihood of establishing educational plans (Scanlon and Page-Adams, 2001). No evaluation of the deadweight loss involved is however available.

Training leaves and part-time study

The analysis of Section 2.C has highlighted the role of *time constraints* in reducing training participation. Meeting the training needs of employed individuals may frequently require them to stop working for a considerable period of time. In many OECD countries access to training under these circumstances is facilitated by statutory or contractual training leave schemes that guarantee employees the right to return to their jobs after completing the training course. Some countries have also facilitated access to training and education on a part-time basis. For instance, in the Australian technical and further education colleges it is possible to study part-time, at distance and on week-ends, and access requirements also take into account previous work experience. As a result, in Australia, 12% of the enrolees in the formal education system are aged 35 and over, which is three times the OECD average (OECD, 2001a).

Wurzburg (2003) suggests that *foregone income* depresses individual rates of return to full-time adult education more than any other factor. This implies that subsidy schemes need to compensate in part for foregone income to reach low-income/low-wealth labour force segments, in particular when training requires a prolonged period of service (and wage) reduction. For this reason, in some countries, special training leave subsidies (Table 5.8) are available, particularly to cover living expenses or partially replace foregone income. In Germany, a special subsidy also exists for part-time workers participating in training. Other policy alternatives include ILAs with large matching funds from a third party and tax incentives, but they have been rarely established in practice by governments. One exception is the possibility for Dutch employees, introduced in 2001, to join a "leave-saving scheme", which allows them to set aside up to 10% of their gross yearly wage in a saving account with privileged tax treatment to finance a personal leave, with training or studies being one of the declared aims of such leave. Provisions for training leaves are also often included in collective agreements, even in countries where statutory schemes do not exist (such as Australia and Portugal).

In most countries that have training leave schemes, however, only a very limited number of employees have participated in them. Belgium and Sweden, where about 1% of workers have been on leave each year since the establishment of the schemes, are two exceptions to this pattern. However, training leaves tend to be more popular among women than men, since they are seen as a flexible way to reconcile further training needs with family responsibilities. For instance, in Denmark there were about 2 000 men and 6 000 women on training leave in the second quarter of the year 2000 (representing about 0.1% and 0.5% of employment, respectively; EIRO, 2001). In Sweden, women take-up training leave twice as frequently as men. In Austria, training sabbaticals were disproportionately used by women until the scheme was reformed and going on training leave soon after maternity leave forbidden. Belgium, where only one-fourth of the employees on training leave were women in mid-1990s, is an exception to this pattern, probably due to the fact that part-time workers are excluded by the Belgian scheme (CEDEFOP, 2001).

Table 5.8. Training-leave schemes in selected OECD countries

Country[a]	Eligibility	Subsidies provided to	Subsidy ranges	Funding mechanism	Numbers of beneficiaries (% of total employment)	Comments
Austria	Workers with a work history of over three years and with the current employer for the past two years	Individual workers	A daily allowance of EUR 14.53 for a period of 3-12 months	Austrian Employment Service	2 263 in 2002 (0.1%)	
Belgium	Full-time workers	Employers	Full wage costs (up to 80-120 hours for general education, 120-180 hours for vocational training, and 180 hours for workers who take both general and vocational courses during the same year) and the direct costs	Social Security Contribution	60 270 during the 2000/2001 academic year (1.5%)	
Finland	Employees with a work history of over ten years	Individual workers	EUR 440 per month plus an earning-related amount covering 15-20% of the last monthly wage up to 1 year	Education and Training Insurance	5 236 in 2002 (0.2%)[b]	
France	Workers with a work history of over 24 months and who worked with the current employer during the last 12 months	Individual workers	80-90% of the foregone wage up to one year or 1 200 hours	Employers' contribution (0.2% of the wage bill) to the accredited bipartite organisations (OPACIF)	26 169 in 2001 (0.1%)	
Japan	Employed persons who are covered by the Employment Insurance	Employers	¼ of the wage costs and ¼ of the direct costs (⅓ for SMEs)	Employment Insurance	3 265 in fiscal year 2002 (0.01%)	A budget of JPY 0.7 billion was made available for fiscal year 2002.
Korea	..	Employers	⅓ of the wage costs and part of direct costs	Employment Insurance	7 756 in 2000 (0.04%)	Total subsidy of KRW 5 589 million in 2000
Norway	Workers with a work history of over three years and with the current employer for the past two years	Individual workers	NOK 80 000 per year, of which 60% is a loan, 25% is an unconditional grant and 15% is converted from loan to grant when the student succeeds in the examination	State Education Loan Fund	..	Only for formal education
Spain	Workers who have been employed by the same firm for at least one year	Individual workers	Full foregone wages up to 200 working hours	Social partners' mandatory contribution to the Tripartite Foundation	1 394 in 2002 (0.01%)[c]	
Sweden	Workers who have been employed for at least six consecutive months or with a work history of over 12 months during the last two years	Individual workers	Grants and loans of SEK 33 880 for 20 weeks full-time studies; a supplementary loan for the workers aged 25 or older if the income of the beneficiary during the 12 months immediately preceding the studies has been above a certain threshold	Study allowance by the government	0.7% in 2002	Only for formal education

.. Information not available.
a) Countries without specific subsidy schemes or where the related schemes are governed by collective agreements, such as Australia, Germany, the Netherlands and Portugal, are not included in the table.
b) The figure refers to the number of employees who have taken alternation leaves, of which only roughly 17% indicate studying was the major reason.
c) The figure refers to the number of individual training permits approved by FORCEM.

Source: OECD Secretariat on the basis of information supplied by the countries in question.

C. Framework conditions

The effectiveness of policies that aim to increase demand by employers and employees (demand in the upstream market) hinges in part on certain *framework conditions* – the policy and institutional environment in which they are implemented. This section will focus on framework conditions that have a primary effect on training outcomes. It must be noted at the outset that other framework conditions, whose primary effect is not on training or education, may have second-order effects on training demand and supply. For instance, institutions in the labour market affecting the distribution of wages, such as the minimum wage and employment protection legislation, modify the incentives of employers and employees to invest in training (see *e.g.* Acemoglu and Pischke, 1999b). Furthermore, the progressiveness of the income tax may have a bearing on individual incentives, to the extent that, on the one hand, it reduces individual appropriability of the benefits from training and, on the other hand, it reduces the opportunity cost of taking unpaid training leaves or opting for part-time work. Finally, a major obstacle for women to participate in adult learning is represented by the fact that the burden of family responsibilities is still unevenly shared within the couple (see Section 2.C). Policies that affect the ability of households to reconcile work with family needs (see OECD, 2002a, 2002c and Chapter 3) can have an impact on the gender-training gap. A detailed analysis of these framework conditions is, however, outside the scope of this chapter.

A number of framework conditions appear to have a primary effect on adult learning. First, barriers to entry of *bona fide* training providers must be relatively low to allow supply shifts accommodating demand needs without raising costs. Second, information on the nature, conditions (location, duration, timing), cost and quality of education and training opportunities must be readily available to individuals and employers in order to ensure efficient allocation of resources for investment in education and training and foster cost-sharing as well as co-operative behaviours. Third, information on the nature and level of skills and competencies that are acquired by individuals through self-financed CVT must be transparently signalled to external labour markets so that workers can capitalise on what they have learned.

Most often, countries have chosen to limit subsidies and other co-financing schemes to training undertaken with accredited providers (see Section 3.B for examples of this kind). Accreditation, however, constrains the capacity of training service supply to respond to sudden changes in demand. Conversely, the entry of new providers can expand training capacity and thus increase the price elasticity of demand for each individual provider. However, massive entry of new providers might raise concerns about quality. In the case of the English ILA initiative, there is evidence that some companies were abusing the system offering low value, poor quality learning (OECD, 2003b). In the case of the Australian levy scheme, many of the new providers were of dubious quality (Fraser, 1996). The implication is that measures to lower barriers to entry need to be introduced in such a way that it is possible to ensure quality. For example, an evaluation of the ILA programme that was carried out in Scotland suggested limiting future ILA initiatives to providers certified through the Scottish Quality Management System as well as small firms for which their Local Enterprise Company is willing to act as a sponsor (York Consulting, 2002).

Smooth functioning of the markets for education and training depends also on adequate information on learning opportunities, particularly for individuals. In the case of the Individual Development Accounts initiative in the United States, counselling and guidance were provided as part of a comprehensive policy package of support services (OECD, 2001b). However, the effectiveness of the strategies for guidance and counselling depends on the extent to which there exist systems for quality assurance by which the quality of education and training opportunities can be evaluated, and systems for assessment and recognition of learning outcomes, to indicate the portability of CVT "qualifications".

In order to foster incentives for individuals to pay for their own training and/or share the cost of CVT with their employers, it is necessary that learning outcomes are transparent and easily signalled to the current or future employer. In contrast to formal education, in which established degrees and diplomas serve as signalling devices, CVT (except where it culminates in a formal degree or diploma) requires mechanisms to assess and recognise smaller increments of learning. However, to function effectively and credibly, such mechanisms need skills "standards" to provide the metric and language for measuring outcomes unambiguously, robust procedures for assessment, and involvement of appropriate stakeholders (Colardyn, 2002).

Many countries have put into place initiatives to certify workers' skills acquired through CVT as well as work experience and, thereby, guarantee portability and market-reward of skills, although evaluations of their effectivenress are scarce. Some initiatives aim to assess outcomes predominantly in terms of labour market skills. For example, in Finland, France, Ireland, the Netherlands and the United Kingdom, governments introduced competence-based qualifications systems, according to which acquisition of qualifications is not conditioned on course attendance in a vocational training or educational institutions. Under this system, workers are allowed to take individual skill tests independently of the way skills are acquired. In many cases, social partners are heavily involved in the elaboration of these certification schemes through "expert groups" (*e.g.* Finland) or joint management/labour bodies (*e.g.* France).

Collective agreements and trade union participation may play an important role in ensuring an equitable distribution of training outcomes, not only by diffusing information and jointly defining curricula, but also by increasing and twisting employers' supply towards more general types of training (see Ok and Tergeist, 2003). For example, a study by the American Society for Training and Development (ASTD) of major joint labour-management training programmes suggests that these joint initiatives do result in a different mix of training activities. While only 2% of firm-supported training addresses basic literacy skills according to the ASTD's benchmarking data base, this figure soars to 15% for the joint programmes (van Buren and Erskine, 2002). The sharing of training costs between employers and individuals can also be fostered by joint CVT agreements to the extent that unions and work councils are in a better place to monitor training content and quality. In most European countries, participation in employer-sponsored training is significantly greater in firms with a joint CVT agreement than in firms without it (Chart 5.9).[31] Differences in training participation rates are particularly large in Mediterranean countries (for which the participation rate in firms with negotiated agreements is more than twice as large as in other firms). Conversely, these differences are not particularly significant in the Nordic countries (except Finland) and the United Kingdom, where however training participation rates are high also in firms without joint CVT agreements.

Chart 5.9. **Training participation is greater in firms with a joint CVT agreement**
Percentage of employees in all enterprises with/without a joint CVT agreement with social partners participating in employer-sponsored CVT courses, 1999[a]

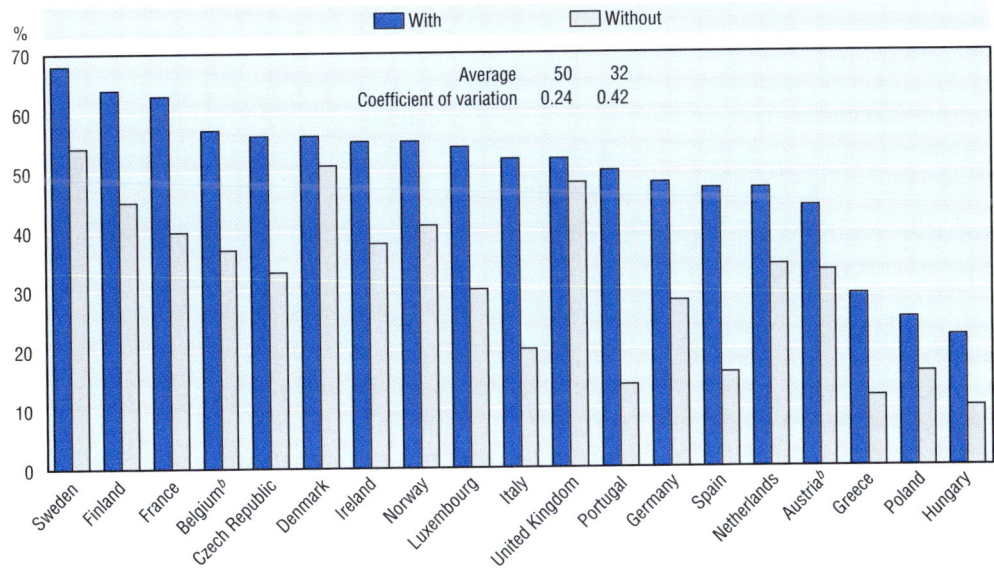

a) Countries are ranked from left to right in descending order of the percentage of employees in all enterprises with a joint CVT agreement participating in employer-sponsored CVT.
b) Estimations include a very small number of non-training enterprises due to missing values.
Source: CVTS2.

Conclusions

It is increasingly acknowledged that education and training of the adult labour force is a key policy issue to meet the challenge posed by technological change and improve career prospects for disadvantaged groups. Although early education is a key aspect of human capital development, the fact that the ageing process will increasingly interest most OECD countries gives a paramount importance to education and training of the adult labour force, since most of the workers who will apply the new technologies will be adults far from their school days. The review of the literature contained in this chapter suggests that, due to market failures in the labour, capital and training markets, training outcomes are likely to fall short of socially desirable levels, although the size of the shortfall remains an open question. Furthermore, the chapter provides empirical evidence that disparities in training outcomes across workers – not necessarily due to market failures – tend to reinforce labour market inequalities insofar as those who are already in a worse position in the labour market tend to receive less employer-sponsored training, leading to worse career prospects, lower wages and less employability.

It is therefore essential to address the thorny issue of how to increase access to education and training for disadvantaged groups by spreading more evenly the costs and benefits, otherwise the life-long learning strategy may remain largely in the realm of rhetoric. Nevertheless, the empirical and policy analysis of this chapter suggests that: i) different policies serve different and sometimes conflicting objectives; ii) policy design is crucial but complex because the identified sources of market failure (e.g. lack of contractibility of training quality) and the risk of inducing inefficient substitution between different types of education and training can equally lead to government failures; and iii) a comprehensive policy strategy involving corporate tax deductions, pay-back clauses, loan schemes and some specific individual subsidy schemes (such as individual learning accounts) is more likely to be effective in reducing both training under-investment and inequalities.

Nevertheless, several important questions remain open for further research:

- More rigorous evaluations of policy initiatives are urgently needed. In this chapter, empirical and theoretical analyses are used to deduce normative implications for policy. However, little or no direct assessments of the various policy schemes are available, only partially due to their novelty and small scale.

- It is necessary to investigate further the role of informal learning in the accumulation of competencies and assess the magnitude of the effect of market failures on both formal and informal training provision. However, the lack of adequate data is, in this area, the main obstacle.

- The policy implications of the relationship between technological or organisational changes and training must be further investigated. For example, by requiring new competencies, technological change induces more rapid human capital scrapping – that is, the phenomenon of obsolescence of previously acquired skills. This might lead certain categories of workers to give up investing in the new competencies since the pay-back period may be too short.

- Different sectors and jobs require different skills. Co-ordination failures can be of paramount importance not only for under-investment in training but also for skill-mismatch. A society may therefore find itself equipped with competencies that are not useful in those sectors for which technological change is more rapid and global demand expanding faster.

- Additional analysis is required to evaluate the effects of off-the-job training on individual productivity and welfare. This assessment will have important bearings not only for demand-side policy strategies based on employees' incentives but also for training policies for individuals at the margin of the labour market, such as the long-term unemployed.

- A comprehensive analysis of the market for training services (the "upstream market" using the terminology of this chapter) would be desirable. This chapter has just pointed out some of the relevant trade-offs (for example between competition and quality). A thorough analysis of these trade-offs – as well as of possible policy innovations to overcome them – is key to put in place an effective co-financing strategy for lifelong learning.

- A more extensive concept of framework conditions should be considered. The analysis of this chapter has shown that market failures in many different markets appear to have an impact on training outcomes. A comprehensive analysis of the effect of policies and institutions on training performance should therefore include the analysis of policies aimed at improving performance in other markets (such as tax policy, labour market flexibility, etc.), but which, nonetheless, affect incentives to train and be trained.

Notes

1. Unless otherwise specified, all the data in this chapter are from the IALS. Data refer to 1994 for Canada, Ireland, the Netherlands, Poland, Switzerland (German and French-speaking regions), and the United States, to 1996 for Australia, Belgium (Flanders only), New Zealand and the United Kingdom and to 1998 for the Czech Republic, Denmark, Finland, Hungary, Italy, Norway and the Italian-speaking regions of Switzerland. Country rankings, as well as discrepancies with the data reported in Table 5.2 for European countries, can be partially ascribed to cross-country differences in the survey years and must be interpreted with great caution.

2. Measured as hours of education and training per employed person aged 26 years or older. Only formal education and training undertaken for career or job-related purposes is considered.

3. Note, however, that language courses are included in the CVT measure.

4. There are several reasons why data from the CVTS are more suitable than IALS data for the analysis of training incidence by firm size: i) employers know better about firm size and employer-sponsored training than employees; ii) employer-provided CVT courses are more precisely defined in the CVTS; and iii) intensity figures from the CVTS are more precise (while the IALS is likely to underestimate training intensity, see Annex 1). IALS data are used, instead of the CVTS, in the other tables, because the latter provides no information on socio-economic and demographic characteristics of the recipients (except gender).

5. Even when employers alone are reported to pay for training, they may not bear the full cost because workers may indirectly pay for these services through wage adjustments and accepting to be trained outside normal working hours. Similarly, newly-hired workers can be offered a contract with lower than usual starting pay combined with the prospect of receiving training and a steeper than usual tenure-earnings profile. The empirical literature shows, however, little evidence that workers accept lower wages to co-finance training (Barron et al., 1999a; Loewenstein and Spletzer, 1998; and Booth and Bryan, 2002), although there is some evidence that workers bear some of the opportunity cost of training by accepting to be trained outside normal working hours, at least under certain circumstances (Autor, 2001).

6. As regards the United States, 76% of respondents in the Employer Opportunity Pilot Project (EOPP; employers) and 73% in the 1993 wave of the National Longitudinal Survey of Youth (NLSY; employees) believe that most of the skills acquired through training would be useful at other firms. Fewer than 8% of respondents reported that the skills gained through training would not be at all useful at other employers (Loewenstein and Spletzer, 1999b). In the United Kingdom, 85% of training recipients in the 1998-2000 waves of the British Household Panel Survey (BHPS) view their training as general (Booth and Bryan, 2002). In Germany, 62% of training recipients in the 1989 wave of the German Socio-Economic Panel (GSOEP) state that they received a certificate from their training (58%, if only training during work hours is considered; see Pischke, 2001).

7. This externality is often associated with the phenomenon of "poaching" – that is, a firm can free ride other firms' investment in training by making better wage offers to trained employees.

8. See Arulampalam et al. (2002) and Bassanini and Brunello (2003) for the EU countries, and Acemoglu and Pischke (2003) for the United States. The evidence for the United States is, however, less conclusive (see Neumark and Wascher, 2001).

9. The price of the latter transaction might be zero – i.e. when the employer bears all the cost.

10. However, while this analysis can track demand and supply factors behind inequality patterns, it cannot identify the role of market imperfections – i.e. whether supply and demand are optimal from the point of view of economic efficiency. The role of market imperfections cannot be directly tested through this identification strategy, but can only be underlined in the discussion of possible explanations of the estimated patterns.

11. These models are estimated subject to the assumption that, by threatening lay-offs and/or offering monetary compensation, an employer can always convince a worker to be trained. For the equilibrium outcome, the dependent variable takes value 1 if the individual participated in employer-sponsored training and 0 otherwise. For demand, the dependent variable takes value 1 if the worker either took training courses that were not sponsored by the employer or would have liked to take training but could not and 0 otherwise. The latter equation is estimated only for workers that did not participate in employer-sponsored training (see Annex 2 for a discussion of the estimation issues involved). Detailed estimation results are presented in Table 5.A1.2 in Annex 1.

12. Both the probability of receiving training in equilibrium and of demanding training at zero cost are estimated to be lower for older workers than for prime-age men. Nevertheless, the shift of the

13. The pay-back period is defined as the number of years an investment needs to yield the expected revenue in order to be profitable.

14. The length of the pay-back period for human capital investments for both employers and employees is likely to depend mainly on individual characteristics that affect the cost of, and total potential benefits from, training. The difference between employers' and employees' pay-back periods is likely to depend on the wage structure, educational attainment and other factors affecting the sharing of the benefits from training, but plausibly not on age. In equilibrium – that is, given a certain division of costs and benefits from training – it is plausible that rates of returns from training are approximately equal for the employee and for the employer. However, the employee retains his/her share of benefits upon quitting, while the employer does not. As a consequence, pay-back periods for general training are likely to be longer for the employee than for the employer because the latter knows that the former has a positive probability of quitting and takes it into account into the calculation of the pay-back period.

15. The only statement that can be made about supply is that it does not increase significantly with educational attainment, but it cannot be established whether it decreases or remains approximately constant. This is due to the fact that the estimated probabilities of demanding training at zero cost and of receiving training in equilibrium increase by approximately the same amount (see Annex 2).

16. In most countries, the mean performance of PISA (Programme for International Student Assessment) students (at age 15) on the IALS literacy scale is greater than the mean performance of IALS individuals both in the whole sample and restricting the comparison to IALS individuals aged 26 to 35 years who completed secondary education (see OECD and Statistics Canada, 2000; and OECD, 2003c). Also, Green and Riddell (2003) find that the coefficient attached to education is altered by literacy in an earnings regression for Canada, while the coefficient attached to experience is not.

17. For five countries (Australia, Canada, Finland, Italy and the United States), the IALS contains a large set of information on parental background that can be used as instruments for literacy in a training regression since their effect on training demand and supply is likely to occur only through literacy and education.

18. In this case, there may be a different explanation. Demand is identified at zero implicit or explicit costs for the worker, including day care for children and relatives. Part-time workers for family reasons are therefore likely to find certain types of training too expensive in terms of their associated day-care costs (see Section 2.C).

19. Given the ambiguity of the question on desired further training ["Since August (Year), was there any training or education that you wanted to take for career or job-related reasons but did not?"] as well as of the definition of this reason in the questionnaire ("too expensive/lack of money"), it is unlikely that all individuals that are credit-constrained reported this reason. Plausibly, this reason is likely to capture direct costs, such as unaffordable course fees, but not issues related to foregone income. The effect of market failures – such as lack of contractibility of training and difficulties to smooth consumption due to individual borrowing constraints – is likely to show up mainly in lower demand at zero cost.

20. The lower level of competition in the market for workers who have acquired transferable skills is the easiest example. In contrast to purely general skills, transferable skills are not valuable at every firm. Therefore, although training in these skills increases potential job opportunities for the worker, finding them may require a long and costly search process.

21. It is true that policy innovations are often tried and evaluated as pilot programs first. However, certain experiences (such as with the British ILAs, see Section 3.B) show that not all the possible implementation problems of mass-scale programs can be anticipated on the basis of small pilot experiments.

22. However, since public policies in this area mainly address formal training, care has to be taken that the low-educated are not forced into a learning environment, which did not work for them in the past. Indeed, lack of appropriate pedagogy is one of the reasons behind school drop-outs (see OECD, 2003a).

23. Since marginal effective training costs for firms that spend more than the legal minimum are not affected by the scheme, these firms are not likely to modify their training expenditure. Still they receive an implicit 100% subsidy up to the legal minimum.

24. To be more precise, in the case of France, a minimum levy of 0.6% of payroll must be paid in all cases. Therefore the 100% implicit subsidy covers only expenditures in excess of 0.6% of payroll (but below 1.5%). As a consequence, the incentive to increase training expenditure for firms that would otherwise invest much less than 0.6% of payroll for that purpose is likely to be extremely small.

25. In many other OECD countries, the costs associated with CVT (*e.g.* fees, instructional material, transportation) are treated by tax regulations as a cost of doing business and deducted from taxable income of employers. As such, however, the treatment is similar to that of investment in fixed assets (where depreciation is deducted from taxable income), and certain forms of investment in intangible capital (such as R&D costs that are deducted from taxable income), but cannot be really considered a tax incentive.

26. The Italian case is more complex since before the "Tremonti-bis" Act (*Legge 383/2001*), training expenditures were not treated as costs of business. As a consequence, the law has introduced a true extra-deduction only for those expenditures that are normally counted as operating costs (such as trainees' and internal trainers' wages) and has only partially caught-up with the legislation of most other countries for other types of training expenditures.

27. Note also that in countries where employment contracts in which the employer can unilaterally change the terms of the contract (*employment at will*) are admissible, such as the United States, pay-back clauses might not be attractive for employers. Stipulating such a clause would transform the employment relationship into a *de facto* long-term relationship and, in the case of long-term relationships, unilateral changes of the terms of contract can be successfully challenged by employees in courts (see Malcomson, 1997).

28. Pay-back clauses might also be more viable if stipulated through collective agreements, since trade unions are in a better position to monitor training contents than individual workers (see Section 3.C).

29. The greater the freedom of choice, the greater is the need that part of the quality monitoring be accomplished by subsidy recipients. Individuals are more likely to be effective in monitoring service quality when the subsidy is a *matched* contribution and they have some own resources at stake. Conversely, monitoring incentives are weak when the subsidy is intended to cover essentially all costs up to a certain limit.

30. For example, the English nation-wide ILA programme was forced to shut down operations prematurely because of allegations of fraud and theft (see Section 3.C).

31. However, to the extent that most grant schemes require previous agreement from trade-unions (see Section 2.B), the causal relationship suggested by Chart 5.9 might be spurious.

ANNEX 1

Data Description and Detailed Estimation Results

A. Data sources

The quantitative analysis in this chapter is based on data from two sources:

a) International Adult Literacy Survey (OECD and Statistics Canada)

The *International Adult Literacy Survey* (IALS) is an individual survey using a common questionnaire. The survey asks whether the workers have received any training or education during the 12 months prior to the survey, but it includes details only about the three most recent courses (purpose, financing, training institution, duration, etc.). For this reason, the number of hours of training is underestimated in the case of workers having taken more than three courses. Data refer to 1994 for Canada, Ireland, the Netherlands, Poland, Switzerland (German and French-speaking regions) and the United States, to 1996 for Australia, Belgium (Flanders only), New Zealand and the United Kingdom and to 1998 for the Czech Republic, Denmark, Finland, Hungary, Italy, Norway and the Italian-speaking regions of Switzerland. For more details, see OECD and Statistics Canada (2000).

b) The second Continuing Vocational Training Survey (Eurostat)

The second *Continuing Vocational Training Survey* (CVTS2) was carried out by Eurostat in 2000 in EU member states, Norway and nine EU candidate countries. This is an enterprise survey covering establishments with at least ten employees. It provides information on employer-sponsored training, which relates to the year 1999, for employed persons, excluding apprentices and trainees. The survey provides a large set of characteristics for the enterprises, but only gender, training participation and total training hours for the employee. For more details, see Eurostat (2000).

B. Data definitions

Continuous Vocation Training (CVT) may entail the following forms of training (see *e.g.* Eurostat, 2000):

a) Courses which take place away from the place of work, *i.e.* in a classroom or training centre, at which a group of people receive instruction from teachers/tutors/lecturers for a period of time specified in advance by those organising the course.

b) Planned periods of training, instruction or practical experience, using the normal tools of work, either at the immediate place of work or in the work situation.

c) Planned learning through job rotation, exchanges or secondments.

d) Attendance at learning/quality circles.

e) Self-learning through open and distance learning, (methods used in this type of learning can include using video/audio tapes, correspondence courses, computer-based methods or the use of a Learning Resources Centre).

f) Instruction at conferences, workshops, lectures and seminars.

In practice, the definition of CVT in different surveys varies and thereby the coverage of the different forms of training is not the same across surveys. In the CVTS2, the definition of CVT conforms strictly with item a) above, including post-graduate education but excluding other types of formal education and initial training – *i.e.* training received by a person when hired in order to make his/her competencies suited to his/her job assignment. In the IALS, there is a distinction between job- or career-related training and training for other purposes. Furthermore, education and training courses are divided into seven mutually exclusive categories: *i)* leading to a university degree/diploma/certificate; *ii)* leading to a college diploma/certificate; *iii)* leading to a trade-vocational diploma/certificate; *iv)* leading to an apprenticeship certificate; *v)* leading to an elementary or secondary school diploma; *vi)* leading to professional or career upgrading; and *vii)* other. For the purpose of this chapter, only job- or career-related training has been considered in the analysis. Moreover, in order to thoroughly exclude formal education courses, only items *iv)*, *vi)*, and *vii)* have been retained in the definition of CVT courses, while items *i)*, *ii)*, *iii)* and *v)* are subsumed into the category of formal education (*cf.* Table 5.1 and Chart 5.1).

The occupation classification used in this chapter corresponds approximately to the one-digit level of the International Standard Classification of Occupations (ISCO-88). In Chart 5.3, data have been grouped as follows: high-skilled occupations corresponding to managers, professionals, technicians and associate professionals (ISCO-88 codes 1 to 3); medium-skilled occupations corresponding to clerks, service and sales workers, craft and related trade workers, plant and machine operators and assemblers (ISCO-88 codes 4 to 8); and low-skilled occupation corresponding to elementary occupations (ISCO-88 code 9).

The average literacy score used in Section 2.B is the simple average of the three literacy scores reported in the IALS that measure proficiency in prose, reading and quantitative skills on a 0-500 quantitative scale (see OECD and Statistics Canada, 2000).

C. Detailed estimation results

Tobit and probit models of the determinants of employer-sponsored training

Maximum likelihood estimations of a probit model for training participation and a tobit model for training hours have been carried out on a pooled sample of 15 countries to provide further evidence on the training gaps discussed in Section 1. Estimates based on these models are reported in Table 5.A1.1. Probit regressions are standard when the dependent variable is a dummy variable. Conversely, tobit regressions are standard when the dependent variable is continuous but censored. In the probit model, the dependent variable takes value one if the individual participated in at least one employer-sponsored CVT course in the 12 months preceding the survey and zero otherwise. The table reports in

Table 5.A1.1. **Probit and Tobit estimates of the determinants of training**

	Training participation	Average hours spent in training
	Probit[a]	Tobit[b]
Gender		
(reference: men)		
Women	–0.011	–0.205*
Age groups		
(reference: aged 36-45)		
Aged 16-25	–0.076*	–0.683*
Aged 26-35	–0.010	–0.070
Aged 46-55	–0.022**	–0.231**
Aged 56-65	–0.065*	–0.711*
Educational attainment		
(reference: upper secondary)		
Less than upper secondary	–0.040*	–0.389*
Tertiary	0.052*	0.411*
Community size		
(reference: urban)		
Rural	–0.001	0.012
Full-time/part-time		
(reference: full-time worker)		
Part-time workers	–0.124*	–1.414*
Country of birth		
(reference: born in country of interview)		
Immigrants	–0.055*	–0.500*
Number of employers (last 12 months)		
(reference: more than one employer)		
One employer only	0.016	0.092
Firm size		
(reference: 100 to 199 employees)		
20 to 99 employees	–0.024***	–0.335**
200 to 499 employees	0.053*	0.433*
500 and more employees	0.099*	0.847*
Industry		
(reference: manufacturing, mining and energy)		
Construction	–0.039***	–0.488**
Wholesale and retail trade	–0.051*	–0.572*
Transport, storage and communications	0.027***	0.283**
Financing, insurance, real estate and business services	0.048*	0.341*
Community, social and personal services	–0.006	–0.104
Occupation		
(reference: clerks)		
Managers	0.110*	1.059*
Professionals	0.053*	0.529*
Technicians and associate professionals	0.056*	0.549*
Service workers and shop and market sales workers	–0.033**	–0.299
Craft and related trades workers	–0.059*	–0.501*
Plant and machine operators and assemblers	–0.113*	–1.181*
Elementary occupations	–0.176*	–2.067*
Country		
(reference: Australia)		
Belgium[c]	–0.162*	–2.418*
Canada	–0.035**	–0.366**
Czech Republic	–0.180*	–2.063*
Denmark	0.180*	1.591*

5. UPGRADING WORKERS' SKILLS AND COMPETENCIES

Table 5.A1.1. **Probit and Tobit estimates of the determinants of training** *(cont.)*

	Training participation	Average hours spent in training
	Probit[a]	Tobit[b]
Finland	0.132*	0.990*
Hungary	–0.197*	–2.454*
Ireland	–0.202*	–2.907*
Italy	–0.166*	–1.888*
New Zealand	0.137*	1.056*
Norway	0.128*	1.113*
Poland	–0.189*	–2.889*
Switzerland	–0.112*	–1.194*
United Kingdom	0.148*	1.048*
United States	–0.017	–0.262
Predicted at vector 0	0.345	–0.830
Log likelihood	–11 138	3 043
Number of observations	19 062	18 853
Number of countries	15	15
Pseudo R²	0.115	0.057

*, **, ***, statistically significant at 1%, 5% and 10% levels respectively.
a) Estimated change in the probability of training participation with respect to the reference individual. The sample population is employees of firms with more than 20 employees, with at least some education, aged 16 to 65 years and not working in the agricultural sector. The reference individual is indicated in the table.
b) The dependent variable is equal to log (1+T) where T stands for hours of training.
c) Flanders only.
Source: OECD estimates based on IALS.

this case the estimated change in the probability of receiving training associated with each specific characteristic for an individual otherwise identical to the reference individual. The tobit model estimates the association of training hours with the characteristics reported in the table, correcting for the sample selection bias due to the fact that individuals with different characteristics have different probabilities of participating in training. The dependent variable in this model is the logarithm of one plus training hours received by the individual. This logarithmic form is chosen to eliminate exponential heteroskedasticity. The argument of the logarithm is augmented by one because otherwise observations for non-participants would be eliminated from the sample. Coefficients can be interpreted as in a standard linear regression.

The reference individual is indicated in the table. Australia is the reference country since it is the country with the largest sample size. Estimations are carried out for a limited number of individual characteristics (including, gender, age, education, country of birth, part-time status and occupation) and firm characteristics (firm size, sector), in order to maximise country coverage. Supervisory role and the distinction between self-employed and employees are not taken into account (the inclusion of these variables would have limited the analysis to only ten countries). As a consequence, the analysis is also restricted to workers of firms with more than 20 employees to eliminate as much as possible self-employment. Moreover, the sample is limited to workers with at least some education (since those without education are an exception and are concentrated in few countries) and not working in the agricultural sector (because of the special character of the agricultural labour market). The sample includes individuals aged 16 to 65 years. This is done for comparison with the empirical results of the analysis of demand and supply of training (Section 2.B) where young individuals are added to preserve a sufficiently large sample size in the case of the estimation of models including literacy as an explanatory variable (see below). All the results presented in this chapter are, however, robust to the elimination of this age class.

Demand and supply of training

Table 5.A1.2 reports complete maximum likelihood estimation results of bivariate probit models of demand and equilibrium outcomes, estimated under two sets of alternative hypotheses (see Annex 2 for a discussion of the identification issues involved). Relative changes of demand and supply derived from these estimates are reported in Table 5.3. Three sets of estimates are considered: a baseline model and two extended specifications (including also supervisory role and temporary contract, respectively) that are estimated on smaller country samples. Countries included in the baseline specification are Australia, Belgium (Flanders only), Canada, the Czech Republic, Denmark, Finland, Hungary, Ireland, Italy, New Zealand, Norway, Poland, Switzerland, the United Kingdom, and the United States. Countries included in the second specification (including dummies for supervisory role) are Canada, Belgium, Czech Republic, Finland, Hungary, Italy, Poland, Switzerland, the United Kingdom and the United States, while in the third specification (including both dummies for supervisory role and temporary contract) are Canada, Finland, Hungary, Italy, Poland, Switzerland, the United Kingdom and the United States. The choice of country samples is motivated by data availability. The summary of results reported in Table 5.3 is based on the baseline specification (when possible), estimated under the hypothesis that, by threatening lay-offs and/or offering monetary compensation, an employer can always convince a worker to be trained (hypothesis A in Table 5.A1.2).

For five countries (Australia, Canada, Finland, Italy and the United States), the IALS contains a large set of information on parental background – namely, educational attainment of parents, father's occupation and a dummy for whether the mother has worked. The effect of parental background on training demand and supply is likely to occur essentially through literacy and education. Accordingly, these background variables can be used as instruments for literacy in a training regression. To instrument literacy, the literacy score is therefore regressed on parental background variables, education and other available characteristics (such as gender, age, community size, country of birth, and country dummies) that are relatively unlikely to be determined by the level of literacy. To avoid reverse-causality bias, other characteristics such as part-time status, industry, occupation, firm size and number of employers are excluded from the instrumental regression. Mother's work status is included separately in the final instrumental variable (IV) regressions estimating the effect of literacy on demand and equilibrium. In fact, mother's work status might not fulfil the orthogonality condition required for an instrument to be valid, to the extent that it affects directly other determinants of training – such as individual motivation and work attachment, particularly of women. This intuition is confirmed by the fact that this is the only parental background variable that is found to be significant when included in demand and equilibrium equations (both with and without the additional inclusion of literacy). Complete estimation results obtained under two sets of alternative hypotheses (see Annex 2) are reported in Table 5.A1.3, but only results obtained under hypothesis A are included in Table 5.3 in the main text.

Table 5.A1.2. **Training demand and supply**
Bivariate probit estimates[a]

	Baseline model			
	Hypothesis A[b]		Hypothesis B[c]	
	Demand	Equilibrium outcome	Demand	Equilibrium outcome
Part-time				
(reference: full-time worker)				
Family and health reasons	–1.74	–9.65*	–8.68*	–10.12*
Still in education	–7.46*	–19.92*	–19.20*	–24.50*
Voluntary part-time for other reasons	–12.05*	–8.55*	–14.45*	–0.17
Involuntary part-time	8.45*	–13.30	–2.17	–22.52*
Gender				
(reference: men)				
Women	2.53**	–1.65**	0.49	–4.32*
Age groups				
(reference: aged 36-45)				
Aged 16-25	2.73	–5.49*	–2.01	–8.66*
Aged 26-35	1.71	–0.74	0.61	–1.93
Aged 46-55	–7.13*	–2.12**	–5.75*	3.13**
Aged 56-65	–15.16*	–6.48*	–13.79*	4.32**
Educational attainment				
(reference: upper secondary)				
Less than upper secondary	–4.91*	–4.07*	–5.92*	–0.79
Tertiary	5.38*	5.16*	6.55*	2.06
Community size				
(reference: urban)				
Rural	–3.66*	–0.18	–2.26**	2.35***
Country of birth				
(reference: born in country of interview)				
Immigrants	2.25	–5.29*	–2.43***	–7.83*
Number of employers (last 12 months)				
(reference: more than one employer)				
One employer only	–9.62*	1.29	–5.35*	6.92*
Firm size				
(reference: 100 to 199 employees)				
20 to 99 employees	1.83	–2.46***	–0.59	–3.69***
200 to 499 employees	0.76	5.57*	4.05**	5.55**
500 and more employees	1.80	9.89*	7.51*	8.79*
Industry				
(reference: manufacturing, mining and energy)				
Construction	6.42**	–3.84***	1.33	–8.97*
Wholesale and retail trade	2.84	–4.31*	–1.64	–5.91*
Transport, storage and communications	0.80	2.52***	2.08	3.41**
Financing, insurance, real estate and business services	–1.18	4.39*	2.42	5.54*
Community, social and personal services	5.33*	–0.57	2.76**	–4.21**
Occupation				
(reference: clerks)				
Managers	1.24	10.74*	8.49*	9.57*
Professionals	6.43*	5.11*	7.08*	1.62
Technicians and associate professionals	3.72**	5.24*	5.55*	3.62***
Service workers and shop and market sales workers	–1.95	–2.92**	–3.23**	–2.00
Craft and related trades workers	–2.88	–5.82*	–5.53*	–5.10**
Plant and machine operators and assemblers	–3.03	–10.99*	–9.96*	–12.56*
Elementary occupations	–8.75*	–16.52*	–18.12*	–16.00*
Predicted at vector 0	39.91	31.48	58.75	55.10
Log likelihood	–6 799	–10 990	–11 591	–6 200
Number of observations	11 763	18 811	18 811	10 709
Number of countries	15	15	15	15
Pseudo R²	0.068	0.117	0.099	0.099

Table 5.A1.2. **Training demand and supply** (cont.)
Bivariate probit estimates[a]

	Including supervisory role		Including temporary contracts	
	Hypothesis A[b]		Hypothesis A[b]	
	Demand	Equilibrium outcome	Demand	Equilibrium outcome
Part-time				
(reference: full-time worker)				
Family and health reasons	–3.95	–6.22*	–6.16***	–5.75**
Still in education	–10.21**	–17.30*	–12.10*	–16.37*
Voluntary part-time for other reasons	–11.33*	–7.86**	–12.16*	–7.27**
Involuntary part-time	1.14	–12.08*	–0.61	–8.98*
Supervisory role				
(reference: some supervisory role)				
No supervisory	–6.63*	–8.52*	–6.47*	–7.51*
Great supervisory	–4.29***	4.75*	–3.45	5.00*
Temporary contract				
(reference: permanent)				
Temporary contract			7.85*	–12.67*
Gender				
(reference: men)				
Women	2.85***	–2.00***	3.49**	–1.22
Age groups				
(reference: aged 36-45)				
Aged 16-25	2.04	–4.17**	2.11	–2.14
Aged 26-35	2.20	0.22	2.28	0.08
Aged 46-55	–6.80*	–2.40***	–7.00*	–4.01*
Aged 56-65	–14.87*	–4.23**	–13.46*	–4.27***
Educational attainment				
(reference: upper secondary)				
Less than upper secondary	–5.10*	–5.29*	–4.93**	–5.09*
Tertiary	7.48*	4.34*	7.05*	4.16*
Community size				
(reference: urban)				
Rural	–1.59	–0.28	–2.67***	–0.27
Country of birth				
(reference: born in country of interview)				
Immigrants	0.10	–5.58*	0.17	–4.96**
Number of employers (last 12 months)				
(references: more than one employer)				
One employer only	–12.74*	0.23	–11.27*	–1.07
Firm size				
(reference: 100 to 199 employees)				
20 to 99 employees	3.23	–1.77	3.56	0.06
200 to 499 employees	–0.65	6.93*	1.04	7.99*
500 and more employees	2.58	11.93*	2.72	14.07*
Industry				
(reference: manufacturing, mining and energy)				
Construction	5.02	–1.51	3.97	–1.55
Wholesale and retail trade	4.22	–5.17*	4.03	–3.72***
Transport, storage and communications	1.96	6.77*	1.85	6.77*
Financing, insurance, real estate and business services	4.28	5.81*	5.16***	8.00*
Community, social and personal services	6.83*	–1.79	7.12*	0.04

Table 5.A1.2. **Training demand and supply** (cont.)

Bivariate probit estimates[a]

	Including supervisory role		Including temporary contracts	
	Hypothesis A[b]		Hypothesis A[b]	
	Demand	Equilibrium outcome	Demand	Equilibrium outcome
Occupation				
(reference: clerks)				
Managers	–1.07	3.26	–2.76	3.50
Professionals	7.81 *	4.02 **	6.61 **	5.35 *
Technicians and associate professionals	5.09 **	3.15 ***	5.72 **	2.71
Service workers and shop and market sales workers	–4.39 ***	–5.12 *	–3.98	–5.39 *
Craft and related trades workers	–5.29 ***	–8.70 *	–5.57 ***	–7.51 *
Plant and machine operators and assemblers	–7.05 **	–11.91 *	–6.50 **	–10.83 *
Elementary occupations	–10.27 *	–18.54 *	–10.19 *	–17.31 *
Predicted at vector 0	45.77	36.96	43.65	34.61
Log likelihood	–3 943	–6 197	–3 432	–5 491
Number of observations	7 228	11 043	6 099	9 623
Number of countries	10	10	8	8
Pseudo R²	0.094	0.129	0.091	0.131

*, **, ***, statistically significant at 1%, 5% and 10% levels respectively.

a) Estimated percentage change in the probability of demanding training (receiving training in equilibrium) with respect to the reference individual. Equations are estimated by maximum likelihood assuming no correlation between residuals. The sample are employees of firms with more than 20 employees, with at least some education, aged 16 to 65 years and not working in the agricultural sector. The reference individual is indicated in the table. The dependent variable for demand takes value 1 if the individual received training or wished to be trained. For the equilibrium outcome the dependent variable takes value 1 if the individual received employer-sponsored training. All equations include country dummies.

b) Employees cannot refuse to be trained. Subject to this hypothesis, the demand equation is estimated only on the sub-sample of those who did not receive employer-sponsored training.

c) Employees can refuse to be trained. Subject to this hypothesis, the equilibrium outcome equation is estimated only on the sub-sample of those who received training or wished they had.

Source: OECD estimates based on IALS.

Table 5.A1.3. **Training supply and demand: the effect of literacy**
Bivariate probit estimates[a]

	Hypothesis A[b]		Hypothesis B[c]	
	Demand	Equilibrium outcome	Demand	Equilibrium outcome
Literacy	0.5	5.0**	3.7	4.0
Mother has worked	5.2**	3.4***	6.6*	–0.5
Gender				
(reference: men)				
Women	1.8	–3.1**	–0.3	–5.1*
Age groups				
(reference: aged 36-45)				
Aged 16-25	–0.4	–9.6*	–6.7*	–9.7*
Aged 26-35	1.9	–2.8***	–0.5	–3.7**
Aged 46-55	–6.2*	–2.2	–6.9*	3.7***
Aged 56-65	–10.2*	–0.6	–9.5*	8.7**
Educational attainment				
(reference: upper secondary)				
Less than upper secondary	–3.4	0.1	–2.7	1.6
Tertiary	5.5**	–1.6	3.2	–5.1***
Community size				
(reference: urban)				
Rural	–0.9	0.6	–0.2	0.4
Full-time/part-time				
(reference: full-time)				
Part-time workers	–0.5	–13.2*	–8.8*	–15.8*
Country of birth				
(reference: born in country of interview)				
Immigrants	3.0	–0.6	1.6	–3.0
Number of employers (last 12 months)				
(reference: more than one employer)				
One employer only	–6.7*	1.6	–5.4*	5.3*
Firm size				
(reference: 100 to 199 employees)				
20 to 99 employees	3.6	–0.1	3.3	–3.6
200 to 499 employees	–1.8	9.7*	4.6	8.4*
500 and more employees	3.1	12.2*	10.3*	7.0*
Industry				
(reference: manufacturing, mining and energy)				
Construction	6.5***	–8.2**	–0.3	–14.0*
Wholesale and retail trade	5.2**	–5.7**	0.0	–9.5*
Transport, storage and communications	2.6	2.9	4.0	2.0
Financing, insurance, real estate and business services	3.3	1.9	3.8	–0.7
Community, social and personal services	7.6*	–1.9	4.6**	–7.6*
Occupation				
(reference: clerks)				
Managers	1.8	6.1**	5.8**	4.2
Professionals	3.4	4.3**	5.6**	1.7
Technicians and associate professionals	5.8**	2.7	6.1*	–0.5
Service workers and shop and market sales workers	0.7	–6.2*	–3.4	–7.3**
Craft and related trades workers	5.5***	–6.9*	0.2	–12.7*
Plant and machine operators and assemblers	–0.3	–14.1*	–10.5*	–16.1*
Elementary occupations	–2.6	–17.8*	–14.0*	–20.4*
Predicted value at the average literacy score[d]	22.5	34.0	48.3	72.3
Average literacy score	291.3	294.4	294.4	298.0
Number of observations	4 437	6 973	6 973	4 141
Log likelihood	–2 760	–4 185	–4 408	–2 530
Number of countries	5	5	5	5
Pseudo R²	0.050	0.084	0.064	0.085

Table 5.A1.3. **Training supply and demand: the effect of literacy** (cont.)

Bivariate probit estimates[a]

*, **, *** statistically significant at 1%, 5% and 10% levels, respectively.

a) Estimated percentage change in the probability of demanding training (receiving training in equilibrium) with respect to the reference individual. For literacy, which is a continuous variable, the effect of a 10% increase in the literacy score from the sample average is reported. Equations are estimated by maximum likelihood assuming no correlation between residuals. Literacy, being potentially endogenous, has been instrumented using parental background characteristics, education, gender, age, community size, country of birth and country dummies. The sample population is employees of firms with more than 20 employees, with at least some education, aged 16 to 65 years and not working in the agricultural sector. The reference individual is indicated in the table. The dependent variable for demand takes value 1 if the individual received training or wished to be trained. For the equilibrium outcome the dependent variable takes value 1 if the individual received employer-sponsored training. All equations include five country dummies.

b) Employees cannot refuse to be trained. Subject to this hypothesis, the demand equation is estimated only on the sub-sample of those who did not receive employer-sponsored training.

c) Employees can refuse to be trained. Subject to this hypothesis, the equilibrium outcome equation is estimated only on the sub-sample of those who received training or wished they had.

d) Predicted probability at the average literacy score for the reference individual.

Source: OECD estimates based on IALS.

ANNEX 2

Identification and Estimation of Training Demand and Supply

Information on workers who would have liked to have taken additional training but could not can be used to identify the demand for training of employed persons. Workers declaring that they could not take all the training they wanted clearly believe that their return from training is non-negative, at least if they do not have to pay for it. It can be said that an individual has a positive demand (at zero cost for the individual) if he/she declares to have taken non-sponsored training courses and/or to desire further training. From this information, the probability of demanding training can be estimated as a function of personal and job characteristics. Taking two different groups of individuals and assuming that demand curves are downward sloped (with respect to the implicit or explicit price of training) and do not cross each other, it is therefore possible to estimate whether one group has greater demand than another by estimating their respective probabilities of desiring further training at zero cost (points A and A' in Chart 5.A2.1).

Chart 5.A2.1. **Demand and supply of training: solving the identification problem**

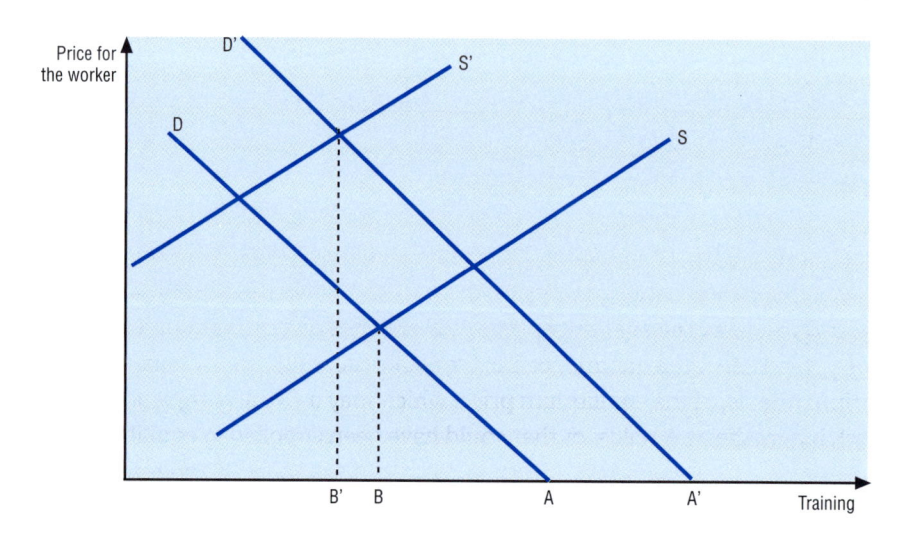

Rigorously speaking, without additional assumptions on employers' behaviour, the demand-identification strategy described above is valid only for employees not receiving employer-sponsored training. Indeed, workers who receive employer-sponsored training may or may not have a positive demand for training, depending on employers' behaviour and training bargaining outcomes. Two extreme alternative assumptions can be selected:

- *Hypothesis A*: by threatening lay-offs and/or offering monetary compensation, an employer can always force a worker to be trained, therefore demand at zero cost for workers receiving employer-sponsored CVT might not be positive and its sign is unobservable; or

- *Hypothesis B*: as assumed by Oosterbeek (1998) in a similar analysis for the Netherlands, employers cannot force their employees to be trained against their will (even at zero cost for the employees, which implies that equilibrium prices in the downstream training market cannot be negative), therefore training takes place only if the worker's demand is non-negative.

Hypothesis B allows the identification of demand on the whole sample while, under hypothesis A, demand can be consistently estimated only on the subsample of those not receiving employer-sponsored training (see Table 5.A2.1). Furthermore, these additional assumptions on employers' behaviour and bargaining outcomes allow deriving the relative positions of supply schedules from the simultaneous estimation of demand and equilibrium outcomes (the training amount corresponding to the intersection between supply and demand, B and B' in Chart 5.A2.1).

Table 5.A2.1. **Samples and dependent variables**

	Demand	Equilibrium outcome
	Dependent variable: 1 for participants in sponsored and non-sponsored CVT or workers who wanted to take further training but did not, and 0 for the others	Dependent variable: 1 for participants in sponsored CVT only, and 0 for the others
Hypothesis A: Employers can always force a worker to be trained through monetary compensation or lay-off threats	Non-participants in sponsored CVT	Whole sample
Hypothesis B: Employers cannot force their employees to be trained against their will	Whole sample	Participants in sponsored and non-sponsored CVT or workers who wanted to take further training but did not

CVT: Continuous vocational training.

More formally, it can be assumed that the equilibrium outcome and demand are described by the following equations:

$y_w = X\beta_w + \varepsilon_w$ if $y_w > 0$ and 0 otherwise,

$y_e = X\beta_e + \varepsilon_e$ if $y_e > 0$ and 0 otherwise,

where y_w represents the quantity of employer-sponsored training demanded by the employee at zero cost borne by him/her (that is if the price of training charged by the employer were zero); y_e represents the quantity of employer-sponsored training demanded and supplied in equilibrium (that is, at the equilibrium price, which may differ across pairs of employers and employees), if hypothesis A holds, or that could have been supplied in equilibrium if there had been no constraint on equilibrium prices, if hypothesis B holds; X represents the vector of observed worker's characteristics; and ε_w and ε_e are error terms. Four different situations can arise: i) $y_w > 0$ and $y_e > 0$; ii) $y_w = 0$ and $y_e > 0$; iii) $y_w > 0$ and $y_e = 0$; and iv) $y_w, y_e = 0$.

In practice, under both hypotheses, the probability of receiving employer-sponsored training in equilibrium and the probability of demanding training at zero cost can be estimated in a bivariate probit framework as a function of personal and firm characteristics. For the equilibrium outcome, the dependent variable takes value one if the worker has received employer-sponsored training – situations i) and ii) – and zero otherwise – situations iii) and iv). For demand, it takes value one if the worker has taken any type of training course or would have liked to – situations i) and iii) – and zero otherwise – situations ii) and iv). However, under hypothesis A, situations i) and ii) cannot be distinguished; therefore demand is estimated only conditional on the fact that the worker has not received any employer-sponsored training – that is, if situations iii) or iv) occur. By contrast the equilibrium outcome is estimated on the whole sample. Symmetrically, under hypothesis B, situations ii) and iv) cannot be distinguished, since the actual equilibrium amount of training can never be greater than the amount demanded at zero cost; therefore the equilibrium outcome is estimated only conditional on the worker having received training or being willing to be trained at zero individual cost, while demand is estimated on the whole sample. In principle, the correlation between the error terms of the demand and equilibrium outcome equations must be taken into account (to avoid selection bias). However, since Oosterbeek (1998), in a similar analysis for the Netherlands, does not find this correlation to be significant, for computational reasons the equations are estimated as if the residuals were incorrelated. Furthermore, Bassanini and Ok (2003) estimate a number of similar models allowing for correlation between unobservable characteristics and obtain similar results.

Under both hypotheses, information on the relative position of employers' supply for different groups can then be derived by comparing demand and equilibrium outcomes, on the basis of the assumption that supply curves are upward sloped and do not cross each other. Table 5.A2.2 summarises all possible combinations of demand and equilibrium estimates and their implications for employers' supply. For example, if training demand for, say, women is estimated to be significantly greater than training demand by men, but no significant difference is estimated for equilibrium outcomes (first row in the table), this can be interpreted as evidence that for any given price of training, employers' supply is greater for men than for women. Equivalently, the supply curve for women is above that for men (compare S and S' with D and D' in the Chart 5.A2.1). To the extent that results are consistent under both hypotheses A and B, some statements on supply and demand can be derived with some confidence. Table 5.3 is based only on estimates under hypothesis A. However, results are similar when estimations are carried over under hypothesis B (see Annex 1).

Table 5.A2.2. **Estimating supply differences across groups from demand and equilibrium estimates**[a]

Demand	Equilibrium outcome	Supply
+	0	–
+	–	–
0	–	–
0	0	0
–	+	+
–	0	+
0	+	+
+	+	Depends on the relative size of differences
–	–	Depends on the relative size of differences

a) +, – and 0 mean that, with respect to the reference individual, a given characteristic is estimated to shift the corresponding curve rightward, leftward and in no significant way, respectively. For example, the first line of the table means that if demand is estimated to shift rightward and no significant shift is estimated for the equilibrium outcome, then the derived supply schedule is estimated to shift leftward.

Finally, under hypothesis A, demand and supply are consistently estimated also if additional hypotheses are made to allow for a more plausible interpretation of respondents' reaction to the question on further training, which is phrased in the IALS as follows: "Since August (Year), was there any training or education that you wanted to take for career or job-related reasons but did not?" In fact, this formulation is somewhat ambiguous, and it can be expected that workers declaring themselves constrained are those who expect positive returns from training even taking part of the (direct or opportunity) cost of training into account (*e.g.* part of the foregone income and leisure time, alternative investment opportunities, displeasure they associate with formal learning due to bad pedagogical experiences, etc.). Nevertheless, the following hypotheses can be made: i) individuals interpret the question on additional desired training as asking whether they would like to receive more training for a fixed implicit or explicit cost borne by them; and ii) this perceived cost (or price) threshold does not depend on observable individual characteristics and can be modelled as a constant plus a standard error term. Subject to these additional hypotheses, the probability of demanding training is identified at the price threshold that is perceived to be implicit in the question on further training, rather than being identified at zero cost supported by the respondent.

Bibliography

ACEMOGLU, D. and J.-S. PISCHKE (1999a), "The Structure of Wages and Investment in General Training", *Journal of Political Economy*, Vol. 107, No. 3, pp. 539-572.

ACEMOGLU, D. and J.-S. PISCHKE (1999b), "Beyond Becker: Training in Imperfect Labour Markets", *Economic Journal*, Vol. 109, No. 453, pp. 112-142.

ACEMOGLU, D. and J.-S. PISCHKE (2003), "Minimum Wage and On-the-Job Training", *Research in Labor Economics*, Vol. 23, forthcoming.

ARULAMPALAM, W., A. BOOTH and M. BRYAN (2002), "Work Related Training and the New National Minimum Wage in Britain", *IZA Discussion Paper No. 595*, October.

AUSTRALIAN BUREAU OF STATISTICS (1990), *How Workers Get Their Training, Australia 1989*, Canberra.

AUTOR, D. H. (2001), "Why Do Temporary Help Firms Provide Free General Skills Training?", *Quarterly Journal of Economics*, Vol. 116, No. 4, pp. 1409-1448.

BARRON, J.M., M.C. BERGER and D.A. BLACK (1997), "How Well Do We Measure Training?", *Journal of Labor Economics*, Vol. 15, No. 3, pp. 507-528.

BARRON, J.M., M.C. BERGER and D.A. BLACK (1999a), "Do Workers Pay for On-the-Job Training?", *Journal of Human Resources*, Vol. 34, No. 2, pp. 235-252.

BARRON, J.M., M.C. BERGER and D.A. BLACK (1999b), "Replacing General with Specific Training: Why Restricting Alternatives Makes Sense", *Research in Labor Economics*, Vol. 18, pp. 281-302.

BASSANINI, A. and G. BRUNELLO (2003), "Is Training More Frequent when Wage Compression is Higher? Evidence from the European Community Household Panel", OECD, Paris, and University of Padua, mimeo.

BASSANINI, A. and W. OK (2003), "The Determinants of the Demand and Supply of Training: Evidence from the IALS", OECD, Paris, mimeo.

BECKER, G.S. (1975), *Human Capital*, 2nd edition, Columbia University Press, New York.

BELLMANN, L. and H. DULL (2001), "Die zeitliche Lage und Kostenaufteilung von Weiterbildungsmassnahmen. Empirische Ergebnisse auf der Grundlage des IAB-Betriebspanels", in R. Dobischat and H. Seifert (eds.), *Lernzeiten neu organisieren*, Hans Böckler Stiftung, Düsseldorf.

BISHOP, J.H. (1997), "What We Know about Employer-Provided Training: A Review of the Literature", *Research in Labor Economics*, Vol. 16, pp. 19-87.

BOOTH, A. and M. BRYAN (2002), "Who Pays for General Training? New evidence for British Men and Women", *IZA Discussion Paper No. 486*, April.

BROYON, M.A., S. HANHART and G. EVÉQUOZ (2002), "Le Chèque de Formation à Genève: rapport descriptif", University of Geneva, mimeo.

CALLENDER, C. (2002), "Loans for Further Education Students", in Mick Fletcher (ed.), *Loans for Lifelong Learning*, Learning and Skills Development Agency, London.

CEDEFOP (2001), *Vocational Education and Training in Belgium*, Thessaloniki.

CINOP (2002), *Dutch Government Policy and Instruments for Co-financing Lifelong Learning Initiated by Government and Employers*, s-Hertogenbosch.

COLARDYN, D. (2002), "Conclusions: Linking Formal and Non-Formal Learning-Towards a Strategy for Lifelong Learning", in D. Colardyn (ed.), *Lifelong Learning: Which Ways Forward?*, 2nd ed., Kenniscentrum EVC, Lemma Publishers, Utrecht.

CROUCH, C., D. FINEGOLD and M. SAKO (1999), *Are Skills the Answer? The Political Economy of Skill Creation in Advanced Industrial Countries*, Oxford University Press, Oxford.

DOBISCHAT, R. and H. SEIFERT (2001), "Betriebliche Weiterbildung und Arbeitszeitkonten", *WSI-Mitteilungen*, No. 2, February.

EIRO (2001), "Working Time Developments and the Quality of Work: Denmark", EIROnline, www.eiro.eurofound.ie/

EUROSTAT (2000), "Continuing Vocational Training Survey (CVTS2): European Union Manual", *Eurostat Population and Social Conditions Working Paper* 3/2000/E/No. 17, Luxembourg.

FOUGERE, D., D. GOUX, E. MAURIN (2001), "Formation continue et carrières salariales: une évaluation sur données individuelles", *Annales d'Economie et de Statistique*, No. 62, pp. 49-69.

FRASER, D. (1996), *The Training Guarantee: Its Impact of and Legacy 1990-1994*, EMB Report 5/96 Department of Employment, Education, Training and Youth Affairs, Australian Government Publishing Service, Canberra.

GASSKOV, V. (1998), "Levies, Leave and Collective Agreements Incentives for Enterprises and Individuals to Invest in Training", *Vocational Training: European Journal*, No. 13.

GASSKOV, V. (2001), "Government Interventions in Private Financing of Training", ILO, Geneva, mimeo.

GIBBONS, R. and M. WALDMAN (1999), "Careers in Organizations: Theory and Evidence", in O. Ashenfelter and D. Card (eds.), *Handbook of Labor Economics*, Vol. 3B, North-Holland, Amsterdam.

GREEN, D.A. and W.C. RIDDELL (2003), "Literacy and Earnings: An investigation of the interactions of cognitive and unobserved skills in earnings generation", *Labour Economics*, Vol. 10, No. 2, pp. 165-184.

HÅKANSON, C., S. JOHANSON and E. MELLANDER (2002), "Firm Training Viewed from Stabilisation and Growth Policy Perspectives", IFAU, Stockholm, mimeo.

HASHIMOTO, M. (1981), "Firm-Specific Human Capital as a Shared Investment", *American Economic Review*, Vol. 71, No. 3, pp. 475-482.

LENGERMANN, P.A. (1999), "How Long Do the Benefits of Training Last? Evidence from Long Term Effects across Current and Previous Employers", *Research in Labor Economics*, Vol. 18, pp. 439-461.

LEUVEN, E. and H. OOSTERBEEK (1999), "The Demand and Supply of Work-Related Training: Evidence from Four Countries", *Research in Labor Economics*, Vol. 18, pp. 303-330.

LEUVEN, E. and H. OOSTERBEEK (2003), "Evaluating the Effect of Tax Deductions on Training", *Journal of Labor Economics*, forthcoming.

LOEWENSTEIN, M.A. and J.R SPLETZER (1998), "Dividing the Costs and Returns to General Training", *Journal of Labor Economics*, Vol. 16, No. 1, pp. 142-171.

LOEWENSTEIN, M.A. and J.R SPLETZER (1999a), "Formal and Informal Training: Evidence from the NLSY", *Research in Labor Economics*, Vol. 18, pp. 403-438.

LOEWENSTEIN, M.A. and J.R SPLETZER (1999b), "General and Specific Training: Evidence and Implications", *Journal of Human Resources*, Vol. 34, No. 4, pp. 710-733.

MALCOMSON, J.M. (1997), "Contracts, Hold-Up, and Labor Markets", *Journal of Economic Literature*, Vol. 35, No. 4, pp. 1916-1957.

MALCOMSON, J. M. (1999), "Individual Employment Contracts", in O. Ashenfelter and D. Card (eds.), *Handbook of Labor Economics*, Vol. 3B, North-Holland, Amsterdam.

MALCOMSON, J.M., J. MAW and B. MCCORMICK (2003), "General Training by Firms, Apprentice Contracts, and Public Policy", *European Economic Review*, Vol. 47, No. 1, pp. 197-227.

MEDEF (2001), *Projet d'un accord national interprofessionnel relatif à l'accès des salariés à la formation professionnelle continue*, October, Paris, mimeo.

NEAL, D. (1995), "Industry-Specific Human Capital: Evidence from Displaced Workers", *Journal of Labor Economics*, Vol. 13, No. 4, pp. 653-677.

NEUMARK, D. and W. WASCHER (2001), "Minimum Wages and Training Revisited", *Journal of Labor Economics*, Vol. 19, No. 3, pp. 563-595.

OECD (1994), *The OECD Jobs Study – Facts, Analysis, Strategies*, Paris.

OECD (1999a), *Implementing the OECD Jobs Strategy – Assessing Performance and Policy*, Paris.

OECD (1999b), *Employment Outlook*, Paris.

OECD (2001a), *The New Economy: Beyond the Hype*, Paris.

OECD (2001b), *The Economics and Finance of Lifelong Learning*, Paris.

OECD (2002a), *Employment Outlook*, Paris.

OECD (2002b), *Education Policy Analysis*, Paris.

OECD (2002c), *Babies and Bosses: Reconciliating Work and Family Life: Australia, Denmark and the Netherlands*, Paris.

OECD (2003a), *Beyond Rhetoric: Adult Learning Policies and Practices*, Paris.

OECD (2003b), *Descriptions and Evaluations of Recent Experience with Mechanisms for Co-financing Lifelong Learning: Reports Prepared by National Authorities and Members of the ELAP Network*, prepared for the "Second International Seminar: Mechanisms for the Co-finance of Lifelong Learning", London, 27-29 November, OECD, Paris.

OECD (2003c), *Reading for Change*, Paris.

OECD and ERNST & YOUNG (1997), *Enterprise Value in the Knowledge Economy: Measuring Performance in the Age of Intangibles*, Ernst & Young Center for Business Innovation, Cambridge, MA.

OECD and STATISTICS CANADA (2000), *Literacy in the Information Age*, Paris and Ottawa.

OK, W. and P. TERGEIST (2003), "Improving Workers' Skills: Analytical Evidence and the Role of the Social Partners", *OECD Social, Employment and Migration Working Papers*, No. 10, Paris.

OOSTERBEEK, H. (1998), "Unravelling Supply and Demand Factors in Work-Related Training", *Oxford Economic Papers*, Vol. 50, No. 2, pp. 266-283.

OWENS, J. (2001), "Evaluation of Individual Learning Accounts – Early Views of Customers and Providers: England", *DfEE Research Brief* No. 294, 28 September.

PARSONS, D.O. (1986), "The Employment Relationship: Job Attachment, Work Effort, and the Nature of Contracts", in O. Ashenfelter, A. Orley and R. Layard (eds.), *Handbook of Labor Economics*, Vol. 2, pp. 789-848, North-Holland, Amsterdam.

PISCHKE, J.-S. (2001), "Continuous Training in Germany", *Journal of Population Economics*, Vol. 14, No. 3, pp. 523-548.

QUARRIE, C. (2002), "Some Thoughts on Career Development Loans", in Mick Fletcher (ed.), *Loans for Lifelong Learning*, Learning and Skills Development Agency, London.

REDDING, S. (1996), "The Low-skill, Low-quality Trap: Strategic Complementarities between Human Capital and R&D", *Economic Journal*, Vol. 106, pp. 458-70.

SCANLON, E. and D. PAGE-ADAMS (2001), "Effects of Asset Holding on Neighbourhoods, Families and Children: A Review of Research", in Boshara, R. (ed.), *Building Assets: A Report on the Asset-Development and IDA Field*, Corporation for Enterprise Development, Washington, D.C.

STEVENS, M. (1994), "A Theoretical Model of On-the-Job Training with Imperfect Competition", *Oxford Economic Papers*, Vol. 46, No. 4, pp. 537-562.

STEVENS, M. (1999), "Human Capital Theory and UK Vocational Training Policy", *Oxford Review of Economic Policy*, Vol. 15, No. 1, pp. 16-32.

STEVENS, M. (2001), "Should Firms Be Required to Pay for Vocational Training?", *Economic Journal*, Vol. 111, No. 473, pp. 485-505.

TERTIARY EDUCATION ADVISORY COMMITTEE (2001), *Shaping the Funding Framework*, Tertiary Education Advisory Committee, November, Wellington.

VAN BUREN, M. and W. ERSKINE (2002), "What Works in Workforce Development: an ASTD/AJLMEP Study of Joint Labor-Management Educational Programs", September.

WURZBURG, G. (2003), "What if? Simulating the Impact of Alternative Policies on the Incentives to Invest in Lifelong Learning for Adults", OECD, Paris, mimeo.

YORK CONSULTING (2002), "Evaluation of Individual Learning Accounts: Final Report", Scottish Executive, Edinburgh.

ISBN 92-64-10061-X
OECD Employment Outlook: 2003
Towards More and Better Jobs
© OECD 2003

Statistical Annex

Sources and definitions

Most of the statistics shown in these tables can be found as well in two other (paper or electronic) publications or references, as follows:

- the annual edition of *OECD Labour Force Statistics, 1982-2002*;
- the OECD On-Line Labour Force Statistics database that shows both raw data (see URL: *www.oecd.org/scripts/cde/members/LFSDATAAuthenticate.asp*) and derived statistics (*www.oecd.org/scripts/cde/members/LFSINDICATORSAuthenticate.asp*), and allows free access to the data.

These publications, which include information on definitions, notes and sources used by member countries, include longer time series and more detailed disaggregations by age group, gender, duration of unemployment, etc., than are shown in this annex.

Sources and definitions for data shown in the statistical annex tables are specified at the bottom of each table.

Please note that the data on employment, unemployment and the labour force are not necessarily the same as the series used for analyses and forecasting by the OECD Economics Department and reproduced in Tables 1.1 and 1.2 of Chapter 1 of this publication.

Interested users can refer to the on-line database, which contains data series describing the labour supply: population, labour force, employment and unemployment disaggregated by gender and age, educational attainment, employment status and sector of activity, participation and unemployment rates, statistics on part-time employment and duration of unemployment. The on-line database contains a number of additional series on labour market results and on features of the institutional and regulatory environment affecting the functioning of labour markets. Among these are the following:

- annual hours of work data for comparisons of trends over time;
- gross earnings by percentile for deriving measures of earnings dispersion for full-time workers by gender;
- gross mean and median earnings of full-time workers by age group and gender;
- statutory minimum wages;
- public expenditure on labour market programmes and labour market participants inflows;
- trade union density rates in OECD member countries.

STATISTICAL ANNEX

Conventional signs

.. Data not available

. Decimal point

| Break in series

– Nil or less than half of the last digit used

Note on the statistical treatment of Germany

In this statistical annex, data up to end-1990 are for western Germany; unless otherwise indicated, they are for the whole of Germany from 1991 onwards.

Table A. Standardised unemployment rates in 27 OECD countries
As a percentage of total labour force

	1990	1991	1992	1993	1994	1995	1996	1997	1998	1999	2000	2001	2002
Australia	6.7	9.3	10.5	10.6	9.5	8.2	8.2	8.3	7.7	7.0	6.3	6.7	6.3
Austria	..	..	..	4.0	3.8	3.9	4.4	4.4	4.5	4.0	3.7	3.6	4.3
Belgium	6.6	6.4	7.1	8.6	9.8	9.7	9.5	9.2	9.3	8.6	6.9	6.7	7.3
Canada	8.1	10.3	11.2	11.4	10.4	9.4	9.6	9.1	8.3	7.6	6.8	7.2	7.7
Czech Republic	..	..	..	4.4	4.4	4.1	3.9	4.8	6.4	8.6	8.7	8.0	7.3
Denmark	7.2	7.9	8.6	9.6	7.7	6.8	6.3	5.3	4.9	4.8	4.4	4.4	4.5
Finland	3.2	6.7	11.6	16.4	16.8	15.2	14.6	12.6	11.4	10.2	9.7	9.1	9.1
France	8.7	9.1	10.0	11.3	11.9	11.4	11.9	11.8	11.4	10.7	9.3	8.5	8.7
Germany[a]	4.8	4.2	6.4	7.7	8.2	8.0	8.7	9.7	9.1	8.4	7.8	7.8	8.2
Greece	6.3	6.9	7.8	8.6	8.9	9.1	9.7	9.6	11.0	11.8	11.0	10.4	9.9
Hungary	..	..	9.9	12.1	11.0	10.4	9.6	9.0	8.4	6.9	6.3	5.6	5.6
Ireland	13.4	14.7	15.4	15.6	14.3	12.3	11.7	9.9	7.5	5.6	4.3	3.9	4.4
Italy	8.9	8.5	8.8	10.1	11.0	11.5	11.5	11.6	11.7	11.3	10.4	9.5	9.0
Japan	2.1	2.1	2.2	2.5	2.9	3.2	3.4	3.4	4.1	4.7	4.7	5.0	5.4
Korea	..	..	..	..	..	..	..	..	..	..	4.4	4.0	3.3
Luxembourg	1.7	1.6	2.1	2.6	3.2	2.9	2.9	2.7	2.7	2.4	2.3	2.0	2.4
Netherlands	5.9	5.5	5.3	6.2	6.8	6.6	6.0	4.9	3.8	3.2	2.8	2.4	2.8
New Zealand	7.8	10.3	10.3	9.5	8.1	6.3	6.1	6.6	7.5	6.8	6.0	5.3	5.2
Norway	5.7	6.0	6.5	6.6	5.9	5.4	4.8	4.0	3.2	3.3	3.4	3.6	3.9
Poland	..	..	..	14.0	14.4	13.3	12.3	10.9	10.2	13.4	16.4	18.5	19.9
Portugal	4.8	4.2	4.3	5.7	6.9	7.3	7.3	6.8	5.2	4.5	4.1	4.1	5.1
Slovak Republic	..	..	..	..	13.7	13.1	11.3	11.9	12.6	16.8	18.7	19.4	18.6
Spain	13.1	13.2	14.9	18.6	19.8	18.8	18.1	17.0	15.2	12.8	11.3	10.6	11.4
Sweden	1.7	3.1	5.6	9.1	9.4	8.8	9.6	9.9	8.2	6.7	5.6	4.9	4.9
Switzerland	..	1.9	2.8	3.8	3.7	3.4	3.7	4.1	3.4	2.9	2.6	2.5	..
United Kingdom	6.9	8.6	9.7	9.9	9.2	8.5	8.0	6.9	6.2	5.9	5.4	5.0	5.1
United States	5.6	6.8	7.5	6.9	6.1	5.6	5.4	4.9	4.5	4.2	4.0	4.7	5.8
European Union[b]	8.1	8.4	9.1	10.1	10.5	10.1	10.2	10.0	9.4	8.7	7.8	7.4	7.6
OECD Europe[b]	8.0	8.2	8.9	10.2	10.5	10.1	10.1	9.8	9.2	9.0	8.5	8.3	8.6
Total OECD[b]	6.1	6.8	7.4	7.8	7.7	7.3	7.2	7.0	6.9	6.7	6.3	6.5	6.9

Note: In so far as possible, the data have been adjusted to ensure comparability over time and to conform to the guidelines of the International Labour Office. All series are benchmarked to labour-force-survey-based estimates. In countries with annual surveys, monthly estimates are obtained by interpolation/extrapolation and by incorporating trends in administrative data, where available. The annual figures are then calculated by averaging the monthly estimates (for both unemployed and the labour force). For countries with monthly or quarterly surveys, the annual estimates are obtained by averaging the monthly or quarterly estimates, respectively. For several countries, the adjustment procedure used is similar to that of the Bureau of Labor Statistics, US Department of Labor. For EU countries, the procedures are similar to those used in deriving the Comparable Unemployment Rates (CURs) of the Statistical Office of the European Communities. Minor differences may appear mainly because of various methods of calculating and applying adjustment factors, and because EU estimates are based on the civilian labour force. For a fuller description, please refer to the following URL: www.oecd.org/oecd/pages/home/displaygeneral/0,3380,EN-document-5-nodirectorate-no-1-29298-5,00.html.

a) Up to and including 1992, western Germany; subsequent data concern the whole of Germany.
b) For above countries only.

Source: OECD (2003), Quarterly Labour Force Statistics, No. 1, Paris.

Table B. Employment/population ratios, activity and unemployment rates[a]

Persons aged 15-64 years (percentages)

	Employment/population ratio						Labour force participation rate						Unemployment rate					
	1990	1998	1999	2000	2001	2002	1990	1998	1999	2000	2001	2002	1990	1998	1999	2000	2001	2002
Australia	67.9	67.2	67.7	69.1	68.9	69.4	73.0	73.0	72.9	73.8	73.8	73.9	7.0	7.9	7.0	6.3	6.7	6.1
Austria	..	67.4	68.2	67.9	67.8	68.2	..	71.3	71.6	71.3	70.7	71.7	..	5.5	4.7	4.7	4.0	4.9
Belgium	54.4|	57.3	58.9	60.9	59.7	59.7	58.7|	63.2	64.6	65.2	63.6	64.1	7.3|	9.4	8.7	6.6	6.2	6.9
Canada	70.3	68.9	70.1	71.1	70.9	71.5	76.6	75.2	75.9	76.3	76.5	77.5	8.2	8.4	7.6	6.9	7.3	7.7
Czech Republic	..	67.5	65.9	65.2	65.3	65.7	..	72.2	72.2	71.6	71.1	70.9	..	6.5	8.7	8.8	8.2	7.3
Denmark	75.4|	75.3	76.5	76.4	75.9	76.4	82.4|	79.3	80.6	80.0	79.2	79.9	8.5|	5.1	5.2	4.5	4.2	4.3
Finland	74.1	64.0	66.0	67.0	67.7	67.7	76.6	72.4	73.6	74.3	74.6	74.5	3.2	11.6	10.3	9.9	9.2	9.1
France	59.9	59.4	59.8	61.1	62.0	61.1	66.0	67.4	67.8	68.0	68.0	68.0	9.2	11.9	11.8	10.1	8.8	10.1
Germany	64.1|	64.7|	65.2	65.6	65.8	65.3	67.4|	71.4|	71.2	71.1	71.6	71.5	4.9|	9.3|	8.5	7.8	7.9	8.6
Greece	54.8|	55.6	55.4	55.9	55.6	56.9	59.1|	62.5	62.9	63.0	62.1	63.1	—	11.0	12.0	11.3	10.4	9.8
Hungary	..	53.8	55.7	56.0	56.2	56.2	..	58.4	59.9	59.9	59.6	59.7	..	7.8	7.0	6.4	5.7	5.8
Iceland[b, c]	79.9	82.2	84.2	84.6	84.6	82.8	82.1	84.5	85.9	86.6	86.6	85.6	2.7	2.7	1.9	2.3	2.3	3.2
Ireland	52.1|	59.6	62.5	64.5	65.0	65.0	60.1|	64.8	66.3	67.4	67.5	67.9	13.3|	8.0	5.8	4.4	3.7	4.3
Italy	52.6	51.6	52.9	53.9	54.9	55.6	59.5	58.5	59.8	60.3	60.7	61.2	11.5	11.8	11.5	10.6	9.6	9.1
Japan	68.6	69.5	68.9	68.9	68.8	68.2	70.1	72.6	72.4	72.5	72.6	72.3	2.2	4.2	4.9	5.0	5.2	5.6
Korea	61.2	59.2	59.6	61.5	62.1	63.3	62.8	63.8	63.8	64.2	64.7	65.4	2.5	7.2	6.6	4.3	3.9	3.2
Luxembourg	59.2|	60.2	61.6	62.7	63.0	63.6	60.1|	61.9	63.1	64.2	64.1	65.3	1.6|	2.8	2.4	2.4	1.8	2.6
Mexico[c]	58.0	61.3	61.2	60.9	60.1	60.1	59.9	63.2	62.5	62.3	61.5	61.6	3.1	3.0	2.2	2.2	2.2	2.5
Netherlands	61.8	69.8	71.3	72.1	72.8	73.2	66.7	73.0	73.9	74.6	74.9	75.6	7.4	4.3	3.5	3.3	2.7	3.2
New Zealand	67.3	69.5	70.0	70.7	71.8	72.4	73.0	75.2	75.2	75.2	75.9	76.4	7.8	7.6	6.9	6.1	5.4	5.3
Norway[b]	73.0|	78.3	78.0	77.9	77.5	77.1	77.1|	80.9	80.6	80.7	80.3	80.3	5.4|	3.2	3.2	3.5	3.5	4.0
Poland	..	58.9	57.5|	55.0	53.5	51.7	..	66.1	65.9|	65.8	65.7	64.8	..	10.9	12.8|	16.4	18.6	20.3
Portugal	67.4|	66.8	67.4	68.3	68.6	68.1	70.9|	70.5	70.7	71.3	71.7	72.0	4.9|	5.2	4.6	4.2	4.3	5.4
Slovak Republic	..	60.5|	58.1|	56.8	56.9	56.9	..	69.3|	69.5|	69.9	70.5	69.9	..	12.6|	16.4|	18.8	19.3	18.6
Spain[b]	51.1	52.4	55.0	57.4	58.8|	59.5	60.9	64.5	65.3	66.7	65.8|	67.1	16.1	18.7	15.7	13.9	10.5|	11.4
Sweden[b]	83.1|	71.5	72.9	74.2	75.3	74.9	84.6|	78.1	78.5	78.9	79.3	79.0	1.8|	8.4	7.1	5.9	5.1	5.2
Switzerland[c]	78.2	78.0	78.4	78.3	79.1	78.9	79.7	81.0	80.9	80.5	81.2	81.3	1.8	3.7	3.1	2.7	2.5	3.0
Turkey	54.5	51.1	51.0	48.2	46.8	45.8	59.4	54.9	55.4	51.8	51.3	51.5	8.2	7.0	7.9	6.8	8.8	10.9
United Kingdom[b]	72.5	71.2	71.7	72.4	72.8	72.7	77.8	75.9	76.3	76.6	76.4	76.6	6.8	6.2	6.1	5.6	4.8	5.1
United States[b]	72.2	73.8	73.9|	74.1	73.1	71.9	76.5	77.4	77.2|	77.2	76.8	76.4	5.7	4.5	4.3|	4.0	4.8	5.9
European Union[d]	61.5|	61.7|	62.6	63.6	64.2|	64.3	67.1|	68.5|	69.0	69.4	69.4|	69.8	8.4|	10.0|	9.3	8.4	7.4|	7.8
OECD Europe[d]	61.0|	60.5|	61.1	61.2	61.4|	61.2	66.5|	66.9|	67.3	67.1	67.0|	67.2	8.2|	9.5|	9.3|	8.7	8.4|	9.0
Total OECD[d]	65.1|	65.2|	65.5|	65.7	65.5|	65.1	69.3|	70.0|	70.1	70.1	69.9|	69.9	6.0|	6.9|	6.7|	6.2	6.3|	6.9

Table B. Employment/population ratios, activity and unemployment rates[a] (cont.)

Men aged 15-64 years (percentages)

	Employment/population ratio							Labour force participation rate							Unemployment rate						
	1990	1998	1999	2000	2001	2002		1990	1998	1999	2000	2001	2002		1990	1998	1999	2000	2001	2002
Australia	78.5	75.2	76.1	76.6	76.0	76.5		84.4	82.1	82.1	82.0	81.7	81.6		6.9	8.4	7.3	6.6		6.9	6.3
Austria	..	75.9	76.7	76.2	75.9	75.3		..	80.2	80.5	80.1	79.0	79.5		..	5.4	4.7	4.8	4.0	5.2
Belgium	68.1|	67.0	67.5	69.8	68.5	68.1		71.3|	72.5	73.0	73.8	72.7	72.6		4.6|	7.6	7.5	5.3	5.7	6.3
Canada	77.8	74.3	75.5	76.3	75.9	76.1		84.9	81.4	82.0	82.1	82.1	82.9		8.3	8.7	7.9	7.0	7.6	8.2
Czech Republic	..	76.3	74.3	73.6	73.6	74.2		..	80.3	80.2	79.4	79.0	78.9		..	5.0	7.3	7.4	6.8	5.9
Denmark	80.1|	80.2	81.2	80.7	80.2	80.2		87.1|	83.5	85.0	84.0	83.3	83.8		8.0|	3.9	4.5	4.0	3.7	4.3
Finland	76.7	66.8	68.4	69.4	70.0	69.2		79.6	75.1	75.9	76.4	76.7	76.2		3.6	11.1	9.8	9.2	8.7	9.1
France	69.7	66.6	66.8	68.1	69.0	68.1		75.0	74.1	74.4	74.4	74.3	74.4		7.0	10.2	10.2	8.5	7.1	8.5
Germany	75.7|	72.9|	72.8	72.9	72.6	71.6		79.0|	79.9|	79.3	78.9	78.8	78.5		4.1|	8.8|	8.1	7.6	7.9	8.8
Greece	73.4|	71.6	70.9	71.3	70.9	71.7		76.8|	77.1	76.9	77.1	76.2	76.6		4.4|	7.2	7.7	7.5	6.9	6.4
Hungary	..	60.6	62.6	62.7	63.0	62.9		..	66.3	67.8	67.5	67.2	67.1		..	8.5	7.5	7.1	6.3	6.2
Iceland[b, c]	85.2	86.0	88.2	88.2	88.0	85.7		87.3	87.9	89.4	89.8	90.0	88.9		2.4	2.3	1.4	1.8	2.1	3.6
Ireland	67.5|	71.0	73.5	75.6	76.0	74.7		77.5|	77.4	78.3	79.1	79.0	78.3		13.0|	8.3	6.1	4.5	3.9	4.7
Italy	69.2	66.8	67.6	68.2	68.7	69.2		75.1	73.5	74.1	74.3	74.2	74.5		7.9	9.1	8.8	8.2	7.4	7.0
Japan	81.3	81.7	81.0	80.9	80.5	79.9		83.0	85.3	85.3	85.2	85.0	84.8		2.1	4.3	5.0	5.1	5.4	5.8
Korea	73.9	71.3	71.3	73.1	73.5	74.9		76.2	77.6	77.0	76.9	76.9	77.7		3.0	8.0	7.4	4.9	4.4	3.6
Luxembourg	76.4|	74.6	74.4	75.0	74.9	75.5		77.4|	76.0	75.7	76.4	76.1	77.0		1.2|	1.9	1.7	1.8	1.6	1.9
Mexico[c]	84.1	84.7	84.6	84.0	83.4	82.6		86.4	87.0	86.2	85.8	85.2	84.7		2.6	2.7	1.9	2.1	2.1	2.5
Netherlands	75.7	79.9	80.8	81.4	81.6	81.5		80.0	82.8	83.1	83.6	83.4	83.9		5.4	3.5	2.8	2.6	2.2	2.8
New Zealand	76.1	77.1	77.3	78.0	78.9	79.6		83.0	83.5	83.2	83.2	83.4	83.9		8.3	7.7	7.1	6.2	5.5	5.1
Norway[b]	78.6|	82.8	82.1	81.7	81.0	80.2		83.4|	85.6	85.0	84.8	84.0	83.8		5.8|	3.2	3.4	3.6	3.6	4.2
Poland	..	65.8	63.6	61.2	59.2	57.0		..	72.8	72.3|	71.7	71.5	70.8		..	9.5	12.0|	14.6	17.2	19.5
Portugal	80.1|	75.6	75.6	76.3	76.5	75.7		82.8|	78.9	78.8	79.0	79.2	v79.3		3.3|	4.2	4.1	3.3	3.4	4.5
Slovak Republic	..	67.8|	64.3|	62.2	62.1	62.5		..	77.2|	76.9|	76.8	77.4	76.7		..	12.2|	16.3|	19.0	19.8	18.6
Spain[b]	71.0	68.3	70.8	72.7	73.8|	73.9		80.4	79.1	79.6	80.4	79.8|	80.4		11.8	13.6	11.0	9.6	7.5|	8.1
Sweden[b]	85.2|	73.5	74.8	76.1	77.0	76.3		86.7|	80.7	80.9	81.2	81.4	80.9		1.8|	8.8	7.5	6.3	5.4	5.7
Switzerland[c]	90.0	87.2	87.2	87.3	87.6	86.1		91.1	90.1	89.6	89.4	89.2	88.7		1.2	3.2	2.7	2.3	1.7	2.9
Turkey	76.9	74.1	72.8	71.0	68.4	66.0		83.6	79.6	79.1	76.2	75.2	74.3		8.0	7.0	8.0	6.8	9.0	11.2
United Kingdom[b]	82.1	78.1	78.4	79.1	79.3	78.9		88.3	83.9	84.1	84.3	83.8	83.7		7.1	6.9	6.8	6.1	5.3	5.7
United States[b]	80.7	80.5	80.5|	80.6	79.4	78.0		85.6	84.2	84.0|	83.9	83.4	83.0		5.7	4.5	4.1	3.9	4.9	6.0
European Union[d]	74.3|	71.6|	72.2	73.0	73.3|	72.9		79.6|	78.4|	78.5	78.6	78.4|	78.5		6.7|	8.7|	8.1	7.2	6.5|	7.0
OECD Europe[d]	74.9|	71.6|	71.7|	71.8	71.6	70.9		80.3|	78.1|	78.1	77.8	77.5|	77.3		6.7|	8.3|	8.3	7.7	7.6|	8.4
Total OECD[d]	78.1|	76.1|	76.1	76.3	75.8|	75.0		82.5|	81.3|	81.2|	81.0	80.6|	80.4		5.4|	6.4|	6.2	5.8	6.0|	6.7

OECD EMPLOYMENT OUTLOOK – ISBN 92-64-10061-X – © OECD 2003

Table B. Employment/population ratios, activity and unemployment rates[a] (cont.)

Women aged 15-64 years (percentages)

	Employment/population ratio							Labour force participation rate							Unemployment rate						
	1990	1998	1999	2000	2001	2002		1990	1998	1999	2000	2001	2002		1990	1998	1999	2000	2001	2002
Australia	57.1	59.2	59.3	61.6	61.7	62.2		61.5	63.9	63.6	65.5	65.8	66.1		7.2	7.3	6.7	5.9	6.3	5.9
Austria	..	59.0	59.7	59.7	59.8	61.1		..	62.5	62.7	62.5	62.3	64.0		..	5.6	4.8	4.6	4.1	4.6
Belgium	40.8|	47.5	50.2	51.9	50.7	51.1		46.1|	53.8	56.0	56.6	54.5	55.4		11.5|	11.7	10.3	8.3	6.9	7.8
Canada	62.7	63.6	64.7	65.8	66.0	66.8		68.3	69.1	69.8	70.5	70.8	71.9		8.1	8.0	7.3	6.7	6.8	7.2
Czech Republic	..	58.7	57.4	56.9	57.0	57.1		..	64.0	64.1	63.7	63.2	62.8		..	8.2	10.5	10.6	9.9	9.1
Denmark	70.6|	70.3	71.6	72.1	71.4	72.6		77.6|	75.1	76.1	75.9	75.0	75.9		9.0|	6.4	5.9	5.0	4.8	4.4
Finland	71.5	61.2	63.5	64.5	65.4	66.1		73.5	69.7	71.2	72.1	72.5	72.7		2.7	12.1	10.8	10.6	9.7	9.1
France	50.3	52.4	53.0	54.3	55.2	54.3		57.2	60.8	61.4	61.7	61.8	61.7		12.1	13.8	13.6	11.9	10.8	12.0
Germany	52.2|	56.3|	57.3	58.1	58.9	59.0		55.5|	62.5|	63.0	63.3	64.0	64.4		6.0|	9.9|	8.9	8.1	8.0	8.4
Greece	37.5|	40.3	40.7	41.3	41.2	42.7		42.6|	48.5	49.7	49.7	48.8	50.2		12.0|	16.8	18.2	16.9	15.6	14.9
Hungary	..	47.3	49.0	49.6	49.8	49.8		..	50.8	52.3	52.6	52.4	52.7		..	6.9	6.3	5.7	5.0	5.4
Iceland[b, c]	74.5	78.3	80.2	81.0	81.1	79.8		76.8	80.9	82.3	83.3	83.1	82.2		3.0	3.3	2.5	2.8	2.5	2.9
Ireland	36.6|	48.2	51.3	53.3	54.0	55.2		42.6|	52.1	54.3	55.7	56.0	57.3		14.0|	7.5	5.5	4.2	3.5	3.7
Italy	36.2	36.4	38.3	39.6	41.1	42.0		44.0	43.5	45.5	46.3	47.3	47.9		17.7	16.3	15.8	14.6	13.1	12.3
Japan	55.8	57.2	56.7	56.7	57.0	56.5		57.1	59.8	59.5	59.6	60.1	59.7		2.3	4.2	4.7	4.7	5.1	5.4
Korea	49.0	47.3	48.1	50.1	51.0	52.0		49.9	50.3	50.8	51.8	52.7	53.4		1.9	5.9	5.3	3.5	3.2	2.7
Luxembourg	41.4|	45.6	48.5	50.0	50.8	51.5		42.4|	47.6	50.2	51.7	52.0	53.5		2.5|	4.2	3.3	3.2	2.2	3.6
Mexico[c]	34.2	40.1	39.8	40.1	39.4	39.9		35.7	41.6	40.9	41.2	40.4	41.0		4.3	3.6	2.7	2.5	2.4	2.5
Netherlands	47.5	59.4	61.6	62.6	63.9	64.7		53.1	62.9	64.5	65.4	66.1	67.1		10.6	5.5	4.5	4.2	3.4	3.6
New Zealand	58.5	62.1	63.0	63.5	64.8	65.4		63.2	67.1	67.4	67.5	68.5	69.1		7.3	7.5	6.6	5.9	5.3	5.4
Norway[b]	67.2|	73.6	73.8	74.0	73.8	73.9		70.7|	76.1	76.1	76.5	76.4	76.7		4.9|	3.3	3.0	3.2	3.4	3.7
Poland	..	52.2	51.6|	48.9	47.8	46.4		..	59.7	59.8|	59.9	59.9	58.9		..	12.6	13.8|	18.4	20.2	21.2
Portugal	55.4|	58.3	59.5	60.5	61.0	60.8		59.6|	62.4	62.9	63.8	64.5	65.0		7.0|	6.5	5.3	5.2	5.4	6.5
Slovak Republic	..	53.5|	52.1|	51.5	51.8	51.4		..	61.7|	62.3|	63.2	63.8	63.2		..	13.2|	16.4|	18.6	18.8	18.7
Spain[b]	31.6	36.5	39.1	42.0	43.8|	44.9		41.8	49.9	50.9	52.9	51.6|	53.7		24.4	26.7	23.2	20.6	15.3|	16.4
Sweden[b]	81.0|	69.4	70.9	72.2	73.5	73.4		82.5|	75.5	76.0	76.4	77.1	77.1		1.8|	8.0	6.7	5.4	4.7	4.7
Switzerland[c]	66.4	68.8	69.6	69.3	70.6	71.6		68.2	71.8	72.2	71.6	73.2	73.9		2.6	4.2	3.6	3.2	3.5	3.1
Turkey	32.9	27.9	29.1	25.3	25.0	25.6		36.0	30.1	31.6	27.2	27.2	28.5		8.7	7.1	7.9	6.8	8.2	10.3
United Kingdom[b]	62.8	64.2	64.9	65.5	66.1	66.3		67.3	67.9	68.4	68.9	69.0	69.3		6.6	5.3	5.1	4.8	4.2	4.4
United States[b]	64.0	67.4	67.6|	67.8	67.1	66.1		67.8	70.7	70.7|	70.7	70.4	70.1		5.6	4.7	4.4|	4.1	4.7	5.7

Table B. **Employment/population ratios, activity and unemployment rates**[a] (cont.)

Women aged 15-64 years (percentages)

	Employment/population ratio							Labour force participation rate							Unemployment rate						
	1990	1998	1999	2000	2001	2002		1990	1998	1999	2000	2001	2002		1990	1998	1999	2000	2001	2002
European Union[d]	48.7	51.7	53.0	54.2	55.1	55.7		54.6	58.5	59.5	60.1	60.3	61.0		10.9	11.7	10.9	9.8	8.7	8.8
OECD Europe[d]	47.2	49.5	50.5	50.6	51.2	51.5		52.7	55.6	56.5	56.4	56.5	57.1		10.4	11.1	10.7	10.2	9.5	9.7
Total OECD[d]	52.4	54.4	55.0	55.3	55.4	55.4		56.3	58.9	59.3	59.4	59.4	59.6		7.0	7.6	7.3	6.9	6.7	7.2

a) Ratios refer to persons aged 15 to 64 years who are in employment or in the labour force divided by the working age population, or in unemployment divided by the labour force.
b) Refers to persons aged 16 to 64.
c) The year 1990 refers to 1991.
d) For above countries only.

Source: OECD database on Labour Force Statistics (see URLs at the beginning of the Annex). For Austria, Belgium, Denmark, Greece and Luxembourg data are from the European Union Labour Force Survey.

Table C. Employment/population ratios, activity and unemployment rates by selected age groups

Both sexes (percentages)

		15 to 24					25 to 54					55 to 64				
		1990	1999	2000	2001	2002	1990	1999	2000	2001	2002	1990	1999	2000	2001	2002
Australia	Unemployment rates	13.2	13.5	12.3	12.7	12.4	5.1	5.4	4.9	5.3	4.7	5.4	5.8	4.0	4.7	3.6
	Labour force participation rates	70.4	68.4	69.0	69.4	68.6	79.9	79.6	80.5	80.6	81.0	44.1	46.9	49.0	48.6	50.1
	Employment/population ratios	61.1	59.2	60.5	60.6	60.0	75.8	75.3	76.5	76.4	77.2	41.8	44.2	47.1	46.3	48.3
Austria	Unemployment rates	..	5.9	6.3	6.0	7.2	..	4.5	4.3	3.6	4.5	..	4.8	6.7	5.6	5.8
	Labour force participation rates	..	58.4	56.1	54.7	55.7	..	85.1	85.3	85.2	86.6	..	30.7	31.4	29.0	29.8
	Employment/population ratios	..	54.9	52.5	51.4	51.7	..	81.3	81.6	82.2	82.7	..	29.2	29.2	27.4	28.1
Belgium	Unemployment rates	14.5|	22.6	15.2	15.3	15.7	6.5|	7.4	5.8	5.4	6.2	3.6|	5.7	3.2	3.0	3.5
	Labour force participation rates	35.5|	32.9	35.7	33.6	33.8	76.7|	82.5	82.8	80.9	81.7	22.2|	26.2	25.9	26.0	26.7
	Employment/population ratios	30.4|	25.5	30.3	28.5	28.5	71.7|	76.4	77.9	76.6	76.6	21.4|	24.7	25.0	25.2	25.8
Canada	Unemployment rates	12.4	14.0	12.6	12.8	13.7	7.3	6.4	5.8	6.2	6.6	6.0	5.9	5.4	5.9	6.2
	Labour force participation rates	69.7	63.5	64.4	64.7	66.3	84.2	84.6	84.8	85.1	85.9	49.3	49.9	51.2	51.3	53.7
	Employment/population ratios	61.1	54.6	56.3	56.4	57.3	78.0	79.2	79.9	79.8	80.2	46.3	46.9	48.4	48.3	50.4
Czech Republic	Unemployment rates	..	17.0	17.0	16.6	16.0	..	7.5	7.7	7.2	6.5	..	4.8	5.2	4.9	4.0
	Labour force participation rates	..	48.3	46.1	43.2	40.1	..	88.6	88.4	88.4	88.2	..	39.4	38.2	39.0	42.5
	Employment/population ratios	..	40.1	38.3	36.1	33.7	..	81.9	81.6	82.1	82.5	..	37.5	36.3	37.1	40.8
Denmark	Unemployment rates	11.5|	10.0	6.7	8.3	7.1	7.9|	4.3	4.1	3.5	3.7	6.1|	4.2	4.0	4.0	4.7
	Labour force participation rates	73.5|	73.3	71.9	67.2	68.8	91.2|	88.2	87.9	87.5	88.0	57.1|	56.6	56.9	58.9	60.1
	Employment/population ratios	65.0|	66.0	67.1	61.7	64.0	84.0|	84.4	84.3	84.5	84.7	53.6|	54.2	54.6	56.5	57.3
Finland	Unemployment rates	9.4	21.5	21.5	19.9	20.7	2.1	8.4	8.0	7.4	7.3	2.3	10.2	9.4	8.9	8.1
	Labour force participation rates	57.5	49.4	50.8	50.4	49.6	89.7	87.7	87.9	88.0	88.1	43.8	43.7	46.6	50.3	52.0
	Employment/population ratios	52.2	38.8	39.8	40.3	39.4	87.9	80.3	80.9	81.5	81.6	42.8	39.2	42.3	45.9	47.8
France	Unemployment rates	19.1	26.5	20.7	18.7	20.7	8.0	10.6	9.2	8.1	9.2	6.7	8.7	7.9	6.1	7.9
	Labour force participation rates	36.4	28.2	29.3	29.9	29.5	84.1	86.2	86.2	86.3	86.2	38.1	37.5	37.3	38.8	37.2
	Employment/population ratios	29.5	20.7	23.2	24.3	23.3	77.4	77.0	78.3	79.3	78.3	35.6	34.2	34.3	36.5	34.2
Germany	Unemployment rates	4.5|	8.6	8.4	8.3	9.7	4.6|	7.6	7.0	7.2	8.2	7.7|	13.5	12.8	11.8	10.6
	Labour force participation rates	59.1|	51.6	51.5	51.1	50.4	77.1|	85.2	85.3	85.6	85.7	39.8|	43.7	43.0	43.0	43.0
	Employment/population ratios	56.4|	47.1	47.2	46.8	45.6	73.6|	78.7	79.3	79.4	78.7	36.8|	37.8	37.6	37.9	38.4
Greece	Unemployment rates	23.3|	31.7	29.5	28.0	25.7	5.1|	9.8	9.6	8.8	8.6	1.6|	4.4	3.8	4.1	3.6
	Labour force participation rates	39.4|	39.3	38.1	36.2	36.3	72.2|	77.6	77.6	77.2	78.2	41.5|	40.2	40.6	39.6	40.7
	Employment/population ratios	30.3|	26.8	26.9	26.0	27.0	68.5|	70.0	70.2	70.4	71.5	40.8|	38.4	39.0	38.0	39.2

Table C. Employment/population ratios, activity and unemployment rates by selected age groups (cont.)

Both sexes (percentages)

		15 to 24					25 to 54					55 to 64				
		1990	1999	2000	2001	2002	1990	1999	2000	2001	2002	1990	1999	2000	2001	2002
Hungary	Unemployment rates	..	12.4	12.7	11.2	12.6	..	6.2	5.7	5.1	5.2	..	2.7	3.0	2.9	3.1
	Labour force participation rates	..	40.7	37.2	34.6	32.6	..	77.1	77.3	77.1	77.0	..	19.9	22.6	24.2	26.4
	Employment/population ratios	..	35.7	32.5	30.7	28.5	..	72.3	73.0	73.1	73.0	..	19.4	21.9	23.5	25.6
Iceland[a, b]	Unemployment rates	4.9	4.4	4.7	4.8	7.2	2.2	1.4	1.7	1.7	2.7	2.1	1.4	1.7	2.0	1.4
	Labour force participation rates	59.5	68.1	71.6	70.2	64.0	90.1	92.1	92.2	92.3	92.5	87.2	87.1	85.7	87.3	88.4
	Employment/population ratios	56.6	65.1	68.2	66.8	59.4	88.1	90.9	90.6	90.7	90.0	85.4	85.9	84.2	85.6	87.2
Ireland	Unemployment rates	17.7	8.5	6.4	6.2	7.7	12.5	5.3	4.0	3.2	3.7	8.4	4.3	2.5	2.6	2.4
	Labour force participation rates	50.3	50.7	51.6	50.1	49.1	68.5	77.3	78.5	78.9	79.5	42.1	45.7	46.3	47.9	49.2
	Employment/population ratios	41.4	46.4	48.2	47.0	45.3	60.0	73.2	75.3	76.4	76.6	38.6	43.8	45.2	46.6	48.0
Italy	Unemployment rates	31.5	31.1	29.7	27.0	26.3	7.3	9.2	8.5	7.9	7.5	1.8	4.8	4.5	4.3	4.1
	Labour force participation rates	43.5	39.6	39.5	37.6	36.3	70.0	73.8	74.3	75.1	75.8	22.3	29.0	29.0	29.2	30.1
	Employment/population ratios	29.8	27.3	27.8	27.4	26.7	64.9	67.1	68.0	69.2	70.1	21.9	27.6	27.7	28.0	28.9
Japan	Unemployment rates	4.3	9.3	9.2	9.7	10.0	1.6	4.0	4.1	4.4	4.9	2.7	5.4	5.6	5.7	5.8
	Labour force participation rates	44.1	47.2	47.0	46.5	45.6	80.9	81.9	81.9	82.2	82.0	64.7	67.1	66.5	65.8	65.4
	Employment/population ratios	42.2	42.9	42.7	42.0	41.0	79.6	78.7	78.6	78.6	78.0	62.9	63.4	62.8	62.0	61.6
Korea	Unemployment rates	7.0	14.0	10.2	9.7	8.1	1.9	5.8	3.7	3.4	2.8	0.8	4.5	2.6	2.1	1.6
	Labour force participation rates	35.0	32.1	32.8	33.3	34.2	74.6	74.6	75.0	75.1	75.5	62.4	61.0	59.4	59.5	60.4
	Employment/population ratios	32.5	27.6	29.4	30.1	31.5	73.2	70.3	72.2	72.6	73.4	61.9	58.2	57.8	58.3	59.5
Luxembourg	Unemployment rates	3.6	6.8	6.4	6.3	7.0	1.4	2.0	2.0	1.4	2.4	0.6	1.0	1.4	0.3	0.2
	Labour force participation rates	44.9	34.0	34.0	34.5	34.7	72.8	78.3	79.8	79.8	81.0	28.4	26.5	27.6	24.9	27.9
	Employment/population ratios	43.3	31.7	31.8	32.3	32.3	71.8	76.7	78.2	78.7	79.1	28.2	26.3	27.2	24.8	27.9
Mexico[b]	Unemployment rates	5.4	3.4	4.4	4.1	4.9	2.2	1.8	1.5	1.6	1.8	1.0	0.8	1.2	1.0	1.3
	Labour force participation rates	52.2	52.3	51.8	49.7	48.4	65.9	69.2	69.3	68.9	69.6	54.6	55.5	53.5	52.6	53.8
	Employment/population ratios	49.3	50.5	49.6	47.7	46.0	64.4	67.9	68.3	67.8	68.4	54.1	55.0	52.8	52.1	53.1
Netherlands	Unemployment rates	11.1	7.0	6.6	5.8	5.9	6.7	2.8	2.7	2.1	2.6	3.7	2.9	2.4	1.9	2.3
	Labour force participation rates	61.4	70.9	71.2	71.1	71.1	76.3	82.7	83.3	83.7	84.2	30.8	36.2	38.9	39.5	42.7
	Employment/population ratios	54.5	66.0	66.5	67.0	66.9	71.2	80.4	81.1	81.9	81.9	29.7	35.1	37.9	38.8	41.8
New Zealand	Unemployment rates	14.1	13.8	13.2	11.8	11.4	6.1	5.4	4.5	4.1	4.0	4.6	4.9	4.7	3.5	3.2
	Labour force participation rates	67.9	63.4	63.0	63.5	64.2	81.2	82.1	82.3	82.7	83.0	43.8	59.8	60.0	62.9	65.5
	Employment/population ratios	58.3	54.6	54.7	56.0	56.8	76.3	77.6	78.6	79.3	79.7	41.8	56.9	57.2	60.7	63.4

Table C. Employment/population ratios, activity and unemployment rates by selected age groups (cont.)

Both sexes (percentages)

		15 to 24					25 to 54					55 to 64				
		1990	1999	2000	2001	2002	1990	1999	2000	2001	2002	1990	1999	2000	2001	2002
Norway[a]	Unemployment rates	11.8	9.6	10.2	10.5	11.5	4.3	2.4	2.6	2.6	3.0	2.5	1.1	1.3	1.6	1.8
	Labour force participation rates	60.5	63.9	64.7	63.1	64.2	85.9	87.6	87.6	87.4	87.1	63.1	68.0	68.0	68.5	69.7
	Employment/population ratios	53.4	57.8	58.1	56.5	56.9	82.2	85.5	85.3	85.1	84.4	61.5	67.3	67.1	67.4	68.4
Poland	Unemployment rates	..	30.0	35.2	41.0	43.9	..	10.8	13.9	15.8	17.5	..	7.7	9.4	9.7	10.5
	Labour force participation rates	..	34.7	37.8	37.4	35.6	..	82.6	82.4	82.2	81.8	..	35.2	31.3	32.1	31.2
	Employment/population ratios	..	24.3	24.5	22.1	20.0	..	73.7	70.9	69.3	67.5	..	32.5	28.4	29.0	27.9
Portugal	Unemployment rates	9.6	8.8	8.6	9.4	11.5	3.8	4.0	3.5	3.5	4.5	2.1	3.1	3.3	3.2	3.7
	Labour force participation rates	60.6	46.7	46.0	47.1	47.3	81.5	84.0	84.7	85.2	85.4	48.0	52.0	52.5	51.7	52.9
	Employment/population ratios	54.8	42.6	42.0	42.7	41.9	78.4	80.6	81.8	82.2	81.5	47.0	50.4	50.8	50.0	50.9
Slovak Republic	Unemployment rates	..	33.8	37.0	39.1	37.4	..	13.1	15.5	15.9	15.3	..	9.5	12.3	12.3	15.3
	Labour force participation rates	..	46.8	46.0	45.8	43.5	..	87.6	88.4	88.9	88.6	..	24.6	24.3	25.4	27.0
	Employment/population ratios	..	31.0	29.0	27.9	27.2	..	76.1	74.7	74.8	75.1	..	22.3	21.3	22.3	22.9
Spain	Unemployment rates	30.1	28.3	25.3	20.8	22.2	13.1	14.0	12.3	9.3	10.2	8.1	9.7	9.4	6.3	7.1
	Labour force participation rates	54.9	48.0	48.5	46.8	47.0	70.3	76.8	78.0	76.5	78.1	40.0	38.8	40.9	41.9	42.7
	Employment/population ratios	38.3	34.4	36.3	37.1	36.6	61.1	66.1	68.4	69.5	70.1	36.8	35.1	37.0	39.2	39.7
Sweden[a]	Unemployment rates	4.5	14.2	11.9	11.8	12.8	1.3	6.2	4.9	4.1	4.2	1.5	6.6	6.1	4.9	4.7
	Labour force participation rates	69.1	51.1	52.3	54.3	53.3	92.8	88.0	88.1	88.2	87.9	70.5	68.6	69.4	70.4	71.7
	Employment/population ratios	66.0	43.8	46.1	47.9	46.5	91.6	82.6	83.8	84.6	84.2	69.4	64.0	65.1	67.0	68.3
Switzerland[b]	Unemployment rates	3.2	5.6	4.8	5.6	5.7	1.6	2.6	2.3	2.1	2.7	1.1	2.5	2.7	1.7	2.0
	Labour force participation rates	71.6	68.6	68.3	67.8	69.2	85.9	87.5	87.4	87.9	88.4	63.8	66.4	65.1	68.2	66.1
	Employment/population ratios	69.3	64.7	65.0	64.0	65.3	84.5	85.2	85.4	86.1	86.0	63.1	64.7	63.3	67.1	64.8
Turkey	Unemployment rates	16.0	15.2	13.2	16.7	19.5	5.4	5.8	5.0	6.7	8.8	3.1	1.8	2.4	2.4	3.7
	Labour force participation rates	54.7	46.4	41.6	40.7	39.9	65.1	62.1	59.3	59.0	59.4	44.1	41.3	36.2	35.5	35.4
	Employment/population ratios	45.9	39.3	36.1	33.9	32.1	61.6	58.5	56.3	55.0	54.2	42.7	40.6	35.3	34.7	34.1
United Kingdom[a]	Unemployment rates	10.1	12.3	11.8	10.5	11.0	5.8	4.9	4.4	3.9	4.1	7.2	5.1	4.4	3.3	3.5
	Labour force participation rates	78.0	69.2	69.7	68.2	68.6	83.9	83.8	84.1	83.9	84.0	53.0	52.1	52.8	54.0	55.2
	Employment/population ratios	70.1	60.7	61.5	61.1	61.0	79.1	79.7	80.4	80.7	80.6	49.2	49.4	50.5	52.2	53.3
United States[a]	Unemployment rates	11.2	9.9	9.3	10.6	12.0	4.6	3.2	3.1	3.8	4.8	3.3	2.7	2.5	3.0	3.9
	Labour force participation rates	67.3	65.5	65.8	64.5	63.3	83.5	84.1	84.0	83.7	83.3	55.9	59.3	59.2	60.4	61.9
	Employment/population ratios	59.8	59.0	59.7	57.7	55.7	79.7	81.4	81.5	80.5	79.3	54.0	57.7	57.8	58.6	59.5

Table C. Employment/population ratios, activity and unemployment rates by selected age groups (cont.)
Both sexes (percentages)

		15 to 24					25 to 54					55 to 64				
	1990	1999	2000	2001	2002	1990	1999	2000	2001	2002	1990	1999	2000	2001	2002
European Union[c] Unemployment rates	16.2|	17.4	15.7	14.1|	14.7	6.8|	8.1	7.3	6.5|	6.9	6.1|	8.3	7.5	6.5|	6.1
Labour force participation rates	53.9|	48.0	48.4	47.6|	47.5	78.0|	82.1	82.4	82.4|	82.8	40.6|	41.1	41.4	42.0|	43.2
Employment/population ratios	45.2|	39.6	40.8	40.8|	40.5	72.7|	75.5	76.4	77.0|	77.1	38.1|	37.7	38.3	39.3|	40.6
OECD Europe[c] Unemployment rates	15.8|	17.6|	16.7	16.6|	17.6	6.5|	8.0|	7.5	7.2|	7.9	5.6|	7.4|	7.0	6.1|	6.0
Labour force participation rates	54.3|	46.8|	46.3	45.4|	44.9	76.7|	80.2|	80.0	79.9|	80.2	41.6|	40.7|	40.4	41.0|	42.0
Employment/population ratios	45.7|	38.6|	38.6	37.9|	37.1	71.7|	73.8|	74.0	74.1|	73.9	39.3|	37.7|	37.6	38.5|	39.5
Total OECD[c] Unemployment rates	11.7|	12.5|	11.8	12.2|	13.1	4.8|	5.7|	5.3	5.4|	6.0	3.9|	5.3|	4.9	4.7|	4.9
Labour force participation rates	55.5|	51.9|	51.8	50.9|	50.3	78.6|	80.4|	80.4	80.2|	80.3	50.6|	50.7|	50.4	50.8|	51.9
Employment/population ratios	49.0|	45.4|	45.7	44.7|	43.7	74.8|	75.9|	76.1	75.9|	75.5	48.7|	48.0|	47.9	48.4|	49.4

Table C. Employment/population ratios, activity and unemployment rates by selected age groups

Men (percentages)

		15 to 24					25 to 54					55 to 64				
		1990	1999	2000	2001	2002	1990	1999	2000	2001	2002	1990	1999	2000	2001	2002
Australia	Unemployment rates	13.9	14.7	13.1	13.3	13.3	4.9	5.5	5.2	5.5	4.7	6.3	6.3	4.9	5.6	4.7
	Labour force participation rates	73.0	70.8	69.8	71.1	70.0	93.1	90.0	90.3	89.9	90.1	63.2	61.7	61.5	60.0	61.1
	Employment/population ratios	62.8	60.3	60.6	61.6	60.7	88.5	85.0	85.6	85.0	85.9	59.2	57.8	58.5	56.7	58.3
Austria	Unemployment rates	..	5.5	6.9	6.2	7.8	..	4.5	4.2	3.4	4.7	..	5.3	7.1	5.7	6.8
	Labour force participation rates	..	62.6	60.7	59.3	60.6	..	93.8	93.6	93.5	93.9	..	43.9	44.5	40.2	40.8
	Employment/population ratios	..	59.2	56.5	55.6	55.9	..	89.6	89.7	90.3	89.5	..	41.6	41.4	37.9	38.1
Belgium	Unemployment rates	10.1 |	22.7	12.9	14.3	16.0	4.0 |	6.1	4.6	4.8	5.4	3.1 |	4.5	3.4	3.9	3.3
	Labour force participation rates	37.0 |	35.5	38.7	37.2	37.3	92.2 |	91.8	92.1	90.9	91.2	35.4 |	36.8	36.3	36.6	36.3
	Employment/population ratios	33.3 |	27.5	33.7	31.8	31.3	88.5 |	86.2	87.9	86.5	86.2	34.3 |	35.1	35.1	35.1	35.1
Canada	Unemployment rates	13.6	15.3	13.9	14.5	15.3	7.2	6.5	5.7	6.3	6.9	6.2	6.3	5.4	6.0	6.5
	Labour force participation rates	72.2	65.3	65.9	66.1	67.7	93.1	91.1	91.1	91.1	91.5	64.3	60.7	61.0	61.2	64.0
	Employment/population ratios	62.3	55.4	56.7	56.5	57.3	86.4	85.1	85.9	85.4	85.3	60.3	56.9	57.7	57.6	59.8
Czech Republic	Unemployment rates	..	15.9	16.7	16.0	15.1	..	5.9	6.0	5.5	4.9	..	4.6	5.0	4.4	3.5
	Labour force participation rates	..	54.2	51.3	48.2	44.8	..	95.1	94.9	95.0	94.9	..	56.2	54.5	55.0	59.4
	Employment/population ratios	..	45.6	42.8	40.5	38.0	..	89.5	89.3	89.7	90.2	..	53.6	51.7	52.6	57.3
Denmark	Unemployment rates	11.4 |	9.5	6.5	7.3	8.8	7.5 |	3.7	3.5	2.9	3.3	5.1 |	3.2	3.9	4.0	5.0
	Labour force participation rates	76.5 |	76.7	75.2	69.4	70.6	94.5 |	92.7	91.5	91.4	91.7	69.1 |	61.9	64.5	65.6	67.6
	Employment/population ratios	67.8 |	69.5	70.3	64.3	64.4	87.4 |	89.3	88.3	88.8	88.7	65.6 |	59.9	61.9	63.0	64.2
Finland	Unemployment rates	10.4	21.0	21.2	19.6	20.9	2.5	7.9	7.2	6.9	7.4	1.8	11.0	9.3	8.9	8.2
	Labour force participation rates	58.1	49.7	50.4	50.0	48.8	92.9	90.6	90.7	91.0	90.6	47.1	45.0	48.1	51.2	52.6
	Employment/population ratios	52.1	39.3	39.8	40.2	38.6	90.6	83.4	84.1	84.7	84.0	46.3	40.1	43.7	46.7	48.3
France	Unemployment rates	15.3	24.2	18.4	16.2	18.4	5.9	8.9	7.5	6.3	7.6	6.0	8.7	7.6	5.6	7.6
	Labour force participation rates	39.6	31.9	32.6	33.1	32.7	95.4	94.1	94.2	94.1	94.1	45.8	42.7	41.7	43.8	41.6
	Employment/population ratios	33.6	24.2	26.6	27.8	26.7	89.8	85.7	87.1	88.1	87.0	43.0	39.0	38.5	41.4	38.4
Germany	Unemployment rates	4.0 |	9.3	9.2	9.3	11.3	3.7 |	7.1	6.6	7.1	8.3	7.0 |	12.8	11.5	11.2	10.0
	Labour force participation rates	61.2 |	54.9	54.7	54.0	53.0	90.2 |	93.6	93.5	93.3	93.0	55.9 |	53.8	52.5	52.2	52.2
	Employment/population ratios	58.7 |	49.8	49.7	49.0	47.1	86.9 |	87.0	87.3	86.7	85.3	52.0 |	46.9	46.4	46.4	47.0
Greece	Unemployment rates	15.1 |	23.0	22.1	21.0	18.7	3.2 |	6.2	6.1	5.5	5.4	1.8 |	4.1	3.5	4.1	3.3
	Labour force participation rates	44.1 |	41.3	41.0	38.5	39.4	94.3 |	94.5	94.3	94.0	94.1	59.5 |	57.1	57.3	57.0	57.0
	Employment/population ratios	37.4 |	31.8	31.9	30.4	32.0	91.3 |	88.7	88.6	88.8	89.0	58.4 |	54.8	55.3	54.6	55.1

Table C. Employment/population ratios, activity and unemployment rates by selected age groups (cont.)

Men (percentages)

		15 to 24					25 to 54					55 to 64				
		1990	1999	2000	2001	2002	1990	1999	2000	2001	2002	1990	1999	2000	2001	2002
Hungary	Unemployment rates	..	13.2	13.8	12.2	13.2	..	6.7	6.2	5.7	5.4	..	3.4	3.7	3.7	3.9
	Labour force participation rates	..	46.2	41.8	39.2	36.0	..	84.4	84.4	84.2	84.3	..	30.8	34.1	35.4	36.9
	Employment/population ratios	..	40.0	36.0	34.4	31.2	..	78.7	79.2	79.4	79.7	..	29.7	32.8	34.1	35.4
Iceland[a, b]	Unemployment rates	5.8	4.4	5.7	5.4	9.7	1.8	0.7	1.1	1.3	2.5	1.0	0.9	0.5	2.0	1.7
	Labour force participation rates	60.1	66.2	70.1	70.3	65.4	97.0	97.1	96.1	96.3	96.6	93.5	94.1	94.7	92.8	91.5
	Employment/population ratios	56.6	63.3	66.1	66.6	59.0	95.2	96.4	95.1	95.0	94.2	92.6	93.2	94.2	91.0	89.9
Ireland	Unemployment rates	19.0 |	8.6	6.1	6.4	8.7	12.0 |	5.7	4.3	3.4	4.1	8.5 |	4.2	2.6	2.6	2.5
	Labour force participation rates	53.2 |	54.4	56.1	55.1	53.1	91.8 |	91.6	92.0	91.8	91.3	65.0 |	64.4	64.7	66.4	66.8
	Employment/population ratios	43.1 |	49.8	52.7	51.5	48.5	80.9 |	86.4	88.1	88.7	87.6	59.5 |	61.7	63.0	64.6	65.1
Italy	Unemployment rates	26.2	26.6	25.4	23.2	22.6	4.5	6.8	6.3	5.8	5.6	1.6	4.7	4.4	4.4	4.0
	Labour force participation rates	46.1	45.1	44.6	42.4	41.4	90.9	90.5	90.6	90.7	91.0	36.0	43.3	42.7	42.3	42.9
	Employment/population ratios	34.0	33.1	33.2	32.6	32.0	86.8	84.4	84.9	85.5	86.0	35.4	41.2	40.9	40.4	41.2
Japan	Unemployment rates	4.5	10.3	10.4	10.7	11.3	1.4	3.7	3.9	4.2	4.7	3.4	6.7	6.8	7.0	7.1
	Labour force participation rates	43.4	47.7	47.4	46.5	46.2	97.5	97.1	97.1	96.9	96.5	83.3	85.2	84.1	83.4	82.8
	Employment/population ratios	41.4	42.8	42.5	41.6	41.0	96.2	93.6	93.4	92.8	92.0	80.4	79.5	78.4	77.5	76.8
Korea	Unemployment rates	9.5	17.5	12.7	12.1	9.9	2.5	6.7	4.3	4.0	3.3	1.2	6.2	3.6	2.9	2.1
	Labour force participation rates	28.4	27.9	28.2	27.6	28.4	94.6	92.3	92.0	91.6	91.7	77.2	73.9	71.0	71.7	73.7
	Employment/population ratios	25.7	23.0	24.6	24.3	25.6	92.2	86.1	88.0	87.9	88.7	76.3	69.3	68.5	69.6	72.1
Luxembourg	Unemployment rates	2.7 |	6.2	5.7	7.1	5.3	1.0 |	1.4	1.4	1.1	1.8	0.6 |	0.7	2.0	0.5	0.3
	Labour force participation rates	45.7 |	36.0	37.4	36.8	38.2	95.0 |	94.2	94.2	94.2	95.0	43.2 |	35.6	38.6	35.5	37.7
	Employment/population ratios	44.5 |	33.7	35.3	34.2	36.1	94.0 |	92.9	92.8	93.2	93.3	42.9 |	35.4	37.9	35.3	37.6
Mexico[b]	Unemployment rates	5.2	2.8	4.2	3.6	4.5	1.5	1.6	1.4	1.6	1.8	1.0	1.0	1.4	1.2	1.7
	Labour force participation rates	71.2	69.4	68.4	66.2	64.4	96.8	96.3	96.3	96.2	96.2	85.9	82.0	80.8	80.4	81.1
	Employment/population ratios	67.5	67.5	65.6	63.8	61.5	95.4	94.8	95.0	94.6	94.5	85.1	81.2	79.7	79.5	79.7
Netherlands	Unemployment rates	10.0	6.3	5.6	5.5	6.3	4.5	2.1	2.0	1.6	2.2	3.2	2.4	2.7	1.9	1.9
	Labour force participation rates	61.8	71.0	72.1	71.8	72.0	93.4	93.5	93.5	93.4	93.3	45.7	48.4	51.4	52.0	55.8
	Employment/population ratios	55.6	66.6	68.1	67.8	67.5	89.2	91.5	91.6	91.9	91.2	44.2	47.3	50.0	51.0	54.7
New Zealand	Unemployment rates	14.9	14.6	14.1	12.1	11.5	6.6	5.5	4.4	4.0	3.8	5.0	5.5	5.4	4.0	3.2
	Labour force participation rates	71.4	66.9	65.9	66.5	67.1	93.4	91.1	91.4	91.3	91.4	56.8	71.6	72.2	74.3	77.3
	Employment/population ratios	60.7	57.2	56.6	58.5	59.4	87.3	86.0	87.3	87.6	88.0	53.9	67.7	68.3	71.3	74.9

Table C. Employment/population ratios, activity and unemployment rates by selected age groups (cont.)

Men (percentages)

		15 to 24					25 to 54					55 to 64				
		1990	1999	2000	2001	2002	1990	1999	2000	2001	2002	1990	1999	2000	2001	2002
Norway[a]	Unemployment rates	12.4|	9.6	9.5	10.6	12.4	4.7|	2.6	2.9	2.7	3.2	3.0|	1.3	1.8	1.7	1.6
	Labour force participation rates	63.9|	66.7	67.5	64.8	64.7	92.3|	91.8	91.4	91.4	91.0	72.8|	74.5	74.4	73.6	74.0
	Employment/population ratios	56.0|	60.2	61.0	57.9	56.6	88.0|	89.4	88.8	88.9	88.1	70.7|	73.6	73.1	72.3	72.8
Poland	Unemployment rates	..	28.3|	33.3	40.1	43.5	..	10.0|	12.1	14.2	16.5	..	8.7|	9.1	10.4	11.2
	Labour force participation rates	..	37.9|	40.9	40.5	39.1	..	88.7|	88.3	88.0	87.6	..	45.8|	40.4	41.5	40.3
	Employment/population ratios	..	27.2|	27.3	24.2	22.1	..	79.8|	77.6	75.5	73.1	..	41.8|	36.7	37.1	35.8
Portugal	Unemployment rates	7.1|	7.1	6.2	7.3	9.7	2.3|	3.5	2.7	2.7	3.5	2.2|	4.0	3.7	3.2	3.7
	Labour force participation rates	66.5|	50.7	50.8	52.1	52.3	94.3|	92.8	92.5	92.7	92.6	66.5|	64.0	64.5	63.3	63.5
	Employment/population ratios	61.8|	47.1	47.7	48.3	47.2	92.1|	89.5	90.0	90.2	89.4	65.0|	61.5	62.1	61.3	61.2
Slovak Republic	Unemployment rates	..	35.3|	39.7	41.8	38.9	..	12.8|	15.2	16.0	14.9	..	10.4|	13.5	12.6	15.6
	Labour force participation rates	..	50.9|	49.4	50.2	47.7	..	93.7|	93.9	94.0	93.4	..	41.1|	41.0	43.0	46.3
	Employment/population ratios	..	32.9|	29.8	29.2	29.2	..	81.7|	79.6	79.0	79.5	..	36.8|	35.4	37.6	39.1
Spain[a]	Unemployment rates	23.2	21.7	19.4	16.1|	18.4	9.3	9.2	8.0	6.3|	6.8	8.3	9.3	8.6	5.6|	5.9
	Labour force participation rates	61.8	53.3	53.6	52.7|	52.4	94.4	92.9	93.0	91.6|	92.1	62.5	57.8	60.5	61.4|	62.2
	Employment/population ratios	47.5	41.8	43.2	44.2|	42.8	85.7	84.3	85.6	85.9|	85.8	57.3	52.4	55.2	57.9|	58.6
Sweden[a]	Unemployment rates	4.5|	14.8	12.3	12.7	13.8	1.3|	6.5	5.2	4.4	4.5	1.3|	7.3	6.9	5.3	5.3
	Labour force participation rates	69.3|	52.6	53.3	54.2	53.0	94.7|	90.3	90.6	90.6	90.0	75.4|	72.3	72.8	73.5	74.7
	Employment/population ratios	66.1|	44.8	46.7	47.3	45.7	93.5|	84.4	85.8	86.6	85.9	74.4|	67.1	67.8	69.6	70.7
Switzerland[b]	Unemployment rates	3.0	5.6	5.6	5.7	7.3	0.8	2.2	1.6	1.0	2.2	1.4	2.5	3.0	1.8	2.1
	Labour force participation rates	72.9	67.9	70.5	68.6	70.7	97.8	97.2	96.7	96.3	96.0	86.4	80.9	79.3	82.4	79.0
	Employment/population ratios	70.7	64.1	66.5	64.7	65.5	97.0	95.1	95.2	95.3	93.8	85.2	78.9	77.0	81.0	77.4
Turkey	Unemployment rates	16.6	15.8	13.7	17.4	20.5	5.2	5.9	5.0	7.1	9.1	4.0	2.6	3.1	3.1	4.8
	Labour force participation rates	71.8	60.3	56.4	54.7	52.1	94.2	91.7	89.4	88.5	88.1	61.3	55.9	52.6	51.5	49.9
	Employment/population ratios	59.9	50.8	48.6	45.2	41.4	89.3	86.3	84.9	82.2	80.1	58.8	54.4	51.0	49.9	47.5
United Kingdom[a]	Unemployment rates	11.1	14.1	13.2	12.0	12.9	5.6	5.4	4.8	4.1	4.4	8.4	6.4	5.5	4.3	4.3
	Labour force participation rates	83.5	73.2	73.7	72.0	72.3	94.8	91.6	91.9	91.3	91.2	68.1	63.5	63.3	64.4	65.0
	Employment/population ratios	74.2	62.9	63.9	63.4	63.0	89.5	86.7	87.5	87.6	87.2	62.4	59.4	59.8	61.6	62.1
United States[a]	Unemployment rates	11.6	10.3|	9.7	11.4	12.8	4.6	3.0|	2.9	3.7	4.8	3.8	2.7|	2.4	3.3	4.3
	Labour force participation rates	71.8	68.0|	68.6	67.0	65.5	93.4	91.7|	91.6	91.3	91.0	67.8	67.9|	67.3	68.3	69.2
	Employment/population ratios	63.5	61.0|	61.9	59.4	57.1	89.1	89.0|	89.0	87.9	86.6	65.2	66.1|	65.7	66.0	66.3

Table C. Employment/population ratios, activity and unemployment rates by selected age groups (cont.)

Men (percentages)

		15 to 24					25 to 54					55 to 64				
		1990	1999	2000	2001	2002	1990	1999	2000	2001	2002	1990	1999	2000	2001	2002
European Union[c]	Unemployment rates	13.9|	16.2	14.5	13.3|	14.5	5.2|	6.8	6.0	5.5|	6.1	6.1|	8.2	7.4	6.4|	6.0
	Labour force participation rates	57.4|	51.8	52.1	51.2|	51.1	93.0|	92.6	92.6	92.3|	92.3	55.2|	52.5	52.4	52.8|	53.8
	Employment/population ratios	49.4|	43.4	44.5	44.4|	43.7	88.2|	86.3	87.0	87.3|	86.7	51.8|	48.2	48.5	49.4|	50.5
OECD Europe[c]	Unemployment rates	14.2|	16.8|	15.8	16.1|	17.7	5.1|	6.9|	6.4	6.3|	7.1	5.7|	7.5|	6.9	6.1|	6.0
	Labour force participation rates	59.9|	52.4|	52.0	50.9|	50.1	93.2|	92.2|	91.9	91.5|	91.4	56.6|	52.5|	51.9	52.3|	53.0
	Employment/population ratios	51.4|	43.6|	43.8	42.7|	41.3	88.5|	85.9|	86.0	85.7|	84.9	53.4|	48.6|	48.3	49.1|	49.8
Total OECD[c]	Unemployment rates	11.2|	12.3|	11.7	12.3|	13.5	4.1|	5.1|	4.7	4.9|	5.6	4.3|	5.7|	5.3	5.2|	5.3
	Labour force participation rates	60.8|	57.1|	57.0	55.9|	55.1	94.1|	92.9|	92.7	92.4|	92.2	66.3|	63.6|	62.8	63.1|	63.8
	Employment/population ratios	54.0|	50.1|	50.3	49.0|	47.6	90.3|	88.1|	88.3	87.8|	87.0	63.5|	59.9|	59.5	59.8|	60.4

Table C. Employment/population ratios, activity and unemployment rates by selected age groups

Women (percentages)

		1990	1999	15 to 24 2000	2001	2002	1990	1999	25 to 54 2000	2001	2002	1990	1999	55 to 64 2000	2001	2002
Australia	Unemployment rates	12.4	12.0	11.5	12.0	11.6	5.5	5.3	4.6	5.0	4.7	3.0	4.7	2.4	3.3	1.8
	Labour force participation rates	67.7	65.9	68.2	67.7	67.1	66.6	69.2	70.7	71.4	71.8	24.9	31.7	36.3	36.9	38.8
	Employment/population ratios	59.3	58.0	60.4	59.5	59.3	62.9	65.6	67.4	67.8	68.5	24.2	30.3	35.4	35.7	38.1
Austria	Unemployment rates	..	6.4	5.6	5.8	6.5	..	4.6	4.4	3.8	4.3	..	3.4	5.9	5.2	3.9
	Labour force participation rates	..	54.2	51.5	50.1	51.0	..	76.3	76.8	76.9	79.2	..	18.3	18.9	18.3	19.4
	Employment/population ratios	..	50.7	48.6	47.2	47.6	..	72.8	73.5	74.0	75.8	..	17.6	17.8	17.4	18.6
Belgium	Unemployment rates	19.2│	22.4	18.2	16.6	15.2	10.3│	9.0	7.4	6.1	7.2	5.0│	8.1	2.8	0.9	3.8
	Labour force participation rates	34.1│	30.1	32.6	30.0	30.2	60.8│	72.9	73.2	70.7	72.0	9.9│	16.1	15.8	15.8	17.4
	Employment/population ratios	27.5│	23.4	26.7	25.0	25.7	54.5│	66.4	67.8	66.4	66.8	9.4│	14.8	15.4	15.6	16.7
Canada	Unemployment rates	11.0	12.6	11.3	11.0	11.8	7.6	6.3	5.8	6.0	6.3	5.7	5.3	5.5	5.6	5.8
	Labour force participation rates	67.3	61.7	62.9	63.3	64.9	75.4	78.2	78.6	79.1	80.2	34.9	39.4	41.6	41.8	43.8
	Employment/population ratios	59.9	53.9	55.8	56.3	57.2	69.7	73.2	74.0	74.3	75.2	33.0	37.3	39.3	39.4	41.3
Czech Republic	Unemployment rates	..	18.5	17.4	17.3	17.3	..	9.5	9.9	9.1	8.3	..	5.1	5.4	5.8	4.9
	Labour force participation rates	..	42.1	40.6	38.0	35.3	..	82.0	81.8	81.8	81.4	..	24.4	23.7	24.6	27.3
	Employment/population ratios	..	34.3	33.6	31.5	29.2	..	74.2	73.7	74.3	74.6	..	23.2	22.4	23.2	26.0
Denmark	Unemployment rates	11.6│	10.5	7.0	9.3	5.2	8.4│	4.9	4.7	4.1	4.2	7.5│	5.6	4.2	4.0	4.2
	Labour force participation rates	70.4│	70.1	68.8	65.0	67.0	87.8│	83.5	84.3	83.5	84.4	45.9│	50.6	48.2	51.9	52.1
	Employment/population ratios	62.2│	62.8	64.0	59.0	63.5	80.3│	79.4	80.4	80.1	80.8	42.4│	47.8	46.2	49.8	49.9
Finland	Unemployment rates	8.3	22.2	21.8	20.2	20.5	1.6	9.0	8.8	8.0	7.3	2.8	9.4	9.4	8.8	8.1
	Labour force participation rates	56.9	49.1	51.1	50.8	50.5	86.5	84.8	85.0	85.0	85.4	40.8	42.4	45.2	49.5	51.4
	Employment/population ratios	52.2	38.2	39.9	40.5	40.1	85.1	77.1	77.6	78.2	79.1	39.7	38.4	40.9	45.1	47.3
France	Unemployment rates	23.9	29.7	23.7	21.8	22.8	10.7	12.6	11.1	10.1	9.4	7.6	8.7	8.3	6.6	5.5
	Labour force participation rates	33.1	24.4	26.0	26.5	26.5	72.9	78.5	78.4	78.7	79.0	31.1	32.6	33.0	34.1	36.6
	Employment/population ratios	25.2	17.1	19.8	20.7	20.4	65.1	68.6	69.6	70.8	71.6	28.8	29.7	30.3	31.8	34.6
Germany	Unemployment rates	5.0│	7.9	7.5	7.1	7.9	6.0│	8.3	7.4	7.5	8.0	9.1│	14.6	13.6	12.7	11.7
	Labour force participation rates	56.8│	48.3	48.2	48.1	47.8	63.4│	76.5	76.9	77.7	78.2	24.7│	33.7	33.5	33.8	33.9
	Employment/population ratios	54.0│	44.5	44.6	44.7	44.0	59.6│	70.2	71.2	71.9	71.9	22.4│	28.8	29.0	29.5	30.0
Greece	Unemployment rates	32.6│	41.0	37.7	35.7	33.7	8.6│	15.2	14.7	13.5	13.2	1.2│	5.0	4.4	4.0	4.3
	Labour force participation rates	35.3│	37.4	35.4	33.9	33.2	51.5│	61.5	61.7	61.3	63.1	24.3│	24.4	25.5	23.7	25.5
	Employment/population ratios	23.8│	22.1	22.0	21.8	22.0	47.1│	52.1	52.6	53.0	54.7	24.0│	23.1	24.4	22.7	24.4

Table C. Employment/population ratios, activity and unemployment rates by selected age groups (cont.)

Women (percentages)

		15 to 24					25 to 54					55 to 64				
		1990	1999	2000	2001	2002	1990	1999	2000	2001	2002	1990	1999	2000	2001	2002
Hungary	Unemployment rates	..	11.3	11.2	10.0	11.9	..	5.6	5.0	4.5	4.9	..	1.3	1.6	1.4	1.9
	Labour force participation rates	..	35.0	32.5	29.9	29.2	..	70.0	70.5	70.1	69.9	..	11.4	13.3	15.1	18.0
	Employment/population ratios	..	31.1	28.8	26.9	25.8	..	66.1	66.9	67.0	66.5	..	11.3	13.1	14.9	17.6
Iceland[a, b]	Unemployment rates	3.9	4.4	3.6	4.3	4.4	2.6	2.1	2.4	2.2	2.9	3.4	1.9	3.2	1.9	1.0
	Labour force participation rates	58.8	70.1	73.2	70.0	62.6	83.0	87.0	88.2	88.1	88.3	81.1	80.3	76.8	81.7	85.3
	Employment/population ratios	56.5	67.0	70.5	67.0	59.8	80.8	85.1	86.0	86.2	85.7	78.3	78.8	74.4	80.2	84.4
Ireland	Unemployment rates	16.1|	8.3	6.9	5.8	6.5	13.5|	4.8	3.6	3.0	3.2	8.3|	4.4	2.4	2.7	2.2
	Labour force participation rates	47.3|	46.9	46.9	44.9	44.9	45.4|	63.0	65.0	66.1	67.8	19.9|	26.9	27.8	29.2	31.4
	Employment/population ratios	39.6|	43.0	43.7	42.3	41.9	39.3|	60.0	62.7	64.1	65.6	18.2|	25.7	27.1	28.4	30.7
Italy	Unemployment rates	37.8	37.4	35.4	32.2	31.4	12.2	13.1	12.1	11.1	10.5	2.3	5.2	4.7	4.1	4.4
	Labour force participation rates	40.8	33.9	34.3	32.6	31.0	49.5	57.1	57.9	59.3	60.3	10.1	15.8	16.1	16.9	18.1
	Employment/population ratios	25.4	21.3	22.1	22.1	21.2	43.5	49.6	50.9	52.8	54.0	9.9	15.0	15.3	16.2	17.3
Japan	Unemployment rates	4.1	8.2	7.9	8.7	8.7	2.1	4.4	4.4	4.7	5.2	1.4	3.3	3.6	3.7	3.6
	Labour force participation rates	44.8	46.7	46.6	46.4	44.8	64.2	66.4	66.5	67.3	67.4	47.2	49.8	49.7	49.2	48.8
	Employment/population ratios	43.0	42.9	43.0	42.4	41.0	62.9	63.6	63.6	64.1	63.9	46.5	48.2	47.9	47.3	47.1
Korea	Unemployment rates	5.5	11.7	8.5	8.1	6.9	0.9	4.4	2.7	2.5	2.0	0.3	2.1	1.2	0.9	0.8
	Labour force participation rates	40.7	35.9	36.8	38.2	39.2	54.2	56.4	57.6	58.2	58.9	49.6	49.2	48.6	48.2	48.0
	Employment/population ratios	38.5	31.7	33.6	35.1	36.5	53.7	53.9	56.0	56.8	57.7	49.4	48.2	48.0	47.8	47.6
Luxembourg	Unemployment rates	4.7|	7.4	7.3	5.4	9.0	2.0|	2.9	2.9	1.9	3.2	0.6|	1.5	0.0	0.0	0.0
	Labour force participation rates	44.0|	31.9	30.6	32.1	31.2	49.7|	62.0	64.9	65.0	66.7	13.8|	17.7	16.8	14.4	18.1
	Employment/population ratios	42.0|	29.5	28.3	30.3	28.4	48.7|	60.2	63.0	63.8	64.5	13.7|	17.5	16.8	14.4	18.1
Mexico[b]	Unemployment rates	5.8	4.5	4.7	5.0	5.6	3.8	2.1	1.7	1.7	1.6	1.0	0.2	0.7	0.5	0.3
	Labour force participation rates	34.5	36.1	36.1	34.3	33.3	38.2	45.0	45.6	45.3	46.5	24.4	29.6	28.6	27.6	29.2
	Employment/population ratios	32.5	34.5	34.4	32.6	31.4	36.8	44.1	44.8	44.6	45.8	24.2	29.5	28.4	27.4	29.1
Netherlands	Unemployment rates	12.3	7.7	7.6	6.1	5.5	10.3	3.8	3.5	2.8	3.2	5.0	3.8	1.9	1.8	2.9
	Labour force participation rates	60.9	70.8	70.3	70.4	70.2	58.5	71.6	72.8	73.8	74.8	16.7	23.8	26.3	26.9	29.5
	Employment/population ratios	53.4	65.3	64.9	66.1	66.3	52.4	68.9	70.2	71.7	72.5	15.9	22.9	25.8	26.5	28.7
New Zealand	Unemployment rates	13.2	12.8	12.1	11.5	11.3	5.4	5.3	4.6	4.1	4.2	4.0	4.1	3.5	2.8	3.3
	Labour force participation rates	64.3	59.6	59.9	60.2	61.1	69.3	73.5	73.8	74.5	75.0	30.7	48.3	48.0	51.8	53.9
	Employment/population ratios	55.8	52.0	52.7	53.3	54.2	65.6	69.6	70.3	71.5	71.8	29.5	46.3	46.3	50.3	52.1

STATISTICAL ANNEX

Table C. Employment/population ratios, activity and unemployment rates by selected age groups (cont.)

Women (percentages)

		15 to 24						25 to 54						55 to 64					
		1990	1999	2000	2001	2002		1990	1999	2000	2001	2002		1990	1999	2000	2001	2002
Norway[a]	Unemployment rates	11.0|	9.5	10.9	10.3	10.5		3.9|	2.2	2.3	2.5	2.8		1.9|	0.8	0.7	1.4	1.9
	Labour force participation rates	56.9|	61.0	61.8	61.3	63.8		79.2|	83.2	83.5	83.3	82.9		53.9|	61.5	61.6	63.2	65.3
	Employment/population ratios	50.7|	55.2	55.0	55.0	57.1		76.1|	81.4	81.6	81.2	80.6		52.8|	61.1	61.2	62.3	64.0
Poland	Unemployment rates	..	32.0|	37.3	42.0	44.4		..	11.8|	16.0	17.6	18.7		..	6.1|	9.7	8.7	9.6
	Labour force participation rates	..	31.5|	34.8	34.4	32.2		..	76.7|	76.5	76.5	76.1		..	26.1|	23.7	24.1	23.3
	Employment/population ratios	..	21.4|	21.8	20.0	17.9		..	67.6|	64.3	63.1	61.9		..	24.5|	21.4	22.0	21.1
Portugal	Unemployment rates	12.8|	10.9	11.6	12.2	13.9		5.8|	4.7	4.4	4.4	5.6		1.8|	1.9	2.7	3.2	3.7
	Labour force participation rates	54.4|	42.7	41.0	42.0	42.2		69.4|	75.6	77.3	78.1	78.3		32.3|	41.5	41.9	41.5	43.5
	Employment/population ratios	47.5|	38.0	36.2	36.9	36.3		65.4|	72.0	73.9	74.6	74.0		31.7|	40.7	40.8	40.2	41.9
Slovak Republic	Unemployment rates	..	32.1|	33.8	35.7	35.5		..	13.4|	15.8	15.8	15.8		..	6.7|	8.7	11.2	14.4
	Labour force participation rates	..	42.8|	42.6	41.5	39.2		..	81.5|	82.9	83.9	83.9		..	11.1|	10.7	11.0	11.2
	Employment/population ratios	..	29.0|	28.2	26.6	25.3		..	70.6|	69.8	70.7	70.6		..	10.3|	9.8	9.8	9.6
Spain[a]	Unemployment rates	39.7	36.9	32.9	27.0|	27.3		21.0	21.2	18.9	13.7|	15.1		7.1	11.0	11.3	8.0|	9.8
	Labour force participation rates	47.7	42.4	43.3	40.7|	41.4		46.9	60.7	62.8	61.2|	63.9		19.4	21.2	22.6	23.6|	24.4
	Employment/population ratios	28.7	26.8	29.0	29.7|	30.1		37.1	47.8	51.0	52.8|	54.2		18.0	18.9	20.1	21.8|	22.0
Sweden[a]	Unemployment rates	4.4	13.6	11.4	10.8	11.9		1.2|	5.9	4.6	3.7	3.8		1.6|	5.9	5.3	4.5	4.0
	Labour force participation rates	68.9|	49.5	51.2	54.4	53.6		90.8|	85.7	85.6	85.6	85.6		65.8|	64.8	65.9	67.3	68.6
	Employment/population ratios	65.9|	42.8	45.4	48.5	47.3		89.7|	80.6	81.7	82.5	82.4		64.8|	61.0	62.4	64.3	65.9
Switzerland[b]	Unemployment rates	3.4	5.7	3.9	5.5	3.9		2.6	3.2	3.1	3.4	3.2		0.6	2.5	2.3	1.6	1.8
	Labour force participation rates	70.3	69.3	66.0	66.9	67.7		73.7	77.6	78.0	79.5	80.7		43.8	52.5	51.3	54.5	53.5
	Employment/population ratios	67.9	65.4	63.4	63.2	65.1		71.8	75.1	75.6	76.8	78.1		43.5	51.1	50.1	53.6	52.5
Turkey	Unemployment rates	15.0	14.2	12.2	15.3	17.8		5.9	5.5	4.7	5.6	7.8		1.0	0.2	0.5	0.5	1.3
	Labour force participation rates	39.4	32.9	27.4	27.1	28.1		36.0	31.5	28.1	28.4	29.8		26.6	27.4	20.5	20.3	21.6
	Employment/population ratios	33.5	28.3	24.0	23.0	23.1		33.9	29.8	26.8	26.8	27.4		26.4	27.4	20.4	20.2	21.3
United Kingdom[a]	Unemployment rates	9.0	10.2	10.1	8.7	8.8		6.0	4.3	4.0	3.6	3.8		5.0	3.2	2.8	1.8	2.3
	Labour force participation rates	72.4	65.0	65.6	64.2	64.8		73.0	75.9	76.1	76.3	76.7		38.7	41.1	42.6	44.0	45.7
	Employment/population ratios	65.9	58.4	58.9	58.6	59.0		68.6	72.6	73.1	73.6	73.8		36.7	39.8	41.4	43.2	44.7
United States[a]	Unemployment rates	10.7	9.5|	8.9	9.6	11.1		4.6	3.4|	3.3	3.9	4.8		2.8	2.6|	2.5	2.7	3.5
	Labour force participation rates	62.9	62.9|	63.0	62.0	61.1		74.0	76.8|	76.7	76.4	75.9		45.2	51.5|	51.9	53.2	55.2
	Employment/population ratios	56.1	57.0|	57.4	56.0	54.3		70.6	74.1|	74.2	73.4	72.3		44.0	50.1|	50.6	51.7	53.2

314   OECD EMPLOYMENT OUTLOOK – ISBN 92-64-10061-X – © OECD 2003

Table C. Employment/population ratios, activity and unemployment rates by selected age groups (cont.)

Women (percentages)

		15 to 24					25 to 54					55 to 64				
		1990	1999	2000	2001	2002	1990	1999	2000	2001	2002	1990	1999	2000	2001	2002
European Union[c]	Unemployment rates	18.8|	18.9	17.2	15.1|	15.1	9.2|	9.8	8.8	7.8|	8.1	6.0|	8.5	7.8	6.6|	6.3
	Labour force participation rates	50.2|	44.1	44.5	43.8	43.7	62.8|	71.5	72.1	72.4|	73.2	27.0|	30.2	30.9	31.7|	33.1
	Employment/population ratios	40.7|	35.7	36.9	37.1|	37.2	57.1|	64.5	65.8	66.7|	67.3	25.4|	27.6	28.5	29.6|	31.0
OECD Europe[c]	Unemployment rates	17.9|	18.7|	17.8	17.1|	17.4	8.7|	9.5|	9.1	8.5|	8.8	5.3|	7.4|	7.1	6.1|	6.0
	Labour force participation rates	48.7|	41.2|	40.5	39.8|	39.7	60.1|	68.0	68.0	68.2|	68.8	27.6|	29.6|	29.5	30.3|	31.5
	Employment/population ratios	40.0|	33.5|	33.3	33.0|	32.8	54.9|	61.6|	61.8	62.4|	62.7	26.1|	27.4|	27.4	28.4|	29.6
Total OECD[c]	Unemployment rates	12.3|	12.7|	12.0	12.0|	12.7	5.9|	6.4|	6.1	6.0|	6.4	3.2|	4.6|	4.4	4.1|	4.2
	Labour force participation rates	50.1|	46.7|	46.6	46.0|	45.5	63.3|	68.1|	68.2	68.3|	68.6	36.1|	38.6|	38.8	39.3|	40.6
	Employment/population ratios	44.0|	40.8|	41.0	40.4|	39.8	59.6|	63.7|	64.1	64.2|	64.1	34.9|	36.8|	37.1	37.7|	38.9

a) Age group 15 to 24 refers to 16 to 24.
b) The year 1990 refers to 1991.
c) For above countries only.

Source: OECD database on Labour Force Statistics (see URLs at the beginning of the Annex). For Austria, Belgium, Denmark, Greece and Luxembourg, data are from the European Union Labour Force Survey.

Table D. Employment/population ratios, activity and unemployment rates by educational attainment, 2001

Persons aged 25-64 (percentages)

		Both sexes			Men			Women		
		Less than upper secondary education	Upper secondary education	Tertiary education	Less than upper secondary education	Upper secondary education	Tertiary education	Less than upper secondary education	Upper secondary education	Tertiary education
Australia	Unemployment rates	7.6	4.7	3.1	8.1	4.5	3.1	7.0	5.2	3.1
	Labour force participation rates	64.8	81.9	85.8	78.5	89.4	91.4	55.0	68.2	80.8
	Employment/population ratios	59.9	78.0	83.1	72.1	85.5	88.6	51.2	64.6	78.3
Austria	Unemployment rates	6.4	3.0	1.5	7.2	2.9	1.4	5.7	3.3	1.8
	Labour force participation rates	57.3	76.9	87.8	70.3	84.3	90.5	49.5	68.7	83.7
	Employment/population ratios	53.6	74.6	86.5	65.3	81.9	89.3	46.7	66.4	82.2
Belgium	Unemployment rates	8.5	5.5	2.7	7.4	4.4	2.5	10.4	6.9	3.0
	Labour force participation rates	53.5	78.2	86.9	68.6	87.1	91.4	38.7	68.6	82.4
	Employment/population ratios	49.0	73.9	84.5	63.5	83.2	89.1	34.7	63.8	80.0
Canada	Unemployment rates	10.2	6.2	4.5	10.2	6.2	4.6	10.2	6.2	4.4
	Labour force participation rates	61.0	80.6	85.8	73.1	87.6	90.4	48.3	72.8	81.8
	Employment/population ratios	54.8	75.6	81.9	65.6	82.2	86.2	43.3	68.3	78.1
Czech Republic	Unemployment rates	19.2	6.2	2.0	19.3	4.7	1.9	19.1	8.0	2.2
	Labour force participation rates	57.8	80.7	89.6	69.7	88.3	94.5	51.7	72.6	82.9
	Employment/population ratios	46.7	75.7	87.8	56.3	84.1	92.7	41.8	66.8	81.0
Denmark	Unemployment rates	5.0	3.3	3.2	4.0	2.7	3.3	6.2	4.0	3.1
	Labour force participation rates	65.2	83.4	90.3	74.5	86.9	92.8	57.0	79.3	88.1
	Employment/population ratios	61.9	80.7	87.3	71.5	84.6	89.7	53.5	76.1	85.3
Finland	Unemployment rates	11.4	8.5	4.4	10.5	7.9	3.8	12.7	9.2	4.9
	Labour force participation rates	65.6	82.5	89.0	69.7	86.1	91.1	61.1	78.6	87.2
	Employment/population ratios	58.2	75.5	85.1	62.4	79.3	87.6	53.3	71.3	82.9
France	Unemployment rates	11.9	6.9	4.8	9.7	5.1	4.2	14.4	9.3	5.3
	Labour force participation rates	65.5	82.2	87.9	75.9	88.0	91.9	56.8	75.6	84.2
	Employment/population ratios	57.7	76.5	83.7	68.6	83.6	88.1	48.6	68.6	79.8
Germany	Unemployment rates	13.5	8.2	4.2	15.6	8.1	3.8	11.5	8.4	5.0
	Labour force participation rates	59.9	76.9	87.1	76.6	83.5	90.1	49.6	70.2	82.4
	Employment/population ratios	51.8	70.5	83.4	64.7	76.7	86.7	43.9	64.3	78.3
Greece	Unemployment rates	7.6	9.8	6.6	4.9	6.2	4.6	12.3	15.1	9.2
	Labour force participation rates	59.5	71.9	85.3	82.0	88.2	88.6	40.2	56.5	81.5
	Employment/population ratios	55.0	64.9	79.7	78.0	82.7	84.5	35.2	48.0	74.0

STATISTICAL ANNEX

Table D. Employment/population ratios, activity and unemployment rates by educational attainment, 2001 (cont.)

Persons aged 25-64 (percentages)

		Both sexes			Men			Women		
		Less than upper secondary education	Upper secondary education	Tertiary education	Less than upper secondary education	Upper secondary education	Tertiary education	Less than upper secondary education	Upper secondary education	Tertiary education
Hungary	Unemployment rates	10.0	4.6	1.2	12.5	4.8	1.1	7.6	4.2	1.3
	Labour force participation rates	40.9	75.4	83.5	49.7	82.5	88.9	34.8	67.3	78.7
	Employment/population ratios	36.8	71.9	82.5	43.5	78.5	88.0	32.1	64.5	77.7
Iceland	Unemployment rates	2.4	1.8	0.9	2.3	1.2	1.0	2.4	2.8	0.8
	Labour force participation rates	89.1	91.1	95.5	95.1	95.4	97.4	85.0	84.4	93.7
	Employment/population ratios	87.0	89.5	94.7	92.9	94.2	96.5	82.9	82.1	92.9
Ireland	Unemployment rates	5.4	2.5	1.7	5.5	2.3	1.6	5.1	2.8	1.8
	Labour force participation rates	60.8	77.3	86.3	79.3	92.9	94.3	40.4	64.1	78.3
	Employment/population ratios	57.6	75.3	84.9	75.0	90.8	92.8	38.4	62.3	77.0
Italy	Unemployment rates	9.1	6.8	5.3	6.9	4.9	3.8	14.0	9.3	7.2
	Labour force participation rates	53.7	77.1	86.2	74.4	86.4	91.0	33.7	67.4	81.4
	Employment/population ratios	48.8	71.9	81.6	69.3	82.2	87.6	29.0	61.2	75.6
Japan	Unemployment rates	5.9	4.8	3.1	6.9	4.8	2.9	4.3	4.7	3.5
	Labour force participation rates	71.8	78.1	83.0	87.2	95.2	97.3	55.9	62.8	66.8
	Employment/population ratios	67.6	74.3	80.4	81.2	90.6	94.5	53.5	59.8	64.4
Korea	Unemployment rates	2.9	3.4	3.3	4.3	3.7	3.6	1.8	2.7	2.4
	Labour force participation rates	69.6	71.8	78.4	83.6	89.0	91.4	61.0	52.6	56.6
	Employment/population ratios	67.5	69.4	75.8	80.0	85.7	88.1	59.9	51.2	55.2
Luxembourg	Unemployment rates	1.9	1.1	1.2	1.6	0.8	1.0	2.4	1.5	1.6
	Labour force participation rates	59.3	75.0	86.6	77.8	86.4	92.4	44.9	61.8	78.4
	Employment/population ratios	58.2	74.2	85.5	76.6	85.7	91.4	43.8	60.9	77.1
Mexico	Unemployment rates	1.4	1.7	2.2	1.4	1.9	2.2	1.4	1.6	2.1
	Labour force participation rates	63.7	65.2	83.3	94.0	95.7	94.2	37.4	56.3	68.9
	Employment/population ratios	62.8	64.1	81.5	92.7	93.9	92.1	36.8	55.4	67.5
Netherlands	Unemployment rates	3.1	1.8	1.3	2.5	1.1	0.7	3.5	2.3	2.0
	Labour force participation rates	60.8	81.4	87.5	77.4	88.6	90.8	46.7	73.5	83.0
	Employment/population ratios	59.0	80.0	86.3	75.5	87.6	90.2	45.0	71.7	81.4
New Zealand	Unemployment rates	6.7	3.2	3.2	7.4	3.0	3.4	5.9	3.6	3.0
	Labour force participation rates	66.9	83.5	84.5	79.6	91.3	91.2	56.1	74.4	79.1
	Employment/population ratios	62.4	80.8	81.7	73.7	88.6	88.1	52.8	71.6	76.7

Table D. Employment/population ratios, activity and unemployment rates by educational attainment, 2001 (cont.)

Persons aged 25-64 (percentages)

		Both sexes			Men			Women		
		Less than upper secondary education	Upper secondary education	Tertiary education	Less than upper secondary education	Upper secondary education	Tertiary education	Less than upper secondary education	Upper secondary education	Tertiary education
Norway	Unemployment rates	3.4	2.7	1.7	3.4	2.9	1.6	3.3	2.5	1.8
	Labour force participation rates	65.5	85.0	91.1	73.7	89.0	93.8	57.7	80.7	88.5
	Employment/population ratios	63.3	82.7	89.6	71.2	86.4	92.3	55.8	78.6	86.9
Poland	Unemployment rates	22.6	15.9	5.0	21.7	14.0	4.0	23.7	18.3	5.9
	Labour force participation rates	53.6	77.0	88.5	64.1	83.1	91.8	44.9	70.6	85.9
	Employment/population ratios	41.5	64.8	84.0	50.2	71.5	88.1	34.3	57.6	80.9
Portugal	Unemployment rates	3.6	3.2	2.8	2.7	3.1	2.1	4.6	3.3	3.2
	Labour force participation rates	76.0	85.5	93.6	86.5	87.3	94.4	65.9	83.6	93.0
	Employment/population ratios	73.3	82.7	91.0	84.2	84.6	92.4	62.8	80.8	90.0
Slovak Republic	Unemployment rates	38.7	14.8	4.2	44.3	14.8	4.6	34.6	14.8	3.9
	Labour force participation rates	49.7	82.4	90.5	62.1	88.4	93.1	43.4	75.8	87.8
	Employment/population ratios	30.5	70.2	86.7	34.6	75.3	88.9	28.4	64.6	84.4
Spain	Unemployment rates	10.2	8.4	6.9	7.3	5.4	4.5	16.1	12.8	9.8
	Labour force participation rates	61.3	78.4	86.7	82.9	89.8	91.6	40.5	66.2	81.5
	Employment/population ratios	55.0	71.7	80.7	76.9	85.0	87.5	34.0	57.7	73.5
Sweden	Unemployment rates	5.9	4.6	2.6	5.6	5.0	3.0	6.4	4.2	2.3
	Labour force participation rates	73.2	85.9	89.3	79.2	88.5	90.3	65.7	83.3	88.4
	Employment/population ratios	68.8	81.9	86.9	74.8	84.0	87.6	61.5	79.8	86.3
Switzerland	Unemployment rates	3.6	2.0	1.3	2.7	1.1	0.7	4.5	2.9	2.8
	Labour force participation rates	72.0	82.8	92.8	87.3	93.3	95.8	62.2	74.5	85.9
	Employment/population ratios	69.4	81.1	91.6	84.9	92.2	95.2	59.4	72.3	83.5
Turkey	Unemployment rates	8.7	8.9	5.8	9.2	8.0	5.6	6.9	13.5	6.1
	Labour force participation rates	53.8	68.0	81.5	82.1	87.3	87.3	22.4	32.0	71.4
	Employment/population ratios	49.1	61.9	76.8	74.5	80.3	82.4	20.8	27.7	67.0
United Kingdom	Unemployment rates	7.6	3.9	2.0	9.4	4.1	2.2	5.7	3.7	1.8
	Labour force participation rates	58.4	82.7	90.1	67.2	87.8	92.9	51.0	76.7	86.7
	Employment/population ratios	54.0	79.5	88.3	60.9	84.2	90.9	48.1	73.9	85.1
United States	Unemployment rates	8.1	3.8	2.1	7.5	4.2	2.1	8.9	3.4	2.1
	Labour force participation rates	63.5	79.2	86.2	75.4	85.8	91.8	51.7	73.1	80.8
	Employment/population ratios	58.4	76.2	84.4	69.8	82.1	89.9	47.1	70.6	79.1

Table D. Employment/population ratios, activity and unemployment rates by educational attainment, 2001 (cont.)

Persons aged 25-64 (percentages)

		Both sexes			Men			Women		
		Less than upper secondary education	Upper secondary education	Tertiary education	Less than upper secondary education	Upper secondary education	Tertiary education	Less than upper secondary education	Upper secondary education	Tertiary education
European Union[a]	Unemployment rates	9.3	6.2	4.0	7.7	5.4	3.3	11.5	7.3	4.8
	Labour force participation rates	60.4	79.5	87.9	77.0	86.4	91.3	45.8	72.1	83.9
	Employment/population ratios	54.8	74.5	84.4	71.0	81.7	88.3	40.5	66.8	79.8
OECD Europe[a]	Unemployment rates	10.2	7.4	3.9	9.3	6.6	3.3	11.8	8.5	4.7
	Labour force participation rates	59.1	79.1	87.8	77.9	86.3	91.3	42.1	71.4	83.7
	Employment/population ratios	53.1	73.3	84.4	70.6	80.6	88.3	37.2	65.3	79.8
Total OECD[a]	Unemployment rates	7.3	5.7	3.1	6.7	5.4	2.8	8.2	6.0	3.4
	Labour force participation rates	61.6	78.5	85.7	81.0	87.5	92.5	44.2	69.4	78.4
	Employment/population ratios	57.1	74.0	83.1	75.5	82.8	89.9	40.6	65.2	75.8

a) For above countries only.

Source: OECD (2003), *Education at a Glance – OECD Indicators*.

Table E. **Incidence and composition of part-time employment**[a]

Percentages

Part-time employment as a proportion of employment

	Men 1990	1999	2000	2001	2002	Women 1990	1999	2000	2001	2002
Australia[b, c]	11.3	14.3	14.8	15.8	16.3	38.5	41.4	40.7	41.6	41.4
Austria	..	2.8	2.6	2.7	3.1	..	24.4	24.4	24.8	26.2
Belgium	4.4	7.3	7.1	5.7	6.0	28.8	36.6	34.5	32.5	32.4
Canada	9.2	10.3	10.3	10.4	10.9	26.9	28.1	27.3	27.1	27.8
Czech Republic	..	1.7	1.6	1.6	1.4	..	5.6	5.4	5.4	4.9
Denmark	10.2	8.9	9.3	9.3	10.3	29.7	22.7	24.0	21.0	23.0
Finland	4.8	6.6	7.1	7.3	7.5	10.6	13.5	13.9	14.0	14.8
France	4.5	5.8	5.5	5.1	5.2	22.5	25.4	24.9	24.4	24.1
Germany	2.3	4.8	4.8	5.1	5.5	29.8	33.1	33.9	35.0	35.3
Greece	4.0	4.6	3.0	2.6	2.9	11.6	13.6	9.5	8.5	10.0
Hungary	..	2.1	1.7	1.7	1.7	..	5.1	4.7	4.0	4.3
Iceland[d]	7.5	9.1	8.8	9.7	10.2	39.7	35.2	33.7	32.6	31.2
Ireland	4.4	7.8	7.8	7.1	7.2	21.2	32.7	33.0	33.4	33.2
Italy	4.0	5.3	5.7	5.4	4.9	18.4	23.2	23.4	23.7	23.5
Japan[b, e]	9.5	13.4	11.6	13.7	14.0	33.4	39.7	38.6	41.0	41.2
Korea[b]	3.1	5.8	5.1	5.2	5.4	6.5	10.4	9.8	10.4	10.6
Luxembourg	1.6	1.7	2.0	2.0	2.3	19.1	28.4	28.4	30.1	28.1
Mexico	..	7.1	7.1	7.5	7.1	..	26.6	25.6	25.7	25.6
Netherlands	13.4	11.9	13.4	13.8	14.7	52.5	55.4	57.2	58.1	58.8
New Zealand	7.9	11.3	11.0	11.0	11.4	34.6	37.1	35.9	36.1	36.1
Norway	6.9	8.2	8.7	9.1	9.2	39.8	35.0	33.4	32.7	33.4
Poland[b]	..	9.8	8.8	7.4	7.5	..	19.2	17.9	16.6	16.7
Portugal	3.9	5.1	4.9	5.1	5.7	12.8	14.7	14.9	14.3	14.4
Slovak Republic	..	0.9	1.0	1.1	1.0	..	2.9	3.0	2.8	2.3
Spain	1.4	2.8	2.6	2.6	2.4	11.5	16.8	16.5	16.6	16.3
Sweden	5.3	7.3	7.3	7.3	7.5	24.5	22.3	21.4	21.0	20.6
Switzerland[c, d]	6.8	7.7	8.4	8.9	7.7	42.6	46.5	44.7	44.7	45.3
Turkey	4.9	4.2	5.5	3.1	3.7	18.8	16.1	19.9	13.4	13.1
United Kingdom	5.3	8.6	8.6	8.3	8.9	39.5	40.6	40.8	40.3	40.1
United States[f]	8.3	8.1	8.0	8.3	8.3	20.0	19.0	18.2	18.3	18.8
European Union[g]	4.3	6.0	6.0	5.9	6.1	27.0	30.0	30.0	30.0	30.0
OECD Europe[g]	4.5	5.9	6.0	5.5	5.8	26.9	27.2	27.5	27.0	27.0
Total OECD[g]	4.9	6.0	5.9	5.9	7.2	20.0	19.0	18.2	18.3	18.8

	Part-time employment as a proportion of total employment 1990	1999	2000	2001	2002	Women's share in part-time employment 1990	1999	2000	2001	2002
Australia[b, c]	22.6	26.1	26.2	27.2	27.4	70.8	68.9	68.3	67.5	66.7
Austria	..	12.3	12.2	12.4	13.5	..	87.2	88.1	88.0	87.3
Belgium	13.5	19.9	19.0	17.0	17.2	79.8	79.0	79.0	80.7	80.1
Canada	17.1	18.5	18.1	18.1	18.7	70.0	69.7	69.3	69.1	68.8
Czech Republic	..	3.4	3.2	3.2	2.9	..	70.9	72.5	72.0	73.4
Denmark	19.2	15.3	16.1	14.7	16.2	71.1	68.5	69.4	66.0	66.2
Finland	7.6	9.9	10.4	10.5	11.0	67.0	64.9	63.8	63.4	64.6
France	12.2	14.6	14.2	13.8	13.7	78.6	78.2	78.8	79.6	79.5
Germany	13.4	17.1	17.6	18.3	18.8	89.7	84.1	84.5	84.6	83.7
Greece	6.7	8.0	5.5	4.9	5.6	60.8	63.9	65.4	66.4	67.8
Hungary	..	3.5	3.2	2.8	2.9	..	68.7	71.2	68.4	69.9
Iceland[d]	22.2	21.2	20.4	20.4	20.1	81.6	77.1	77.0	74.5	73.1
Ireland	10.0	17.9	18.1	17.9	18.1	70.3	74.1	74.4	76.5	77.0
Italy	8.9	11.8	12.2	12.2	11.9	70.5	71.5	70.5	72.6	74.4

Table E. **Incidence and composition of part-time employment**[a] (cont.)

Percentages

	\multicolumn{5}{c	}{Part-time employment as a proportion of total employment}	\multicolumn{5}{c}{Women's share in part-time employment}
	1990	1999	2000	2001	2002	1990	1999	2000	2001	2002
Japan[b, e]	19.2	24.1	22.6	24.9	25.1	70.5	67.0	69.7	67.5	67.0
Korea[b]	4.5	7.7	7.0	7.3	7.6	58.7	55.5	57.7	58.8	58.3
Luxembourg	7.6	12.1	12.4	13.3	12.6	86.6	91.3	90.0	90.7	89.1
Mexico	..	13.7	13.5	13.7	13.5	..	65.4	65.1	63.8	65.6
Netherlands	28.2	30.4	32.1	33.0	33.9	70.4	77.4	76.2	76.3	75.4
New Zealand	19.6	23.0	22.3	22.4	22.6	77.1	73.3	72.9	73.2	72.5
Norway	21.8	20.7	20.2	20.1	20.6	82.7	78.8	77.0	76.0	76.2
Poland[b]	..	14.0	12.8	11.6	11.7	..	61.2	61.7	64.7	65.0
Portugal	7.6	9.4	9.4	9.2	9.6	70.3	70.5	71.5	69.9	67.8
Slovak Republic	..	1.8	1.9	1.9	1.6	..	73.2	71.2	68.3	66.1
Spain	4.6	7.8	7.7	7.8	7.6	79.2	76.8	78.5	79.0	80.1
Sweden	14.5	14.5	14.0	13.9	13.8	81.1	73.7	72.9	72.7	71.8
Switzerland[c, d]	22.1	24.8	24.4	24.8	24.7	82.4	82.6	80.6	80.1	82.8
Turkey	9.2	7.6	9.0	5.9	6.3	62.5	60.6	55.1	61.2	57.9
United Kingdom	20.1	22.9	23.0	22.7	23.0	85.1	79.4	79.4	79.8	78.8
United States[f]	13.8	13.3	12.9	13.1	13.4	68.2	68.4	68.2	67.6	68.2
European Union[g]	13.3	16.1	16.2	16.2	16.4	80.6	78.6	78.7	79.2	78.8
OECD Europe[g]	13.2	14.7	14.8	14.5	14.7	79.3	76.6	76.3	77.6	77.2
Total OECD[g]	11.1	12.3	12.3	12.2	14.7	74.1	72.2	72.1	72.4	72.3

a) Part-time employment refers to persons who usually work less than 30 hours per week in their main job. Data include only persons declaring usual hours.
b) Data are based on actual hours worked. For Poland until 2000 only.
c) Part-time employment based on hours worked at all jobs.
d) Data 1990 refer to 1991.
e) Less than 35 hours per week.
f) Data are for wage and salary workers only.
g) For above countries only.

Sources and definitions: OECD database on Labour Force Statistics (see URLs at the beginning of the Annex). For Austria, Belgium, Denmark, France, Germany, Greece, Ireland, Italy, Luxembourg, the Netherlands, Portugal, Spain and the United Kingdom, data are from the European Union Labour Force Survey. See OECD the "Definition of Part-time Work for the Purpose of International Comparisons", Labour Market and Social Policy Occasional Paper No. 22, available on Internet (www.olis.oecd.org/olis/1997doc.nsf/linkto/ocde-gd(97)121).

Table F. **Average annual hours actually worked per person in employment**[a]

	1979	1983	1990	1998	1999	2000	2001	2002
Total employment								
Australia	1 904	1 853	1 866	1 856	1 860	1 855	1 837	1 824
Belgium	..	1 684	1 677	1 609	1 553	1 530	1 547	1 559
Canada	1 832	1 780	1 788	1 799	1 806	1 807	1 790	1 778
Czech Republic	..	..	..	2 075	2 088	2 092	2 000	1 980
Denmark	..	..	1 491	1 511	1 539	1 504	1 516	1 499
Finland[b]	..	1 809	1 763	1 761	1 765	1 721	1 694	1 686
Finland[c]	1 837	1 787	1 728	1 736	1 737	1 727	1 720	1 711
France	1 806	1 712	1 657	1 603	1 596	1 587	1 564	1 545
Germany[d]	..	..	1 541	1 489	1 479	1 463	1 451	1 444
Western Germany	1 708	1 674	1 561	1 465	1 456	1 443	1 433	1 428
Greece	..	1 990	1 919	1 925	1 943	1 924	1 933	1 934
Iceland	..	..	..	1 817	1 873	1 885	1 847	1 812
Ireland	..	1 910	1 920	1 721	1 692	1 690	1 677	1 668
Italy	1 717	1 694	1 675	1 639	1 634	1 631	1 620	1 619
Japan	2 126	2 095	2 031	1 842	1 810	1 821	1 809	..
Mexico	..	..	..	1 879	1 923	1 888	1 864	1 888
Netherlands	..	..	1 437	1 366	1 348	1 371	1 327	1 340
New Zealand	..	..	1 820	1 825	1 842	1 817	1 817	1 816
Norway	1 514	1 485	1 432	1 400	1 398	1 380	1 360	1 342
Portugal	..	..	1 881	1 747	1 761	1 718	1 718	1 719
Slovak Republic	..	..	..	2 034	2 022	2 023	2 026	1 979
Spain	2 022	1 912	1 824	1 834	1 816	1 814	1 816	1 807
Sweden	1 517	1 520	1 549	1 638	1 647	1 625	1 602	1 581
Switzerland	..	..	..	1 589	1 597	1 568	1 541	..
United Kingdom	1 815	1 713	1 767	1 731	1 719	1 708	1 711	1 707
United States	1 838	1 824	1 837	1 850	1 847	1 834	1 821	1 815
Dependent employment								
Belgium	..	1 549	1 558	1 490	1 451	1 439	1 455	1 463
Canada	1 801	1 762	1 771	1 789	1 797	1 800	1 781	1 774
Czech Republic	..	..	..	1 995	2 014	2 018	1 922	1 896
Denmark	..	..	1 421	1 454	1 490	1 446	1 467	1 448
Finland[b]	..	..	1 666	1 672	1 673	1 638	1 616	1 609
France	1 669	1 570	1 543	1 501	1 499	1 491	1 471	1 453
Germany[d]	..	..	..	1 408	1 397	1 381	1 369	1 361
Western Germany	1 623	1 590	1 485	1 380	1 369	1 356	1 347	1 342
Greece	..	1 765	1 763	1 810	1 815	1 825	1 837	1 830
Hungary	..	1 829	1 710	1 788	1 795	1 795	1 766	1 766
Iceland	..	..	..	1 762	1 810	1 820	1 779	1 740
Ireland	..	1 709	1 720	1 610	1 602	1 602	1 599	1 589
Italy	..	1 626	1 599	1 568	1 564	1 566	1 552	1 552
Japan[e]	2 114	2 098	2 052	1 879	1 842	1 859	1 848	1 837
Japan[f]	..	..	2 064	1 871	1 840	1 853	1 836	1 825
Korea	..	2 734	2 514	2 390	2 497	2 474	2 447	2 410
Mexico	..	..	..	1 942	1 977	1 935	1 915	1 945
Netherlands	1 591	1 530	1 433	1 340	1 343	1 331	1 330	..
Portugal	..	..	1 792	1 713	1 732	1 696	1 705	1 710
Slovak Republic	..	..	..	1 998	1 984	1 986	1 993	1 950
Spain	1 936	1 837	1 762	1 767	1 753	1 753	1 757	1 748
United Kingdom	1 750	1 652	1 704	1 703	1 695	1 684	1 686	1 683
United States	1 816	1 809	1 819	1 833	1 829	1 817	1 805	1 802

Table F. **Average annual hours actually worked per person in employment**[a] *(cont.)*

a) The concept used is the total number of hours worked over the year divided by the average numbers of people in employment. The data are intended for comparisons of trends over time; they are unsuitable for comparisons of the level of average annual hours of work for a given year, because of differences in their sources. Part-time workers are covered as well as full-time.
b) Data estimated from the Labour Force Survey.
c) Data estimated from national accounts.
d) The year 1990 refers to 1991.
e) Data refer to establishments with 30 or more regular employees.
f) Data refer to establishments with five or more regular employees.

Sources and definitions:

Secretariat estimates for Belgium, Denmark, Greece, Ireland, Italy, Netherlands (for total employment only) and Portugal for annual hours worked for the total economy based on the European Labour Force Survey. Estimates of annual working time per employed persons are based on the Spring European Labour Force Survey (EULFS) as the main source of data for various components of working time (overtime, illness, maternity leave, etc.). The data from the EULFS correspond to one single reading in the year, which requires the use of external sources for hours not worked due to public holidays and annual leave. A correction is also made to account for an estimated 50 per cent underreporting, on average, of hours lost due to illness and maternity leave in the EULFS. In sum, the estimates are computed by multiplying weekly usual hours worked by the number of effective weeks worked during the year (taking into account vacation and time not worked due to other reasons).

Australia: Data supplied by the Australian Bureau of Statistics from the Labour Force Survey. Annual hours are adjusted to take account of public holidays occuring during the reporting period. The method of estimation is consistent with the national accounts.

Canada: Data series supplied by Statistics Canada, based mainly on the monthly Labour Force Survey supplemented by the Survey of Employment Payrolls and Hours, the annual Survey of Manufacturers and the Census of Mining.

Czech Republic: Data supplied by the Czech Statistical Office and based on the quarterly Labour Force Sample Survey. Main meal breaks (one half hour a day) are included.-

Finland: Data supplied by Statistics Finland. National accounts series based on an establishment survey for manufacturing, and the Labour Force Survey for other sectors and for the self-employed. Alternative series based solely on the Labour Force Survey.

Germany and western Germany: Data series from 1991 onward that extend coverage of part-time work with few hours of work. Data supplied by the Institut für Arbeitsmarkt- und Berufsforschung, calculated within a comprehensive accounting structure, based on establishment survey estimates of weekly hours worked by full-time workers whose hours are not affected by absence, and extended to annual estimates of actual hours by adjusting for a wide range of factors, including public holidays, sickness absence, overtime working, short-time working, bad weather, strikes, part-time working and parental leave. Data prior to 1991 are spliced with old annual hours of work estimates for 1991.

France: Data series supplied by the Institut National de la Statistique et des Études Économiques (INSEE), produced within the framework of the national accounts. Estimates for years 2000 to 2002 made by the Secretariat by prolonging the trend in data based on alternative estimates derived from the European Labour Force Survey (see notes for Belgium, Denmark, etc.).

Iceland: Data are provided by Statistics Iceland and are based on the Icelandic Labor Force Survey. Annual actual hours worked per person in employment are computed by multiplying daily actual hours worked by annual actual working days net of public holidays and annual vacations. The latter are for a typical work contract by sector of activity.

Italy: Data are Secretariat estimates based on the European Labour Force Survey for 1985 to 1999 (see notes for Belgium, Denmark, etc.). From 1960 to 1985, the trend in data is taken from the series provided by ISTAT and based on a special establishment survey on total employment discontinued in 1985.

Japan: Data for total employment are Secretariat estimates based on data from the Monthly Labour Survey of Establishments, extended to agricultural and government sectors and to the self-employed by means of the Labour Force Survey. Data for dependent employment supplied by Statistics Bureau, Management and Coordination Agency, from the Monthly Labour Survey, referring to all industries excluding agriculture, forest, fisheries and government services. Total employment data for 2001 is provisional.

Korea : Data supplied by the Ministry of Labour from the Report on monthly labour survey.

Mexico: Data supplied by STPS-INEGI from the bi-annual National Survey of Employment, based on the assumption of 44 working weeks per year.

Netherlands: From 1977 onwards, figures are "Annual Contractual Hours", supplied by Statistics Netherlands, compiled within the framework of the Labour Accounts. Overtime hours are excluded. For 1970 to 1976, the trend has been derived from data supplied by the Economisch Instituut voor het Midden en Kleinbedrijf, referring to persons employed in the private sector, excluding agriculture and fishing.

New Zealand: Data supplied by Statistics New Zealand and derived from the quarterly Labour Force Survey, whose continuous sample design avoids the need for adjustments for public holidays and other days lost.

Norway: Data supplied by Statistics Norway, based on national accounts and estimated from a number of different data sources, the most important being establishment surveys, the Labour Force Surveys and the public sector accounts.

Slovak Republic: Data supplied by the Statistical Office of the Slovak Republic and based on the continuous labour force survey with quarterly results. Hours worked cover the main meal break until 2001 and are exluded thereafter.

Table F. **Average annual hours actually worked per person in employment**[a] *(cont.)*

Spain: New series supplied by Instituto Nacional de Estadística and derived from the quarterly Labour Force Survey. Series break at 1986/87 due to changes in the survey.

Sweden: New series from 1996 are supplied by Statistics Sweden derived from national accounts data, based on both the Labour Force Survey and establishment surveys.

Switzerland: Data supplied by the Office fédéral de la statistique. The basis of the calculation is the Swiss Labour Force Survey which provides information on weekly hours of work during one quarter of the year. The estimates of annual hours are based also on supplementary, annual information on vacations, public holidays and overtime working and have been extended to correspond to national accounts concepts.

United Kingdom: Since 1994, data refer to the United Kingdom (including Northern Ireland). Break in series 1994/95 are due to small change in the way estimates of employment are derived. For 1992 to 1995, the levels are derived directly from the continuous Labour Force Survey. For 1984 to 1991, the trend in the data is taken from the annual Labour Force Survey. From 1970 to 1983, the trend corresponds to estimates by Professor Angus Maddison.

United States: Secretariat estimates are based on unpublished data supplied by the Bureau of Labor Statistics (BLS). Estimates of annual hours actually worked per job on the basis of the Current Employment Statistics (CES) and the Current Population Survey (CPS) are multiplied by one plus the rate of multiple jobholding from the CPS to produce estimates of annual working time on a per worker basis, as it is the case for most countries.

STATISTICAL ANNEX

Table G. Incidence of long-term unemployment[a, b, c, d, e]
As a percentage of total unemployment

	1990 6 months and over	1990 12 months and over	1999 6 months and over	1999 12 months and over	2000 6 months and over	2000 12 months and over	2001 6 months and over	2001 12 months and over	2002 6 months and over	2002 12 months and over
Australia	41.0	21.6	48.4	29.4	43.6	27.9	38.7	21.5	39.8	22.1
Austria	..	..	44.2	29.2	39.7	25.8	36.1	23.3	33.5	19.2
Belgium	81.4	68.5	73.5	60.5	71.8	56.3	66.5	51.7	67.3	49.6
Canada	20.2	7.2	21.4	11.6	19.5	11.2	16.8	9.5	18.7	9.7
Czech Republic	..	..	61.9	37.1	69.9	48.8	71.3	52.7	70.3	50.7
Denmark	53.2	29.9	38.5	20.5	38.1	20.0	38.5	22.2	33.3	19.7
Finland[f]	32.6	9.2	46.4	29.6	46.5	29.0	42.2	26.2	41.7	24.4
France	55.6	38.1	55.6	40.4	62.0	42.6	57.2	37.6	53.4	33.8
Germany	64.7	46.8	67.2	51.7	67.6	51.5	66.2	50.4	64.8	47.9
Greece	72.0	49.8	74.3	55.3	73.5	56.4	69.0	52.8	69.0	52.4
Hungary	..	..	70.4	49.5	69.8	49.0	67.9	46.6	67.4	44.8
Iceland[f]	13.6	6.7	20.2	11.7	18.6	11.8	21.0	12.5	24.8	11.1
Ireland	81.0	66.0	76.1	55.3	..	..	50.3	33.1	50.3	29.3
Italy	85.2	69.8	77.2	61.4	77.6	61.3	77.4	63.4	75.7	59.2
Japan	39.0	19.1	44.5	22.4	46.9	25.5	46.2	26.6	49.0	30.8
Korea	13.9	2.6	18.7	3.8	14.3	2.3	13.0	2.3	13.9	2.5
Luxembourg[g]	(68.4)	(47.4)	(53.8)	(32.3)	(37.0)	(22.4)	(44.9)	(28.4)	(46.8)	(27.4)
Mexico	..	..	6.9	1.7	5.0	1.1	4.1	1.1	5.4	0.9
Netherlands	63.6	49.3	80.7	43.5	..	..	..	..	43.2	26.7
New Zealand	39.5	20.9	39.1	20.9	36.2	19.2	31.3	16.8	28.5	14.4
Norway	40.8	20.4	16.1	7.1	16.6	5.3	16.1	5.5	20.0	6.4
Poland[h]	62.8	34.7	57.1	34.8	63.0	37.9	66.1	43.1	70.0	48.4
Portugal	62.3	44.9	63.8	41.2	60.0	42.9	58.0	38.1	54.4	35.5
Slovak Republic	..	..	69.2	47.7	74.4	54.6	73.4	53.7	77.5	59.8
Spain	70.2	54.0	67.8	51.2	64.8	47.6	61.8	44.0	59.2	40.2
Sweden	22.2	12.1	45.2	30.1	41.5	26.4	36.7	22.3	36.2	21.0
Switzerland[f]	27.5	17.0	61.2	39.6	45.7	29.0	47.3	29.9	37.2	21.8
Turkey	72.6	47.0	49.9	28.3	35.9	21.1	35.5	21.1	45.7	29.6
United Kingdom	50.3	34.4	45.4	29.6	43.2	28.0	43.6	27.8	38.8	23.1
United States	10.0	5.5	12.3	6.8	11.4	6.0	11.8	6.1	18.3	8.5
European Union[i]	65.3	48.7	63.8	47.5	63.8	46.9	61.8	45.3	59.0	41.4
OECD Europe[i]	65.4	46.2	61.9	44.3	61.8	43.7	60.2	42.7	59.8	41.6
Total OECD[i]	46.3	31.3	47.2	31.8	46.9	31.6	44.0	29.7	45.0	29.6

a) While data from labour force surveys make international comparisons easier, compared to a mixture of survey and registration data, they are not perfect. Questionnaire wording and design, survey timing, differences across countries in the age groups covered, and other reasons mean that care is required in interpreting cross-country differences in levels.

b) The duration of unemployment database maintained by the Secretariat is composed of detailed duration categories disaggregated by age and sex. All totals are derived by adding each component. Thus, the total for men is derived by adding the number of unemployed men by each duration and age group category. Since published data are usually rounded to the nearest thousand, this method sometimes results in slight differences between the percentages shown here and those that would be obtained using the available published figures.

c) Data are averages of monthly figures for Canada, Sweden and the United States, averages of quarterly figures for the Czech Republic, Hungary, Norway, New Zealand, Poland, the Slovak Republic and Spain, averages of semi annual figures for Turkey until 1999 and quarterly averages since 2000. The reference period for the remaining countries is as follows (among EU countries it occasionally varies from year to year): Australia, August; Austria, March; Belgium, April; Denmark, April-May; Finland, autumn prior to 1995, spring between 1995 and 1998, and averages of monthly figures since 1999; France, March; Germany, April; Greece, March-July; Iceland, April; Ireland, May; Italy, April; Japan, February; Luxembourg, April; Mexico, April; the Netherlands, March-June; Portugal, February-April; Switzerland, second quarter; and the United Kingdom, March-May.

Table G. Incidence of long-term unemployment among men[a, b, c, d, e] (cont.)
As a percentage of male unemployment

	1990 6 months and over	1990 12 months and over	1999 6 months and over	1999 12 months and over	2000 6 months and over	2000 12 months and over	2001 6 months and over	2001 12 months and over	2002 6 months and over	2002 12 months and over
Australia	42.6	24.4	50.9	31.8	45.9	30.6	40.3	24.0	43.3	25.9
Austria	..	..	38.8	27.8	39.0	28.1	34.0	23.7	32.1	16.4
Belgium	79.5	66.1	73.2	60.1	70.2	55.9	68.2	52.5	66.6	45.9
Canada	20.4	7.9	23.3	12.8	20.9	12.2	17.9	10.5	19.7	10.3
Czech Republic	..	..	58.0	32.7	68.4	47.5	70.0	52.0	69.2	50.3
Denmark	48.9	27.8	38.6	20.9	36.5	20.1	39.1	26.2	30.3	17.2
Finland[f]	36.8	9.7	49.2	33.1	49.6	32.2	45.0	30.0	44.8	27.3
France	53.2	35.5	53.7	39.0	60.6	41.2	56.9	37.6	52.5	32.2
Germany	65.2	49.1	65.3	49.9	65.9	50.1	64.0	48.4	63.4	46.0
Greece	61.8	39.9	69.0	48.6	67.1	49.4	61.8	47.0	68.0	47.1
Hungary	..	..	70.9	50.6	71.4	51.2	69.9	48.2	69.2	47.0
Iceland[f]	5.1	1.3	13.9	6.6	17.4	8.7	17.2	11.2	19.4	9.5
Ireland	84.3	71.1	77.8	59.5	..	..	57.9	40.8	57.6	35.9
Italy	84.1	68.6	76.6	62.1	76.8	61.4	76.1	63.7	74.0	58.2
Japan	47.6	26.2	49.5	27.4	52.8	30.7	53.2	32.1	54.5	36.2
Korea	16.0	3.3	21.3	4.7	16.7	3.1	15.4	2.9	16.3	3.1
Luxembourg[g]	(80.0)	(60.0)	(61.6)	(38.6)	(40.0)	(26.4)	(53.3)	(32.8)	(39.3)	(28.6)
Mexico	..	..	6.1	2.7	4.3	0.5	4.3	1.1	5.5	1.2
Netherlands	65.6	55.2	75.1	47.7	..	..	..	..	39.5	26.9
New Zealand	44.0	24.5	42.7	23.1	39.5	23.1	34.4	19.6	31.8	16.9
Norway	37.9	19.0	17.8	7.9	20.5	6.9	18.5	6.8	23.1	8.3
Poland[h]	60.2	33.3	52.4	31.4	59.3	34.1	62.7	39.9	67.4	45.1
Portugal	56.3	38.2	63.5	39.5	60.1	46.7	53.8	35.7	52.4	34.8
Slovak Republic	..	..	67.5	45.3	74.1	54.1	71.6	52.1	76.6	58.5
Spain	63.2	45.8	62.1	45.4	58.5	41.0	56.0	37.9	52.9	34.3
Sweden	22.2	12.3	48.5	33.3	44.3	29.3	39.0	24.2	38.9	23.1
Switzerland[f]	28.8	15.9	59.3	40.6	47.6	28.2	38.8	20.6	36.8	19.3
Turkey	71.2	44.9	47.4	25.1	33.0	18.1	32.1	18.2	43.7	27.3
United Kingdom	56.8	41.8	50.1	34.5	48.1	33.7	48.6	33.0	43.8	26.9
United States	12.1	7.0	13.0	7.4	12.1	6.7	12.1	6.4	18.9	8.9
European Union[i]	63.5	47.0	61.8	46.1	61.9	45.5	60.3	44.4	57.3	39.5
OECD Europe[i]	63.7	44.5	59.2	41.9	58.8	41.2	57.0	40.1	57.3	38.9
Total OECD[i]	45.1	30.0	45.9	30.5	45.4	30.2	42.6	28.4	44.1	28.5

d) Data refer to persons aged 15 and over in Australia, Austria, Belgium, Canada, the Czech Republic, Denmark, France, Germany, Greece, Ireland, Italy, Japan, Luxembourg, Mexico, the Netherlands, New Zealand, Poland, Portugal, the Slovak Republic, Switzerland and Turkey; and aged 16 and over in Iceland, Spain, the United Kingdom and the United States. Data for Finland refer to persons aged 15-64 (excluding unemployment pensioners). Data for Hungary refer to persons aged 15-74, for Norway to persons aged 16-74 and for Sweden to persons aged 16-64.
e) Persons for whom no duration of unemployment was specified are excluded.
f) Data for 1990 refer to 1991.
g) Data in brackets are based on small sample sizes and, therefore, must be treated with care.
h) Data for 1990 refer to 1992.
i) For above countries only.

Table G. Incidence of long-term unemployment among women[a, b, c, d, e] (cont.)

As a percentage of female unemployment

	1990 6 months and over	1990 12 months and over	1999 6 months and over	1999 12 months and over	2000 6 months and over	2000 12 months and over	2001 6 months and over	2001 12 months and over	2002 6 months and over	2002 12 months and over
Australia	38.8	17.8	44.9	25.8	40.2	24.0	36.5	18.0	35.2	17.1
Austria	..	..	51.1	30.9	40.6	22.8	38.8	22.9	35.5	23.3
Belgium	82.5	70.0	73.8	60.9	73.1	56.7	64.5	50.8	68.0	53.6
Canada	19.8	6.2	18.9	10.2	17.8	10.0	15.3	8.2	17.5	8.8
Czech Republic	..	..	65.3	40.9	71.2	49.8	72.5	53.4	71.2	51.1
Denmark	57.7	32.0	38.5	20.1	39.6	20.0	38.0	18.8	36.7	22.4
Finland[f]	26.3	8.4	43.7	26.2	43.7	26.2	39.6	22.6	38.3	21.2
France	57.5	40.0	57.4	41.7	63.2	43.7	57.5	37.6	54.3	35.2
Germany	64.2	44.5	69.4	54.0	69.5	53.1	68.9	52.9	66.7	50.3
Greece	78.2	55.9	77.7	59.5	77.7	61.0	73.7	56.6	75.5	55.7
Hungary	..	..	69.7	47.9	67.4	45.7	64.8	44.1	64.9	41.7
Iceland[f]	21.1	11.5	24.5	15.2	19.5	14.1	24.7	13.8	24.7	13.3
Ireland	75.0	56.8	72.9	47.5	..	..	38.6	21.3	37.9	18.0
Italy	86.0	70.7	77.7	60.7	78.3	61.2	78.5	63.1	77.2	60.1
Japan	26.3	8.8	36.9	14.8	37.4	17.1	35.7	18.3	40.3	22.4
Korea	8.8	0.9	13.1	2.0	9.3	0.8	8.3	1.2	9.3	1.2
Luxembourg[g]	(55.6)	(33.3)	(47.5)	(27.2)	(34.3)	(18.8)	(35.8)	(23.7)	(52.6)	(26.5)
Mexico	..	..	8.0	0.3	6.1	2.0	3.9	1.0	5.1	0.4
Netherlands	62.0	44.6	84.9	40.4	..	..	..	..	47.0	26.4
New Zealand	32.6	15.5	34.3	17.9	32.0	14.3	27.5	13.4	24.8	11.5
Norway	45.0	22.5	13.9	6.0	11.5	3.3	13.3	3.9	16.0	3.9
Poland[h]	65.2	36.0	61.9	38.3	66.6	41.3	69.5	46.2	72.8	52.0
Portugal	66.4	49.4	64.2	42.9	60.0	40.0	61.0	39.9	56.1	36.2
Slovak Republic	..	..	71.3	50.5	74.8	55.1	75.6	55.7	78.7	61.2
Spain	76.5	61.5	72.0	55.5	69.3	52.2	66.1	48.6	63.8	44.5
Sweden	22.2	11.8	41.2	26.1	37.9	22.8	33.8	20.0	32.7	18.2
Switzerland[f]	26.6	17.8	63.1	38.7	44.0	29.7	52.3	35.5	37.7	24.5
Turkey	75.6	51.2	56.2	36.4	44.1	29.5	46.1	30.3	51.6	36.4
United Kingdom	40.8	23.7	37.6	21.5	35.6	19.0	35.7	19.5	30.8	17.1
United States	7.3	3.7	11.6	6.2	10.6	5.3	11.5	5.8	17.6	8.1
European Union[i]	67.0	50.2	65.7	48.9	65.6	48.2	63.2	46.2	60.7	43.3
OECD Europe[i]	67.0	47.9	64.8	46.8	64.9	46.4	63.7	45.5	62.7	44.7
Total OECD[j]	47.6	32.6	48.7	33.3	48.5	33.1	45.8	31.2	46.1	30.9

Source: OECD database on Labour Force Statistics (see URLs at the beginning of the Annex).
Data for Belgium, Denmark, Germany, Greece, Ireland, Italy, Luxembourg, the Netherlands, Portugal and the United Kingdom are based on the uropean Union Labour Force Survey and were supplied by Eurostat.

STATISTICAL ANNEX

Table H. **Public expenditure and participant inflows* in labour market programmes in OECD countries**

	Australia[a]								Austria								Belgium						
	Public expenditure as a percentage of GDP				Participant inflows as a percentage of the labour force				Public expenditure as a percentage of GDP				Participant inflows as a percentage of the labour force				Public expenditure as a percentage of GDP				Participant inflows as a percentage of the labour force			
Programme categories and sub-categories	1998-99	1999-00	2000-01	2001-02	1998-99	1999-00	2000-01	2001-02	1999	2000	2001	2002	1999	2000	2001	2002	1998	1999	2000	2001	1998	1999	2000	2001
1. Public employment services and administration	0.20	0.20	0.20	0.20					0.13	0.13	0.14	0.14					0.21	0.20	0.18	0.20				
2. Labour market training	0.02	0.02	0.02	0.02	0.79	0.96	0.95	0.78	0.18	0.17	0.19	0.21	3.01	3.00	3.74	4.42	0.25	0.24	0.25	0.26	9.63	10.18	10.73	13.30
a) Training for unemployed adults and those at risk	0.02	0.02	0.02	0.02	0.58	0.77	0.72	0.58	0.16	0.16	0.18	0.19	..	..	..	..	0.16	0.16	0.16	0.16	2.82	2.99	3.02	3.63
b) Training for employed adults	–	–	–	–	0.21	0.19	0.23	0.20	0.02	0.02	0.02	0.02	..	..	..	..	0.09	0.09	0.09	0.10	6.81	7.19	7.70	9.66
3. Youth measures	0.05	0.06	0.07	0.07	0.53	0.78	3.08	2.96	0.05	0.04	0.03	0.02	0.20	0.11	0.10	0.10	–	–	–	–	–	–	0.32[c]	0.93[c]
a) Measures for unemployed and disadvantaged youth	–	0.01	0.01	–	–	0.23	0.61	0.88	0.16	0.02	0.02	0.02	0.01	..	..	..	..	–	–	–	–	–	–	0.32[c]	0.93[c]
b) Support of apprenticeship and related forms of general youth training	0.05	0.05	0.07	0.07	0.31	0.17	2.21	2.81	0.03	0.02	0.01	0.01	..	..	..	..	–	–	–	–	–	–	–	–
4. Subsidised employment	0.09	0.11	0.11	0.10	0.77	1.07	1.31	1.51	0.09	0.11	0.11	0.10	0.64	0.56	0.64	0.67	0.82	0.75	0.76	0.69	7.28[c]	6.84[c]	7.46[c]	7.26[c]
a) Subsidies to regular employment in the private sector	0.01	0.01	0.01	0.01	–	–	0.07	0.08	0.05	0.05	0.06	0.04	..	..	..	..	0.35	0.27	0.27	0.28	4.37[c]	3.75[c]	3.89[c]	4.04[c]
b) Support of unemployed persons starting enterprises	0.02	0.02	0.01	0.02	0.07	0.08	0.07	0.06	0.01	0.02	0.02	0.02	..	..	..	..	–	–	–	–	–	–	–	–
c) Direct job creation (public or non-profit)	0.07	0.09	0.09	0.08	0.70	0.95	1.17	1.37	0.03	0.04	0.03	0.04	..	[b]	[b]	[b]	0.47	0.48	0.48	0.41	2.91[c]	3.08[c]	3.56[c]	3.20[c]
5. Measures for the disabled	0.06	0.05	0.05	0.05	0.80	0.74	0.80	0.83	0.06	0.05	0.06	0.06	..	[b]	[b]	[b]	0.12	0.12	0.12	0.12	..	..	..	..
a) Vocational rehabilitation	0.02	0.02	0.02	0.01	0.28	0.19	0.19	0.17	0.02	0.02	0.03	0.05	..	..	..	..	0.02	0.02	0.02	0.01	..	..	..	..
b) Work for the disabled	0.04	0.04	0.04	0.04	0.52	0.56	0.62	0.65	0.03	0.03	0.02	0.02	..	..	..	..	0.10	0.10	0.10	0.11	..	..	..	..
6. Unemployment compensation	1.17	1.04	0.98	0.98	..	8.48	8.49	8.45	1.15	1.01	1.00	1.12	18.88	18.13	18.93	19.92	1.90	1.80	1.70	1.78	16.92[d]	17.02[d]	18.52[d]	21.48[d]
7. Early retirement for labour market reasons	–	–	–	–	–	–	–	–	0.04	0.04	0.06	0.13	0.59	0.78	1.11	1.41	0.56	0.52	0.49	0.46	..	..	..	..
TOTAL	1.60	1.49	1.43	1.42	..	12.04	14.63	14.53	1.71	1.55	1.59	1.79	23.32	22.59	24.51	26.52	3.85	3.64	3.50	3.52	..	..	..	..
Active measures (1-5; for inflows, 2-5)	0.43	0.45	0.46	0.45	2.90	3.55	6.14	6.09	0.52	0.50	0.53	0.53	3.84	3.68	4.48	5.19	1.40	1.32	1.32	1.28	..	..	..	..
Passive measures (6 and 7)	1.17	1.04	0.98	0.98	..	8.48	8.49	8.45	1.19	1.05	1.06	1.25	19.47	18.91	20.03	21.33	2.46	2.32	2.18	2.24	..	..	..	..

.. Data not available.
– Nil or less than half of the last digit used.
* Data for participant inflows are reported only for categories 2 to 7 since data for category 1 "Public employment services and administration" are commonly incomplete and non-comparable. Totals shown must be interpreted with caution.
a) Fiscal years starting on July 1.
b) Participant inflows for category 5 "Measures for the disabled" are included in category 2 "Labour market training".
c) Data for categories 3 and 4 refer to stocks.
d) Participant inflows for category 5 "Measures for the disabled" are not included.

Table H. Public expenditure and participant inflows* in labour market programmes in OECD countries (cont.)

Programme categories and sub-categories	Canada[a] Public expenditure as a percentage of GDP 1998-99	1999-00	2000-01	2001-02	Participant inflows as a percentage of the labour force 1998-99	1999-00	2000-01	2001-02	Czech Republic Public expenditure as a percentage of GDP 1999	2000	2001	2002	Participant inflows as a percentage of the labour force 1999	2000	2001	2002	Denmark Public expenditure as a percentage of GDP 1997	1998	1999	2000	Participant inflows as a percentage of the labour force 1997	1998	1999	2000
1. Public employment services and administration	0.22	0.20	0.19	0.20					0.09	0.08	0.07	0.07					0.12	0.12	0.12	0.12				
2. Labour market training	0.15	0.15	0.15	0.15	1.40[b]	1.18[b]	1.09[b]	1.21[b]	0.01	0.02	0.02	0.02	0.44	0.64	0.68	0.70	0.93	0.97	0.99	0.86	18.47	20.62	19.72	15.90
a) Training for unemployed adults and those at risk	0.15	0.15	0.15	0.15	1.40	1.18	1.09	1.21	0.01	0.02	0.02	0.02	0.44	0.64	0.68	0.70	0.64	0.72	0.78	0.67	8.82	12.46	11.64	5.76
b) Training for employed adults	–	–	–	–	..	..	..	..	–	–	–	–	–	–	–	–	0.28	0.25	0.21	0.18	9.65	8.16	8.09	10.15
3. Youth measures	0.03	0.02	0.02	0.02	0.58	0.55	0.48	0.42	0.02	0.02	0.02	0.02	0.21	0.22	0.19	0.15	0.10	0.08	0.12	0.10	1.50	1.50	1.88	1.83
a) Measures for unemployed and disadvantaged youth	0.02	0.01	0.01	0.01	0.24	0.21	0.17	0.10	0.02	0.02	0.02	0.02	0.21	0.22	0.19	0.15	0.10	0.08	0.12	0.10	1.50	1.50	1.88	1.83
b) Support of apprenticeship and related forms of general youth training	0.01	0.01	0.01	0.01	0.35	0.34	0.31	0.32	–	–	–	–	–	–	–	–	–	–	–	–	–	–	–	–
4. Subsidised employment	0.08	0.05	0.03	0.03	0.56	0.41	0.34	0.31	0.05	0.09	0.09	0.06	0.60	0.90	0.80	0.58	0.30	0.27	0.23	0.17	1.11	1.05	1.00	0.82
a) Subsidies to regular employment in the private sector	0.01	0.01	–	–	0.20	0.16	0.18	0.17	0.02	0.04	0.04	0.02	0.24	0.41	0.33	0.20	0.02	0.02	0.02	0.02	0.22	0.25	0.22	0.20
b) Support of unemployed persons starting enterprises	0.01	0.01	0.01	0.01	0.11	0.09	0.07	0.07	0.01	0.01	0.01	–	0.06	0.11	0.09	0.06	0.06	0.04	0.02	–	0.10	–	–	–
c) Direct job creation (public or non-profit)	0.05	0.04	0.02	0.02	0.25	0.15	0.08	0.06	0.03	0.04	0.04	0.03	0.31	0.38	0.39	0.32	0.22	0.21	0.19	0.15	0.78	0.78	0.78	0.62
5. Measures for the disabled	0.02	0.02	0.02	0.02	..	..	..	..	0.01	0.01	0.01	0.01	–	–	–	–	0.21	0.25	0.33	0.34	2.28	2.51	3.05	2.58
a) Vocational rehabilitation	0.02	0.02	0.02	0.02	..	..	..	..	0.01	0.01	0.01	0.01	–	–	–	–	0.21	0.25	0.33	0.34	2.28	2.51	3.05	2.58
b) Work for the disabled	–	–	–	–	–	–	–	–	0.01	0.01	0.01	0.01	–	–	–	–	–	–	–	–	–	–	–	–
6. Unemployment compensation	0.94	0.78	0.71	0.81	..	..	..	..	0.30	0.29	0.24	0.27	..	..	..	..	2.12	1.69	1.44	1.37	24.42	23.08	21.15	19.61
7. Early retirement for labour market reasons	–	–	–	–	..	..	..	..	–	–	–	–	1.11	1.09	0.99	0.39	1.71	1.72	1.71	1.67	1.06	1.06	0.58	0.98
TOTAL	1.44	1.23	1.12	1.24	..	2.56[b,c]	2.18[b,c]	1.93[b,c] 1.96[b,c]	0.48	0.50	0.45	0.44	..	..	..	..	5.49	5.09	4.94	4.62	48.86	49.83	47.39	41.72
Active measures (1-5; for inflows, 2-5)	0.50	0.45	0.41	0.43	..	..	..	..	0.18	0.21	0.21	0.17	1.27	1.76	1.69	1.43	1.66	1.68	1.79	1.58	23.37	25.69	25.66	21.13
Passive measures (6 and 7)	0.95	0.78	0.71	0.81	..	..	..	..	0.30	0.29	0.24	0.27	..	..	..	..	3.83	3.41	3.15	3.04	25.48	24.15	21.72	20.59

.. Data not available.
– Nil or less than half of the last digit used.
* Data for participant inflows are reported only for categories 2 to 7 since data for category 1 "Public employment services and administration" are commonly incomplete and non-comparable. Totals shown must be interpreted with caution.
a) Fiscal years starting on April 1.
b) Participant inflows for category 2b "Training for employed adults" are not included.
c) Participant inflows for category 5a "Vocational rehabilitation" are not included.

STATISTICAL ANNEX

Table H. Public expenditure and participant inflows* in labour market programmes in OECD countries (cont.)

Programme categories and sub-categories	Finland Public expenditure as a percentage of GDP 1999	2000	2001	2002	Finland Participant inflows as a percentage of the labour force 1999	2000	2001	2002	France Public expenditure as a percentage of GDP 1998	1999	2000	2001	France Participant inflows as a percentage of the labour force 1998	1999	2000	2001	Germany Public expenditure as a percentage of GDP 1999	2000	2001	2002	Germany Participant inflows as a percentage of the labour force 1999	2000	2001	2002
1. Public employment services and administration	0.15	0.11	0.12	0.12					0.16	0.17	0.18	0.18					0.23	0.23	0.23	0.23				
2. Labour market training	0.40	0.30	0.29	0.30	4.22	3.40	2.95	2.95	0.31	0.29	0.25	0.24	2.85	2.64	2.39	2.27	0.35	0.34	0.34	0.32	1.34	1.51	1.23	1.24
a) Training for unemployed adults and those at risk	0.37	0.27	0.26	0.27	2.33	2.55	2.35	2.51	0.28	0.25	0.22	0.21	2.24	2.11	1.85	1.73	0.35	0.34	0.34	0.32	1.34	1.51	1.23	1.24
b) Training for employed adults	0.04	0.03	0.03	0.03	1.89	0.85	0.60	0.44	0.04	0.04	0.03	0.03	0.61	0.53	0.54	0.54	–	–	–	–	–	–	–	–
3. Youth measures	0.20	0.18	0.16	0.17	2.49	2.28	2.00	2.11	0.33	0.40	0.42	0.43	2.95	2.96	2.81	2.69	0.08	0.08	0.09	0.10	1.02	1.03	1.11	1.25
a) Measures for unemployed and disadvantaged youth	0.08	0.06	0.06	0.07	1.25	1.05	1.07	1.01	0.14	0.21	0.24	0.25	0.80	0.70	0.56	0.44	0.07	0.07	0.08	0.09	0.62	0.67	0.67	0.74
b) Support of apprenticeship and related forms of general youth training	0.13	0.11	0.10	0.11	1.23	1.23	0.93	1.10	0.19	0.19	0.18	0.18	2.15	2.26	2.25	2.25	0.01	0.01	0.01	0.02	0.41	0.36	0.44	0.51
4. Subsidised employment	0.38	0.31	0.29	0.33	2.74	2.24	2.23	1.73	0.43	0.43	0.38	0.35	3.75	3.52	3.10	2.45	0.40	0.32	0.25	0.22	1.62	1.26	1.06	0.97
a) Subsidies to regular employment in the private sector	0.16	0.15	0.14	0.16	1.06	0.91	0.85	0.42	0.24	0.23	0.18	0.16	2.14	1.95	1.65	1.20	0.03	0.03	0.03	0.03	0.10	0.11	0.13	0.08
b) Support of unemployed persons starting enterprises	0.03	0.03	0.03	0.03	0.17	0.16	0.44	0.43	–	–	–	–	0.15	0.16	0.16	0.14	0.04	0.04	0.04	0.05	0.25	0.23	0.24	0.31
c) Direct job creation (public or non-profit)	0.19	0.13	0.12	0.14	1.51	1.17	0.94	0.88	0.18	0.19	0.18	0.18	1.39	1.36	1.23	1.06	0.33	0.25	0.19	0.15	1.27	0.91	0.69	0.58
5. Measures for the disabled	0.10	0.09	0.09	0.08	0.83	0.90	0.88	0.83	0.09	0.09	0.09	0.09	0.26[a]	0.37[a]	0.44[a]	0.55[a]	0.27	0.28	0.29	0.32	0.33[a]	0.39[a]	0.34[a]	0.34[a]
a) Vocational rehabilitation	0.06	0.05	0.05	0.05	0.83	0.90	0.88	0.83	0.02	0.02	0.03	0.03	0.26	0.37	0.44	0.55	0.12	0.12	0.13	0.15	0.33	0.39	0.34	0.34
b) Work for the disabled	0.05	0.04	0.04	0.04	–	–	–	–	0.06	0.06	0.06	0.07	..	..	..	..	0.15	0.15	0.16	0.17	..	..	..	..
6. Unemployment compensation	1.88	1.65	1.51	1.53	..	..	..	..	1.47	1.46	1.38	1.40	6.60	6.58	6.35	7.12	2.12	1.88	1.89	2.10	..	..	..	..
7. Early retirement for labour market reasons	0.47	0.48	0.50	0.53	..	..	..	..	0.32	0.30	0.27	0.24	0.34	0.29	0.25	0.17	0.01	0.01	0.02	0.03	..	..	..	..
TOTAL	3.57	3.13	2.95	3.07	..	..	..	..	3.11	3.13	2.96	2.94	16.75	16.36	15.35	15.26	3.45	3.14	3.12	3.33	..	..	..	..
Active measures (1-5; for inflows, 2-5)	1.23	1.00	0.94	1.01	10.27	8.82	8.07	7.61	1.31	1.38	1.32	1.30	9.81[a]	9.49[a]	8.75[a]	7.96[a]	1.33	1.25	1.21	1.20	4.31[a]	4.18[a]	3.74[a]	3.80[a]
Passive measures (6 and 7)	2.34	2.13	2.01	2.06	..	..	..	..	1.80	1.75	1.65	1.64	6.94	6.87	6.60	7.30	2.12	1.89	1.92	2.13	..	..	..	..

.. Data not available.
– Nil or less than half of the last digit used.
* Data for participant inflows are reported only for categories 2 to 7 since data for category 1 "Public employment services and administration" are commonly incomplete and non-comparable. Totals shown must be interpreted with caution.
a) Participant inflows for category 5b "Work for the disabled" are not included.

Table H. Public expenditure and participant inflows* in labour market programmes in OECD countries (cont.)

Greece

Programme categories and sub-categories	Public expenditure as a percentage of GDP				Participant inflows as a percentage of the labour force			
	1995	1996	1997	1998	1995	1996	1997	1998
1. Public employment services and administration	0.14	0.14	0.12	0.06	..	..	..	..
2. Labour market training	0.13	0.09	0.06	0.21	2.01	2.09	..	..
a) Training for unemployed adults and those at risk	..	..	..	0.12	0.13	0.19	..	..
b) Training for employed adults	..	..	..	0.07	1.88	1.91	..	..
3. Youth measures	0.10	0.09	0.09	0.10	0.32	0.38	..	..
a) Measures for unemployed and disadvantaged youth	0.03	0.03	0.02	–	–	–	..	..
b) Support of apprenticeship and related forms of general youth training	0.07	0.07	0.07	0.10	0.32	0.38	..	..
4. Subsidised employment	0.08	0.10	0.06	0.08	0.91	0.54	..	..
a) Subsidies to regular employment in the private sector	0.05	0.07	0.04	0.05	0.73	0.45	..	..
b) Support of unemployed persons starting enterprises	0.02	0.02	0.02	0.03	0.18	0.09	..	..
c) Direct job creation (public or non-profit)	–	–	–	–	–	–	..	..
5. Measures for the disabled	–	0.03	0.01	0.01	–	–	..	..
a) Vocational rehabilitation	–	..	..	0.01	–	–	..	..
b) Work for the disabled	–	..	..	–	–	–	..	..
6. Unemployment compensation	0.42	0.44	0.49	0.47	7.87	8.26	..	..
7. Early retirement for labour market reasons	–	–	–	–	–	–	..	–
TOTAL	0.87	0.88	0.84	0.93	11.13	11.28	..	..
Active measures (1-5; for inflows, 2-5)	0.45	0.44	0.35	0.46	3.26	3.02	..	..
Passive measures (6 and 7)	0.42	0.44	0.49	0.47	7.87	8.26	..	..

Hungary

Programme categories and sub-categories	Public expenditure as a percentage of GDP				Participant inflows as a percentage of the labour force				
	1999	2000	2001	2002[a]	1999	2000	2001	2002[a]
1. Public employment services and administration	0.11	0.11	0.11	0.12				
2. Labour market training	0.07	0.07	0.07	0.06	1.35	1.34	1.62	1.17
a) Training for unemployed adults and those at risk	0.07	0.06	0.07	0.06	1.24	1.25	1.57	1.09
b) Training for employed adults	–	–	–	–	0.11	0.09	0.06	0.09
3. Youth measures	–	–	–	–	–	–	–	–
a) Measures for unemployed and disadvantaged youth	–	–	–	–	–	–	–	–
b) Support of apprenticeship and related forms of general youth training	–	–	–	–	–	–	–	–
4. Subsidised employment	0.22	0.21	0.29	0.34	4.07	4.02	5.10	6.71
a) Subsidies to regular employment in the private sector	0.09	0.07	0.09	0.08	1.03	0.98	1.15	0.66
b) Support of unemployed persons starting enterprises	–	–	0.01	0.01	0.09	0.09	0.24	0.22
c) Direct job creation (public or non-profit)	0.13	0.15	0.19	0.25	2.96	2.95	3.72	5.82
5. Measures for the disabled	–	–	–	–	–	–	–	–
a) Vocational rehabilitation	–	–	–	–	–	–	–	–
b) Work for the disabled	–	–	–	–	–	–	–	–
6. Unemployment compensation	0.47	0.43	0.37	0.37	7.44	7.02	7.16	7.10
7. Early retirement for labour market reasons	0.09	0.04	0.01	–	–	–	–	–
TOTAL	0.97	0.86	0.86	0.88	12.86	12.38	13.88	14.98
Active measures (1-5; for inflows, 2-5)	0.40	0.39	0.47	0.51	5.42	5.36	6.73	7.88
Passive measures (6 and 7)	0.57	0.47	0.38	0.37	7.44	7.02	7.16	7.10

Ireland

Programme categories and sub-categories	Public expenditure as a percentage of GDP		Participant inflows as a percentage of the labour force	
	2000	2001	2000	2001
1. Public employment services and administration	..	0.24	..	..
2. Labour market training	..	0.15	..	1.43
a) Training for unemployed adults and those at risk	..	0.15	..	1.43
b) Training for employed adults	..	0.01	..	..
3. Youth measures	..	0.18	..	1.73
a) Measures for unemployed and disadvantaged youth	..	0.08	..	0.73
b) Support of apprenticeship and related forms of general youth training	..	0.10	..	1.00
4. Subsidised employment	..	0.53	..	5.00
a) Subsidies to regular employment in the private sector	..	0.17	..	2.52
b) Support of unemployed persons starting enterprises	..	..	..	–
c) Direct job creation (public or non-profit)	..	0.36	..	2.48
5. Measures for the disabled	..	0.03	..	..
a) Vocational rehabilitation	..	0.03	..	..
b) Work for the disabled	..	0.01	..	..
6. Unemployment compensation	..	0.63	..	7.34
7. Early retirement for labour market reasons	..	0.07	..	0.66
TOTAL	..	1.84	..	..
Active measures (1-5; for inflows, 2-5)	..	1.14	..	..
Passive measures (6 and 7)	..	0.70	..	8.00

.. Data not available.
– Nil or less than half of the last digit used.
* Data for participant inflows are reported only for categories 2 to 7 since data for category 1 "Public employment services and administration" are commonly incomplete and non-comparable. Totals shown must be interpreted with caution.
a) Provisional data.

Table H. Public expenditure and participant inflows* in labour market programmes in OECD countries (cont.)

Italy

Programme categories and sub-categories	Public expenditure as a percentage of GDP 1998	1999	2000	2001	Participant inflows as a percentage of the labour force 1998	1999	2000	2001
1. Public employment services and administration	0.12	..	0.05	0.04				
2. Labour market training	..	0.07			1.26	0.77	–	0.10
a) Training for unemployed adults and those at risk	..	..	..	..	..	..	..	..
b) Training for employed adults	..	..	..	..	..	..	..	..
3. Youth measures	0.22	0.24	0.23	0.21	3.45	3.43	3.33	3.12
a) Measures for unemployed and disadvantaged youth	0.01	0.01	0.01	0.01	–	–	–	–
b) Support of apprenticeship and related forms of general youth training	0.21	0.23	0.21	0.20	3.45	3.43	3.33	3.12
4. Subsidised employment	0.24	0.27	0.32	0.38	2.69	4.44	4.55	4.52
a) Subsidies to regular employment in the private sector	0.17	0.19	0.24	0.27	2.09	3.79	4.01	4.08
b) Support of unemployed persons starting enterprises	–	0.01	0.04	0.07	–	–	–	0.06
c) Direct job creation (public or non-profit)	0.06	0.07	0.05	0.05	0.59	0.63	0.50	0.38
5. Measures for the disabled	..	..	..	..	..	..	..	..
a) Vocational rehabilitation	..	..	..	..	..	..	..	..
b) Work for the disabled	..	..	..	..	..	..	..	..
6. Unemployment compensation	0.59	0.56	0.52	0.53	10.50	11.35	11.29	12.74
7. Early retirement for labour market reasons	0.18	0.13	0.11	0.08	1.73	1.68	1.70	1.66
TOTAL	1.34[a]	1.26[a]	1.22[a]	1.25[a]	19.63[a]	21.68[a]	20.92[a]	22.15[a]
Active measures (1-5; for inflows, 2-5)	0.58[a]	0.58[a]	0.60[a]	0.64[a]	7.40[a]	8.65[a]	7.92[a]	7.75[a]
Passive measures (6 and 7)	0.76	0.68	0.62	0.61	12.23	13.03	12.99	14.40

Japan[b]

	Public expenditure as a percentage of GDP 1998-99	1999-00	2000-01	2001-02
1.	0.17	0.17	0.17	0.17
2.	0.03	0.03	0.03	0.03
a)	0.03	0.03	0.03	0.03
b)	–	–	–	–
3.	–	–	–	–
a)	–	–	–	–
b)	–	–	–	–
4.	0.05	0.08	0.07	0.07
a)	–	–	–	–
b)	–	–	–	–
c)	–	–	–	–
5.	0.01	0.01	0.01	0.01
a)	0.01	0.01	0.01	0.01
b)	–	–	–	–
6.	0.47	0.51	0.55	0.46
7.	–	–	–	–
TOTAL	0.72	0.80	0.83	0.74
Active	0.26	0.29	0.28	0.28
Passive	0.47	0.51	0.55	0.46

Korea

	Public expenditure as a percentage of GDP 1999	2000	2001	2002	Participant inflows as a percentage of the labour force 1999	2000	2001	2002
1.	0.04	0.04	0.05	0.05				
2.	0.11	0.09	0.08	0.08	5.37	6.82	8.09	8.24
a)	0.08	0.06	0.04	0.04	1.73	1.26	1.15	0.88
b)	0.02	0.03	0.04	0.04	3.64	5.56	6.94	7.35
3.	0.04	0.03	0.02	0.02	0.36	0.42	0.34	0.19
a)	0.01	0.01	0.01	0.01	0.14	0.16	0.18	0.15
b)	0.03	0.02	0.01	–	0.22	0.26	0.16	–
4.	0.51	0.31	0.15	0.11	9.28	5.66	4.51	3.99
a)	0.02	0.01	0.01	0.01	2.24	1.64	1.94	1.73
b)	0.01	0.01	0.01	0.01	–	–	–	–
c)	0.48	0.29	0.12	0.09	7.04	4.01	2.57	2.25
5.	0.01	0.01	0.02	0.02	0.11	0.12	0.14	0.28
a)	0.01	0.01	0.02	0.02	0.11	0.11	0.11	0.20
b)	–	–	–	–	–	–	–	0.08
6.	0.19	0.09	0.16	0.14	2.14	1.38	1.67	1.78
7.	–	–	–	–	–	–	–	–
TOTAL	0.89	0.58	0.47	0.42	17.26	14.40	14.75	14.48
Active	0.70	0.49	0.31	0.28	15.13	13.02	13.08	12.70
Passive	0.19	0.09	0.16	0.14	2.14	1.38	1.67	1.78

Mexico

	Public expenditure as a percentage of GDP 1998	1999	2000	2001	Participant inflows as a percentage of the labour force 1998	1999	2000	2001
1.	–	–	–	–				
2.	0.04	0.04	0.04	0.03	2.92	3.42	3.39	1.87
a)	0.03	0.03	0.03	0.03	1.32	1.44	1.52	1.01
b)	0.01	0.01	0.01	0.01	1.60	1.98	1.88	0.85
3.	–	–	–	–	–	–	–	–
a)	–	–	–	–	–	–	–	–
b)	–	–	–	–	–	–	–	–
4.	0.03	0.04	0.03	0.02	1.19	1.76	1.37	1.43
a)	–	–	–	–	–	–	–	–
b)	–	–	–	–	–	–	–	–
c)	0.03	0.04	0.02	0.02	0.16	0.12	0.10	0.07
5.	–	–	–	–	1.04	1.64	1.27	1.36
a)	–	–	–	–	–	–	–	–
b)	–	–	–	–	–	–	–	–
6.	–	–	–	–	–	–	–	–
7.	–	–	–	–	–	–	–	–
TOTAL	0.07	0.08	0.06	0.06	4.12	5.18	4.76	3.30
Active	0.07	0.08	0.06	0.06	4.12	5.18	4.76	3.30
Passive	..	..	..	..	..	..	..	..

.. Data not available.
– Nil or less than half of the last digit used.
* Data for participant inflows are reported only for categories 2 to 7 since data for category 1 "Public employment services and administration" are commonly incomplete and non-comparable. Totals shown must be interpreted with caution.
a) Only active categories 2-4 are taken into account.
b) Fiscal years starting on April 1.

STATISTICAL ANNEX

Table H. **Public expenditure and participant inflows* in labour market programmes in OECD countries** (cont.)

	Netherlands								New Zealand[b]								Norway							
Programme categories and sub-categories	Public expenditure as a percentage of GDP				Participant inflows as a percentage of the labour force				Public expenditure as a percentage of GDP				Participant inflows as a percentage of the labour force				Public expenditure as a percentage of GDP				Participant inflows as a percentage of the labour force			
	1998	1999	2000	2001	1998	1999	2000	2001	1998-99	1999-00	2000-01	2001-02	1998-99	1999-00	2000-01	2001-02	1999	2000	2001	2002	1999	2000	2001	2002
1. Public employment services and administration	0.31	0.28	0.27	0.26	–	–	–	–	0.12	0.15	0.13	0.13	–	–	–	–	0.15	0.12	0.12	0.13	–	–	–	–
2. Labour market training	0.39	0.45	0.45	0.47	3.00	3.46	3.62	3.82	0.23	0.18	0.16	0.12	2.98	5.43	3.34	2.87	0.05	0.08	0.06	0.05	1.03	1.05	0.86	0.99
a) Training for unemployed adults and those at risk	0.35[a]	0.40[a]	0.38[a]	0.39[a]	1.20	1.37	1.34	1.37	0.23	0.18	0.16	0.12	2.98	5.43	3.34	2.87	0.05	0.08	0.06	0.05	1.03	1.05	0.86	0.99
b) Training for employed adults	0.05	0.06	0.07	0.08	1.80	2.09	2.28	2.44	–	–	–	–	–	–	–	–	–	–	–	–	–	–	–	–
3. Youth measures	0.04	0.04	0.04	0.04	0.59	0.64	0.63	0.64	0.12	0.13	0.14	0.16	3.22	0.11	4.76	4.95	0.01	0.01	0.01	0.01	0.39	0.41	0.41	0.51
a) Measures for unemployed and disadvantaged youth	–	–	–	–	–	–	–	–	0.07	0.07	0.07	0.08	0.54	0.11	1.22	0.71	0.01	0.01	0.01	0.01	0.39	0.41	0.41	0.51
b) Support of apprenticeship and related forms of general youth training	0.04	0.04	0.04	0.04	0.59	0.64	0.63	0.64	0.05	0.07	0.07	0.08	2.67	–	3.54	4.24	–	–	–	–	–	–	–	–
4. Subsidised employment	0.41	0.38	0.38	0.38	1.91	1.88	1.88	1.77	0.09	0.11	0.09	0.08	1.34	2.63	1.96	1.61	0.01	0.01	0.01	0.01	0.25	0.26	0.27	0.24
a) Subsidies to regular employment in the private sector	0.08	0.05	0.05	0.05	1.47	1.39	1.43	1.41	0.04	0.06	0.05	0.04	0.71	1.06	0.91	0.93	0.01	0.01	0.01	0.01	0.19	0.22	0.22	0.21
b) Support of unemployed persons starting enterprises	–	–	–	–	–	–	–	–	0.03	0.03	0.03	0.03	0.40	0.35	0.36	0.24	–	–	–	–	0.06	–	–	–
c) Direct job creation (public or non-profit)	0.33	0.33	0.33	0.34	0.44	0.49	0.45	0.36	0.03	0.02	0.01	0.01	0.22	1.22	0.68	0.44	–	–	–	–	–	–	–	–
5. Measures for the disabled	0.52	0.56	0.55	0.58	0.39	0.73	0.77	0.99	0.05	0.05	0.05	0.05	0.62	1.33	1.31	–	0.57	0.52	0.59	0.66	1.84	2.29	2.54	2.74
a) Vocational rehabilitation	–	–	–	–	–	–	–	–	0.03	0.03	0.01	0.01	0.43	1.00	0.40	–	0.39	0.37	0.43	0.50	1.26	1.58	1.78	..
b) Work for the disabled	0.52	0.56	0.55	0.58	0.37	0.71	0.77	0.99	0.02	0.02	0.04	0.04	0.19	0.33	0.90	..	0.18	0.15	0.17	0.17	0.58	0.72	0.76	..
6. Unemployment compensation	2.58	2.30	2.03	1.88	7.46	5.72	4.77	4.33	1.55	1.58	1.40	1.16	13.68	10.21	8.64	7.98	0.45	0.43	0.44	0.53	4.70	4.46	4.20	5.37
7. Early retirement for labour market reasons	–	–	–	–	–	–	–	–	–	–	–	–	–	–	–	–	–	–	–	–	–	–	–	–
TOTAL	4.25	4.02	3.73	3.62	13.35	12.43	11.67	11.55	2.17	2.21	1.97	1.70	21.84	19.70	20.01	17.41[c]	1.24	1.17	1.23	1.39	8.20	8.47	8.26	9.85
Active measures (1-5; for inflows, 2-5)	1.67	1.72	1.70	1.74	5.90	6.71	6.90	7.22	0.61	0.62	0.57	0.54	8.16	9.49	11.37	9.43[c]	0.79	0.74	0.79	0.86	3.50	4.02	4.06	4.48
Passive measures (6 and 7)	2.58	2.30	2.03	1.88	7.46	5.72	4.77	4.33	1.55	1.58	1.40	1.16	13.68	10.21	8.64	7.98	0.45	0.43	0.44	0.53	4.70	4.46	4.20	5.37

.. Data not available.
– Nil or less than half of the last digit used.
* Data for participant inflows are reported only for categories 2 to 7 since data for category 1 "Public employment services and administration" are commonly incomplete and non-comparable. Totals shown must be interpreted with caution.
a) Incorporates a revised estimate for unemployment benefits paid to participants in training.
b) Fiscal years starting on July 1.
c) Participant inflows for category 5 "Measures for the disabled" are not included.

STATISTICAL ANNEX

Table H. Public expenditure and participant inflows* in labour market programmes in OECD countries (cont.)

Poland

Programme categories and sub-categories	Public expenditure as a percentage of GDP 1998	1999	2000	2001	Participant inflows as a percentage of the labour force 1998	1999	2000	2001
1. Public employment services and administration	..	..	..	..				
	0.02	0.02	0.01	0.01				
2. Labour market training					0.80	0.74	0.57	0.27
a) Training for unemployed adults and those at risk	0.02	0.02	0.01	0.01	0.80	0.74	0.57	0.27
b) Training for employed adults	–	–	–	–	–	–	–	–
3. Youth measures	0.10	0.09	0.07	0.08	2.56	2.37	..	..
a) Measures for unemployed and disadvantaged youth	0.04	0.04	0.03	0.03	0.82	0.81	..	..
b) Support of apprenticeship and related forms of general youth training	0.06	0.05	0.04	0.05	1.74	1.56	..	..
4. Subsidised employment	0.16	0.11	0.06	0.05	1.51	1.19	0.90	0.41
a) Subsidies to regular employment in the private sector	0.07	0.05	0.03	0.02	0.84	0.74	0.58	0.23
b) Support of unemployed persons starting enterprises	0.02	0.02	0.01	0.01	0.06	–	–	–
c) Direct job creation (public or non-profit)	0.06	0.03	0.02	0.02	0.60	0.40	0.29	0.17
5. Measures for the disabled	0.18	0.14	0.10	..	0.23	0.23	0.21	..
a) Vocational rehabilitation	–	0.01	0.01	..	–	–	0.06	..
b) Work for the disabled	0.18	0.13	0.09	..	0.20	0.20	0.15	..
6. Unemployment compensation	0.55	0.64	0.84	1.01	3.01	3.58	4.58	5.26
7. Early retirement for labour market reasons	–	–	–	–	–	–	–	–
TOTAL	..	..	..	..	8.11	8.12	..	..
Active measures (1-5; for inflows, 2-5)	..	..	..	..	5.11	4.53	..	..
Passive measures (6 and 7)	0.55	0.64	0.84	1.01	3.01	3.58	4.58	5.26

Portugal

	Public expenditure as a percentage of GDP 1997	1998	1999	2000	Participant inflows as a percentage of the labour force 1997	1998	1999	2000
1.	0.11	0.11	0.11	0.11				
2.	0.27	0.29	0.29	0.15	10.77	14.96	..	..
a)	0.08	0.08	0.08	0.07	0.60	0.61	0.81	..
b)	0.19	0.22	0.21	0.09	10.17	14.35	..	..
3.	0.28	0.24	0.28	0.22				
a)	0.05	0.07	0.09	0.10	0.27	0.41	0.56	0.50
b)	–	–	–	–	–	–	–	–
4.	0.22	0.18	0.19	0.12	..	..	..	..
	0.09	0.09	0.10	0.09	1.02	1.06	1.13	1.07
a)	0.01	0.01	0.01	0.01	–	0.06	0.08	0.05
b)	0.02	0.03	0.03	0.03	0.13	0.11	0.12	0.09
c)	0.05	0.05	0.05	0.05	0.84	0.89	0.94	0.92
5.	0.03	0.04	0.04	0.04	0.15	0.17	0.14	0.16
a)	0.02	–	–	–	0.13	..	–	–
b)	0.01	0.01	–	–	–	–	–	–
6.	0.69	0.65	0.65	0.69	3.40	3.26	3.18	3.18
7.	0.14	0.15	0.15	0.21	0.50	0.55	0.53	0.81
TOTAL	1.60	1.57	1.62	1.51	..	..	..	..
	0.77	0.77	0.81	0.61	..	3.81	3.71	3.98
	0.83	0.80	0.81	0.90	3.90	3.81	3.71	3.98

Slovak Republic

	Public expenditure as a percentage of GDP 1999	2000	2001	2002	Participant inflows as a percentage of the labour force 1999	2000	2001	2002
1.	0.16	0.16	0.15	0.16				
	0.01	0.01	0.02	0.04	0.23	0.19	0.95	1.91
a)	0.01	–	0.02	0.04	0.22	0.18	0.93	1.86
b)	–	–	–	–	–	–	–	–
3.	–	–	–	0.01	–	–	–	0.50
a)	–	–	–	0.01	–	–	–	0.50
b)	–	–	–	–	–	–	–	–
4.	0.03	0.14	0.17	0.21	0.27	2.64	2.29	2.63
a)	0.01	–	0.01	0.06	–	–	0.21	0.74
b)	–	–	0.01	0.06	–	–	0.09	0.35
c)	0.01	0.14	0.15	0.10	0.22	2.59	1.99	1.54
5.	0.02	0.02	0.03	0.04	0.11[a]	0.10[a]	0.12[a]	0.19[a]
a)	–	–	–	–	–	–	–	–
b)	0.01	0.02	0.02	0.04	0.11	0.10	0.12	0.19
6.	0.87	0.68	0.48	0.49	10.64	7.93	7.46	7.36
7.	0.18	0.19	0.07	0.01	0.82	0.32	–	–
TOTAL	1.27	1.20	0.93	0.96	12.06	11.18	10.83	12.58
	0.21	0.33	0.38	0.47	0.61[a]	2.93[a]	3.37[a]	5.22[a]
	1.06	0.87	0.56	0.49	11.45	8.25	7.46	7.36

.. Data not available.
– Nil or less than half of the last digit used.
* Data for participant inflows are reported only for categories 2 to 7 since data for category 1 "Public employment services and administration" are commonly incomplete and non-comparable. Totals shown must be interpreted with caution. Participant inflows for category 5a "Vocational rehabilitation" are not included.
a)

334

OECD EMPLOYMENT OUTLOOK – ISBN 92-64-10061-X – © OECD 2003

Table H. Public expenditure and participant inflows* in labour market programmes in OECD countries (cont.)

Programme categories and sub-categories	Spain[a] Public expenditure as a percentage of GDP 1999	2000	2001	2002[b]	Participant inflows as a percentage of the labour force 1999	2000	2001	2002[b]	Sweden Public expenditure as a percentage of GDP 1999	2000	2001	2002	Participant inflows as a percentage of the labour force 1999	2000	2001	2002	Switzerland Public expenditure as a percentage of GDP 1999	2000	2001	2002	Participant inflows as a percentage of the labour force 1999	2000	2001	2002
1. Public employment services and administration	0.06	0.09	0.09	0.09	–	–	–	–	0.29	0.30	0.36	0.38	–	–	–	–	0.15	0.11	0.10	0.12	–	–	–	–
2. Labour market training	0.21	0.25	0.23	0.22	10.12	10.45	15.05	15.27	0.47	0.29	0.30	0.29	3.79	2.84	2.68	2.50	0.14	0.11	0.09	0.13	1.73	1.37	1.22	1.71
a) Training for unemployed adults and those at risk	0.10	0.10	0.10	0.10	1.95	2.14	2.20	2.16	0.46	0.29	0.29	0.28	3.21	2.42	2.32	2.40	0.13	0.10	0.09	0.13	1.70	1.34	1.19	1.71
b) Training for employed adults	0.11	0.11	0.09	0.08	8.17	8.31	12.85	13.10	0.01	0.01	0.01	0.01	0.58	0.42	0.36	0.10	–	–	–	–	–	–	–	–
3. Youth measures	0.07	0.07	0.06	0.05	2.41	1.98	..	..	0.03	0.02	0.02	0.02	0.73	0.62	0.55	0.61	–	0.01	0.01	0.01	0.06	0.06	0.06	0.07
a) Measures for unemployed and disadvantaged youth	0.06	0.05	0.04	0.04	0.98	0.80	..	..	0.03	0.02	0.02	0.02	0.73	0.62	0.55	0.61	–	0.01	0.01	0.01	0.06	0.06	0.06	0.07
b) Support of apprenticeship and related forms of general youth training	0.01	–	–	..	1.43	1.18	..	..	–	–	–	–	–	–	–	–	–	–	–	–	–	–	–	–
4. Subsidised employment	0.44	0.48	0.43	0.44	5.09	5.17	5.42	5.69	0.44	0.26	0.23	0.21	3.33	2.97	2.11	1.95	0.25	0.14	0.11	0.14	3.02	2.14	1.67	2.00
a) Subsidies to regular employment in the private sector	0.30	0.30	0.25	0.26	3.20	3.64	4.07	4.47	0.17	0.14	0.18	0.17	2.78	2.66	1.89	1.70	0.07	0.06	0.04	0.04	2.05	1.53	1.16	1.38
b) Support of unemployed persons starting enterprises	0.04	0.05	0.05	0.05	0.20	0.17	0.19	0.12	0.07	0.05	0.04	0.04	0.36	0.30	0.22	0.25	0.01	–	–	0.01	0.06	0.57	0.48	0.58
c) Direct job creation (public or non-profit)	0.09	0.09	0.08	0.08	1.69	1.37	1.17	1.10	0.20	0.07	–	–	0.19	–	–	–	0.17	0.08	0.07	0.09	0.92	..	..	..
5. Measures for the disabled	0.03	0.03	0.03	0.03	0.17	0.23	0.24	0.25	0.55	0.50	0.49	0.50	0.85	0.90	0.87	0.99	0.14	0.14	0.14	0.15	6.86	5.29	5.06	7.32
a) Vocational rehabilitation	–	–	–	–	–	–	–	–	0.03	0.03	0.03	0.03	0.51	0.55	0.43	0.50	0.14	0.14	0.14	0.15	–	–	–	–
b) Work for the disabled	0.03	0.03	0.03	0.03	0.17	0.23	0.24	0.25	0.52	0.47	0.46	0.47	0.34	0.34	0.44	0.48	–	–	–	–	–	–	–	–
6. Unemployment compensation	1.40	1.34	1.32	1.56	1.39	1.37	1.47	1.59	1.53	1.27	0.92	0.92	..	..	..	..	0.90	0.56	0.49	0.79	6.86	5.29	5.06	7.32
7. Early retirement for labour market reasons	–	–	–	–	–	–	–	–	0.09	0.06	0.03	0.01	..	..	..	..	–	–	–	–	–	–	–	–
TOTAL	2.22	2.27	2.17	2.41	19.17	19.21	22.20[c]	22.80[c]	3.39	2.70	2.35	2.34	8.69	7.33	6.22	6.05	1.58	1.07	0.94	1.33	11.68[d]	8.87[d]	8.02[d]	11.10[d]
Active measures (1-5; for inflows, 2-5)	0.82	0.94	0.84	0.85	17.78	17.83	20.72[c]	21.21[c]	1.77	1.37	1.39	1.41	7.33	6.22	6.05		0.68	0.50	0.45	0.54	4.81[d]	3.58[d]	2.96[d]	3.78[d]
Passive measures (6 and 7)	1.40	1.34	1.32	1.56	1.39	1.37	1.47	1.59	1.62	1.33	0.96	0.93	..	..	..	..	0.90	0.56	0.49	0.79	6.86	5.29	5.06	7.32

.. Data not available.
– Nil or less than half of the last digit used.
* Data for participant inflows are reported only for categories 2 to 7 since data for category 1 "Public employment services and administration" are commonly incomplete and non-comparable. Totals shown must be interpreted with caution.
a) Data by category and for total expenditure include expenditure on LMPs administered by the Autonomous Communities and by the municipalities with at least 20 000 inhabitants. The figures by sub-category, which do not include such disbursements, do not add up to the totals by category. Public expenditure data for labour market training have been revised.
b) Provisional data.
c) Participant inflows for category 3 "Youth measures" are not included.
d) Participant inflows for category 5 "Measures for the disabled" are not included.

STATISTICAL ANNEX

Table H. **Public expenditure and participant inflows*** **in labour market programmes in OECD countries** (cont.)

Programme categories and sub-categories	United Kingdom[a] Public expenditure as a percentage of GDP 1998-99	1999-00	2000-01	2001-02	United Kingdom[a] Participant inflows as a percentage of the labour force 1998-99	1999-00	2000-01	2001-02	United States[b] Public expenditure as a percentage of GDP 1998-99	1999-00	2000-01	2001-02	United States[b] Participant inflows as a percentage of the labour force 1998-99	1999-00	2000-01	2001-02
1. Public employment services and administration	**0.13**	**0.13**	**0.13**	**0.16**					**0.06**	**0.04**	**0.04**	**0.04**				
2. Labour market training	0.05	0.05	0.04	0.03	0.49	0.52	0.51	0.31	0.04	0.04	0.04	0.04	0.59	–	0.97	0.94
a) Training for unemployed adults and those at risk	0.04	0.04	0.04	0.02	0.44	0.46	0.45	0.25	0.04	0.04	0.04	0.04	0.59	–	0.97	0.94
b) Training for employed adults	0.01	0.01	0.01	0.01	–	0.06	0.07	0.06	–	–	–	–	–	–	–	–
3. Youth measures	**0.14**	**0.15**	**0.15**	**0.13**	..	..	..	..	**0.03**	**0.03**	**0.03**	**0.03**	**0.56**	..	**0.44**	**0.44**
a) Measures for unemployed and disadvantaged youth	0.03	0.04	0.04	0.04	..	..	..	..	0.03	0.03	0.03	0.03	0.48	..	0.36	0.35
b) Support of apprenticeship and related forms of general youth training	0.11	0.11	0.11	0.09	0.98	1.03	1.07	0.94	–	–	–	–	–	–	–	–
4. Subsidised employment	**0.01**	**0.01**	**0.02**	**0.03**	..	..	..	..	**0.01**	**0.01**	**0.01**	**0.01**	**0.08**	..	**0.09**	**0.09**
a) Subsidies to regular employment in the private sector	–	–	–	0.02	..	..	..	..	–	–	–	–	0.38	0.37	0.38	0.35
b) Support of unemployed persons starting enterprises	–	0.01	0.01	0.01	..	..	..	..	–	–	–	–	0.31	0.37	0.33	0.29
c) Direct job creation (public or non-profit)	–	–	–	–	–	–	–	–	0.01	0.01	0.01	0.01	0.07	..	..	..
5. Measures for the disabled	**0.02**	**0.02**	**0.02**	**0.02**	**0.20**	**0.19**	**0.18**	**0.17**	**0.04**	**0.03**	**0.03**	**0.04**	..	..	..	**0.06**
a) Vocational rehabilitation	–	0.01	0.01	0.01	0.12	0.10	0.09	0.09	0.04	0.03	0.03	0.04	..	..	..	..
b) Work for the disabled	0.02	0.02	0.02	0.02	0.08	0.08	0.08	0.08	–	–	–	–	–	–	–	–
6. Unemployment compensation	**0.63**	**0.56**	**0.44**	**0.42**	**10.67**	**10.39**	**9.67**	**9.27**	**0.25**	**0.23**	**0.30**	**0.56**	..	..	..	..
7. Early retirement for labour market reasons	–	–	–	–	–	–	–	–	–	–	–	–	–	–	–	–
TOTAL	**0.97**	**0.92**	**0.81**	**0.80**					**0.42**	**0.38**	**0.45**	**0.70**				
Active measures (1-5; for inflows, 2-5)	0.34	0.36	0.37	0.38	..	..	..	..	0.17	0.15	0.15	0.15	1.53[c]	..	1.80[c]	1.74[c]
Passive measures (6 and 7)	0.63	0.56	0.44	0.42	10.67	10.39	9.67	9.27	0.25	0.23	0.30	0.56	–	–	–	–

.. Data not available.
– Nil or less than half of the last digit used.
* Data for participant inflows are reported only for categories 2 to 7 since data for category 1 "Public employment services and administration" are commonly incomplete and non-comparable. Totals shown must be interpreted with caution.
a) Excluding Northern Ireland. Fiscal years starting on April 1.
b) Fiscal years starting on October 1.
c) Participant inflows for category 5 "Measures for the disabled" are not included.

Source: OECD database on Labour Market Programmes.

Index of previous issues of the OECD Employment Outlook, 1983-2002

1983

The Employment Imperative and Labour Market Policies

Part I. The Labour Market in the Latest Recession

    Chapter 1. Labour Market Developments

    Chapter 2. Labour Market Prospects

Part II. Employment and Unemployment: Selected Medium-term Developments

    Chapter 3. The Determinants of Working Hours

    Chapter 4. Part-time Employment in OECD Countries

    Chapter 5. Long-term Unemployment in OECD Countries

    Chapter 6. The Nature of Youth-Adult Unemployment Differentials

1984

Jobs, Efficiency and Equity in Today's Labour Market

Part I. The Labour Market in the Recovery

    Chapter 1. Labour Market Developments

    Chapter 2. Labour Market Prospects

Part II. Selected Medium-term Developments in Employment and Unemployment

    Chapter 3. The Contribution of Services to Employment

    Chapter 4. The Importance of Long-term Job Attachment in OECD Countries

    Chapter 5. Do Relative Wage Levels Affect Youth Employment?

    Chapter 6. Unemployment and Family Income

1985

Employment Growth, Flexibility and Job Security: A Challenge for All

Part I. Labour Market Developments in the OECD Area

    Chapter 1. Short-term Labour Market Developments and Prospects

    Chapter 2. Medium-term Labour Market Developments

Part II. Detailed Analyses of Key Labour Market Issues

    Chapter 3. The Labour Market Implications of International Migration in Selected OECD Countries

Chapter 4. Employment in Small and Large Firms: Where Have the Jobs Come from?

Chapter 5. Relative Wages, Industrial Structure and Employment Performance

Chapter 6. Moving In and Out of Unemployment: The Incidence and Patterns of Recurrent Unemployment in Selected OECD Countries

1986

Policies for Employment in a Changing Economy

Part I. Labour Market Developments in the OECD Area

Chapter 1. Short-term Labour Market Developments and Prospects

Part II. Detailed Analyses of Key Labour Market Issues

Chapter 2. Self-employment in OECD Countries

Chapter 3. Concealed Employment

Chapter 4. Non-wage Labour Costs and Employment

Chapter 5. The Youth Labour Market Problem: Age and Generational Crowding

1987

Editorial: Activity for All in Tomorrow's Society

Part I. Labour Market Developments in the OECD Area

Chapter 1. Recent Labour Market Trends

Chapter 2. Labour Market Prospects

Part II. Detailed Analyses of Key Labour Market Issues

Chapter 3. Occupational Differentials in Earnings and Labour Demand

Chapter 4. The Process of Job Creation and Job Destruction

Chapter 5. Who Are the Unemployed? Measurement Issues and their Policy Implications

Chapter 6. On the Margin of the Labour Force: An Analysis of Discouraged Workers and Other Non-participants

Chapter 7. Long-term Unemployment

1988

Editorial: Steps towards an Active Society

Chapter 1. Labour Market Trends and Prospects in the OECD Area

Chapter 2. Longer-run Labour Market Issues

Chapter 3. Profiles of Labour Market Budgets 1985-1987

Chapter 4. Description of Unemployment Benefit Systems in OECD Countries

Chapter 5. Women's Activity, Employment and Earnings: A Review of Recent Developments

Chapter 6. Technology and Employment

1989

Editorial: *The Path to Full Employment: Structural Adjustment for an Active Society*

    Chapter 1. Labour Market Trends and Prospects

    Chapter 2. Educational Attainment of the Labour Force

    Chapter 3. Regional Unemployment in OECD Countries

    Chapter 4. Occupational Accidents in OECD Countries

    Chapter 5. Characteristics of Employment in Growing and Declining Industries

1990

Editorial: *Labour Markets in the 1990s: Challenges and Opportunities*

    Chapter 1. Labour Market Trends and Prospects in the OECD Area

    Chapter 2. Displacement and Job Loss: The Workers Concerned

    Chapter 3. Supply and Demand in Regional Labour Markets: Population Growth, Migration, Participation and Earnings Differentials

    Chapter 4. Occupational Illness in OECD Countries

    Chapter 5. Child Care in OECD Countries

    Chapter 6. Employer *versus* Employee Taxation: The Impact on Employment

    Chapter 7. Involuntary Part-time Work as a Component of Underemployment

1991

Editorial: *Labour Market Reform: Staying the Course*

Part I. Labour Market Developments and Prospects

    Chapter 1. Recent Labour Market Developments and Prospects

    Chapter 2. A Review of Labour Markets in the 1980s

    Chapter 3. Labour Markets in Dynamic Asian Economies

Part II. Key Issues for Labour Market and Social Policies

    Chapter 4. Trends in Trade Union Membership

    Chapter 5. Enterprise-related Training

    Chapter 6. Absences from Work Reported in Labour Force Surveys

    Chapter 7. Unemployment Benefits Rules and Labour Market Policy

1992

Editorial: *Fighting Unemployment: Action on Labour Market Reforms*

Part I. Labour Market Prospects and Developments

    Chapter 1. Recent Labour Market Developments and Prospects

    Chapter 2. Monitoring Labour Market Developments

    Chapter 3. The Public Employment Service in Japan, Norway, Spain and the United Kingdom

Part II. Key Issues for Labour Market and Social Policies

Chapter 4. Recent Developments in Self-employment

Chapter 5. Labour Market Participation and Retirement of Older Workers

Chapter 6. Reforming Labour Markets in Central and Eastern Europe and the Rise of Unemployment

1993

Editorial: Growth and Employment: A Key Role for Human Resource Development

Part I. Monitoring Labour Market Prospects and Developments

Chapter 1. Labour Market Prospects and Recent Developments

Chapter 2. Active Labour Market Policies: Assessing Macroeconomic and Microeconomic Effects

Part II. Key Issues for Labour Market and Social Policies

Chapter 3. Long-term Unemployment: Selected Causes and Remedies

Chapter 4. Enterprise Tenure, Labour Turnover and Skill Training

Chapter 5. Earnings Inequality: Changes in the 1980s

1994

Editorial: Creating Viable and Productive Jobs

Part I. Labour Market Prospects and Developments

Chapter 1. Recent Labour Market Developments and Prospects

Chapter 2. Medium-term Perspectives on Labour Supply and Occupational Change

Part II. Key Issues for Labour Market and Social Policies

Chapter 3. Job Gains and Job Losses in Firms

Chapter 4. Labour Standards and Economic Integration

Chapter 5. Collective Bargaining: Levels and Coverage

1995

Editorial: Making Active Labour Market Policies more Effective

Part I. Labour Market Prospects and Developments

Chapter 1. Recent Labour Market Developments and Prospects

Chapter 2. Supplementary Measures of Labour Market Slack: An Analysis of Discouraged and Involuntary Part-time Workers

Part II. Key Issues for Labour Market and Social Policies

Chapter 3. The Public Employment Service in Denmark, Finland and Italy

Chapter 4. Profit-sharing in OECD Countries

Chapter 5. Long-term Leave for Parents in OECD Countries

1996

Editorial: Countering the Risks of Labour Market Exclusion

Chapter 1. Recent Labour Market Developments and Prospects

Chapter 2. Making Work Pay

Chapter 3. Earnings Inequality, Low-paid Employment and Earnings Mobility

Chapter 4. Growing into Work: Youth and the Labour Market over the 1980s and 1990s

Chapter 5. Employment Adjustment, Workers and Unemployment

1997

Editorial: Low-wage Jobs: Stepping Stones to a Better Future or Traps?

Chapter 1. Recent Labour Market Developments and Prospects

Chapter 2. Earnings Mobility: Taking a Longer Run View

Chapter 3. Economic Performance and the Structure of Collective Bargaining

Chapter 4. Trade, Earnings and Employment: Assessing the Impact of Trade with Emerging Economies on OECD Labour Markets

Chapter 5. Is Job Insecurity on the Increase in OECD Countries?

1998

Editorial: Towards an Employment-centred Social Policy

Chapter 1. Recent Labour Market Developments and Prospects – *Special focus on patterns of employment and joblessness from a household perspective*

Chapter 2. Making the Most of the Minimum: Statutory Minimum Wages, Employment and Poverty

Chapter 3. Getting Started, Settling In: The Transition from Education to the Labour Market

Chapter 4. Work-force Ageing in OECD Countries

Chapter 5. Working Hours: Latest Trends and Policy Initiatives

1999

Editorial: Giving Youth a Better Start

Chapter 1. Recent Labour Market Developments and Prospects – *Special focus on the quality of part-time jobs*

Chapter 2. Employment Protection and Labour Market Performance

Chapter 3. Training of Adult Workers in OECD Countries: Measurement and Analysis

Chapter 4. New Entreprise Work Practices and their Labour Market Implications

2000

Editorial: Rewarding Work

Chapter 1. Recent Labour Market Developments and Prospects – *Special focus on the evolution of employment in the new OECD Member countries*

Chapter 2. Disparities in Regional Labour Markets

Chapter 3. Employment in the Service Economy: A Reassessment

Chapter 4. Eligibility Criteria for Unemployment Benefits

Chapter 5. The Partial Renaissance of Self-employment

2001

Editorial: Reconciling Social and Employment Goals

Chapter 1. Recent Labour Market Developments and Prospects – *Special focus on labour market policies: how the money has been spent*

Chapter 2. When Money is Tight: Poverty Dynamics in OECD Countries

Chapter 3. The Characteristics and Quality of Service Sector Jobs

Chapter 4. Balancing Work and Family Life: Helping Parents into Paid Employment

Chapter 5. The Employment of Foreigners: Outlook and Issues in OECD Countries

2002

Editorial: Surveying the Jobs Horizon

Chapter 1. Recent Labour Market Developments and Prospects – *Special focus on "A Better Start for Youths?"*

Chapter 2. Women at Work: Who Are They and How Are They Faring?

Chapter 3. Taking the Measure of Temporary Employment

Chapter 4. The Ins and Outs of Long-Term Unemployment

Chapter 5. And the Twain Shall Meet: Cross Market Effects of Labour and Product Market Policies

The following publications are also available through the OECD on-line bookshop (www.oecd.org)

Ageing and Employment Policies/Vieillissement et politiques de l'emploi – Sweden
Language: English. Published in 2003
ISBN: 926419996-9

Vieillissement et politiques de l'emploi/Ageing and Employment Policies – Suisse
Language: French. Published in 2003
ISBN: 926410257-4

Vieillissement et politiques de l'emploi/Ageing and Employment Policies – Belgique
Language: French. Published in 2003
ISBN: 926429996-3

Transforming Disability into Ability: Policies to Promote Work and Income Security for Disabled People
Published in 2003
ISBN: 926419887-3

Combating Child Labour: a Review of Policies
Forthcoming September 2003
ISBN: 9264102930

Beyond Rhetoric: Adult Learning Policies and Practices
Published in 2003
ISBN: 926419943-8

Babies and Bosses – Reconciling Work and Family Life (Vol. 1): Australia, Denmark and the Netherlands
Published in 2002
ISBN: 926419843-1

Babies and Bosses: Reconciling Work and Family Life (Vol. 2): Austria, Ireland and Japan
Forthcoming October 2003
ISBN: 926410418-6

Innovations in Labour Market Policies: The Australian Way
Published in 2001
ISBN: 9264187359-9

If you want to keep up with the latest research on international trends in social, employment, migration and health policies,
you can sign up for free email alerts on our two recently launched Working Papers Series:
"**OECD Social, Employment and Migration**" or "**Health**"
www.oecd.org/employment/emailalerts
Papers cover such wide-ranging topics as employment policies, child labour, human capital, pharmaceutical use, pension entitlements and family policies.
www.oecd.org/employment/workingpapers

OECD PUBLICATIONS, 2, rue André-Pascal, 75775 PARIS CEDEX 16
PRINTED IN FRANCE
(81 2003 09 1 P 1) ISBN 92-64-10061-X – No. 52991 2003